AF167588

Communications
in Computer and Information Science 2255

Series Editors

Gang Li, *School of Information Technology, Deakin University, Burwood, VIC, Australia*
Joaquim Filipe, *Polytechnic Institute of Setúbal, Setúbal, Portugal*
Zhiwei Xu, *Chinese Academy of Sciences, Beijing, China*

Rationale
The CCIS series is devoted to the publication of proceedings of computer science conferences. Its aim is to efficiently disseminate original research results in informatics in printed and electronic form. While the focus is on publication of peer-reviewed full papers presenting mature work, inclusion of reviewed short papers reporting on work in progress is welcome, too. Besides globally relevant meetings with internationally representative program committees guaranteeing a strict peer-reviewing and paper selection process, conferences run by societies or of high regional or national relevance are also considered for publication.

Topics
The topical scope of CCIS spans the entire spectrum of informatics ranging from foundational topics in the theory of computing to information and communications science and technology and a broad variety of interdisciplinary application fields.

Information for Volume Editors and Authors
Publication in CCIS is free of charge. No royalties are paid, however, we offer registered conference participants temporary free access to the online version of the conference proceedings on SpringerLink (http://link.springer.com) by means of an http referrer from the conference website and/or a number of complimentary printed copies, as specified in the official acceptance email of the event.

CCIS proceedings can be published in time for distribution at conferences or as post-proceedings, and delivered in the form of printed books and/or electronically as USBs and/or e-content licenses for accessing proceedings at SpringerLink. Furthermore, CCIS proceedings are included in the CCIS electronic book series hosted in the SpringerLink digital library at http://link.springer.com/bookseries/7899. Conferences publishing in CCIS are allowed to use Online Conference Service (OCS) for managing the whole proceedings lifecycle (from submission and reviewing to preparing for publication) free of charge.

Publication process
The language of publication is exclusively English. Authors publishing in CCIS have to sign the Springer CCIS copyright transfer form, however, they are free to use their material published in CCIS for substantially changed, more elaborate subsequent publications elsewhere. For the preparation of the camera-ready papers/files, authors have to strictly adhere to the Springer CCIS Authors' Instructions and are strongly encouraged to use the CCIS LaTeX style files or templates.

Abstracting/Indexing
CCIS is abstracted/indexed in DBLP, Google Scholar, EI-Compendex, Mathematical Reviews, SCImago, Scopus. CCIS volumes are also submitted for the inclusion in ISI Proceedings.

How to start
To start the evaluation of your proposal for inclusion in the CCIS series, please send an e-mail to ccis@springer.com

Hani Hagras · Younes Bennani ·
Mohamed Nemiche
Editors

Intelligent Systems and Advanced Computing Sciences

4th International Conference, ISACS 2023
Taza, Morocco, October 26–27, 2023
Proceedings

 Springer

Editors
Hani Hagras (ORCID)
University of Essex
Colchester, UK

Younes Bennani (ORCID)
Sorbonne Paris Nord University
Villetaneuse, France

Mohamed Nemiche (ORCID)
University Sidi Mohamed Ben Abdellah
Fes, Morocco

ISSN 1865-0929   ISSN 1865-0937 (electronic)
Communications in Computer and Information Science
ISBN 978-3-031-93447-6   ISBN 978-3-031-93448-3 (eBook)
https://doi.org/10.1007/978-3-031-93448-3

This Springer imprint is published by the registered company Springer Nature Switzerland AG
The registered company address is: Gewerbestrasse 11, 6330 Cham, Switzerland

If disposing of this product, please recycle the paper.

Artificial Intelligence and Smart Computer

About this book

This work brings together the peer-reviewed proceedings of the 4th International Conference on Intelligent Systems and Advanced Computing Sciences ISACS2023, held in Taza, Morocco, October 26–27, 2023. For this edition of the conference, each reviewer received an average of 3.5 papers to review, while each paper in the conference proceedings was reviewed by an average of approximately 3 reviewers in a single-blind process

The 30 full papers and 8 short papers included in these proceedings underwent a rigorous evaluation and were selected from 131 submissions. These papers are organized into three topic sections: Artificial Intelligence, Computer Vision, and Security and Information Processing.

Papers in the Artificial Intelligence section cover a wide range of topics, including: Machine Learning, Natural Language Processing, Robotics and Expert Systems.

Computer Vision papers cover topics such as: Image Processing, Pattern Recognition, Video Analysis and Object Detection. The papers in the Security and Information Processing section cover topics such as: Cryptography, Network Security, Data Privacy and Information Forensics

The proceedings are a valuable resource for researchers and practitioners in the fields of artificial intelligence, computer vision, and security and information processing. The papers provide a snapshot of the latest research in these areas and offer new insights and solutions to a wide range of problems.

Keywords

Track 1: Artificial Intelligence
AI for Computer Architecture
Big Data Analytics
Cloud Computing
Deep Learning
Intelligent Control Systems
Fuzzy Systems
Internet of Things
Machine Learning
Multi-Agent Systems
Neural Networks

Track 2: Computer vision
3D reconstruction
AI in Computer Vision

Applied Mathematics
Fuzzy Pattern Recognition
Image Analysis
Internet of Things and Cloud Computing
Algebra and Computer Science
Video Processing
Video Security

Track 3: Security and Information Processing
Assessment in e-Learning
Coding Theory
Computer Security and Cryptography
Data Analytics & Big Data in Education
Emerging Technologies in Education
Information Security
Intelligent Learning Systems
Learning Based on Serious Games
Mobile Learning
Numerical Computer Simulations

October 2023

Hani Hagras
Younes Bennani
Mohamed Nemiche

Organization

General Chairs

Majid Ben Yakhlef   Sidi Mohamed Ben Abdellah University, Morocco
Chakir El-kasri   Sidi Mohamed Ben Abdellah University, Morocco

Program Committee Chairs

Hani Hagras   University of Essex,UK
Younes Bennani   Paris 13 University, France
Mohamed Nemiche   Sidi Mohamed Ben Abdellah University, Morocco

Steering Committee

Aziza El Ouaazizi   Sidi Mohamed Ben Abdellah University, Morocco
Abdelkarim Boua   Sidi Mohamed Ben Abdellah University, Morocco
El Habib Nfaoui   Sidi Mohamed Ben Abdellah University, Morocco
Michel Aillerie   University of Lorraine, France
Soulaimane El Hazzat   Sidi Mohamed Ben Abdellah University, Morocco
Younes Oubenaalla   Sidi Mohamed Ben Abdellah University, Morocco
Kaarim Elmoutaoukil   Sidi Mohamed Ben Abdellah University, Morocco
J. Boumhidi   Sidi Mohamed Ben Abdellah University, Morocco
Malik Muhammad Yousaf   Quaid-I-Azam University Islamabad, Pakistan
Mohammed Ouriagli   Sidi Mohamed Ben Abdellah University, Morocco
Fernando Tadeo   University of Valladolid, Spain
Khalid Satori   Sidi Mohamed Ben Abdellah University, Morocco

Program Committee

Ahlem Aboud   University of Sfax, Tunisia
Abdelkaher Aitabdelouahad   Ibn Zohr University, Morocco
Ahmed Azouaoui   National School of Computer Science and
                                Systems Analysis, Morocco
Aziz Baataoui   Moulay Ismail University, Morocco
Abdelhak Bahri   Abdelmalek Essaâdi University, Morocco

Anouar Benamor	University of Manouba, Tunisia
Adil Ben-Hdec	Abdelmalek Essaâdi University, Morocco
Abdelkarim Boua	Sidi Mohamed Ben Abdellah University, Morocco
Aziz Boukenter	Jean Monnet University, France
Abderrazak Bouzid	Moulay Ismail University, Morocco
Amine Dhraief	University of Manouba, Tunisia
Antonio Javier Gallego	University of Alicante, Spain
Anibran Kundu	Universiti Teknologi PETRONAS, Malaysia
Ahmad Taher Azar	Benha University, Egypt
Abdelhakim Chillali	Sidi Mohamed Ben Abdellah University, Morocco
Abdelhak Boulaalam	Sidi Mohamed Ben Abdellah University, Morocco
Abdessamad Benlahbib	Sidi Mohamed Ben Abdellah University, Morocco
Anas El Affar	Sidi Mohamed Ben Abdellah University, Morocco
Abderrahim El Kadi	Mohammed V University in Rabat, Morocco
Asmae El Kassiri	Mohammed V University in Rabat, Morocco
Ahmed Elngar	Beni Suef University, Egypt
Abdelghani El Ougli	Sidi Mohamed Ben Abdellah University, Morocco
Abdelouhad Essahlaoui	Sidi Mohamed Ben Abdellah University, Morocco
Abdelaziz Hallaoui	Sidi Mohamed Ben Abdellah University, Morocco
Akram Halli	Moulay Ismail University, Morocco
Amina Housni	Sidi Mohamed Ben Abdellah University, Morocco
Amer Karam	Lebanese University, Lebanon
Asmae Labzour	Sidi Mohamed Ben Abdellah University, Morocco
Abdelhgni Lakehal	Abdelmalek Essaâdi University, Morocco
Abderrahmane Laraqui	Chouaib Doukkali University, Morocco
Ali Mouhib	Sidi Mohamed Ben Abdellah University, Morocco
Akhloufi Moulay	Université de Moncton, Canada
Abderrahmane Nitaj	University of Caen Normandy, France
Abdelhakim Qachar	Chouaib Doukkali University, Morocco
Abdelhamid Rabhi	University of Amiens, France
Abdelouhad Sabri	Sidi Mohamed Ben Abdellah University, Morocco
Amin Shoukry	Alexandria University, Egypt
Adam Slowik	Koszalin University of Technology, Poland
Ali Soltani	University of Lille, France
Ahmed Taher Azar	Prince Sultan University, Saudi Arabia
Abdelkrim Talbi	University of Lille, France
Adil Tannouche	Moulay Ismail University, Morocco
Amal Tmiri	Chouaib Doukkali University, Morocco
Abdessamad Tridane	UAE University, UAE
Ahmad Yahya Dawod	Chiang Mai University, Thailand
Ali Yahyaouy	Sidi Mohamed Ben Abdellah University, Morocco
Abdelaziz Ahaitouf	Sidi Mohamed Ben Abdellah University, Morocco

Badraddine Aghoutane	Moulay Ismail University, Morocco
Brahim Aksass	Moulay Ismail University, Morocco
Boukili Bensalem	Sidi Mohamed Ben Abdellah University, Morocco
Badr Bossoufi	Sidi Mohamed Ben Abdellah University, Morocco
Bouchaib Cherradi	Hassan II University of Casablanca, Morocco
Bouzid El Amine	Mohamed I University, Morocco
Cezar Collazos	Universidad del Cauca, Colombia
Chakir El-kasri	Sidi Mohamed Ben Abdellah University, Morocco
Cemil Tunc	Van Yüzüncü Yil University, Turkey
Driss Achemlal	Sidi Mohamed Ben Abdellah University, Morocco
Djemel Ziou	Université de Sherbrooke, Canada
Driss Bennis	Mohamed V University in Rabat, Morocco
Dirk Thorleuchter	Fraunhofer Institute for Technological Trend Analysis INT, Germany
Dounia El Bourkadi	Sidi Mohamed Ben Abdellah University, Morocco
Delfim F. M. Torres	University of Aveiro, Portugal
El-Mahjoub Boufounas	Moulay Ismail University, Morocco
Valentina Emilia Balas	Aurel Vlaicu University of Arad, Romania
El Hassan Abdelwahed	Cadi Ayyad University, Morocco
Edvard Kokanyan	ASP University, Armenia
El Habib Nfaoui	University of Sidi Mohamed Ben Abdellah, Morocco
Edgar Martínez-Moro	University of Valladolid, Spain
El Mustapha Mouaddib	University of Picardie Jules Verne, France
El Bachir Tazi	University of Sidi Mohamed Ben Abdellah, Morocco
Fatima Amounas	Moulay Ismail University, Morocco
Faouzi Boufarès	University of Paris 13, France
Faouzi Boussedra	Chouaib Doukkali University, Morocco
Fouad Khalil	Sidi Mohamed Ben Abdellah University, Morocco
Faten Kharbat	Al Ain University, UAE
Fatima Lakrami	Chouaib Doukkali University, Morocco
Fernando Moreira	Universidade Portucalense, Portugal
Fernando Tadeo	University of Valladolid, Spain
Fatima Zahra Fagroud	Hassan II University of Casablanca, Morocco
Gábor Péter Nagy	University of Szeged, Hungary
Guillaume Caron	University of Picardy Jules Verne, France
Hassan Ali Barkad	University of Djibouti, Djibouti
Habib Dhahri	King Saud University, Saudi Arabia
Hani Hagras	University of Essex, UK
Hachem Kadari	Aix-Marseille University, France
Huizilopoztli Luna-Garcia	Universidad Autónoma de Zacatecas, Mexico

Sumit Kumar Jha	University of Central Florida, USA
Soumia Lalaoui Rhali	Sidi Mohamed Ben Abdellah University, Morocco
S. Sudheer Mangalampalli	VIT-AP University, India
Srikanta Patnaik	SOA University, India
Salaheddine A. Kammouri	Sidi Mohamed Ben Abdellah University, Morocco
Sicong Shao	University of Arizona, USA
Tarik Lakhlifi	Moulay Ismail University, Morocco
Tomasz Kisielewicz	Warsaw University of Technology, Poland
Vani Rajasekar	Kongu Engineering College, India
Wiem Chebil	University of Monastir, Tunisia
Walid Gomaa	Egypt-Japan University of Science and Technology, Egypt
Xiang-ling Deng	Southeast University, China
Youssef Akdim	Sidi Mohamed Ben Abdellah University, Morocco
Younès Bennani	Paris 13 University, France
Youness Dhassi	Sidi Mohamed Ben Abdellah University, Morocco
Younes El khchine	Moulay Ismail University, Morocco
Youssef Hamdaoui	Mohammed V University in Rabat, Morocco
Youssef Hanyf	Ibn Zohr University, Morocco
Youness Oubenaalla	Sidi Mohamed Ben Abdellah University, Morocco

Contents

Security and Information Processing

Artificial Intelligence

Integrating Machine Learning and Optimisation for Parkinson's Detection: A Study of SMOTE, Featurewiz, Genetic Algorithm and Grid Search

Abd Allah Aouragh[(✉)] [ID] and Mohamed Bahaj [ID]

Faculty of Sciences and Techniques, Hassan 1st University, Settat, Morocco
abdallahaouragh@gmail.com

Abstract. Parkinson's disease is a chronic, progressive neurological disorder affecting principally the motor system. It is distinguished by symptoms such as muscular rigidity and slowness of movement. As per statistics provided by the World Health Organization, Parkinson's disease affects around 6 million individuals globally. The incidence of this pathology increases with age, and it mainly affects people over 60. The consequences of Parkinson's disease on patients' quality of life are significant, causing functional limitations, communication problems, and psychological impacts. As a result, early diagnosis of this condition is critical to ensure appropriate treatment and boost the overall life satisfaction of patients. In this paper, we suggest a method based on machine learning techniques for recognizing Parkinson's disease within a clinical dataset. To overcome the imbalanced classes in the dataset, we applied the SMOTE method to generate synthetic examples of the minority class. Next, we employed Featurewiz and the genetic algorithm to identify the most relevant attributes. Finally, we optimized the hyperparameters of the models with Grid Search. The experimental findings demonstrate that our strategy outperforms traditional approaches and significantly boosts the efficiency of the various performance metrics that exceed 96%. This promising approach provides new prospects for early and accurate diagnosis of Parkinson's disease, enabling earlier therapeutic intervention and enhancing patients' life satisfaction.

Keywords: Parkinson's Disease · Classification · Machine Learning · SMOTE · Featurewiz · SVM · Genetic Algorithm · Feature Selection · Grid Search

1 Introduction

Parkinson's disease is a chronic neurological condition characterized by the gradual breakdown of nerve cells within a distinct brain region designated as the substantia nigra. This degeneration causes a decline in the production of dopamine, a critical neurotransmitter crucial for the organization and supervision of movement [1]. The common signs of Parkinson's disease include muscular stiffness, bradykinesia (slowness of motion), rest tremor, and balance problems. However, Parkinson's disease can also lead to non-motor problems such as sleep disorders, depression, cognitive problems, and gastrointestinal issues [1, 2]. It is also important to emphasize that Parkinson's illness can

H. Hagras et al. (Eds.): ISACS 2023, CCIS 2255, pp. 3–15, 2025.
https://doi.org/10.1007/978-3-031-93448-3_1

vary considerably from person to person in terms of symptom severity, disease development and treatment effectiveness [2]. In statistical terms, as indicated by the World Health Organization's reports, about 6 million individuals worldwide deal with Parkinson's disease. The frequency of the condition rises with age, especially among those over 60. As a result of the aging population in many countries, the rate of Parkinson's condition is predicted to rise significantly over the next few decades [3]. The detection of Parkinson's disorder is grounded in an extensive clinical assessment of the patient's symptoms in addition to his medical history. The detection can be complex, as there is no specific test to definitively confirm the presence of the disease. Clinicians, in turn, rely on established diagnostic criteria, such as the criteria of the International Parkinson's Disease Movement (MDS), which include observation of motor symptoms, elimination of other possible causes, and response to treatment.

In some cases, additional tests, such as brain scans like magnetic resonance imaging (MRI) or positron emission tomography (PET), might be utilized to rule out other comparable conditions [3]. It is important to highlight that early recognition of Parkinson's disorder is crucial for appropriate management and adequate supervision.

Artificial intelligence, in particular machine learning algorithms, has opened up new prospects for promoting the detection of Parkinson's disorder. Through these technological advances, it is now possible to exploit techniques such as SMOTE, Featurewiz, genetic algorithm, and Grid Search to enhance the precision and consistency of diagnosis [4]. Within the context of Parkinson's disease, these algorithms have the capacity to process extensive medical datasets, including symptoms, clinical tests, and brain imaging results, to identify patterns and characteristics that are associated with the disease. By combining these artificial intelligence advancements, it is possible to develop more accurate and reliable Parkinson's detection models. This would lead to an earlier and more accurate diagnosis, enabling faster therapeutic intervention and improved life quality for Parkinson's patients [5].

To illustrate the various stages involved in our study, the subsequent sections of this paper will follow this structure: In Sect. 2, we outline the pertinent literature concerning the utilization of artificial intelligence techniques for Parkinson's disorder detection, and in Sect. 3, we present the used dataset and its distribution. In Sect. 4, we describe the methodology and materials utilized. Then, in Sect. 5, we provide the results obtained at every level of our process. Finally, in Sect. 6, we conclude our findings and raise prospects for improvement and future development in the application of artificial intelligence techniques for identifying Parkinson's disorder.

2   Related Work

Analysis of Parkinson's condition based on artificial intelligence has received great attention from researchers. The outcomes of these studies hold promise for enhancing our comprehension of the condition and implementing more efficient management strategies for this intricate neurodegenerative disorder.

Mei et al. [6] conducted a literature assessment on a total of 209 studies in this regard. Their study shows a strong potential for machine learning methods and new biomarkers to be used in health care decisions, leading to a more methodical and informed diagnosis of Parkinson's illness. Huang et al. [7] conducted a comparative assessment between several machine learning algorithms and several CNN architectures on a dataset of 196 patients and found that for the machine learning algorithms, the random forest recorded the leading accuracy, and for the CNN architectures, the model based on VGG16 outperformed the other models. Karan et al. [8] suggested an Intrinsic Mode Function Cepstral Coefficient (IMFCC) to effectively express Parkinson's speech characteristics; their new method provides an accuracy superior to that of usual acoustic features and the Mel Frequency Cepstral Coefficient (MFCC). Wang et al. [9] developed a deep learning framework to quickly identify whether or not an individual has Parkinson's disorder based on premotor characteristics. An assessment of the suggested deep learning framework compared to twelve alternative machine learning and other ensemble learning approaches revealed that the created model had greater detection capability, achieving the top accuracy of 96.45% on average.

Nahar et al. [10] investigated new methods for the identification of non-motor symptoms within the initial phases of Parkinson's illness. A detection technique based on machine learning was proposed, employing feature selection and classification approaches. Four classification algorithms were examined: bagging, gradient boosting, the extra tree classifier, and extreme gradient boosting. Bagging combined with recursive feature elimination surpassed the other methods, showcasing an accuracy of 82.35%. Lamba et al. [11] introduced a hybrid diagnostic method for Parkinson's illness relying on speech signals. Several feature selection techniques and classification algorithms were evaluated in various combinations. With an accuracy of 95.58%, the fusion of the genetic algorithm and the random forest model demonstrated the most impressive performance. Pahuja et al. [12] compared existing computational intelligence techniques, namely multi-layer perceptron, nearest neighbor, and support vector machine, on the reference speech dataset to see which of them was the most effective and precise Parkinson's disease categorization model. The best classifier was determined to be the multi-layer perceptron using the Levenberg-Marquardt method, with the greatest accuracy of 95.89%. Polat et al. [13] introduced a hybrid approach for identifying Parkinson's disorder utilizing characteristics extracted from speech signals. The method comprises two steps: data pre-processing and classification. The results showed that this hybrid method produced promising classification results with an accuracy of 94.89%. Martinez-Eguiluz et al. [14] evaluated nine machine learning techniques to discriminate patients with Parkinson's illness. The findings revealed that the majority of the algorithms could recognize people with Parkinson's disease with superior accuracy (>80%). The support vector machine and multilayer perceptron emerged as the top performers, achieving accuracies of 86.3% and 84.7%, respectively.

3 Dataset

The quality of the datasets used in machine learning projects is crucial to ensure dependable and widely applicable detection performance. Representative, well-annotated datasets containing records from different categories are needed to train and evaluate machine learning models effectively. Within the scope of our research, we relied on the Oxford Parkinson's Disease Detection Dataset (OPDDD), which is a widely used dataset in Parkinson's detection research. This dataset contains 195 movement recordings from both affected and healthy participants. In terms of attributes, the dataset consists of 24 attributes linked to participants' movement recordings and measurements of acceleration, speed, orientation, and other kinematic characteristics [15]. Table 1 provides an overview of the attributes.

Table 1. Dataset Attributes

Attribute	Type attribute	Description
name	Nominal	Name of the subject and recording identifier
mdvp:fo(hz)	Numerical	Mean vocal fundamental frequency
mdvp:fhi(hz)	Numerical	Peak vocal fundamental frequency
mdvp:flo(hz)	Numerical	Lowest vocal fundamental frequency
mdvp:jitter(%)	Numerical	indicators of fluctuations in fundamental frequency
mdvp:jitter(abs)	Numerical	
mdvp:rap	Numerical	
mdvp:ppq	Numerical	
jitter:ddp	Numerical	
mdvp:shimmer	Numerical	Numerous metrics quantifying amplitude variability
mdvp:shimmer(db)	Numerical	
shimmer:apq3	Numerical	
shimmer:apq5	Numerical	
mdvp:apq	Numerical	
shimmer:dda	Numerical	
nhr	Numerical	Two indices of ratio of noise to tonal components in the voice
hnr	Numerical	
rpde	Numerical	A duo of nonlinear dynamical complexity metrics
d2	Numerical	
dfa	Numerical	Fractal scaling exponent of the signal
spread1	Numerical	Three non-linear metrics for fundamental frequency fluctuation
spread2	Numerical	
ppe	Numerical	
status	Nominal	1 = affected, 0 = healthy

The distribution of classes in the dataset is unbalanced: 147 (75.38%) have Parkinson's disease and 48 (24.62%) are healthy. This imbalance can present difficulties in learning models, as they may develop a tendency to predict the majority class without fully taking into account examples of the smaller class. Therefore, it is crucial to take appropriate measures to balance the distribution and carefully evaluate the performance of the models to ensure accurate and reliable results.

4 Methods and Materials

In the following section, we will introduce the various material and methodological elements of our study, including dataset balancing, machine learning algorithms, feature selection techniques, hyperparameter optimization, an overview of the architecture adopted, and the involved evaluation metrics.

4.1 Balancing Dataset: SMOTE

The SMOTE (Synthetic Minority Over-sampling Technique) method is a technique applied to oversample the minority category in unbalanced datasets. When a significant imbalance occurs between classes, machine learning models tend to be biased in favor of the majority class, resulting in a decrease in performance in identifying the minority class. The SMOTE principle relies on the creation of new synthetic instances by interpolating attributes from existing samples of the minority class. By selecting an example from the minority class, SMOTE identifies the k nearest neighbors based on a similarity measure such as Euclidean distance. Then, for each selected neighbor, SMOTE performs an interpolation between the selected example and the neighbor by adding a fraction of the difference between their attributes to the selected example. This generates a new synthetic example for the minority class [16].

4.2 Machine Learning

Machine learning has become a major area of research and application in many fields, particularly in data classification. Classification involves assigning class labels to instances based on their characteristics, and supervised machine learning algorithms play an essential role in building models capable of accurately predicting the appropriate class on new data. The use of these algorithms enables valuable patterns and information to be extracted from the data, facilitating decision-making and the automation of classification tasks. In our study, we used the following algorithms [17]:

- Logistic regression (LR): is a binary classification supervised machine learning technique. It is based on a logistic function that transforms a linear combination of features into a probability between 0 and 1. Logistic regression is used to estimate the probability of being assigned to a given category using a set of labeled training examples to learn the optimal weights and coefficients. It is appreciated for its simplicity and interpretability [17].
- The k nearest neighbors (KNN): is a machine learning technique built upon the fundamental principle that similar instances tend to belong to the same category or produce comparable output values. The central concept of KNN is to determine the k closest instances of a given instance in feature space, where similarity is usually measured using distance measures such as Euclidean distance. One of the key advantages of KNN is its simplicity and ease of implementation. It can be used with different distance metrics, allowing the specific nature of the problem and the characteristics of the data to be taken into account [17].

- Support Vector Machine (SVM): The primary goal of SVM is to determine the ideal hyperplane that best separates the various classes in the feature space. SVM can also project training data into a higher-dimensional space, where it's easier to find a separating hyperplane. For this purpose, the SVM employs a kernel function that calculates the scalar products between pairs of instances in the higher-dimensional space without requiring explicit computation. One of the advantages of SVM is its ability to handle high-dimensional datasets, making it an appropriate choice for problems having an extensive set of features [17].
- Random Forest (RF): is a supervised machine learning technique constructed on a collection of decision trees, each with a random sample of training data and feature variables. The main concept behind Random Forest is to combine numerous decision trees' predictions to obtain a more robust and accurate prediction. Random Forest can handle large datasets with great efficiency. Moreover, it can handle both linear and non-linear problems, and it is also outlier-insensitive [17].
- AdaBoost (AB): is an algorithm that belongs to the family of ensemble methods, which combine the forecasts of several simpler models to obtain a more robust model. AdaBoost combines the predictions of weak models weighted by their individual performance. Weaker models with better performance contribute more to the final prediction. AdaBoost does not require any prior knowledge of weak model parameters, making it easy to use and adapt to different problems [17].
- Gradient Boosting (GB): is an ensemble approach that merges various elementary models to build a more powerful one. The basic principle of Gradient Boosting is to build successive models by focusing on the residual errors of preceding models. Gradient Boosting utilizes a gradient descent approach to reduce a loss function, which evaluates the difference between actual values and predictions. It is also effective for managing high-dimensional datasets with a large number of feature variables [17].

4.3 Feature Selection

During the analysis of complex data, it is common to be confronted with a large number of feature variables that can potentially influence the results of a machine learning model. However, not all these variables are necessarily relevant to the prediction or analysis task. Feature selection is a process that aims to identify the most informative variables and include them in the model while excluding redundant, irrelevant, or noisy variables. Different feature selection methods can be used depending on the specific needs of the application. In our study, we applied the following techniques [18, 19]:

- Featurewiz: is an advanced feature selection technique that automates the selection process using machine learning algorithms. In contrast to traditional feature selection methods, which require manual intervention to select variables, Featurewiz uses machine learning algorithms to assess the importance of variables and select them objectively. Featurewiz uses an iterative approach to evaluate the importance of variables. It starts by training an initial model on the feature set and measures the importance of each variable based on coefficients, scores, or other measures of model performance. Then, the least important variables are eliminated, and the process is executed until a predefined criterion is accomplished, such as the desired number of variables or an importance threshold [18].

- Genetic algorithm: Genetic algorithm is a prevalent approach of feature selection that is derived from the principles of biological evolution. This approach uses a population of potential solutions, represented as chromosomes, and evolves them over generations to find the ideal combination of attributes. The genetic algorithm evaluates the quality of each solution in the population using an evaluation function, which measures the performance of models built from each combination of features. The best-performing solutions are favored and have a greater probability of reproducing and passing on their characteristics to subsequent generations. Reproduction in the genetic algorithm involves operations such as selecting parents, crossovering characteristics between parents, and introducing random variation (mutation) to maintain genetic diversity [19].

4.4 Hyperparameter Optimization: Grid Search

Grid search is a widely utilized method for optimizing hyperparameters in machine learning algorithms. Hyperparameters are external model parameters that must be set prior to training in order to optimize model performance. Grid search works by defining a grid or list of possible values for each hyperparameter to be set. Then, all possible combinations of these values are evaluated using a specific performance metric, such as precision, recall, or accuracy. Each combination is evaluated using a cross-validation technique, where he dataset is partitioned into training and validation partitions. The advantage of grid search is that it systematically explores the space of hyperparameters and finds the best combinations to optimize model performance. However, Grid search can be costly in terms of computing time, especially if the hyperparameter grid is large or the dataset is voluminous [20].

4.5 Architecture Overview and Evaluation Metrics

- Global Overview: Our Parkinson's detection method was based on a comprehensive approach involving machine learning algorithms in association with techniques such as SMOTE for data balancing, feature selection to pinpoint the most pertinent features, and grid search for hyperparameter optimization. We have used a variety of supervised machine learning algorithms, to construct powerful classification models. SMOTE was implemented to tackle the uneven distribution of classes in our dataset. Next, feature selection techniques such as Featurewiz and genetic algorithm are employed to pinpoint the most informative attributes and reduce dimensionality. Finally, grid search was applied to search for optimal combinations of hyperparameters for each algorithm. The proposed architecture is illustrated in Fig. 1.

- Evaluation Metrics: Evaluating classification model performance is critical for determining their accuracy and reliability in class prediction [21]. Various metrics are used to measure the proficiency. In our study, we chose the following metrics:

  - Accuracy: calculates the fraction of accurate predictions relative to the total sample size [21].

$$\text{accuracy} = \frac{\text{correct predictions}}{\text{all predictions}} \tag{1}$$

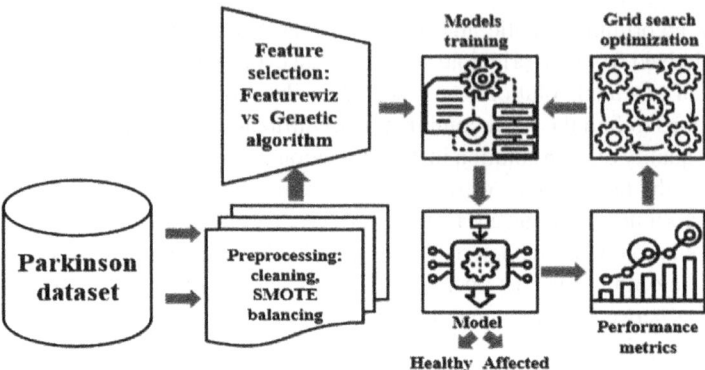

Fig. 1. Model architecture

– Precision: calculates the percentage of true positives among positive forecasts [21].

$$precision = \frac{true\ positive}{true\ positive + false\ positive} \tag{2}$$

– Recall: measures the proportion of true positives among true positives and false negatives [21].

$$recall = \frac{true\ positive}{true\ positive + false\ negative} \tag{3}$$

– F1-score: combines the last two metrics to provide a balanced measure [21].

$$F1 - score = 2 * \frac{precision * recall}{precision + recall} \tag{4}$$

– AUC-ROC (Area Under the Receiver Operating Characteristic Curve) computes the area beneath the ROC curve, illustrating the correlation between the true positive rate and false positive rate across various classification thresholds [21].

5 Results and Discussion

In this section, we reveal the detailed findings obtained using the various machine learning algorithms and optimization techniques. Tables 2, 3, 4, 5, 6 and 7 illustrate the detailed results for each algorithm, including accuracy, precision, recall, F1-score, and AUC-ROC.

The techniques involved in our approach considerably improve the efficiency of the various classification algorithms, with significant gains ranging from 1% to 10%. In particular, the combination of the genetic algorithm and Grid Search led to outstanding performance, with the best accuracy and AUC-ROC recorded at 96.53% and 96.84, respectively. These results clearly demonstrate the positive impact of these approaches on the efficiency of models in accurately detecting Parkinson's disease.

Table 2. Original dataset

	LR	KNN	SVM	RF	AB	GB
accuracy	87.58%	85.16%	63.96%	88.24%	85.99%	90.38%
precision	89.49%	90.65%	60.71%	91.25%	93.06%	92.36%
recall	95.18%	91.09%	76.27%	94.18%	88.45%	96.00%
F1-score	92.09%	90.25%	67.47%	92.52%	90.60%	93.94%
AUC-ROC	89.66%	84.54%	64.42%	92.89%	91.86%	92.87%

Table 3. SMOTE balanced dataset

	LR	KNN	SVM	RF	AB	GB
accuracy	82.02%	88.76%	84.27%	94.28%	91.01%	94.38%
precision	96.65%	97.45%	92.78%	94.98%	97.56%	97.57%
recall	65.96%	78.72%	70.21%	89.36%	85.11%	89.36%
F1-score	78.41%	87.09%	79.93%	92.09%	90.91%	93.29%
AUC-ROC	82.98%	89.36%	85.11%	94.63%	91.36%	94.68%

Table 4. SMOTE + Featurewiz

	LR	KNN	SVM	RF	AB	GB
accuracy	81.86%	88.76%	86.52%	94.38%	92.13%	95.51%
precision	94.29%	97.44%	93.57%	98.54%	98.25%	97.85%
recall	70.21%	80.85%	74.47%	89.36%	85.11%	91.49%
F1-score	80.49%	88.37%	82.93%	93.73%	91.21%	94.56%
AUC-ROC	82.73%	89.24%	87.23%	94.68%	92.55%	95.74%

Table 5. SMOTE + Genetic algorithm

	LR	KNN	SVM	RF	AB	GB
accuracy	85.39%	88.76%	86.52%	94.38%	92.13%	95.63%
precision	92.50%	97.44%	89.96%	98.51%	97.85%	91.96%
recall	78.72%	80.85%	74.47%	89.36%	85.11%	91.49%
F1-score	85.06%	88.37%	81.48%	93.71%	91.03%	91.72%
AUC-ROC	85.79%	89.24%	85.23%	96.68%	92.55%	95.74%

Table 6. SMOTE + Featurewiz + Grid Search

	LR	KNN	SVM	RF	AB	GB
accuracy	80.90%	92.13%	95.91%	93.26%	94.38%	95.58%
precision	91.67%	96.23%	98.65%	96.21%	97.06%	97.08%
recall	70.21%	85.11%	91.69%	87.23%	89.36%	91.49%
F1-score	79.52%	90.33%	94.93%	91.50%	93.05%	94.20%
AUC-ROC	81.54%	92.55%	95.86%	93.62%	94.68%	95.74%

Table 7. SMOTE + Genetic algorithm + Grid Search

	LR	KNN	SVM	RF	AB	GB
accuracy	83.15%	92.13%	96.53%	93.26%	94.38%	95.87%
precision	94.34%	97.15%	94.36%	98.68%	95.47%	96.36%
recall	72.34%	85.11%	91.97%	87.23%	89.36%	91.49%
F1-score	81.93%	90.73%	93.90%	92.60%	92.31%	93.86%
AUC-ROC	83.79%	92.55%	96.84%	93.62%	94.68%	95.74%

In Table 2, we present the effectiveness of the algorithms on the initial dataset without any additional pre-processing or optimization. The gradient boosting algorithm achieved the best accuracy, recall, and F1-score with values of 90.38%, 96.00%, and 93.94%, respectively. For precision and AUC-ROC, the best values were recorded, respectively, by the adaboost and the random forest with the following values: 93.06% and 92.89%. SVM recorded the worst values for all metrics with the following values: accuracy: 63.96%, precision: 60.71%, recall: 76.27%, F1-score: 67.47%, and AUC-ROC: 64.42%. In Table 3, we illustrate the results after applying the SMOTE balancing technique. The gradient boosting dominated the best results for all metrics, with the following values: accuracy: 94.38%, precision: 97.57%, recall: 89.36%, F1-score: 93.29%, and AUC-ROC: 94.68%. For the worst values, logistic regression obtained the worst results for the following measures: accuracy: 82.02%, recall: 65.96%, F1-score: 78.41%, and AUC-ROC: 82.98%. For precision, the worst value was recorded by SVM with a value of 92.78%. Table 4 shows the results after applying the Featurewiz feature selection method to the dataset. Once again, gradient boosting achieved the best results for the following metrics: accuracy: 95.51%, recall: 91.49%, F1-score: 94.56%, and AUC-ROC: 95.74%. For precision, the best value was recorded by random forest with a value of 98.54%. Again, as in Table 3, logistic regression recorded the following worst-case values: accuracy: 81.86%, recall: 70.21%, F1-score: 80.49%, and AUC-ROC: 82.73%. For precision, the worst value was recorded by SVM with a value of 93.57%. In Table 5, we use the genetic algorithm to perform feature selection on the dataset. This time the gradient boosting only recorded the best values in the following metrics: accuracy: 95.63% and recall: 91.49%; for precision, the adaboost recorded the best value of 97.85%; for F1-score and AUC-ROC, the random forest recorded the best values of 93.71% and 96.68%, respectively. For the worst values, logistic regression recorded the worst accuracy with 85.39%, and for the other metrics, SVM recorded the following worst values: precision: 89.96%, recall: 74.47%, F1-score: 81.48%, and AUC-ROC: 85.23%.

Table 6 shows the results after applying the grid search method on Featurewiz to optimize the hyperparameters of the classification algorithms. SVM dominated the best results for all metrics, with the following values: accuracy: 95.91%, precision: 98.65%, recall: 91.69%, F1-score: 94.93%, and AUC-ROC: 95.86%. Logistic regression recorded the worst values for all metrics with the following values: accuracy: 80.90%, precision: 91.67%, recall: 70.21%, F1-score: 79.52%, and AUC-ROC: 81.54%. Finally, Table 7 shows the results after applying the grid search method to the genetic algorithm for hyperparameter optimization. This time, the SVM once again dominated the following metrics: accuracy: 96.53%, recall: 91.97%, F1-score: 93.90%, and AUC-ROC: 96.84%. For precision, the random forest recorded the best value at 98.68%. Once again, Logistic regression recorded the worst values for all metrics, with the following values: accuracy: 83.15%, precision: 94.34%, recall: 72.34%, F1-score: 81.93%, and AUC-ROC: 83.79%. Figure 2 shows a graphical comparison between the different algorithms discussed above.

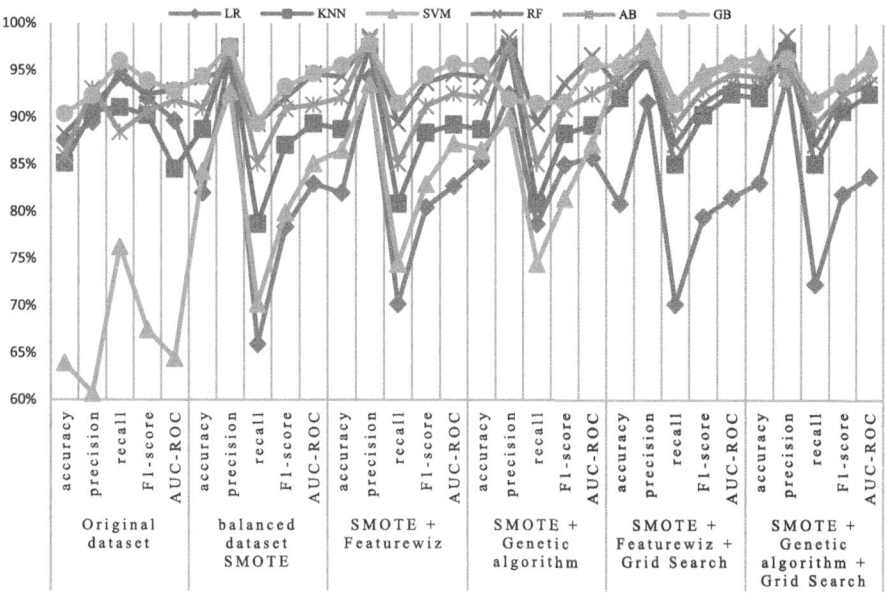

Fig. 2. Comparative Visualization of Algorithm Performance Metrics

6 Conclusion

To conclude, our study demonstrated the effectiveness of artificial intelligence techniques, particularly machine learning algorithms, in improving Parkinson's detection. Utilizing approaches such as SMOTE for class balance, Featurewiz and the genetic algorithm for feature selection, and Grid Search for hyperparameter fine-tuning, we achieved promising classification performance. These approaches offer new prospects to enhance the early detection and treatment of Parkinson's disorder.

However, further research is needed to explore other pre-processing, feature selection, and optimization techniques, as well as to evaluate model performance on larger, more diverse datasets. Moreover, the integration of new variables or characteristics could enrich the models and improve their predictive capacity. By continuing to develop these approaches and collaborating with clinical experts, we can advance the recognition and control of Parkinson's disease, aiding in the advancement of patients' quality of life.

References

1. Parkinson disease [Internet]. https://www.who.int/news-room/fact-sheets/detail/parkinson-disease
2. https://www.facebook.com/NIHAging. National Institute on Aging. Parkinson's Disease: Causes, Symptoms, and Treatments. https://www.nia.nih.gov/health/parkinsons-disease
3. Statistics | Parkinson's Foundation [Internet]. https://www.parkinson.org/understanding-parkinsons/statistics
4. Belić, M., Bobić, V., Badža, M., Šolaja, N., Đurić-Jovičić, M., Kostić, V.S.: Artificial intelligence for assisting diagnostics and assessment of Parkinson's disease—A review. Clin. Neurol. Neurosurg. 1(184), 105442 (2019)
5. Moon, S., Song, H.J., Sharma, V.D., Lyons, K.E., Pahwa, R., Akinwuntan, A.E., et al.: Classification of Parkinson's disease and essential tremor based on balance and gait characteristics from wearable motion sensors via machine learning techniques: a data-driven approach. J. NeuroEng. Rehabil. 17(1), 125 (2020)
6. Mei, J., Desrosiers, C., Frasnelli, J.: Machine Learning for the Diagnosis of Parkinson's Disease: A Review of Literature. Frontiers in Aging Neuroscience. https://doi.org/10.3389/fnagi.2021.633752
7. Huang, G.H., Lin, C.H., Cai, Y.R., Chen, T.B., Hsu, S.Y., Lu, N.H., et al.: Multiclass machine learning classification of functional brain images for Parkinson's disease stage prediction. Stat. Anal. Data Mining: ASA Data Sci. J. 13(5), 508–523 (2020)
8. Karan, B., Sahu, S.S., Mahto, K.: Parkinson disease prediction using intrinsic mode function based features from speech signal. Biocybern. Biomed. Eng. 40(1), 249–264 (2020)
9. Wang, W., Lee, J., Harrou, F., Sun, Y.: Early detection of Parkinson's disease using deep learning and machine learning. IEEE Access 8, 147635–147646 (2020)
10. Nahar, N., Ara, F., Neloy, M.A.I., Biswas, A., Hossain, M.S., Andersson, K.: Feature selection based machine learning to improve prediction of Parkinson Disease. In: Mahmud, M., Kaiser, M.S., Vassanelli, S., Dai, Q., Zhong, N. (eds.) Brain Informatics: 14th International Conference, BI 2021, Virtual Event, September 17–19, 2021, Proceedings, pp. 496–508. Springer International Publishing, Cham (2021). https://doi.org/10.1007/978-3-030-86993-9_44
11. Lamba, R., Gulati, T., Alharbi, H.F., Jain, A.: A hybrid system for Parkinson's disease diagnosis using machine learning techniques. Int. J. Speech Technol. 25(3), 583–593 (2022)

12. Pahuja, G., Nagabhushan, T.N.: A comparative study of existing machine learning approaches for Parkinson's Disease detection. IETE J. Res. **67**(1), 4–14 (2021)
13. Polat, K.: A hybrid approach to Parkinson Disease classification using speech signal: the combination of SMOTE and random forests. In: 2019 Scientific Meeting on Electrical-Electronics & Biomedical Engineering and Computer Science (EBBT), pp. 1–3 (2019)
14. Martinez-Eguiluz, M., Arbelaitz, O., Gurrutxaga, I., Muguerza, J., Perona, I., Murueta-Goyena, A., et al.: Diagnostic classification of Parkinson's disease based on non-motor manifestations and machine learning strategies. Neural Comput. Applic. **35**(8), 5603–5617 (2023)
15. Little, M.: Parkinsons [Internet]. UCI Machine Learning Repository (2007). https://archive.ics.uci.edu/dataset/174
16. Fernandez, A., Garcia, S., Herrera, F., Chawla, N.V.: SMOTE for learning from imbalanced data: progress and challenges, marking the 15-year anniversary. J. Artific. Intell. Res. **20**(61), 863–905 (2018)
17. Sarker, I.H.: Machine learning: algorithms, real-world applications and research directions. SN Comput. Sci. **2**(3), 160 (2021)
18. Zaki S, Ghali NI, Abo-Elfetoh A, Idrees AM.: Predictive Analysis of Big data in Egypt Census 2017 Comparison of Four ML Predictive Models [Internet]. Rochester, NY (2022). https://papers.ssrn.com/abstract=4225813
19. Halim, Z., et al.: An effective genetic algorithm-based feature selection method for intrusion detection systems. Comput. Secur. (2021). https://doi.org/10.1016/j.cose.2021.102448
20. Belete, D.M., Huchaiah, M.D.: Grid search in hyperparameter optimization of machine learning models for prediction of HIV/AIDS test results. Int. J. Comput. Appl. **44**(9), 875–886 (2022)
21. Ferrer, L.: Analysis and Comparison of Classification Metrics [Internet]. arXiv. http://arxiv.org/abs/2209.05355

Kernel Adaptive Filters for Machine Learning-Based System Identification with Binary Output Data

Rachid Fateh[1]([✉])(iD), Hicham Oualla[2], Es-said Azougaghe[3](iD), Anouar Darif[1](iD), Ahmed Boumezzough[4], Said Safi[1](iD), Mathieu Pouliquen[2], and Miloud Frikel[2](iD)

[1] Laboratory of Innovation in Mathematics, Applications and Information Technologies, Sultan Moulay Slimane University, Beni Mellal, Morocco
`rachid.fateh@usms.ac.ma`
[2] Laboratory of Engineering Systems, UNICAEN, ENSICAEN, Normandie University, Caen, France
[3] Laboratory of Information Processing and Decision Support, Sultan Moulay Slimane University, Beni Mellal, Morocco
[4] Laboratory of Research in Physics and Engineering Sciences, Sultan Moulay Slimane University, Beni Mellal, Morocco

Abstract. Kernel methods constitute a category of machine learning algorithms extensively employed in the realm of classification, regression, identification, and other tasks. Our paper addresses the challenging problem of identifying the finite impulse response (FIR) of single-input single-output nonlinear systems under the influence of perturbations and binary-valued measurements. To overcome this challenge, we exploit two algorithms that leverage the framework of reproducing kernel Hilbert spaces (RKHS) to accurately identify the impulse response of the Proakis C channel. Additionally, we introduce the application of these kernel methods for estimating binary output data of nonlinear systems. We demonstrate the efficacy of kernel adaptive filters for identifying nonlinear systems with binary output measurements through experimental results presented in this work.

Keywords: Nonlinear systems identification · Kernel adaptive filtering · Finite impulse response · Proakis C channel · Machine Learning

1 Introduction

A particular category of digital filters called linear adaptive filters has the ability to adjust its parameters according to the input data. These filters find widespread usage in signal processing duties like reducing noise, canceling out echoes, and achieving equalization [1–4]. The key technique of adaptive linear filters has always been to employ an algorithm capable of updating the filter coefficients in time with changes in their input values. [5,6]. The most widely approach applied

H. Hagras et al. (Eds.): ISACS 2023, CCIS 2255, pp. 16–29, 2025.
https://doi.org/10.1007/978-3-031-93448-3_2

for these tasks is the least mean squares (LMS) algorithm [7], it iteratively adapts the filter coefficients in order to reduce the mean square error between the filter output and the desired output. Intelligent linear adaptive filter performance relies on a number of critical factors, notably the selection of the filter structure, the approach used to update the filter coefficients, and the configuration of the input signal. Overall, these filters perform better with stationary or slowly time-varying input signals, and when the filter framework is selected to match the characteristic statistical properties of the signal.

Linear adaptive filters are widely used in various fields, such as communications, control systems, and biomedical signal processing, due to their versatility and effectiveness in handling complex signals. They are often used in conjunction with other signal processing techniques, such as Fourier analysis and wavelet transforms, to achieve more sophisticated processing of signals [1]. For instance, in the field of biomedical signal processing, adaptive filtering has been utilized to remove noise and artifacts from electroencephalogram (EEG) signals [8]. In communication systems, adaptive filters have been applied to mitigate channel impairments and improve signal quality. In control systems, adaptive filtering has been used to identify and estimate system parameters, and to compensate for time-varying disturbances [9].

Kernel methods represent a family of machine learning technologies extensively exploited for classification, regression, channel estimation and many other purposes [10,11]. In order to isolate or analyze data more easily, they work by translating it into an area with greater dimensions, without explicitly computing the coordinates of the data in that space [12–15]. These methods are based on the concept that a decision boundary in the reproducing kernel Hilbert space (RKHS) [12] can be represented as a linear boundary in a lower-dimensional space, making it possible to capture complex, non-linear relationships between input features and the output variable [16]. Support vector machines (SVMs) are one of the most widely used kernel methods, especially for classification tasks [17]. Kernel ridge regression, on the other hand, is often used for regression tasks due to its ability to capture non-linear relationships between variables. Additionally, kernel principal component analysis (PCA) is used for data analysis, allowing for non-linear feature extraction and dimensionality reduction [18]. In addition to their performance, kernel methods are also highly interpretable, allowing users to understand how the algorithm is making predictions and adjust the model accordingly. For example, SVMs can be visualized by plotting the decision boundary in the input feature space, which can provide insight into the characteristics of the data and the model [19].

Recently, kernel methods have been successfully applied in channel identification tasks, particularly in the context of blind channel identification, where the channel parameters are estimated without prior knowledge of the channel. Kernel-based blind channel identification methods typically use a kernel function to map the received signal into a high-dimensional space, where the channel parameters can be estimated using linear regression techniques. The estimated parameters can then be used to equalize the received signal and improve the accuracy of the communication system (see e.g. [20–24]). At present, there are many adaptive kernel filtering algorithms that have been exploited for channel identification in wireless communication systems: The following are some of them: (i) kernel least mean squares (KLMS) is a kernel-based adaptive filter that can be used for channel identification in wireless communication systems [25]. In KLMS, a kernel function is used to map the input data into a higher-dimensional space, where the linear regression problem is easier to solve. The KLMS algorithm updates the filter coefficients based on the difference between the predicted output and the actual output. The Gaussian kernel is a popular choice for this purpose. (ii) kernel normalized least mean squares (KNLMS) is a variant of KLMS that includes a normalization factor in the update rule. This helps to prevent the filter coefficients from becoming too large and unstable [27]. KNLMS can be used for channel identification in wireless communication systems, and it has been shown to be effective in reducing the computational complexity of KLMS. (iii) kernel extended improved proportionate NLMS (KE-IPNLMS) [28], this algorithm employs a radial basis function (RBF) kernel to perform an implicit mapping of the data using the kernel trick to estimate the impulse response parameters for single-input single-output (SISO) nonlinear system identification.

In this paper, we present an investigation of a non-linear system identification problem in the presence of noise. Section 2 provides a detailed description of the problem. In Sect. 3, we introduce fundamental notations of kernel methods, followed by a discussion of two algorithms: KLMS, and KNLMS. We then evaluate the effectiveness of kernel methods using binary-valued output by analyzing simulation results in Sect. 4. Our findings are summarized in Sect. 5, which concludes the paper.

2   System Descriptions

We introduce a few notations and assumptions in this part that will be utilized along the rest of the work. Specifically, we consider the Hammerstein system shown in Fig. 1, which is composed of a nonlinear static function followed by a finite impulse response (FIR) filter of known order.

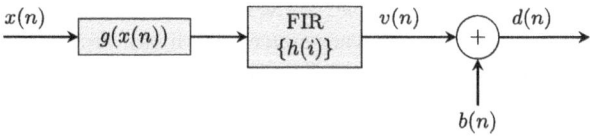

Fig. 1. Block diagram of Hammerstein system

As shown in Fig. 1, the desired system output can be obtained using the following expression:

$$\begin{cases} v(n) = & \sum_{i=0}^{L-1} h(i)g(x(n-i)) \\ d(n) = & v(n) + b(n), \quad n = 0, 1, 2, ..., N \end{cases} \tag{1}$$

where $x(k)$ is the input signal, $h(i)_{(i=0,1,...,L-1)}$ represents the channel impulse response, L refers to the FIR system order, $g(.)$ denotes the nonlinearity and $b(k)$ is the measurement noise.

The Hammerstein system was adopted under the following fundamental assumptions:

- The input sequence $x(n)$, is i.i.d. (independent and identically distributed) bounded random process with zero mean,
- The additive noise $b(n)$ is suggested, Gaussian and independent of $x(n)$ (bounded) and d(n) (bounded),
- Let $g(.)$ be invertible and continuous for any finite x.

The hypotheses listed above are formulated to simplify system analysis and to achieve the best results in terms of mean square error. The primary objective of this paper is to present a comparison of the kernel methods that have been proposed in the literature for identifying the output d generated by (1).

3   Kernel Methods

Here, we introduce the kernel approaches, which are a class of techniques that allow us to extend classic linear algorithms to work with non-linear data. The main idea behind kernel methods is to apply the linear algorithm on a projection of the data in a higher-dimensional space. This projection enables us to separate the data into classes that were not linearly separable in the original space

Kernel methods represent a family of machine learning technologies that use kernel functions to transform input data into a higher dimensional space. These algorithms are most often used to address classification and regression problems.

A function $\kappa : \mathcal{X} \times \mathcal{X} \longmapsto \mathbb{R}_{\setminus}$ is a similarity measure if the following conditions are satisfied:

- $x, y \in \mathcal{X} \; \kappa(x, y) \geq 0$,
- $x, y \in \mathcal{X} \; \kappa(x, y) = \kappa(y, x)$,
- $\forall y \in \mathcal{X}, y \neq x \; \kappa(x, y) > \kappa(x, x)$,
- $\kappa(x, y) = \kappa(x, x) \Leftrightarrow x = y$,

3.1   Positive Definite Kernel

Theorem 1. *Let $\mathcal{X}$ be a compact in $\mathbb{R}_{\setminus}$ (compact = closed and bounded) and $K : \mathcal{X} \times \mathcal{X} \longmapsto \mathbb{R}_{\setminus}$ a symmetric function. We also assume that $\forall f \in \mathcal{L}_2(\mathcal{X})$:*

$$\int_{\mathcal{X}} K(x, y)f(x)f(y)dxdy \geqslant 0 \quad (Mercer\ condition) \tag{2}$$

Then there exists a Hilbert space $\mathcal{H}$ and Φ : $\mathcal{X} \longrightarrow \mathcal{H}$ such that $\forall (x,y) \in \mathcal{X}^2$:

$$K(x,y) = \langle \Phi(x), \Phi(y) \rangle \tag{3}$$

The function $K(x,y)$ is called positive definite kernel.

An equivalent condition for the function $K : \mathcal{X} \times \mathcal{X} \longmapsto \mathbb{R}\setminus$ to be a definite positive kernel is the following:

- $\forall n \in \mathbb{N}\ltimes$ and $\{x_i\}i = 1, ..., n \subset \mathcal{X}$ the Gramm matrix

$$K = [K_{i,j}]i = 1, ..., n = [K(x_i, x_j)]i = 1, ..., n \tag{4}$$

  is positive definite, that is:

$$\forall c \in \mathbb{R}\setminus^n, \ c \neq 0, \ \text{we have} \ c^\top Kc > 0 \tag{5}$$

A valid kernel, therefore, ensures the existence of $\mathcal{H}$ and can be expressed as a scalar product in Hilbert space $\mathcal{H}$. A good kernel also guarantees the convexity of the quadratic optimization problem under inequality constraints encountered for SVM.

3.2 Conditionally Positive Definite Kernel

A kernel is conditionally positive definite (CPD) if $\forall n \in \mathbb{N}\ltimes$ and $\{x_i\}i = 1, ..., n \subset \mathcal{X}$ the Gramm matrix

$$K = [K_{i,j}]i = 1, ..., n = [K(x_i, x_j)]i = 1, ..., n \tag{6}$$

is conditionally positive definite, i.e.

$$\forall c \in \mathbb{R}\setminus^n, \ c \neq 0 \ \text{such as} \ \sum_{i=1}^{n} c_i = 0, \ \text{we have} \ c^\top Kc > 0 \tag{7}$$

This definition extends the class of kernel functions for which the SVM optimization problem is guaranteed convex.

Given a positive conditionally defined symmetric kernel, there exists:

- a vector space $\mathcal{V}$
- a transformation Φ : $\mathcal{X} \longrightarrow \mathcal{V}$
- a bilinear form Q : $\mathcal{V} \times \mathcal{V} \longmapsto \mathbb{R}\setminus$

Such as :

$$K(x,y) = Q(\Phi(x), \Phi(y)) \tag{8}$$

- If K is not defined positive, then Q is not a scalar product.

3.3   KLMS Algorithm

Kernel Least Mean Square (KLMS) is an online machine learning algorithm that is designed for non-linear regression problems. KLMS uses a kernel function to transform the input data into a high-dimensional feature space, where a linear relationship between inputs and outputs can be learned using a simple linear model. Here is the description of the KLMS algorithm [25]:

$$\theta(0) = 0$$
$$e(n) = d(n) - \theta(n-1)^\top \Phi(x(n))$$
$$\theta(n) = \theta(n-1) + \mu e(n)\Phi(x(n)) \tag{9}$$

The KLMS algorithm works by transforming the input data into a high-dimensional feature space using a kernel function. The kernel function measures the similarity between two data points and maps them into a high-dimensional space, where they can be linearly separable. The output $\theta(n-1)^\top \Phi(x(n))$ is then predicted using the inner product of the kernel function and the weight vector θ. The error $e(n)$ is computed as the difference between the predicted output $\theta(n-1)^\top \Phi(x(n))$ and the actual output $d(n)$.

The KLMS algorithm updates the weight vector w using the error e and the kernel function κ to compute the update. The update rule follows the same principle as the LMS algorithm, where the weight vector is updated in the direction that reduces the error. The update rule includes the kernel function to account for the non-linear relationship between inputs and outputs.

3.4   KNLMS Algorithm

The KNLMS algorithm is a variation of the NLMS [26] algorithm that uses a kernel function to map the input signal to a higher-dimensional space, where it is easier to separate linearly. This makes the algorithm more powerful and versatile, with applications in nonlinear filtering and prediction.

The basic idea behind the KNLMS algorithm is to apply a nonlinear mapping to the input signal using a kernel function, such as a Gaussian or polynomial function. The mapped signal is then used as the input to the standard NLMS algorithm, which updates the filter weights based on the difference between the predicted output and the actual output. The weight update step is normalized based on the power of the mapped signal, similar to the NLMS algorithm.

The formula for the weight update in the KNLMS algorithm is [27]:

$$\theta(n+1) = \theta(n) + \frac{\mu}{\varepsilon + \|\Phi(x(n))\|^2} e(n)\Phi(x(n)) \tag{10}$$

where $\theta(n)$ is the filter weights at iteration n, μ is the step-size parameter, $e(n)$ is the error signal at iteration n, $\Phi(x(n))$ is the mapped input signal at iteration n, ε refers to a small constant mobilized to avoid numerical problems, and $\|\Phi(x(n))\|^2$ is the power of the mapped input signal.

The KNLMS algorithm has several advantages over the NLMS algorithm, including its ability to handle nonlinear signals and its improved performance in high-dimensional spaces. However, it can be computationally expensive and may require careful selection of the kernel function and its parameters to achieve good performance.

4   Simulation Results and Discussion

To validate the efficacy of the presented algorithms in the presence of Gaussian additive noise, simulations were performed on nonlinear system identification with binary-valued output, utilizing the Gaussian kernel.

$$\kappa(x,y) = exp\left(-\frac{\|x-y\|^2}{2\sigma^2}\right), \quad \forall(x,y) \in \mathcal{X}^2 \tag{11}$$

where $\sigma > 0$ represent the smoothing parameter.

The simulations involve passing a signal $x(n)$ from a normal distribution with mean 0 and variance 1 through a Hammerstein system. This system consists of a nonlinearity tanh(x) followed by a linear finite impulse response (FIR) channel. The linear channel uses an impulse response h of length $L = 5$ known as the Proakis C channel, with coefficients of $[0.227, 0.460, 0.688, 0.460, 0.227]$. Additionally, Gaussian white noise with a power of $20dB$ is added to the channel output during each of the 1024 iterations. Finally, using a binary detector $I[.]$ equipped with a predefined threshold $C \in \mathbb{R}\setminus$, the output of the system $d(k)$ becomes measurable. The quantized output data $s(k)$ could be expressed by the following mathematical formula:

$$s(k) = I_{[d(n)\geq C]} = \begin{cases} 1 & \text{if } d(n) \geq C \\ -1 & \text{otherwise}. \end{cases} \tag{12}$$

4.1   Proakis C Channel Identification

Figure 2 shows the impulse response parameters of the Proakis C channel estimated using both algorithms (KLMS and KNLMS). The estimates were obtained for an SNR of 20 dB and $N = 1024$ input signal samples, using 50 Monte Carlo iterations. The results indicate that the kernel normalised least mean squares (KNLMS) algorithm accurately estimates the response parameters, while the kernel least mean squares (KLMS) algorithm produces estimated values that differ significantly from the measured values.

To assess the frequency domain performance of both algorithms, we visualize the estimated amplitude and phase response of the Proakis C channel's impulse response for a sample size of $N = 1000$ and $SNR = 20$ dB. The Fig. 3 highlights the estimates of the amplitude and phase of the Proakis C channel, using the

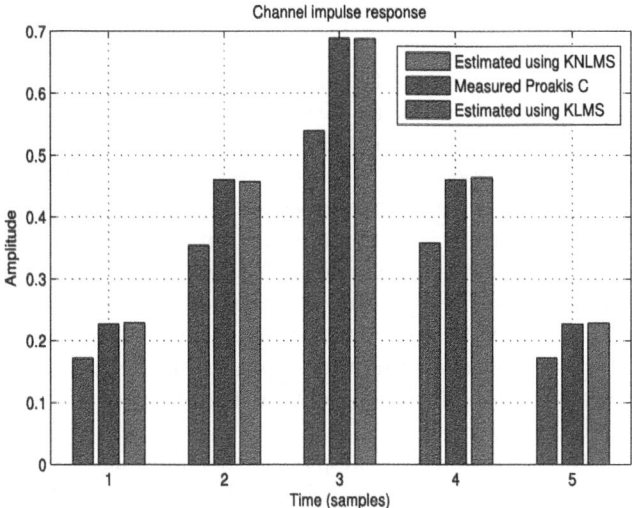

Fig. 2. Proakis C channel impulse response estimation for data length of $N = 1000$ and $SNR = 20$ dB.

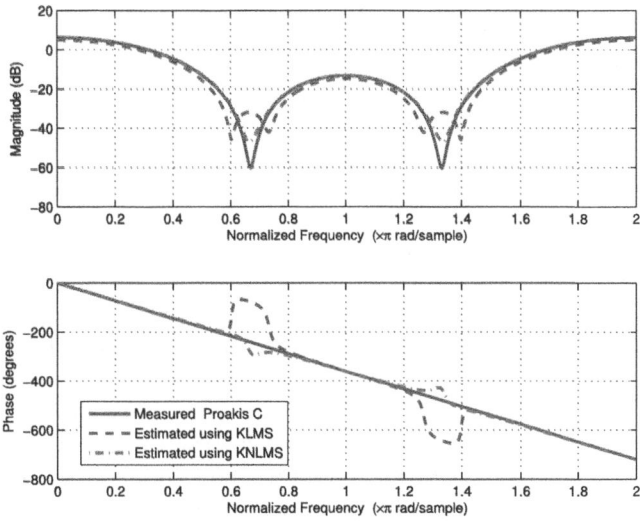

Fig. 3. Estimation of the Proakis C amplitude, for a data length $N = 3000$ and $SNR = 20$ dB.

KLMS and KNLMS algorithms. Based on these results, the KNLMS algorithm proves to be more effective than the KLMS algorithm, as it allows obtaining the same shapes of the estimated values in terms of amplitude and phase as those measured.

4.2   Output Data Estimation

In Figs. 4 and 5, the estimation of the output $d(k)$ for nonlinear system identification without binary-valued output observations is demonstrated using KLMS and KNLMS. The lower graphs depict the complete signal form for a data length of $N = 1000$, while the upper graphs focus on data lengths between 590 and 640 to provide a more detailed view of the processed signals. It should be noted that with the KNLMS algorithm, the estimated output $d(k)$ follows the true model in perfect agreement with the measured data (Fig. 5). In comparison, with the KLMS algorithm, we observe that the estimated output $d(k)$ follows the variations of the real output with some fluctuations. The performance of the KLMS algorithm degrades when estimating the output for small sample sizes $N < 100$, and we have a significant difference between the shape of the estimated and measured output (Fig. 4).

To illustrate the performance of adaptive kernel filter algorithms (KLMS and KNLMS) based on binary data output, the identification is applied to Hammerstein models with different complexities and binary output. The estimation of the binary output $s(k)$ as a function of the number of samples is presented in Figs. 6 and 7 using kernel algorithms (KNLMS and KLMS) for a signal-to-noise ratio (SNR) of $20dB$. It appears that the estimated binary output takes the same form as the measured output data. The estimation of the binary output is done with high accuracy using the KNLMS algorithm. In the case of the KLMS algorithm, we observe a difference in some samples (Fig. 6).

The KNLMS algorithm is often considered more effective than the KLMS algorithm for system identification because it can produce more accurate estimates of the output data. The main reason for this is that the KNLMS algorithm includes a normalization step that improves the stability and convergence of the algorithm. This is particularly important in noisy environments, where the impact of noise on the estimated impulse response can be reduced, leading to improved accuracy in the channel identification process.

Based on the results obtained, it can be concluded that kernel adaptive filters are effective for identifying nonlinear systems with binary output measurements. Nonlinear systems with binary output can offer various advantages. Firstly, binary output is easier to process and interpret compared to continuous output due to its simplicity, which results in lower computational and storage requirements. Secondly, binary output is more robust to noise and interference than continuous output. Binary signals are less affected by small variations or fluctuations in the input signal, thus enhancing the accuracy and reliability of the system.

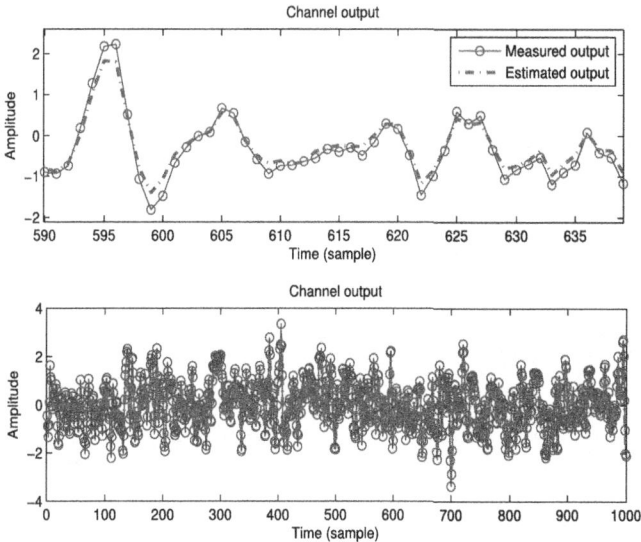

Fig. 4. Output $d(k)$ estimation using KLMS algorithm, Top: zoomed-in, between $590-640$ samples. Bottom: full 1000 samples.

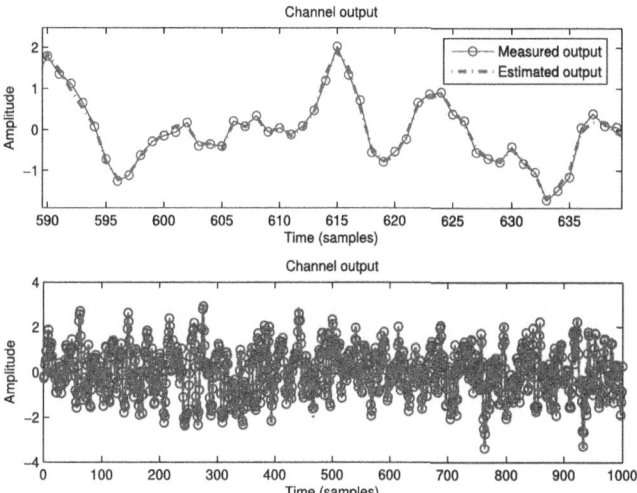

Fig. 5. Output $d(k)$ estimation using KNLMS algorithm, Top: zoomed-in, between $590-640$ samples. Bottom: full 1000 samples.

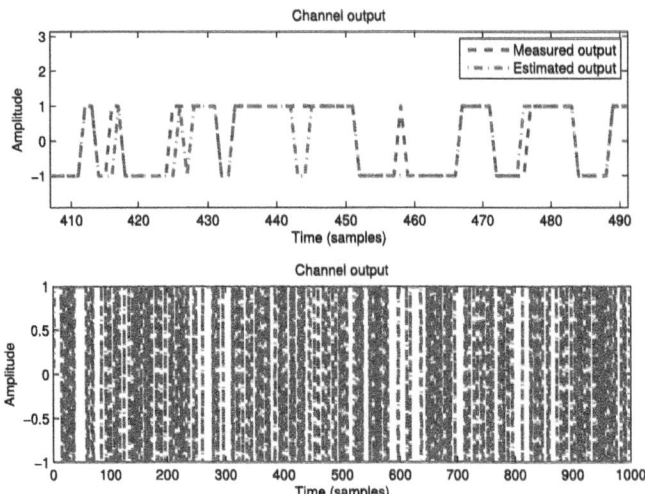

Fig. 6. Binary output $s(k)$ estimation using KLMS algorithm, Top: zoomed-in, between $410 - 590$ samples. Bottom: full 1000 samples.

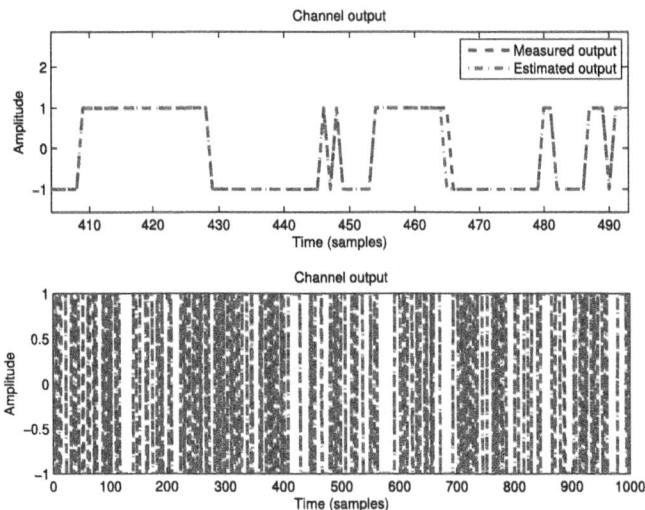

Fig. 7. Binary output $s(k)$ estimation using KNLMS algorithm, Top: zoomed-in, between $410 - 590$ samples. Bottom: full 1000 samples.

5 Conclusion

In our paper, we addressed the problem of identifying nonlinear systems with binary output data using adaptive kernel filtering algorithms. Specifically, we applied these algorithms to estimate the parameters of the Proakis channel. Through simulation, we found that the KNLMS algorithm outperformed KLMS for the Hammerstein system identification problem with binary output data, both in terms of binary output data estimation and channel impulse response parameter estimation.

In the future, we will concentrate on expanding the kernel algorithm to enable the identification of measurable frequency-selective fading radio channels.

References

1. Haykin, S.: Adaptive Filter Theory, 4th edn. Prentice Hall, Delhi (2002). ISBN: 9780130901262
2. Sondhi, M.M.: The history of echo cancellation. IEEE Signal Process. Mag. **23**(5), 95–102 (2006)
3. Sayed, A.H.: Fundamentals of Adaptive Filtering. Wiley, New York (2003)
4. Diniz, P.: Adaptive Filtering: Algorithms and Practical Implementations, 3rd edn. Springer, New York (2008)
5. Fateh, R., Darif, A., Safi, S.: Kernel and linear adaptive methods for the BRAN channels identification. In: International Conference on Advanced Intelligent Systems for Sustainable Development, pp. 579–591. Springer, Cham (2020)
6. Fateh, R., Darif, A., Safi, S.: Identification of the linear dynamic parts of wiener model using kernel and linear adaptive. In: International Conference on Advanced Intelligent Systems for Sustainable Development, pp. 387–400. Springer, Cham (2020)
7. Ferrara, E.: Fast implementations of LMS adaptive filters. IEEE Trans. Acoust. Speech Signal Process. **28**(4), 474–475 (1980). https://doi.org/10.1109/tassp.1980.1163432
8. Sanei, S., Chambers, J.A.: EEG Signal Processing. Wiley, Hoboken (2013)
9. Krstic, M., Kanellakopoulos, I., Kokotovic, P.V.: Nonlinear and Adaptive Control Design. Wiley (1995)
10. Fateh, R., Darif, A., Safi, S.: Channel identification of non-linear systems with binary-valued output observations based on positive definite kernels. In: E3S Web of Conferences, EDP Sciences, vol. 297 (2021). https://doi.org/10.1051/e3sconf/202129701020
11. Fateh, R., Darif, A., Safi, S.: Hyperbolic functions impact evaluation on channel identification based on recursive kernel algorithm. In: 2022 8th International Conference on Optimization and Applications (ICOA), Genoa, Italy, pp. 1–6 (2022). https://doi.org/10.1109/ICOA55659.2022.9934118
12. Xu, J.W., Paiva, A.R., Park, I., Principe, J.C.: A reproducing kernel Hilbert space framework for information-theoretic learning. IEEE Trans. Signal Process. **56**(12), 5891–5902 (2008)
13. Liu, W., Principe, J.C., Haykin, S.: Kernel Adaptive Filterng: A Comprehensive Introduction. Wiley, Hoboken (2011)
14. Shawe-Taylor, J., Cristianini, N.: Kernel Methods for Pattern Analysis. Cambridge University Press (2004)
15. Aronszajn, N.: Theory of reproducing kernels. Trans. Am. Math. Soc. **68**(3), 337–404 (1950)
16. Schölkopf, B., Smola, A.: Learning with Kernels: Support Vector Machines, Regularization, Optimization, and Beyond. MIT Press (2002)
17. Cortes, C., Vapnik, V.: Support-vector networks. Mach. Learn. **20**(3), 273–297 (1995). https://doi.org/10.1007/bf00994018

18. Scholkopf, B., Smola, A., Muller, K.R.: Kernel principal component analysis. In: International Conference on Artificial Neural Networks (ICANN), pp. 583–588. Springer, Heidelberg (1997)
19. Hearst, M.A., Dumais, S.T., Osuna, E., Platt, J., Scholkopf, B.: Support vector machines. IEEE Intell. Syst. Appl. **13**(4), 18–28 (1998)
20. Zidane, M., Dinis, R.: A new combination of adaptive channel estimation methods and TORC equalizer in MC-CDMA systems. Int. J. Commun. Syst. **33**(11), e4429 (2020). https://doi.org/10.1002/dac.4429
21. Zidane, M., Safi, S., Sabri, M.: Measured and estimated data of non-linear BRAN channels using HOS in 4G wireless communications. Data Brief **17**, 1136–1148 (2018)
22. Fateh, R., Darif, A., Safi, S.: Performance evaluation of MC-CDMA systems with single user detection technique using kernel and linear adaptive method. J. Telecommun. Inf. Technol. (4), 1–11 (2021). https://doi.org/10.26636/jtit.2021.151621
23. Zidane, M., Safi, S., Sabri, M.: Compensation of fading channelsusing partial combining equalizer in MC-CDMA systems. J. Telecommun. Informat. Technol. (1), 5–11 (2017). http://dlibra.itl.waw.pl/dlibra-webapp/Content/1962/ISSN_1509-4553_1_2017_5.pdf
24. Safi, S., Frikel, M., Zeroual, A., M'Saad, M.: Higher order cumulants for identification and equalization of multicarrier spreading spectrum systems. J. Telecommun. Informat. Technol. **2**(1), 74–84 (2011). https://www.itl.waw.pl/czasopisma/JTIT/2011/2/74.pdf
25. Liu, W., Pokharel, P.P., Principe, J.C.: The kernel least-mean-square algorithm. IEEE Trans. Signal Process. **56**(2), 543–554 (2008). https://doi.org/10.1109/tsp.2007.907881
26. Ciochină, S., Paleologu, C., Benesty, J.: An optimized NLMS algorithm for system identification. Signal Process. **118**, 115–121 (2016)
27. Richard, C., Bermudez, J., Honeine, P.: Online prediction of time series data with kernels. IEEE Trans. Signal Process. **57**(3), 1058–1067 (2009)
28. Fateh, R., Darif, A., Safi, S.: An extended version of the proportional adaptive algorithm based on kernel methods for channel identification with binary measurements. J. Telecommun. Inf. Technol. (3), 47–58 (2022). https://doi.org/10.26636/jtit.2022.161122
29. Ljung, L.: System Identification: Theory for the User. Prentice Hall PTR, Upper Saddle River (1999)
30. Ding, F.: System Identification-Performances Analysis for Identification Methods. Science Press, Beijing (2014)
31. Zhang, X., Ding, F., Alsaadi, F.E., Hayat, T.: Recursive parameter identification of the dynamical models for bilinear state space systems. Nonlinear Dyn. **89**(4), 2415–2429 (2017). https://doi.org/10.1007/s11071-017-3594-y
32. Xu, L.: Application of the Newton iteration algorithm to the parameter estimation for dynamical systems. J. Comput. Appl. Math. **288**, 33–43 (2015)
33. Song, Q.: Recursive identification of systems with binary-valued outputs and with ARMA noises. Automatica **93**, 106–113 (2018)
34. Guo, J., Wang, X., Xue, W., Zhao, Y.: System identification with binary-valued observations under data tampering attacks. IEEE Trans. Autom. Control **66**(8), 3825–3832 (2020)
35. Li, L., Wang, F., Zhang, H., Ren, X.: A novel recursive learning estimation algorithm of Wiener systems with quantized observations. ISA Trans. **112**, 23–34 (2021)

36. Zhang, L., Zhao, Y., Guo, L.: Identification and adaptation with binary-valued observations under non-persistent excitation condition. Automatica **138**, 110158 (2022)
37. Fateh, R., Darif, A.: Mean square convergence of reproducing kernel for channel identification: application to bran D channel impulse response. In: Fakir, M., Baslam, M., El Ayachi, R. (eds.) CBI 2021. LNBIP, vol. 416, pp. 284–293. Springer, Cham (2021). https://doi.org/10.1007/978-3-030-76508-8_20
38. Liu, W., Principe, J.C.: Kernel affine projection algorithms. EURASIP J. Adv. Signal Process. **2008**, 1–12 (2008). https://doi.org/10.1155/2008/784292

Application of Machine Learning to Additive Manufacturing Tasks: The State of the Art

Mohamed Achraf El Youbi EL Idrissi[1]($\boxtimes$) ⓘ, Loubna Laaouina[2] ⓘ, Adil Jeghal[3] ⓘ,
Hamid Tairi[1] ⓘ, and Moncef Zaki[1] ⓘ

[1] LISAC Laboratory, Faculty of Sciences Dhar EL Mehraz, Sidi Mohamed Ben Abdellah University, Fez, Morocco
achraf.elyoubi@usmba.ac.ma, {htairi,zaki.moncef}@yahoo.fr

[2] LISA Laboratory National School of Applied Sciences Sidi Mohamed Ben Abdellah University Fez, Fez, Morocco
loubna.laaouina@usmba.ac.ma

[3] LSATE Laboratory, National School of Applied Sciences, Sidi Mohamed Ben Abdellah University, Fez 30000, Morocco
adil.jeghal@usmba.ac.ma

Abstract. In Industry 4.0, additive manufacturing (AM) is increasingly turning to artificial intelligence technology and in particular to the use of Machine Learning algorithms, given their beneficial contributions, enabling among other things, to improve the manufacturing process, offer AM designers a means of doing their studies before launching into manufacturing, help manufacturers categorize part quality and study the parameters that impact the processes used in manufacturing, etc. In this synthesis article, we present a study of the applicability of Machine Learning algorithms in the field of Additive Manufacturing, with the main aim of reviewing the main tasks to which these algorithms are applied: Processing Parameter Optimization, Property Prediction, Quality Prediction, Closed-Loop Control, Geometric Deviation Control, Defect Detection and the cost estimation. To achieve this, we have focused our research on articles published mainly Pin the last five years. In addition, this manuscript paves the way for future work on the applicability of ML to other processes, other materials that can be used in manufacturing and other tasks that are related to additive manufacturing.

Keywords: Additive Manufacturing (AM) · Machine Learning (ML) ·
Processing Parameter Optimization · Quality Prediction · Closed-Loop Control ·
Cost estimation. Geometric Deviation Control · Defect Detection

1 Introduction

Additive Manufacturing (abbreviated to AM), also known as Rapid Prototyping (RP), is a 3D printing process that encompasses several classes of processes, layer by layer, and computer-guided assistance (CAD). The field of application of AM has broadened to include medical, automotive, aerospace, and other fields [1]. Due to advances in artificial intelligence (AI), and more specifically, machine learning, AM has effectively benefited

H. Hagras et al. (Eds.): ISACS 2023, CCIS 2255, pp. 30–44, 2025.
https://doi.org/10.1007/978-3-031-93448-3_3

from these contributions, resolving a number of problems that can impact the manufacturing process. In this study, we will review the application of ML to the most popular Additive Manufacturing tasks. To this end, we have organized this work as follows: in Sect. 2, we present the seven classes of AM according to the recommendation of the "American Standards Organization of Technical Material"; in Sect. 3, we discuss Machine Learning; and in Sect. 4, we present the latest research in the literature concerning the applicability of ML to the main AM tasks. The last section is reserved for discussion and conclusion.

2 Classification of AM Processes

In AM, several approaches are used to classify AM processes. The classical approach is based on the technology used in printing, such as the type of printer, the lasers used and whether extrusion is applied in the manufacturing process or not applied [2, 3].The second approach groups processes according to the materials used [4, 5]. The process classification based on the two approaches poses a problem, as it can lead to a bizarre combination of technology and material used. This is the case when we are confronted with processes with similarities concerning the machine or material used, which has a negative impact on the passage of information at the educational level. For this reason, the American Society for Testing and Materials (ASTM) and the International Organization for Standardization (ISO) have published a report classifying processes into seven types in accordance with standard 52.900 [6, 7]. In the figure below, materials are grouped according to three types (powder, solid and liquid materials) (Fig. 1):

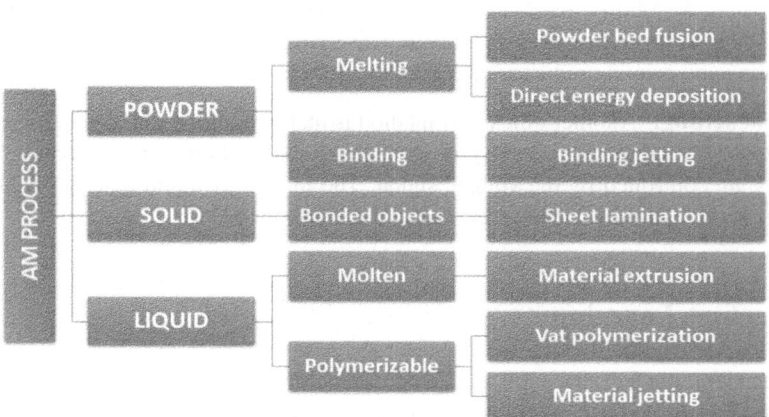

Fig. 1. Types of AM processes

In the following, we briefly present the seven AM manufacturing processes:

Powder Bed Fusion (PBF): Considered one of the first AM technologies, this process is versatile since it can be adapted to metals and polymers and can even be fabricated on ceramics or composite materials. On the market, several types of machine with distinct energy sources are used in this field, the most widely exploited being "metal powder bed fusion" with lasers as the energy source (PBF-LB/M). For PBF manufacturing, thin layers are created, each containing fine powder particles that are deposited serenely and uniformly on a platform [8].

Direct Energy Deposition (DED): Is a process whereby the substrate and material are melted and fused together in a "substrate melt", and the parts are built up in successive layers. This process is carried out by applying a targeted energy source, such as electron or laser-based beams or plasma arc beams. The material used by DED is somewhat limited, generally being either a powder or a wire [9, 10].

Binding Jetting: It's considered one of the first AM techniques created for polymer powder-based materials. The liquid binder is sprayed onto the powdered polymer with an inkjet print head. By chemical reaction bonding at a reasonable rate, the powder material solidifies in the produced part's section layer by layer [11].

Sheet Lamination: Ultrasonic Additive Manufacturing (UAM) and Laminated Object Manufacturing (LOM) are two types of additive manufacturing based on sheet lamination (SL). The bonding of the sheets of material is performed with the help of a fusion resource, such as ultrasound [12].

Material Extrusion: The most popular AM method on the market right is now material extrusion (ME), in which the materials are typically forced out through a nozzle under constant pressure in a semisolid state. The materials are then solidified and joined to the materials that were previously extruded to create a solid structure [13].

Vat Polymerization: UV light is mostly used in vat photopolymerization (VP) procedures to cure or solidify materials which may be either "photopolymers", "liquids" or "resins". These procedures can produce massive parts with submillimeter details, and the coating and printing industries frequently use them [14].

Material Jetting: Another quick AM method is material jetting (MJ), which employs ultraviolet (UV) light to primarily power solid-liquid photopolymer droplets, these droplets are controlled by the voltage signal. The melted or liquid material is blasted onto the surface of the created object through the print head [15].

3 Machine Learning

In artificial intelligence, the subfield of machine learning is considered to be a technique that uses data to perform automated learning to make predictions, control the process performed in real life, make decisions in situ, etc., among other things. ML algorithms can generally be divided into three main categories: supervised, unsupervised and reinforcement [16]. For the Supervised Learning, a pair of input-output data are available to the system, and the required result is to predict functions that are unknown. Supervised algorithms can be used for either regression or classification [17]. About Unsupervised Learning, This is a class whose input data are unlabelled and unsorted. These data are not clustered as a whole, so they have no output values. The scope of application of unsupervised approaches mainly consists of clustering data based on similarity measures, and they are also used to reduce the dimensions of data [18]. For Reinforcement Learning, This is based on training an agent to act in relation to an environment carrying a set of observations. The system's evaluated states provide either a reward or a cost in return. One of the problems encountered with these algorithms is how to assign credit and how to determine which actions lead to a reward [19].To overcome this problem, a local reward system is beneficial since global environments require a sample set with a certain number of participant-nodes [20].

4   Application of Machine Learning to AM Tasks

In what follows, we review a few articles mainly published over the last five years, whose common topic concerns the application of ML techniques to the most common AM tasks by extending another work we had done concerning the applicability of ML Fused Deposition Modeling (FDM) algorithms [21]. This review is carried out by targeting four main task categories: "process parameter optimization and property prediction", "quality prediction and closed-loop control", "geometric deviation control and defect detection" and "cost estimation". The major aim of our study can be summarized as follows: Identification of the most popular tasks related to additive manufacturing, classifying the studies according to tables showing the applicability of ML algorithms in AM and opening an avenue for discussion of the works cited.

4.1   Processing Parameter Optimization and Property Prediction

Manufacturing quality in AM is only uncertain when the part is printed according to precise parameters, and to judge the quality of the printed element, it is necessary to print a few samples and verify test performance. This requires a great deal of effort, with costs associated with the verification operation. This is why ML algorithms remain a wise choice to help designers find a close relationship between system parameters and the quality to be achieved. In other words, ML aims to solve the problem of optimizing parameters for better manufacturing quality [22]. In the table below, we present a literature review of recent works concerning the application of ML algorithms for the optimization of AM process parameters and Property Prediction (Table 1):

From the results in Table 4, we note that optimization of processing parameters can be achieved using several ML algorithms (the autoencoder, a combination of models (SMOF), RFN, GP and reinforcement learning), this study covered three processes (SLS, PBF and DED). While the algorithms (GA-ANFIS, LSTM, GBR) showed their effectiveness for part property prediction, targeting the FFF, WAAM and PBF processes. Although ML algorithms can be effectively used to optimize parameters related to the AM process, the applicability of these algorithms needs to be extended to several other additive manufacturing processing parameters in order to improve the quality of the final part.

Table 1. Some recent research into the application of ML techniques in Processing Parameter Optimization and Property Prediction tasks.

Brief introduction	Task	ML-algorithms, Measures/Output	Refs
Optimization of AM parameters using conventional autoencoders by segmenting high quality images representing these optimal parameters used during scanning and optimum laser spot distance	Processing Parameter optimization	-CNN-AutoEncoder: CNN to reduce the dimension and Autoencoder for parameters optimization -8 features on input -Optimal parameters: speed laser = 500 mm/s, thickness at 30 μm and points distance: 50 μm	[23]
An optimized metamodel based on sub-models composed of weighted techniques with study of the effect of 3 parameters: "Scan spacing", "Variable Values" and "Pulse frequency" on "relative density of the parts"	Processing Parameter optimization	-Kriging, Polynomial Regression (PR), ANN and SMOF (the best model) -Average Relative Error Magnitude (AREM) = 5.47%	[24]
Optimization of L-PBF manufacturing parameters with study of the effect of 3 parameters on porosity: "position", "orientation relative to the part" and "recycled powder fraction"	Processing Parameter optimization	-Random Forest Network (RFN) -Pore population influenced by orientation effect -Relative median pore size and distribution are influenced by the position applied to the plate	[25]
Development of an ML model to predict the depth of track remelting, taking into account the combination of laser speed and power	Processing Parameter optimization	-Gaussian Process (GP) -MAE (Mean Absolute Error) = 0,6 μm -Optimum powder bed thickness: 30 μm -Test on 24 data samples	[26]
Model for predicting the depth of the molten pool as a function of scanning speed, size and power of the laser beam	Processing Parameter optimization	-Gaussian Process (GP) -Mean Absolute Percentage Error MAPE = 6 μm	[27]
Optimization of scan speed "V", laser power "P" and melt depth using reinforcement learning approach for metal AM while maintaining melt depth in a stable state	Processing Parameter optimization	-Reinforcement learning: Q-learning approach -The optimum combination obtained by 1 mm depth of SS316-L: P = 888,9 W, V = 566,7 mm by min	[28]
Ensemble learning model for surface roughness prediction of 3D printed specimens	Property Prediction	-RF, Adaboost, Classification and Regression Trees (CART), SVR (Support vector regression), Ridge Regression, RVFL And hybrid model based on the 6 algorithms (best model) -For 40 inputs used and 90% of training data:Root mean square error (RMSE) = 0.294 and Relative error (RE) = 0.046	[29]
Development of a surface roughness prediction model using 5 ML models and based on three parameters derived from a laser sensor	Property Prediction	-ELM (Extreme learning machine), SVR, "Adaptive Neuro-Fuzzy Inference System": ANFIS, Genetic Algorithm ANFIS (GA-ANFIS) and "Particle swarm optimization ANFIS": PSO-ANFIS and GA-ANFIS (the best model) -Inputs: "Welding speed", "Overlap ratio" and "Wire feed speed" -RMSE = 0,0694, MAE = 0,0574, R2 = 0,93516 and MAPE = 14,15%	[30]

(continued)

Table 1. (*continued*)

Brief introduction	Task	ML-algorithms, Measures/Output	Refs
Proposal of a new surface roughness prediction model based on a hybrid method for selecting features relevant to ground surface roughness, also using grinding signals	Property Prediction	-RF and Long short-term memory network (LSTM), which is the best model -R2 = 0.995, RMSE (μm) = 0.013, Hardware cost = 52,500$ and Time cost = 0.640 sc	[31]
Prediction of "Tensile Modulus", "the Nominal Stress Modulus" and "Elongation at break" using five ML algorithms	Property Prediction	-Linear regressor, Gradient Boost Regressor (GBR), Decision Tree (DT) and AdaBoost regressor -GBR (is the best model) -434 parts on input -For the Tensile Modulus: R2 = 0.888 and Mean Square Error (MSE) = 916.721 -For the Nominal Stress: R2 = 0. 964 and MSE = 1.537 -For the Elongation and break: R2 = 0.987 and MSE = 0.284	[32]

4.2   Quality Prediction and Closed-Loop Control

Closed-loop control and detection of defects in manufactured parts are tasks that need to be monitored in real time, so an AM control and data acquisition system is used to improve the manufacturing process [33]. On the other hand, the choice of materials and their characteristics have an impact on the quality of the part to be manufactured; therefore, quality control of the material is desired to ensure its adequacy with the desired functionality of the product [34]. In Table 2, we review some recent research on Quality Prediction and Closed-Loop Control for AM:

Table 2. Presentation of ML algorithms used for Quality Prediction and Closed-Loop Control.

Brief introduction	Task	ML-algorithms, Measures/ Output	Refs
Prediction and control of WAAM manufacturing quality using ML with analysis and optimization of process parameters	Quality Prediction	-Regression, ANN models and Multidimensional Variability Neural Network Model (the best model) -Accuracy: "Bead Width Model" have 99,8% in prediction, "Bead Height" have 99,6% and 99,8% for "Depth of Penetration" -3 inputs: current, speed and voltage	[35]
Quantification of repeatability to L-PBF manufacturing quality using ML and standard deviation calculation, to preserve the static and mechanical properties of parts by studying the causes influencing repeatability	Quality Prediction	-Linear Regression, Support Vector Machine, Decision Tree CART (DT), RF, XGBoost, Multilayer Perceptron, K-Nearest Neighbors and Linear Discriminant Analysis -DT-CART and RF: the best models -13 parameters on input -F1-Score of DT-CART and RF > 0,9	[36]

(*continued*)

Table 2. (*continued*)

Brief introduction	Task	ML-algorithms, Measures/ Output	Refs
Development of a deep learning (DL) approach for monitoring the manufacturing process to overcome the problem of sparse or low-quality images of manufactured metal parts by adding coherent images	Quality Prediction	-Proposed deep neural network optimization architecture (best model) -Accuracy in task 1–1 (using different amounts of supervised data): 100% for beautiful weld and under melt, with 99,3% for type of over melt -Accuracy pour task 2–4 (using images that are noisy or blurred): 94% for beautiful weld, 72,8% for under melt and 54,3% for type of over melt	[37]
Inspecting droplet behavior and stabilizing the printing process (online monitoring and in situ correction) using neural networks with a vision technique	Closed Loop Control	-Neural network approach -MSE: 0.012388 at epoch 6	[38]
A closed-loop deep learning approach to failure detection and improvement for metal fabricated parts	Closed Loop Control	-Deep Convolutional Neural Networks (DCNN) and simple logistic regression -The best model is DCNN -with three data sets of 100, 150, 200 images: the accuracy using "inception v.3.0" is 93%, 95% and 98.8% -for "simple logistic regression" the precision is: 67%, 50% and 47%	[39]
Study of the change in melt bath size in real time and its impact on part manufacturing based on DL	Closed Loop Control	-CNN -2763 melt pool images -Accuracy is 91% -Time reduction of up to 90% compared with traditional approaches	[40]

ML algorithms have proved effective for in-situ closed-loop control and for predicting the mechanical properties of parts manufactured in AM. From this and the results of the above study, we deduce that deep learning (DL) is particularly used in closed-loop control, while DL and regression algorithms were used to predict part quality. We also note that only three processes were targeted in this study (WAAM, PBF and LMJP). However, the applicability of ML could also be extended to several types of process other than those cited in our study, taking into account several types of material, thus opening up a new avenue of research in this field.

4.3 Geometric Deviation Control and Defect Detection

Poor surface integrity and low precision geometry are fairly common defects encountered in AM, which hinder the manufacturing process. In this respect, ML techniques have proven their worth in helping users of AM to identify part defects and quantify the degree of geometric deviation. These algorithms can be used either to identify and detect defects in parts manufactured in AM or to optimize process parameters in real time. With the aim of providing AM designers with solutions for defects that may have an impact on sensitive areas such as medical prototypes and aerospace, where the margin of defects is always present [8, 41]. In the following, we have focused on recent articles concerning the application of ML in tasks relating to Geometric Deviation Control and fault detection (Table 3):

Table 3. Application of ML to defect detection and geometric deviation control.

Brief introduction	Task	ML-algorithms, Measures/Output	Refs
Prediction of process parameters and geometrical deviations for several parts of different shapes to optimize the design	Geometric Deviation	-CNN -98.944% of the variance e in the original deviation data of the square part, and 98.467% in that of the cylindrical part	[42]
New automated approach for intelligent control and efficient prediction of geometric deviations based on ML	Geometric Deviation	-Bayesian neural networks (the best model) and Bayesian extreme learning machine (BELM) methods: For stereolithography process A, for deviations in the plane of the test cylinder, RMSE = 0.066 and for process B, for deviations in the plane of the half-test cylinder, RMSE = 0.041	[43]
Use of DL to identify distortion defects in LBAM manufacturing based on thermal data and manufacturing process parameters	Geometric Deviation	-Developped model: CAMP (Convolutional and Artificial Neural Network for AM Prediction using Big Data) -RMSE = 24 μm at epoch 260	[44]
Use of ML to identify in situ geometric defects parts by exploring a technique called "patch" which captures data from the nearest source and target clouds	Defect Detection	-Bagging of Trees, Gradient Boosting, RF, KNN and Linear SVM -best models: Bagging and RF -the best precision was obtained on detection effectiveness on the "Plane" and "barrel" by Bagging and RF, for example on Detection Effectiveness on the "Plane" we have:F-measure = 0.7391, Accuracy 99,78% and G-mean = 0.7656	[45]
Detection and classification of manufacturing defects with part quality control using DL	Defect Detection	-CNN:VGG16, VGG16 Grad-CAM, Xception and Xception Grad-CAM -best architecture: VGG16 -Accuracy = 0.958, Precision = 0.939, Recall = 0.980 and F1 Score = 0.959	[46]

(continued)

Table 3. (*continued*)

Brief introduction	Task	ML-algorithms, Measures/Output	Refs
incremental learning model from HD images for in situ detection of geometric defects (incomplete fusion, porosity, cracks or inclusions)	Defect Detection	-Support Vector Machine (SVM) -In-situ defect detection measurements: Accuracy > 85%, Precision > 64% and Recall exceeds 60%	[47]
Classification of 3D polymer parts according to good or defective products on 3294 parts	Defect Detection	-Principal Component Analysis (PCA), Support Vector Machine (SVM) and CNN (best model) - Accuracy = 99,5%	[48]
Use of ML to detect the porosity in parts based on light signals induced in situ by melting, with localization of geometrical defects linked to the disturbed signals	Defect Detection	-Self Organizing Map (SOM) for prediction and classification (main algorithm) -K-Means for clustering -Sensitivity (true positive rates) is 61% to 94 and specificity (true negative rates) is 69% to 93%	[49]
Use of Acoustic Emission for in-situ monitoring of LPBF manufacturing based on four ML algorithms and with fault detection of "316L" data	Defect Detection	-K-means (to classify 3 types of defects: low, medium and high quality), Deep learning for classification to detect specific defects, PCA and Gaussian Mixture Models (GMM) for data dimensionality reduction and rapid anomaly detection and Variational auto-encoder (VAE): the best model for defect detection -Defect prediction rates of to the 3 quality categories respectively high, medium and low: Minimum defects (89.1% 77.4% 63.6%) Porosity (8.7% 8.4% 24.1%) and Cracks (2.2% 14.2% 12.3%)	[50]
Identification of signal disturbances in WAAM manufacturing to detect defects in parts	Defect Detection	-Support Vector Machine (SVM) - F1 Score > 90%	[51]

From the results of this study, we note that LD algorithms (neural networks in particular) are particularly used to detect geometric and. Several regression algorithms were used for defect detection (Bagging, RF, VGG16, SVM, CNN, SOM and VAE) as well as other clustering algorithms to reduce data dimensionality (PCA, GMM and K-Means). We also note that this study covers several types of process (SLM, stereolithography, LBAM, FFF, SLS, PBF and WAAM). In the literature, several works have focused on geometric deviation prediction and defect detection, but there are virtually no works combining both tasks at the same time, where the application of ML algorithms can provide several solutions in this sense.

4.4   Cost Estimation

Estimating the cost of AM remains a central element in the design of Industry 4.0.design, and Additive Manufacturing is no exception, since depending on the type of process or the type of material used, manufacturers can record very significant values for energy consumption, machine cost or even post-processing and labor. Applying ML algorithms to this type of task could help AM designers find solutions to minimize the cost of additive manufacturing. In Table 4, some recent work on the applicability of ML algorithms for predicting the cost of additive manufacturing:

Table 4. Application of ML algorithms to predict the cost in AM.

Brief introduction	Task	ML-algorithms, Measures/ Output	Refs
cost prediction based on historical data containing permanent characteristics of additive manufacturing using ML algorithms	Cost estimation	-Dynamic clustering method (based on k-means) for "variance reduction", Lasso Regressor and Elastic Net Regressor for "prediction" -135 images of input and 17 features -The prediction error of the total cost according to 4 used images for the validation are: $4.45, $0.15, $4.39 and $1.89 And for errors we have respectively: 6.51%, 0.93%, 2.1% and 5.58%	[52]
prediction of part manufacturing costs using DL and study of the effects of voxels on cost	Cost estimation	-2D CNN and 3D CNN (the best model) -120990 images -MAPE = 10,02% for optimum RGB voxel resolution of up to 256 to the power of 3	[53]
Energy consumption prediction using a set of 12 ML models	Cost estimation	-Gaussian Process Regressor (GPR) is the best model using 68 images -Explained-Variance = 99.16%,RSquared = 99.14%, MAE = 3.88 and RMSE = 5.79	[54]
Study of energy consumption in stereolithography manufacturing based on multiple part geometric parameters while using mask image projection and ML algorithms	Cost estimation	-PCA, linear regression, shallow neural network and Stacked autoencoders (SAE) -the best model is SAE -RMSE of test = 0.85%	[55]
In-situ control and stimulation of AM process behavior with heat consumption prediction using ML methods	Cost estimation	-Linear Regression, Lasso Regression, Ridge Regression, AutoRegressive Integrated Moving Average (ARIMA), DT, RF, AdaBoost and XGBoost. The best model based on bagged decision trees (50 trees) -MAE < 1% and R-Square = 0,99	[56]

(continued)

Table 4. (*continued*)

Brief introduction	Task	ML-algorithms, Measures/ Output	Refs
Energy consumption prediction in AM using hybrid ML approaches	Cost estimation	Hybrid approach: "Extreme Gradient Boosting": XGBoost) for prediction. In addition, "Density-Based Spatial Clustering Of Applications With Noise": DBSCAN for dimentionality reduction -RMSE = 130,783 kWh/kg and Model Correlation Coefficient (MCC) = 0,708	[57]
modeling and optimization of energy costs and printing time based on the multilayer perceptron	Cost estimation	-SVM, RF, XGBoost and MLP (the best model) -R2-squared > 99%, EV > 99%, MAE < 0.99%, MSE < 0.02% and RMSE < 1.36% -Dataset with 168 images	[58]

In the literature found, we find that the application of ML algorithms contributes effectively to cost reduction efforts, we also deduce that several types of algorithms can be used for this purpose, these algorithms are regression type (Net Regression, Lasso Regression, bagged decision trees), neural networks (3D CNN and SAE) or hybrid approaches. In addition, several other algorithms can be used to reduce data dimensionality (PCA, DBSCAN and K-means). However, we note that in recent research, the cost of materials, the cost of machines, the cost of labor, etc. are not found, which opens up a research avenue in this direction.

5   Discussion and Conclusion

Additive manufacturing is a vast field whose use has soared. According to the latest AM ranking, there are seven main processes according to the ASTM and ISO standards. At the same time, machine learning has covered many fields of application, including additive manufacturing, where its effectiveness has been investigated in a number of research studies covering, among other things, the tasks of: "Processing Parameter Optimization and Property Prediction", "Quality Prediction and Closed-Loop Control", "Geometric Deviation Control and Defect Detection" and "Cost estimation". In this work, we attempt to review recent work mainly from the last five years concerning the above tasks, however we note and believe that the applicability of machine learning algorithms can cover several additive manufacturing tasks.

References

1. Bahnini, I., Rivette, M., Rechia, A., Siadat, A., Elmesbahi, A.: Additive manufacturing technology: the status, applications, and prospects. Int. J. Adv. Manuf. Technol. **97**(1–4), 147–161 (2018). https://doi.org/10.1007/s00170-018-1932-y
2. Burns, M.: Automated Fabrication: Improving Productivity in Manufacturing. PTR Prentice Hall, Englewood Cliffs, N.J. (1993)
3. Kruth, J.-P., Leu, M.C., Nakagawa, T.: Progress in additive manufacturing and rapid prototyping. CIRP Ann. **47**(2), 525–540 (1998). https://doi.org/10.1016/S0007-8506(07)632 40-5
4. Kai, C.C., Fai, L.K.: Rapid Prototyping: Principles & Applications in Manufacturing. Wiley (1998)

5. Chua, C.K., Leong, K.F., Lim, C.S.: Rapid Prototyping: Principles and Applications, 2e éd. World Scientific (2003). https://doi.org/10.1142/5064

6. Godec, D., et al.: Introduction to Additive Manufacturing. In: Godec, D., Gonzalez-Gutierrez, J., Nordin, A., Pei, E., Ureña Alcázar, J. (eds.) A Guide to Additive Manufacturing, pp. 1–44. Springer International Publishing, Cham (2022). https://doi.org/10.1007/978-3-031-058 63-9_1

7. Pérez, M., Carou, D., Rubio, E.M., Teti, R.: Current advances in additive manufacturing. Procedia CIRP **88**, 439–444 (2020). https://doi.org/10.1016/j.procir.2020.05.076

8. Mahesh, M., Wong, Y.S., Fuh, J.Y.H., Loh, H.T.: Benchmarking for comparative evaluation of RP systems and processes. Rapid Prototyping J. **10**(2), 123–135 (2004). https://doi.org/10.1108/13552540410526999

9. Gibson, I., Rosen, D., Stucker, B., Khorasani, M.: Additive Manufacturing Technologies. Springer International Publishing, Cham (2021). https://doi.org/10.1007/978-3-030-56127-7

10. Shim, D.-S., Baek, G.-Y., Seo, J.-S., Shin, G.-Y., Kim, K.-P., Lee, K.-Y.: Effect of layer thickness setting on deposition characteristics in direct energy deposition (DED) process. Optics Laser Technol. **86**, 69–78 (2016). https://doi.org/10.1016/j.optlastec.2016.07.001

11. Gokuldoss, P.K., Kolla, S., Eckert, J.: Additive manufacturing processes: selective laser melting, electron beam melting and binder jetting—selection guidelines. Materials **10**(6), 672 (2017). https://doi.org/10.3390/ma10060672

12. Bhatt, P.M., Kabir, A.M., Peralta, M., Bruck, H.A., Gupta, S.K.: A robotic cell for performing sheet lamination-based additive manufacturing. Addit. Manuf. **27**, 278–289 (2019). https://doi.org/10.1016/j.addma.2019.02.002

13. Park, S.-I., Rosen, D.W., Choi, S., Duty, C.E.: Effective mechanical properties of lattice material fabricated by material extrusion additive manufacturing. Addit. Manuf. **1–4**, 12–23 (2014). https://doi.org/10.1016/j.addma.2014.07.002

14. Chartrain, N.A., Williams, C.B., Whittington, A.R.: A review on fabricating tissue scaffolds using vat photopolymerization. Acta Biomaterialia **74**, 90–111 (2018). https://doi.org/10.1016/j.actbio.2018.05.010

15. Udroiu, R., Braga, I.C., Nedelcu, A.: Evaluating the quality surface performance of additive manufacturing systems: methodology and a material jetting case study. Materials **12**(6), 995 (2019). https://doi.org/10.3390/ma12060995

16. Wang, C., Tan, X.P., Tor, S.B., Lim, C.S.: Machine learning in additive manufacturing: State-of-the-art and perspectives. Additi. Manuf. **36**, 101538 (2020). https://doi.org/10.1016/j.addma.2020.101538

17. Bonetto, R., Latzko, V.: Machine learning. In: Computing in Communication Networks, pp. 135–167. Elsevier (2020). https://doi.org/10.1016/B978-0-12-820488-7.00021-9

18. Verbraeken, J., Wolting, M., Katzy, J., Kloppenburg, J., Verbelen, T., Rellermeyer, J.S.: A survey on distributed machine learning. ACM Comput. Surv. **53**(2), 1–33 (2021). https://doi.org/10.1145/3377454

19. Kaelbling, L.P., Littman, M.L., Moore, A.W.: An introduction to reinforcement learning. In: Steels, L. (ed.) The Biology and Technology of Intelligent Autonomous Agents, pp. 90–127. Springer Berlin Heidelberg, Berlin, Heidelberg (1995). https://doi.org/10.1007/978-3-642-79629-6_5

20. Bagnell, J., Ng, A.: On Local Rewards and Scaling Distributed Reinforcement Learning (2005)

21. El Youbi El, M.A., Idrissi, L., Laaouina, A., Jeghal, H., Tairi, M. Zaki.: Application of machine learning in fused deposition modeling: a review. In: Motahhir, S., Bossoufi, B. (eds.) Digital Technologies and Applications: Proceedings of ICDTA'23, Fez, Morocco, vol. 1, pp. 114–124. Springer Nature Switzerland, Cham (2023). https://doi.org/10.1007/978-3-031-29857-8_12

22. Doshi, M., Mahale, A., Kumar Singh, S., Deshmukh, S.: Printing parameters and materials affecting mechanical properties of FDM-3D printed Parts: perspective and prospects. Mater. Today: Proc. **50**, 2269–2275 (2022). https://doi.org/10.1016/j.matpr.2021.10.003
23. Silbernagel, C., Aremu, A., Ashcroft, I.: Using machine learning to aid in the parameter optimisation process for metal-based additive manufacturing. Rapid Prototyp. J. **26**(4), 625–637 (2019). https://doi.org/10.1108/RPJ-08-2019-0213
24. Yang, Z., Eddy, D., Krishnamurty, S., Grosse, I., Lu, Y.: A super-metamodeling framework to optimize system predictability. In: Volume 1A: 38th Computers and Information in Engineering Conference, p. V01AT02A009. American Society of Mechanical Engineers, Quebec, Canada (2018). https://doi.org/10.1115/DETC2018-86055
25. Kappes, B., Moorthy, S., Drake, D., Geerlings, H., Stebner, A.: Machine learning to optimize additive manufacturing parameters for laser powder bed fusion of inconel 718. In: Ott, E., et al. (eds.) Proceedings of the 9th International Symposium on Superalloy 718 & Derivatives: Energy, Aerospace, and Industrial Applications, pp. 595–610. Springer International Publishing, Cham (2018)
26. Meng, L., Zhang, J.: Process design of laser powder bed fusion of stainless steel using a Gaussian process-based machine learning model. JOM **72**(1), 420–428 (2020). https://doi.org/10.1007/s11837-019-03792-2
27. Tapia, G., Khairallah, S., Matthews, M., King, W.E., Elwany, A.: Gaussian process-based surrogate modeling framework for process planning in laser powder-bed fusion additive manufacturing of 316L stainless steel. Int. J. Adv. Manuf. Technol. **94**(9–12), 3591–3603 (2018). https://doi.org/10.1007/s00170-017-1045-z
28. Dharmadhikari, S., Menon, N., Basak, A.: A reinforcement learning approach for process parameter optimization in additive manufacturing. Addit. Manuf. **71**, 103556 (2023). https://doi.org/10.1016/j.addma.2023.103556
29. Li, Z., Zhang, Z., Shi, J., Wu, D.: Prediction of surface roughness in extrusion-based additive manufacturing with machine learning. Robot. Comput.-Integrated Manuf. **57**, 488–495 (2019). https://doi.org/10.1016/j.rcim.2019.01.004
30. Xia, C., Pan, Z., Polden, J., Li, H., Xu, Y., Chen, S.: Modelling and prediction of surface roughness in wire arc additive manufacturing using machine learning. J. Intell. Manuf. **33**(5), 1467–1482 (2022). https://doi.org/10.1007/s10845-020-01725-4
31. Guo, W., Wu, C., Ding, Z., Zhou, Q.: Prediction of surface roughness based on a hybrid feature selection method and long short-term memory network in grinding. Int. J. Adv. Manuf. Technol. **112**(9–10), 2853–2871 (2021). https://doi.org/10.1007/s00170-020-06523-z
32. Baturynska, I.: Application Of Machine Learning Techniques To Predict The Mechanical Properties Of Polyamide 2200 (PA12) in additive manufacturing. Appl. Sci. **9**(6), 1060 (2019). https://doi.org/10.3390/app9061060
33. Everton, S.K., Hirsch, M., Stavroulakis, P.I., Leach, R.K., Clare, A.T.: Review of in-situ process monitoring and in-situ metrology for metal additive manufacturing. Mater. Des. **95**, 431–445 (2016). https://doi.org/10.1016/j.matdes.2016.01.099
34. Lanzetta, M., Sachs, E.: Improved surface finish in 3D printing using bimodal powder distribution. Rapid Prototyping J. **9**(3), 157–166 (2003). https://doi.org/10.1108/13552540310477463
35. Xiao, X., Waddell, C., Hamilton, C., Xiao, H.: Quality prediction and control in wire arc additive manufacturing via novel machine learning framework. Micromachines **13**(1), 37 (2022). https://doi.org/10.3390/mi13010137
36. Huang, D.J., Li, H.: A machine learning guided investigation of quality repeatability in metal laser powder bed fusion additive manufacturing. Mater. Des. **203**, 109606 (2021). https://doi.org/10.1016/j.matdes.2021.109606

37. Li, X., Jia, X., Yang, Q., Lee, J.: Quality analysis in metal additive manufacturing with deep learning. J. Intell. Manuf. **31**(8), 2003–2017 (2020). https://doi.org/10.1007/s10845-020-015 49-2

38. Wang, T., Kwok, T.-H., Zhou, C., Vader, S.: In-situ droplet inspection and closed-loop control system using machine learning for liquid metal jet printing. J. Manuf. Syst. **47**, 83–92 (2018). https://doi.org/10.1016/j.jmsy.2018.04.003

39. Razaviarab, N., Sharifi, S. Banadaki, Y.M.: Smart additive manufacturing empowered by a closed-loop machine learning algorithm », in Nano-, Bio-, Info-Tech Sensors and 3D Systems III. In: . Kim, J (éd.), Denver, United States: SPIE, p. 17 (2019). https://doi.org/10.1117/12. 2513816

40. Yang, Z., Lu, Y., Yeung, H., Krishnamurty, S.: Investigation of deep learning for real-time melt pool classification in additive manufacturing. In: 2019 IEEE 15th International Conference on Automation Science and Engineering (CASE), pp. 640–647. IEEE, Vancouver, BC, Canada (2019). https://doi.org/10.1109/COASE.2019.8843291

41. Grasso, M., Colosimo, B.M.: Process defects and in situ monitoring methods in metal powder bed fusion: a review. Meas. Sci. Technol. **28**(4), 044005 (2017). https://doi.org/10.1088/1361-6501/aa5c4f

42. Zhu, Z., Ferreira, K., Anwer, N., Mathieu, L., Guo, K., Qiao, L.: Convolutional Neural Network for geometric deviation prediction in Additive Manufacturing. Procedia CIRP **91**, 534–539 (2020). https://doi.org/10.1016/j.procir.2020.03.108

43. de Souza Borges, R., Ferreira, A Sabbaghi, Huang, Q.: Automated geometric shape deviation modeling for additive manufacturing systems via bayesian neural networks. IEEE Trans. Automat. Sci. Eng. **17**(2), 584–598 (2020). https://doi.org/10.1109/TASE.2019.2936821

44. Francis, J., Bian, L.: Deep learning for distortion prediction in laser-based additive manufacturing using big data. Manuf. Lett. **20**, 10–14 (2019). https://doi.org/10.1016/j.mfglet.2019. 02.001

45. Li, R., Jin, M., Paquit, V.C.: Geometrical defect detection for additive manufacturing with machine learning models. Mater. Des. **206**, 109726 (2021). https://doi.org/10.1016/j.matdes. 2021.109726

46. Westphal, E., Seitz, H.: A machine learning method for defect detection and visualization in selective laser sintering based on convolutional neural networks. Addit. Manuf. **41**, 101965 (2021). https://doi.org/10.1016/j.addma.2021.101965

47. Gobert, C., Reutzel, E.W., Petrich, J., Nassar, A.R., Phoha, S.: Application of supervised machine learning for defect detection during metallic powder bed fusion additive manufacturing using high resolution imaging. Addit. Manuf. **21**, 517–528 (2018). https://doi.org/10. 1016/j.addma.2018.04.005

48. Narayanan, B.N., Beigh, K., Loughnane, G., Powar, N.U.: Support vector machine and convolutional neural network based approaches for defect detection in fused filament fabrication. In: Zelinski, M.E., Taha, T.M., Howe, J., Awwal, A.A., Iftekharuddin, K.M. (eds.) Applications of Machine Learning, San Diego, United States: SPIE, p. 36 (2019). https://doi.org/10. 1117/12.2524915

49. Taherkhani, K., Eischer, C., Toyserkani, E.: An unsupervised machine learning algorithm for in-situ defect-detection in laser powder-bed fusion. J. Manuf. Proc. **81**, 476–489 (2022). https://doi.org/10.1016/j.jmapro.2022.06.074

50. Ghayoomi Mohammadi, M., Mahmoud, D., Elbestawi, M.: On the application of machine learning for defect detection in L-PBF additive manufacturing. Optics Laser Technol. **143**, 107338 (2021). https://doi.org/10.1016/j.optlastec.2021.107338

51. Li, Y., et al.: A defect detection system for wire arc additive manufacturing using incremental learning. J. Ind. Inform. Integrat. **27**, 10029 (2022). https://doi.org/10.1016/j.jii.2021.100291

52. Chan, S.L., Lu, Y., Wang, Y.: Data-driven cost estimation for additive manufacturing in cybermanufacturing. J. Manuf. Syst. **46**, 115–126 (2018). https://doi.org/10.1016/j.jmsy.2017.12.001

53. Ning, F., Shi, Y., Cai, M., Xu, W., Zhang, X.: Manufacturing cost estimation based on a deep-learning method. J. Manuf. Syst. **54**, 186–195 (2020). https://doi.org/10.1016/j.jmsy.2019.12.005

54. Idrissi, M.A.E.Y.E., Laaouina, L., Jeghal, A., Tairi, H., Zaki, M.: Energy consumption prediction for fused deposition modelling 3D printing using machine learning. Appl. Syst. Innov. **5**(4), 86 (2022). https://doi.org/10.3390/asi5040086

55. Yang, Y., He, M., Li, L.: Power consumption estimation for mask image projection stereolithography additive manufacturing using machine learning based approach. J. Cleaner Product. **251**, 119710 (2020). https://doi.org/10.1016/j.jclepro.2019.119710

56. Paul, A., et al.: A real-time iterative machine learning approach for temperature profile prediction in additive manufacturing processes (2019)

57. Li, Y., Hu, F., Qin, J., Ryan, M., Wang, R., Liu, Y.: A hybrid machine learning approach for energy consumption prediction in additive manufacturing. In: Del Bimbo, A., et al. (eds.) Pattern Recognition. ICPR International Workshops and Challenges: Virtual Event, January 10–15, 2021, Proceedings, Part IV, pp. 622–636. Springer International Publishing, Cham (2021). https://doi.org/10.1007/978-3-030-68799-1_45

58. Idrissi, M.A.E.Y.E., Laaouina, L., Jeghal, A., Tairi, H., Zaki, M.: Modeling of energy consumption and print time for FDM 3D printing using multilayer perceptron network. J. Manuf. Mater. Process. **7**(4), 128 (2023). https://doi.org/10.3390/jmmp7040128

Sentiment Analysis for Moroccan Dialect Using the Model of Machine Learning

Sara El Ouahabi[1][✉], Safâa El Ouahabi[2][ID], and El Wardani Dadi[1]

[1] SOVIA Team, LSA, National School of Applied Sciences, Abdelmalek Essaadi University, Tétouan, Morocco
saraelouahabi18@gmail.com
[2] Laboratory of Applied Mathematics and Information Systems, Polydisciplinary Faculty of Nador, Mohammed First University, Oujda, Morocco

Abstract. Since the advent of social networks, the scientific community working on NLP has been increasingly interested in developing automatic sentiment analysis and opinion-mining tools. Currently, most of the proposed works deal with Indo-European languages, especially English. However, a large community of people who use dialectics is not yet targeted. In this work, we are interested in the Moroccan Arabic dialect (MAD). Our primary focus, in this sense, is to determine the polarity of a given text statement. For the dataset, we have used data that are collected from different social networks (Facebook, Twitter, YouTube, Instagram, and Websites). Indeed, to our knowledge, there is no publicly available MAD dataset based on all social networks for the sentiment analysis task. Moreover, our collected data dataset is the largest Moroccan dataset created for sentiment analysis. It is characterized by its size, its quality, and its variety. We describe the methodology we evolved for collecting, preprocessing, feature extraction, and polarity classification using various supervised machine learning algorithms.

Keywords: Sentiment Analysis · Machine learning · Moroccan Dialect dataset · Natural language processing (NLP)

1 Introduction

With the growing number of online reviews, opinions, and ratings, analysis of expression of opinion has taken on great importance of companies looking to identify the strengths and the weaknesses of their products and services to adjust their offer accordingly. Studying online opinion trends allows companies to better position their products, identify consumer demands and measure their brand image. The first studies on sentiment analysis in texts appeared in 2001 [1], has proven the impact of social media on human behavior, which is reflected in their decisions. Therefore, extracting news from social media platforms and analyzing feelings guide companies to make appropriate decisions.

Sentiment analysis refers to opinions mining, which is a field that researchers use to analyze opinions, trends, evaluations, behavior, feelings, and attitudes

H. Hagras et al. (Eds.): ISACS 2023, CCIS 2255, pp. 45–58, 2025.
https://doi.org/10.1007/978-3-031-93448-3_4

of people towards a specific thing, such as services, issues, events, and topics, according to a body of text. This is done by applying different methods of Natural language processing and, textual analysis and information extracted from unstructured texts [2,3]. Over the last two decades, Morocco has experienced a clear transition from traditional modes of expression to digital media, which is represented by the use of social networking pages. The Internet has become the global system of interconnected computer networks for the dissemination and circulation of information, discussion, and dialogue. The number of Internet users in Morocco is 20 million people out of 35 million inhabitants [4], also the use of social media applications (YouTube, Facebook, Instagram, TikTok, Twitter, and Snapchat) has grown remarkably in recent years, with, the spread of smartphones and fourth generation Internet connections.

Numerous studies have explored sentiment analysis in Arabic dialects across various Arab countries [5–27]. However, when focusing on the Moroccan context, a handful of works have delved into sentiment analysis for Darija [27–31]. These studies have primarily concentrated on Twitter posts and have employed machine learning algorithms to categorize sentiment in Moroccan Arabic text. Additionally, some efforts have been directed toward crafting sentiment analysis tools tailored specifically for the Moroccan Arabic dialect.

To our knowledge, there are no data sets available to the public for sentiment analysis tasks. These challenges led us to develop a large-scale and multi-domain dataset for the Moroccan Arabic dialect sentiment analysis. We propose in this work the application of the supervised approach, this approach involves four consecutive tasks: Data collection, text preprocessing, feature extraction, and sentiment classification. We used almost all kinds of supervised machine learning methods (LinearSVC, Random Forest, Decision Tree, etc.).

The paper is organized as follows: Sect. 2 presents the sentiment analysis and the characteristics of the Arabic Language, the specificities of Modern Standard Arabic, and the Moroccan Arabic dialectal. Sections 3 and 4 present data collection and data annotation, then, we present in Sect. 5, the different NLP pre-processing steps for the Arabic language. Sections 6 and 7 define the set of machine learning techniques (BOW and TFIDF) that aim at representing the words or sentences of a text by vectors of real numbers and the models of machine learning that we use. Finally, we discuss the obtained result and present our future work.

2   Sentiment Analysis and the Moroccan Arabic Dialect

The Arabic community has recognized an evolution in the use of the Web and especially social networks(Facebook, Tweeter, YouTube, Instagram...). These technologies are considered the most platform in which users post a lot of comments to express their opinions, feelings, and other information. This makes the social media platform a rich source of data for data mining and sentiment analysis. It is important to mention that the Arabic language is among the most spoken languages in the world. It is one of the six official languages of the world [32]. It is the official language of 26 countries and is spoken by over 245 million people in the Arab world [33]. On the web, Arabic is ranked as the fourth most used language [34]. The Arabic language is classified as a Semitic language and can be divided into three general types (Classical Arabic al Arabiya al Fusha; Modern or standard Arabic, al-luga al Fusha, and Dialectal Arabic).

Dialectal Arabic is the third type of Arabic language [27], and is used in the daily interactions of Arabic speakers and is the most used on the web, the majority of Arabic speakers express their feelings and opinions in dialect. This type differs from country to country or even region to region. Also Arabic dialectal differs from MSA syntactically, morphologically, and phonologically. Moreover, dialects do not have standard spellings. With the spread of online social interaction in the Arab world, dialects have begun to find their way into online social interaction. Several factors make dialects different. Different dialects may make different lexical choices to express concepts, although in many cases the lexical choices have their Arabic language [35]. The Fig. 1 shows the difference between three dialects (Moroccan, Egyptian, Iraqi) for saying 'want'.

MSA	Orid اريد
Maroc	Bghit بغيت
Egypte	Awiz عاوز
Iraq	Abi ابى

Fig. 1. The table shows the difference between three dialects (Moroccan, Egyptian, Iraqi) for saying 'want'

In our research, we focus our interest on the study of the Moroccan Arabic dialectal or Darija. It is the native and natural language of Arabic speakers in Morocco [9]. There are different regional varieties of darija, which makes it gives great vitality. Darija is the language of communication used in Morroco in its private and informal forms. Indeed, the darija has gained ground over several levels: from educational to religious, from private to public, from artistic to cultural, and from political to virtual. In short, the darija is much more visible than it was before. This work aims to perform an analysis of the sentiments extracted from Moroccan darija texts, using supervised machine learning approaches. To do this, we have to perform and follow several steps, starting with data collection, then data preprocessing, feature extraction, sentiment classifications, and finally model evaluation. In the following sections, we will give details for each step.

3   Data Collection

The data collection phase consists in assembling a corpus which is considered the primary key of sentiment analysis, as it is used to train and evaluate the system. Although one of the main challenges of sentiment analysis in Arabic is the lack of sentiment analysis corpora. Our main contribution to this work is to create a large dataset of Moroccan dialect dataset extracted from different social networks and annotated. As far as we know, this dataset is the largest Moroccan dataset created for sentiment analysis. It is featured by its size, its given quality, and variety. First, we used the website statista.com, to obtain statistics on the most popular and most used networks in the world in January 2022. Facebook, the market leader, was the first social network to surpass one billion registered accounts and had more than two billion monthly active users. The video hosting and social media website YouTube, with 2,562 billion active users, and the photo-sharing application Instagram, ranked fourth, had 1.47 billion active accounts. The Fig. 2 shows the ranking of the most popular social networks in the world in January 2022, according to the number of active users.

To gather a large amount of data through multiple social media platform and websites, we use Python libraries and tools. Python is an ideal programming language for web scraping because of its user readability, and a wide range of Python web scraping libraries and tools that make web scraping seamless. Python has become the most popular language for web scraping because of its built-in libraries specifically designed for web scraping. With libraries like Numpy, Matplotlib, and Pandas, Python provides developers with an extensive range of tools and services to scrape and manipulate web data.

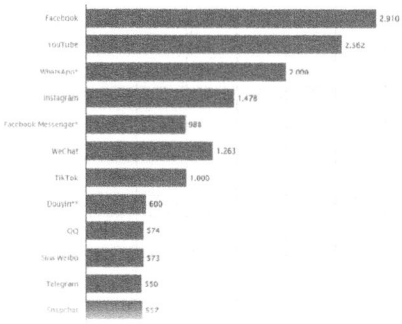

Fig. 2. Figure represents the ranking of the most popular social networks in the world in January 2022

Then, we used tools to extract data from these social media pages (Facebook, Twitter, YouTube, Instagram), and collect all the comments, tweets and store them in CSV format. Figure 3 showcases data statistics gathered from various social networks. The collection includes approximately 23,843 entries from

YouTube, 11,658 from Facebook, 11,422 from Instagram, 1,619 from Twitter, and additional data from various other websites. We were able to collect 50,341 messages (positive,négative and neutral) over several weeks.

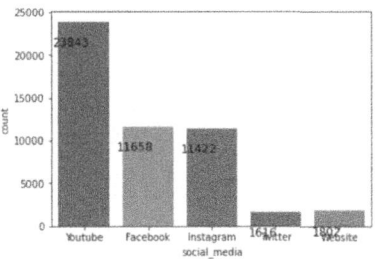

Fig. 3. Statistics on data collected from different types of social networks

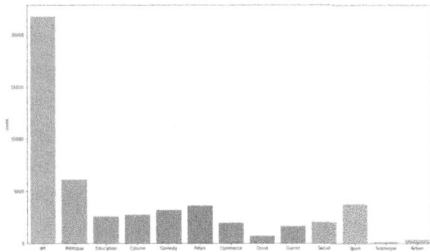

Fig. 4. Statistics derived from data collected across various social media platforms.

The data are collected from different types of social networks Facebook, YouTube, Instagram, Twitter, and Websites, written only in Morrocan Arabic dialect, related to different domains islamic, political, social, and sport.

To illustrate the frequency of tokens in the dataset corresponding to a specific domain, we use graphical representations of word frequency that give greater prominence to words that appear more frequently in a source text. The larger the word in the visual the more common the word was in the document. The Figs. 6, 7, 8, and 9 show the occurrences of words for the domains.

4 Data Annotation

Data annotation is the process of labeling or tagging data with specific information or attributes to make it useful for training machine learning models. It involves manually or automatically adding annotations or metadata to raw data to provide context, meaning, or classification to the data points.

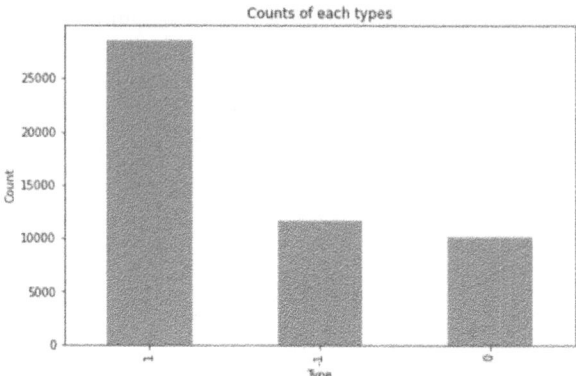

Fig. 5. Word occurrences for the three classes

Data annotation is the most important task in machine learning. If the data is poorly annotated, the performance of our learning system will decrease. For message annotation, the manual annotation method was chosen.

The manual annotation allowed us to ensure the quality of the data and its labels. It involves human experts carefully reviewing and labeling data based on specific guidelines or criteria. Manual annotation is often preferred when dealing with complex or subjective data that requires human judgment, such as semantic understanding, sentiment analysis, or nuanced classifications.

In situations where resources and tools are limited, such as for languages like Darija, manual annotation may be the sole feasible option for dataset creation and is crucial for safeguarding endangered languages. While manual annotation offers benefits, it entails a significant expenditure of time and financial resources.

Classification is always easier to do with a minimum number of categories because the more classes there are, the more chances the algorithm has to make mistakes. For the sake of simplification, we have chosen to use positive, negative, and neutral annotations.Figure 5 illustrates the class distribution, with a notable prevalence of the positive class compared to the negative and neutral classes.

We managed to collect data that covers all types of text such as social media (Facebook, Twitter, YouTube, Instagram), in the Arabic dialect, and that our data is representative of the actual distribution of feelings (positive, negative, neutral). We were able to annotate 50,341 messages over several weeks related to the different domains of art, comedy, commerce, Covid, cooking, education, parties, war, islam, politics, social, and sport and all trends from 2020 to now as shown in Fig. 4. The data collected come from different types of social networks of users written in Arabic dialect.

Fig. 6. Occurrence of words for the field of social

Fig. 7. Occurrence of words for the political domain

5   Data Pre-processing

Pre-processing techniques are an essential step for Arabic text, especially dialectal Arabic due to its unstructured form. Indeed, texts generated by social media include informal writing, errors, the use of abbreviations, and non-compliance with grammatical rules. So we need to deal with unstructured text.

The aim is to remove everything that is not useful for our sentiment analysis study. The pre-processing step includes the removal of punctuation, stop words, hashtags, numbers, emojis, latin words, arabizi, and normalization.

By analyzing our data, we noticed that it contained a high content of noise, which makes it very difficult to process them automatically. We have stored this data in .csv format (Fig. 10), ready to be analyzed in more detail.

We start the preprocessing of the data by converting the polarities, 1 for pos and −1 for neg, and 0 for neu. The rest of the data preprocessing steps are presented in the following paragraphs.

- Normalization: also known as the standardization process, which consists of converting the document into a standard format that is easy to handle. normalization aims at normalizing some letters that have different shapes in the same word to a shape. For example, normalization of [آ][aleph mad], [إ][aleph with hamza below] and [أ][aleph with hamza above] to [ا][aleph]. Another example, the normalization of [ئ][hamza over yae] and [ؤ][hamza over waw]

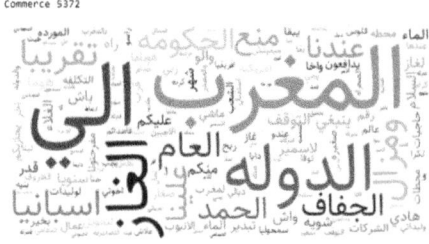

Fig. 8. Occurrence of words for the field of commerce

Fig. 9. Occurrence of words for the field of sport

	text	sentiment	word_count	char_count	avg_char_per_word	stopwords	emoji_count
8117	...قاع الناس اللي ساهمو في إنتاج ونشر هذا العمل س	1	442	2280	4.378571	82	0
46431	خي ايا بعلي دخم Adam Amin 01 01 à 17 03	0	330	1506	5.117391	13	4
16475	...باريي نفرج همكم ديروني هتكم أوحدة منكم مثلو	0	278	1366	4.500000	36	0
37328	...سلام جيت نحاوز لكم واحد الحاجة بالنسبة لكاتلب	0	224	751	3.940299	21	0
9152	...انا على حسب ما فهمت هو القصة ديال سيرة ناكية د	0	219	939	3.659898	55	0
24273	...سلام عليكم انا اليوم جيت قاصداكم و المقصود ال	0	215	1079	4.042056	55	0
38223	...بعيدت عير نفهم تقي اش باعا كفاش الانسان مكمرش	-1	211	1105	4.282297	35	0
48804	الجهل عند البعض عرب المغرب سيستغل محطة لنحو	-1	207	982	4.409091	37	0
36501	...سلام عليكم انا اليوم جيت قاصداكم و المقصود ال	0	205	1030	4.049020	51	0
39013	...الجماااااااااال باحني	1	192	215	12.000000	0	0

Fig. 10. The figure represents the text before cleaning

to [ء][hamza]. Normalization of [ى] to [ي]. Removing diacritics such as «آ ، أ ، أَ» because These signs placed above or below the Arabic letters can modify the meaning of a single word.

- Remove repetitions.
- Convert text written in Latin to Arabic.
- Removal of stop words: are words that add no feeling to the text and do not convey information such as (since منذ) (for لاجل), which appear in sentences

and have no meaning or indication of the context; we have created a list containing specific Arabic and Moroccan stop words, which we have eliminated from our dataset. we have also retained certain negative prepositions.

- Punctuation removal: aims to remove punctuation symbols.
- Removal of hashtags: aims to remove hashtags (phrases that start with the # symbol), as they are not useful in our approach.
- Removal of numbers and URLs.
- Transformation of emojis into words: aims to transform emojis into words, replace each emoji with a word [حب، مضحك، عادي، محزن], so we used a CSV file that contains emojis with their transformations into Arabic words. In this way, we do not lose the feeling expressed by these emojis.
- Emoji removal: aims to remove emojis that were not translated in the emoji-to-word transformation step.
- Remove all usernames (ex, @username), hashtags, URLs (ex, https://www.example.com/ re-tweet signs (ex, RT), punctuation marks, extra whitespace, and non-Arabic word. After cleaning, the cleaned data is saved in a new .csv file.
- Tokenization by splitting texts into a sequence of tokens based on white-space characters. This step allows us to model a text as a vector of words that can be treated in the next stages of the processing phase.

The Fig. 11 represents the text after cleaning.

6   Features Extraction

It is important to remember that the development of a classification model requires the identification of relevant features in the data set. Hence, the feature extraction phase is a very important step in the process of text classification based on machine learning, this feature extraction step aims at transforming the data from textual data to numerical data. In addition, feature extraction transforms the original features into more meaningful features. The vector representation of features enables the classifier to perform the classification process efficiently. In this work, we will use BOW(bag-of-words) and TFIDF (term frequency-inverse document frequency) feature extraction techniques.

	text	sentiment	word_count	char_count	avg_char_per_word	stopwords	emoji_count
8117	...عاع الناس ساهمو انتاج ونشر العمل سواء مباشر عبر	1	314	1803	4.745223	0	0
46431	...ادام امين خلي ابلا بغيلي لخدمي الدار تحمي احلا	0	216	1173	4.435185	17	0
16475	...ياربي افرج همكم ديرولي خلكم اوحده منكم مظلومتي	0	189	1100	4.825397	3	0
38223	...يخيت لهم لتي اش باها كهاش كهادش الانسان مكهدرش النع	-1	154	900	4.850649	0	0
36665	...كثره التفكير وتضخيم الامور سب كامل المشاكل الن	0	146	914	5.267123	0	0
37356	...سلام اخوتي مزاوكه فيكوم شوف حالتي راني تغيره	0	136	757	4.573529	0	0
49846	...اولا الاخ كمال انت تخلط امرين علاقه بينهما فحا	0	131	764	4.839695	0	0
24273	...لسلام جيت قاصداكم المقصود نتمنا منصحكوش عليا ان	0	130	754	4.807692	0	0
48685	...سوال بسيط يوحدو فالعالم ضاهش الشدا عاش الدول	-1	129	830	5.441860	1	0
24362	...فلتها مرارا وتكرارا واكرها مره اخرا يجب طبينا	0	129	907	6.038760	0	0
48918	...جراء فا موريداتيا لادمول مشروع الوهم اليوب الغ	0	127	847	5.677165	0	0
9152	فهمت القصه سيره داتيه مصطفا ناس جنب الحيط المج...	0	127	686	4.409449	0	0

Fig. 11. The figure represents the text after cleaning

7   Sentiment Classification

The next step after feature extraction is the sentiment classification step. Sentiment classification, also known as sentiment analysis, is a natural language processing (NLP) task that involves determining the sentiment or subjective opinion expressed in a piece of text. The goal of sentiment classification is to classify text into predefined sentiment categories such as positive, negative, or neutral.

In the context of sentiment analysis, there are multiple approaches to determining the emotional tone of sentences. In our specific approach, we rely on Machine Learning Classification. This involves training a sentiment classifier using a labeled dataset. A variety of machine learning algorithms, and deep learning models or Transformers, can be utilized for this purpose. Once the model is trained, it becomes capable of predicting the sentiment polarity of new sentences based on their distinctive features, which may encompass word embedding's, n-grams, or other linguistic characteristics.

We used five classifiers: Decision Tree, MultinomialNB, LinearSVC, RandomForest, Logistic Regression. We test each classifier with two different feature extraction techniques (TF-IDF, BOW) to compare the impact of features.

8   Results and Discussion

For the classification step, the constructed datasets were randomly distributed in the subset training with 80% and the test subset with the remaining 20%, to test the performance of the developed models.

Several algorithms have been used for classification and discrimination, including DecisionTree, MultinomialNB, LinearSVC RandomForest and Logistic Regression.

Table 1. the results obtained after applying the algorithms

Classifier	BOW	TFIDF
Decision Tree Classifier	74%	72%
Multinomial NB	74%	73%
Linear SVC	74%	79%
Random Forest Classifier	56%	76%
Logistic Regression Classifier	75%	78%

Table 1 presents the accuracy obtained by applying our five classifiers for the two vectorization methods (BOW, TF-IDF), which were tested on data collected in the framework of this project.

- LinearSVC with TF-IDF appears to be the best-performing model in terms of accuracy, achieving 79%. It seems that TF-IDF, with its ability to capture the importance of words, works well for this dataset.
- Naive Bayes models, both MultinomialNB with BOW and TF-IDF, performed consistently well with accuracies of 74% and 73%, respectively.
- Decision Trees, whether using BOW or TF-IDF, yielded similar accuracy scores, but they were slightly outperformed by other models.
- Random Forest performed better with TF-IDF than BOW, suggesting that TF-IDF features may have helped in better feature selection.
- Logistic Regression showed competitive performance with both BoW and TF-IDF.

In terms of performance, the best-developed models are those obtained with the classifier Logistic Regression for the two vectorization methods BOW and TFIDF, and the LinearSVC classifier for the TFIDF method. Against the Decision Tree model which showed less performance with an accuracy of 72% than MultinomialNB. Indeed, the highest accuracy, 79%, was given from the LinearSVC experiment + TFIDF.

The choice of the best model ultimately depends not only on accuracy but also on other metrics (e.g., precision, recall, F1-score) and the specific objectives of our project. It's also important to consider model interpretability, computational resources, and the potential need for further hyperparameter tuning when selecting the final model. Those different parameters will be treated in futures works.

Remember that the Moroccan dialect is a rich and culturally significant language variant, and working with it requires attention to linguistic details and a deep understanding of its nuances. It's also an exciting area for NLP research and applications, as it can help support communication and information access for Moroccan Arabic speakers.

There are instances in our dialect where sentences may appear positive at first glance but, in reality, convey a different meaning. This phenomenon can be attributed to various factors:

- Sarcasm and Irony: Dialects, much like standard languages, frequently employ sarcasm or irony as a means of indirectly expressing opinions or emotions. In such cases, a sentence that appears positive may actually serve as a form of mockery or criticism.
- Linguistic Idiosyncrasies: Certain dialects may possess distinctive linguistic characteristics or idiomatic expressions that may be perplexing to individuals not familiar with them. These peculiarities can lead to sentences appearing positive when they are, in fact, not.

Due to these reasons, we find it necessary to explore other approaches in our future works, such as Hybrid Approaches and Probabilistic Models, particularly when addressing dialectal variations or situations involving ambiguous sentiments.

The results obtained are very satisfactory even if the corpus is imbalanced.

9   Conclusion

In this paper, we focus our study on Moroccan dialect sentiment analysis in different social networks, we have collected and manually annotated a rich dataset from different social media (Facebook, Twitter, YouTube, Instagram, and website). Our dataset is characterized by its size (50,341), quality, and variety (covering a lot of domains). To determine the sentiment polarity of Moroccan Arabic dialect text statements, we tested a range of machine learning algorithms. The results obtained from these experiments show promise and are encouraging.

In future work, we intend to expand the dataset further, explore deep learning models, and investigate techniques for extracting additional features to enhance the accuracy of multi-class classification.

References

1. Liu, B.: Sentiment Analysis and Opinion Mining. Morgan & Claypool Publishers (2012)
2. Khader, M., Awajan, A., Al-Naymat, G.: Sentiment analysis based on mapreduce: a survey. In: ACM International Conference on Proceeding, pp. 1–8 (2018). https://doi.org/10.1145/3291280.3291795
3. Oueslati, O., Cambria, E., HajHmida, M.B., Ounelli, H.: A review of sentiment analysis research in Arabic language. Futur. Gener. Comput. Syst. **112**, 408–430 (2020). https://doi.org/10.1016/j.future.2020.05.034
4. Kemp, S.: Digital 2022: morocco. https://datareportal.com/reports/digital-2022-morocco. Accessed 2022
5. Shoukry, A., Rafea, A.: Preprocessing Egyptian dialect tweets for sentiment mining. In: Fourth Workshop on Computational Approaches to Arabic-Script Based Languages, pp. 47–56 (2012). https://aclanthology.org/2012.amta-caas14.7
6. Mazari, A.C., Djeffal, A.: Sentiment analysis of Algerian dialect using machine learning and deep learning with word2vec. Informatica (2022). https://doi.org/10.31449/inf.v46i6.3340

7. Al-Horaibi, L., Khan, M.: Sentiment analysis of Arabic tweets using text mining techniques, p. 100111F (2016). https://doi.org/10.1117/12.2242187

8. Al-Twairesh, N., Al-Khalifa, H., Al-Salman, A., Al-Ohali, Y.: Arasentitweet: a corpus for Arabic sentiment analysis of Saudi tweets. Procedia Comput. Sci. **117**, 63–72 (2017). https://doi.org/10.1016/j.procs.2017.10.094

9. Al-Ayyoub, M., Essa, S.B., Alsmadi, I.: Lexicon-based sentiment analysis of Arabic tweets. Int. J. Soc. Netw. Mining **2**, 101–114 (2015). https://doi.org/10.1504/IJSNM.2015.072280

10. Baly, R., El-Khoury, G., Moukalled, R., Aoun, R., Hajj, H., Shaban, K.B., El-Hajj, W.: Comparative evaluation of sentiment analysis methods across Arabic dialects. Procedia Comput. Sci. **117**, 266–273 (2017). https://doi.org/10.1016/j.procs.2017.10.118

11. Ben Salamah, J., Elkhlifi, A.: Microblogging opinion mining approach for Kuwaiti dialect. In: International Conference of Computer Technology and Information Management, pp. 388–396 (2014)

12. Duwairi, R., Al-Refai, M., Khasawneh, N.: Stemming versus light stemming as feature selection techniques for Arabic text categorization. In: 2007 Innovations in Information Technologies (IIT), pp. 446–450 (2007). https://doi.org/10.1109/IIT.2007.4430403

13. Duwairi, R.: Sentiment analysis for dialectical Arabic (2015). https://doi.org/10.1109/IACS.2015.7103221

14. El-Beltagy, S.R., El Kalamawy, M., Soliman, A.B.: NileTMRG at SemEval- 2017 task 4: Arabic sentiment analysis. In: Proceedings of the 11th International Workshop on Semantic Evaluation (SemEval-2017), pp. 790–795 (2017). https://doi.org/10.18653/v1/S17-2133

15. El-Masri, M., Altrabsheh, N., Mansour, H., Ramsay, A.: A web-based tool for Arabic sentiment analysis. Procedia Comput. Sci. **117**, 38–45 (2017). https://doi.org/10.1016/j.procs.2017.10.092

16. Heikal, M., Torki, M., El-Makky, N.: Sentiment analysis of Arabic tweets using deep learning. Procedia Comput. Sci. **142**, 114–122 (2018). https://doi.org/10.1016/j.procs.2018.10.466

17. Akerkar, R., Sajja, P.: Knowledge-Based Systems. Jones & Bartlett Publishers (2009)

18. Bettiche, M., Mouffok, M.Z., Zakaria, C.: Opinion mining in social networks for Algerian dialect. In: Medina, J., Ojeda-Aciego, M., Verdegay, J.L., Perfilieva, I., Bouchon-Meunier, B., Yager, R.R. (eds.) IPMU 2018. CCIS, vol. 855, pp. 629–641. Springer, Cham (2018). https://doi.org/10.1007/978-3-319-91479-4_52

19. Mataoui, M., Zelmati, O., Boumechache, M.: A proposed lexicon-based sentiment analysis approach for the vernacular Algerian Arabic. Res. Comput. Sci. **110**, 55–70 (2016)

20. Mdhaffar, S., Bougares, F., Esteve, Y., Hadrich-Belguith, L.: Sentiment analysis of Tunisian dialects: linguistic resources and experiments. In: Third Arabic Natural Language Processing Workshop (WANLP), pp. 55–61 (2017)

21. Abdul-Mageed, M.: Subjectivity and sentiment analysis of Arabic as a morphologically-rich language. Ph.D. thesis, Indiana University (2015)

22. Nabil, M., Aly, M., Atiya, A.: ASTD: Arabic sentiment tweets dataset. In: Proceedings of the 2015 Conference on Empirical Methods in Natural Language Processing, pp. 2515–2519 (2015)

23. Abdulla, N.A., Ahmed, N.A., Shehab, M.A., Al-Ayyoub, M.: Arabic sentiment analysis: lexicon-based and corpus-based. In: 2013 IEEE Jordan Conference on

Applied Electrical Engineering and Computing Technologies (AEECT), pp. 1–6. IEEE (2013)

24. Brachemi-Meftah, S., Barigou, F., Djendara, A., Zaoui, O.: Impact of dimensionality reduction on sentiment analysis of Algerian dialect. In: 2022 IEEE 9th International Conference on Sciences of Electronics, Technologies of Information and Telecommunications (SETIT), pp. 433–440. IEEE (2022)

25. Alnawas, A., Arici, N.: The corpus based approach to sentiment analysis in modern standard Arabic and Arabic dialects: a literature review. Politeknik Dergisi **21**, 461–470 (2018)

26. Abu Kwaik, K., Saad, M., Chatzikyriakidis, S., Dobnik, S.: LSTM-CNN deep learning model for sentiment analysis of dialectal Arabic. In: Smaïli, K. (ed.) ICALP 2019. CCIS, vol. 1108, pp. 108–121. Springer, Cham (2019). https://doi.org/10.1007/978-3-030-32959-4_8

27. Ridouane, T., Bouzoubaa, K., Harrat, S., Smaïli, K.: Arabic dialects morphological analyzers: a survey, pp. 189–203 (2022). https://doi.org/10.1007/978-3-031-14748-7_11

28. Abdelminaam, D.S., Neggaz, N., Gomaa, I., Ismail, F.H., Elsawy, A.A.: Arabicdialects: an efficient framework for Arabic dialects opinion mining on twitter using optimized deep neural networks. IEEE Access **9**, 97079–97099 (2021)

29. El Abdouli, A., Hassouni, L., Anoun, H.: Mining tweets of Moroccan users using the framework Hadoop, NLP, K-means and basemap. In: 2017 Intelligent Systems and Computer Vision (ISCV), pp. 1–7. IEEE (2017)

30. Mihi, S., Ait, B., El, I., Arezki, S., Laachfoubi, N.: MSTD: Moroccan sentiment twitter dataset. Int. J. Adv. Comput. Sci. Appl. **11**, 363–372 (2020)

31. Garouani, M., Chrita, H., Kharroubi, J.: Sentiment analysis of Moroccan tweets using text mining. In: Motahhir, S., Bossoufi, B. (eds.) ICDTA 2021. LNNS, vol. 211, pp. 597–608. Springer, Cham (2021). https://doi.org/10.1007/978-3-030-73882-2_54

32. Berlitz: Digital 2022: Morocco. https://www.berlitz.com/blog/most-spokenlanguages-world. Accessed 2022

33. Wikipedia: List of countries where Arabic is an official language. https://en.wikipedia.org/wiki/List_of_countries_where_Arabic_is_an_official_language. Accessed 2022

34. Communicate: This is the 4th most used language online. https://communicateonline.me/category/industry-insights/post-details/this-is-the-4th-most-used-language-online-but-has-only-1-content. Accessed 2018

35. Darwish, K.: Arabic information retrieval. Parlux (2005)

Combining CNNs and Transformers Networks for Improved Breast Ultrasound Image Segmentation

Jaouad Tagnamas$^{(\boxtimes)}$, Hiba Ramadan, Ali Yahyaouy, and Hamid Tairi

Faculty of Sciences Dhar El Mahraz, Department of Informatics, University of Sidi Mohamed Ben Abdellah, B.P. 1796, Atlas-Fez, 30000 Fez, Morocco
`jaouad.tagnamas@usmba.ac.ma`

Abstract. Breast cancer is a major global health issue that particularly affects women. Many breast ultrasound (BUS) segmentation methods have been developed based on convolution neural networks (CNNs) due to the need for accurate diagnosis of medical images. Nevertheless, CNNs have restrictions in modeling long-range relationships, which can lead to reduced accuracy in BUS segmentation. Transformers, which can obtain global information, also have limitations in extracting local details and require training on huge datasets. In this paper, we propose a Hybrid CNNs-Transformer architecture for segmenting BUS images. Our proposed method is built upon the U-Net architecture and comprises of two encoders. The first encoder utilizes pure CNN blocks to extract local and fine-grained features, while the second encoder leverages the powerful Swin-Transformer architecture to effectively model global dependencies. The decoder part of the architecture utilizes the merged extracted features and leverages skip-connections to reconstruct the segmented BUS images. Through experimentation and evaluation on two publicly available BUS datasets, it has been demonstrated that our proposed method outperforms recent BUS image segmentation methods.

Keywords: Breast Ultrasound segmentation · Convolutional Neural Networks · Swin-Transformer

1 Introduction

Breast cancer is the most frequently detected form of cancer in women [1] and has the highest mortality rate after lung cancer. The treatment of advanced-stage tumors poses significant challenges, emphasizing the importance of early detection and precise diagnosis. Breast ultrasound imaging (BUS) has became a widely accepted and cost-effective method for detecting breast tumors [2]. The use of BUS has increased significantly due to its ability to detect tumors at an early stage without any harmful side effects. Researchers have shown considerable interest in enhancing the objectivity and precision of breast ultrasound (BUS) diagnosis through the development of computer-aided diagnostic (CAD)

© The Author(s), under exclusive license to Springer Nature Switzerland AG 2025
H. Hagras et al. (Eds.): ISACS 2023, CCIS 2255, pp. 59–70, 2025.
https://doi.org/10.1007/978-3-031-93448-3_5

systems. Automated image segmentation is a crucial aspect that significantly impacts the reliability and accuracy of diagnostic results, making it imperative to develop advanced segmentation technology for BUS. By detecting and diagnosing tumors accurately at an early stage, clinicians can intervene with appropriate treatment plans, improving patient survival rates.

Deep learning methods have gained important attention in medical image processing, with U-Net [3] emerging as a leading architecture for the segmentation of medical image. These techniques have the capacity to improve both the effectiveness and precision of medical image analysis, resulting in improved patient outcomes. While convolutional neural networks (CNNs) have been the leading approach for computer vision tasks, the introduction of Transformers in natural language processing (NLP) has generated interest in their potential applications in medical imaging. Researchers are actively exploring the use of Transformer [4] in medical imaging, particularly in the areas of detection, segmentation, and classification. The use of these advanced deep learning methods has the potential to revolutionize medical image analysis and improve the accuracy of medical diagnoses.

Despite CNNs have been the go-to architecture for processing image data due to their ability to extract local features, however, CNNs are not well-suited for capturing global dependencies within images. Transformers in the other hand, have shown great promise in capturing long-range dependencies in natural language processing tasks, but their use in computer vision has been limited due to their high computational cost [5]. The recently proposed Swin-Transformer architecture [6] aims to address this limitation by utilizing a hierarchical structure that allows for efficient computation of SA mechanisms. The success of the Swin-Transformer in different image tasks, Swin-Unet [7] was proposed a Unet-shaped pure Transformer architecture that leverages the Swin-Transformer blocks for segmenting medical images.

Drawing inspiration from the significant accomplishments of Swin-Transformers in various computer vision tasks, in addition to the pure transformer architecture Swin-Unet specifically developed for medical imaging segmentation, we propose a novel hybrid method in this paper. Our approach combines the strengths of both CNNs and Transformers to enable improved segmentation of BUS images.

We propose a two-encoder architecture comprising a CNN encoder for extracting local and fine-grained features, and a Swin-Transformer encoder to capture global features from BUS images. The two encoders are integrated through a decoder that upsamples the merged features to reconstruct the segmentation of the input BUS image, utilizing skip-connections from the CNN encoder. Our work contributes in two ways: Firstly, we present a hybrid CNN-Swin-Transformer U-shaped network to segment BUS images. Secondly, we demonstrate that our approach significantly enhances the segmentation performance of BUS images.

2   Related Works

CNN-based techniques [3,8,9] have been extensively utilized in medical image segmentation over time because of their proficiency in extracting features from images. Transformer-based methods, on the other hand, are gaining popularity due to their superior performance in capturing global dependencies in the data. In recent years, efforts have been made to combine the strengths of both CNNs and Transformers to achieve better segmentation performance in BUS images.

2.1   CNNs Based Methods

Recently, with the advancements of deep learning architectures, multiple CNNs architectures have been proposed. Mainly, the work in [10] developed a residual convolutional network to segment BUS images that consists of a deep supervision module, missed detection residual network and a false detection residual network. Yap et al. [11] proposed a CNN based method for BUS lesion detection. For the same task [12] introduced a method by combining a dilated CNN with a phase-based active contour. In the study [13] a multi-stage BUS segmentation method is proposed, where a residual U-Net feature selection network named RFS-UNet is employed to solely segment abnormal images using the BTEC-Net.

2.2   Transformers Based Methods

The fundamental concept behind the Transformer architecture is to leverage SA mechanisms to extract long-range dependencies in images. In the literature, Mo et al. [14] presented the HoVer-Trans network that employs the Transformer architecture for BUS images diagnosis. Similarly, in the segmentaion of medical images contexte, Cao et al. [7] proposed a pure Transformer-based Unet-like architecture known as Swin-Unet. This approach utilized encodes the feature maps using a hierarchical Swin-Transformer with shifted windows. Despite its potential advantages, the Transformer architecture requires training on huge datasets and is computationally complex, resulting in significant overhead during both training and inference. For this reason, few studies have focused solely on Transformers, with many opting for CNN-Transformer fusion-based approaches.

3   Proposed Method

3.1   Network Architecture

Figure 1 depicts an overview of the proposed segmentation network. The suggested model is built upon the U-Net architecture, which includes two encoders and a decoder. The BUS image is inputted into both encoders to extract feature maps. The CNN encoder captures shallow structural information from the input BUS image. Whereas the Transformer encoder extracts deep global features. These feature maps are then combined into a single vector. This merging of feature maps facilitates the integration of both local and global information captured by the CNN encoder and the Swin-Transformer encoder, respectively. After the feature map fusion, the combined vector is passed to the decoder, which plays a vital role in reconstructing the segmented image. The decoder employs a series of upsample and convolutional layers to gradually increase the spatial resolution of the feature vector. This upsampling process helps restore the fine details lost during the downsampling stage of the encoders, allowing for a more accurate reconstruction of the segmented image. To further enhance the reconstruction process and facilitate information flow, skip connections are incorporated in the decoder. Skip connections establish direct connections between the feature maps of the corresponding encoding and decoding stages. This methodology is effective in accurately segmenting medical images, such as BUS images. The initial encoder in the proposed model consists of five CNN blocks, with each block serving as a feature extractor. Each CNN block comprises a Conv2D layer, a BatchNormalization layer, and a LeakyReLU activation function, which are performed twice on the input tensors. Following each CNN block is a MaxPooling2D layer, which downsamples the spatial information of the image and increases the number of channels. Further, The CNN blocks have varying numbers of filters, with the first block having 64 filters and the subsequent blocks having 128, 256, 512, and 1024 filters, respectively. The varying number of filters in the CNN-encoder is used to extratct different types of feature from low-level features to higher-level and abstract features. To improve the accuracy of segmentation, the proposed network utilizes a pure pre-trained Transformer architecture with base configuration, Swin-Transformer [6], to extract deep global features, while a CNNs are used to extract shallow structural information. The second encoder leverages the pre-trained Swin-Transformer to model the feature maps obtained by the first encoder globally. Further details on the Swin-Transformer architecture will be presented in the following subsection.

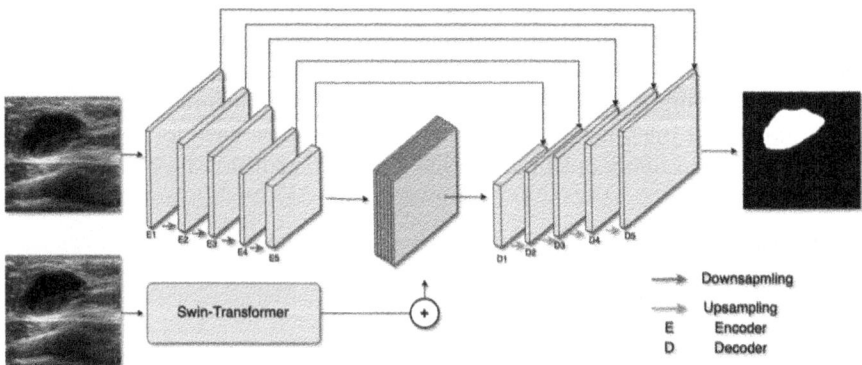

Fig. 1. Overview of the proposed segmentation architecture

3.2   Review of Swin-Transformer

The performance of the ViT [5] in image classification tasks has been promising. However, its practical utility is limited due to certain drawbacks. Firstly, it is not optimized for dense prediction tasks including segmentation. Secondly, the global attention computation in ViT leads to a quadratic computational complexity with respect to the input size, which is highly resource-intensive. The Swin-Transformer [6] was developed to overcome the challenges encountered by the original ViT and introduced two essential ideas: hierarchical feature maps and shifted window attention. Like ViT, Swin-Transformer splits the input image into non-overlapping patches of 4×4. A linear embedding layer is applied on the flattened pixels in each patch to project it to an arbitrary dimension C. Several Transformer blocks with modified SA computation (Swin-Transformer blocks) are applied on these patch tokens. Swin-Transformer uses Hierarchical Feature Maps, where the number of tokens is reduced by using patch merging layers. The patch merging layers groups each $n \times n$ neighboring patches and concatenates them depth-wise. This operation is used to downsample the input by a factor of n, transforming the input from a shape of $\frac{H}{n} \times \frac{W}{n} \times n^2 C$, where W, H and C refers to the width, height and number of channels respectively. The Swin-Transformer is composed of multiple blocks, and each block contains two types of multi-head self-attention (MSA) modules: W-MSA (window-based MSA) and SW-MSA (shifted-window-based MSA), which replace the standard MSA module as presented in the left part of Fig. 2 represents. The right part of Fig. 2 transformer block demonstrates the W-MSA method, where the input image is divided into M x M windows, and the SA is computed locally for each window. Consequently, using W-MSA results in improved computational complexity compared to global MSA, which has a quadratic computational complexity with respect to the number of patches. However, the local computation of SA within each window has limitations in terms of the network's ability to learn connections between different windows. To address this issue, the paper proposes the SW-MSA approach, which maintains computational efficiency while introducing interconnections between neighboring windows.

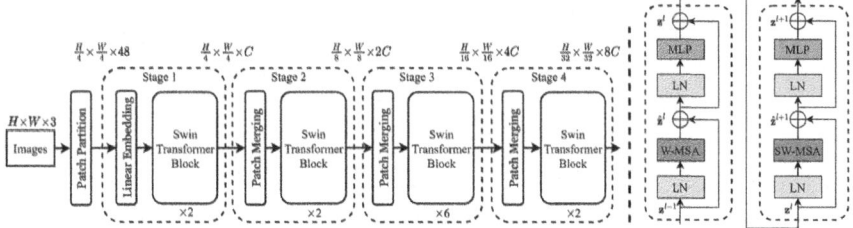

Fig. 2. Left: Overview of the Swin-Transformer architecture. Right: Swin-Transformer Blocks. The figure is taken from the original paper [6]

4   Experiments

4.1   Datasets

In this study, we assessed the performance of our approach on two available datasets of breast ultrasound (BUS) images. The first dataset, BUSI, was provided online by Al-Dhabyani et al. [15] and consists of 780 PNG format images of BUS scans from 600 female patients, along with corresponding masks. The average image size in this dataset is 500 px * 500 px. The dataset is divided into three classes, with 487 images in the benign class and 210 images in the malignant class. In our work, we focused on the two classes of malignant and benign, as the first phase of our approach involves tumor region segmentation and normal class images do not contain any tumor regions. The second dataset, UDIAT [16], was gathered by the Diagnostic Center of the Parc Tauli Corporation, Sabadell (Spain) and contains 110 benign and 53 malignant BUS images, collected using a Siemens ACUSON Sequoia C512 system 17L5 HD linear array transducer. By evaluating our approach on these datasets, we were able to provide a comprehensive analysis of its effectiveness and robustness. The use of publicly accessible datasets ensures the reproducibility and generalizability of our findings and enables comparison with other methods and techniques in the field.

4.2   Evaluation Metrics

In order to evaluate the effectiveness of our segmentation models, we utilized established metrics, including Accuracy, Dice coefficient (DC), Jaccard index (IoU), recall and precision. We utilized the true positive (TP), true negative (TN), false positive (FP), and false negative (FN) rates to compute the evaluation metrics. By employing these commonly used metrics, we were able to conduct a thorough evaluation of the segmentation model performance and compare our findings with other reported results in recents works in the field.

$$Accuracy = \frac{TP + TN}{TP + TN + FP + FN} \tag{1}$$

$$Dice = \frac{2 \times TP}{2 \times TP + FP + FN} \tag{2}$$

$$Iou = \frac{TP}{TP + FP + FN} \tag{3}$$

$$Precision = \frac{TP}{TP + FP} \tag{4}$$

$$Recall = \frac{TP}{TP + FN} \tag{5}$$

4.3   Implementation Details

Throughout this study, we used a 5-fold cross-validation method using the same dataset partition to conduct our experiments. During the training process, the dataset was split in this manner: 80% of BUS images for training, while 20% of the images were reserved for testing. Additionally, 20% of the training data was used for validation. All images were resized to 224×224 pixels. We utilized two encoders in our approach. The first encoder is composed of five CNN blocks, where each block consists of a Conv2D layer, a BatchNormalization layer, and a LeakyReLU activation function. The second encoder is based on the pretrained Swin-Transformer [6]. We explored various combinations of batch sizes, learning rates and epochs. The best results were reported using the Adam optimizer [17] with an initial learning rate of $1e^{-4}$ and $\beta_1 = 0, 9$, $\beta_2 = 0.999$ and $1e^{-7}$. We trained the model for 200 epochs with a batch size of 8 and early stopping enabled. Data augmentation techniques were applied to the training set to improve the robustness of the model. All methods and experiments were implemented on MSI workstation, 12th Gen Core i5 processor and 16Gb of RAM, using Tensorflow v2.10, and performed using a single NVIDIA GeForce RTX 3060 12-GB GPU. The choice of loss function had a significant impact on the outcomes of our study, and to address the challenge of imbalanced class distribution in the dataset, we employed a custom loss function that combines the Dice loss and binary cross-entropy (BCE). This combined loss function, denoted as L_T, is defined as:

$$L_{BCE} = -\frac{1}{N} \sum_{i=1}^{N} [y_i \log(p_i) + (1 - y_i) \log(1 - p_i)] \tag{6}$$

$$L_{Dice} = 1 - \frac{2 \sum_{i=1}^{N} y_i p_i + \epsilon}{\sum_{i=1}^{N} (y_i + p_i) + \epsilon} \tag{7}$$

$$L_T = L_{Dice} + L_{BCE} \tag{8}$$

4.4   Results and Discussion

In this section we present the findings of our proposed method as well as its discussion. After training the proposed segmentation method using the details in the previous section, the results are presented in Table 1. Further, we trained our proposed method on the BUSI [15] dataset and tested on UDIAT [16] dataset, reported results are diplayed in Table 2.

Our segmentation results were compared with existing methods in the literature. To ensure a fair comparison, we ensured that the training environment and data preprocessing methods for both training and testing were identical. Specifically, we compared our segmentation results with those reported in the work [18]. Podda et al. performed the segmentation of BUS images using a CNN ensembles with soft voting, where they adopted a U-Net architecture with different backbones, mainly they used Resnet50 [19], Densenet121 [20], VGG19 [21], Inception [22] as backbones for the U-Net and a custom U-Net architecture developed in their work. Table 3 reports the comparaison between our segmentation results with their findings. The findings demonstrates that our proposed method ameliorate the performance of the BUS segmentation with 1.44% in terms of dice coefficient. These results demonstrates that the proposed segmentation network can segment BUS images more accurately than previous networks and detect edge information more precisely. Further, the results obtained are due to the use of two encoders. The CNN-encoder excels at capturing local details and low-level features, while the Swin-Transformer encoder effectively models long-range dependencies and global context. Therefore by combining the strengths of both encoders, the network leverages comprehensive information from various scales and levels of complexity, leading to more accurate and robust segmentation results.

Figure 3 illustrates a visual representation of segmentation examples for both Dataset BUSI and Dataset UDIAT. The figure presents the input images (A), actual masks (B), predicted masks (C) and the overlay of the predicted mask on the original image (D). The proposed model demonstrates efficient segmentation of both malignant and benign lesions, exhibiting marginally superior performance in segmenting benign tumors. Nevertheless, it encounters specific difficulties in segmenting malignant tumors, particularly within the UDIAT dataset. Although the suggested approach presents remarkable segmentation efficacy, its precision may be constrained for certain BUS images. Figure 3 illustrates several instances of unsuccessful segmentation, where the technique fails to accurately detect specific areas of breast lesions present in BUS images, predominantly for malignant tumors. These scenarios emphasize the challenges in precisely segmenting lesion tissue when confronted with indistinct lesion boundaries and regions exhibiting heterogeneous intensities. Similar to alternative segmentation methodologies, the neural network may experience difficulty in identifying the target breast lesion region when the intensity values are insubstantial or boundaries remain indistinct. In forthcoming researches, we intend to explore more proficient feature extraction modules, such as incorporating CNNs into transformers or developing more robust variant transformer-based methods to augment the segmentation of BUS images.

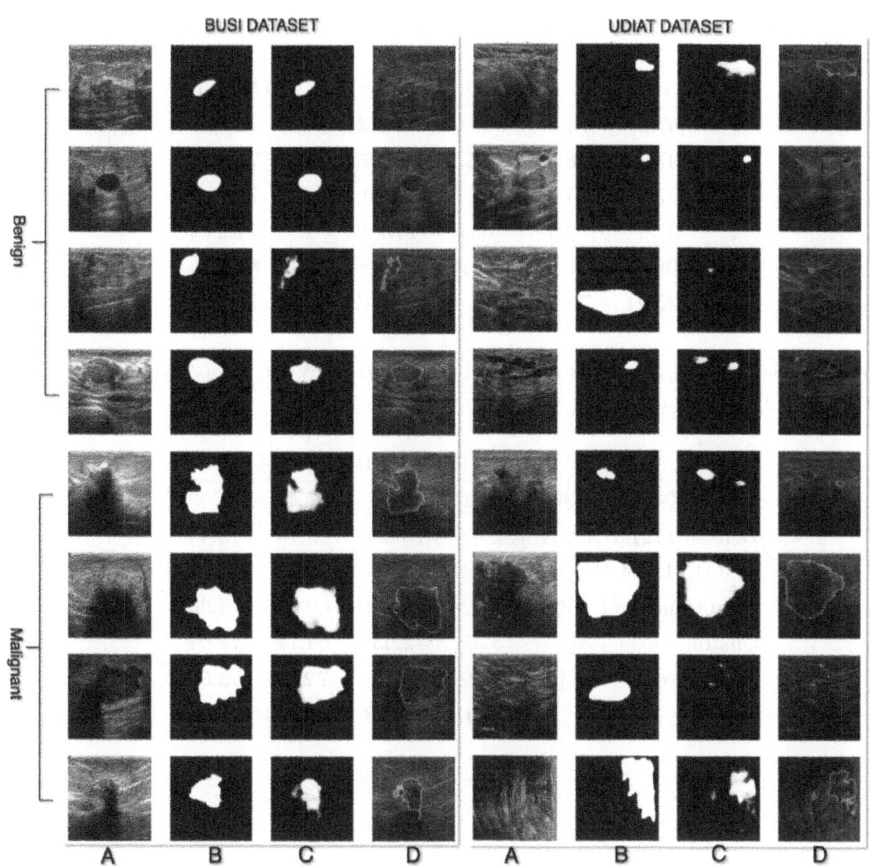

Fig. 3. Examples of predicted masks by our proposed method on BUSI [15] and UDIAT [16]. A) the original image, B) the actual mask, C) the predicted mask and D) the overlay of the predicted mask on the original image.

Table 1. Segmentation results reported by the proposed model on BUSI [15] dataset

Fold	Acc (%)	Dice (%)	IoU (%)	Precision (%)	Recall (%)
1	96.1	80.9	68.8	**78.4**	84.7
2	96.0	79.5	67.0	75.0	87.0
3	95.8	79.5	67.0	76.6	84.9
4	**96.2**	**81.3**	**69.0**	76.6	**88.2**
5	95.9	79.7	66.8	74.1	88.2
Mean	96.0	80.18	67.72	76.14	86.6

Table 2. Segmentation results reported by the proposed model trained on BUSI [15] dataset and tested on UDIAT [16]

Fold	Acc (%)	Dice (%)	IoU (%)	Precision (%)	Recall (%)
1	97.6	76.7	63.0	**83.2**	72.8
2	97.9	**78.1**	**65.2**	78.9	78.6
3	97.5	75.1	61.5	79.9	73.1
4	97.6	74.6	60.8	76.9	74.2
5	**98.1**	77.7	65.1	73.2	**85.5**
Mean	97.94	76.44	63.12	78.42	76.34

Table 3. Segmentation results comparaison reported by our proposed model trained on BUSI [15] dataset and [18]

Model	Acc (%)	Dice (%)	IoU (%)	Recall (%)
Resnet50-UNet [18]	80.41	74.31	67.49	74.19
Densenet121-UNet [18]	82.48	76.80	69.74	79.44
VGG19-UNet [18]	77.64	73.26	66.19	73.88
Inception-UNet [18]	82.72	75.82	69.03	74.96
Custom UNet [18]	75.39	72.03	64.77	72.04
SEG_{LN} ensemble [18]	87.59	78.74	**72.44**	78.52
Ours	**96.0**	**80.18**	67.72	**86.6**

5   Conclusions

In this paper introduces a novel approach for segmenting breast ultrasound (BUS) images that combines convolutional neural networks (CNNs) and Swin-Transformer architectures. The proposed U-shaped architecture comprises two branches, with each branch serving as a features encoder. The first encoder employs CNNs to capture fine-grained local features, while the second encoder leverages the Swin-Transformer's ability to model global, long-range dependencies. This architecture allows the network to capture both fine-grained local features and global, long-range dependencies, ensuring a comprehensive understanding of the complex structures present in BUS images. To reconstruct the segmented images, our decoder section employs CNN blocks to upsample the merged features obtained from the two encoders. This fusion of features preserves both local and global information, allowing for precise and detailed segmentation results. Additionally, the decoder benefits from the skip-connections originating from the first encoder, which enhance the network's ability to capture fine details and maintain spatial coherence. We evaluate the performance of our proposed network on two distinct BUS image datasets and compare it against recent methods. The experimental findings indicate that our method outperforms all competitors in accurately segmenting BUS images.

References

1. Siegel, R.L., Miller, K.D., Fuchs, H.E., Jemal, A.: Cancer statistics, 2022. CA: A Cancer J. Clin. **72**, 7–33 (2022)
2. Stephanie, S., Krithika, M., Adam, L., Sachita, S.: Review article: use of ultrasound in the developing world. Int. J. Emerg. Med. **4**, 72 (2011)
3. Ronneberger, O., Fischer, P., Brox, T.: U-Net: convolutional networks for biomedical image segmentation. In: Navab, N., Hornegger, J., Wells, W.M., Frangi, A.F. (eds.) MICCAI 2015. LNCS, vol. 9351, pp. 234–241. Springer, Cham (2015). https://doi.org/10.1007/978-3-319-24574-4_28
4. Vaswani, A., et al.: Attention is all you need (2017)
5. Dosovitskiy, A., et al.: An image is worth 16x16 words: transformers for image recognition at scale (2020)
6. Liu, Z., et al.: Swin transformer: hierarchical vision transformer using shifted windows (2021)
7. Cao, H., et al.: Swin-unet: unet-like pure transformer for medical image segmentation (2021)
8. Zhou, Z., Siddiquee, M.M.R., Tajbakhsh, N., Liang, J.: Unet++: a nested U-net architecture for medical image segmentation (2018)
9. Chen, L.-C., Papandreou, G., Schroff, F., Adam, H.: Rethinking atrous convolution for semantic image segmentation (2017)
10. Chen, G., Dai, Y., Zhang, J.: Rrcnet: refinement residual convolutional network for breast ultrasound images segmentation. Eng. Appl. Artif. Intell. **117**, 105601 (2023)
11. Yap, M.H., et al.: Automated breast ultrasound lesions detection using convolutional neural networks. IEEE J. Biomed. Health Inform. **22**(4), 1218–1226 (2018)
12. Hu, Y., et al.: Automatic tumor segmentation in breast ultrasound images using a dilated fully convolutional network combined with an active contour model. Med. Phys. **46**(1), 215–228 (2019)
13. Cho, S.W., Baek, N.R., Park, K.R.: Deep learning-based multi-stage segmentation method using ultrasound images for breast cancer diagnosis. J. King Saud Univ. Comput. Inf. Sci. **34**(10), 10273–10292 (2022)
14. Mo, Y., et al.: Hover-trans: anatomy-aware hover-transformer for ROI-free breast cancer diagnosis in ultrasound images. IEEE Trans. Med. Imaging **42**(6), 1696–1706 (2022)
15. Al-Dhabyani, W., Gomaa, M., Khaled, H., Fahmy, A.: Dataset of breast ultrasound images. Data Brief **28**, 2 (2020)
16. Yap, M.H., et al.: Automated breast ultrasound lesions detection using convolutional neural networks. IEEE J. Biomed. Health Inform. **22**(4), 1218–1226 (2017)
17. Kingma, D.P., Ba, J.: Adam: a method for stochastic optimization (2014)
18. Podda, A.S., Balia, R., Barra, S., Carta, S., Fenu, G., Piano, L.: Fully-automated deep learning pipeline for segmentation and classification of breast ultrasound images. J. Comput. Sci. **63**, 101816 (2022)
19. He, K., Zhang, X., Ren, S., Sun, J.: Deep residual learning for image recognition. In: Proceedings of the IEEE Conference on Computer Vision and Pattern Recognition, pp. 770–778 (2016)
20. Huang, G., Liu, Z., Van Der Maaten, L., Weinberger, K.Q.: Densely connected convolutional networks. In: Proceedings of the IEEE Conference on Computer Vision and Pattern Recognition, pp. 4700–4708 (2017)

21. Simonyan, K., Zisserman, A.: Very deep convolutional networks for large-scale image recognition (2015)
22. Szegedy, C., Vanhoucke, V., Ioffe, S., Shlens, J., Wojna, Z.: Rethinking the inception architecture for computer vision. In: Proceedings of the IEEE Conference on Computer Vision and Pattern Recognition, pp. 2818–2826 (2016)

Tiny Machine Learning for IoT-Enabled Embedded Systems: A Review

Azzedine El mrabet[1]([✉]) [iD], Ayoub Tber[1] [iD], Rachida Elmousaid[1] [iD],
Laamari Hlou[2] [iD], and Rachid El gouri[1] [iD]

[1] Laboratory of Advanced Systems Engineering, National School of Applied Sciences,
Ibn Tofail University, Kenitra, Morocco
{Azzedine.elmrabet,ayoub.tber,rachid.elgouri}@uit.ac.ma
[2] Laboratory of Electronic Systems, Information Processing, Mechanics and Energetics,
Faculty of Sciences, Ibn Tofaïl University, Kenitra, Morocco
laamari.hlou@uit.ac.ma

Abstract. Tiny Machine Learning (TinyML) is an emerging field that combines embedded systems and machine learning, with a focus on empowering resource-constrained devices such as smartphones, microcontrollers (MCUs), and sensors. By enabling on-device machine learning applications, TinyML eliminates the need for cloud services and external power sources. This review provides a comprehensive overview of TinyML, discussing its definition, benefits, and challenges. It explores techniques like model quantization, pruning, clustering, and cascading architectures that make TinyML feasible. The review also emphasizes the importance of hardware-software co-design and presents methodologies and tools for implementing TinyML. Recent advances in TinyML across various domains, including image processing, natural language processing, and robotics, are discussed, highlighting the potential impact on embedded system capabilities and performance. The transformative potential of TinyML is explored, uncovering new possibilities for previously unattainable use cases and applications.

Keywords: TinyML · Tiny Machine learning · Embedded Systems · IoT · On-device Machine Learning · Resource-constrained Devices

1 Introduction

The IoT has emerged as a rapidly expanding domain that interconnects billions of devices [1], empowering us with a wealth of data to improve efficiency, safety, and convenience in our daily lives [2]. However, a substantial proportion of IoT devices have resource constraints [3], such as limited processing power, memory, and energy capabilities. These limitations make it difficult to run conventional machine learning models on such devices [4].

TinyML is an emerging discipline that tackles the hurdles of deploying machine learning models on resource-constrained IoT devices [5]. TinyML techniques aim to optimize machine learning models, minimizing their size, complexity, and power consumption, thereby rendering them suitable for deployment in the IoT ecosystem [6].

© The Author(s), under exclusive license to Springer Nature Switzerland AG 2025
H. Hagras et al. (Eds.): ISACS 2023, CCIS 2255, pp. 71–84, 2025.
https://doi.org/10.1007/978-3-031-93448-3_6

TinyML technologies have the potential to revolutionize the IoT landscape, enabling a wide range of applications in various fields, including healthcare [7, 8], agriculture [9], and transportation [10]. With the deployment of TinyML models, IoT devices can perform complex tasks such as image recognition [11] and voice processing [12], without the need for cloud connectivity or high computing power. This opens up new possibilities for the development of efficient and autonomous IoT systems.

As TinyML is a relatively new field, there are still challenges that need to be addressed, such as the development of efficient training methods and the creation of TinyML-specific hardware. However, with the rapid growth of the IoT industry, the demand for TinyML technologies is expected to increase significantly.

In this comprehensive review, we explore the landscape of Tiny Machine Learning for IoT-enabled embedded systems. We discuss the definition and benefits of TinyML, while addressing the challenges of implementing it in resource-constrained environments. Additionally, we highlight the various techniques, hardware-software co-design approaches, and recent advances in TinyML.

2   Overview of TinyML

TinyML is an incredibly exciting and rapidly expanding area of research. With a focus on creating machine learning (ML) models specifically designed for deployment on compact, low-powered devices like MCUs, TinyML presents an innovative solution to the growing demand for ML-powered applications in the Internet of Things (IoT) space.

2.1   Definition of TinyML

TinyML is a field of machine learning that focuses on developing algorithms and models that can run on small, low-power devices, such as battery-powered sensors and actuators. This allows devices to analyze data and make decisions locally, without having to send data to a cloud server. With a focus on battery-powered embedded devices that can be used in large-scale IoT or wireless sensor network applications [13].

TinyML can revolutionize embedded devices by enabling them to analyze data and make decisions locally, without needing to send data to a cloud server. This can accelerate the decision-making process and enhance device independence. TinyML is versatile and applicable in various domains, ranging from healthcare to transportation.

2.2   TinyML Benefits and Challenges

TinyML technologies have the potential to offer several benefits in various applications and domains, including low power consumption, small size, low latency, customizability, and edge computing. However, implementing TinyML in embedded systems also poses notable challenges that hinder its growth and adoption, such as constraints on battery power, limited processor capabilities, restricted memory capacity, and costs of large-scale deployment (see Table 1 for a summary of key benefits and challenges with TinyML implementation on resource-constrained IoT devices).

Table 1. Summary of key benefits and challenges with TinyML implementation on resource-constrained IoT devices

Benefits	Challenges
Low power consumption – Optimized for milliwatts/microwatts power budget. Enables prolonged battery life	Battery power consumption – High aggregate current draw reduces battery life of IoT devices
Low latency – Enables real-time edge processing, reduces system response time	Processor capacity – 10-1000MHz clock speeds limit complex model execution
Low cost – Avoids expensive hardware and cloud costs. Lowers deployment and maintenance expenses	Memory limitations – Typical < 1MB capacity restricts model complexity
Customizability – Models can be tailored for specific applications	Cost of large-scale deployments – Expenses must be addressed for mass IoT edge deployment

3   TinyML Techniques

There are a number of techniques that can be used to optimize machine learning models for TinyML. These techniques include:

3.1   Model Quantization

Model quantization is a critical technique for enabling the deployment of neural networks (NNs) on resource-constrained MCUs in IoT-enabled embedded systems. In traditional NN implementations, weights, biases, and activations are typically represented as 32-bit floating-point values [14]. However, this approach presents two significant challenges when deploying NNs on MCUs.

Firstly, not all MCUs feature built-in hardware support for floating-point operations, thereby limiting computational capabilities. Secondly, the extensive use of 32-bit values consumes a significant portion of the limited memory available on MCUs. For instance, popular MCUs like the Arduino Nano 33 BLE [15] Sense provides only 256 KB of RAM, leaving room for approximately 64,000 weights, biases, and activations. This capacity falls short when considering modern NN architectures like AlexNet and Resnet-50, which consist of over one million weights, biases, and activations.

To address these challenges, researchers have explored the technique of quantization [16], which involves converting NN parameters from 32-bit floating-point representations to more memory-efficient 8-bit integers. Operations involving 8-bit integers are generally faster on most hardware platforms [17], rendering them suitable for TinyML models deployed on MCUs. The quantization process entails mapping the minimum and maximum values of the 32-bit floating-point weights to the corresponding values of 8-bit integers [18]. This mapping preserves the intervals between them. However, it's important to note that multiplying or adding two 8-bit integers might lead to overflow, as the mapping of the largest 32-bit weight to the maximum 8-bit integer value can result in exceeding the range of representable values.

To mitigate potential accuracy loss introduced by quantization, researchers have introduced quantization-aware training [14]. This approach involves training the model with the awareness that it will undergo quantization later, which helps preserve model performance even after quantization.

Furthermore, researchers have explored advanced techniques beyond traditional quantization, such as further quantization [19] and binarization of NNs. These techniques can achieve even greater reductions in model size, up to 32 times, and significantly improve inference time, up to 52 times [20].

3.2 Model Pruning

Model pruning is indeed a widely adopted technique in NNs to reduce model size and computational complexity. In the context of IoT-enabled embedded systems, where resource constraints are a critical concern, model pruning offers a promising approach to achieve efficient and lightweight machine learning models. By selectively pruning redundant or less significant weights, connections, and neurons, pruning can significantly reduce the memory footprint and computational requirements of NNs.

One common pruning approach is based on quantization, which can result in some weights becoming zero and, therefore, irrelevant for inference. In this case, zero-weight connections can be pruned, and if all incoming connections to a neuron are pruned, the neuron itself can also be eliminated along with its outgoing connections. This further reduces the model size and improves computational efficiency. Alternatively, non-zero weight connections can be pruned based on threshold pruning, which involves pruning connections below a certain threshold value. This approach has been successfully employed in previous studies, where pruning reduced the size of NNs by a factor of 9 to 13 [21].

Pruning not only aids in removing connections but also provides a systematic approach to eliminate neurons that have no input connections or zero output connections, commonly known as dead neurons. During retraining, these neurons are automatically pruned, contributing to a further reduction in model size. The effectiveness of pruning in reducing network size by up to 13 times without sacrificing accuracy has been demonstrated [22].

3.3 Model Clustering

Model clustering is an optimization technique closely related to both quantization and pruning, offering a unique approach to reduce the size of neural networks for IoT-enabled embedded systems.

Model clustering involves grouping weights within a neural network into clusters, where all weights within a particular cluster are assigned the same value. This is in contrast to pruning, which removes weights from the network, and quantization, which reduces the precision of weights. Clustering can achieve significant reductions in model size without significantly impacting computational efficiency.

The pioneering work by [23] introduced the concept of clustering in the context of neural network optimization. The authors claimed that their clustering approach achieved a remarkable reduction in model size, reporting a reduction of 27 to 31 times compared to the original network size. This reduction was achieved after pruning had already reduced the model size by 9 to 13 times.

Model clustering can be seen as a complementary technique to quantization and pruning, offering an additional dimension of model optimization. However, it is important to carefully analyze the trade-offs between model size reduction and the potential impact on computational efficiency when considering clustering for IoT-enabled embedded systems.

3.4 Knowledge Distillation

Knowledge distillation is a promising technique for enabling efficient machine learning on embedded systems, where limited computational resources and power constraints make it challenging to deploy large neural network models. In the context of tinyML, knowledge distillation offers a solution to leverage the structure and performance of larger models while deploying smaller, resource-constrained models.

The concept behind knowledge distillation involves training a smaller model, referred to as the "student", not only using ground truth labels but also by incorporating the predictions of a larger model, known as the "teacher". This process transfers the knowledge learned by the teacher model to the student model, allowing the student to benefit from the teacher's ability to understand the complex relationships within a dataset.

To achieve this, the loss function of the student model is altered to incorporate the similarity between its predictions and the predictions of the teacher model. This is done by adding a "distillation loss" term to the loss function, which measures the distance between the students' predictions and the teacher's predictions. By incorporating this additional knowledge, the student model can capture the intricate patterns and structures present in the data, despite its smaller size and limited computational capabilities.

3.5 Removing Operations

Removing operations is a technique specifically applicable to the TensorFlow Lite for MCUs interpreter, offering a solution to address the size constraints of machine learning models in IoT-enabled embedded systems. This technique involves selectively deciding which neural network operations the interpreter should execute, resulting in a reduction in the interpreter's size and memory footprint [24].

The process of removing operations requires careful consideration of the specific requirements and constraints of the target system. It involves analyzing the neural network model to identify operations that are not essential for the intended functionality or can be approximated or replaced with alternative techniques. By removing these operations from the interpreter, unnecessary computational overhead and memory consumption can be minimized.

It is important to note that the process of removing operations should be performed judiciously to strike a balance between model size reduction and maintaining the desired performance. Careful analysis and profiling of the model's operations are necessary to ensure that the removed operations do not significantly impact the model's accuracy or functionality.

3.6 Cascading Architectures

Cascading architectures provide a compelling approach to address the challenges of reducing model size and enhancing inference speed in tinyML for IoT-enabled embedded systems. This technique involves splitting a model into multiple models of increasing size, where a smaller model acts as a filter or pre-processing stage before activating a larger model [25].

The concept of cascading architectures finds practical application in various scenarios, one of which is exemplified by the operation of Google Home devices. In this case, a small model runs locally on the device, continuously listening for wake-up keywords such as "Hey Google." Once these keywords are detected, the remaining speech data is forwarded to a larger model hosted in the cloud for further processing and interpretation of the user's request [26].

It is worth noting that cascading architectures are typically associated with reducing model size and alternative system configurations. However, research has also explored the concept of cascading hardware utilization within a system. This approach involves sequentially activating different internal hardware components based on the specific processing requirements of the task at hand. By dynamically utilizing internal hardware resources in a cascading manner, overall system efficiency can be enhanced, leading to optimized resource utilization and improved energy efficiency [26].

4   Hardware and Software Co-Design

Deploying ML models in constrained environments like MCUs poses additional challenges. The execution of numerous weight multiplications, non-linear functions, and gradient computations, coupled with the need for frequent updates during training, demands considerable computational power. Moreover, the limited memory of MCUs necessitates longer training durations and consumes significant power. Therefore, the post-training ML algorithm undergoes a process of compression and optimization to create a compact representation compatible with MCUs. This involves making trade-offs between model accuracy, memory requirements, and performance.

To address these challenges, various TinyML tools and techniques have been proposed, including deep quantization techniques, memory-aware neural architecture searches, optimization frameworks (e.g., TensorFlow Lite, or TFL), and dedicated inference libraries. Among these, deep compression has emerged as a prominent area of research in the TinyML field. Deep compression focuses on reducing the size and complexity of ML models to make them suitable for inference on MCUs.

Figure 1 illustrates the comprehensive architecture of TinyML. It encompasses the entire process, beginning with data collection from the physical world, followed by ML model development on high-end processors, and culminating in the compression of the model to accommodate MCUs for inference [27].

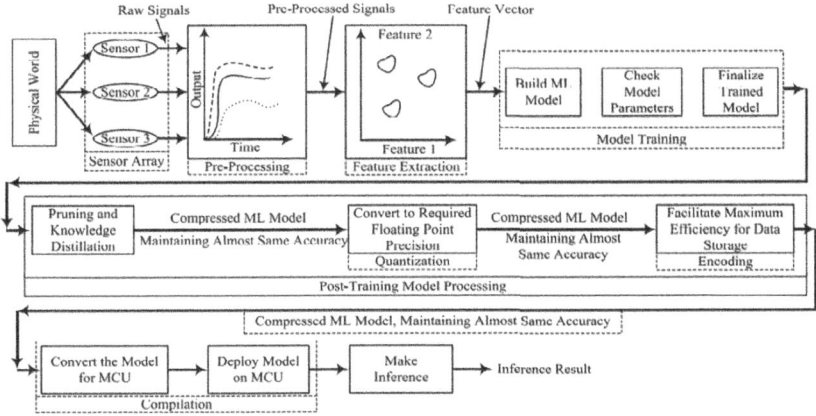

Fig. 1. Overview of a typical TinyML system architecture for IoT devices [27].

4.1 Methodology and Procedures

The deployment process encompasses key phases such as system design, data processing, model training, and model deployment inference (see Fig. 2). Throughout these phases, various optimization techniques can be applied, including quantization, pruning, clustering, and knowledge distillation.

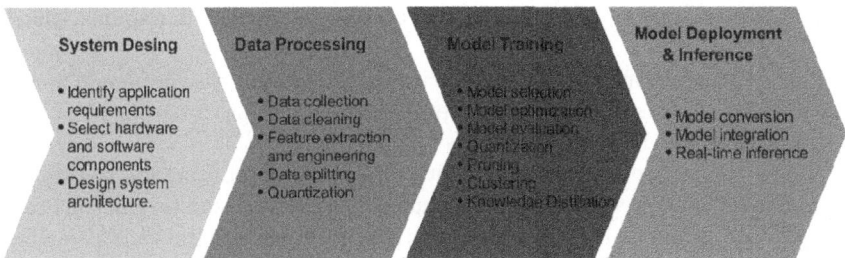

Fig. 2. TinyML Deployment Process.

System Design Phase. The primary objective of the system design phase is to comprehend the specific requirements of the target application and devise a TinyML system capable of effectively fulfilling those requirements. This phase encompasses a series of crucial steps that guide the design process.

Initially, it is essential to define the application requirements by identifying the precise task or problem that the TinyML system aims to address. This involves determining the sources of input data, specifying the desired output, and acknowledging any constraints or limitations imposed by the target embedded system.

Following this, the selection of appropriate hardware and software components becomes imperative. Careful consideration must be given to choosing embedded boards or microcontrollers that align with the computational, power, and connectivity requirements of the application. Similarly, the software stack must be assessed, encompassing operating systems, libraries, and frameworks suitable for TinyML development and deployment.

Lastly, the system architecture must be meticulously designed, encompassing the integration of sensors, actuators, and any external devices or services. Factors such as communication protocols, interfaces, and data flow between the components of the system should be taken into account to ensure a seamless and efficient operation of the TinyML system within IoT-enabled embedded systems.

The Data Processing Phase. Data preprocessing is a vital stage in preparing the dataset for training the TinyML model, involving procedures to ensure data quality and relevance. The process includes data collection from various sources, such as sensors or publicly available datasets. Collected data undergoes cleaning to remove inconsistencies, outliers, and missing values. Feature extraction and engineering enhance the model using domain-specific knowledge and selection techniques. Data is then divided into subsets – training, validation, and testing sets. The training set trains the TinyML model, the validation set aids hyperparameter tuning and model selection, and the testing set evaluates the final model's real-world performance.

The Model Training Phase. Involves training the TinyML model using the preprocessed dataset. This phase consists of several essential steps that guide the training process. The following steps outline the key procedures involved in model training:

Firstly, model selection is performed, where an appropriate TinyML model architecture is chosen based on the specific requirements of the target application and the constraints of the embedded system. Factors such as model complexity, computational requirements, and memory footprint are taken into consideration during this selection process.

After selecting the model, the next step is model initialization. The chosen model is initialized with suitable initial weights or parameters to establish a starting point for the training process.

Model optimization is then carried out to train the model using the preprocessed dataset. Optimization techniques such as gradient descent or stochastic gradient descent are employed to minimize the loss function and iteratively update the models' parameters. This process enables the model to learn from the data and improve its performance over time. Additionally, advanced techniques such as model quantization, pruning, clustering, and knowledge distillation can be applied during the model training phase to further optimize the TinyML model.

Once the model is trained, it undergoes evaluation using the validation dataset. Performance metrics such as accuracy, precision, recall, or mean squared error are calculated to assess the model's performance. This evaluation provides insights into the model's ability to generalize to unseen data and make reliable predictions.

The Deployment and Inference. The subsequent step involves deploying the model onto the embedded system for real-time inference. The deployment and inference procedures encompass the following steps:

Firstly, the trained TinyML model needs to be converted into a format that is compatible with the target hardware and software stack. Specialized tools or frameworks designed for TinyML deployment can be employed to ensure compatibility and efficiency during the conversion process.

Following the conversion, the transformed TinyML model is integrated into the software environment of the embedded system. This encompasses writing code or scripts to load the model, establish the necessary inference pipelines, and manage input/output interfaces with sensors or actuators. The integration process guarantees the seamless interaction of the model with the remaining software components within the embedded system.

Once the model is both deployed and integrated, real-time inference can be executed. Fresh data samples obtained from sensors or external sources are fed through the deployed TinyML model to yield predictions or outputs. It is imperative to optimize the inference process to minimize latency and maximize energy efficiency, particularly given the resource-constrained nature of embedded systems.

By adhering to these model deployment and inference procedures, the trained TinyML model becomes operational within the embedded system. The steps involving model conversion, integration, and real-time inference ensure the systems capability to efficiently process incoming data and generate predictions or outputs. This functionality facilitates real-time decision-making and actions based on the embedded systems inherent capacities.

5 TinyML Tools

The successful implementation of TinyML systems relies on carefully selecting appropriate hardware and software components that align with the computational, power, and connectivity requirements of the application. Considerations for hardware and software play a crucial role in achieving efficient and effective deployment of TinyML models within IoT-enabled embedded systems.

5.1 Hardware

When selecting hardware components for a TinyML system, several factors must be taken into account. Firstly, assess the computational capabilities of the hardware to ensure its ability to efficiently handle the workload of running the TinyML model. Microcontrollers or embedded boards with integrated AI accelerators, such as specialized neural network processors or digital signal processors, can significantly enhance inference performance and energy efficiency.

The current market offers numerous options suitable for TinyML application development. Some popular hardware platforms designed for TinyML include Raspberry Pi 4B, Nvidia Jetson Nano, STM32F Discovery, Arduino Nano 33 BLE Sense, Apollo3, Arduino Portenta H7, and Nicla Sense ME. These platforms provide a range of features and capabilities that can be explored to determine their suitability for specific TinyML applications.

The majority of hardware boards used in TinyML applications are equipped with processors operating at frequencies below 100 MHz, making them well-suited for low-power and resource-constrained environments. Typically, these boards have less than 1 MB of flash memory and less than 1 MB of SRAM. Connectivity options such as Bluetooth

Low Energy and Wi-Fi are commonly supported, enabling seamless communication with other devices or cloud services.

Considering power consumption is crucial, particularly for battery-powered or energy-constrained devices. Hardware boards designed for TinyML applications typically exhibit power consumption in the milliwatt range, allowing for extended battery life. These boards can be powered by various sources, including Li-Po batteries, coin batteries, or regular DC power supplies, offering flexibility in powering the embedded system.

5.2 TinyML Frameworks

In the realm of TinyML development and deployment, a range of specialized tools and frameworks cater to the requirements of resource-constrained devices. Notable among these are: TensorFlow Lite [28], an open-source deep learning framework by Google, designed for low-power devices; NanoEdge AI Studio [29] (formerly cartesiam.ai), facilitating library selection with emulation and optimization features; uTensor [30], an open-source platform for rapid embedded learning application development; Edge Impulse [31], a cloud service for TinyML model development and deployment; PyTorch Mobile [32], supporting training and deployment of models on mobile devices; Microsoft's Embedded Learning Library [33], enabling internet-independent models on embedded devices; STM32Cube.AI [34], simplifying AI implementation on STM32 ARM Cortex M-based boards. These frameworks provide optimization, compatibility, and ease of implementation for TinyML on embedded devices, aiding developers in selecting suitable components for their applications. A summary comparison of TinyML frameworks is provided in the Table 2.

Table 2. Summary comparison of TinyML frameworks.

Framework	Key Features	Hardware Compatibility	Optimizations Offered
TensorFlow Lite	Lightweight ML inference, model conversion	Microcontrollers, smartphones, IoT devices	Quantization, latency, memory footprint
uTensor	Inference engine, graph tool, data collection	Mbed, STM32, K64 boards	Small footprint, customization via Python SDK
Edge Impulse	AutoML, training to deployment workflow	Various boards incl. Smartphones	Memory optimization, frequency filtering
PyTorch Mobile	Training to deployment, mobile pre-processing	Android, iOS, GPUs, DSPs, NPUs	Quantization, mobile interpreter
Embedded Learning Library	Internet-independent models	Raspberry Pi, Arduino, micro:bit	-
STM32Cube.AI	Code generation, model conversion	STM32 Cortex M boards	Memory optimization, integrates with STM32CubeMX
NanoEdge AI Studio	Benchmarking, emulator testing, optimization	STM32 Nucleo, Arduino Nano	Library selection, frequency filtering

6   Recent Advances in TinyML

TinyML is rapidly advancing and proving to be a valuable tool in a wide range of IoT applications. This section provides an overview of recent progress in ML algorithms designed specifically for TinyML and explores the modifications made to ML paradigms for seamless integration into MCUs. Furthermore, we discuss well-established use cases of TinyML. However, the current landscape of TinyML lacks maturity due to the absence of a unified benchmarking scheme. While this hinders systematic comparison and evaluation across different TinyML frameworks, the diverse methodologies proposed by researchers offer a strong foundation for the development of benchmarking strategies.

Researchers in [35] have identified the challenges and directions for benchmarking TinyML. Key issues like low power, limited memory capacity, hardware heterogeneity, and software heterogeneity need to be addressed to establish an appropriate benchmark. Additionally, an analysis [36] focused on TinyML in the context of frugal smart objects. The performance of popular ML algorithms, including Support Vector Machines, Multilayer Perceptron, decision trees, and Random Forest, was evaluated on an Arduino Uno board using a synthetic dataset of 10,000 training samples for classification tasks. The findings demonstrated the superior performance of decision trees and RF classifiers.

In the autonomous navigation of mini vehicles, Prado et al. [37] deployed tiny CNNs based on the LeNet 5 architecture on ultra-low-power MCUs, namely GAP8, STM32 L476, and NXP K64f. A comparison with the STM platform integrated with CMISIS-NN showed that GAP8 achieved significantly reduced latency and higher accuracy. Another study [38] proposed YOLO Nano, a highly compact CNN paradigm for object detection tasks. Experimental results revealed its superior computation efficiency compared to existing frameworks.

Recent advancements include achieving competitive classification accuracy in CNNs by limiting weights to a binary format. Andri et al. [39] introduced YodaNN, an accelerator optimized for binary weight CNNs, which demonstrated impressive energy and area efficiency. In reducing memory footprint, Liberis et al. [40] developed a tool to optimize operator order in NN models created using the TensorFlow Lite framework.

For real-time Deep Neural Network (DNN) execution, Niu et al. [41] proposed PatDNN, an end-to-end framework that outperformed existing frameworks in terms of speed without compromising accuracy. Wong et al. [42] introduced AttendNets, a compact and low-precision DNN designed for on-device image recognition, which exhibited higher accuracy, low power consumption, and minimal memory usage compared to state-of-the-art methodologies.

Furthermore, TinyML has found successful applications in audio analysis, image recognition, psychological/behavioral metrics, and industry telemetry. Integrating kilobyte-sized ML models into tiny IoT devices, detecting eating behaviors, estimating parameters of Li-Ion batteries, and medical face mask detection are among the notable applications. The TinyML community shows particular interest in computer vision, sound recognition, and the development of low-power, accurate ML models.

These advancements, along with the availability of free resources from communities, industries, and websites, have accelerated the adoption of TinyML in IoT-enabled embedded systems. By further exploring complex ML applications and evaluating their performance in challenging environments, we can unlock the full potential of TinyML.

7 Conclusion

In conclusion, our analysis highlights the future prospects of TinyML and its potential impact on the IoT industry. Despite the challenges posed by resource-constrained IoT devices, such as limited processing power, memory, and energy, TinyML techniques offer effective solutions. By reducing model size and complexity, leveraging quantization techniques, employing pruning strategies, and optimizing for low power consumption, TinyML addresses these challenges head-on. The transformative potential of TinyML is immense, revolutionizing the IoT landscape by enabling the deployment of machine learning on a wide range of resource-constrained devices. This paradigm shift opens doors to innovative IoT applications in domains like healthcare, manufacturing, transportation, and beyond. The remarkable possibilities presented by TinyML hold great promise for shaping the future of the IoT industry.

References

1. Alsharif, M.H., Jahid, A., Kelechi, A.H., Kannadasan, R.: Green IoT: a review and future research directions. Symmetry **15**(3), 757 (2023). https://doi.org/10.3390/sym15030757
2. Zaheeruddin, Gupta, H.: Foundation of IoT: An overview. Internet of Things (IoT): Concepts Appl. (2020) https://doi.org/10.1007/978-3-030-37468-6_1/COVER
3. Ali, S.A., Ansari, M, Alam, M.: Resource management techniques for cloud-based IoT environment. Internet of Things (IoT): Concepts Appl. (2020) https://doi.org/10.1007/978-3-030-37468-6_4/COVER
4. Imteaj, A., Thakker, U., Wang, S., Li, J., Amini, M.H.: A survey on federated learning for resource-constrained IoT devices. IEEE Internet Things J. **9**, 1–24 (2022)
5. Janapa Reddi, V., et al.: Widening Access to Applied Machine Learning with TinyML. In: Proceedings of TinyML Research Symposium, vol. 1
6. Ray, P.P.: A review on TinyML: state-of-the-art and prospects. J. King Saud Univ. – Comput. Inform. Sci. **34**, 1595–1623 (2022)
7. Ahmed, K., Hassan, M.: TinyCare: A tinyml-based low-cost continuous blood pressure estimation on the extreme edge. In: 2022 IEEE 10th (ICHI), pp. 264–275. IEEE (2022). https://doi.org/10.1109/ICHI54592.2022.00047
8. Ferreyro, L.P., et al.: An implementation of a channelizer based on a goertzel filter bank for the read-out of cryogenic sensors. J. Inst. **18**(06), P06009 (2023). https://doi.org/10.1088/1748-0221/18/06/P06009
9. Gutti, V., Karthi, R.: Real time classification of fruits and vegetables deployed on low power embedded devices using tiny ML. In: Iong-Zong Chen, J., Manuel, J., Tavares, R.S., Shi, F. (eds.) Third International Conference on Image Processing and Capsule Networks: ICIPCN 2022, pp. 347–359. Springer International Publishing, Cham (2022). https://doi.org/10.1007/978-3-031-12413-6_27
10. Giordano, M., et al.: Design and performance evaluation of an Ultralow-power smart IoT device with embedded TinyML for asset activity monitoring. IEEE Trans. Instrum. Meas. **71**, 1–11 (2022)
11. Sudharsan, B., Salerno, S., Ranjan, R.: TinyML-CAM: 80 FPS Image Recognition in 1 kB RAM. In: Proceedings of the Annual International Conference on Mobile Computing and Networking, MOBICOM 862–864 (2022). https://doi.org/10.1145/3495243.3558264
12. Maayah, M., Abunada, A., Al-Janahi, K., Ahmed, M.E., Qadir, J.: LimitAccess: on-device TinyML based robust speech recognition and age classification. Discover Artific. Intell. **3** (2023)

13. Xie, J., Ding, H., Alajlan, N.N., Ibrahim, D.M.: TinyML: enabling of inference deep learning models on ultra-low-power IoT edge devices for AI applications. Micromachines **13**, 851 (2022)
14. Jacob, B., et al.: Quantization and training of neural networks for efficient integer-arithmetic-only inference. In: Proceedings of the IEEE Computer Society Conference on Computer Vision and Pattern Recognition, pp. 2704–2713 (2018). https://arxiv.org/abs/1712.05877v1
15. Kurniawan, A.: Arduino nano 33 BLE sense board development. In: Kurniawan, A. (ed.) IoT Projects with Arduino Nano 33 BLE Sense: Step-By-Step Projects for Beginners, pp. 21–74. Apress, Berkeley, CA (2021). https://doi.org/10.1007/978-1-4842-6458-4_2
16. Nagel, M., et al.: A White Paper on Neural Network Quantization (2021)
17. Yang, Y., et al.: Towards efficient full 8-bit integer DNN online training on resource-limited devices without batch normalization. Neurocomputing **511**, 175–186 (2022)
18. Kuzmin, A., et al.: FP8 Quantization: The Power of the Exponent (2022)
19. Kung, H.T., Mcdanel, B., Zhang, S.Q.: Term Revealing: Furthering Quantization at Run Time on Quantized DNNs
20. Rastegari, M., Ordonez, V., Redmon, J., Farhadi, A.: Enabling AI at the edge with XNOR-networks. Commun. ACM **63**, 83–90 (2020)
21. Han, S., Pool, J., Tran, J., Dally, W.J.: Learning both Weights and Connections for Efficient Neural Networks. (2015)
22. Geng, L., Niu, B.: Pruning convolutional neural networks via filter similarity analysis. Mach. Learn. **111**, 3161–3180 (2022)
23. Han, S., Mao, H., Dally, W.J.: Deep compression: compressing deep neural networks with pruning, trained quantization and huffman coding. In: 4th ICLR 2016 – Conference Track Proceedings (2015)
24. David, R., et al.: TensorFlow Lite Micro: Embedded Machine Learning on TinyML Systems (2020)
25. Warden, P., Situnayake, D.: TinyML: machine learning with TensorFlow Lite on arduino and ultra-low-power microcontrollers. 504
26. Zalewski, P., et al.: From bits of data to bits of knowledge—an on-board classification framework for wearable sensing systems. Sensors **20**(6), 1655 (2020)
27. Dutta, D.L., Bharali, S.: TinyML meets IoT: a comprehensive survey. Internet of Things **16**, 100461 (2021)
28. TensorFlow Lite | ML for Mobile and Edge Devices. https://www.tensorflow.org/lite
29. NanoEdgeAIStudio – Automated Machine Learning (ML) tool for STM32 developers – STMicroelectronics. https://www.st.com/en/development-tools/nanoedgeaistudio.html
30. microTensor. https://utensor.github.io/website/
31. Edge Impulse. https://www.edgeimpulse.com/
32. Home | PyTorch. https://pytorch.org/mobile/home/
33. The Embedded Learning Library – Embedded Learning Library (ELL). https://microsoft.github.io/ELL/
34. STM32Cube Development Software – STM32 Open Development Environment – STMicroelectronics. https://www.st.com/en/ecosystems/stm32cube.html
35. Banbury, C.R., et al.: Benchmarking TinyML Systems: Challenges and Direction (2020)
36. Sanchez-Iborra, R., Skarmeta, A.F.: TinyML-enabled frugal smart objects: challenges and opportunities. IEEE Circuits Syst. Mag. **20**, 4–18 (2020)
37. de Prado, M., et al.: Robustifying the deployment of tinyML Models for autonomous mini-vehicles. In: Proceedings – IEEE International Symposium on Circuits and Systems (2020)
38. Wong, A., et al.: YOLO nano: a highly compact you only look once convolutional neural network for object detection. In: Proceedings – 5th Workshop on Energy Efficient Machine Learning and Cognitive Computing, EMC2-NIPS 2019, pp. 22–25 (2019). https://doi.org/10.1109/EMC2-NIPS53020.2019.00013

39. Andri, R., Cavigelli, L., Rossi, D., Benini, L.: YodaNN: an architecture for ultra-low power binary-weight CNN acceleration. IEEE Trans. Comput. Aided Des. Integr. Circuits Syst. **37**, 48–60 (2016)
40. Liberis, E., Lane, N.D.: Neural networks on microcontrollers: saving memory at inference via operator reordering (2019)
41. Niu, W., et al.: PatDNN: Achieving real-time DNN execution on mobile devices with pattern-based weight pruning. In: International Conference on Architectural Support for Programming Languages and Operating Systems – ASPLOS 907–922 (2019). https://doi.org/10.1145/3373376.3378534
42. Wong, A., Famouri, M., Shafiee, M.J.: AttendNets: tiny deep image recognition neural networks for the edge via visual attention condensers (2020)

New Deep Steganography Model Based on Josephus Confusion

Mohamed Htiti[1]([✉])[iD], Aziza El Ouaazizi[2][iD], Ismail Akharraz[3][iD], and Abdelaziz Ahaitouf[1][iD]

[1] Laboratory of Engineering Sciences (LSI), Polydisciplinary Faculty of Taza, Sidi Mohamed Ben Abdellah University, B.P. 1223, Taza, Morocco
{mohamed.htiti1,abdelaziz.ahaitouf}@usmba.ac.ma
[2] Laboratory of Artificial Intelligence, Data Sciences and Emergent Systems (LIASSE), National School of Engineers (ENSA), Sidi Mohamed Ben Abdellah University, Fez, Morocco
aziza.elouaazizi@usmba.ac.ma
[3] Mathematical and Informatics Engineering Laboratory (IMI), Agadir Faculty of Science, Ibnou Zohr University, Agadir, Morocco
i.akharraz@uiz.ac.ma

Abstract. With the rapid advancements in computers and the internet, digital media has emerged as a preferred medium for concealing information. This paper explores the field of steganography, focusing specifically on image steganography due to the widespread availability and abundance of data within images. The process of image steganography involves two key components: hiding a secret message within a cover image and extracting it from the image. Traditional techniques operate in either the spatial or frequency domain, directly modifying pixel intensities or embedding information in wavelets, respectively. In contrast, deep steganography utilizes neural networks to generate images containing hidden information, leveraging the power of machine learning for more robust concealment and automated learning processes. Further research is required to fully explore its implications in terms of security, detection resistance, and efficiency. Existing work in deep steganography demonstrates promise in terms of information security, as it preserves the visual and statistical properties of the cover image while offering potential resistance to detection. To enhance this work, we propose the addition of a Josephus confusion layer with a novel architecture, presenting promising and satisfactory results.

Keywords: Deep Steganography · CNN Neural Networks · Deep Learning · Josephus Confusion · Image Steganography · Digital Data Security

1 Introduction

The steganography word is composed of two Greek words: Steganos meaning "covered" and Graphia meaning "written". It is a field of computer science

H. Hagras et al. (Eds.): ISACS 2023, CCIS 2255, pp. 85–97, 2025.
https://doi.org/10.1007/978-3-031-93448-3_7

research that focuses on algorithms for hiding confidential secret information within other information. The origin of steganography goes back to ancient civilizations [1]. Indeed, the ancient Egyptians communicated secretly using the hieroglyphic language which is composed of a series of symbols. The hieroglyphic message simply looks like a drawing, although it may contain in some cases hidden information that only the person conscious of the presence of this secret can reveal it. The Greeks also used the technique of steganography to send secret text messages. In fact, in the fifth century BC, the governor Histaiacus tattooed a message on a slave's skull after shaving the slave's head and then sent him with the message after hair had grown back. [2].

The Chinese also used an ancient method of steganography [3] in which a paper mask with holes is placed on a blank paper, the secret message to be sent is written through the holes, then the mask is removed and the rest of the text is written to hide the secret message.

Other traditional examples of steganography can be found in the writings of the Roman poet Ovid, who tells the story of the Greek soldier Demaratus. He hid a message on a wooden tablet covered with wax. The message remained hidden under the wax and only someone who knew where to look could read it [4]. Linguistic steganography, known as acrostics, was also one of the most well known antiquated steganographic methods. The first letters of succeeding phrases or tercets of a poem were used to encrypt secret communications. One of the most famous examples is "Amorosa visione" by Giovanni Boccaccio [5]. After the great technical development of computers and the internet in the last decades, digital media such as: images, sounds and texts, have become the best choice to hide information. These digital media must have two characteristics: the medium must be popular, and any change made to it must be invisible to any unauthorized person [6]. Images are the most used in steganography. One of the reasons for this is the wide distribution on the internet and the large number of bits in each image. For this reason we will focus on images in this work.

An image steganography approach has two parts. The first part serves the purpose of concealing a confidential message within the cover image. The second part is an extraction algorithm designed for the effortless retrieval of the secret message from the composite image (comprising both the cover and the concealed secret) [7]. There are two commonly employed techniques for concealing information that do not involve artificial intelligence (AI)(spatial domain and frequency domain). Within the spatial domain, the information bit is directly incorporated and embedded into the pixel intensities of the cover image. Conversely, in the frequency domain, the initial step involves transforming the cover image into the frequency domain, and the information is then concealed within the wavelet [8].

Deep Steganography, differs from classical approaches in several ways. While classical steganography often focuses on modifying the features or pixels of the cover image to incorporate hidden data, deep steganography uses neural networks to generate images containing hidden information. This allows potentially more robust and sophisticated concealment capabilities, as neural networks can learn complex patterns and representations. Additionally, deep steganography takes advantage of machine learning automation, enabling automated learning of the process of concealing and extracting secret data. This adaptability, combined with the potential for better detection resistance by preserving the visual and statistical properties of the cover image, makes it a promising approach in the field of information security. However, further research is needed to fully explore its implications in terms of security, detection resistance, and efficiency.

The work proposed by Baluja [9] is an example of deep steganography. It involves hiding a color image within another image. However, if the cover image is available, there is a risk that an attacker, in case of suspicion, may compare the original with the one that was sent to at least get an idea of the secret. This issue is partially addressed by Sharma [10] when adding a block permutation layer of the secret image before incorporating it into the auto-encoder training procedure. To improve this work, we add a Josephus confusion layer with a new architecture; the results demonstrate its efficacy and provide good outcomes.

The paper is structured as follows: Sect. 2 introduces the deep steganography approach. In Sect. 3, we address the problematic aspects related to the topic and highlight our specific contributions. The results and discussions are presented in Sect. 4. Finally, in Sect. 5, we provide the conclusion of our study.

2 Deep Steganography Approach

In the field of steganography, particular attention has been paid to the use of deep learning approaches. Among the techniques commonly used in this approach are generative adversarial networks (GANs) and convolutional neural networks (CNNs).

2.1 Generative Adversarial Networks (GANs)

In the deep steganography and steganalysis approach, some works use Generative Adversarial Networks GANs. Two elements known as a generator and a discriminator are included in this network. In order to trick the discriminator, the generator goes through training to produce new samples. At the same time, the discriminator acquires the ability to avoid being deceived by the generator, involving a classification task of distinguishing genuine inputs from counterfeit ones.

The (Secure steganography) SSGAN model, presented in [11], is one of the first models of this type; It uses the generator to produce cover pictures and the discriminator to assess them. In [12], the authors designed the (Automatic steganographic distortion learning) ASDL-GAN, which applies distortions to the cover images in order to maximize the concealment of the message once it is embedded.

In [13], an evolving GAN architecture for steganography enhancement is proposed, where the learning process pursues a set of modifications that, once applied to the bitmap image, lead to a more robust steganographic method. In other words, GAN prepares an input picture for the eventual insertion of a steganographic message that will deceive the steganographic analysis model, represented by the discriminator, by a sequence of small, precise adjustments to the bitmap image. The image should also be modified as little as possible, to the point where these changes cannot be seen.

2.2 Convolutional Neural Networks (CNNs)

Convolutional Neural Networks (CNNs) have played an important role in advancing the field of steganography. They have been used in a variety of steganography related tasks, including steganographic message embedding and steganalysis (the detection of hidden information in images). They were introduced by LeCun et al. in 1990 [14].

The success of CNNs can be attributed not only to their architecture, but also to two crucial factors: data preprocessing and training strategy. Data preprocessing plays an essential role in increasing the size of the training set and improving network performance. By employing effective preprocessing techniques, CNNs can extract meaningful features from input images, improving their ability to analyze and classify them. In addition, the learning strategy of CNNs involves splitting the learning process into two different streams and running each stream on a separate GPU (Graphics Processing Unit). This parallelization technique speeds up the training process and improves computational efficiency.

CNNs have become the most widely used algorithms for a variety of image analysis tasks, including image classification and segmentation, and hiding secret images in others. A CNN consists of one or more convolutional layers that apply a number of filters to the input image. The role of these filters is to detect relevant features in the image, such as contours or textures. The convolutional layers are followed by one or more probing layers that reduce the dimensionality of the feature maps by sampling the data.

3 Proposed Steganographic Model

3.1 Problematic

Baluja [9] has successfully hidden an original color image (S) within another cover image (C). However, it is possible for someone to obtain the original cover image (C) without the embedded secret image. In this case, it becomes possible to partially reveal the secret image by comparing the original cover image (C) with the sent cover image (C') by calculating their difference.

The goal of resolving this problem is to minimize the difference between C and C' and make sure that the histograms of the two are as similar as possible. This histogram similarity preserves the main characteristic of steganography, which is to hide the existence of the communication, unlike cryptography, which aims to secure a secret public communication. Hence we need also to keep the correlation between the pixels of C and C' as close as possible.

Sharma [10] proposed a solution by adding a block permutation to the secret image before its incorporation into the learning process. Since he considered the permutation he made as cryptography, he sought to subject his results to cryptographic criteria.

In this work we propose a new architecture that incorporates Josephus confusion of the secret image before subjecting it to the learning process. Regarding image processing, confusion refers to altering the positions of pixels without modifying their values. This proposition aims to achieve better dissimulation while preserving much of the histogram of (C') similar to that of (C). It also keeps the pixel correlation intact.

3.2   Josephus Confusion

The Josephus problem is a mathematical enigma that arises in the fields of computer science and mathematics [15]. Its various origins can be summarized by the following mathematical model: A group of N individuals form a circle and are assigned numbers from 1 to N. From a specified position within the circle, individuals are counted in a sequence until the person at position M is eliminated from the circle. The counting process then continues from the next position after the one that has been eliminated. This problem can be expressed mathematically by the Josephus function q = Josephus(n, s, p), where n is the total number of individuals in the circle, s is the starting position, p is the counting period, and q is the resulting Josephus sequence.

To illustrate the Josephus operation, consider the case where n = 10, s = 2, and p = 3. The resulting Josephus sequence q would be [2, 5, 8, 1, 6, 10, 7, 4, 9, 3]. Figure 1 provides a visual illustration of the generation process. In this example, counting starts from position 2, with step of 3. Therefore, the first individual to leave the array is 2, and counting continues from the position immediately following 2. The Josephus sequence is the result of this procedure, which is repeated until the final element is reached. Figure 2 shows 6 Josephus confusion results as a function of the step value equal p.

3.3   Architecture

The architecture of the network in question bears a certain resemblance to CNN Autoencoders [16]. CNN Autoencoders, in general, aim to generate an output that closely matches the input after a series of transformations. This process allows them to learn the fundamental characteristics of the input image. However, in our case, Instead of only reproducing images, the network has the additional task of hiding an image while simultaneously generating another image. Figure 3) illustrates the proposed architecture.

The initial layer, Josephus-Layer, introduces confusion to all the pixels of the secret images. The second layer consists of the hiding network, which takes the output of the Josephus layer and the cover image as inputs to generate the container image. It includes five convolution layers, each consisting of three parallel sub-layers with 30, 60, and 90 filters of sizes (3 × 3), (4 × 4), (5 × 5) respectively. The third layer is the Reveal Network, which exclusively takes the Container image as input (without the cover or secret image). This network is

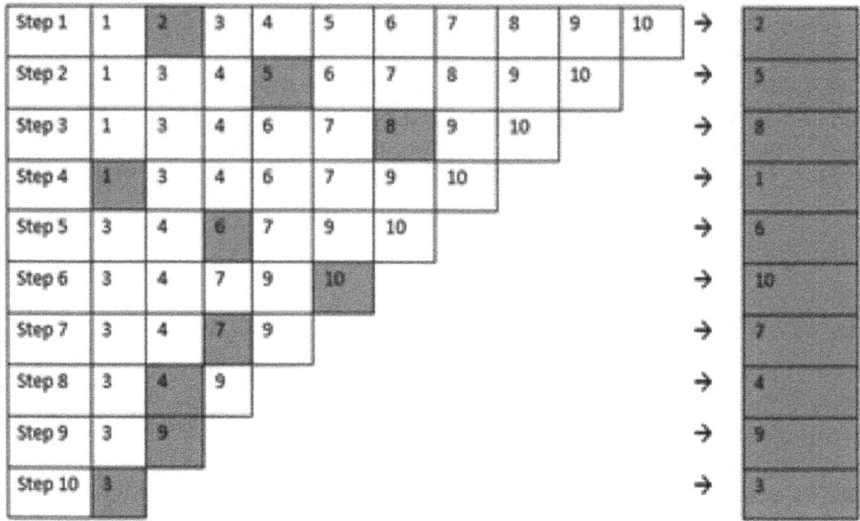

Fig. 1. An example of Josephus sequence.

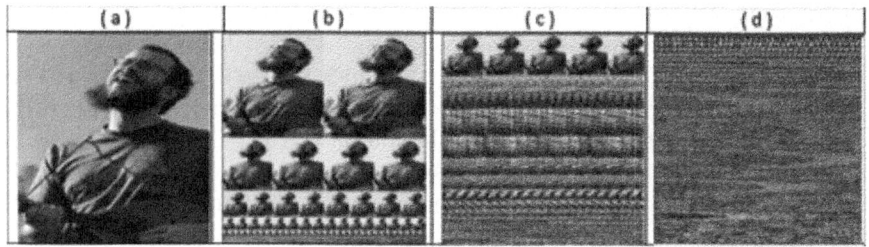

Fig. 2. Josephus Confusion on an Image Based on Step p: (a) Original Image, (b) p = 2, (c) p = 5, (d) p = 10, (e) p = 15, (f) p = 25, (g) p = 35.

responsible for removing the cover image to unveil the secret image. Lastly, the Reverse-Josephus layer is applied to re-confuse the output of the reveal network in order to extract the secret image.

3.4   Experimental Configuration

The model was trained using the Python 3 Google Compute Engine on the Google Colab platform, which provides access to additional resources, including GPU and RAM. The GPU acceleration offered by Google significantly speeds up the process of training deep learning models by harnessing the power of parallel processing. The increased RAM capacity enables larger datasets and more complex models to be processed, resulting in more robust and resource-intensive training. Google Colab provides a JupyterLab environment in which model development and training took place. This environment also provided

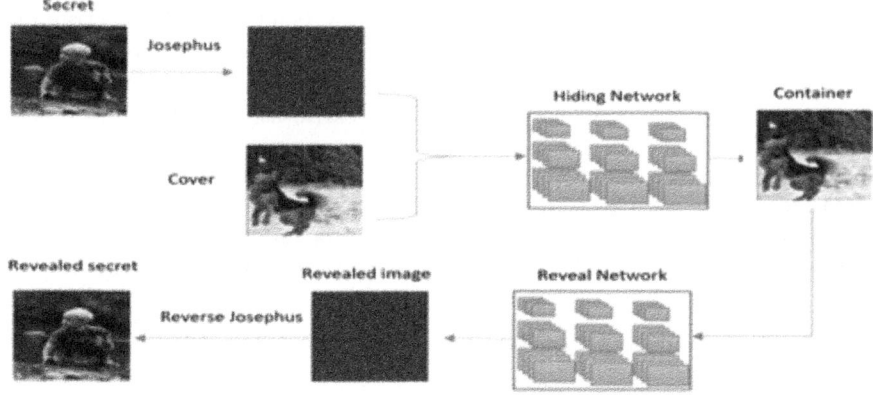

Fig. 3. Architecture of the proposed system.

access to all the essential libraries for artificial intelligence and machine learning, including Keras, Matplotlib, Numpy, Scipy, and more.

3.5 Preparing Datasets

The Flickr30k dataset was used to train the model and prepare the dataset. The photos in the dataset were reduced to 256×256 in line with our training model because their sizes were irregular throughout the dataset. In total, 2000 covers and 2000 secrets were used in the learning process. The datasets are available in [17]. In addition, as part of the confusion process, each image in the dataset was subjected to a Josephus operation with a step size of 3500 and a pixel index start of 10.

3.6 Model Training

The training process for a machine learning model is crucial for achieving good results.

Batch Size: The model is trained using a batch size of 32 images. This means that during each training iteration, 32 images are processed together before the model's parameters are updated. Batch size can affect training efficiency and model generalization.

Epochs: The training process runs for a total of 250 epochs. An epoch is one complete pass through the entire training dataset. Training for 250 epochs means the model has seen the entire dataset 250 times. This is a common training setup. We decide to limit the training to 250 epochs to minimize the training duration. After 250, additional training epochs may not significantly improve the model's performance.

Training Duration: The model took approximately 10 h to complete its training. This is a crucial piece of information, as it indicates the computational resources and time investment required for this specific training run. It's important to consider the hardware specifications, such as GPU(s) used, in this context.

Model Summary: A summary of the full model is provided in Table 1. This suggests that there is likely to be a more detailed description of the model architecture, including the number of layers, types of layers, and number of parameters. This information is essential for understanding the model's complexity.

Table 1. Detailed representation of the full model.

Layer (type)	Output Shape	Param	Connected to
input-1 (InputLayer)	[(None, 256, 256, 1)]	0	[]
input-2 (InputLayer)	[(None, 256, 256, 1)]	0	[]
Encoder (Functional)	(None, 256, 256, 1)	2,532,243	['input-1[0][0]', 'input-2[0][0]']
Decoder (Functional)	(None, 256, 256, 1)	2,521,803	['Encoder[0][0]']
concatenate-15 (Concatenate)	(None, 256, 256, 2)	0	['Decoder[0][0]', 'Encoder[0][0]']
Total params	5,054,046		
Trainable params	5,054,046		
Non-trainable params	0		

4   Results and Discussion

Table 2 shows the trainable parameters of our model and those of Baluja [9] and Sharma [10]. Trainable parameters refer to the number of model parameters that can be adjusted during the training process. These parameters are usually learned from the data and play a crucial role in model training and prediction.

In terms of total number of parameters, our model is the highest with 5,054,046 parameters. Baluja's model has 3,782,406 parameters, while Sharma's has the least with 488,661 parameters.

Table 2. Number of the trainable and non trainable parameter.

	Trainable params	Non-trainable params
Our model	5,054,046	0
Baluja [9]	3,782,406	0
Sharma [10]	293,273	195,388

Figure 4(a) and (b) provide the cover and stegano image, respectively. The histogram comparison and correlation between C and C'respectively are shown in (c) and (d). Figure 4 illustrates that our model has effectively preserved the shape of the histogram and the correlation of the "cover" image. Indeed, if someone obtains the sent cover image and suspects something, by comparing the histogram or correlation distribution of the intercepted image with that of the original image, he will not detect that there is a secret hidden inside.

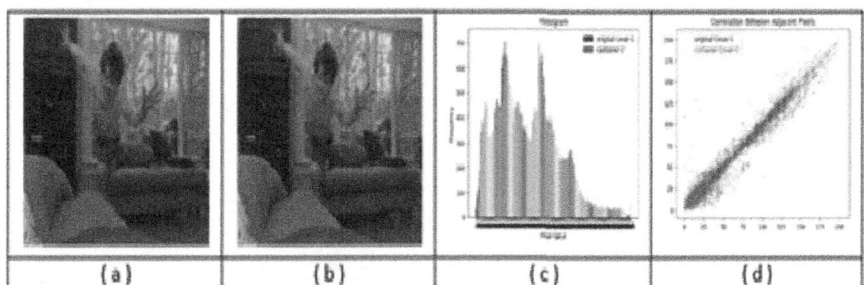

Fig. 4. Histogram and correlation result: (a) original cover C, (b) container cover C', (c) histogram of C and C', (d) correlation distribution between adjacent pixel for C and C'.

Figure 5 illustrates the process of hiding and recovering a secret image. The first row shows the original cover image used to hide the confused secret image shown in the third row. By integrating the confused secret image, the fourth line represents the reconstructed cover image. Finally, in the sixth row, we see the revealed secret image. The result confirms the successful concealment and recovery of the secret image.

Figure 6 shows a comparison between the results obtained with our model and those obtained with Baluja's model. The first line shows the original cover image used to hide the secret image, which appears in the second line. The third and fourth lines show the reconstructed cover images, each incorporating the secret image using our model and Baluja's, respectively. Finally, the amplified difference |C-C'| between our model and Baluja's model is shown in the fifth and sixth rows, respectively. The results confirm the success of secret image masking and the retrieval with our model compared to Baluja's. If someone obtains the cover image sent and gets suspicious, by displaying the difference between the intercepted image and the original image, he will not suspect that there is a secret hidden inside. However, with Baluja's results, it is clear that we can be certain that the intercepted image contains a secret and get an idea of its nature.

Quality Metrics of Steganographic Images. The most commonly used measures for comparing steganographic images (S) and original images (C) of size M × N are [18]:

Fig. 5. Results of integrating neural networks with a Josephus confusion.

Peak-Signal-to-Noise Ratio (PSNR). PSNR is a statistical estimate of image quality used to measure the distortion between the original image and the steganographic image. Low PSNR results in noticeable alterations in the steganographic pictures, which may be easily identified by the human visual system, whereas high PSNR values suggest a low level of distortion and great visual quality. The PSNR is given by [19]:

$$PNCR = 20 \times \log_{10}(255/\sqrt{MSE}) \tag{1}$$

Fig. 6. Results obtained by combining neural networks with a Josephus confusion technique, presenting a comparison between our model and the Baluja model.

where the mean square error (MSE) is given by:

$$MSE = \frac{1}{M \times N} \sum_{i=0}^{M-1} \sum_{j=0}^{N-1} (S - C)^2 \qquad (2)$$

Normalized-Cross-Correlation (NCC). The NCC indicates the strength of the correlation between the steganographic image and the original image. NCC values range from 0 to 1. A value of 1 indicates that steganographic images are completely robust to various image processing attacks [20]. The NCC is calculated as follows:

$$NCC = \frac{\sum_{i=0}^{M-1} \sum_{j=0}^{N-1} (S(i,j) \times C(i,j))}{\sum_{i=0}^{M-1} \sum_{j=0}^{N-1} S(i,j)^2} \tag{3}$$

Structural Similarity Index Measurement (SSIM). SSIM is a metric used to assess the quality of pictures that looks for similarities between steganographic and original images. As described below:

$$SSIM(C,S) = \frac{(2\mu_C \mu_S + c_1)(2\sigma_{CS} + c_2)}{(\mu_C^2 + \mu_S^2 + c_1)(\sigma_C^2 \cdot \sigma_S^2 + c_2)} \tag{4}$$

where μ_C is the pixel mean of the original image C. μ_S is the pixel mean of the steganographic image S, σ_c^2 is the variance of C. σ_S^2 is the variance of S; σ_{CS} is the covariance of C and S, $c_1 = (K_1 \times L)^2$, $c_2 = (K_2 \times L)^2$ are two variables that stabilize the division with a low denominator, L is the dynamic range of pixel values, and $K_1 = 0.01$ and $K_2 = 0.03$ by default.

Table 3 shows the results for the three dissimilation quality metrics. The data clearly show that our model significantly outperforms Baluja's for all three metrics.

Table 3. Results for the three dissimilation quality metrics.

test	Baluja Model [9]	Our Model
PSNR	31.0509	32.7722
NCC	0.9993	0.9995
SSIM	0.9355	0.9710

5   Conclusion

This article presents a new, more secure method for hiding secret information in images. By combining deep steganography with Josephus confusion, our method becomes difficult to break. The added confusion layer, implemented with deep neural networks, provides an additional level of security. The results obtained show that our model effectively preserves the original image and hides secret information. The shape of the image and its correlation are maintained, making it difficult for someone to suspect the presence of a hidden secret. The successful process highlights the superiority of our method in terms of hiding and recovering the secret image over other approaches. The noticeable difference between the intercepted and the original image in Baluja's results clearly indicates the presence of a secret, whereas our method effectively hides the secret and avoids suspicion. But our model effectively hides the secret and avoids suspicion. These conclusions are supported by the three most commonly used dissimulation quality metrics: PSNR, NCC, and SSIM.

References

1. Cox, I., Miller, M., Bloom, J., Fridrich, J., Kalker, T.: Digital Watermarking and Steganography. Morgan Kaufmann (2007)
2. Provos, N., Honeyman, P.: Hide and seek: an introduction to steganography. IEEE Secur. Priv. **1**(3), 32–44 (2003)
3. Fridrich, J.: Steganography in Digital Media: Principles, Algorithms, and Applications. Cambridge University Press (2009)
4. Kipper, G.: Investigator's Guide to Steganography. CRC Press (2003)
5. Tacticus, A.: How to Survive Under Siege. Clarendon Press (1990)
6. Zamir, R., Shamai, S., Erez, U.: Nested linear/lattice codes for structured multi-terminal binning. IEEE Trans. Inf. Theory **48**(6), 1250–1276 (2002)
7. Kasapbaşi, M.C.: A new chaotic image steganography technique based on Huffman compression of Turkish texts and fractal encryption with post-quantum security. IEEE Access **7**, 148495–148510 (2019)
8. Khosravi, B., Khosravi, B., Khosravi, B., Nazarkardeh, K.: A new method for pdf steganography in justified texts. J. Inf. Secur. Appl. **45**, 61–70 (2019)
9. Baluja, S.: Hiding images in plain sight: deep steganography. In: Advances in Neural Information Processing Systems, vol. 30 (2017)
10. Sharma, K., Aggarwal, A., Singhania, T., Gupta, D., Khanna, A.: Hiding data in images using cryptography and deep neural network. arXiv preprint arXiv:1912.10413 (2019)
11. Shi, H., Dong, J., Wang, W., Qian, Y., Zhang, X.: SSGAN: secure steganography based on generative adversarial networks. In: Zeng, B., Huang, Q., El Saddik, A., Li, H., Jiang, S., Fan, X. (eds.) PCM 2017. LNCS, vol. 10735, pp. 534–544. Springer, Cham (2018). https://doi.org/10.1007/978-3-319-77380-3_51
12. Tang, W., Tan, S., Li, B., Huang, J.: Automatic steganographic distortion learning using a generative adversarial network. IEEE Signal Process. Lett. **24**(10), 1547–1551 (2017)
13. Martín, A., Hernández, A., Alazab, M., Jung, J., Camacho, D.: Evolving generative adversarial networks to improve image steganography. Expert Syst. Appl. **222**, 119841 (2023)
14. Le Cun, Y., et al.: Handwritten digit recognition with a back-propagation network. Adv. Neural. Inf. Process. Syst. **2**, 396–404 (1990)
15. Schumer, P.: The Josephus problem: once more around. Math. Mag. **75**(1), 12–17 (2002)
16. Hinton, G.E., Salakhutdinov, R.R.: Reducing the dimensionality of data with neural networks. Science **313**(5786), 504–507 (2006)
17. Kaggle: Flickr Image Dataset. https://www.kaggle.com/datasets/hsankesara/flickr-image-dataset
18. He, L., Gao, F., Hou, W., Hao, L.: Objective image quality assessment: a survey. Int. J. Comput. Math. **91**(11), 2374–2388 (2014)
19. Wang, Z., Bovik, A.C.: Modern image quality assessment. Ph.D. thesis, Springer (2006)
20. Thiyagarajan, P., Aghila, G.: Reversible dynamic secure steganography for medical image using graph coloring. Health Policy Technol. **2**(3), 151–161 (2013)
21. Wang, Z., Bovik, A.C., Sheikh, H.R., Simoncelli, E.P.: Image quality assessment: from error visibility to structural similarity. IEEE Trans. Image Process. **13**(4), 600–612 (2004)

Intelligent Deep Learning Model for Disease Detection in Plants: Leveraging Particle Swarm Optimization in Intelligent Agriculture

Krim Hajar$^{(\boxtimes)}$ (ID) and Assir Abdelhadi (ID)

Faculty of Sciences and Techniques, Hassan First University of Settat, RMI Laboratory Settat, Settat, Morocco
{h.krim,abdelhadi.assir}@uhp.ac.ma

Abstract. Intelligent agriculture, also known as smart farming, is an emerging field that integrates advanced technologies and data-driven approaches to optimize agricultural practices. By leveraging artificial intel- ligence, the Internet of Things (IoT), and big data analytics, intelligent agriculture aims to enhance crop yield, minimize resource consumption, and improve overall sustainability. In this context, the accurate detection of diseases in plants holds significant importance for ensuring optimal crop health and productivity. This research proposes an intelligent deeplearning model based on PSO for disease detection in intelligent agriculture. PSO and deep learning are combined to automatically search for the optimal architecture. Utilizing CNNs as the base architecture, the model leverages PSO to determine hyperparameters. Extensive experiments perform better than manual design, with high accuracy, precision, and recall. The model demonstrates robustness and generalizability across diverse datasets, promising practical applications in intelligent agriculture. This research automates architecture design, improving crop management and enabling early disease detection.

Keywords: Intelligent agriculture · Deep learning · Particle swarm optimization · Disease detection · Convolutional neural networks

1 Introduction

Intelligent agriculture, also known as smart farming, has emerged as a transformative approach to optimize agricultural practices using advanced technologies and data-driven methodologies [1]. With the integration of artificial intelligence (AI) and deep learning techniques [2], intelligent agriculture has the potential to revolutionize crop management, resource allocation, and disease detection in plants.

This research introduces a novel approach in the realm of intelligent agriculture by proposing an intelligent deep-learning model based on particle swarm optimization (PSO) for accurate disease detection in plants. By combining the optimization capabilities of PSO with the power of deep learning, the proposed model aims to automatically search for the optimal architecture to achieve superior performance in disease detection tasks. The foundation of the proposed model lies in convolutional neural networks

H. Hagras et al. (Eds.): ISACS 2023, CCIS 2255, pp. 98–109, 2025.
https://doi.org/10.1007/978-3-031-93448-3_8

(CNNs), a powerful deep-learning architecture widely recognized for its efficacy in image classification and object detection. Leveraging the inherent capabilities of CNNs, the intelligent deep learning model employs PSO to determine the optimal configuration of hyper-parameters, including the number of layers, filter sizes, and activation functions. This integration enables the model to dynamically adapt and optimize its architecture specifically for the task of disease detection in plants.

To assess the effectiveness of the proposed approach, extensive experiments were conducted on diverse plant disease datasets. The results of these experiments demonstrated that the intelligent deep learning model based on PSO surpasses traditional manual design approaches, exhibiting exceptional accuracy, precision, and recall in detecting plant diseases. Furthermore, the model showcases robustness and generalizability across different datasets, signifying its potential for practical applications in intelligent agriculture. The significance of this research lies in its contribution to automating the architecture design process in disease detection systems within the context of intelligent agriculture. By eliminating the need for manual intervention, this approach streamlines the process and enhances crop management practices. Early and accurate detection of plant diseases facilitated by the proposed model can lead to improved disease management strategies, optimized resource allocation, and enhanced agricultural productivity and sustainability. In the subsequent sections of this paper, we present the methodology employed for developing the intelligent deep learning model based on PSO, discuss the experimental setup, and provide an in-depth analysis of the results. Additionally, we explore the implications of this research and its potential for transforming intelligent agriculture practices in the near future.

This paper has the following structure: Sect. 1 introduces intelligent agriculture in the context of plant disease detection. Section 2 presents significant related work conducted in the field of intelligent agriculture for disease detection in plants. Section 3 provides background information on the proposed solution. Moreover, Sect. 4 describes the methodology and materials used in the study. Section 5 presents the proposed deep learning-based solution for disease detection in plants. Section 5 presents the obtained results and a performance evaluation of the proposed solution. Finally, Section 6 concludes this paper by summarizing the key findings and discussing future directions for research in the field of intelligent agriculture for plant disease detection.

2   Related Work

The field of intelligent agriculture has witnessed remarkable advancements in recent years [3], leveraging cutting-edge technologies to address challenges related to crop health and productivity. Among these technologies, deep learning models have emerged as powerful tools for disease detection in plants [4, 5]. By harnessing the capabilities of neural networks [6, 7], these models can analyze large volumes of plant data, extract intricate patterns, and accurately identify disease symptoms. In this paper, we delve into the realm of deep learning-based disease detection in plants, aiming to provide a comprehensive review of the related work conducted in this domain. By examining the existing literature, we aim to highlight the various approaches, methodologies, and achievements in employing deep learning models for the early and accurate diagnosis of plant diseases. Through this exploration, we aim to identify potential research gaps and suggest directions for future advancements in intelligent agriculture. In this research paper [8], the authors address the challenge of enhancing plant disease classification in Low-Resolution (LR) images for smart agriculture. They propose two contributions: first, fine-tuning the Dense Convolutional Network (DenseNet), a low-complexity classifier, using High-Resolution (HR) plant leaf images to detect tomato leaf diseases. Secondly, they introduce a novel Super-Resolution (SR) algorithm called Wideractivation for Attention Mechanism based on a Generative Adversarial Network (WAGAN) to enhance LR tomato image classification. Evaluation results show the efficacy of the proposed SR method, achieving 97.63% accuracy with 3.6 times lower complexity compared to the state-of-the-art. The SR model focuses on critical information, enabling DenseNet to accurately recognize plant diseases. This research demonstrates the potential of leveraging fine-tuned DenseNet and the Wideractivation SR algorithm to improve disease classification in LR images, providing an efficient and accurate approach for smart agriculture. However, Agriculture, a vital contributor to economic growth, Faces challenges with population, climate, and resources. Precision agriculture, or smart farming, emerges as a solution, Powered by machine learning (ML) and cutting-edge technology, ML and IoT-driven machinery shape the future of agriculture. The authors in paper [9] review ML applications in agriculture's domain, Focusing on soil parameter prediction, crop yield estimation, Detecting diseases, weeds, and species with ML and computer vision, Monitoring crop quality and yield through image classification, Integration for livestock production improvements, predicting fertility, ML models diagnose disorders, analyze cattle behavior through sensors, and Intelligent irrigation and harvesting reduce human labor, Knowledge-based agriculture enhances sustainability and quality.

Furthermore, the authors in paper [10], introduce an intelligent solution known as deep learning, A modern technique for image processing and data analysis with great potential, Its successful application in various domains now extends to agriculture, The paper conducts a survey of 40 research efforts utilizing deep learning in agriculture, Examining agricultural challenges addressed, models employed, data sources and preprocessing, Overall performance is assessed based on specific metrics for each study. Comparisons are made between deep learning and other popular techniques, Highlighting differences in classification or regression performance. The findings reveal deep learning's superiority, providing high accuracy and outperforming commonly used image processing techniques in agriculture. In another research paper [11], the proposed solution is described as follows: Combining machine learning, big data technologies, and high-performance computing, Creating opportunities for data-intensive science in the agri-technologies domain, The paper presents a comprehensive review of machine learning applications in agricultural production systems, Categorized into crop management, livestock management, water management, and soil management, Crop management applications include yield prediction, disease and weed detection, crop quality, and species recognition, Livestock management applications cover animal welfare and livestock production, Water management and soil management are also discussed, The analysis showcases the benefits of machine learning in agriculture, Sensor data enables real-time AI-enabled farm management systems, Providing rich recommendations and insights for farmer decision-support and action.

In contradiction to the cited work, our research aims to address the challenge of disease detection by proposing an optimized deep learning architecture based on Particle Swarm Optimization (PSO). By leveraging PSO, we seek to enhance the performance and efficiency of the deep learning model for accurate disease identification in the context of intelligent agriculture. This approach combines the strengths of deep learning in feature extraction and PSO in optimizing model parameters, leading to improved disease detection capabilities.

3 Background

3.1 Convolutional neural networks (CNNs)

Convolutional Neural Networks (CNNs) have revolutionized the field of computer vision by demonstrating remarkable performance in tasks such as image classification [12], object detection, and semantic segmentation. Unlike traditional neural networks, CNNs excel at processing structured grid-like data, particularly images, due to their unique architectural design [13]. By leveraging convolutional layers, pooling operations, and non-linear activation functions, CNNs can automatically learn hierarchical representations of visual features. These features enable them to capture spatial relationships, detect patterns, and extract meaningful information from images [14].

3.2 Particle Swarm Optimization (PSO)

Particle Swarm Optimization (PSO) is a metaheuristic optimization algorithm inspired by the social behavior of bird flocking or fish schooling [15, 16]. It is widely used for solving optimization problems in various domains [17, 18]. In PSO, a population of particles represents potential solutions, with each particle representing a candidate solution in the search space [19]. These particles explore the search space by adjusting their positions based on their individual best-known positions and the best-known positions of the entire population. The mechanism of this algorithm can be described as follow At each iteration, particles update their velocities by considering both their previous velocities and the distances to their best-known positions and the global best-known position [20]. This allows particles to move toward promising regions in the search space.

Through iterations, particles share information about their local and global best positions, leading to a cooperative search behavior that aims to converge toward the optimal solution [21].

4 Research Methodology

4.1 Dataset

The dataset employed in this study is a subset derived from the larger database available on Kaggle [22]. The Kaggle database comprises approximately 174,000 images depicting infected and healthy leaves from various plant species, including tomato, orange, and maize. However, this paper focuses exclusively on images of maize plants. This particular subset was selected due to its extensive range of conditions and a sufficient number of images in each category. The subset consists of four distinct categories, encompassing a total of 12,332 images for the training set and 3,076 images for the test set.

4.2 Metrics

Evaluation metrics play a crucial role in assessing the performance and effectiveness of deep learning models for disease detection in the context of intelligent agriculture. Accurate evaluation metrics provide valuable insights into the model's ability to correctly identify and classify plant diseases, enabling researchers and practitioners to make informed decisions. One commonly used metric is accuracy (ACC), which measures the overall correctness of the model's predictions. It helps determine the percentage of correctly classified disease samples, providing a general assessment of the model's performance. Additionally, precision (PRE) and recall (REC) are vital metrics for disease detection as they provide insights into the model's ability to minimize false positives and false negatives, respectively. Precision measures the proportion of correctly identified disease samples out of all samples predicted as positive, while recall measures the proportion of correctly identified disease samples out of all actual disease samples. These metrics are essential for evaluating the model's reliability in identifying true positive cases and avoiding misclassifications that could have significant consequences for agricultural practices. Furthermore, the F1 score (F), which combines precision and recall, provides a balanced measure of the model's overall performance. It offers a single value that represents both the model's precision and recall, making it a useful metric for comparing different models and selecting the most suitable one. Overall, these evaluation metrics play a vital role in quantifying the accuracy, precision, and reliability of deep learning models in disease detection, enabling researchers and practitioners to gauge the performance of their intelligent agriculture systems and make data-driven decisions for effective disease management. Here is the formulation of the proposed evaluation metrics

$$ACC = \frac{TN + TP}{TN + FP + TP + FN} \tag{1}$$

$$REC = \frac{TP}{FP + TP} \tag{2}$$

$$REC = \frac{TP}{FN + TP} \tag{3}$$

$$F = \frac{2 * (PER) * (REC)}{(PER) + (PER)} \tag{4}$$

Within the scope of machine learning evaluation, the outputs TP, FP, FN, and TN correspond to the quantities that indicate the classification results for fraud transactions. TP (True Positive) represents the number of accurately identified fraud transactions, FP (False Positive) indicates the count of incorrectly identified legitimate transactions, TN (True Negative) signifies the accurate identification of legitimate transactions, and FN (False Negative) represents the number of fraud transactions that were incorrectly predicted.

4.3 Proposed Solution

The proposed approach follows a systematic methodology for identifying plant diseases using deep learning with Particle Swarm Optimization (PSO). Initially, a diverse dataset of plant images containing healthy and diseased crop leaves is collected. The dataset is then preprocessed using standard techniques to enhance the model's performance. A customized Convolutional Neural Network (CNN) architecture is designed, consisting of convolutional, pooling, and fully connected layers. PSO is employed to optimize the hyperparameters of the CNN model, including learning rate, batch size, number of filters, and kernel sizes. The model is trained using the preprocessed dataset, and its performance is evaluated using standard evaluation metrics. Validation and testing are conducted on separate datasets to ensure the model's generalization capability. The results are analyzed and compared with existing methods to assess the proposed approach's effectiveness. The proposed solution aims to provide accurate and efficient plant disease identification, contributing to the field of intelligent agriculture. Figure 1 describes the pipeline of the proposed solution. From this figure, it's clear that in the first step, the dataset is divided into three parts: training (50%), validation (20%), and testing (30%). Following, a CNNs architecture is used in an optimization process based on the particle swarm algorithm, and the training and validation sets are used to search for an optimized CNNs model. The outcome-optimized process is then used to classify the testing set and calculate the used evaluation metrics.

In every deep learning architecture, optimizing hyperparameters is essential to achieve better performance. In this paper, our focus is on enhancing the performance of our convolutional neural network (CNN). We aim to accomplish this by utilizing the Particle Swarm Optimization (PSO) algorithm to select the optimal hyperparameters. Specifically, we aim to determine the best values for the following hyperparameters:

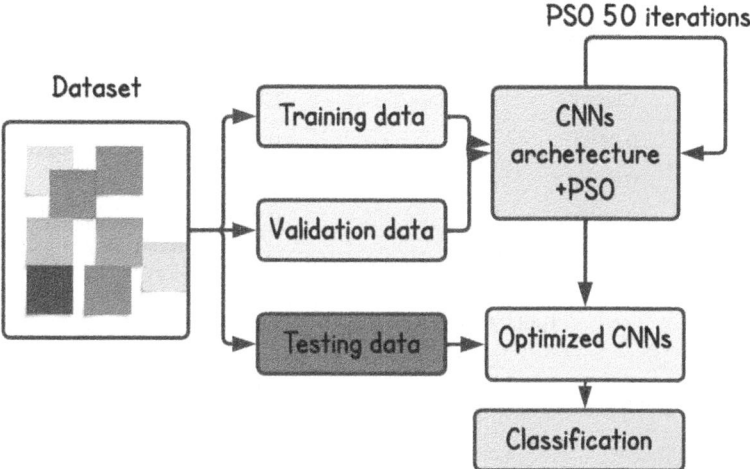

Fig. 1. Proposed solution

1. Learning Rate: The learning rate determines the step size at each iteration during the training process. It controls how much the weights are updated based on the gradient. Typical range: [0.001, 0.1].

2. Activation Function: The activation function introduces non-linearity into the neural network. Common choices include ReLU (Rectified Linear Unit), sigmoid, and tanh. The selection depends on the specific problem and the behavior required. No specific range, as it depends on the chosen activation function.
3. Batch Size: Batch size determines the number of samples processed at each iteration during training. It affects the speed of training and the memory requirements. Typical range: [8, 256].
4. Dropout Rate: Dropout is a regularization technique that randomly sets a fraction of input units to zero during training to prevent overfitting. The dropout rate controls the fraction of units to drop. Typical range: [0.1, 0.5].

5   Results and Analysis

Table 1. The Achieved Outcomes from Optimized CNNs

Metrics	Class 1	Class 2	Class 3	Class 4
PRE	0.9491	1	0.95641	1
REC	0.9142	1	0.9746	1
F	0.9313	1	0.9654	1

Table 2. The Achieved Outcomes from CNNs

Metrics	Class 1	Class 2	Class 3	Class 4
PRE	0.9590	1	0.9313	1
REC	0.8602	1	0.9809	1
F	0.9069	1	0.9555	1

Table 3. The Accuracy score obtained

Model	Accuracy
CNNs	0.9765
Optimized CNNs	0.98211

The provided tables present the performance results of two different CNN models: the original CNNs (Table 1) and the optimized CNNs (Table 2). The metrics evaluated for each class include Precision (PRE), Recall (REC), and F1-score (F).

Comparing the results, it can be observed that the optimized CNNs consistently outperform the original CNNs across all metrics and classes. In terms of Precision, the optimized CNNs achieve high values in all classes, with Class 2 achieving perfect precision (1.0). The original CNNs also show good precision but slightly lower compared to the optimized CNNs.

Regarding Recall, the optimized CNNs exhibit excellent performance, achieving high values close to 1.0 for all classes, indicating the ability to effectively detect positive instances. On the other hand, the original CNNs demonstrate lower recall in Class 1, suggesting a higher rate of false negatives.

The F1-score, which combines precision and recall, provides a balanced measure of the models' performance. The optimized CNNs achieve near-perfect F1-scores of 1.0 for all classes, indicating their ability to achieve a harmonious balance between precision and recall. The original CNNs, although showing reasonable F1-scores, demonstrate comparatively lower values in Class 1.

Additionally, the overall accuracy score of the models is provided in Table 3. The optimized CNNs achieve an accuracy of 0.98211, outperforming the original CNNs with an accuracy of 0.9765. This indicates that the optimized CNNs are more accurate in classifying instances across all classes, resulting in fewer mis-classifications. In conclusion, the optimized CNNs exhibit superior performance compared to the original CNNs in terms of Accuracy, Precision, Recall, and F1- score for each class. These findings highlight the effectiveness of optimizing the CNN hyperparameters in achieving improved performance in disease detection within the context of intelligent agriculture.

Figures 2, 3, and 4 present a comprehensive analysis of the performance of Convolutional Neural Networks (CNNs) and Optimized CNNs in a classification task involving four distinct classes, Class 1 represents Gray Leaf Spot, Class 2 represents Common rust, Class 3 represents Northern Leaf Blight, and Class 4 represents Healthy. The key evaluation metrics—Precision, Recall, and F1-Score, have been meticulously examined for each class to provide insights into the models' effectiveness. The Precision comparison graph reveals that Optimized CNNs consistently outperform CNNs across all four classes, showcasing their superior ability to make accurate positive predictions. In terms of Recall, the graph illustrates that Optimized CNNs exhibit higher sensitivity, particularly for Class 1 and Class 3, indicating their proficiency in correctly identifying true positives. Furthermore, the F1-Score comparison graph synthesizes both Precision and Recall, demonstrating that Optimized CNNs consistently achieve a higher harmonic mean of Precision and Recall, affirming their overall better performance in achieving the delicate balance between precision and recall. These findings underscore the significance of optimization techniques in enhancing the classification capabilities of CNNs, with potential implications for various real-world applications requiring precise and reliable predictions across multiple classes. Figure 5, we illustrate the model accuracy of two distinct neural network architectures: CNNs (Convolutional Neural Networks) and Optimized CNNs. The y-axis represents accuracy values, while the x-axis denotes the models being compared. For CNNs, we observe an accuracy of approximately 0.9765, indicating a strong predictive performance. In contrast, the Optimized CNNs exhibit a slightly higher accuracy, with a value of approximately 0.98211, suggesting that optimization techniques have contributed to further enhancing the model's accuracy. Circular markers in blue highlight the data points for each model, allowing for a direct visual comparison of their respective accuracies. This plot provides a concise yet informative representation of model performance, emphasizing the subtle differences in accuracy between the two neural network configurations.

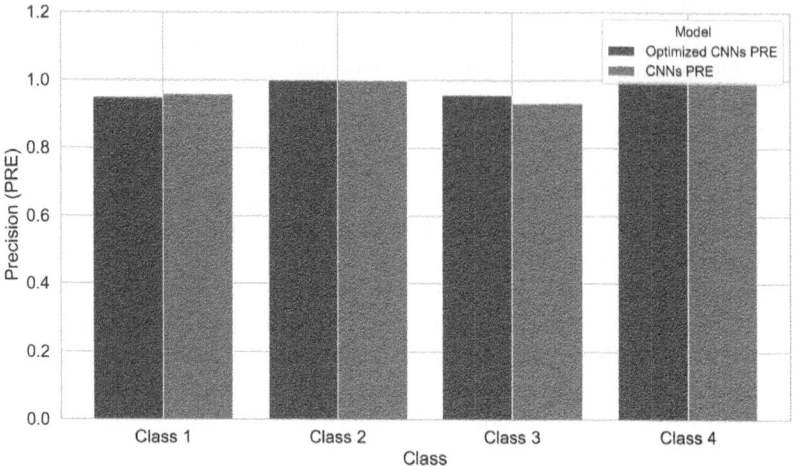

Fig. 2. Comparison of Precision (PRE) for Classes 1–4: Optimized CNNs vs. CNNs

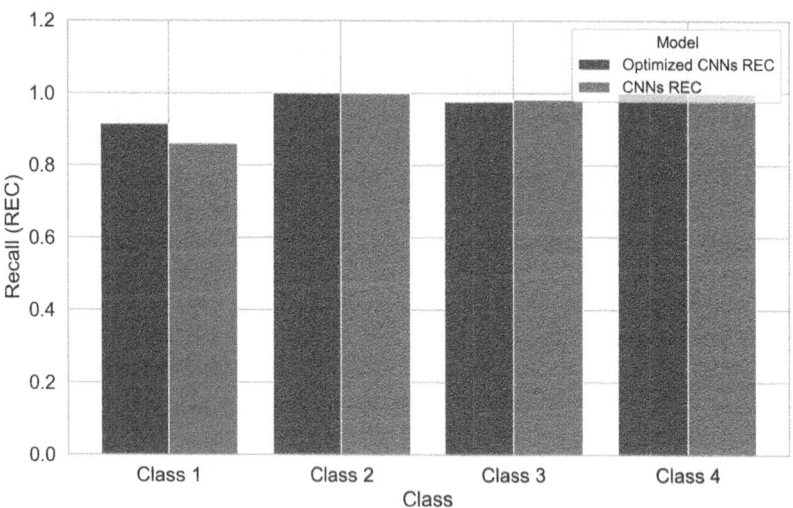

Fig. 3. Comparison of Recall (REC) for Classes 1–4: Optimized CNNs vs. CNNs

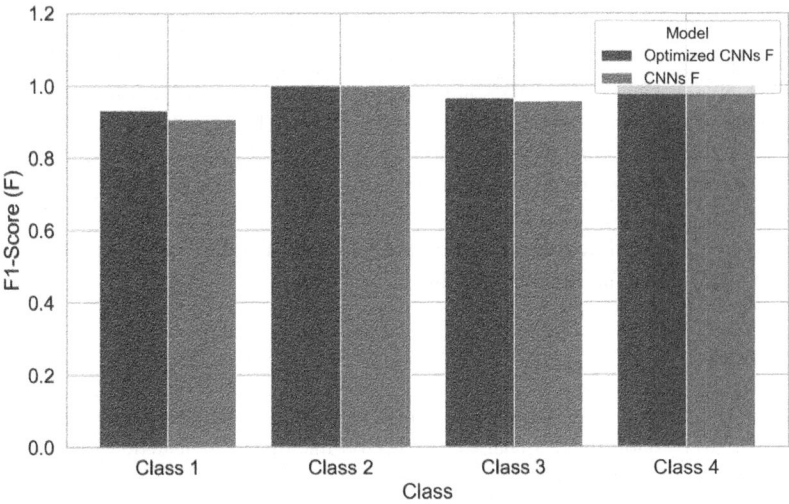

Fig. 4. Comparison of F1-Score (F) for Classes 1–4: Optimized CNNs vs. CNNs

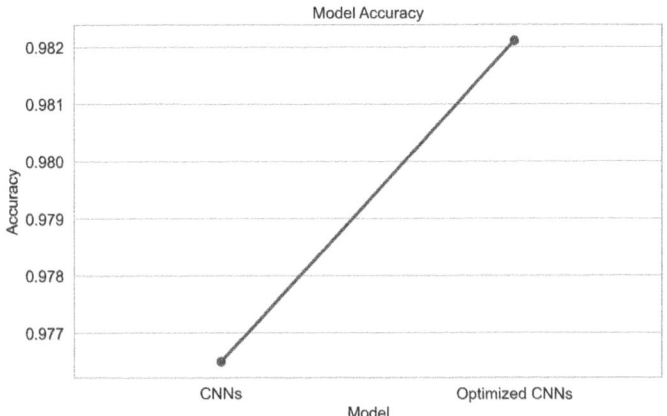

Fig. 5. Model Accuracy Comparison: CNNs vs. Optimized CNNs

6 Conclusion and Future Works

In conclusion, this research paper presented a novel approach for disease detection in intelligent agriculture by leveraging a CNN architecture and optimizing its hyperparameters using the PSO algorithm. The obtained results clearly demonstrate the superiority of the proposed optimized CNNs in accurately identifying and classifying plant diseases. Through the application of PSO, the optimized CNNs outperformed the baseline CNN models in terms of accuracy, precision, recall, and F1-score. The higher precision values indicate a reduced number of false positives, while the higher recall values reflect a decreased number of false negatives. This combination resulted in improved F1-scores, showcasing a more balanced trade-off between precision and recall.

The success of the optimized CNNs can be attributed to the power of the PSO algorithm in fine-tuning the hyperparameters of the models. By efficiently exploring the parameter space, PSO effectively identified the optimal values for key hyperparameters, leading to improved convergence and superior model performance. Looking ahead, future work could explore the utilization of other metaheuristic algorithms, such as Genetic Algorithms or Simulated Annealing, to further optimize the hyperparameters of the CNN models. Additionally, the investigation of different hyperparameters and variations in CNN architectures can provide valuable insights into improving disease detection accuracy in intelligent agriculture.

References

1. Yan-e, D.: Design of intelligent agriculture management information system based on IoT. In: 2011 Fourth International Conference on Intelligent Computation Technology and Automation, vol. 1. IEEE (2011)
2. Mekonnen, Y., et al.: Review—machine learning techniques in wireless sensor network based precision agriculture. J. Electrochem. Soc. **167**(3), 037522 (2019). https://doi.org/10.1149/2.0222003JES
3. Sharma, A., et al.: Machine learning applications for precision agriculture: a comprehensive review. IEEE Access **9**, 4843–4873 (2021)
4. Sarker, I.H.: Machine learning: Algorithms, real-world applications and research directions. SN Comput. Sci. **2**(3), 160 (2021). https://doi.org/10.1007/s42979-021-00592-x
5. Reddy, K.S.P., et al. : IoT based smart agriculture using machine learning. In: 2020 Second International Conference on Inventive Research in Computing Applications (ICIRCA). IEEE (2020)
6. Katarya, R., et al.: Impact of machine learning techniques in precision agriculture. In: 2020 3rd International Conference on Emerging Technologies in Computer Engineering: Machine Learning and Internet of Things (ICETCE). IEEE (2020)
7. Treboux, J., Genoud, D.: High precision agriculture: an application of improved machine-learning algorithms. In: 2019 6th Swiss Conference on Data Science (SDS). IEEE (2019)
8. Salmi, A., Benierbah, S.: Development of image analysis techniques using machine learning. Diss. Université Frères Mentouri-Constantine 1 (2022)
9. Sharma, A., Jain, A., Gupta, P., Chowdary, V.: Machine learning applications for precision agriculture: a comprehensive review. IEEE Access **9**, 4843–4873 (2020)
10. Kamilaris, A., Prenafeta-Boldú, F.X.: Deep learning in agriculture: a survey. Comput. Electron. Agric. **147**, 70–90 (2018)
11. Liakos, K.G., Busato, P., Moshou, D., Pearson, S., Bochtis, D.: Machine learning in agriculture: a review. Sensors **18**(8), 2674 (2018)
12. Koushik, J.: Understanding convolutional neural networks. arXiv preprint arXiv:1605.09081 (2016)
13. O'Shea, K., Nash, R.: An introduction to convolutional neural networks. arXiv preprint arXiv:1511.08458 (2015)
14. Lu, J., Tan, L., Jiang, H.: Review on convolutional neural network (CNN) applied to plant leaf disease classification. Agriculture **11**(8), 707 (2021)
15. Marini, F., Walczak, B.: Particle swarm optimization (PSO). A tutorial. Chemom. Intell. Lab. Syst. **149**, 153–165 (2015)
16. García-Gonzalo, E., Fernández-Martínez, J.L.: A brief historical review of particle swarm optimization (PSO). J. Bioinform. Intell. Control **1**(1), 3–16 (2012). https://doi.org/10.1166/jbic.2012.1002

17. Tayebi, M., El Kafhali, S.: Deep neural networks hyperparameter optimization using particle swarm optimization for detecting frauds transactions. In: Saeed, F., Al-Hadhrami, T., Mohammed, E., Al-Sarem, M. (eds.) Advances on Smart and Soft Computing: Proceedings of ICACIn 2021, pp. 507–516. Springer Singapore, Singapore (2022). https://doi.org/10.1007/978-981-16-5559-3_42

18. Tayebi, M., El Kafhali, S.: Performance analysis of metaheuristics based hyperparameters optimization for fraud transactions detection. Evol. Intel. (2022). https://doi.org/10.1007/s12065-022-00764-5

19. Eberhart, R., Kennedy, J.: Particle swarm optimization. In: Proceedings of the IEEE International Conference on Neural Networks, vol. 4 (1995)

20. Zhu, H., Wang, Y., Wang, K., Chen, Y.: Particle Swarm Optimization (PSO) for the constrained portfolio optimization problem. Expert Syst. Appl. **38**(8), 10161–10169 (2011). https://doi.org/10.1016/j.eswa.2011.02.075

21. Lazinica, A. (ed.) Particle swarm optimization. BoD–Books on Demand (2009)

22. Raj Sharma, S.: https://www.kaggle.com/saroz014/plant-diseases

A Scenario Case Study of a Recommender System Designed Using Various Collaborative Filtering Algorithm Techniques

Oumaima Stitini[1,2]([envelope]) [ID], Soulaimane Kaloun[2] [ID], and Omar Bencharef[2] [ID]

[1] Cadi Ayyad University, Higher Normal School, Department of Computer Science, Marrakesh, Morocco
o.stitini@uca.ac.ma
[2] Cadi Ayyad University, Faculty of Sciences and Technologies, L2IS Laboratory, Marrakesh, Morocco
so.kaloun@uca.ac.ma, o.bencharef@uca.ma

Abstract. Recommender systems are software applications that offer customers suggestions for products based on their previous purchases or item evaluations. Collaborative filtering (CF), among the most effective recommendation techniques, has garnered substantial attention and practical implementation across academic and business settings. A prime strategy for constructing recommender systems is through collaborative filtering (CF), a method that extrapolates forecasts or recommendations about future user preferences by analyzing the collective preferences of a user group, all without delving into the specifics of the content itself. In collaborative filtering recommender systems, user inclinations are conveyed as ratings assigned to items, with each new rating augmenting the system's knowledge and influencing the accuracy of its suggestions. Generally, as customers contribute more ratings, the impact of the suggestions grows. Nevertheless, the significance of each individual rating may differ significantly; various ratings can supply diverse quantities and types of information about a user's preferences. This article delves into the recent innovations suggested for collaborative filtering and the most up-to-date uses within the realm of recommendation systems. Furthermore, it conducts a hypothetical case study involving a recommendation system that employs diverse collaborative filtering algorithm techniques. The aim is to distinguish the appropriate quality metrics and indicators for evaluating both categories of collaborative filtering algorithms: memory-based and model-based.

Keywords: Collaborative Filtering · Memory-based Collaborative Filtering · Model-based Collaborative Filtering · Rating Prediction · User rating matrix

1 Introduction

In today's world, our daily decisions are often based on suggestions from those around us (friends, colleagues, relatives). Nowadays, we find many possibilities

H. Hagras et al. (Eds.): ISACS 2023, CCIS 2255, pp. 110–127, 2025.
https://doi.org/10.1007/978-3-031-93448-3_9

for online research, and we may have difficulty choosing what we need. Usually, when we have to decide, we compare articles, read comments written by anonymous users [7], and search for relevant information [1]. However, it is hard to find information quickly because of the exponential growth of the information rate in the digital world. The growth of the web requires the use of new technologies to help and assist users to quickly find what they want and show them that information exists. These techniques are called recommender systems. Recommender systems are divided in two kinds: personnalized and non personnalized recommendations. All users receive the same recommendations while using non-personalized recommendations. Examples of non-personalized recommendations include top-rated hotels, most-watched movies, and current music hits. A recommender system is a computational technique used to estimate the probability of a particular item being selected by a specific individual. Recommendation approaches are categorized into eight distinct categories based on the methodology used to generate recommendations. These categories include: Collaborative Filtering System, Content-Based Filtering System, Hybrid Filtering System, Demographic Recommender System, Knowledge-Based Recommender System, Risk-Aware Recommender System, Social Network Recommender System, and Context-Aware Recommender System. Collaborative filtering (CF) is a technique that focuses on capturing user opinions and expressions. It operates on the fundamental concept of mimicking the "word of mouth" principle, a historical way humans have used to form opinions about unfamiliar goods or services. The core idea behind this approach is that the opinions and preferences of other users can be used to make a reasonable prediction of what might interest a particular user in unranked items [3]. These methods assume that users with similar preferences for a certain set of products are likely to share similar preferences for other unrated items. CF employs two distinct mechanisms, namely memory-based CF and model-based CF, to generate recommendations. Different users get different recommendations when using customized recommendations. Although we will utilize non-personalized suggestions as a starting point. Better suggestions than non-personalized approaches are the aim of a customized recommender. We will also see some circumstances in which non-individualized recommendations are still a wise decision. For instance, you will propose movies that most people like if you suggest the most well-liked films. Various categories may be used to divide up personalized recommendation strategies further. Multiple decisions are to be made based on recommendations, such as which product to buy, what type of music to listen to, which movie to watch, which restaurant to choose, which doctor to visit, or where to read credible news [16]. Recommender systems are practical personalization tools. They consistently stay current and come highly recommended, tailored to users real actions. These systems find primary use within large online platforms. Notable instances encompass friend proposals across social apps like Facebook, Twitter, and LinkedIn, suggested profiles on Instagram, item recommendations on Amazon, video suggestions on YouTube, and news pointers on Google News. Various techniques for recommendation systems are classified by the method they employ. The collaborative filtering (CF) approach, for instance, suggests products to users based on their past preferences and the behaviors of other users with similar patterns [5]. In collaborative filtering, users provide ratings for items to indicate their preferences, which are then used to create profiles [10]. Using their similarity [12,14], these scores are compared to those supplied by other users to determine which users are the most similar. In other words, the suggestions sent to users are determined by their behavior and preferences compared to other users. Collaborative filtering methods use "user behavior" to make recommendations. The utility matrix is often used in industries because it is independent of additional information. This paper examines the current level of collaborative filtering recommender systems. This paper makes the following significant contributions: In the first section, we present the systematic literature review we conducted. We define the objective of our research in Sect. 2.3. Subsequently, in Sect. 3, we provide detailed explanations of our scenario cases for different types of collaborative filtering. Our experimental outcomes are deliberated in Sect. 4. Finally, we wrap up and summarize our work in Sect. 6.

2   State-of-the-Art

2.1   Procedure Used

When creating a recommender system, software developers must select a certain recommender algorithm from the available options. This decision substantially impacts the system logic, the user data and suggestion items that will be required, and performance problems. This decision-making process is difficult due to the literature's abundance of algorithm combinations and modifications.

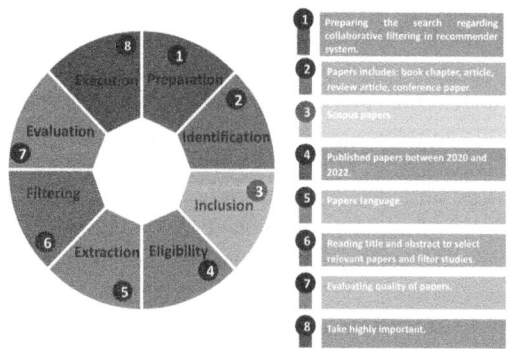

Fig. 1. Flow chart diagram for the proposed paper.

It is challenging to construct tools that will make recommender systems easier since new research must be done to continuously monitor new open problems and trends and expand the knowledge base. Due to these factors, this study aims to find the most recent works that compromise the eight phases outlined Fig. 1 in the collaborative filtering field.

2.2   Research Problematic

Exploring the collaborative approach to recommendation systems can be a multifaceted endeavor due to the wide array of algorithms and similarity methods available. These algorithms and methods are designed with distinct principles and are better suited for specific types of recommendation scenarios. This diversity poses an intriguing research problem in the field of recommendation systems. The central challenge lies in discerning which algorithm or similarity method should be employed in a particular recommendation scenario to achieve the best results. In essence, researchers and practitioners face the task of finding the most appropriate tool from this toolbox of techniques to tailor recommendations to the unique needs and characteristics of users and items. This research problem underscores the importance of understanding the strengths and weaknesses of different collaborative filtering algorithms and similarity metrics. It also necessitates the development of guidelines or automated approaches that can assist in selecting the most suitable method based on factors like data characteristics, user behavior, and domain-specific requirements. Solving this problem can lead to more effective and personalized recommendation systems, ultimately enhancing the user experience in various application domains.

2.3   Aim of the Study

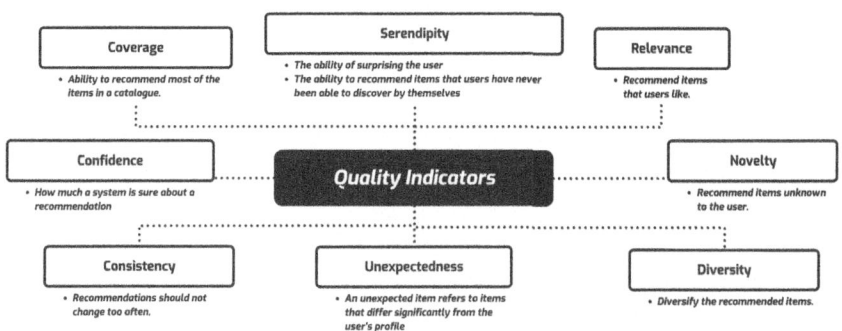

Fig. 2. Quality indicators of recommender system.

In collaborative filtering approach, the user's profile is built by filtering information from user behaviors such as ratings [11], assigned tags, and comments, or implicit rating by liking the items. The user's preference is expressed in two categories:

–   Explicit rating: entails the most straightforward user feedback, involving a user's assignment of a score on a sliding scale or the allocation of a tag to an item.

– Implicit rating: is a rating given by users who express their preference indirectly, such as purchase records, clicks, likes, number of page views, etc.

There are several ways to gauge what a consumer thinks of a product without directly asking for an opinion. Implicit ratings are the names given to the implicit judgments gathered in this manner [17]. A few examples are the length of time spent watching a film, the number of times a user has listened to a piece of music or the fact that a user has made a purchase. When it comes to watching movies, we may infer that if a user stops after 20 to 30 min, they do not like it. Instead, if the watching time roughly matches the film's duration, the viewer has likely loved it. We will now examine a few practical indications that will enable us to evaluate the effectiveness of a recommender system as mentioned in Fig. 2.

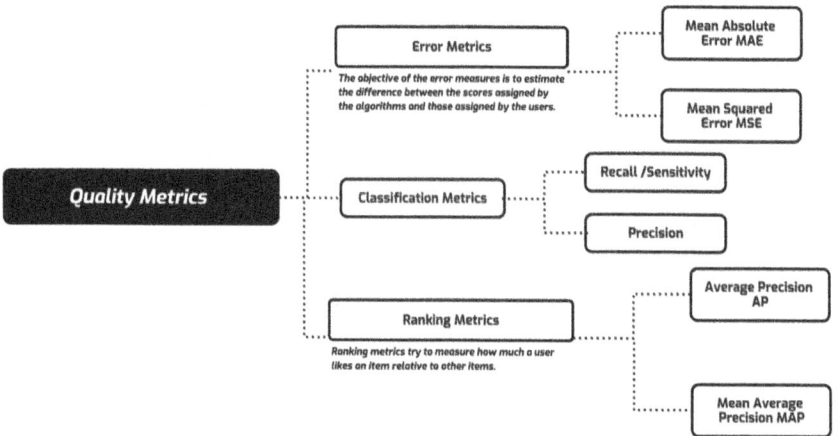

Fig. 3. Quality metrics of recommender system.

Consider a system like Netflix that wishes to suggest movies [13] to its viewers as an example [9]. The total quality of the recommendation would be quite low if it had a high relevance but low originality. If the algorithm recommends the most well-liked movies and offers nothing new, we will likely become bored and switch to another platform after a while. We will look at a few useful metrics that can help assess a recommender system's quality as mentioned in Fig. 3. Three basic categories of quality measures may be used to assess recommender systems metrics for classification, ranking, and errors. [19] introduce an innovative recommendation system that enhances precision and personalization for users by combining sentiment analysis of textual data with collaborative filtering methods. They constructed the system through a three-step process. Firstly, they employed unsupervised "GloVe" vectorization to improve classification performance and constructed a sentiment model utilizing Bidirectional Long Short-Term Memory (Bi-LSTM). Secondly, they formulated a recommendation model based on collaborative filtering techniques. Finally, they seamlessly integrated sentiment analysis model into the recommendation system.

Otherwise, the primary innovation in some researchers like [22] is the evaluation approach, which focuses on assessing potential recommendation lists instead of individual items before composing the final recommendation list.

The paper [2] outlines the process of evaluating these item-based stereotypes through a series of statistical tests before their implementation in the recommendation system. Our proposed approach enhances recommendation quality across various metrics and significantly reduces the complexity of the recommendation model.

The paper [23] introduces a collaborative filtering algorithm named UI2vec, which leverages embedding representation and word embedding techniques. UI2vec is designed to embed users and items into a shared latent space and utilize item similarity to predict user preferences effectively.

In this research [24], they have taken steps to enhance the K-nearest neighbor (KNN)-based collaborative filtering algorithm employed in recommendation systems. The proposed enhancement focuses on considering the similarity in user cognition to achieve greater accuracy in grouping users and generating more pertinent recommendations for active users.

3   Foundational Knowledge for Collaborative Filtering

Many academics are interested in collaborative filtering (CF), which aims to improve recommender system efficiency by reducing its limitations. The basic concept of CF is to recognize the expectations of the customers by taking into account their evaluations of the objects. CF can be divided into two categories memory-based approach and model-based approach. Memory-based approaches can be categorised to item-based and user-based approach. Model-based approaches is divided to SVD, Matrix Factorization, and Non Negative Matrix Factorization.

Due to the often noticeable interconnections between observed ratings among various users and items, collaborative filtering methods are grounded on the idea that predicting the ratings a user hasn't expressly provided for items is feasible. These approaches depend on user preferences rather than any particular item characteristic. The matrix employed to depict product ratings is termed the user rating matrix (URM), constituting the core input for a collaborative filtering mechanism.

In Table 1, the matrix's rows, labeled as 'u', represent users, while its columns, labeled as 'i', represent objects. The elements of the matrix, denoted as 'r', u, and i, signify the past interactions between user u and object i. Explicit ratings are one type of interaction in the user rating matrix. When a user rates something expressly, it signifies that they have given their honest assessment of it. The number of stars a user assigned to an item is an example of an explicit rating. The comparable number in the URM is 0 if a user has not given an item a rating. Implicit ratings are still another form of interaction that might occur, according to the URM.

Table 1. User rating matrix representation.

	i_1	i_2	i_n
u_1	r_{11}	?	r_{1n}
u_n	?	r_{n2}	r_{nn}

Implicit ratings merely indicate that a user interacted with a certain item. The only possible values for implicit ratings are zero or one. Zero represents no information, whereas one indicates user interaction with the object, although it is theoretically conceivable to create an algorithm that can employ both explicit and implicit ratings. Most straightforward algorithms are created to only function with either implicit or explicit ratings.

The most successful approach in recommender systems is collaborative filtering (CF). It recommends items by identifying other users who share similar preferences with the current user and leveraging their feedback to suggest items to the current user. There are several points to take into consideration to elaborate on a sound CF system:

1. **Formal model**: let X is the set of customers, and S is the set of items. The utility function modelized by

$$u : X \times S \to R \qquad (1)$$

R means the set of ratings. It is a totally ordered set between 0 and 5 stars.
2. **Utility matrix**: the utility matrix is represented by the rating that user attribute to a specific items as mentioned in Table 2.

Table 2. Data representation for user-item rating matrix.

	a	b	c	d	e
u1	5	?	2	3	?
u2	?	5	?	3	4
u3	4	?	5	3	?

3. **Key problems**: we have three major issues to carry into regard:
   - Obtaining existing ratings from the utility matrix.
   - Make assumptions about unknown ratings based on known ones: the utility matrix U is sparse [18], and the majority of customers haven't given most goods a rating. Additionally, because new products do not yet have ratings and because new users do not yet have histories, the cold start problem can affect collaborative filtering.
   - Evaluating prediction strategies by measuring the recommendation technique's success and performance.

3.1 Scenario 1: Memory-Based Recommendation

The similarty between two users is found only using the rating data for movies that has been rated by both the users in common. Memory-based approaches were the first collaborative filtering algorithms as mentioned in Fig. 4, it predicted ratings based on user neighbourhoods [15].

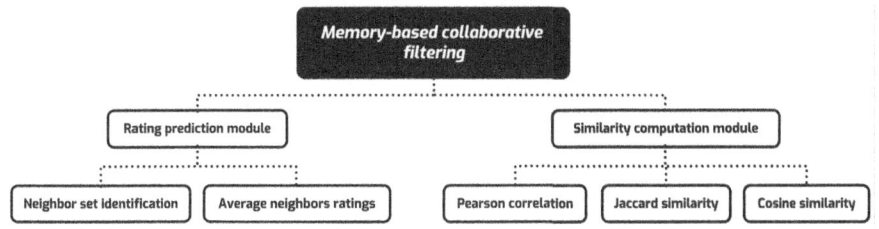

Fig. 4. Memory-based collaborative filtering.

They are simpler to implement and directly employ the user rating matrix, or URM, ratings, in the production. On the other hand, model-based strategies pull data from the dataset to create a model rather than relying on the entire dataset when recommendations are derived. Building the model is the first phase in these approaches two-step prediction process. The two functions that make up the model receive a matrix as input: the URM for collaborative filtering and the ICM for content-based filtering. The user profile and the previously defined model are inputs into a function called g in the second stage, which estimates ratings. The method's memory-based or model-based nature is determined by the user profile, the second parameter of the function g. If the user profile is not a part of the URM, the method is memory-based.

Architecture of a User-Based CF Recommender System

The fundamental concept underlying user-based collaborative filtering is to identify individuals who have akin preferences and propose the items that hold the highest value for those users.

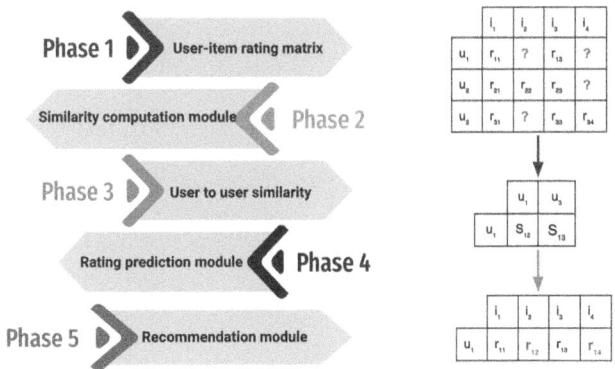

Fig. 5. Architecture of user-user collaborative filtering.

The first difficulty is coming up with a way to gauge user similarity. Based on user evaluations, we may compare user preferences. If two users give comparable ratings to a number of different objects, we may infer that they share a similar viewpoint on those two items. Similarly, if two users have similar viewpoints on a large number of different items, we can infer that these two users are similar. Figure 5 describe the general architecture followed in user-user collaborative filtering. Algorithm 1 show the followed algorithm on user-to-user technique.

Algorithm 1. User-based algorithm.

1: **Input:** Comparable user inclinations
2: **Output:** Recommendation
3: Compute user resemblance
4: Identify users that exhibit likeness to user u.
5: Estimate user ratings for unrated items.
6: Recommendation.

Similarity Metrics

1. Pearson Correlation Coefficient:

$$r = \frac{\sum_{i=1}^{n}(x_i - \bar{x})(y_i - \bar{y})}{\sqrt{\sum_{i=1}^{n}(x_i - \bar{x})^2}\sqrt{\sum_{i=1}^{n}(y_i - \bar{y})^2}} \tag{2}$$

2. Cosine Similarity measure:

$$\cos(\mathbf{t}, \mathbf{e}) = \frac{\mathbf{te}}{\|\mathbf{t}\|\|\mathbf{e}\|} = \frac{\sum_{i=1}^{n}\mathbf{t}_i\mathbf{e}_i}{\sqrt{\sum_{i=1}^{n}(\mathbf{t}_i)^2}\sqrt{\sum_{i=1}^{n}(\mathbf{e}_i)^2}} \tag{3}$$

3. Jaccard Similarity measure:

$$JCS(u, v) = \frac{A}{B} \tag{4}$$

$A = |I_u| \cap |I_v|$ and $B = |I_u| \cup |I_v|$

Scenario Case 1: Movies Example
Our illustration presents a display of 7 users who have provided ratings for 6 movies, as outlined in Table 3.

Table 3. Data representation: movie to user ratings.

	u_1	u_2	u_3	u_4	u_5	u_6	u_7
m_1	5	5	2	?	4	3	?
m_2	3	3	?	?	4	?	?
m_3	3	5	5	5	4	4	4
m_4	3	5	3	4	?	5	4
m_5	2	3	?	?	2	3	1
m_6	3	3	4	4	3	3	?

The symbol **?** denotes instances where a user has not yet assigned a rating to the particular movie, while other values range between 1 and 5.

1. Calculate User Similarity As an instance, it is necessary to assess the likeness between u_7 and the remaining individuals. Table 4 illustrates the comparability between user u_7 and other users through various similarity metrics.

Table 4. Similarity between user 7 and other users using different similarity metrics.

	u_1	u_2	u_3	u_4	u_5	u_6
Pearson Correlation	0.99	1	0	0	1	0.87
Cosine Similarity	0.31	0.53	0.76	**0.83**	0.40	**0.82**
Jaccard Similarity	0	0	0.33	**0.5**	0.4	0.4

2. Finding similar users Using Pearson correlation, the most similar users for user 7 are user 2 and 5. Otherwise using cosine similarity similar users are 4 and 6, because the problem on cosine similarity is that treats missing ratings as "negative". Jaccard similarity ignores the value of the rating that's why we have different result in comparison with other metrics.

3. Rating Predictions Collaborative filtering is a popular technique used in recommendation systems to predict ratings and make recommendations based on the preferences of similar users or items (Table 5).

Table 5. Rating predictions for user 7 regarding movies 1, 2, and 6.

	m_1	m_2	m_6
Pearson Correlation	4.29	3.33	3
Cosine Similarity	2.68	1.13	3.44
Jaccard Similarity	2.12	1	3.50

4. Recommendation Based on the previous step we notice that the predicted rating for movie 6 is approximately similar using different similarity metrics. Table 6 compare between our related works datasets.

Table 6. Summarization of contributions.

Contribution	Domain	Dataset used	similarity metric
[8]	Tourism	[20]	Pearson Correlation
[21]	Education	Books dataset	Pearson Correlation
[9]	Movie	Movies dataset	Cosine Similarity

Item-Based Collaborative Filtering
To produce rating predictions for the target item using item-based approaches, we must first determine the group of objects that are most comparable to the target item [4]. The goal is to determine how similar they are according to how many people have evaluated each pair of things [3]. Then, to determine if the user would enjoy the target items, we utilize the ratings provided by the user in that item. Figure 6 and 2 illustrate steps used in the item-to-item approach.

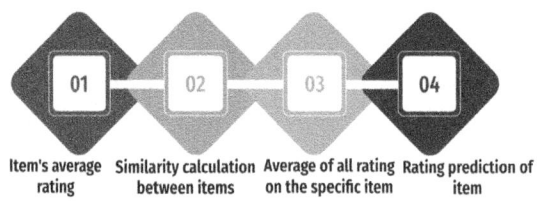

01	02	03	04
Item's average rating	Similarity calculation between items	Average of all rating on the specific item	Rating prediction of item

Fig. 6. Steps of item-to-item-based collaborating filtering.

3.2   Scenario 2: Model-Based Recommendation

K-Nearest Neighbors

Algorithm 2. Item-based algorithm.

1: **Input:** User inclinations
2: **Output:** Recommendation
3: Discover analogous items for item i.
4: Utilizing ratings for comparable items, predict the rating for item I.
5: It is possible to utilize identical similarity metrics and prediction methods as those employed in the user-user model.

A simple collaborative filtering algorithm is KNNBasic. Based on the KNN supervised classification method, the KNNWithMeans algorithm is a straight-forward collaborative filtering system that considers each user's mean ratings. User or Item-based collaborative filtering will arise from changing the user-based parameter of the sim settings, according to [6]. K-NN concentrates primarily on the similarity, proximity, and distance of the pieces of data. Because there are no costs associated with learning, K-NN is particularly effective when training with larger datasets. Since K-NN cannot, by definition, handle missing value issues, choosing the K value (the appropriate number of neighbors) is crucial when cat-egorizing the new sample. Cross-validation may be used to select the value of K, or it may be done randomly. The choice of distance measure is another prob-lem. Cosine similarity and Euclidean distance are the most often used distance measures (Tables 7 and 8).

Table 7. Rating predictions for user 7 regarding movies 1, 2, and 6 using KNN.

	m_1	m_2	m_6
KNN	3.5	3.50	3.28
RMSE	0.90	1.02	1.07

Table 8. Rating predictions for user 7 regarding movies 1, 2, and 6 using KNNBaseline.

	m_1	m_2	m_6
KNNBaseline	4.03	3.32	3.31
RMSE	1.05	1.08	0.87

Singular Value Decomposition. The item-user rating matrix is reduced using the matrix decomposition technique known as SVD to two lower-dimensional matrices. The SVD technique reduces the dimensionality of the matrix using linear algebra. The primary goal of SVD, a matrix factorization approach, is to minimize the number of features in the dataset, which lowers the dimensionality space from N to k, where k is fewer than N. A given model may fit a dataset more accurately the lower the RMSE. To decide if a certain RMSE score is low or not, however, depends on the range of the dataset we are using.

Non-negative Matrix Factorization. A cutting-edge feature extraction app-roach is factorization. When there are many qualities and the attributes are unclear or have poor predictability, Non-Negative Matrix Factorization NMF is helpful. NMF may create significant patterns, subjects, or themes by combin-ing characteristics. The original attribute collection is linearly combined into each feature produced by NMF. Each feature contains a set of coefficients that represent the relative importance of each attribute to the feature as a whole. Each numerical attribute and each unique value of each category attribute has a unique coefficient. All of the coefficients are positive (Tables 9, 10, 11 and 12).

Table 9. Rating predictions for user 7 regarding movies 1,2, and 6 using KNNWith-Means.

	m_1	m_2	m_6
KNNWithMeans	5.00	3.95	2.01
RMSE		1.65	0.91	0.97

Table 10. Rating predictions for user 7 regarding movies 1,2, and 6 using KNNWith-ZScore

	m_1	m_2	m_6
KNNWithZScore	2.44	4.28	3.31
RMSE	0.98	0.92	1.68

Table 11. Rating predictions for user 7 regarding movies 1, 2, and 6 using NMF.

	m_1	m_2	m_6
NMF	3.15	3.21	2.42
RMSE	0.71	1.19	1.11

4   Experimental Findings and Results

We employed RMSE, MAE, Recall, Precision, and F-measure five statistical techniques for calculating error, to evaluate the effectiveness of a recommender system.

Fig. 7. Model-based collaborative filtering using SVD.

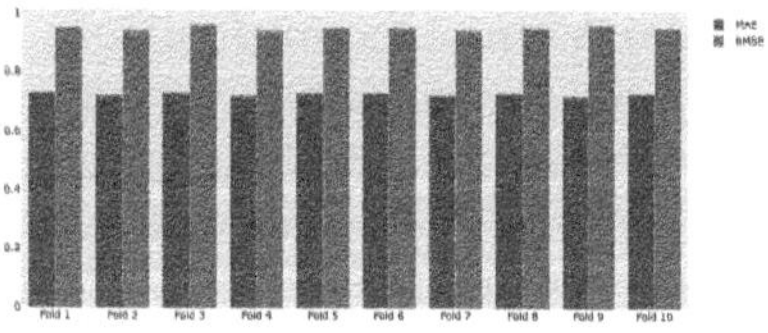

Fig. 8. Model-based collaborative filtering using KNN.

Figures 8 and 7 illustrate the error (RMSE, MAE) analysis performed using 10 Folds and the MovieLens dataset.

Figures 10 and 11 illustrate the error (RMSE, MAE) analysis performed using 10 Folds and the Amazon products dataset. Figure 9 show the error MAE achieved for Negative Matrix Factorization (Tables 13, 14 and 15).

Table 12. Rating predictions for user 7 regarding movies 1, 2, and 6 using SlopeOne.

	m_1	m_2	m_6
SlopeOne	3.25	2.11	2.87
RMSE	1.05	1.23	1.52

Table 13. Rating predictions for user 7 regarding movies 1,2, and 6 using SVD.

	m_1	m_2	m_6
SVD	3.57	3.22	3.39
RMSE	0.80	0.79	0.87

Fig. 9. Model-based collaborative filtering using NMF.

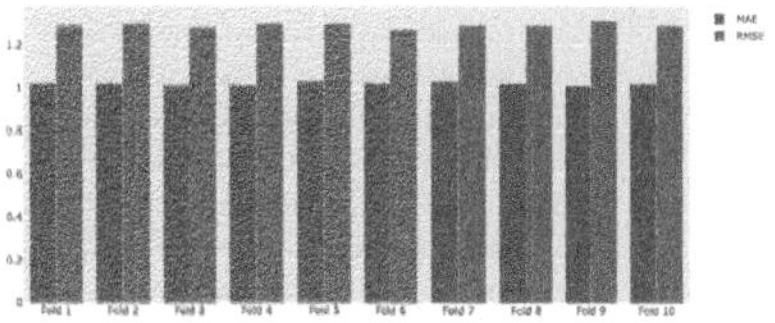

Fig. 10. Model-based collaborative filtering using SVD for Amazon products dataset.

Table 14. Rating predictions for user 7 regarding movies 1,2, and 6 using SVDpp.

	m_1	m_2	m_6
SVDpp	3.60	3.35	3.26
RMSE	0.75	0.92	0.90

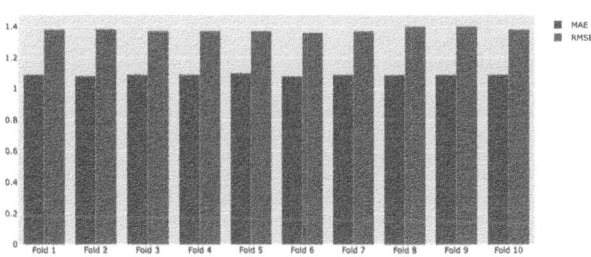

Fig. 11. Model-based collaborative filtering using NMF for Amazon products dataset.

5   Distinctions and Comparisons

Table 15. Comparisons between our proposed approach and other approaches.

Reference	Goal	Handled Issues	Advantages
[24]	The goal of this research is to introduce and evaluate the ExtKNNCF, an adaptive KNN-based collaborative filtering model that incorporates user cognition parameters. This model aims to enhance the quality of recommendations by accurately capturing user preferences	The main issue addressed in this paper is the improvement of collaborative filtering recommendations by integrating user cognition parameters into the ExtKNNCF model	– Enhanced Recommendations – Comparison with Benchmarks – Future Cross-Domain Application – Performance Analysis. – Validation with Diverse Datasets
[23]	The main goal of this research is to introduce and evaluate a collaborative filtering algorithm called UI2vec, which is based on embedding representation and word embedding techniques. The research also aims to address issues related to data sparsity and implicit feedback uncertainty in recommendation systems	The research addresses the challenges of data sparsity and implicit feedback uncertainty in collaborative filtering recommendation systems, offering UI2vec as a potential solution	– Embedding Representation – Simultaneous Learning – Incorporation of Global Information
[19]	The primary goal of this research is to enhance recommendation systems (RSs) in the e-commerce domain by combining sentiment analysis with collaborative filtering techniques. The objective is to provide more accurate and personalized product recommendations to improve conversion rates in online shopping	The research addresses the limitation of traditional RSs, which rely solely on numerical ratings, by incorporating sentiment analysis from user reviews to gain a deeper understanding of user opinions and emotions	– Improved Accuracy – Enhanced Performance
[18]	The primary goal of this research is to enhance the performance of Recommender Systems by addressing two common limitations: the cold start problem and data sparsity. This is achieved through the analysis and implementation of Collaborative Filtering (CF)-based recommendation approaches	The research focuses on mitigating the drawbacks of Recommender Systems, specifically the challenges posed by the cold start problem and data sparsity, using CF-based methods	– Diverse CF Approaches – User-Item Similarity and Prediction – Relevance of Recommendations
Our proposed approach	The main goal of this discussion is to provide an overview of recommender systems and the role of collaborative filtering in generating recommendations. Additionally, it highlights the diversity of collaborative filtering algorithms and similarity methods, leading to the research problem of determining the most appropriate approach for specific recommendation scenarios	The discussion addresses the challenge of selecting the right collaborative filtering algorithm and similarity method to tailor recommendations effectively to users and items in diverse recommendation scenarios	– Diverse Recommendation Approaches – Explanation of Collaborative Filtering: – Memory-Based and Model-Based CF – Significance of User Ratings – Innovation and Case Study

6   Conclusion and Future Work

Collaborative filtering algorithms are the predominant choice within recommender systems. In today's landscape, these CF algorithms face challenges related to handling vast datasets, addressing sparsity in evaluation matrices, and managing cold start issues. In this paper, we delve into the objectives and motives of pertinent research, conducting an in-depth evaluation of advancements in the realm of recommender systems, with a specific emphasis on collaborative filtering, spanning the period from 2019 to 2023. We introduce a framework for classification that categorizes different scenarios pertinent to each variant of collaborative filtering. Additionally, we delve into valuable metrics that streamline the assessment of recommender system efficacy, alongside quality indicators tailored to gauge system performance. The primary goal of this study is to elucidate noteworthy progress, pinpoint promising avenues for future exploration, and furnish researchers with a comprehensive comprehension of the objectives underpinning recommender techniques.

References

1. Sallam, R.M., Hussein, M.F., Mousa, H.M.: An enhanced collaborative filtering-based approach for recommender systems. Int. J. Comput. Appl. **176**(41), 9–15 (2020). https://doi.org/10.5120/ijca2020920531
2. AlRossais, N., Kudenko, D., Yuan, T.: Improving cold-start recommendations using item-based stereotypes. User Model. User-Adap. Inter. **31**(5), 867–905 (2021). https://doi.org/10.1007/s11257-021-09293-9
3. Atashkar, M., Safi-Esfahani, F.: Item-based recommender systems applying social-economic indicators. SN Comput. Sci. **1**(2), 1–31 (2020). https://doi.org/10.1007/s42979-020-0115-8
4. Singh, P.K., Sinha, M., Das, S., Choudhury, P.: Enhancing recommendation accuracy of item-based collaborative filtering using Bhattacharyya coefficient and most similar item. Appl. Intell. **50**(12), 4708–4731 (2020). https://doi.org/10.1007/s10489-020-01775-4
5. Chen, J., Zhao, C., Uliji, Chen, L.: Collaborative filtering recommendation algorithm based on user correlation and evolutionary clustering. Complex Intell. Syst. **6**(1), 147–156 (2019). https://doi.org/10.1007/s40747-019-00123-5
6. Zhao, W., Tian, H., Wu, Y., Cui, Z., Feng, T.: A new Item-Based Collaborative filtering algorithm to improve the accuracy of prediction in sparse data. Int. J. Comput. Intell. Syst. **15**(1), 15 (2022). https://doi.org/10.1007/s44196-022-00068-7
7. Stitini, O., Kaloun, S., Bencharef, O.: An improved recommender system solution to mitigate the Over-Specialization problem using genetic algorithms. Electronics **11**(2), 242 (2022). https://doi.org/10.3390/electronics11020242
8. Munaji, A.A., Emanuel, A.: Restaurant recommendation system based on user ratings with collaborative filtering. IOP Conf. Ser. **1077**(1), 012026 (2021). https://doi.org/10.1088/1757-899x/1077/1/012026

9. Gupta, M., Thakkar, A., Aashish, Gupta, V., Rathore, D.P.S.: Movie recommender system using collaborative filtering. In: 2020 International Conference on Electronics and Sustainable Communication Systems (ICESC) (2020). https://doi.org/10.1109/icesc48915.2020.9155879

10. Li, C., Ma, L.: Item-based collaborative filtering algorithm based on group weighted rating. In: 13th International Symposium on Computational Intelligence and Design (ISCID), Hangzhou, China, 2020, pp. 114–117 (2020). https://doi.org/10.1109/ISCID51228.2020.00032

11. Nam, L.: Towards comprehensive approaches for the rating prediction phase in memory-based collaborative filtering recommender systems. Inf. Sci. **589**, 878–910 (2022). https://doi.org/10.1016/j.ins.2021.12.123

12. Gazdar, A., Hidri, L.: A new similarity measure for collaborative filtering based recommender systems. Knowl. Based Syst. **188**, 105058 (2020). https://doi.org/10.1016/j.knosys.2019.105058

13. Bhalse, N., Thakur, R.: WITHDRAWN: algorithm for movie recommendation system using collaborative filtering. Mater. Today: Proc. (2021). https://doi.org/10.1016/j.matpr.2021.01.235

14. Fkih, F.: Similarity measures for collaborative filtering-based recommender systems: review and experimental comparison. J. King Saud Univ. Comput. Inf. Sci. **34**(9), 7645–7669 (2022). https://doi.org/10.1016/j.jksuci.2021.09.014

15. Khojamli, H., Razmara, J.: Survey of similarity functions on neighborhood-based collaborative filtering. Expert Syst. Appl. **185**, 115482 (2021). https://doi.org/10.1016/j.eswa.2021.115482

16. Nudrat, S., Khan, H.U., Iqbal, S., Talha, M.M., Alarfaj, F.K., Almusallam, N.: Users' rating predictions using collaborating filtering based on users and items similarity measures. Comput. Intell. Neurosci. **2022**, 2347641 (2022). https://doi.org/10.1155/2022/2347641

17. Aljunid, M.F., Huchaiah, M.D.: IntegrateCF: integrating explicit and implicit feedback based on deep learning collaborative filtering algorithm. Expert Syst. Appl. **207**, 117933 (2022). https://doi.org/10.1016/j.eswa.2022.117933

18. Chen, J., Zhao, C., Anwar, T., Uma, V., Hussain, M.I., Pantula, M.: Collaborative filtering and kNN based recommendation to overcome cold start and sparsity issues: a comparative analysis. Multimedia Tools Appl. **12**, 1–19 (2022). https://doi.org/10.1007/s11042-021-11883-z

19. Karabila, I., Darraz, N., El-Ansari, A., Alami, N., El Mallahi, M.: Enhancing collaborative filtering-based recommender system using sentiment analysis. Future Internet **15**(7), 235 (2023). https://doi.org/10.3390/fi15070235

20. Restaurant consumer data Data Set. https://archive.ics.uci.edu/ml/datasets/Restaurant+

21. Devika, P., Jyothisree, K., Rahul, P., Arjun, S., Narayanan, J.: Book recommendation system. In: 2021 12th International Conference on Computing Communication and Networking Technologies (ICCCNT), pp. 1–5 (2021). https://doi.org/10.1109/ICCCNT51525.2021.9579647

22. Alhijawi, B., Kilani, Y.: A collaborative filtering recommender system using genetic algorithm. Inf. Process. Manag. **57**(6), 102310 (2020). https://doi.org/10.1016/j.ipm.2020.102310

23. Alharbe, N., Rakrouki, M.A., Aljohani, A.: A collaborative filtering recommendation algorithm based on embedding representation. Expert Syst. Appl. **215**, 119380 (2023). https://doi.org/10.1016/j.eswa.2022.119380

24. Nguyen, L.V., Vo, Q.-T., Nguyen, T.-H.: Adaptive KNN-based extended collaborative filtering recommendation services. Big Data Cogn. Comput. **7**(2), 106 (2023). https://doi.org/10.3390/bdcc7020106

Classifying Authenticity of Prophet's Statements Using Artificial Intelligence Techniques

Moulay Abdellah Kassimi$^{(\boxtimes)}$ (ID), Abdessalam Essayad (ID), and Khalid Tatane (ID)

Ibn Zohr University, National School of Applied Sciences, Agadir, Morocco
abdellahkasimi@gmail.com, a.essayad@edu.uiz.ac.ma,
k.tatane@uiz.ac.ma

Abstract. The authenticity of Hadiths, or sayings and actions attributed to the Prophet Muhammad peace be upon him, is a critical issue in Islamic scholarship. In this paper, we present a method for classifying Prophet's statements as authentic or unauthentic using artificial intelligence (AI) techniques in our newly created corpus. Our corpus is composed of a collection of wordings separated from the text (Maten) and chain of narrators and, then, labelled based on their authenticity. In the first step, we will focus on analyzing the style of the Prophet Muhammad's wordings and evaluating the performance of machine learning (ML) techniques for the classification of hadith authenticity. Second, we use a BERT-based model, which is a ML framework for natural language processing (NLP) designed to capture the contextual relationships between the words in the hadith. The results of our experiments show that the hybrid approach is able to achieve high accuracy in authenticating Hadiths, outperforming machine learning based methods.

Keywords: Authenticity · Hadith · AI · ML · BERT · Natural Language Processing · Fine-Tuning

1 Introduction

The sayings of Prophet Muhammad peace be upon him, also known as Hadiths, play a vital role in the Islamic tradition. They are considered as the second most important source of Islamic law and teachings after the Quran. However, one of the major challenges in studying and understanding Hadiths is the issue of authenticity. Many Hadiths have been fabricated over the centuries [1], making it difficult to distinguish authentic Hadiths from unauthentic ones. Moreover, Hadith specialists have gathered hadith in various collections with differing criteria, therefore, not all hadith in all collections are necessarily authentic. Therefore, authenticating Hadiths is a crucial task in the field of Islamic studies.

Traditionally, the authenticity of Hadiths has been determined by using various methods such as the study of the chain of narrators, the content of the Hadith, and the comparison with other authentic Hadiths [2]. However, these methods are time-consuming and require a high level of expertise. Moreover, the increasing number of Hadiths available online has made it even more challenging to authenticate them manually. In recent years,

H. Hagras et al. (Eds.): ISACS 2023, CCIS 2255, pp. 128–136, 2025.
https://doi.org/10.1007/978-3-031-93448-3_10

natural language processing (NLP) techniques have been applied to authenticate Hadiths [3, 4]. However, most of the existing approaches use machine learning techniques and rely on a small dataset of labelled Hadiths. In this paper, we propose a novel approach for authenticating Hadiths using a transformer language model, BERT [5] in our newly created corpus. Our corpus is composed of a large collection of Hadiths in Arabic language, which are labelled based on their authenticity. We use a BERT-based model to classify the Hadiths into authentic and unauthentic categories by analyzing the style of the Prophet Muhammad's sayings peace be upon him, also known as Lafd_al_hadith or wordings. We evaluate our approach on a test set of Hadiths and compare the results with machine learning based techniques. The main contributions of this paper are:

- The creation of a large corpus of labelled Hadiths in Arabic language
- The use of an Arabic BERT-based model to classify Hadiths into authentic and unauthentic categories
- The evaluation of the proposed approach on a test set of Hadiths and comparing BERT models with each other, and then comparing the best model with the machine learning based techniques.

The rest of the paper is organized as follows: In Sect. 2, we describe the related work on authenticating Hadiths using AI techniques. In Sect. 3, we present our approach for authenticating Hadiths using Arabic BERT in our new corpus. In Sect. 4, we evaluate our approach and present the results. Finally, in Sect. 5, we conclude the paper and discuss future work.

2 Related Work

In the past, the authenticity of hadiths has primarily been determined through manual inspection by experts in Islamic studies. This process is time-consuming and subject to human error, and has limited the ability to efficiently evaluate large volumes of hadiths [6]. In recent years, NLP techniques have been applied to authenticate Hadiths [1, 4, 8]. The main aim of these approaches is to automatically classify Hadiths into authentic and unauthentic categories based on various features such as the chain of narrators, the content of the Hadith, and the comparison with other authentic Hadiths. After reviewing many studies that dealt with AI in the criticism of hadith, the most important of them were collected, which try to answer some of our questions. One of the early works in this field is by Desouki et al. [7]. In this paper, the authors aim to simulate the application of author attribution on the texts of Hadiths, relying on the accepted Hadiths to learn the Style of the Prophet Muhammad peace be upon him, and then judge about the its correctness. This work is similar to our paper in that it also uses author attribution techniques for hadith authenticity classification. However, our paper focuses specifically on the use of Arabic BERT, which allows for a more comprehensive analysis of the language and context of the hadith.

M. Khedher [8] confirmed that AI can also help in imitating the work of the first hadith scholars and applying the rules of wounding and modification. He also confirmed that fuzzy logic applications can be used in the applications of hadith science, especially if huge classified data are available. What was stated in this research remains theoretical and lacks the application and construction of the expert system model for hadith criticism.

In the research [6], the author tried to provide an alternative to the traditional method of criticizing hadiths, as he considered that judgment is based on limited human knowledge and therefore the existence of errors, in addition to the draining of time and effort and sometimes changing the judgment on hadith. The researcher believes that the solution lies in the employment of AI in processing data and benefiting from it in the service of the Sunnah, and the expert system can criticize the hadith and judge it as valid or weak based on what he understood from the sources of the Sunnah and the experience of scholars. In the paper [9], the researcher proposed hidden Markov model (HMM) to authenticate Hadiths by analyzing the chain of narrators. The study found that the hybrid approach to process Isnads of Hadiths achieved good performance in authenticating Hadiths 86%. The researcher in the article, like other authors, focused on implementing algorithms that analyze the chain of narrators only and pass judgment on it.

In the article [10], the author used, in a stylistic measurement experiment to attribute authorship, a set of ML classifiers to Qur'anic and Hadith passages. Although the Qur'an and the hadith were attributed without error, the author used the hadith in its two parts: the chain of narrators and the text, which raised significant critical observations in this study.

One approach that has shown promise in the NLP field is the use of transformer-based models, such as BERT (Bidirectional Encoder Representations from Transformers) [5]. These models have achieved state-of-the-art results in many NLP tasks and have been applied to a variety of languages, including Arabic [11]. K. GAANOUN in this paper proposes a BERT-based model for automated Hadith classification to achieve a 92.47% $F1_{MH}$ score in detecting Mawdu Hadiths. However, authors rely on a small dataset of labelled Mawdu Hadiths.

Due to its remarkable performance in Authorship Attribution tasks [12], we experimented with the popular BERT model [5], taking advantage of the Arabic BERT base model and our Hadiths dataset for automating the process of hadith authentication.

3   Method

In this section, we present our approach for authenticating Hadiths using Arabic BERT in our new corpus. Our corpus is composed of a large collection of Hadiths in Arabic language, which are labeled based on their authenticity. The corpus is divided into two sets: a training set and a test set. The training set is used to train the BERT-based model, and the test set is used to evaluate the performance of the model.

3.1   Approach

The first step in our approach is to pre-process the Hadiths in the corpus [11]. This includes cleaning the text and removing any irrelevant information such as the actions, the silent approval of the prophet Muhammad peace be upon him and chain of narrators. The pre-processed Hadiths are then passed through a BERT-based model. BERT is a transformer-based model that is pre-trained on a large corpus of text and fine-tuned for specific tasks such as text classification.

The BERT-based model is fine-tuned on the training set of Hadiths to classify them into authentic and unauthentic categories. The model is trained to identify the style of the Prophet Muhammad's sayings peace be upon him, which is considered to be a unique feature of authentic Hadiths. The fine-tuned model is then used to classify the Hadiths in the test set into authentic and unauthentic categories.

3.2 Data Collection

In this research, we faced several challenges in the data collection process due to the lack of open-source data for NLP in the field of hadith studies. Specifically, we were unable to find data that separated the wording from the Maten of the hadith (Fig. 1), which made it difficult to analyze the language and style of the Hadiths.

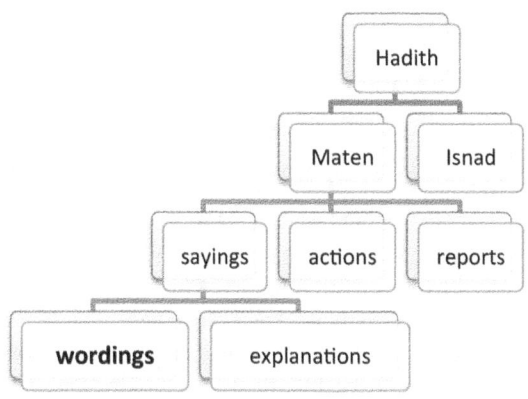

Fig. 1 Wordings from Hadith

Fortunately, in our database, the type of hadith was specified: Marfua [17] (a hadith attributed to the Prophet Muhammad peace be upon him and a companion narrates it), Maktua, Mawqoof or Qudsi. The type of the Sunnah was also described as: sayings, actions and reports [13]. It was confirmed to be free from errors manually by our experts, especially the most reliable and authentic books of Hadiths: Sahih al-Bukhari, Sahih Muslim, Sunan Abu Dawood, Sunan al-Tirmidhi, Sunan al-Nasa'i, Sunan ibn Majah, Muwatta Imam Malik, Sunan ad-Darimi, Musnad Ahmad ibn Hanbal. We also worked to remove any extraneous information that was not part of the actual hadith, such as explanations or interpretations by narrators. This included removing phrases like "He means...", "he wants...", or "some of what he said, then he recited this verse...", as well as references to gestures or other actions taken by the Prophet. This process was expensive and required specialized knowledge and expertise in hadith studies. However, it was necessary in order to provide the correct data for AI and to ensure that the data was properly prepared for training.

Overall, the data collection process was a major challenge in this research and high-lights the need for more open-source data and resources for NLP in the field of hadith studies.

In order to collect data for this study, we used web crawler techniques to browse and index the content of websites available on the internet. We focused on trusted websites that contained reliable hadith data. Using websites, we were able to access hundreds of thousands of Hadiths with annotated rulings on their authenticity. We were able to search for Hadiths using the API service, allowing us to choose to search within the authentic or unauthentic Hadiths. In total, we collected 34,324 Hadiths (see Table 1).

Table 1. Total Hadiths before pre-processing

Database	Number of Hadiths	Annotated
Jawamea-Kalem [13]	463,733	yes
Dorar-saniya [21]	331,536	yes
hadith-json [20]	38,102	yes
LK-Hadith-Corpus [19]	32,577	yes
Total	**865,948**	**yes**

Web crawler techniques were an effective way for us to access large amounts of hadith data from trusted sources, which allowed us to accurately and efficiently collect the data needed for our study. Fortunately, authors in [13, 20, 21] create library to collect large data from websites using scraping library. This annotated data is, then, saved in JSON or binary format, so it is easily read and processed.

By carefully cleaning and pre-processing the data in this way, we were able to focus on the language and wording of the Hadiths themselves, rather than any additional context or interpretation provided by narrators. This allowed us to more accurately analyze the language and style of the Hadiths and to identify patterns and characteristics that are indicative of authenticity. Moreover, in this paper, we relied on what was confirmed manually by our team, due to the difficulty and responsibility of working on the hadith of the Prophet Muhammad peace be upon him.

4   Results and Evaluation

In this section, we evaluate our approach for authenticating Hadiths using Arabic BERT in our new corpus and present the results. To carry out this article, we chose just the hadiths Marfua which contains Lafd_al_hadith and, to remain faithful to the text of the hadith, we diligently checked and verified our data with a dedicated team. We have done our best to provide the most authentic and exact hadith possible. We therefore adopted, initially, the six books on authentic Hadiths. For unauthentic Hadiths, we relied on the books of Shaykhs al-Arna'ut, Al-Albani's books (series of weak Hadiths and their impact on the nation) and fake hadith from dorar website [18] reviewed and approved by the site's general supervisor. The final corpus is composed of 19,019 Hadiths Marfua after pre-processing step, with 9802 labeled as authentic and 9217 labeled as unauthentic. The corpus is divided into a training set of 15,215 Hadiths and a test set of 3804 Hadiths.

The BERT-based model is fine-tuned on the training set of Hadiths using a batch size of 32 and a learning rate of 2e-5. The models are trained for 3 epochs and the best model is selected based on the performance on the validation set. The performance of the model is evaluated on the test set of Hadiths using accuracy metric and F1-score. The results are shown in Table 2.

Table 2. Comparison of accuracy scores for different Arabic BERT models

Model	Accuracy	F1_Score
CAMeLBERT_ca	89.43%	89.38%
Arabic_BERT	83.52%	83.48%
AraBERT	81.49%	81.49%
QARiB	84.73%	84.69%
Multilingual	58.19%	58.14%

As can be seen from the above tables, CAMeLBERT_ca [14] model, pre-trained on classical Arabic texts, performs the best in terms of accuracy and F1-score. Other Arabic models also show good performance, but with slightly lower accuracy. CAMeLBERT_ca model is therefore selected for use in our authenticity classification system. In this table, also, we can see that Arabic BERT models outperform the multilingual BERT model in terms of accuracy and F1 score. This suggests that using a model specifically trained on Arabic language data is more effective for hadith authenticity classification.

To further evaluate the system, we also compared its performance to that of a baseline approach using word TF-IDF [15]. The Arabic BERT system outperformed the baseline approach, achieving an accuracy of 89.43% compared to 84.56% for the baseline (Table 3).

Table 3. Results of baseline TF-IDF model

Model	Accuracy	F1_Score
Nearest Neighbors	0.625131	0.557625
Random Forest	0.845689	0.84547
Decision Trees	0.807308	0.806383
Logistic Regression	0.754206	0.753754
Support Vector Machine	0.720557	0.720043

As shown in the tables above, the Arabic BERT model outperforms the baseline TF-IDF model in all evaluation metrics.

Additionally, we incorporate stylometric, TF-IDF and N_gram [16] to Arabic BERT (Table 4). Classification is then done using a Logistic Regression algorithm.

Table 4. Results adding stylometric and hybrid features

Model	Accuracy	F1_Score
BERT	89.43%	89.38%
TF-IDF	84.56%	84.54%
style	75.53%	75.48%
N-gram	79.39%	79.36%
BERT + IDF	89.80%	89.77%
BERT + Style	89.72%	89.68%
BERT + N-Gram	89.70%	89.66%
BERT + Style + N-Gram	89.96%	89.93%

Table 4 shows that, adding hybrid features to CAMeLBERT_ca can improve the F1-score by 0.54% on average.

Overall, the results of our experiments show that the use of Arabic BERT is effective for classifying the authenticity of hadith with a high degree of accuracy. This represents a significant improvement over previous approaches, which relied on chain of narrators or Maten and Isnad. The use of our system allows for the automatic and efficient evaluation of large volumes of hadith, facilitating the dissemination of authentic teachings to the wider Muslim community.

5   Discussion

The results of our study demonstrate that using Arabic BERT model can be a highly effective approach for classifying the authenticity of hadith. The system achieved an accuracy of 89.96%, which represents a significant improvement over previous methods that relied on chain of narrators.

One of the key advantages of our approach is these models are monolingual and were originally trained on Arabic vocabulary using various Arabic language resources. The CAMeLBERT_ca model performed relatively well when compared to other models. This is particularly important given the vast number of hadith that exist. Another benefit of our approach is that it allows for a more comprehensive analysis of the language and context of the hadith. By considering the contextual information factor, our system is able to make more accurate judgement about the authenticity of the hadith.

However, there are also limitations to our approach. One potential issue is that the accuracy of the system may be affected by the quality of the training data. If the training data is biased or contains errors, this could impact the accuracy of the system. Additionally, the system may not perform as well on hadith that are less common or more difficult to classify.

Despite these encouraging results, employing artificial intelligence in criticizing the hadith of the Prophet faces a number of difficulties, the most important of which are:

• Narrating some Hadiths by meaning, not by wording;

- The narrator's narration of the same hadith with different wording;
- The great similarity between authentic and unauthentic Hadiths;
- Judging hadiths when removing or adding a word only;
- Judging hadiths through the chain of narrators;
- The type of stemming used to extract the vocabulary;

Overall, our results suggest that Arabic BERT can be a valuable tool for classifying the authenticity of hadith. Future research could focus on improving the system by using the structure of the BERT model and training it from scratch on our own data: books of Hadith, history or the translations written in Classical Arabic, and also relying on a large database by adding other hadiths, and then adjusting them with BERT using the fine-tuning approach. Additionally, further research could explore the use of Arabic BERT for other tasks related to hadith, such as translation or summarization.

6 Conclusion

This paper presented a novel approach for authenticating Hadiths in Arabic using BERT and stylometry. We used Arabic BERT-based model fine-tuned on a corpus of labeled Hadiths in Arabic language to analyze the wording of the Hadith and identify the unique language patterns and writing behaviors of the Prophet Muhammad peace be upon him. We also used stylometry to classify Hadiths into authentic and unauthentic categories. The system was trained on a database of hadith for authenticity and achieved an accuracy of 89.96%. This represents a significant improvement over previous approaches, which relied on chain of narrators or all text of hadith. In future work, we plan to expand the database training BERT from scratch on our own data of books written in Classical Arabic, and then adjusting them with BERT using the fine-tuning approach.

References

1. de Oliveira, N.R., Pisa, P.S., Lopez, M.A., et al.: Identifying fake news on social networks based on natural language processing: trends and challenges. Information **12**(1), 38 (2021). https://doi.org/10.3390/info12010038
2. Savoy, J.: Machine Learning Methods for Stylometry: Authorship Attribution and Author Profiling. Springer International Publishing, Cham (2020)
3. Ouamour, S., Sayoud, H. : Authorship attribution of short historical Arabic texts based on lexical features. In: 2013 International Conference on Cyber-Enabled Distributed Computing and Knowledge Discovery. IEEE (2013).
4. Haque, F., Orthy, A.H., Siddique, S.: Hadith authenticity prediction using sentiment analysis and machine learning. In: 2020 IEEE 14th International Conference on Application of Information and Communication Technologies (AICT). IEEE (2020).
5. Devlin, J., Chang, M.-W., Lee, K., et al.: Bert: Pre-training of deep bidirectional transformers for language understanding. arXiv preprint arXiv:1810.04805 (2018).
6. Kashur, A.S.: Artificial Intelligence in Serving Sunna. Malaysia: Al-Madinah International University (2014).
7. Desouki. M.S.: Simulating the Application of Authorship Attribution for Hadith Sharif Texts. IMAN Conference (2021).

8. Khedher, M.Z.: Artificial Intelligence in Serving Hadith and its Sciences. International Journal on Islamic Applications in Computer Science and Technology, IJASAT (2018).

9. Najeeb, M.M.A.: A Hidden Markov Model-Based Tagging Approach for Arabic Isnads of Hadiths. Math. Problem. Eng. (2022).

10. Ouamour, S., Khennouf, S., Bourib, S., Hadjadj, H., Sayoud, H.: Effect of the text size on stylometry—application on Arabic religious texts. In: Nguyen, T.B., van Do, T., Thi, H.A.L., Nguyen, N.T. (eds.) Advanced Computational Methods for Knowledge Engineering: Proceedings of the 4th International Conference on Computer Science, Applied Mathematics and Applications, ICCSAMA 2016, 2-3 May, 2016, Vienna, Austria, pp. 215–228. Springer International Publishing, Cham (2016). https://doi.org/10.1007/978-3-319-38884-7_16

11. Gaanoun, K., Alsuhaibani, M.: Fabricated hadith detection: a novel matn-based approach with transformer language models. IEEE Access **10**, 113330–113342 (2022). https://doi.org/10.1109/ACCESS.2022.3217457

12. Fabien, M., Villatoro-Tello, E., Motlicek, P., et al.: BertAA: BERT fine-tuning for Authorship Attribution. In: Proceedings of the 17th International Conference on Natural Language Processing, ICON (2020).

13. Jawamea-alKalem Homepage: https://waqfeya.net/book.php?bid=6366. Last accessed 16 May 2023

14. Go, I., Bashar, A., Nurpeiis, B.. Houda, B., Nizar, H.: The interplay of variant, size, and task type in arabic pre-trained language models. In: Proceedings of the Sixth Arabic Natural Language Processing Workshop (2021).

15. Yun-tao, Z., Ling, G., Yong-cheng, W.: An improved TF-IDF approach for text classification. J. Zhejiang Univ.-Sci. A **6**(1), 49–55 (2005)

16. Khreisat, L.: Arabic text classification using N-gram frequency statistics a comparative study. In: Conference on Data Mining| DMIN (2006).

17. Mughal, M.A:. Al- Marfu' A Term of Science of Hadith. (2016). https://ssrn.com/abstract=2733470

18. fake-hadith Homepage. https://dorar.net/fake-hadith. Last accessed 20 May 2023

19. Altammami, S., Atwell, E., Alsalka, A.: Constructing a bilingual hadith corpus using a segmentation tool. In: Proceedings of the 12th Conference on Language Resources and Evaluation (2020).

20. hadith-json Homepage: https://github.com/A7med3bdulBaset/hadith-json. Last accessed 20 May 2023

21. tnqeeb Homepage: https://github.com/ARBML/tnqeeb. Last accessed 20 May 2023

Pre-treatment Proposal for Effective Forecasting of Used Car Pricing

Charlène Béatrice Bridge-Nduwimana[1]([✉])(iD), Aziza El Ouaazizi[1,2](iD), and Majid Benyakhlef[2](iD)

[1] Laboratory of Artificial Intelligence, Data Sciences and Emerging Systems (LIASSE), Sidi Mohamed Ben Abdellah University, Fez, Morocco
{charlenebeatrice.bridgenduwimana,aziza.elouaazizi}@usmba.ac.ma
[2] Laboratory of Engineering Sciences (LSI), Sidi Mohamed Ben Abdellah University, Fez, Morocco
majid.benyakhlef@usmba.ma

Abstract. Due to the increase in the price of new cars and the lack of funds among users, the sales/purchases of used cars are increasing overall. Predicting the price of used cars attracts a lot of interest in the field of research because it requires considerable effort and knowledge from the expert in the field where the main objective is to use all data generated by vehicle sellers. For the same purpose, specific characteristics are taken into account for precise predictions. The suggested pre-treatment model utilizes a dataset that includes information on the make and model of the vehicle, the year it was produced, its miles, its condition, and other elements that affect used-car prices. To estimate the cost of used cars, the Light Gradient Boosted Machine, Extreme Gradient Boosting, Gradient Boosting Regressor, Random Forest, and Bagging Regressor models are used. Each model was trained using market information gathered from websites. The used techniques to improve predictions are processing techniques on data set and processing regulations by models. We present two different types of data-driven data processing. As a result, we have a new data frame to analyze. We evaluate and compared the data frame with each other of the machine learning models to find the model that works most effectively and consistently. Putting time and effort into preparing the dataset and optimizing the regularization resulted in a decent score with Gradient Boosting Regressor.

Keywords: Data Pre-treatment · Prediction · Ensemble Machine Learning · Price Forecasting

1 Introduction

Used car sales is one of the common active sectors. This market could be worth 460 billion dollars with an average annual growth rate of more than 10% over the forecast period [1], revealing the more important issue of pricing. The valuation methods in the used car market remains unclear and unreliable for customers. In

H. Hagras et al. (Eds.): ISACS 2023, CCIS 2255, pp. 137–150, 2025.
https://doi.org/10.1007/978-3-031-93448-3_11

this sense, it is obvious to have a vehicle cost estimation framework to adequately determine the real value of the vehicle using its characteristics.

There are websites [2] which provide tools calculating the estimated value of a used car. They offer solutions for some problems. For the Consumer Reports tool [2], the user enters information such as the year of manufacturing, the manufacturer and the car's model created and the tool provides in return a summary of the car's resale value. Such as the AutoTrader [2] valuation system, those websites are data-driven which are integrated in their systems which allowing user's data to be evaluated. Only the benefits of using these tools are frequently emphasized with no mention of their limitations (TüvSüd tool [2]). The system proposed by Ifthkar [3] presents a solution to overcome the irregularities of an existing system based on rule-based data integration, filtering of data extracted from websites, formation and prediction of training data on models, and adjustment on the vehicle's "condition" characteristic prior to final evaluation of the proposed system. The used car system is gaining popularity as people choose this option because of its low cost and availability. In order to estimate used automobile prices, Monburinon et al. [4] used sophisticated algorithms such as gradient boosting and random forest and compared their results to more conventional regression models like multiple linear regression. When compared to other models, such as Random Forest (mse: 0.35) and Multiple Linear Regression (mse: 0.55), gradient boosting (mse: 0.28) performs better. Because of system limitations, authors in this work converted categorical data using label encoding. Even though the values of the specific column are discrete when utilizing label encoding, it is assumed that there is some relationship between the values after conversion. While building the model, it might provide some incorrect information. In the approach we proposed, we use one-hot-encoding technique for category conversion to address this issue.

In this paper, we conducted a comparative study on pre-treatment to machine learning methods, then to find the most efficient model for used car price identification. The models were implemented using data extracted from www.kaggle.com [5] website. Due of its status as one of the largest databases of used cars for sale, we chose the Craigslist dataset. Each used car listing on Craigslist in the US is included. How quickly and accurately a query is answered depends on the type of data processing you employ. This necessitates careful selection of the strategy. In scenarios where availability is essential, there is an easier way and more powerful techniques to improve model accuracy than meticulous algorithm selection: models function like ensembles [6]. Light Gradient Boosted Machine, Extreme Gradient Boosting, Gradient Boosting Regressor, Random Forest, and Bagging Regressor are the ensemble approaches in concern. As an alternative, Lasya et al. [7] decide to forecast used car prices using artificial neural network models (penalized models, linear regression, and regression trees). The primary focus here is continuing forward with pre-treatment while keeping in mind that careful selection of characteristics clearly shown a major advantage over multiple works (e.g. Srinivasan et al. [8]). To improve the value of our data pre-treatment proposition, we tune their behavior. This paper is organised as follows: Sect. 2

contains related works in the field of price prediction of used cars. In Sect. 3, the used steps descriptive research on Data are presented. Section 4 describes the implemented machine learning methods. Section 5 presents the data, expose the two proposed pre-treatment on data and finally discusses their respective performances on the prediction of the used cars price.

2   Related Works

Many studies have already been carried out to predict the value of used vehicles. Some authors provide papers in which the main objective is to present models or systems that estimate the price of cars with high accuracy. Anderson [9] examines car safety and the safety limit in Sweden. He used a semi-logarithmic hedonic regression model for car prices. Some characteristics into account for his model are: model's annual fuel bill, the number of deaths recorded, the number of injuries recorded, power, payload and fuel type. According to the study's findings, Swedish automobile buyers pay a safety premium for safer vehicles, there is less desire to pay for more car safety. Cumhur and Senturk [10] article use the hedonic regression technique to determine the factors influencing used car pricing in Turkey. Regression models were constructed using the semi-log, log-linear, and Box-Cox transformation methods on a dataset of 1074 cars. According to the results, although having a diesel engine, black and grey hues, an automatic transmission, a sunroof, the country and the year of manufacturing, and engine cylinder name have positive effects. In fact, the quantity of official vehicle servicing and sales locations in Istanbul affect negatively used cars prices. Different used car attributes imply diverse price premiums. One major limitation was the body style. The two examples above show that the selection of relevant features [11] is important in studies like ours.

Some various models and systems can help predict the true market value of a used car. For Gegic et al. [12] proposed model, three machine learning approaches (artificial neural network, support vector machine, and random forest) are employed to create a model for predicting the price of used cars in Bosnia and Herzegovina. However, the both of those strategies were used in ensemble way. The prediction model that best fits the data was put into the Java program to create a system. However, the suggested system demand significantly more computational resources than a single machine learning method. Longani et al. [13] present a system to forecast a fair price for any used car. To construct models that can predicted an appropriate price for used cars, ensemble techniques in machine learning such as random forest or extreme gradient boost (XGBoost) algorithms, are applied. Both approaches performed similarly with Extreme Boost surpassing the random forest algorithm. In contrast to XGBoost, which is fast to execute and provides substantial accuracy, Random Forest minimizes overfitting by using more trees with the flexibility to accommodate missing information. According to Chigateri et al. [14], for a successfully detected car, extra information on the car model and its review can be provided. Their accurate and efficient neural network-based model was designed to recognize the car model and make. It also categorizes a car video based on its model. To train the network, about 16,000 pictures of cars from over 30 different automobile types and manufacturers were employed. The convolutional neural network (CNN) model and additionally resnet34 were used, with the last layer changed with a customized layer that ended up generating less classifications. Pal et al. [15] use a Random Forest supervised learning model to estimate the price of used cars. After careful analysis of exploratory data, this model was selected to evaluate the impact of each characteristic on price. Accuracy was 95.82% in training and 83.63% in testing. The model was able to accurately estimate car prices by selecting the most appropriate characteristics. In the article [16], Noor and Jan propose a vehicle price prediction system that uses supervised machine learning. In their research, they use multiple linear regression as an estimation method, which gives them a prediction accuracy of 98%. In their application, there were several independent variables and one dependent variable to compare with the actual and predicted accuracy values of the score level. This article proposes a system where price is the predicted variable by using vehicle model, make, city, equipment, color, mileage, alloy wheels, and power steering as features.

In contrast to either simple multiple regression or multivariate regression, Listiani in his thesis [17] demonstrated that the regression mode built using support vector machines (SVM) can predict the residual value of chartered cars with superior accuracy. SVM will prevent both over-fitting and under fitting and it will better suited to handle highly dimensional information (number of features used to forecast pricing). The study showed one flaw: the SVM couldn't be assessed using metrics like mean deviation or variance. Pudaruth [18] employed multiple linear regression, k nearest neighbors, naive Bayes, and decision trees to assess the worth of used automobiles in Mauritius; nevertheless, their results were not intelligent for prediction due to a limited number of observations. He came to the conclusion that naive Bayes and decision trees cannot be used to continuous valued data. To predict the residual value of used personal cars, Gonggi [19] developed a new model based mostly on artificial neural networks, taking into account the vehicle's expected useful life, manufacturer, and mileage. The proposed model is optimized to address non-linear relationships that cannot be handled by the simple regression techniques.

3   Descriptive Research on Data

In this section, we present the main steps for discovering datasets, data pre-treatment and thus extracting explanatory data until their usage [20]. The steps are:

Selection: Define data sources.

Pre-Processing/Pre-treatment: Improvement of the dataset, analysis of variables, definition of their importance and their interaction.

Data Mining or Exploration: Involves the use of statistical and machine learning algorithms to extract structures, correlations, patterns and rules from

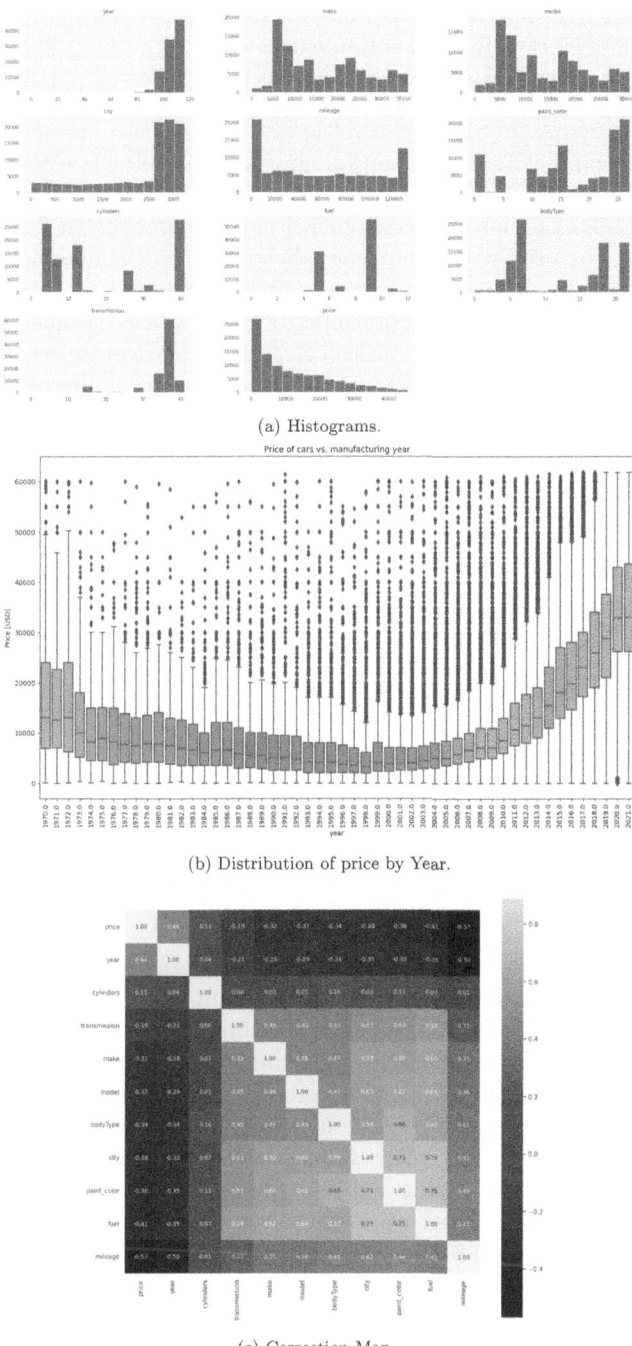

(a) Histograms.

(b) Distribution of price by Year.

(c) Correction Map.

Fig. 1. (a) Features histograms – (b) Distribution of price by year – (c) Correlation Map.

the data. Prediction is one of the fundamental tasks of data mining which are classification, clustering, association, summarizing.

Interpretation/Evaluation: Reveals whether the detected patterns are really interesting or not.

The Fig. 1 exposes data exploration charts Fig. 1a, 1b, 1c. We have an histogram (Fig. 1a) that illustrates the data distribution by showing the number of observations belonging into each category. Figure 1b presents the mean distribution of pricing features across the years allowing us to examine how it changes over time. That means encoding methods on values in the pre-treatment stage is important to capture the relationships between values because the number of observations in each category varies considerably. A feature with a high correlation coefficient frequently, but not always, has more influence on the prediction variable for datasets in predictive statistics and machine learning cases. In chart Fig. 1a, the correlation is presented. It is a statistical method for illustrating the relationship between variables. If it equals 0, there is no correlation, but values of 1 and −1 imply positive and negative relationships respectively. The variables "year" and "cylinders" appear to be positively connected with the variable "price" according to the correlation map, while others appear to be negatively correlated.

4   Machine Learning Methods

We conduct data collecting and preparation phase. After we do price forecasting using machine learning algorithms and performance analysis for our system. The chosen algorithm to use should be moderately stable. We work with ensemble-based prediction models [21]. To enhance the greatest performance and robustness on our data, we selected five of them. Here we present in this section the used regression models:

1. LGBM: Light Gradient Bossting Machine is a gradient reinforcement approach that uses a tree-based learning algorithm. It grows the tree vertically whereas other algorithms grow trees horizontally, which means that it grows the tree by leaf whereas the other algorithm grows by level. It will choose the leaf with the maximum delta loss to grow. When growing the same leaf, the per-leaf algorithm can reduce more loss than a per-level algorithm.
2. Extra Tree Regressor: Extremely Randomized Trees is an ensemble of decision trees and is related to bagging and random forest. From the training dataset, it generates a large number of non-truncated decision trees. In the case of regression, predictions are made by averaging the predictions of the decision trees to increase predictive accuracy and reduce overfitting.
3. XGradient Boosting Regressor: It is commonly used in a variety of machine learning problems. The success of XGBoost is primarily due to its scalability in all situations. On a single machine, the system operates more than 10 times quicker than currently used solutions, and in distributed or memory-constrained environments, it scalable to billions of samples.

4. Random Forest Regressor: It is the most well-liked decision tree method. In comparison to any single tree in the model, performance is improved when predictions from the trees are averaged over all decision trees in order to reduce overfitting after fitting numerous classification decision trees to different dataset sub-samples.

5. Bagging Regressor: A machine learning ensemble algorithm, that integrates the forecasts from numerous decision trees. Regression problems are predicted by averaging the forecast across all of the decision trees.

5   Results and Discussion

In this section, we will discuss the results of the most popular regression models presented in Sect. 4. To determine which approach better fits the data set, algorithm performance was compared. We use the r2-score (Eq. (1)) to evaluate performance. The coefficient of determination, usually referred to as R-squared or R2 [22,23], is a regression metric that makes it easier to compare models. This metric is a 'standardised' version of MSE (Mean Squared Error). The R2 value increases with model performance and approaches 100% when all predictions are accurate. On the other hand, it is difficult to understand and does not provide details of the typical inaccuracy of the model. It often needs to be paired with other metrics, such as the MSE or MAE values [22,23], to better understand the performance of the model. We will consider the calculation of the MAE metric in our situation (Eq. (2)). The difference between the value measured and the "true" value is known as the "absolute error," and the average absolute error (MAE) is the average of all absolute errors.

$$R^2 = 1 - \frac{\sum_{i=1}^{n}(y_i - \hat{y}_i)^2}{\sum_{i=1}^{n}(y_i - \bar{y}_i)^2} \tag{1}$$

$$MAE = \frac{1}{n}\sum_{i=1}^{n}|x_i - x| \tag{2}$$

Dataset. We collect the data from Kaggle [5] and it has values prior to cleaning. This data is scraped every few months and comprises nearly all essential information offered on car sales. There are numerous missing rows in the dataset. If these missing rows were eliminated, we would have less data to work, and in data science, the more data there is, the better the algorithm will be. We will perform two distinct kinds of preprocessing on our dataset. We will explore them in more detail below.

Data Collection. Using the information provided by Mokin [5], we established a collection of data. Mokin's dataset [5] contains 525839 rows and 22 features. We often referred to as source (a). From Krishnamoorthy's kaggle account [5], we use two of its datasets, we call them source (b) and source (c). Each of the two sources has respectively 3 million lines and 66 features (source (b)) and 426880 lines and 26 features (source (c)). We extract 500,000 rows from sources (a) and (b) and maintain all of the rows of source (c). The designers of these dataset did not assign identical names for features, we locate their names in all three datasets and get finally a dataset with 1426880 rows and 14 columns of features.

Features. Here are the main factors of our second-hands cars dataset. They are used in the input pattern in training and price forecasting procedure. The 'price' variable is the target. 'city', 'make', 'model', 'cylinders', 'fuel', 'transmission', 'vin', 'bodyType' and 'paint_color' are the categorical features and the numerical features are 'year', 'mileage', 'longitude' and 'latitude'.

- Price - The cost calculated in US dollars.
- Year - The year that the automobile was made.
- Manufacturer - 42 distinct variables are used to represent manufacturers.
- Make - The exact model of the vehicle.
- Condition - Car's condition: excellent, good, fair, like new, salvaged, new.
- Cylinders - The engine of a car has somewhere between 3 and 12 cylinders. 'Other' is another category that is present.
- Fuel - Five groups: 'diesel', 'gas', 'electric', 'hybrid' and 'other'.
- Mileage - Mileage is the odometer which displays the distance the vehicle has covered since being acquired.
- Transmission - Three varieties: automatic, manual, and 'other' acquired.
- VIN - Vehicle Identification Number.
- City - The data set contains the name of the city as well as the short form of the state, such as "fl" for the State of Florida, which is a political territory.
- bodyType - This attribute lets you know whether a car is a 'bus' or a 'minivan'. There are 13 different values for this quality.
- Paint_color - The color of the car.
- Latitude and Longitude - Provide information on car's sales location.

5.1   Proposed Data Cleaning Methods

Data Cleaning Steps. We remove several non-fillable columns from our dataset for first (Sect. 5.1 (a)) and second (Sect. 5.1 (b)) preprocessing step to keep the most significant features, such as 'url', 'city_url', 'title_status', 'image_url', 'size', 'drive' and 'desc', that we don't need for the analysis stage. We work with Python language and its Pandas, Scikit-learn, Numpy and Matplotlib libraries. In relation to the pre-treatment kinds proposed, we have the following python functions we use: dropna(), LabelEncoder(), OrdinalEncoder(), OneHotEncoding(), StandardScaler().

(a) First Way of Preprocessing Stage. 'nan' (Not Available Number) in Python is used to describe missing values. We use dropna() to remove the values. OrdinalEncoder() is used to encode categorical characteristics and LabelEncoder() is used to encode the target variable, we do not touch numerical features at this stage. Our data collection gets reorganized by reset his index. Since the variables 'VIN', 'lat' for latitude, and 'long' for longitude make the training set excessively cumbersome, we remove them at this point. To reduce time consuming during training, we encode all the categorical variables using OrdinalEncoding() and scale the numerical variables using StandardScaler(). Before segregating the data to test our models, we use drop_duplicated(keep='first') to remove duplicates and then we have 648890 rows. The test set is 30% and train set takes 70%.

(b) Second Way of Preprocessing Stage. For the second and last suggestion, we verify that the categorical variables are correctly registered. Using "astype()", "lower()", "replace(' ', '_')" and "replace('-','_')", we adjust the features 'make', 'vin', 'model', 'city'. We organise the variables 'fuel', 'transmission', 'cylinders', 'colors', 'bodyType'. We proceed for example as follows:

```
1  ## For "paint_color"
2  white = {'white', 'WHite', 'WHITE'}
3  def function(x):
4    if x in white:
5      return 'white'
6  df['paint_color'] = df['paint_color'].apply(function)
```

We take into account rows with prices between 100$ and 100,000$ because the information is unclear beyond these values. We consider the years between 1970 and 2020 because we want to benefit from an understanding of the characteristics. Vehicles produced after 2019 are considered 'new', while those produced between 2017 and 2019 are considered 'like new'. We calculate the average mileage for each state. Every vehicle, whether new, nearly new, excellent, good, passable or salvage, will have a mileage that is either close to or far from the average we calculate. We classify these qualities using a set of conditional rules.

```
1  fair_odo_mean = data[data['condition'] == 'fair']['odometer'].mean()
2  print('Fair average odometer:', round( fair_odo_mean,2))
3
4  data.loc[data['odometer'] >= fair_odo_mean, 'condition'] =
   ↪  data.loc[data['odometer'] >= fair_odo_mean,
   ↪  'condition'].fillna('fair')
```

Following this actions, the fill method ('ffill') is used to replace the category variables with missing values by their most prevalent modal value. This method replaces null values with the value of the previous line. The mean value of the numerical variables is used as a replacement for the missing values. For the variables 'odometer', 'vin', 'lat', and 'long', if there are some rows with missing values in them, we choose to use dropna() to get rid of them. After that, we employ the same methods as for our first pre-treatment: LabelEncoder() is used to encode the target variable, while OrdinalEncoder() is used to encode categorical features. We reorganize the rows by reset index method. With the drop() function, we also eliminate the variables "vin", "lat", "city" and "long"; they are time-consuming because of many distinct and unique values. Then, we use OrdinalEncoding() to encode all category variables and StandardScaler() to scale all numerical variables. We apply drop_duplicated(keep='first') to erase the duplicates. We divide up data set: 70% for training and 30% for testing.

5.2 Discussion

For all models (mentioned in Sect. 4), the mean absolute error is then used as the comparison criterion to compare the outcomes. The MAE outcomes for the test are represented by the red curve, while those for the training are shown by the green curve Fig. 2. We can choose any model if the two MAE values for test and training are evaluated similarly or closely. For the first pre-treatment proposal where we drop missing values and duplicates, we see in Fig. 2a that Gradient Boosting Regressor is more suitable for our dataset. We have LGBM and XGB regressors that are performing particularly well. We present results in Table 2 (see Proposal 1) the MAE score values for Gradient Boosting Regressor model and the r2-score criterion are represented in Table 1 (see Proposal 1). In addition, the second pre-treatment proposal increase the performance score for Gradient Boosting Regressor model which learn also effectively. In terms of performance and error requirements, LGBM and XGB operate similarly to Gradient Boosting Regressor (see curve Fig. 2b). Bagging Regressor and Random Forest, on the other hand, reveal that the pre-treatments are not in their favor due to the percentage of errors (see curve Fig. 2b), they had poor learning capabilities and overlearning in training.

Table 1. R2-Score

Pre-treatment	Training	Testing
Proposal 1	82.15%	81.16%
Proposal 2	85.77%	83.18%

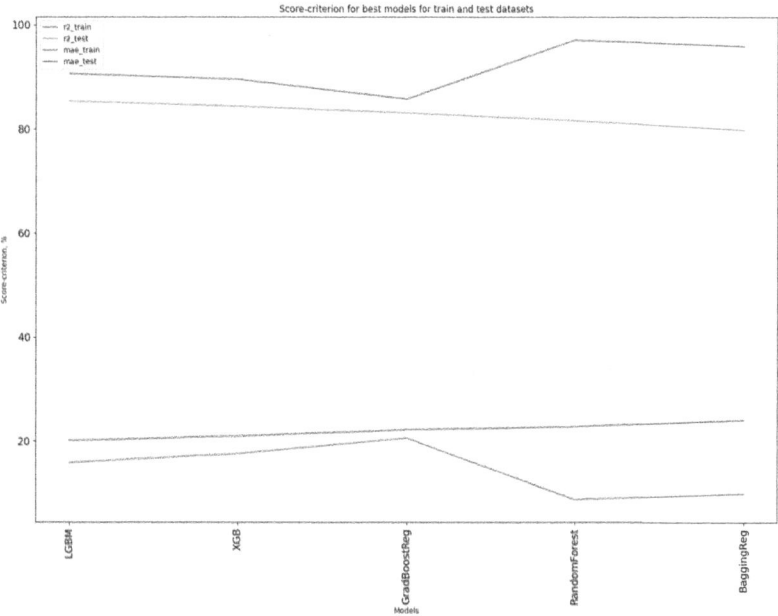

(a) First Pre-treatment Proposal.

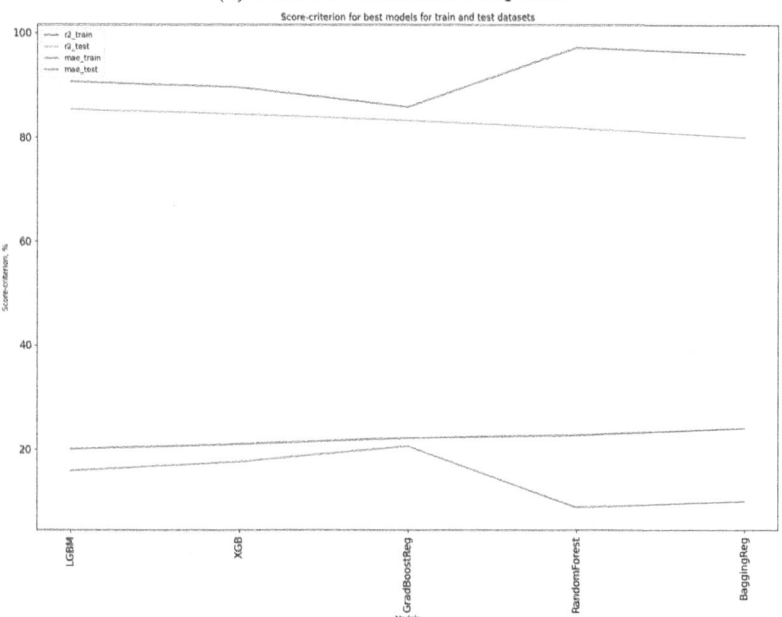

(b) Second Pre-treatment Proposal.

Fig. 2. Performance Results

Table 2. MAE score

Pre-treatment	Training	Testing
Proposal 1	21.93%	22.24%
Proposal 2	20.62%	22.20%

6   Conclusion

This research attempts to estimate the price of used cars using five different machine learning techniques. The dataset was subjected to exploratory data analysis and the relationships between the dependent variable and the independent factors were shown on graphs. The data wasn't comprehensive or ordered. In order to improve the performance of the model, we propose two pre-processing approaches to create a new cleaned dataset. The data were then prepared and cleaned before being used for testing and training. According to the results, the Gradient Boosting Regressor outperformed every model with an R2 value greater than 80%. At this point we can confirm that using large datasets, advanced models, fine-tuning the hyperparameters and developing additional attributes can improve the performance of the models, as these steps were taken throughout the project. In the future, we plan to explore new attributes and data preprocessing methods.

References

1. Mordor Intelligence. https://www.mordorintelligence.com/industry-reports/global-used-car-market-growth-trends-and-forecast-2019-2024. Accessed 20 May 2023
2. ConsumerReports tool. https://www.consumerreports.org/cars/car-value-estimator/. AutoTrader tool. https://www.autotrader.co.uk/cars/valuation. TüvSüd tool. https://www.tuvsud.com/en/industries/mobility-and-automotive/retail-and-leasing/automotive-remarketing/it-tools/car-pricing-tool
3. Ifthikar, A., Vidanage, K.: Valuation of used vehicles: a computational intelligence approach. In: Intelligent Systems Modelling & Simulation (2018). https://doi.org/10.1109/ISMS.2018.00011
4. Monburinon, N., Chertchom, P., Kaewkiriya, T., Rungpheung, S., Buya, S., Boonpou, P.: Prediction of prices for used car by using regression models. In: 5th International Conference on Business and Industrial Research (ICBIR), pp. 115–119 (2018)
5. Kaggle. www.kaggle.com. Mokin V.: https://www.kaggle.com/code/vbmokin/used-cars-fe-eda-with-3d-abnormals-filter/input?select=craigslistVehicles.csv. Krishnamoorthy, A.: https://www.kaggle.com/code/adikrishnamoorthy/notebookf7cc1611bc/input

6. Kathiravan, M., Ramya, M., Jayanthi, S., Reddy, V.V., Ponguru, L., Bharathiraja, N.: Predicting the sale price of pre-owned vehicles with the ensemble ML model. In: 4th International Conference on Electronics and Sustainable Communication Systems (ICESC), pp. 1793–1797 (2023). https://doi.org/10.1109/ICESC57686.2023.10192988

7. Lasya, C.L., Pooja, S., Jeyashree, S., Ambhika, C., Eswari, G.: Forecasting pre-owned car prices using machine learning. In: 2nd International Conference on Smart Technologies and Systems for Next Generation Computing (ICSTSN), pp. 1–6 (2023). https://doi.org/10.1109/ICSTSN57873.2023.10151632

8. Srinivasan, P., Reddy, R.O., Sai, K.A., Naidu, J.: Predictive analysis and application of various machine learning algorithms to forecast used car prices. In: International Conference on Sustainable Computing and Smart Systems (ICSCSS), pp. 190–194 (2023). https://doi.org/10.1109/ICSCSS57650.2023.10169183

9. Andersson, H.: The value of safety as revealed in the Swedish car market: an application of the hedonic pricing approach. J. Risk Uncertain. **30**(3), 211–239 (2005)

10. Cumhur, E., Senturk, I.: A hedonic analysis of used car prices in Turkey. Int. J. Econ. Perspect. **3**(2), 141–149 (2009)

11. Matas, A., Raymond, J.L.: Hedonic prices for cars: an application to the Spanish car market, 1981–2005. Appl. Econ. **41**, 2887–2904 (2009)

12. Gegic, E., Isakovic, B., Keco, D., Masetic, Z., Kevric, J.: Car price prediction using machine learning techniques. TEM J. **8**(1), 113–118 (2019)

13. Longani, C., Potharaju, S.P., Deore, S.: Price prediction for pre-owned cars using ensemble machine learning techniques. In: Recent Trends in Intensive Computing, pp. 178–187 (2021). https://doi.org/10.3233/APC210194

14. Chigateri, K.B., Suryavamshi, S., Rajendra, S.: System for detecting car models based on machine learning. Mater. Today: Proc. **52**(3), 1697–1701 (2022). https://doi.org/10.1016/j.matpr.2021.11.335

15. Pal, N., Arora, P., Kohli, P., Sundararaman, D., Palakurthy, S.S.: How much is my car worth? A methodology for predicting used cars' prices using random forest. In: Arai, K., Kapoor, S., Bhatia, R. (eds.) FICC 2018. AISC, vol. 886, pp. 413–422. Springer, Cham (2019). https://doi.org/10.1007/978-3-030-03402-3_28

16. Noor, K., Jan, S.: Vehicle price prediction system using machine learning techniques. Int. J. Comput. Appl. **167**(9), 27–31 (2017)

17. Listiani, M.: Support Vector Regression Analysis for Price Prediction in a Car Leasing Application. Thesis (MSc), Hamburg University of Technology (2009)

18. Pudaruth, S.: Predicting the price of used cars using machine learning techniques. Int. J. Inf. Comput. Technol. **4**(7), 753–764 (2014)

19. Gonggi, S.: New model for residual value prediction of used cars based on BP neural network and non-linear curve fit. In: Proceedings of the 3rd IEEE International Conference on Measuring Technology and Mechatronics Automation (ICMTMA), vol. 2, pp. 682–685 (2011)

20. Safhi, H.M., Frikh, B., Hirchoua, B., Ouhbi, B., Khalil, I.: Data intelligence in the context of big data: a survey. J. Mobile Multimedia **13**, 1–27 (2017)

21. Mohammed, A., Kora, R.: A comprehensive review on ensemble deep learning: opportunities and challenges. J. King Saud Univ. Comput. Inf. Sci. **35**(2), 757–774 (2023)

22. Alnajim, T., Alshahrani, N., Asiri, O.: A survey on used vehicle price estimation systems using artificial intelligence methods. J. Theor. Appl. Inf. Technol. **101**(11), 4425–4432 (2023)

23. Kumar, A.: Machine learning based solution for asymmetric information in prediction of used car prices. In: International Conference on Intelligent Vision and Computing (ICIVC 2022), pp. 409–420 (2023). https://doi.org/10.1007/978-3-031-31164-2_34

Overview of Self-Sovereign Identity for Blockchain-Based Authentication

Youssef Achir[1]([✉]) [iD], Ayman Nait Cherif[1] [iD], Mohamed Youssfi[2] [iD],
Mouhcine Elgarej[1] [iD], and Omar Bouattane[3] [iD]

[1] 2IACS Laboratory ENSET, Hassan II University Casablanca, Adria B-TCasablanca, Morocco
youssef.achir1-etu@etu.univh2c.ma
[2] 2IACS Laboratory ENSET, Hassan II University Casablanca, Casablanca, Morocco
[3] EESS Laboratory ENSET, Hassan II University Casablanca, Casablanca, Morocco

Abstract. The current state of identity systems faces a multitude of challenges that have significant implications for user privacy and security. Data duplication, fragmented credentials, and vulnerabilities within these systems create an environment ripe for identity theft and privacy breaches. To address these pressing issues, the concept of Self-Sovereign Identity (SSI) has emerged as a decentralized identification service that harnesses the power of blockchain technology. By leveraging the decentralized ledger of blockchain, SSI enables individuals to reclaim control over their digital identities. This paradigm shift from centralized authorities to user-centric control is at the core of SSI's principles. Through SSI, individuals gain the ability to manage their personal information securely and efficiently, while enjoying the convenience of accessing service from anywhere. This article aims to provide an in-depth exploration of SSI, shedding light on its fundamental principles and architectural components necessary for implementing a functional SSI service. By understanding the core concepts of SSI, readers can grasp the potential of this innovative approach to revolutionize identity systems.

Keywords: Self-Sovereign Identity · Decentralization · Blockchain · Digital Identity · Data Privacy · User Centric

1 Introduction

Blockchain technology has garnered a significant following in recent years for its tremendous potential to reshape the landscape of many industries using decentralized and distributed systems. Credited with introducing this technology through the publication of Bitcoin: A Peer-to-Peer Electronic Cash System [1], in the paper Nakamoto presented the concept of a decentralized electronic cash system, famously known as Bitcoin, which is based on blockchain technology to record transactions securely and transparently without the need for a central authority that controls and oversees them. Considering its growth, blockchains decentralized consensus protocol applications are not limited to the financial industry but extend to other fields such as identity management.

Self-sovereign identity (SSI) is a concept in the field of digital identity that refers to a system whose individuals have complete sovereignty, in other words, control over their

H. Hagras et al. (Eds.): ISACS 2023, CCIS 2255, pp. 151–160, 2025.
https://doi.org/10.1007/978-3-031-93448-3_12

digital credentials, rather than having their identities controlled by third-party services. In recent years, SSI has emerged as a promising solution to establish a portable, secure, and controllable identity for individuals or organizations. By leveraging decentralized technologies such as blockchain and the decentralized Identifiers (DIDs) concept [2], SSI guarantees the integrity, immutability, and security of identity credentials. This allows individuals and organizations to prove their authenticity or attribute possession of a particular credential in a verifiable and secure manner, without the need to reveal any personally sensitive information.

As such, SSI has the potential to play a significant role in shaping the future of digital trust and identity.

In this paper, we review the current state of the art in the field of SSI, including its principles, key concepts, and the currently proposed architecture. We also discuss the challenges and opportunities that SSI presents and outline future research directions in this quickly evolving area.

The paper's structure is as follows. Section 2 provides an overview of the research topic's background. In Sect. 3 related research is discussed. Section 4 delineates the Key Concepts of SSI and its Main Actors. SSI Architecture is elaborated upon in Sect. 5, while Sect. 6 outlines the benefits and challenges associated with SSI. Finally, Sect. 7 concludes the paper.

2 Background

2.1 Blockchain and Decentralized Ledgers

Blockchain technology has gained significant traction in the past decade due to its prospective to revolutionize various industries. The concept of a blockchain, which is a decentralized and distributed database [3] that stores a growing list of records secured by cryptography, was first introduced in 2008 in a white paper detailing the design of Bitcoin, a decentralized digital currency. In addition to being used for cryptocurrency, the decentralized nature of blockchain technology makes it well-suited for use in a variety of industries, including finance, supply chain management [4], voting systems, and authentication and identity management. The combination of a distributed ledger and computing infrastructure allows for the creation of decentralized applications that have the potential to improve upon traditional systems in terms of security, transparency, and efficiency.

The data structure of a blockchain consists of a linked list of identifiable blocks that contain transactions. These blocks are linked to each other using cryptographic hashes, forming an immutable chain of data storage. The immutability and transparency of a blockchain allow for the maintenance of data integrity, and the decentralization of the network improves its availability. However, in public blockchains, data privacy and scalability can be issues due to the open nature of the network, as anyone can join and access the information without the need for privileges, moreover, the scalability challenge stems from the decentralized nature of the network, which can make it difficult to process many transactions. This is because every node in the network must validate and record each transaction, which can lead to bottlenecks and delays as the number of transactions increases, the scalability issue can also vary depending on the blockchain network due to the adopted consensus protocol [5].

2.2   The Evolution of Identity Management Models

In the current landscape of online identity models, SSI is characterized as the latest new and revolutionizing model. Before SSI, identity management systems have continuously progressed from centralized, federated then user-centric models.

Centralized identity refers to a model in which a single authority or hierarchy holds administrative control over the issuance and management of digital identities. This model is often associated with online platforms that use a traditional pair of usernames and passwords to identify an individual and store and manage all related personal and sensitive information in their databases. In this model, the platform acts as the central authority controlling access to and managing the individual's digital identity.

Federated identity [6], on the other hand, involves service providers that delegate their users' credential management to a trusted identity provider so they can access their services securely with a single set of login credentials, for example, if you log in to your *Gmail* account, you can use those credentials to access other services that support federated identities such as *Google Drive* or *Google Calendar*.

In the user-centric identity model, the individual user is in control of their own identity and can use it across multiple authorities without the need for a central federation to manage it. This means that the user can use the same identity credentials to access different services and applications without having to go through the separate process of authentication and authorization.

SSI represents the next iteration in identity management progress, as it allows individuals to have complete control of their digital identities across any number of authorities, devices, and services.

Overall, the progression from centralized to self-sovereign identity reflects a shift towards greater individual control in the context of digital identity.

3   Related Work

SSI is closely linked to decentralized identifiers they are usually perceived as equivalents, and always associated with blockchain technology and to a lesser degree with distributed systems, for this reason, in the current landscape of SSI systems, the concept of SSI is still loosely defined as there is no official consensus among experts in the field. Despite this, several key properties have been established. For example, on July 19, 2022, the World Wide Web Consortium (W3C) announced that DIDs v1.0 is now an official Web Standard.

The Sovrin Foundation, a non-profit organization that is a pioneer in the decentralized identity sphere, governs the Sovrin network. Its goal is to offer a global, publicly available infrastructure for self-sovereign identity and to promote its use for the benefit of individuals and organizations. In its white paper [7], the foundation has laid out the foundational principles required for an SSI system, which we will be discussed further in the section on SSI key concepts.

Mühle et al. have conducted a comprehensive survey on the fundamental components of SSI systems [8] that provides valuable insight into the different options available for building SSI systems, and the trade-offs that need to be considered when choosing a particular approach, focusing on proposed solutions for implementing identification, authentication, managing verifiable claims, and attribute storage, they have also presented the two main approaches for SSI systems, the identifier registry model architecture, and the claims registry model architecture. The former is characterized by the identity claims being stored in user-controlled storage. This approach allows users to have complete control over their data and the ability to share it selectively with trusted parties. This model is often associated with the use of decentralized identifiers. On the other hand, the claims registry model architecture uses the blockchain as a registry for the identifiers and cryptographic fingerprints of every associated claim of a particular identity. This model is often associated with the use of smart contracts, which are self-executing contracts with the terms of the agreement written directly into code, to manage the registration and verification of identity claims [9].

In the study by Liu et al., they proposed 12 design patterns for blockchain-based SSI identity systems [10], and these patterns were classified into three main categories: Key management, DID management, and credential design patterns. The key management patterns focus on using cryptographic keys based on symmetric or asymmetric encryption, to secure and manage identity-related transactions and storage, these patterns aim to ensure the confidentiality and integrity of identity-related information, as well as the authenticity of transactions. The DID management patterns associate unique decentralized identifiers with an individual's identity and attributes, these patterns enable individuals to have control over their own identities, rather than relying on centralized systems. The credential design patterns are designed to give holders full control over their credentials, also known as verifiable claims, these patterns enable individuals to choose and limit the sharing of their credentials, which can include information such as educational qualifications, employment history, and other personal information. The patterns aim to provide a secure transparent, and privacy-preserving way for individuals to share their credentials with other entities usually called verifiers, this interchange will be further discussed in the SSI actors' interactions section.

4 Key Concepts of SSI

4.1 Principles of SSI

The Sovrin Foundation has extended and organized Christopher Allen's [11] core principles of the SSI ecosystem into three primary categories: *Agency, Control* and *Protection* as detailed in Table 1.

These principles aim to enable any entity, including humans, legal entities, and natural or physical objects, to be represented by digital identities that can be exchanged, secured, and verified using open and public standards. SSI ecosystems should be decentralized and allow entities to control their digital identity data and interact with agents of their choice. The systems should be accessible and consistent for all users and allow for the portability of identity data. Additionally, SSI should prioritize security, verifiability, and authenticity, as well as protect the privacy of identity data and minimize disclosure.

Finally, SSI ecosystems should be transparent, allowing all stakeholders to access and verify information about the incentives, rules, and policies under which the systems operate.

Table 1. Sovrin's Foundational Principles of SSI

Agency	Control	Protection
Representation	Participation	Security
Delegation	Decentralization	Verifiability
Equity	Interoperability	Authenticity
Inclusion	Portability	Privacy
Usability		Minimal Disclosure
Accessibility		Transparency
Consistency		

4.2 Main Actors of SSI

An SSI system typically operates based on the Issuer-Holder-Verifier Trust Triangle, consisting of three main actors: *holders*, *issuers*, and *verifiers* (see Fig. 1).

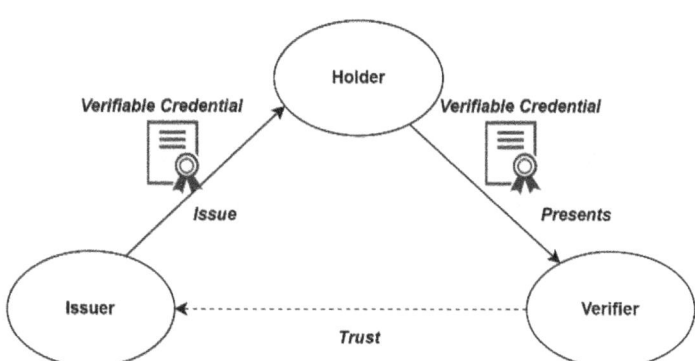

Fig. 1. SSI actors' interactions.

Holders are individuals or entities that create and manage their own DID use a digital wallet application and receive verifiable credentials (VCs). DIDs are unique identifiers that are stored in a distributed ledger and are controlled by the holder, allowing them to have full ownership and agency over their identity data. VCs are digital documents that are issued by issuers and contain information about the holder's identity, such as their name, age, gender, address or qualifications, or any other piece of private information that concerns the individual's identity. Holders can use their DID and VCs to prove their identity by relying on parties called verifiers in various transactions or interactions.

Issuers are parties with the authority to issue VCs to holders. They are responsible for verifying the authenticity and accuracy of the identity information contained in VCs before issuing them. Issuers may be government agencies, educational institutions, private companies, or other organizations that have the necessary information and resources to verify identity data.

Verifiers are actors that are responsible for checking the authenticity and accuracy of VCs when they are presented by holders. They may be involved in various interactions with holders and may need to verify the holder's identity to proceed. Verifiers may be relying parties, such as banks, and insurance companies, or they may be independent third parties that are hired to verify VCs on behalf of relying parties.

Overall, the roles of holders, issuers, and verifiers are crucial to the functioning of an SSI system, as they enable individuals and organizations to leverage this system to fully control their identity and guarantee its authenticity and privacy in a decentralized manner.

5   SSI Architecture

There are many different approaches for implementing SSI architectures, one focusing solely on an entity's identifier with uses a DID registry to store and manage identifiers, while other approaches extend this by also storing cryptographic fingerprints of verifiable claims made by entities (see Fig. 2).

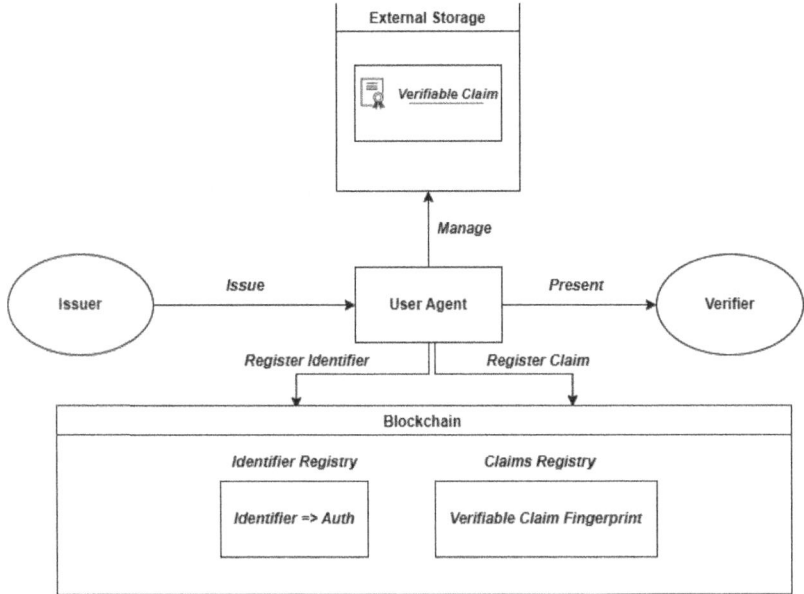

Fig. 2. SSI architecture

Typically, the architecture of an SSI ecosystem is based on the use of a distributed ledger, such as a blockchain, to store and manage identity information. The distributed ledger serves as a substitute for the central registration authority which is usually found in traditional management systems. It is where the pairing of identification and authentication is maintained, allowing individuals to store and manage their identity data in a secure and decentralized manner.

In a self-sovereign identifier registry model, the identifier and verifiable claims are directly managed by the user. The identifier is tied to the specific user by an authentication method, with asymmetric cryptography and public key infrastructures (PKIs) being the most desired choices among SSI systems due to their zero-knowledge proof properties, this, however, begs the question of how the user should keep the private key associated with his key pair. The most popular solution in the landscape currently is employing smartphones for key storage, thanks to their commodity usage and portability. Another challenge that comes to mind here is that there needs to be trust placed in a third party assigning and verifying the key pairs. For this task, a centralized Certificate Authority must be employed and be trusted to correctly map the pairing of identity and public key. Though, not only does this centralization carry a risk through attacks and coercion, but it also shatters a significant part of the desired decentralization aspect of an SSI system, with that being the case, numerous research is also conducted to propose new decentralized public key infrastructure (DPKIs) models based on blockchain solutions [12] leveraging consensus protocols and digital signatures to ensure the trustworthiness and integrity of public keys without the need of a central certificate authority.

When it comes to the actual identity claims of an individual, they are usually stored in a user-controlled storage location. This location is often placed off-chain, meaning it is not stored on the blockchain itself due to privacy concerns, off-chain storage can take a variety of forms, such as a personal device or a cloud-based storage service.

Regarding the verification of identity claims, the entity relying on the claim's validity, referred to as the claim-verifier, can access a publicly accessible identifier linked to the individual. This identifier is stored on the blockchain and serves to uniquely recognize the individual and their associated identity assertions. Subsequently, the verifier can compare this openly accessible identifier within the presented claim provided by the user. After authenticating the user using the blockchain-stored authentication method, the verifier can then assess the claim's accuracy and decide whether to validate it.

The legitimacy of the claim hinges on both the furnished information and the credibility of the third-party entity attesting to it. This systematic approach ensures a secure and efficient process of identity verification, all without necessitating a central authority to govern and retain identity data.

6   Benefits and Challenges of SSI Ecosystems

In this section, we will discuss the key benefits and the challenges [13, 14] that still constrain the adoption of SSI as an authentication model. At the end of the section, Table 2 will act as a comprehensive summary of these benefits and challenges.

6.1 Benefits of SSI Ecosystems

As a decentralized approach to identity management, SSI offers many benefits and opportunities to the digital identity landscape. As discussed previously, SSI provides individuals greater control and autonomy over their data and its management. For example, users have the freedom to choose not only which pieces of their data to share but also with whom, thereby allowing them to safeguard their privacy.

Another crucial advantage originates from the decentralized nature of the SSI ecosystem, meaning that personal data is not stored in a single location, but rather distributed across a network of nodes. This makes it increasingly difficult for malicious attackers to compromise the system, as they would need to target multiple nodes simultaneously to be successful, as such, the SSI system is more resilient and less vulnerable to a single point of failure, making it less likely that a technical issue or cyberattack to result in data loss, thus ensuring data integrity and security.

Streamlining identity-related processes and increasing efficiency is yet another added benefit of SSI systems, as they inherently reduce the number of necessary intermediaries to verify and authenticate identities by allowing individuals to directly manage and share their data. This can potentially lead to cost savings and faster transaction times, as there is no need to involve additional parties in the process. In addition, SSI systems can reduce reliance on physical documents, such as driver's licenses, diplomas, and passports. These documents can be easily lost, stolen, or even forged, and may require periodic renewals. With SSI systems, individuals can use a digital equivalent that is easily verifiable and tamper-proof. This can make it quicker and more convenient to complete transactions and verify identities, while also reducing the need for physical documents.

6.2 Challenges in Adopting SSI Ecosystem

SSI in its current state is still regarded as a relatively new concept, thus it is still facing several challenges and limitations that are preventing its widespread adoption.

From an organization's point of view, SSI is perceived as being in its infancy and not yet mature enough for widespread deployment, particularly due to its lack of interoperability with legacy systems and the various technological components that need to be integrated to ensure decentralization.

One of the major challenges facing SSI is the lack of clear and well-established standards that can be universally agreed upon to coordinate the necessary steps to establish trust and connectivity between the different actors participating in the system, such as issuers and verifiers. This lack of clear standardization makes it difficult for organizations to comply with existing regulations, such as the European Regulation on electronic identification and trust services (eIDAS) [15] and the General Data Protection Regulation (GDPR) [16].

Another challenge is the lack of clear and common consensus about the technical, behavioural, functional, and regulatory features of SSI systems, which leads to uncertainty among organizations and concerns about the risk and challenges associated with the adoption of an SSI system for authentication.

Furthermore, while the collaboration among the different actors is a crucial aspect of SSI, it also presents an important challenge, as various types of organizational structures (e.g., profit and non-profit, private, and public institutions, service providers, and end-users) need to interact with one another to ensure transparency, trust, and data integrity. However, these different actors view the usefulness of SSI from a different lens, which makes it difficult to reach a common ground and induce beneficial partnerships and support the adoption of ecosystems.

Lastly, the implementation of SSI systems presents a significant challenge for organizations due to their complex nature. These systems rely heavily on the understanding of decentralized systems and blockchain, which require a high level of expertise. This presents a significant barrier to entry for organizations that are interested in investing in SSI technology, as this complexity can make it rigorous for organizations to use the technology effectively and efficiently, which does not justify the necessary initial investment required to replace their existing authentication services with the recent decentralized SSI based services, therefore leading to a strong reluctance of adoption.

Table 2. Key benefits and challenges of SSI

Benefits	Challenges
Increased control and autonomy	Interoperability with legacy systems
Enhanced Security, Data Integrity, and transparency	Standardization
Resilient to a single point of failure	Lack of Regulations compliance
Cost and time savings in the long term	Required collaboration of different actors
	Complexity and high barrier to entry

7 Conclusion

Self-sovereign identity is a promising concept that has the potential in the long term to revolutionize the way we perceive and manage identity, since it leverages blockchain technology and decentralization, it can give control to individuals over their own digital identity, rather than relying on centralized systems, it also improves privacy and security as well the ability to efficiently and transparently verify identity, moreover it turns authentication systems resilient to single point of failures, however, the technology still has many challenges needed to be addressed before it can be widely used, as issues such as scalability, interoperability, and the need for standardization are causes of organizations unwillingness to adopt this new and upcoming identity management solution, nevertheless, these challenges can be regarded as important research gaps offering new opportunities and areas of research in the fields of blockchain, identity and authentication management, and more broadly speaking security to overcome the presented challenges and improve the overall SSI system.

References

1. Nakamoto, S.: Bitcoin: A Peer-to-Peer Electronic Cash System (2008)

2. A Primer for Decentralized Identifiers, https://w3c-ccg.github.io/did-primer/. Last accessed 16 May (2022)
3. Six, N., Herbaut, N., Salinesi, C.: Blockchain software patterns for the design of decentralized applications: a systematic literature review. Blockchain: Research and Applications **3**, 100061 (2022). https://doi.org/10.1016/j.bcra.2022.100061
4. Chang, S.E., Chen, Y.: When blockchain meets supply Chain: a systematic literature review on current development and potential applications. IEEE Access. **8**, 62478–62494 (2020). https://doi.org/10.1109/ACCESS.2020.2983601
5. Zhang, S., Lee, J.-H.: Analysis of the main consensus protocols of blockchain. ICT Express. **6**, 93–97 (2020). https://doi.org/10.1016/j.icte.2019.08.001
6. Chadwick, D.W.: Federated identity management. In: Aldini, A., Barthe, G., Gorrieri, R. (eds.) Foundations of Security Analysis and Design V, pp. 96–120. Springer Berlin Heidelberg, Berlin, Heidelberg (2009). https://doi.org/10.1007/978-3-642-03829-7_3
7. Tobin, A., Reed, D., Windley, F.P.J., Foundation, S.: The Inevitable Rise of Self-Sovereign Identity 24 (2017)
8. Mühle, A., Grüner, A., Gayvoronskaya, T., Meinel, C.: A survey on essential components of a self-sovereign identity. Computer Science Review. **30**, 80–86 (2018). https://doi.org/10.1016/j.cosrev.2018.10.002
9. Alharby, M., Moorsel, A. van: Blockchain based smart contracts: a systematic mapping study. In: Computer Science & Information Technology (CS & IT), pp. 125–140. Academy & Industry Research Collaboration Center (AIRCC) (2017). https://doi.org/10.5121/csit.2017.71011
10. Liu, Y., Lu, Q., Paik, H.-Y., Xu, X.: Design Patterns for Blockchain-based Self-Sovereign Identity http://arxiv.org/abs/2005.12112 (2020)
11. Allen, C.: The Path to Self-Sovereign Identity, http://www.lifewithalacrity.com/2016/04/the-path-to-self-soverereign-identity.html
12. Toorani, M., Gehrmann, C.: A Decentralized Dynamic PKI based on Blockchain. arXiv:2012.15351 [cs] (2020)
13. Laatikainen, G., Kolehmainen, T., Abrahamsson, P.: Self-Sovereign Identity Ecosystems: Benefits and Challenges (2021)
14. Bernal Bernabe, J., Canovas, J.L., Hernandez-Ramos, J.L., Torres Moreno, R., Skarmeta, A.: Privacy-Preserving Solutions for Blockchain: Review and Challenges. IEEE Access. **7**, 164908–164940 (2019). https://doi.org/10.1109/ACCESS.2019.2950872
15. Schwalm, S., Alamillo Domingo, I.: Self-Sovereign-Identity & eIDAS: a Contradiction? Challenges and Chances of eIDAS 2.0. European Review of Digital Administration & Law. 89–108 (2022). https://doi.org/10.53136/979125994752910
16. Kondova, G., Erbguth, J.: Self-sovereign identity on public blockchains and the GDPR. In: Proceedings of the 35th Annual ACM Symposium on Applied Computing, pp. 342–345. ACM, Brno Czech Republic (2020). https://doi.org/10.1145/3341105.3374066

Comparison of Performance of Feature Engineering Techniques for Text Classification

Meryem Amri[(✉)] and Khalid Haddouch

Laboratory of Engineering, Systems and Applications, ENSA, USMBA, Fez, Morocco
{meryem.amri,khalid.haddouch}@usmba.ac.ma

Abstract. Feature engineering is a crucial step for natural language processing (NLP) applications, involving the extraction of pertinent features from unprocessed text data and their subsequent conversion into a format suitable for machine learning models. In this study, we compare feature engineering techniques using two datasets. These datasets concern the medical domain, where we applied widely used feature engineering techniques to convert textual documents into numerical vectors representing textual features. The three techniques TF-IDF, GloVe and Word2Vec were used to be applied to both cancer text documents and Symptom2Disease datasets. Then, we trained some classification models and evaluated the performance of each model using standard evaluation metrics. The results indicate that the performance differs depending on the used feature extraction techniques. The LR model with TF-IDF features achieved the highest accuracy for the first dataset compared to the other models, and the KNN model using TF-IDF features obtained the best accuracy for the second dataset. Furthermore, these results demonstrate that the TF-IDF features outperform GloVe and Word2Vec.

Keywords: NLP · Feature engineering · TF-IDF · GloVe · Word2Vec · Text classification

1 Introduction

Natural language processing (NLP) is a rapidly evolving domain with many varied applications such as text classification, sentiment analysis, speech recognition and machine translation. Text classification, which involves classifying texts according to their topic, theme or intent, is a major challenge for NLP [1]. The use of NLP techniques for text classification in the medical domain offers the potential to automate the sorting and categorization of medical documents, which benefits tasks such as disease surveillance, disease classification, and medical research. This use holds promise for improving efficiency and advancing healthcare-related applications.

The feature extraction process holds significant importance in text classification, as it transforms unstructured textual content into organized data. This

© The Author(s), under exclusive license to Springer Nature Switzerland AG 2025
H. Hagras et al. (Eds.): ISACS 2023, CCIS 2255, pp. 161–173, 2025.
https://doi.org/10.1007/978-3-031-93448-3_13

structured format enables the use of machine learning algorithms for data processing. Thus, the selection of an appropriate and efficient feature extraction method is crucial. It can have an impact on the classification performance [2].

The initial phase of text classification involves preprocessing the text to convert unstructured data containing noise into a structured form. Preprocessing tasks include removal of accented and special characters, lemmatization, removal of stop words, tokenization, etc. The next phase involves feature extraction, in which the text is converted into numerical vectors that can be used as inputs for the machine learning models. Various techniques can be used for feature extraction, including bag-of-words (BOW), TF-IDF, as well as word embeddings like Word2Vec, Doc2Vec, FastText and GloVe [1]. Finally, machine learning algorithms are applied to the processed and extracted text.

This study focuses on the use of feature engineering techniques based on natural language processing (NLP), with the goal of extracting features from textual data, and then evaluate the performance of text classification using machine learning (ML) approaches. We used two datasets, the first one focuses on textual documents on cancer, it contains 7569 documents, with 3 classes of target variables, and the second dataset includes 24 different diseases classes, and each disease has symptoms descriptions. These datasets were available online on the official Kaggle website [3].

The key points of our work are summarised as follows:

- Applying a preprocessing technique to document corpora to have the same corpora with cleaned text documents.
- Three feature engineering approaches such as TF-IDF, GloVe and Word2Vec will be applied to extract features from the training and test datasets. Afterwords analyze and compare the performance of the classifiers.
- The application of supervised ML classification algorithms.

This paper focuses on evaluating and comparing the performance of text document classification models using three different feature extraction techniques in the field of biomedical research. These techniques are: TF-IDF, GloVe, and Word2Vec.

We cite a few examples of work involving the use of feature extraction techniques and performance comparisons. Ahuja et al. [2] applied six different classification algorithms to the SS-Tweet dataset using two types of features extraction, namely N-Gram and TF-IDF. After their analyses, they observed that TF-IDF features produce better results than N-Gram features. For Cahyani and Patasik research [4], the performance of Word2Vec and TF-IDF techniques in feature representation for emotional text classification was examined. Three approaches were considered, that is, SVM using Word2Vec, SVM using TF-IDF and MNB using TF-IDF and the results showed that SVM using TF-IDF achieved the greatest accuracy when contrasted with other approaches, and the TF-IDF features outperformed Word2Vec. In the Hossein et al. research [5], the study focused on the classification of news into different groups, the proposed method based on the use of TD-IDF and the SVM model, shows promising results with high classification accuracies on two evaluated data sets. The study presented by Zhu et al. [6] focused on unstructured clinical data. In this research, they introduced a new approach to represent clinical records using Word2Vec and TF-IDF techniques. The methods were compared using four distinct classifiers: KNN, SVM, Decision Tree, and Random Forest. The results showed that the proposed method performed well. In the Shao et al. study [7], they evaluated Word2Vec and Doc2Vec features extraction for clinical text classification and compared them to the bag-of-words (BOW) features extraction. The results showed that the Word2Vec of features extraction approach were superior compared to the others.

This paper is organized as follows: In Sect. 2, we will present features engineering techniques. Section 3 of the research methodology describes various aspects, including data collection, data preprocessing, feature extraction, text classification models, and evaluation parameters. Lastly, in Sect. 4, we present and discuss the results of the study, and Sect. 5 contains the conclusion.

2   Features Engineering Techniques

Feature engineering is essential for developing more efficient ML models, its goal being to extract useful characteristics from the dataset that can be utilized by machine learning classification algorithms [8]. Representing features as vectors can have a significant impact on the overall performance of machine learning. In this section, we will present three common features engineering techniques: TF-IDF, GloVe and Word2Vec.

2.1   TF-IDF

TF-IDF, which stands for Term Frequency-Inverse Document Frequency, is an approach employed to extract features from textual data that measures the significance of a word according to its frequency in a document. TF-IDF works as a method of assigning weights to individual terms in a document, taking into account the terms' frequency in the document itself and in the set of documents. This technique is commonly used in areas such as information retrieval, text classification and content recommendation.

The TF-IDF combines two measures: term frequency (tf) and inverse document frequency (idf). Mathematically, tf-idf is the product of these two measures, represented by:

$$tfidf = tf \times idf \tag{1}$$

- The term frequency (tf) refers to the occurrence count of a specific term in a given document. It could be denoted as $tf(w, D) = f_{w_D}$, where f_{w_D} is the frequency of term w in document D.
- The inverse document frequency (idf) is a metric used to determine the significance of a term within a corpus. By dividing the total amount of documents

in the corpus by the document frequency of each term and applying a logarithmic transformation can the *idf* be obtained. The formula for calculating *idf* is represented by:

$$idf(w, D) = 1 + log\frac{N}{1 + df(w)} \tag{2}$$

$df(w)$ indicates the number of documents where the term w appears, and N is the total number of documents in the corpus.

Thus, to obtain the TF-IDF, we multiply the term frequency by the inverse document frequency.

2.2 GloVe

GloVe is an unsupervised learning model that uses co-occurrence statistics to create vector representations of words [9]. Developed in 2014 by researchers from Stanford University, GloVe is notable for its ability to incorporate global statistics based on word co-occurrences and probability ratios.

GloVe relies on the likelihood ratios extracted from the matrix of word co-occurrences, which is a matrix of size $V \times V$, with V representing the vocabulary size. Each element of the matrix represents the frequency of two specific words appearing together in a predefined pop-up window, which moves through the corpus [10].

The construction of the (X) word-word co-occurrence matrix is necessary for the creation of GloVe embeddings. The number of occurrences of word j in the context of word i is given by X_{ij}. The count of a word is present in the context of word i is denoted by $X_i = \sum_k X_{ik}$. The probability that word j appears in the context of word i is computed by:

$$P_{ij} = P(j|i) = \frac{X_{ij}}{X_i} \tag{3}$$

In order to deduce embeddings, GloVe uses the probability ratio presented by the following equation:

$$f(w_i, w_j, \tilde{w}_k) = \frac{P_{ik}}{P_{jk}} \tag{4}$$

where w represents vectors of words, $\tilde{w}$ represents vectors of distinct contextual words, and f is a weighting function [11].

The GloVe model aims to learn embeddings in a way that minimizes the reconstruction error between the actual and predicted co-occurrence statistics [9,10]. Specifically, the following loss function must by minimized:

$$J = \sum_{i,j=1}^{V} f(X_{ij})(w_i^T \tilde{w}_j + b_i + \tilde{b}_j - log X_{ij})^2 \tag{5}$$

The empirical term co-occurrence matrix's X_{ij} value denotes the number of co-occurrences that were actually seen. While b_i and $\tilde{b}_j$ represent the biases for words i and j, respectively, w_i and w_j represent the vector embeddings of words i and j.

2.3   Word2Vec

Word2Vec, developed in 2013 by Tomas Mikolov and other Google researchers, is a commonly used method for creating word embeddings, wherein similar words that are present in related contexts are assigned comparable representations [12]. In this method, each word is represented as a vector of real numbers in a dense, low-dimensional vector space. Word2Vec transforms words into numerical representations, grouping similar words and separating them from those that are not semantically related.

To build the word vectors, Word2Vec uses a neural network. In this process, each word in the vocabulary is represented by a neuron in the input layer, where a given term is evaluated as 1 and the others as 0, creating a binary vector. The number of neurons in the hidden layer corresponds to the dimensions of the word vectors. The value of a neuron in the hidden layer is determined by multiplying the input value by its corresponding weight, due to the linear activation function of this layer. Next, the hidden layer's value is multiplied by separate weights in the output layer. The output layer, which has the same number of neurons as the input layer representing the target word, applies the Softmax activation function [4].

The Word2Vec prediction method can be used in two different ways: continuous bag of words (CBOW) and skip-gram (SG). In the CBOW approach, the neural network takes, as input, a set of words and tries to predict the central word. In the SG approach, the neural network takes, as input, a word and tries to predict the surrounding words.

3   Proposed Methodology

This section presents an overview of the methodology employed. In other words, we provide an overview of the collected data, the preprocessing steps applied to the text data, the feature extraction techniques employed, the machine learning classifiers and the used evaluation parameters. The general approach of this study is illustrated in Fig. 1. Data collection via the Kaggle website is the first

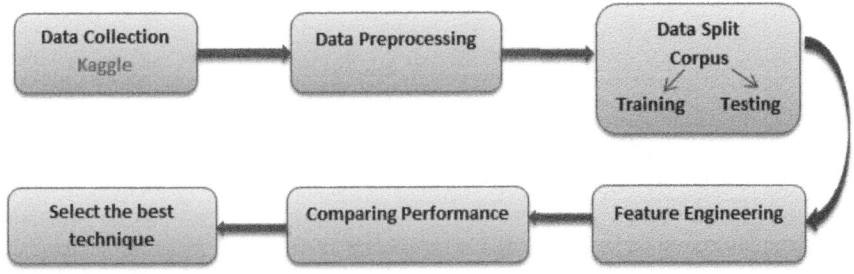

Fig. 1. Proposed Methodology

step, then data preprocessing is applied to the acquired data. In order to construct a machine learning system, it is necessary to develop models using training data, followed by testing and evaluating their performance on separate test data. Therefore, the dataset is divided into training and test sets, with a split ratio of 80% and 20% respectively. The model is trained using the training set, which contains 80% of the available data, while the remaining 20% is designated for performance testing. Once the data is prepared for testing, feature engineering methods are applied to extract features from the training and testing datasets. Then, classification techniques are used and the parameters are evaluated.

3.1 Data Collection

In this study, the initial step in our methodology was to download two datasets "Cancer Text Documents" and "Symptom2Disease". To do this, we used Kaggle as our main source, a reputable online platform offering a variety of datasets from different fields.

The "Cancer Text Documents" dataset is devoted to full-length research papers longer than six pages, specifically addressing different types of cancer, including "Thyroid Cancer", "Colon Cancer", and "Lung Cancer" [13]. With a total of 7569 publications, this dataset is classified into three distinct categories. Each category contains a specific number of samples: Colon Cancer (2579 samples), Lung Cancer (2180 samples) and Thyroid Cancer (2810 samples). Figure 2.a) illustrates the distribution of data in the different categories.

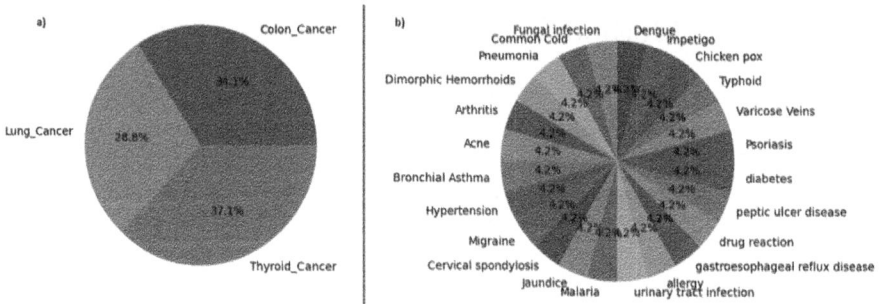

Fig. 2. Distribution of data

The dataset "Symptom2Disease" [14] encompasses 1200 data points and is structured with two columns: 'label' and 'text'. The 'label' column contains disease labels, while the 'text' column contains symptom descriptions expressed in natural language. This dataset encompasses 24 distinct diseases, with each disease accompanied by 50 symptom descriptions, resulting in a total of 1200 data points. Figure 2.b) illustrates the distribution of data in the 24 different classes of diseases.

3.2   Data Preprocessing

Text preprocessing involves cleaning, normalizing and formatting the text into a standard format, so that it can be easily used for feature extraction. The main goal is to produce clean text documents by eliminating extraneous content from one or more corpus-based text documents. For these data sets, the following preprocessing steps were performed:

⋆ **Removal of accented characters.** This step consists in replacing the accented characters of a text by their non-accented equivalents. In particular, characters with accents are transformed and normalized into ASCII characters.

⋆ **Removing special characters.** Special characters and symbols in unstructured text are generally characters that are not letters or numbers, such as punctuation symbols, mathematical symbols and many others, which add extra interference. In general, simple regular expressions (regex) can be used to eliminate them.

⋆ **Lemmatization.** This process involves removing affixes from a word to obtain its basic form, known as a lemma. The lemma is the canonical or standardized form of a word that represents its basic meaning. Lemmatization involves using a dictionary or morphological analysis to determine the basic form of a word.

⋆ **Removal of stop words.** When processing text, stop words, that is, words with little or no meaning, are usually eliminated in order to preserve the most contextual and meaningful words. These include words such as "the", "a", "are", "at", "in" and "and". To get a superior prediction, they must be attenuated. Although there is no single collection of all stop words, we use the standard NLTK stop word list for the English language [1].

⋆ **Case Normalization.** This process involves converting text to a consistent case, usually upper or lower case. We convert all words to lower case as various words carry identical meanings. However, it is important to note that the machine learning models differ from human learning processes.

We have integrated all these components and combined them into a function that accepts a corpus of documents as input and outputs the identical corpus, but with its textual documents cleaned and standardized.

3.3   Feature Extraction

For the "Cancer Text Documents" dataset, we used the feature engineering techniques TF-IDF and GloVe, presented in the previous section, to extract features from training and test datasets, and for "Symptom2Disease", we used TF-IDF, GloVe and Word2Vec.

– **TF-IDF**. The Scikit-Learn library's TfidfVectorizer was used to compute the TF-IDF vectors. This vectorizer internally calculates both term frequencies and inverse document frequencies, taking the raw documents as input directly.
– **GloVe**. The renowned spaCy framework offers the ability to take advantage of GloVe embeddings built on several language models.
– **Word2Vec**. The Word2Vec model, which we will use for our corpus, is implemented reliably and efficiently by the Gensim framework.

3.4   Text Classification Models

Machine learning classification models are used to classify or assign labels to data points using prior observations. These models require training data and can be trained using different text features. In this study, several supervised machine learning models were employed, including Logistic Regression (LR), Support Vector Machine (SVM), Gradient Boosting (GB), Naive Bayes (NB), K-Nearest Neighbors (KNN), Random Forest (RF), and Decision Tree (DT).

3.5   Evaluation Parameters

For the evaluation, we adopted the most commonly used evaluation parameters, namely accuracy, precision, recall and F-measure. These performance metrics play a fundamental role in assessing classification algorithms, providing a detailed and balanced view of their efficiency. Accuracy measures the proportion of correct predictions among all predictions, giving an overall idea of performance. Precision focuses on the accuracy of positive predictions by indicating the ratio of correctly predicted positive instances to all instances predicted as positive. Recall is the measure of the number of true positives predicted out of all positives in the dataset. Lastly, F-measure combines both precision and recall through their harmonic mean.

$$\text{Accuracy} = \frac{TP + TN}{TP + TN + FP + FN} \quad (6) \qquad \text{Precision} = \frac{TP}{TP + FP} \quad (7)$$

$$\text{Recall} = \frac{TP}{TP + FN} \quad (8) \qquad \text{F-measure} = 2 * \frac{Precsion * Recall}{Precision + Recall} \quad (9)$$

4   Results and Discussions

For the cancer text document dataset (Dataset 1), we used the TF-IDF, GloVe and Word2Vec features to train the classification models to analyze the performance of these three features on this dataset. Tables 1, 2 and 3 present the results of five classification models (LR, SVM with SGDClassifier, NB, KNN, and GB) using the TF-IDF, GloVe and Word2Vec features. The performance metrics that were evaluated comprise accuracy, precision, recall, and F-measure.

Table 1. Results of classification models using TF-IDF features on first dataset.

Dataset 1 - (TF-IDF)				
ML Models	Accuracy	Precision	Recall	F-measure
Logistic Regression	0.955	0.958	0.958	0.958
SVM with SGD	0.945	0.948	0.948	0.948
Gradient Boosting	0.935	0.939	0.936	0.937
Naïve Bayes	0.921	0.931	0.926	0.926
KNN	0.835	0.838	0.845	0.841

Table 2. Results of classification models using GloVe features on first dataset.

Dataset 1 - (GloVe)				
ML Models	Accuracy	Precision	Recall	F-measure
Logistic Regression	0.884	0.892	0.889	0.890
Gradient Boosting	0.834	0.837	0.838	0.838
KNN	0.817	0.831	0.823	0.826
SVM with SGD	0.803	0.876	0.810	0.804
Naïve Bayes	0.647	0.656	0.654	0.654

Table 3. Results of classification models using Word2Vec features on first dataset.

Dataset 1 - (Word2Vec)				
ML Models	Accuracy	Precision	Recall	F-measure
Logistic Regression	0.883	0.890	0.891	0.891
SVM with SGD	0.879	0.890	0.888	0.887
KNN	0.855	0.859	0.865	0.861
Gradient Boosting	0.843	0.851	0.848	0.848
Naïve Bayes	0.674	0.718	0.683	0.691

According to these results, as can be seen in the three tables (Table 1, Table 2 and Table 3), for TF-IDF features, the Logistic Regression model generates the highest accuracy with a score of (0.955), followed by SVM (0.945), Gradient Boosting (0.935), Naive Bayes (0.921) and finally KNN (0.835). Similarly in the case of GloVe, the Logistic Regression model generates the highest accuracy with a score of (0.884), followed by the Gradient Boosting model (0.834), KNN (0.817), SVM (0.803), then Naive Bayes (0.647). For Word2Vec, the Logistic Regression model generates the highest accuracy with a score of (0.883), followed by SVM (0.879), KNN (0.855), Gradient Boosting (0.843) and finally Naive Bayes (0.674). These results show that the Logistic Regression model using the TF-IDF technique gives the highest level of accuracy when compared to the other approaches.

For the Symptom2Disease dataset (Dataset 2), we used the TF-IDF, GloVe, and Word2Vec features to train the classification models to analyze the performance of these three features on this dataset. Tables 4, 5 and 6 present the results of five classification techniques (LR, SVM with SGDClassifier, KNN, RF, and DT) using these features. The evaluated performance metrics include accuracy, precision, recall and F-measure.

Table 4. Results of classification models using TF-IDF features on second dataset.

Dataset 2 - (TF-IDF)				
ML Models	Accuracy	Precision	Recall	F-measure
KNN	0.954	0.957	0.963	0.958
SVM with SGD	0.946	0.949	0.956	0.949
Logistic Regression	0.925	0.926	0.945	0.929
Random Forest	0.896	0.905	0.915	0.900
Decision Tree	0.817	0.839	0.832	0.822

Table 5. Results of classification models using GloVe features on second dataset.

Dataset 2 - (GloVe)				
ML Models	Accuracy	Precision	Recall	F-measure
Logistic Regression	0.933	0.934	0.939	0.932
KNN	0.900	0.901	0.913	0.900
Random Forest	0.846	0.847	0.865	0.846
SVM with SGD	0.792	0.901	0.785	0.797
Decision Tree	0.550	0.560	0.570	0.553

Table 6. Results of classification models using Word2Vec features on second dataset.

Dataset 2 - (Word2Vec)				
ML Models	Accuracy	Precision	Recall	F-measure
KNN	0.833	0.854	0.842	0.837
Random Forest	0.792	0.797	0.812	0.795
SVM with SGD	0.700	0.781	0.722	0.709
Decision Tree	0.658	0.666	0.682	0.663
Logistic Regression	0.642	0.629	0.701	0.626

For the second dataset, as can be seen in the three tables, for TF-IDF features, the KNN model generates the highest accuracy with a score of (0.954), followed by SVM (0.946), Logistic Regression (0.925), Random Forest (0.896) and finally Decision Tree (0.817). Similarly in the case of GloVe, the Logistic Regression model generates the highest accuracy with a score of (0.933), followed by the KNN model (0.900), Random Forest (0.846), SVM (0.792), then Decision Tree (0.550). For Word2Vec, the KNN model generates the highest accuracy with a score of (0.833) followed by Random Forest (0.792), SVM (0.700), Decision Tree (0.658) and finally Logistic Regression (0.642). These results show that the KNN model using TF-IDF technique gives the highest accuracy compared to the other approaches.

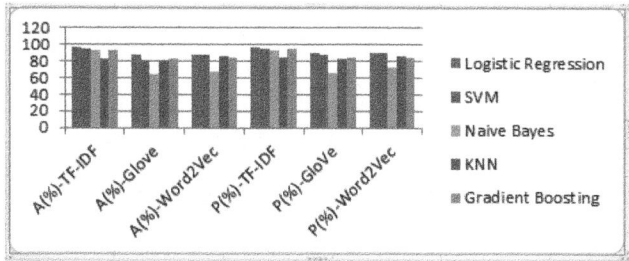

Fig. 3. Comparison of Word2Vec, GloVe and TF-IDF approch on Cancer Text Documents

Figures 3 and 4 show a comparison of the Word2Vec, GloVe and TF-IDF approaches for the first dataset, while Figs. 5 and 6 show a comparison of the Word2Vec, GloVe and TF-IDF approaches for the second dataset. The purpose of this comparison is to identify the best-performing features. Precision, recall and F-measure were additionally evaluated during classification. According to the results presented in these figures, the LR model with TF-IDF features yields the best scores for the first dataset, and the KNN model using TF-IDF features gives the best scores for the second dataset.

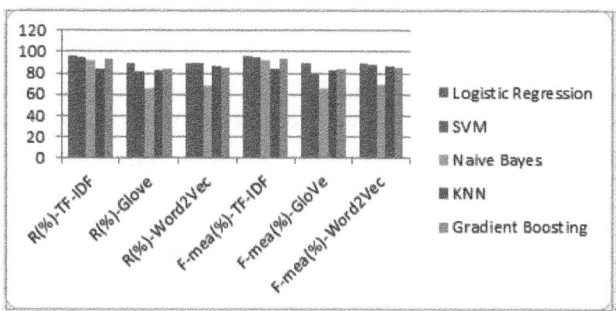

Fig. 4. Comparison of Word2Vec, GloVe and TF-IDF approch on Cancer Text Documents dataset.

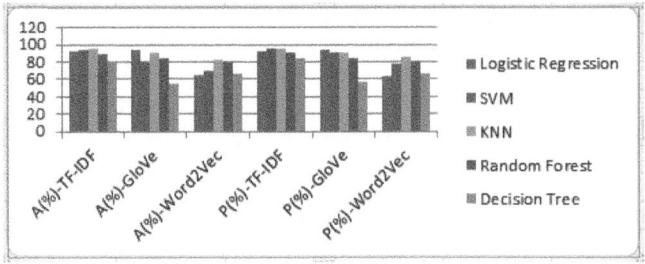

Fig. 5. Comparison of Word2Vec, GloVe and TF-IDF approch on Symptom2Disease dataset.

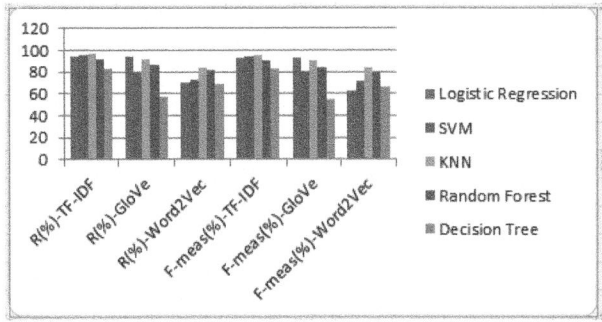

Fig. 6. Comparison of Word2Vec, GloVe and TF-IDF approch on Symptom2Disease dataset.

5   Conclusion

The comparison of TF-IDF, GloVe, and Word2Vec feature extraction techniques used in both datasets allows us to conclude that, for these two collected datasets, the TF-IDF method outperforms the others in terms of performance for machine learning models. While GloVe and Word2Vec are also good feature extraction techniques that yield satisfactory results, they do not surpass TF-IDF in terms of accuracy on the test set for these datasets. For our future research, we intend to collect other datasets related to the medical domain and utilize more sophisticated word representation models.

References

1. Sarkar, D.: Text Analytics with Python, A Practitioner's Guide to Natural Language Processing, 2nd edn. India (2019)
2. Ahuja, R., et al.: The impact of features extraction on the sentiment analysis. Procedia Comput. Sci. **152**, 341–348 (2019)
3. https://www.kaggle.com/datasets

4. Cahyani, D.E., Patasik, I.: Performance comparison of TF-IDF and Word2Vec models for emotion text classification. Bull. Electr. Eng. Inf. **10**(5), 2780–2788 (2021)

5. Hossein, S.M., Araghi, M.S., Farahani, M.M.: A novel text mining approach based on TF-IDF and support vector machine for news classification. In: IEEE International Conference on Engineering and Technology (ICETECH), pp. 1–5. IEEE (2016)

6. Zhu, W, et al.: A study of damp-heat syndrome classification Using Word2vec and TF-IDF. In: IEEE International Conference on Bioinformatics and Biomedicine (BIBM), pp. 1415–1420. IEEE 2016)

7. Shao, Y, et al.: Clinical text classification with word embedding features vs. bag-of-words features. In: 2018 IEEE International Conference on Big Data (Big Data), pp. 2874–2878. IEEE (2018)

8. Amaar, A., et al.: Detection of fake job postings by utilizing machine learning and natural language processing approaches. Neural Process. Lett. **54**, 2219–2247 (2022)

9. Pennington, J, Socher, R, Manning, C.D.: GloVe: global vectors for word representation. In: Proceedings of the 2014 Conference on Empirical Methods in Natural Language Processing (EMNLP), pp. 1532–1543 (2014)

10. Khattak, F.K., et al.: A survey of word embeddings for clinical text. J. Biomed. Inf. **100S**, 100057 (2019)

11. Habib, M., et al.: AltibbiVec: a word embedding model for medical and health applications in the arabic language. IEEE Access **9**, 133875–133888 (2021)

12. Mikolov, T, et al.: Efficient estimation of word representations in vector spac. arXiv preprint arXiv:1301.3781 (2013)

13. https://www.kaggle.com/datasets/falgunipatel19/biomedical-textpublication-classification

14. https://www.kaggle.com/datasets/niyarrbarman/symptom2disease

Measuring the Effectiveness of Serious Games Intended for Use in Teaching

Farida Bouroumane$^{(\boxtimes)}$ ⓘ and Mustapha Abarkan ⓘ

Laboratory of Engineering Sciences, Faculty Polydisciplinaire of Taza, Sidi Mohamed Ben Abdellah University, Fez, Morocco
`{farida.bouroumane,mustapha.abarkan}@usmba.ac.ma`

Abstract. In recent years, there has been a growing interest in digital games in the educational community. Today, serious gaming is a powerful learning and teaching tool. However, the most important limitation to the pedagogical use of this tool is the appropriateness of the choice of game to be used in the classroom. The process of adopting a game-based pedagogy also requires the teacher to be supported by tools that facilitate the understanding and effective implementation of this strategy in a specific learning situation, in order to offer learners games that meet their pedagogical needs. In this context, we describe in this paper a scale for measuring the ludic and pedagogic effectiveness of a serious game. This scale enables the teacher to gather precise and exhaustive information on the level of compliance of the serious game content with a specific learning context so that it can be accepted and implemented effectively in the classroom.

Keywords: Serious games · Teaching · Scale

1 Introduction

The research on the integration of serious games (SGs) in education has significantly evolved a lot in recent years. Several studies [1–3] have confirmed that SGs can motivate, engage, and stimulate higher thinking skills in learners. Indeed, research studies [4, 5] have shown that the integration of classroom games improves learners' learning. Today, a new generation of students is heavily influenced by digital and continuously relies on technology in their daily lives. In addition, the rapid development of the gaming industry has hugely impacted this new generation. Also, the existence of features that can be used for purposes the interest of the educational community for the use of games increased over the last decade, especially in the field of education. However, a recently published study by Hébert et al. [6] confirms the need for experimental research that addresses the implementation of game-based pedagogy in various classroom contexts, taking into account the obstacles faced by teachers themselves are confronted for this methodology. The authors in [7], stated that the general objective of the evaluation of the SG is to validate the effectiveness and adequacy of the game in relation to its designated objective and the context of application.

Based on the (GameFlow) proposed model by the authors in [8], the researchers in [9] developed (EGameFlow), a scale that measures learners' enjoyment specific to educational games. The scale consists of eight dimensions: immersion, interaction, challenge, clarity of objectives, feedback, control, and improvement of knowledge. EGameFlow is an effective tool for evaluating the level of pleasure provided by e-learning games to their users. However, the authors stated that the study did not focus on the factors that determine the enjoyment of online games. In addition, the study [10] specifies that the evaluation of a SG must take into account the ludic aspect as well as the serious aspect. In addition, the study [11] asserts that evaluating SGs involves ascertaining beforehand that the pedagogical objectives have been achieved. In addition, the study [12] developed a scale to assess the quality of any SG according to three criteria, which are enjoyment, learning, and usability. The scale can be used by teachers to identify the quality of SGs. However, the authors point out that usability is not yet included in the scale. Furthermore, the study does not present the scale and it is considered to be under development. The Game User Experience Satisfaction Scale (GUESS) proposed by the authors in [13], assesses user satisfaction with different types of video games. However, the GUESS authors point out that the games in their study were primarily commercial games and popular purely for entertainment. Based on this hypothesis, the study [14] developed a scale designed specifically to evaluate educational games (E-GUESS). They introduce changes aimed at educational issues and educational content, as well as simplification and reduction factors considered redundant in the original GUESS. However, the authors of this study have indicated that the validation of (E-GUESS) is part of the future work of this research.

Most of these works are dedicated to game designers and are applied during the game design and development process. Also, the relevance of the choice of game to use in class constitutes the most important limitation to SG adoption in education [1, 2, 6, 15–18].

The objective of this research work is to propose an approach for measuring the educational effectiveness of SGs through a specific learning situation in order for teachers to integrate them effectively into their pedagogy and offer games that meet their educational needs.

Our study research aims to answer the questions:

- What aspects of SG must be taken into account to evaluate their educational value and justify their relevance in teaching?
- On what criteria do teachers select educational and motivating SGs?

After this introduction, the second section presents our proposed scale and the evaluation protocol to evaluate this scale. Then, the third section is reserved for the analysis of the results obtained during the experimental phase and the discussion of these results. Finally, the fourth section is a conclusion.

2 Research Method

2.1 Serious Games for Learning

Several researchers have shown that the integration of SG into had a positive impact on learners' learning. The study [19] indicates that SGs are valuable tools to facilitate classroom dialogue. However, according to the author in [20], we must think about how teachers position themselves in relation to the game.

For these reasons, we decided to analyze the game from the angle of its use by teachers wishing to apply game-based pedagogy.

Based on Jean Houssaye's model of pedagogical understanding [21], which defined the pedagogical act as the space between three vertices of a triangle: the teacher, the learner and knowledge, we defined the position of the game within this model and identified the relationships that exist between the teacher, the learner, knowledge and the game (see Fig. 1).

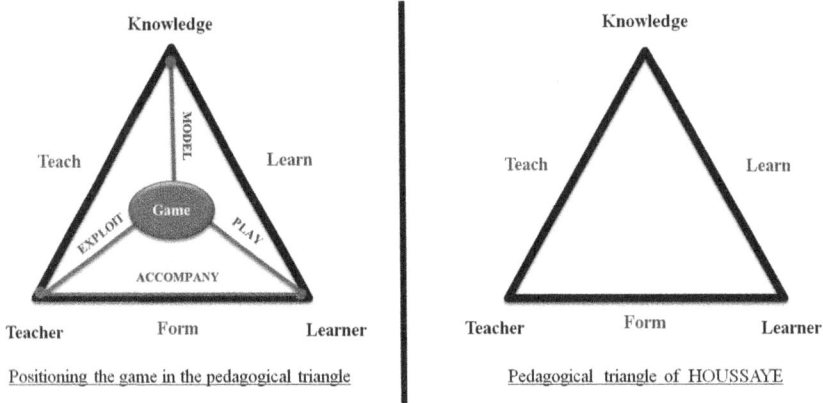

Positioning the game in the pedagogical triangle   Pedagogical triangle of HOUSSAYE

Fig. 1. A serious game's pedagogical triangle.

Knowledge is hidden behind the game. The teacher EXPLOITS the game to teach and promote specific educational concepts. He or she must have sufficient knowledge of the used games to know which areas of knowledge and cross-curricular skills these games address. As for the learner, he or she PLAYS games to acquire knowledge through ludic learning situations in which they can experiment with knowledge in order to build it up in the best possible way. The learner is ACCOMPANY by the teacher during the acquisition of knowledge through game. Knowledge can be MODELLED as meaningful, easy-to-understand objects. This modeling represents a pedagogical structure in a ludic context.

2.2 Teachers and Serious Games

A game-based pedagogy can contribute to the modern conception of teaching where the emphasis is placed on where experimentation is valued and where the right to is granted.

However, the use of games in a pedagogical context requires teachers to ask questions (see Table 1) about the components of the pedagogical and ludic aspects (What? and Who?), the functioning of the game universe (How? and Why?), and the conditions of use of the game (When? How much? and Where?).

Table 1. Questions for the verification of a serious game.

Structure of the pedagogical and ludic aspects	-What is it all about? -Who is involved?
Universe of the game	-In what way? -For what purpose?
Conditions of use	-When? -How many times? -What resources?

In general, a double-check is necessary to integrate SG into the educational process. On the one hand, the content of the game must correspond to the knowledge of the learner and, on the other hand, the content of the game must correspond to the educational needs of the teacher. If we want to encourage the adoption of games as pedagogical technology, teachers must also be able to find games that meet their educational needs.

2.3 Proposed Scale

The evaluation of SGs requires putting into two different balances, the serious aspect, which is generally intended for learning, and the ludic aspect, which is intended for entertainment. For this mix of fun and seriousness to work, we must to use game evaluation approaches that meet the needs of both parties. Indeed, the effectiveness of SGs needs to be evaluated not only in terms of their purpose but also in terms of the characteristics and particularities linked to the educational needs met. Defining evaluation criteria is very important if teachers are to accept the use of SGs in specific learning situations. These criteria support the teacher's decision-making process. In addition, the criteria can describe the parameters of the game to simplify the elements which interact within SG. This enables teachers to explain game mechanisms to learners and give clear answers to questions. The learning process when using SGs begins by observing the game features. However, learning and a deep understanding of educational content occur when completing the given tasks in a cyclical manner. In addition, for the learner to be able to carry out the iterations, the game must engage and motivate them.

The Serious Game Evaluation Scale (SGEScale) developed in this study is composed of three dimensions (Observation, Interaction, and Performance), and each dimension is analyzed under three aspects (Motivate, Divert, and Educate). The Fig. 2 describes our scale.

- Observing the interface of the game: the learner can look at the game scenario and develop knowledge; this phase therefore depends on the representation of the game components in the game scene.

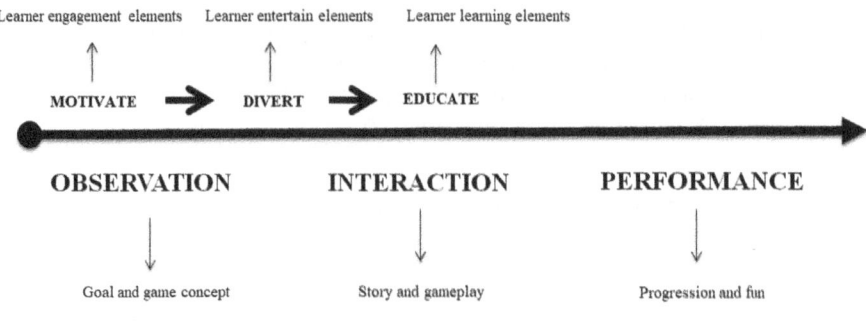

Fig. 2. Proposed scale.

– Interacting with game components: the learner interacts with the game and develops knowledge; this phase therefore depends on the gameplay strategy and the story scenario.
– Perform tasks: the learner performs the game and develops knowledge; this phase therefore depends on tasks that the learner is required to carry out. To be able to do it, the learner must have knowledge of the properties and relationships between the components of the game.

To construct the grid for our evaluation scale, we drew inspiration from the study [22], which defines the pedagogical elements that can be constructed using SGs and that can be used for teaching purposes; also the "Enroll, Entertain, Educate" (3E) model proposed by Sanchez [23], which enables us to design ludic situations for epistemic games.

The scale developed in this research is divided into the following nine criteria. Table 2 presents a description of the criteria for the Serious Game Evaluation Scale proposed.

2.4 Evaluation

We conducted two experimental studies. The first experiment was devoted to the verification of the elements of our scale by experienced game teachers. The second experiment focused on the clarity and utility of our scale. Figure 3 describes the test procedure that we carried out.

First Experiment
The grid was checked for completeness by eight teachers. Six of the teachers are experienced users of the games and have been using them for several years. The other two used the SG (THE MAGIC SOLDIER OF THE HUMAN BODY) [24] in class for the first time. They read the first version of the questionnaire and freely expressed their understanding of the items they commented on one by one. They were interviewed at the end of the school year, just after the game experience. Several follow-up questions were prepared in advance to ensure that all key points of the grid were covered. The interview lasted between 30 and 45 min. This phase enabled us to identify certain elements of our scale and propose new ones.

Table 2. Evaluation criteria for the Serious Game Evaluation Scale.

	Motivate	Divert	Educate
Observation	**Universe**: the story, graphics, and sounds contribute to creating an atmosphere and/or a game world that motivates players to play the SG	**Attraction**: the game offers elements to capture the learner's emotions	**Easy to learn**: simple tasks can be completed quickly and easily
Interaction	**Gameplay**: the game mechanics are fun and addictive enough to encourage players to play the SG	**Ease of use**: game elements are immediately identifiable, and the information contained in the game is clear, organized, user-friendly and easy to use	**Feedback**: the game provides clear information on how learners respond
Performance	**Progression**: the game offers a challenge that motivates the player to progress through the SG	**Pleasure**: The game offers a sense of enjoyment and appreciation while playing	**Skill**: Players should realize that their skills are at a level where it is possible to overcome the game's challenges. As difficulty increases, the challenges should require the player to develop his or her skills in order to progress through the game

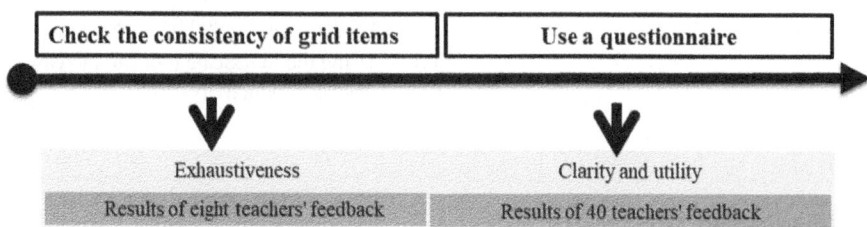

Fig. 3. Evaluation process.

Second Experiment

In order to better analyze the obtained results in the first phase, we also carried out a survey evaluation with 40 teachers from public open-access higher education establishments, to study the clarity and utility of our scale. The survey (see Table 3) consists of 12 closed questions. The evaluation results are calculated on a scale with 5 performance levels ranging from 1 (strongly disagree) to 5 (strongly agree) for three aspects: time, efficiency, and appreciation.

Table 3. Survey to assess the clarity and utility of our scale.

A	The relevance of the SGEScale tool in terms of the needed time to choose the right SG	A_1	I found the SGEScale tool easy to use and effective in helping me find the game
		A_2	Workload in SGEScale is adequate
		A_3	Using SGEScale will help me get the job done faster
		A_4	I familiarized myself with the SGEScale tool very quickly
B	Relevance of SGEScale activities	B_1	Most of the activities in the SGEScale tool are linked to tasks that enable understanding of the game
		B_2	SGEScale tool helps teachers find effective, suitable games
		B_3	SGEScale activities are linked to tasks that lead to decisions about choosing the right SG
		B_4	SGEScale tool motivates teachers to improve teaching strategies
C	Teachers' assessment of the activities proposed by the SGEScale tool	C_1	The SGEScale tool motivates teachers to use games in teaching
		C_2	The SGEScale tool offers content that stimulates my attention
		C_3	Using the SGEScale tool can improve teachers' professional performance
		C_4	Using the SGEScale tool can increase teacher productivity

3   Results and Discussion

3.1   Results

The response averages and standard deviation values (see Table 4) calculated from these data demonstrate that teachers' attitudes are positive overall.

3.2   Discussion

Of the 40 teachers, 90% did not use SGs in teaching, and more than 65% said that our scale helped them change their assessment of the need to use games in learning situations.

Table 4. Mean and standard deviation of survey results.

Criteria	Mean	Standard deviation
A_1	3,63	,586
A_2	3,63	,868
A_3	4,45	,639
A_4	4,2	,687
B_1	3,8	,823
B_2	3,35	,893
B_3	4,23	,62
B_4	4,55	,504
C_1	4,23	,768
C_2	4,2	,687
C_3	3,63	,868
C_4	3,75	,954

Over 70% of experimenters were satisfied with the evaluation criteria specified in our scale. Thus, 62.5% declare that the SGEScale tool helps determine whether the game's objectives are consistent with the intended pedagogical goals and, consequently, whether the game is effective in helping learners. The results of the questionnaire we sent to teachers were conclusive. Almost all questionnaire items scored above average. Overall, the questionnaire results showed that the SGEScale tool provided to teachers was deemed useful.

4 Conclusion

The effectiveness of using a serious game in a learning activity depends heavily on the teacher, who must choose a game that is adapted to the learners and compatible with the pedagogical objectives to be achieved. In fact, this type of application must meet two contradictory requirements. It must be engaging and offer learners a pedagogically relevant learning experience. In this article, we have proposed and described a scale for describing the components of a serious game in order to clearly verify the game's pedagogical and ludic content, thus facilitating the teacher's work through the effective implementation of the serious game in a particular learning situation. Overall, the evaluation protocol for our scale produced positive results in terms of its utility.

References

1. Leblanc, G.L.: Analyse comparative d'une formation en présentiel et d'une formation mixte (jeu sérieux et une journée en présentiel) à Hydro-Québec (2020)
2. Kaimara, P., Deliyannis, I.: Why should I play this game? The role of motivation in smart pedagogy. In: Didactics of smart pedagogy, pp. 113–137. Springer (2019)

3. Antit, S., et al.: Evaluation of students' motivation during the gamification of electrocardio-gram interpretation learning. Tunis. Med. **98**, 776–782 (2020)
4. Ding, D., Guan, C., Yu, Y.: Game-Based Learning in Tertiary Education: A New Learning Experience for the Generation Z. Int. J. Inf. Educ. Technol. **7**, 148–152 (2017)
5. Gentry, S.V., et al.: Serious gaming and gamification education in health professions: systematic review. J. Med. Internet Res. **21**, e12994 (2019)
6. Hébert, C., Jenson, J., Terzopoulos, T.: Access to technology is the major challenge: Teacher perspectives on barriers to DGBL in K-12 classrooms. E-Learning Digit. Media **18**, 307–324 (2021)
7. Emmerich, K., Bockholt, M.: Serious games evaluation: processes, models, and concepts. In: Entertainment Computing and Serious Games: International GI-Dagstuhl Seminar 15283, Dagstuhl Castle, Germany, July 5–10, 2015, Revised Selected Papers 265–283 (2016)
8. Sweetser, P., Wyeth, P.: GameFlow: a model for evaluating player enjoyment in games. Comput. Entertain. **3**, 3 (2005)
9. Fu, F.-L., Su, R.-C., Yu, S.-C.: EGameFlow: A scale to measure learners' enjoyment of e-learning games. Comput. Educ. **52**, 101–112 (2009)
10. Bellotti, F., et al.: A gamified short course for promoting entrepreneurship among ICT engineering students. In: 2013 IEEE 13th International Conference on Advanced Learning Technologies, pp. 31–32 (2013)
11. Taipe, M.S.A., Pesántez, D.Á., Rivera, L., Vizueta, D.O. : Juegos Serios en el Proceso de Aprendizaje. UTCiencia" Cienc. y Tecnol. al Serv. del pueblo" **4**, 111–122 (2017)
12. Ak, O.: A game scale to evaluate educational computer games. Procedia-Social Behav. Sci. **46**, 2477–2481 (2012)
13. Phan, M.H., Keebler, J.R., Chaparro, B.S.: The development and validation of the game user experience satisfaction scale (GUESS). Hum. Factors **58**, 1217–1247 (2016)
14. Silveira, A.C., Martins, R.X., Vieira, E.A.O.: E-Guess: Usability evaluation for educational games (2021)
15. Nousiainen, T., Kangas, M., Rikala, J., Vesisenaho, M.: Teacher competencies in game-based pedagogy. Teach. Teach. Educ. **74**, 85–97 (2018)
16. Hanghøj, T., Brund, C.E.: Teacher roles and positionings in relation to educational games. In: Proceedings of the 4th European conference on games based learning, pp. 116–122 (2010)
17. Kebritchi, M.: Factors affecting teachers' adoption of educational computer games: a case study. Br. J. Educ. Technol. **41**, 256–270 (2010)
18. Becker, K.: Choosing and using digital games in the classroom. Springer (2017)
19. Silseth, K.: The multivoicedness of game play: Exploring the unfolding of a student's learning trajectory in a gaming context at school. Int. J. Comput. Collab. Learn. **7**, 63–84 (2012)
20. Molin, G.: The role of the teacher in game-based learning: A review and outlook. Serious games edutainment Appl. 649–674 (2017)
21. Houssaye, J., Hameline, D., Hameline, D.: Le triangle pédagogique (1988)
22. Tang, S., Hanneghan, M., El-Rhalibi, A.: Pedagogy elements, components and structures for serious games authoring environment. In: 5th International Game Design and Technology Workshop (GDTW 2007), pp. 26–34. Liverpool, UK (2007)
23. Sanchez, E.: A model for the design of digital epistemic games. In: VIIe colloque {\guillemotleft}Questions de pédagogies dans l'enseignement supérieur{\guillemotright} (2013)
24. Bouroumane, F., Abarkan, M.: A serious game about Covid-19: design and evaluation study. Int. J. Inf. Commun. Technol. **12**, 195–204 (2023)

Impact of Spectrogram Resizing for Automatic Speech Recognition Case of Amazigh Isolated Word

Mohamed Daouad[1]([✉]) [iD], Fadoua Ataa Allah[2] [iD], and El Wardani Dadi[1] [iD]

[1] SOVIA Team, LSA Laboratory, ENSAH, University of Abdelmalek Essaadi, Tetouan, Morocco
mohamed.daouad@etu.uae.ac.ma, w.dadi@uae.ac.ma
[2] CEISIC, The Royal Institute of Amazigh Culture, Rabat, Morocco
ataaallah@ircam.ma

Abstract. In recent years, speech technology has received increasing attention from the scientific community, particularly when integrated into consumer products like home assistants and smartphones. However, it is important to emphasize that the efficiency of automatic speech recognition systems heavily depends on the preprocessing techniques used for the speech signal. Among these techniques, spectrogram resizing plays a crucial role in improving recognition accuracy. In this study, our objective is to investigate the impact of spectrogram resizing on the accuracy of a speech recognition system based on a convolutional neural network. We focused on the extraction and classification of an Amazigh isolated word corpus comprising 18 classes, which was collected from speakers in the Rif region of Morocco. The initial size of the Mel spectrogram was 96×96, and we explored resizing it to various dimensions. Additionally, we assessed the influence of different resizing interpolation techniques on speech recognition performance, including Bilinear, Lanczos, Gaussian, and others. Our findings indicate that resizing the Mel spectrogram to a resolution of 64×64 pixels using Bilinear interpolation yielded optimal performance, achieving a speech recognition accuracy of 93.66%. However, alternative interpolation techniques such as Lanczos 5 and area interpolation also produced viable options, offering reasonably high accuracy scores.

Keywords: Speech recognition · Neural network · Resizing spectrogram · CNN · Amazigh language

1 Introduction

Automatic Speech Recognition (ASR) system is an incredibly fascinating and promising technology, finding applications in diverse areas including interactive voice response, transcription, and aiding disabled individuals [1]. It serves as a means of simplifying human-machine interaction by converting acoustic waveforms into word sequences uttered by the speaker. The effectiveness of ASR systems heavily depends on the preprocessing techniques employed for the speech signal. Notably, spectrogram resizing

H. Hagras et al. (Eds.): ISACS 2023, CCIS 2255, pp. 183–194, 2025.
https://doi.org/10.1007/978-3-031-93448-3_15

plays a crucial role in enhancing recognition accuracy. By appropriately adjusting the spectrogram representation, valuable information can be extracted, leading to improved performance in ASR tasks.

The spectrogram serves as a visual depiction of the changing frequency content of a speech signal over time. It is widely utilized as an input feature in ASR systems. This work would like to examine the impact of spectrogram resizing on the accuracy of an ASR system, specifically for recognizing Amazigh isolated words.

Amazigh, also referred to as Tamazight or Berber, is a historic Afro-Asiatic language spoken by millions in North Africa [2], characterized by diverse dialects and phonetic variations. In Morocco, the Amazigh language is divided into three principal regional varieties: Tarifite in the north, Tamazight in Central Morocco and the south-east, and Tachelhite in the south-west and the High Atlas regions [3]. The language has been integrated into the Moroccan school system since 2003 and officially recognized in 2011. However, due to its limited resources and documentation, developing accurate ASR systems for Amazigh poses many challenges.

Consequently, we hypothesize that resizing the speech signal spectrograms can further augment their effectiveness. To verify this hypothesis, we investigate the optimal resizing parameters that maximize the performance of the ASR system for Amazigh. This entails exploring different resizing interpolation techniques and resolutions for the Mel spectrogram audio representation. To evaluate the effectiveness of different spectrogram resizing techniques, we employ a comprehensive experimental setup. Specifically, we utilize a corpus of Amazigh isolated word speech collected from native speakers and construct a robust ASR system using a deep learning model, specifically a 2D convolutional neural network. To enhance the model's performance, parameters such as the number of convolution layers, fully-connected layers, activation function, and epochs were tuned. By manipulating these parameters, we aim to enhance the discriminative power of the acoustic features and achieve improved recognition accuracy. Indeed, the findings of this work hold practical implications for the development of ASR systems tailored to under-resourced languages like Amazigh. By comprehending the impact of spectrogram resizing on the accuracy of ASR systems, we can provide valuable insights for designing efficient and effective recognition pipelines specific to different languages and tasks.

In the following sections, we provide an overview of the related work in Sect. 2, highlighting previous research and advancements in the field of image and spectrogram resizing. Section 3 details our experimental setup, beginning with the presentation of collected datasets for Amazigh isolated word recordings. We then delve into the creation and analysis of spectrograms, exploring different resizing interpolation techniques. Additionally, we discuss the selection of appropriate deep neural network models that were implemented to effectively capture the complex patterns and features present in Amazigh speech. In Sect. 4, we present and discuss the results of our experiments, analyzing the impact of spectrogram resizing interpolation on the performance of CNN models. Finally, in Sect. 5, we conclude the study by summarizing our key findings and discussing the implications for improving ASR systems, specifically within the context of Amazigh isolated word recognition.

2 Related Work

In the context of image classification using convolutional neural networks (CNNs), maintaining consistent image sizes is essential. A recent study proposed zero-padding as an alternative to the traditional approach of scaling images up with interpolation [4]. The study found that zero-padding had no impact on the accuracy of classification. It significantly decreased the duration of training. Furthermore, exploring interpolation-based image resizing techniques for uniformly sized time-frequency representations, the study of Sharan and Moir assesses various interpolation methods and examines a database comprising 50 sound event classes of different durations [5]. The results indicate that employing Bicubic and Lanczos kernel interpolation significantly enhances the classification performance compared to conventional representations. Similarly, a comprehensive evaluation of audio signal representation techniques for CNN-based classification was conducted in the study of Sharan et al. [6]. This study examines various methods for sound events and speech commands classification and identifies the cochleagram representation as the most effective. Moreover, within the context of image resizing techniques for time-frequency representations, the study compares different interpolation methods. The results highlight the superior performance of Bicubic and Lanczos kernel interpolations. In addition, an assessment of progressive training in CNN for audio events classification is discussed in the study of Colangelo et al. [7]. This study introduces a resizing process that gradually incorporates more Mel filters and compares it to a bilinear resize-based procedure on two audio event classification datasets. The results reveal a slight advantage of Mel-based resizing over bilinear resizing. Moreover, the study Roszkowiak et al. evaluates and compares nine interpolation methods for resizing whole slide images [8]. The evaluation incorporates general test images as well as specialized biological immunohistochemically stained tissue sample images. Based on the performance analysis, the sinc, Catmull-Rom, and Lagrange interpolation methods are identified as optimal for image resizing. However, considering calculation time, the study suggests utilizing the nearest neighbor algorithm, which is the fastest option. Additionally, in the context of user recognition system utilizing feature extraction, the study of Choi et al. presents an approach that employs 2D resizing based on Bicubic interpolation [10]. This approach enhances the calculation speed while preserving the original data values, specifically in the analysis of electrocardiogram (ECG) signals. The resizing process enables the extraction of multi-dimensional features, leading to improved efficiency and accuracy in user recognition. Furthermore, a novel approach to image resizing is introduced in the study of Danon et al. [9], where resizing is performed in the feature space of a neural network. The researchers directly manipulate the image feature maps, extracted from a pre-trained classification network, and employ neural network-based optimization to reconstruct the resized image.

3 Experimental Setup

The next section presents the construction and characteristics of the datasets used in the proposed system, aiming to analyze the impact of different spectrogram resizing techniques on the performance of an Amazigh isolated word recognition system. It begins by describing how spectrograms were extracted from audio files, resulting in 2000 spectrograms of equal size (96 × 96). The section then proceeds to explain the process of resizing the spectrograms to serve as the input for the subsequent component of the system, which is the 2D CNN neural network. By providing these details, the section establishes the foundation for the upcoming sections, which will delve into further aspects of the proposed methodology (see Fig. 1).

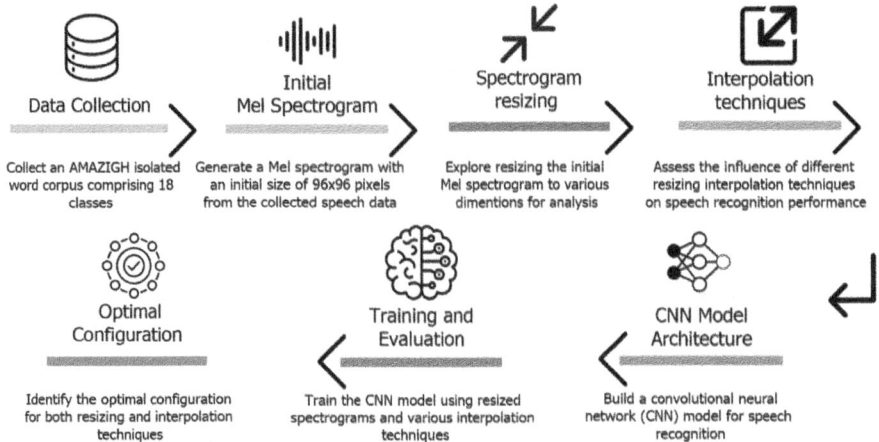

Fig. 1. General architecture of the proposed approach

3.1 Datasets

To assess the impact of resizing on speech recognition systems, we conducted an extensive study using various resized spectrograms. Our analysis centered around a database containing 18 distinct isolated words, as outlined in Table 1. These words were articulated by a panel of 25 native speakers from the Amazigh-Tarifit community, located in the Rif region of Morocco. The contributors' ages ranged from 15 to 30 years, encompassing a wide range of vocal characteristics. The compilation included recordings from both male and female voices, meticulously captured at a high sampling frequency of 48 kHz, as detailed in. Our data acquisition adhered to the industry-standard WAV file format, ensuring superior audio quality.

To ensure robustness and reliability under real-life conditions, each word was pronounced five times by each individual speaker, with each pronunciation saved as a separate audio file. The audio recordings, captured in normal life situations, varied in duration, with an average length of around one second.

Upon completing the recording process, a manual verification and classification were performed, resulting in a meticulous organization of the recordings into 18 distinct files, each clearly labeled to indicate the corresponding word. These file names followed a unique nomenclature, combining a class_id and record_id, exemplified by the format "1--10.wav." Any disrupted or silent recordings were eliminated, resulting in the curation

Table 1. The speech corpus.

Word's identifier	Amazigh Words	Latin notation (Rifain accent)	English correspondence
0	ⵄⵛⵄⴻⵄⵇ [Amḥdar]	Amḥda	Student
1	ⵄⵔⵒⵔⵄ [Asqsi]	Asqsi	Question
2	ⵜⵄⵔⵄ [Tira]	Tira	Writing
3	ⵜⵄⵔⵔⵄⵍⵔⵉ [Tiṭṭawin]	Tiṭṭawin	Eyes
4	ⵄⴷⵛⵔ [Afus]	Fus	Hand
5	ⵜⵄⵛⵔⵔⵄ [Timssi]	Timssi	Fire
6	ⵄⵕⵕⵛⴷ [Akkuḥ]	Akkuḥ	Small
7	ⵄⵛⵛⵄⵎ [Acmlal]	Acmrar	White
8	ⵄⵯⵯⵯⵄⵃ [Azggʷaɣ]	Azggʷaɣ	Red
9	ⵄⵍⵔⵄⵃ [Awraɣ]	Awraɣ	Yellow
10	ⵜⵔⵛⴻ [Tṣmd]	tṣmḍ	Cold
11	ⵇⴷⵛⵛ [Rḥmu]	Rḥmu	Hot
12	ⵄⵔⵛ [Ari]	Ari	Write
13	ⵇⵯⴻ [Rẓm]	Aẓm	Open
14	ⵔⵒⵔⵄ [Sqsa]	Sqsa	ask
15	ⵔⵔⵛⵉⵛ [Ssili]	Ssiri	Raise
16	ⵔⵔⵛⵣⵃ [Ssufɣ]	Ssufɣ	Take out
17	ⵉⵛⵂ [Lmd]	Rmd	Learn

of a pristine collection of 2000 audio files. In the results, each word class comprised over 100 repetitions, attesting the diversity and comprehensiveness of our database (Table 2).

Table 2. Records' attributs.

Records' attributs and dataset details	Value
Sampling rate	48 kHz
Bit-depth	32 bits
Channels	1 (Mono)
Audio file format	Wav
Corpus	18 distinct Amazigh words
Condition of noise	Normal life
Number of repetitions per person	5

For our experimental setup, we partitioned the database, allocating 80% of the data for training purposes and reserving the remaining 20% for testing. This partitioning ensured a balanced distribution of data and provided a reliable evaluation framework to assess the impact of resizing on speech recognition performance.

3.2 Spectrogram

The input of a CNN requires an image format. Therefore, a preprocessing step of the audio signal is necessary. We accomplish this process by transforming each audio sample into a 2D time-frequency matrix, resulting in a spectrogram, an image-like representation, as depicted in Fig. 2.

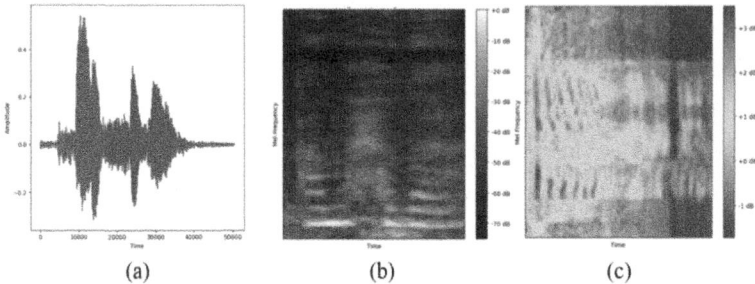

(a)   (b)   (c)

Fig. 2. Waveform (a), Mel spectrogram (b), transposed log Mel spectrogram (c) representation of recording word 'Amaḥda'.

To obtain this representation, the audio signal was divided into short overlapping frames. Each frame undergoes transformation into the frequency domain using the Fast Fourier Transform (FFT) [10], resulting in a power spectrum. The subsequent step involves mapping the power spectrum onto a Mel scale, which is a perceptually motivated frequency scale. The Mel scale is nonlinear, emphasizing lower frequencies more in line with human auditory perception. For each frame, it computes the energy within each Mel-frequency band by summing the power spectrum values weighted by the filter response. These energies across all Mel-frequency bands constitute the Mel spectrogram. Following the extraction of audio features using the Mel spectrogram method provided by Librosa, we obtain features consisting of 96 Mel bands. To ensure equal-sized Mel spectrograms, we employ a condition: If the feature length is less than 96, we pad the features with zeros to match the desired length; otherwise, we discard the remaining parts. Subsequently, a power-to-decibel transformation is applied to the features, yielding a logarithmic spectrogram representation. The resulting spectrogram is then transposed, arranging the dimensions as (n_samples, n_features). Lastly, we normalize the spectrogram features by subtracting the mean and dividing by the standard deviation. This normalization step ensures that the features have zero mean and unit variance, which can be advantageous for training machine learning models.

3.3 Resizing

Resizing images plays a critical role as a pre-processing step in computer vision, particularly when it comes to accelerating the training of deep learning models using smaller images. Image interpolation, a widely employed technique, is used to map each pixel in the resized image back to the original image by utilizing diverse algorithms that interpolate between neighboring pixels (see Fig. 3). In fact, this interpolation process often includes the image convolution with a small kernel comprised of weight coefficients. For this purpose, various kernels such as nearest neighbor, Lanzos, Bicubic, and Gaussian are used [5].

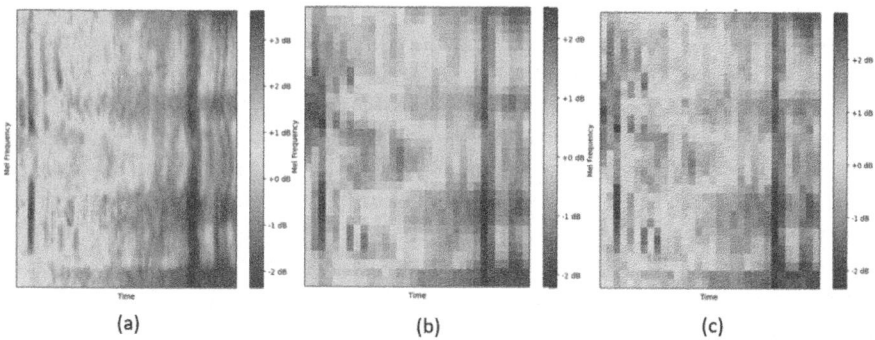

Fig. 3. Transposed log Mel spectrogram (a) of word "Amaḥda", resized to 32 × 32 using Area (b) and nearest (c) interpolation.

The main objective of employing these methods is to adjust the size of the input image while ensuring the preservation of important visual regions, such as salient objects, and reducing the occurrence of visual artifacts [9].

- **Nearest Neighbor:** Nearest Neighbor interpolation involves replacing an interpolated point with the value of the nearest neighboring pixel in the original image. This technique works by approximating the coordinates of the intended interpolation point to find the closest corresponding pixel [11].
- **Bilinear:** Bilinear interpolation involves computing a weighted average of the four adjacent pixels in order to determine the interpolated value. This technique results in a significantly smoother image compared to the original. In cases where the distances between the known pixels are equal, the interpolated value is obtained by summing these values and dividing the total by four [12].
- **Bicubic:** Bicubic take into account the nearest 4 × 4 block of known pixels, encompassing a total of 16 pixels. As these pixels are positioned at different distances from the target pixel, those in closer proximity carry more significance and are accorded greater importance during the calculation process [12].
- **Area:** The theory behind this interpolation technique involves redistributing the pixel values of an image when resizing it to a different size. When scaling an image up or down, the Area-Based Resampling method calculates the contribution of each neighboring pixel based on the proportion of its area that overlaps with the target pixel [13].
- **Lanczos:** In Lanczos interpolation, the algorithm applies a windowed sinc function, known as the Lanczos kernel, to calculate the weighted average of neighboring pixels. The sinc function is designed to minimize aliasing and preserve the sharpness of edges in the image [14].
- **Gaussian:** Gaussian interpolation utilizes the convolution of an image with a Gaussian kernel, which is a bell-shaped curve characterized by its standard deviation [15].

The Gaussian kernel determines the weighting of neighboring pixels by considering their distances from the target pixel.

3.4 Deep Neural Network Models

The proposed architecture (see Fig. 4) for the neural network model is comprised of multiple layers that are designed to efficiently process and classify audio data. The initial layer is a resizing layer that takes an input of shape (96, 96, 1) and resizes it. The model comprises two main parts: feature extraction and classification. The feature extraction part consists of three groups of layers. Each group consists of a convolutional layer, followed by a ReLU activation function, batch normalization, and a max pooling operation with a pool size of 3 × 3. The number of filters increases progressively from 32 to 64 and finally to 128, enhancing the complexity of the learned features. After the convolutional layers, a flatten operation is applied to reshape the output. To prevent overfitting and improve generalization, a dropout layer with a rate of 50% is utilized, randomly disabling half of the neurons. This helps regularize the model and reduce its dependency on specific features.

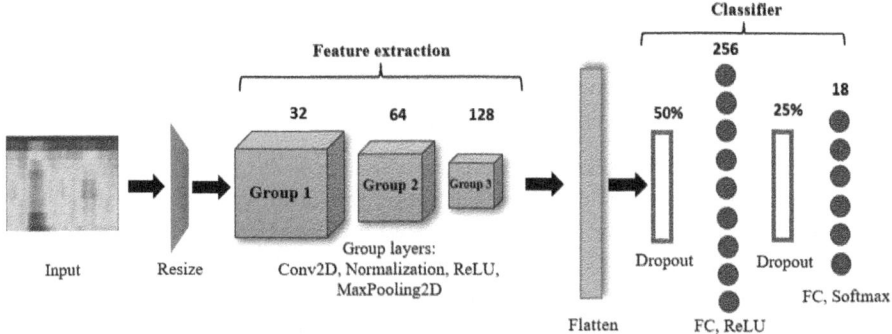

Fig. 4. 2D Convolutional neural network architecture.

Following the feature extraction, the classification part begins. It starts with a dense layer that applies the ReLU activation function, transforming the features into a higher-dimensional space. To further regularize the model, another dropout layer with a rate of 25% is added, increasing its robustness. Finally, a dense layer with softmax activation is applied, generating the final output shape of (None, 18), representing the classification probabilities for 18 different classes. The softmax function normalizes the outputs, ensuring they sum up to 1 and can be interpreted as probabilities. This allows the model to make predictions and assign a class label to the input data based on the highest probability.

4   Results and Discussion

In our work, we utilized a PC equipped with an NVIDIA GeForce MX 330 to carry out all the preprocessing and training tasks. We employed TensorFlow GPU on Windows 11 with Anaconda, CUDA Toolkit 11.2, and cuDNN 8.1 to accelerate the computations required for training a Convolutional Neural Network (CNN) model on a dataset of 2000 Amazigh isolated words. The dataset was divided into an 80% training split, consisting of 1600 audio files, and a 20% test split.

We investigated the impact of resizing on speech recognition performance by applying different resizing interpolation techniques and resolutions to the Mel spectrogram audio representation.

- Resizing with Different Resolutions:

We observed in Table 3 that resizing the Mel spectrogram to different resolutions had varying effects on the speech recognition accuracy. Among the different resolutions tested, the highest accuracy was achieved when the Mel spectrogram was resized to 64 × 64 pixels, with an accuracy of 93.66%. This indicates that downsampling the Mel spectrogram to a resolution of 64 × 64 pixels had a positive impact on the speech recognition performance compared to the original size of 96 × 96 pixels.

Table 3. Precision, Recall, F1-score and Accuracy for CNN model with different resolution.

Size	Precision	Recall	F1 score	Accuracy
32 × 32	92,63	91,46	91,54	91,46
64 × 64	**94,47**	**93,66**	**93,72**	**93,66**
96 × 96	92,93	92,28	92,27	92,29
112 × 112	92,66	91,73	91,89	91,74
128 × 128	92,93	91,18	91,34	91,18

- Resizing with Different Interpolation Techniques:

Among these techniques presented in Table 4, the Bilinear interpolation method resulted in the highest accuracy, with an accuracy of 93.66%. This suggests that Bilinear interpolation was most effective in preserving the essential features of the Mel spectrogram during the resizing process. Furthermore, we found that Lanczos 5 and area interpolation techniques also performed well, achieving accuracies of 93.39% and 92.86%, respectively. These findings indicate that these interpolation methods are suitable alternatives for resizing Mel spectrograms without significant degradation in speech recognition performance. On the other hand, Nearest, Bicubic, and Gaussian interpolation techniques showed lower accuracy scores compared to the other methods. This suggests that these techniques might not preserve the fine details and nuances of the Mel spectrogram adequately during resizing, leading to a drop in speech recognition performance.

Throughout the training process (see Fig. 5), we monitored the model's loss and accuracy on both the training and test data, observing their convergence with increasing epochs, ultimately leading to stable model performance.

In terms of execution time, the selection of an interpolation technique plays a significant role in influencing the training duration of the model. This is particularly evident due

Table 4. Precision, Recall, F1-score, Accuracy and Execution time for CNN model with different interpolation algorithms.

Interpolation	Precision	Recall	F1 score	Accuracy	Execution time
Nearest	92,85	91,73	91,83	91,74	52 s 65 ms
Bilinear	**94,47**	**93,66**	**93,72**	**93,66**	57 s 98 ms
Bicubic	92,18	91,18	91,14	91,18	68 s 58 ms
Lanzos 3	93,63	93,11	93,12	93,11	74 s 02 ms
Lanzos 5	94,38	93,38	93,45	93,39	79 s 87 ms
Area	93,05	92,56	92,55	92,86	74 s 94 ms
Gaussian	93,31	91,73	91,80	91,74	67 s 39 ms

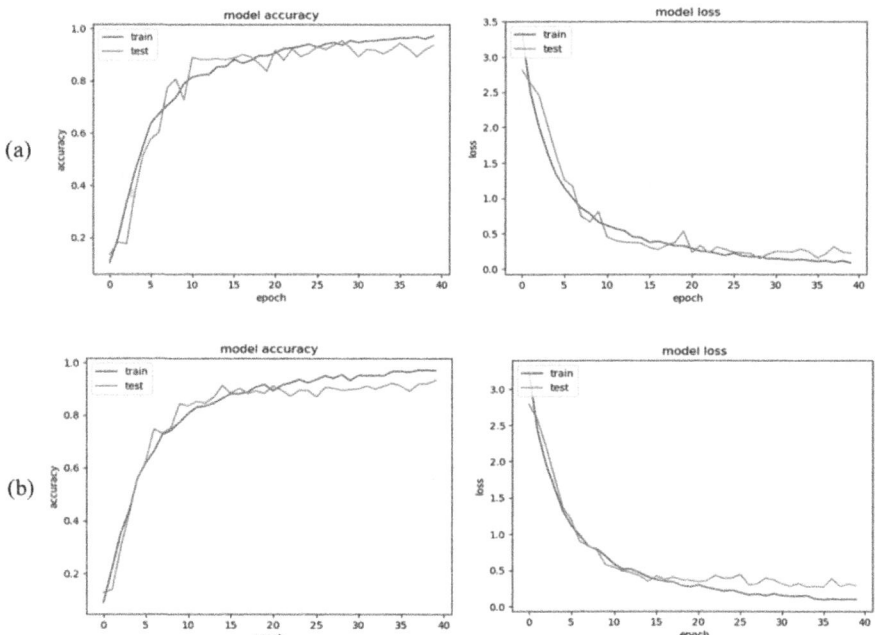

Fig. 5. Training and validation accuracy of model using resized data with Bilinear (a) and Lanzos interpolation (b).

to the batch-based processing that occurs during training. If an interpolation technique demands significant computational resources, it has the potential to decelerate the speed of batch processing, subsequently elongating the overall training period. In our case, it's worth noting that Lanczos 5 and Area interpolations demonstrate slightly lengthier training times when contrasted with alternative techniques such as Nearest, Bilinear, and Gaussian. This discrepancy could be attributed to the inherently more computationally demanding nature of these techniques.

we compared our results with findings from several related research works. Ronnel et al. proved that resizing Mel spectrograms with Bilinear kernel interpolation significantly improved classification accuracy [6], which aligns with our own results. Similarly, Sharan et al. observed enhanced classification performance with Lanzos interpolation technique [5]. Additionally, our study concurs with Saponara et al. observations regarding the trade-off between resolution and performance. They noted that downscaling images led to faster computation times [16]. Furthermore, the application of bicubic interpolation to electrocardiogram (ECG) signals in another study [17] emphasizes the versatility of this technique. Overall, our results contribute to the growing body of evidence supporting the benefits of careful resizing and interpolation methods in enhancing data representations for various applications.

5 Conclusion

In summary, our experiment's results provide valuable insights into the relationship between interpolation techniques, spectrogram sizes, model performance, and training time complexity. We highlight the impact of different interpolation techniques and spectrogram sizes on the performance of the CNN model. Looking at the recall, F1 score, precision, and accuracy metrics, it's clear that the choice of interpolation technique can influence the model's predictive capabilities. Bilinear interpolation with a resolution of 64×64 pixels appears to offer a promising option that balances accuracy and time complexity. However, other interpolation techniques such as Lanczos 5 and Area interpolation also offer viable alternatives with reasonably high accuracy scores. The choice ultimately depends on the specific requirements of the application and the trade-offs willing to make between training time and model performance. These results stress the importance of selecting appropriate resizing techniques when applying speech recognition systems to different resolutions. In essence, our investigation of spectrogram resizing interpolation contributes to the understanding of its efficacy and potential benefits for ASR, opening avenues for further research and development in this area.

References

1. Zealouk, O., Satori, H., Hamidi, M.., Satori, K.: Pathological detection using HMMSpeech Recognition-Based AmazighDigits. In: Embedded Systems and Artificial Intelligence, pp. 281–289. Springer Singapore, Fez, Morocco (2019)
2. Boukous, A.: Société, langues et cultures au Maroc : enjeux symboliques. Publ. la Fac. des lettres des Sci. Hum. Univ. Mohamed V. Série Essais études no. **8**, 239 (1995)
3. Fadoua, A.A., Siham, B.: Natural language processing for Amazigh language: Challenges and future directions. Lang. Technol. Norm. Less-Resourced Lang. 19–23 (2012)
4. Hashemi, M.: Enlarging smaller images before inputting into convolutional neural network: zero-padding vs. interpolation. J. Big Data. 6 (2019). https://doi.org/10.1186/s40537-019-0263-7
5. Sharan, R.V., Moir, T.J.: Time-Frequency Image Resizing Using Interpolation for Acoustic Event Recognition with Convolutional Neural Networks. Proc. - 2019 IEEE Int. Conf. Signals Syst. ICSigSys 2019, pp. 8–11 (2019). https://doi.org/10.1109/ICSIGSYS.2019.8811088

6. Sharan, R.V., Xiong, H., Berkovsky, S.: Benchmarking audio signal representation techniques for classification with convolutional neural networks. Sensors 21 (2021). https://doi.org/10.3390/s21103434

7. Colangelo, F., Battisti, F., Neri, A.: Progressive training of convolutional neural networks for acoustic events classification. In: 28th European Signal Processing Conference (EUSIPCO), pp. 26–30. IEEE (2020)

8. Roszkowiak, L., Korzynska, A., Zak, J., Pijanowska, D., Swiderska-Chadaj, Z., Markiewicz, T.: Survey: interpolation methods for whole slide image processing. J. Microsc. **265**, 148–158 (2017). https://doi.org/10.1111/jmi.12477

9. Danon, D., Arar, M., Cohen-Or, D., Shamir, A.: Image resizing by reconstruction from deep features. Comput. Vis. Media. **7**, 453–466 (2021). https://doi.org/10.1007/s41095-021-0216-x

10. Badshah, A.M., et al.: Deep features-based speech emotion recognition for smart affective services. Multimed. Tools Appl. **78**, 5571–5589 (2019). https://doi.org/10.1007/s11042-017-5292-7

11. Prajapati, A., Naik, S., Mehta, S.: Evaluation of different image interpolation algorithms. Int. J. Comput. Appl. **58**, 6–12 (2012). https://doi.org/10.5120/9332-3638

12. Parsania, M.P.S., Virparia, D.P.V.: A Comparative Analysis of Image Interpolation Algorithms. Ijarcce. **5**, 29–34 (2016). https://doi.org/10.17148/ijarcce.2016.5107

13. Amanatiadis, A., Andreadis, I., Konstantinidis, K.: Fuzzy area-based image scaling. Conf. Rec. - IEEE Instrum. Meas. Technol. Conf., pp. 1–6 (2007). https://doi.org/10.1109/imtc.2007.379084

14. Parsania, S., Virparia, P.V.: A review: image interpolation techniques for image scaling. Int. J. Innov. Res. Comput. Commun. Eng. **02**, 7409–7414 (2015). https://doi.org/10.15680/ijircce.2014.0212024

15. Lehmann, T.M., Gönner, C., Spitzer, K.: Survey: Interpolation methods in medical image processing. IEEE Trans. Med. Imaging **18**, 1049–1075 (1999). https://doi.org/10.1109/42.816070

16. Saponara, S., Elhanashi, A.: Impact of image resizing on deep learning detectors for training time and model performance. Lect. Notes Electr. Eng. 866 LNEE, pp. 10–17 (2022). https://doi.org/10.1007/978-3-030-95498-7_2

17. Choi, G.H., Bak, E.S., Pan, S.B.: User identification system using 2D resized spectrogram features of ECG. IEEE Access. **7**, 34862–34873 (2019). https://doi.org/10.1109/ACCESS.2019.2902870

Recommender Systems Based on Matrix Factorization: Comparative Analysis

Lamyae El Youbi El Idrissi[1]([✉]), Ismail Akharraz[2] [ID], and Abdelaziz Ahaitouf[1] [ID]

[1] Engineering Sciences Laboratory, Polydisciplinary Faculty of Taza, Sidi Mohamed Ben Abdellah University, 35000 Taza, Morocco
{lamyae.elyoubielidrissi,abdelaziz.ahaitouf}@usmba.ac.ma
[2] Mathematical and Informatics Engineering Laboratory, Faculty of Science Agadir, Ibnou Zohr University, 80000 Agadir, Morocco
i.akharraz@uiz.ac.ma

Abstract. The growing need for personalized information has resulted in the development of recommender systems (RS), which are widely used to predict user preferences and generate appropriate recommendations through the adoption of different techniques and algorithms. These systems can achieve the recommendation process using techniques based on Artificial Intelligence (AI). It can determine what users prefer based on their preferences and past behavior. Our work aims to make a comparative study of three matrix factorization (MF) methods, namely, singular value decomposition (SVD), singular value decomposition plus plus (SVD++) and non-negative matrix factorization (NMF), to identify the most efficient algorithm in terms of prediction in a movie recommender system based on collaborative filtering. The performance of these methods is experimentally verified over the MovieLens 100 K dataset by using the mean absolute error (MAE) and root mean square error (RMSE). The results showed the efficiency of SVD++ with a reduced values of MAE and RMSE.

Keywords: Recommender system · collaborative filtering · Matrix factorization (MF)

1 Introduction

With the massive amount of data generated and shared on the internet every day. Users have been submerged by data flow. It is increasingly difficult to discover what users want or need. Recommander systems (RS) are information-filtering tools that assist users in identifying relevant elements, by lowering the information surcharge. These tools enable the provision of personalized recommendations that can assist users in making decisions [1]. Figure 1 illustrates the operation of recommendation systems in a simplified form.

RS have proven their effectiveness in a wide range of applications [2]. E-commerce sites have used recommendation algorithms to enhance purchasing new items. With the arrival of streaming movie and music services, such as Netflix and Spotify, providers of services must maintain their clients interested or risk losing customers and income [3].

© The Author(s), under exclusive license to Springer Nature Switzerland AG 2025
H. Hagras et al. (Eds.): ISACS 2023, CCIS 2255, pp. 195–204, 2025.
https://doi.org/10.1007/978-3-031-93448-3_16

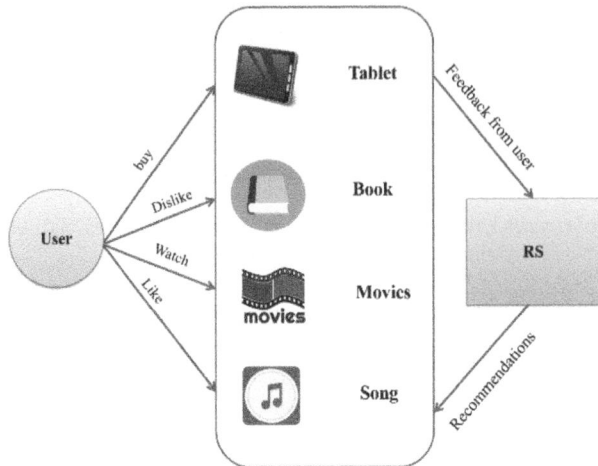

Fig. 1. Process of RS

Machine learning (ML) [4] has made it possible for robots to learn from their prior experiences with the aid of an enormous amount of data and several algorithms. RS gather information about a user's prior behavior on a collection of items and use it to make recommendations. The information can be explicit (such as user ratings), implicit (such as browsing history), contextual (such as time, location), demographic, or social (such as tags, friends, trusters, trustees) [5]. With the use of different ML algorithms, the system generates recommendations for users.

There are three main popular strategies of RS:content-based recommendations, collaborative recommendations, and hybrid recommendations [6]. The user will recommend items that are similar to his previous favorites in the first method. In contrast, with the collaborative approach, suggestions are based on items that users who share the user's tastes and preferences have consumed. Finally, because the two types of recommendations can complement each other, combining content-based recommendations with collaborative recommendations results in hybrid approaches that can improve the system's prediction capabilities [6].

The most widely used method for implementing RS is collaborative filtering [7]. There are two different categories of collaborative filtering methods, namely "memory-based collaborative filtering" and "model-based collaborative filtering" [6]. The first technique groups users or items into neighborhoods to produce rating predictions using similarity indices and known ratings. The second technique creates a system model by matrix factorization (MF) using the known ratings.

MF is a commonly used method to address the sparsity problem in model based collaborative filtering because only few items are assessed for each user [8]. This method produces a user-item rating matrix with significantly fewer dimensions than the original one by learning the latent user and item and removing uncharacteristic elements. We studied the performance of three MF approaches often employed in RS based on collaborative filtering: "singular value decomposition (SVD)", "singular value decomposition plus plus (SVD++)", and "non-negative matrix factorization (NMF)".

The performance of these approaches will be evaluated by two standard metrics: RMSE and MAE. The objective of this work consist to examine and analyse the three models to assist practitioners and researchers and in identifying effective solutions in RS.

The rest of this paper is structured as follows: Sect. 2 contains related works. Section 3 includes a description of the examined models. The data set, evaluation metrics, and experimental setup are presented in Sect. 4. A comparison of the three models is provided in Sect. 5. Finally, the study's conclusion is presented in Sect. 6.

2 Literature Survey

The various domains of application of RS have allowed the development of several recommendation models over time, demonstrating the adaptability of RS to different fields. This section examines the state of the art in RS based on MF algorithms.

MF is one of the most widely used collaborative filtering techniques in RS, thanks to a competition organized by Netflix, which revealed a winning team that came up with a method based on MF [9]. Several works have been carried out on the (RS) using the MF. Mhammedi et al. [10] propose a recommender system using the MF algorithm of collaborative filtering based on the dimensional reduction method and, more specifically, NMF combined with ontology. The authors tested the model and compared the results to other traditional methods. The results demonstrated that the applied approach effectively reduces the sparsity of collaborative filtering suggestions, increases their accuracy and provides more relevant items as recommendations. Nurrahmi et al. [11] Have proposed a model based on the NMF algorithm, which uses the implicit feedback that are: "View Product Detail", "View Review Detail", and "Add to Wishlist" from the Female Daily mobile application for product recommendation. In this context, the "surprise" library was used to implement the NMF algorithm with two implicit evaluation weighting scenarios: cumulative weighting and maximum weighting. Numerous NMF parameters were tested and 5-fold cross-validation were applied to evaluate the model, in order to find the right MSE (mean squared error), RMSE (root mean square error) and MAE (mean absolute error) measures for cumulative and maximum weighting. Christina & Baizal Applied in [12], the "Slope-SVD" algorithm to implement a book recommendation approach using rating information extracted from the Goodreads website. In this context, the SVD algorithm was combined with the Slop-one algorithm to complete the empty ratings. In this way, the "Slope-SVD" method improved the accuracy of the system. In order to evaluate the accuracy of the system, the MAE metric was used, and the results showed the effectiveness of the "Slope-SVD" algorithm. Andika et al. [13] collected collaborative filtering -related publications using a systematic literature review technique, and 28 studies were ultimately taken into account for the analysis using KNN, deep learning, and SVD. According to the review's findings, the majority of the datasets used in collaborative filtering to test the recommendation model were movie datasets, and most of the models showed good results for item recommendation. The Most existing works combine many techniques to overcome or lessen the effects of collaborative filtering difficulties (cold-start, sparsity, shilling attacks, etc.), which might affect the performance of the recommendation to produce good results. Al-Ghamdi et al.

[14] compared a set of collaborative filtering algorithms to assess their performance. The K-Nearest Neighbor ("KNN"), "Slope", "Co-clustering" and "NMF" methods are specifically evaluated. The MovieLens dataset is used with six evaluation measures: MAE, RMSE, Fraction of Concordant Pairs (FCP), coverage, training time and testing time for experimentation. The results proved that the KNN method for item-based collaborative filtering outperforms all the other algorithms studied. Shi et al. [15] created a "user embedding" based rating prediction model (UE-SVD++) using SVD++. They took advantage of explicit user feedback via evaluation data and created a "user integration" matrix to enrich the user model with explicit information by exploring mutual information suggested by the user. Furthermore, to enhance the accuracy of their model, the matrix of "user embedding" was added to SVD++ 's current user bias and implicit parameters. Massimo & Ricci [16] employed NMF to group users' POI visiting trajectories through geographic and temporal factors in their location-based recommendation system. They also suggested an NMF-based point of interest RS model that integrates geographical influence and textual data.

3   The Algorithms

This study aims to evaluate and compare three techniques: "NFM", "SVD" and "SVD++". The first technique, NFM, aims to decompose the original matrix into two smaller ones with non-negative elements. SVD is used to solve complex real metrics. The third technique, called SVD++, uses the advantages of latent and neighbourhood. The SVD, SVD++ and NMF methods applied in this work are presented below.

3.1 SVD

SVD is commonly used to produce approximations having a lower rank [17]. Let $B \in R^{m \times n}$ with r the rank of B, by decomposing the matrix into singular values, we obtain:

$$B = P * Q * S^T \tag{1}$$

P and S are two orthogonal matrices and Q is a diagonal matrix containing r non-zero elements that are singular values of the matrix B. We have $P \in R^{m \times m}$, $S \in R^{n \times n}$ and $Q \in R^{m \times n}$, and the columns of the matrices P and S are the eigenvectors of BB^T and $B^T B$, respectively.

Thus, the three matrices P, S and Q have the effective dimensions: $m \times r$, $n \times r$ and $r \times r$, respectively. The orthogonal values $(\sigma_1, \sigma_2, \ldots, \sigma_r)$ of S have the following characteristic: $\sigma_1 \geq \sigma_2 \geq \ldots \geq \sigma_r > 0$.

The SVD technique has the property of providing an optimal approximation of the initial matrix B by decomposing it into three small matrices while retaining k first largest singular values of Q, keeping in addition the smaller values at the value zero. This reduced matrix of Q will be noted by Q_k. In addition, we denote P_k and S_k as the two reduced matrices of P and S, which have k columns. Thus, formula (1) can be changed by:

$$B_k = P_k Q_k S_k^T \tag{2}$$

Thus, B_k is the closest approximation to the initial matrix B.

In this work, we investigated and assessed the usage of SVD in a movies recommender system.

3.2 SVD++

By minimizing the dimensions, SVD++ maps high-dimensional sample data to low-dimensional semantic space, and it additionally eliminates redundant and noise information from the sample data, representing the valuable part of the data [18]. SVD++ is a developed version of SVD. The distinction is that SVD++ considers implicit feedback, whereas the SVD technique solely considers user ratings ('explicit feedback') [19]. The 'implicit feedback' from users could often be traced on the base of user's behaviour or "user-item" interactions, showing implicitly their interest in the elements they have interacted with. For example, if a user frequently watches artist's movies, it's reasonable to assume that he likes that artist. Similarly, if a user has bought a tablet and doesn't return it, we can assume it is because he likes it. The 'implici feedback' from users may be especially useful when users have provided very few explicit ratings.

In this work, we compared SVD++ to other algorithms in a movies recommender system.

3.3 NMF

NMF is a new MF method that is exploited to perform high-dimensional data analysis [20]. In contrast to SVD and SVD++, which can allow negative values, this method automatically extracts the characteristics of several non-negative data vectors. SVD generates unique factors, but NMF generates non unique factors, which gives NMF the advantage of being especially ideal when privacy and protection are required [21]. X is a matrix that has been factored into two other matrices P and Q, with non-negative elements on all three matrices, we have:

$$X = PQ^T \tag{3}$$

In this work, we compare NMF to other algorithms and examine its application in a movies RS.

4 Experimentation

4.1 Dataset Design

The dataset chosen to train the recommender system is the MovieLens 100 K [22]. This dataset collected by the GroupLens research project at the University of Minnesota is freely available and widely used in the field of RS. It includes 100,000 ratings at scale [1–5] of 943 users on 1682 movies where each user has rated at least twenty movies. Additionally, there are some demographic data for users, such as (gender, age, occupation, zip code).

4.2 Evaluation Metrics

There are numerous approaches for evaluating recommendation systems in the literature. A general partition of these quantities gives the two types of evaluation measures presented as follows [23]:

-Accuracy statistical measures assess a filter recommender system's accuracy by comparing predicted ratings to actual user ratings. RSME, MAE, and Correlation are the most commonly used measures.

-Decision support accuracy measurements enable users to choose extremely high-quality products from a selection of available items. The Precision-Recall curve, Receiver Operating Characteristics (ROC), Recall, Precision and F-measure are the most commonly utilized measures.

In this article, the RMSE and the MAE are two metrics applied to calculate the accuracy of recommendations. RMSE and MAE. In RS, the MAE is frequently used to calculate the average of all absolute value deviations between the actual and predicted ratings. The following formula is used to calculate the MAE [24]:

$$MAE = \frac{1}{N} \sum_{j=1}^{n} |rj - pj| \tag{3}$$

The RMSE is employed for evaluating multiple RS by calculating the average of all absolute value deviations between the predicted and true ratings. The following equation can be used to calculate the RMSE [24]:

$$RMSE = \sqrt{\frac{1}{N} \sum_{j=1}^{n} (rj - pj)^2} \tag{4}$$

where N, rj and pj determined respectively; the number of ratings, the actual ratings and the prediction ratings.

4.3 Comparison Methodology

The procedure adopted in this study is described in Fig. 2. to analyze the effectiveness of the recommender methods. In Step 1, we chose the MovieLens 100 K as dataset. In Step 2, we split the dataset into 60% training and 40% testing, as well as 70:30 and 80:20 ratios. Three recommendation models, SVD, SVD++, and NMF, were implemented in Step 3 using the Surprise library [25], which includes an integrated implementation of the various recommender system algorithms. Ultimately, in step 4, we used the RMSE and MAE measures to evaluate the recommendation models.

5 Performance Comparison

The implemented RS uses the collaborative filtering technique to predict the user's evaluation based on previous evaluations. To achieve this, we chose 20% for the test and 80% for the training. In addition, we took into account the ratios 70:30 and 60:40. We applied the system to the recommendation methods listed in Sect. 3, and evaluated these algorithms using the "MAE" and "RMSE" values mentioned above. Tables 1, 2 and 3 indicate respectively the performance of recommendation models based on RMSE and MAE.

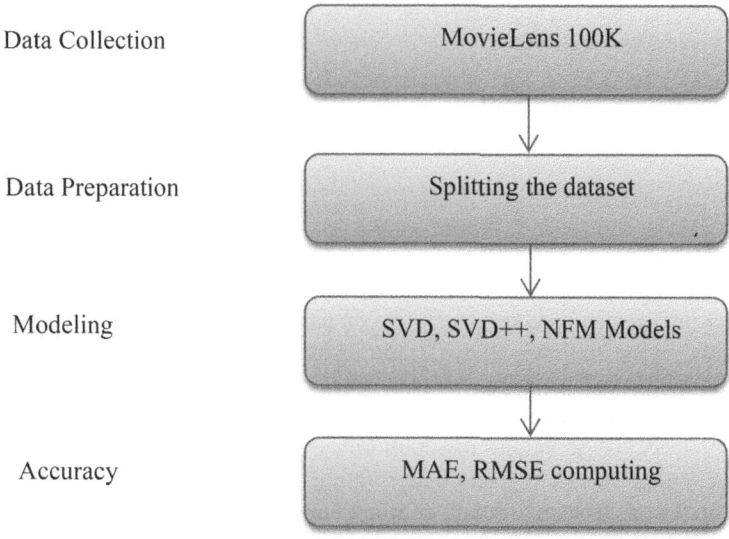

Data Collection	MovieLens 100K
Data Preparation	Splitting the dataset
Modeling	SVD, SVD++, NFM Models
Accuracy	MAE, RMSE computing

Fig. 2. Architecture for analysing the recommendation techniques.

Table 1. Performance evaluation of recommendation models based on the MAE and RMSE for training-testing situations at 60:40

Model	MAE	RMSE
SVD	0.751692	0.950068
SVD++	0.734238	0.932059
NMF	0.776211	0.985900

Table 2. Performance evaluation of recommendation models based on the MAE and RMSE for training-testing situations at 70:30

Model	MAE	RMSE
SVD	0.748444	0.949942
SVD++	0.719678	0.918192
NMF	0.765876	0.974204

6   Discussion

The results provided by the Tables 1, 2 and 3 indicate that SVD++ consistently outperforms the other models (SVD and NMF) across all scenarios (60:40, 70:30, and 80:20), demonstrating the lowest MAE and RMSE values. The NMF model is unable to produce better recommendations than the SVD and SVD++ models in these cases. SVD

Table 3. Performance evaluation of recommendation models based on the MAE and RMSE for training-testing situations at 80:20

Model	MAE	RMSE
SVD	0.734233	0.930018
SVD++	0.724326	0.924490
NMF	0.757620	0.964619

can deliver intermediate recommendation compared to NMF and SVD++ algorithms. Interestingly, as the "training-testing" ratio increases (60:40, 70:30, 80:20), the MAE and RMSE values tend to decrease for all three methods. This is expected, as having more data for training usually leads to better predictive performance. However, even with varying ratios, SVD++ maintains its superiority, emphasizing its effectiveness in recommendation systems across different data splitting scenarios. These findings underscore the significance of appropriate data splitting strategies and highlight that employing SVD++ for collaborative filtering to predict movie evaluations appears to be efficient.

SVD++ tries to combine the "neighborhood" and "latent factor techniques". The Neighborhood approach is used to calculate the relationships that may exist between items and users, while at the same time evaluating a user's preference for a given item based on the same user's evaluation of similar items. The latent factor approach converts items and users into the same latent factor space, and makes them comparable. Additionally, SVD++ makes use of both explicit feedback, which includes user input about their interests in items or products, and implicit feedback, which comprises indirect opinions by observing user behavior.

7 Conclusion

In this paper, we have compared three different MF algorithms namely "SVD", "SVD++" and "NMF" on MovieLens 100 K. The principal objective of the developed recommendation system is to predict the ratings of each user's movies. This experience was assessed using two accuracy evaluation measures: RMSE and MAE in 60:40, 70:30 and 80:20 training–testing situation.

The SVD++ model has demonstrated it effectiveness by obtaining the lowest MAE and RMSE values.

Future directions for our study include employing alternative MF approaches, like hybrid MF that integrates two techniques content filtering and collaborative filtering to produce more pertinent and precise recommendations. Furthermore, deeplearning MF might be studied to get predictions that are more accurate.

References

1. Naghiaei, M., Rahmani, H.A., Deldjoo, Y.: Cpfair: Personalized consumer and producer fairness re-ranking for recommender systems. In: Proceedings of the 45th International ACM SIGIR Conference on Research and Development in Information Retrieval, p. 770–779 (2022)

2. Pawlicka, M.P., Kozik, R., Choraś, R.S.: A systematic review of recommender systems and their applications in cybersecurity. Sensors **21**(15), 5248 (2021)
3. Mahyari, P.P., LeBlanc, J.A.: Real-Time Learning from an Expert in Deep Recommendation Systems with Application to mHealth for Physical Exercises. IEEE J. Biomed. Health Inform. **26**(8), 4281–4290 (2022)
4. Sen, P.C., Hajra, M., Ghosh, M.: Supervised classification algorithms in machine learning: A survey and review. In: Emerging Technology in Modelling and Graphics: Proceedings of IEM Graph 2018, pp. 99–111. Springer (2020)
5. Mehta, R., Rana, K.: A review on matrix factorization techniques in recommender systems. In: 2017 2nd International Conference on Communication Systems, Computing and IT Applications (CSCITA), pp. 269–274. IEEE (2017)
6. Casillo, M., et al.: Context-aware recommender systems and cultural heritage: a survey. J. Ambient Intell. Humaniz. Comput. **14**(4), 3109–3127 (2023)
7. Borges, R., Stefanidis, K.: On measuring popularity bias in collaborative filtering data (2020)
8. Duan, R., Jiang, C., Jain, H.K.: Combining review-based collaborative filtering and matrix factorization: A solution to rating's sparsity problem. Decis. Support Syst. **156**, 113748 (2022)
9. Pujahari, D.S., Sisodia: Pair-wise Preference Relation based Probabilistic Matrix Factorization for Collaborative Filtering in Recommender System. Knowl.-Based Syst. **196**, 105798 (2020)
10. Mhammedi, S., El Massari, H., Gherabi, N., Amnai, et M.: CF Recommender System Based on Ontology and Nonnegative Matrix Factorization (NMF). In: Farhaoui, Y., Rocha, A., Brahmia, Z., Bhushab, B. (éds.) Artificial Intelligence and Smart Environment, in Lecture Notes in Networks and Systems, vol. 635, pp. 313–318. Springer International Publishing, Cham (2023)
11. Nurrahmi, H., Wibowo, A.T., Meliana, S.: Non-Negative Matrix Factorization Based Recommender System using Female Daily Implicit Feedback. Indones. J. Comput. Indo-JC **7**(1), 1–14 (2022)
12. Christina, Z.K., Baizal, A.: Book Recommender System Using Singular Value Decomposition Combined with Slope One Algorithm. In: 2022 10th International Conference on Information and Communication Technology (ICoICT), pp. 346–350 (2022)
13. Andika, H.G., Hadinata, M.T., Huang, W., Anderies, I., Iswanto, A.: Systematic Literature Review: Comparison on Collaborative Filtering Algorithms for Recommendation Systems. In: 2022 IEEE International Conference on Communication, Networks and Satellite (COMNETSAT), pp. 56–61 (2022)
14. Al-Ghamdi, M., Elazhary, H., Mojahed, A.: Evaluation of Collaborative Filtering for Recommender Systems. Int. J. Adv. Comput. Sci. Appl. **12**(3) (2021)
15. Shi, W., Wang, L., Qin, J.: User embedding for rating prediction in SVD++-based collaborative filtering. Symmetry **12**(1), 121 (2020)
16. Massimo, D., Ricci, F.: Clustering Users' POIs Visit Trajectories for Next-POI Recommendation. In: Pesonen, J., Neidhardt, J. (éds.) Information and Communication Technologies in Tourism 2019, pp. 3–14. Springer International Publishing, Cham (2019)
17. Zhou, X., He, J., Huang, G., Zhang, Y.: SVD-based incremental approaches for recommender systems. J. Comput. Syst. Sci. **81**(4), 717–733 (2015)
18. Liu, Y., Zhong, X., Li, L., Yuan, J.: A novel algorithm for group recommendation based on combination of recessive characteristics. In: 2018 5th International Conference on Behavioral, Economic, and Socio-Cultural Computing (BESC), pp. 10–13. IEEE (2018)
19. Al Sabaawi, H.K., Yenice, Y.: Two models based on social relations and SVD++ method for recommendation system (2021)
20. Gan, J. , Liu, T., Li, L., Zhang, J.: Non-negative Matrix Factorization: A Survey. Comput. J. **64**(7), 1080–1092 (2021)

21. Athanasiadis, C., Hortal, E., Koutsoukos, D., Lens, C.Z., Asteriadis, S.: Personalized, affect and performance-driven computer-based learning. in CSEDU (1), 132–139 (2017)
22. Harper, F.M., Konstan, J.A.: The MovieLens Datasets: History and Context. ACM Trans. Interact. Intell. Syst. **5**(4), 1–19 (2016)
23. De Medio, C., Limongelli, C., Sciarrone, F., Temperini, M.: MoodleREC: A recommendation system for creating courses using the moodle e-learning platform. Comput. Hum. Behav. **104**, 106168 (2020)
24. Salam Patrous, Z., Najafi, S.: Evaluating prediction accuracy for collaborative filtering algorithms in recommender systems (2016)
25. Hug, N.: Surprise: a python library for recommender systems. J. Open Source Softw. **5**(52), 2174 (2020)

Artificial Intelligence Approaches for Smart Anomaly Detection in Solar Power Systems

Naima El Yanboiy[1,2,3](✉), Mohamed Khala[1,2,3], Ismail Elabbassi[1,2,3] (iD),
Nourddine Elhajrat[1,2,3], Omar Eloutassi[1,2,3] (iD), Youssef El Hassouani[1,2,3] (iD),
and Choukri Messaoudi[1,2,3]

[1] Optoelectronics and Applied Energy Techniques, Faculty of Science and Technology, Moulay
Ismail University of Meknes, Errachidia, Morocco
naima.elyanboiy@gmail.com, {mo.khala,
ism.elabbassi}@edu.umi.ac.ma
[2] Materials and Modelling Laboratory, Department of Physics, Faculty of Science, Moulay
Ismail University of Meknes, Meknes, Morocco
[3] New Energies and Materials Engineering, Faculty of Science and Technology, Ismail
University of Meknes, MoulayErrachidia, Morocco

Abstract. The renewable energy sector is becoming more important to cover the current demand of electricity. Solar energy is a promising source of renewable energy, especially in the last few years. However, like any other industrial processes, a photovoltaic (PV) system is susceptible to diverse defaults and anomalies that might occur during its operational functioning. The system's performance is affected by the interaction between the climate and material properties of photovoltaic panels, leading to a decrease in performance. Therefore, fault detection and identification in PV systems are essential tasks to achieve optimal operating performance. They provide operators with relevant informations about system operation. In this paper, smart detection algorithms of anomalies in solar plants are proposed based on Artificial intelligence techniques. We have proposed two approaches: The first one is based on Machine Learning (ML) methods for multi-class classification and the second one is based on Deep Learning (DL) methods for anomaly detection in the dataset. By comparing the performance of various anomaly detection models in two solar power plants, the experimental results showed that the AE-LSTM method outperforms XGBOOST in detecting anomalies in data. Concerning the machine learning methods KNeighborsClassifier, Support Vector Classifier (SVC) and ExtraTreesClassifier are more efficient, they achieve an accuracy more than 97% compared to the AdaBoostClassifier method which provides a low accuracy less than 47%.

Keywords: Fault Detection · Machine learning · Deep Learning · Solar Power System · LSTM · Autoencoder

1 Introduction

In recent years, solar energy is emerging as a particularly promising renewable energy alternative to meet escalating global energy demand and simultaneously reduce greenhouse gas emissions [1]. It is an alternative source to traditional fossil fuel production

H. Hagras et al. (Eds.): ISACS 2023, CCIS 2255, pp. 205–215, 2025.
https://doi.org/10.1007/978-3-031-93448-3_17

[2]. However, solar energy can be affected by several defects that can reduce the efficiency of solar energy production [3]. The main faults are shading, cracks, accumulation of dirt on the solar panels, unfavorable weather conditions, and accidents which reduces their efficiency. If these faults are not detected and repaired early, they can lead to a significant reduction in solar energy production and increased maintenance costs [4, 5]. This is the reason why detecting faults in solar panels is extremely important. Fault detection techniques can be depending on the nature of the fault and the particular type of solar panel under consideration, which include visual inspections, electrical testing, thermography, data analysis, and Artificial intelligence [6]. However, the above-mentioned defect detection techniques have certain limitations:

- The conventional method of visual inspection necessitates maintenance and operations personnel to individually examine solar cells using tools. This technique is both time-intensive and expensive, relying heavily on the subjective expertise of the inspector.
- Thermography can detect solar panel failures by measuring temperature changes, but it does not always provide accurate results due to environmental factors.
- Electrical testing does not always reveal the primary cause of the failure and it can be difficult to identify the precise location of the fault.
- Data analysis requires a large dataset to train the algorithm, and the accuracy of the results can be affected by the quality and quantity of the data collected. In addition, some defects might be unidentifiable by data analysis only, requiring additional inspection techniques.

AI methods can provide an efficient solution for early detection of defects in solar panels, They are able to analyze large amounts of data with high accuracy and optimal computation time. Several researches have been carried out on the detection of anomalies in PV systems. S.Hempelmannand et al. [7] utilized distinct state-of-the-art unsupervised methods for anomaly detection methods on photovoltaic monitoring data such as Locally Selective Combination of Parallel Outlier Ensembles(LSCP), Variational Autoencoder(VAE) and Multiple-Objective Generative Adversarial Active Learning (MOGAAL), which identified the most common faults. A. Mehmood et al. [8] proposed an algorithm that can effectively detect, classify, and locate line-to-ground (L-G) and line-to-line (L-L) faults in the PV array, irrespective of the degree of mismatch and the array's scale, the provided algorithm remains uncomplicated, precise, and not reliant on expensive hardware components. In [9], A Convolutional Neural Network (CNN) is employed to analyze the surface of the photovoltaic (PV) panel and identify any anomalies present. Transfer learning with AlexNet CNN is employed, resulting in a very promising performance for detecting various defects on the surface of solar panels. In [10] a methodology was introduced that relies on monitoring the rate of voltage variation and current trajectory in the transient phase following a fault occurrence. This algorithm demonstrates the capability to identify various fault scenarios, encompassing issues like cell-to-cell faults, string-to-string faults, and partial-to-complete shadow-related faults. M.,Ibrahim et al. [11] evaluated the efficacy of three distinct machine learning models in order to ascertain the model with the highest level of accuracy. For detecting anomalies in PV system by analyzing the correlation coefficients between the internal and external parameters of the installations, the AutoEncoder Long Short-Term

Memory (AE-LSTM) model was found to be effective in detecting anomalies and distinguishing healthy signals. Kim et al. [12] presents a novel approach to detect anomalies in PV systems by analyzing power generation data from renewable energy housing support project sites. Mellit et al. [13] present a method for detecting and classifying faults in PV arrays. The method is based on two machine learning approaches and successfully detected, classified a variety of faults, incorporating elements such as the accumulation of dust on the surface of PV modules, continuous shading, and the detachment of a PV module, and the presence of a short-circuited bypass diode in a PV module. The method achieved an accuracy of 98% for fault detection and 96% for classification, demonstrating its feasibility and effectiveness.

The literature review we conducted in this study allowed us to identify some challenges. Overall, effective use of AI for solar array anomaly detection requires careful consideration of such limitations. AI models can detect an anomaly when there is none, or false negatives (not detecting an anomaly that exists), which can reduce the effectiveness of anomaly detection systems. This issue can be caused either by the choice of the detection method or by the quality and quantity of the data collected. This study aims to compare the performance of various anomaly detection models in two solar power plants. Multi-class classification techniques are performed based on the various machine learning methods available, or by using anomaly detection techniques in a dataset using ML and DL methods like AE-LSTM and XGBOOS. Our research offers the following notable contributions:

- **Methodological insights:** Through a systematic comparison of various anomaly detection methods, we offer a comprehensive understanding of the advantages and constraints associated with each approach. This information assists professionals in choosing the optimal technique for the specific context of their solar power plant.
- **Improved anomaly detection:** The exploration of AE-LSTM and XGBoost introduces new approaches to anomaly detection, potentially more efficient than conventional methods. This extension of the detection system contributes to more accurate and reliable anomaly detection.
- **Performance evaluation:** Comprehensive evaluation of multi-class classification algorithms and advanced ML/DL techniques provides benchmarks for anomaly detection efficiency. This enables researchers and industry professionals to set reasonable performance targets for their systems.

The remainder of this paper is described as follows, Sect. 2 describes data pre-processing and analysis. Section 3 presents the proposed methods for detection anomalies and results. The last section concludes the paper.

2 Data Pre-Processing and Analysis

2.1 Data Description

In this study we trained and assessed the proposed models by utilizing a publicly available dataset sourced from github website [14]. This database is mainly composed by the electrical characteristics of the two solar panels which are current, voltage, and power, also it contains the data related to the weather such as temperature, irradiation and weather state, the Fig. 1 shows the correlation between the different dataset parameters. This dataset is mainly based on two types of faults which are line to line and open-circuit faults. The data was published, authorized, and made available according to [14].

	S1(Amp)	S2(Amp)	S1(Volt)	S2(Volt)	Light(kiloLux)	Temp(degC)	PUISSANCE
S1(Amp)	1.000000	0.184263	0.721077	-0.156457	0.648651	0.648658	0.783447
S2(Amp)	0.184263	1.000000	-0.153432	0.722047	0.581881	0.559998	0.744845
S1(Volt)	0.721077	-0.153432	1.000000	-0.292398	0.121130	0.229861	0.389163
S2(Volt)	-0.156457	0.722047	-0.292398	1.000000	0.145018	0.124232	0.330049
Light(kiloLux)	0.648651	0.581881	0.121130	0.145018	1.000000	0.844760	0.777043
Temp(degC)	0.648658	0.559998	0.229861	0.124232	0.844760	1.000000	0.798278
PUISSANCE	0.783447	0.744845	0.389163	0.330049	0.777043	0.798278	1.000000

Fig. 1. Correlation between the different dataset parameters.

2.2 Programming Language

Fault detection and classification models are implemented through the use of Python 3.7.13 in an online environment using Google Colab [15], and also, we implemented Scikit-Learn [16] and Keras [17] packages for the proposed models.

2.3 Performance Metrics

To assess the performance of the fault detection method using the machine learning algorithms, the frequently used confusion matrix (CM) technique was applied [18]. The set of metrics within the confusion matrix comprises four components: true positives (TP), true negatives (TN), false positives (FP), and false negatives (FN).From these metrics, several evaluation metrics can be derived, including the following [18]:

Precision: Represents the ratio of accurate positive predictions among all predictions marked as positive. This metric system measures the model's proficiency in accurately recognizing positive samples.

$$Precision = TP/(TP + FP) \tag{1}$$

Recall: Often referred to as sensitivity, is a metric that gauges a model's ability to identify all positive instances in the dataset. It quantifies the ratio of correctly predicted positive cases to the total actual positives. A higher recall score signifies the model's proficiency in sensitively detecting positive instances.

$$Recall = TP/(TP + FN) \tag{2}$$

F1-score: Is a significant classification metric, representing the harmonic mean of precision and recall. This single value encapsulates the balance achieved between precision's specificity and recall's sensitivity, offering a comprehensive assessment of a model's classification performance.

$$F1 - score = 2*(Precision * Recall)/(Precision + Recall) \qquad (3)$$

Accuracy: Is a crucial metric that gauges a model's performance by calculating the ratio of correct predictions to the total predictions. It offers a comprehensive overview of the model's ability to make accurate classifications.

$$Accuracy = (TP + TN)/(TP + TN + FP + FN) \qquad (4)$$

3 Proposed Methods for Detection Anomalies and Results

The problem of detecting faults in PV panels can be modeled as a multiclass classification problem, among the various ML methods available, or can be detected by using anomaly detection techniques in a dataset, among the various ML and DL approaches.

3.1 Machine Learning Classification Methods

A selection of diverse machine learning (ML) methods has been employed in this study to address the task of classifying and detecting faults within photovoltaic (PV) systems. The chosen ML models encompass a range of techniques, including Gaussian Naive Bayes (GaussianNB), K-Nearest Neighbors, Support Vector Classification (SVC), RandomForestClassifier, ExtraTreesClassifier, and AdaBoostClassifier. These models are harnessed to accurately categorize and identify specific PV faults, such as line-to-line (short-circuit) and open-circuit faults. Each model brings its unique strengths and intricacies to the classification task, contributing to a comprehensive analysis of PV system performance. The subsequent summarized overview provides a glimpse into the array of sophisticated ML models utilized in this work, underscoring the versatility and potential of these techniques in enhancing fault detection methodologies for PV systems.

Gaussian Naive Bayes: Is a probabilistic classification technique commonly used in classification tasks. It constructs a probability model from category descriptions for training dataset feature vectors. Despite making unrealistic assumptions, it remains effective, especially with limited data [19].

K-Nearest Neighbors: Classifies data points based on their proximity to others. It assigns class labels using the majority class of the k nearest neighbors in the feature space. This method works well for small datasets, offering versatility without assuming specific data distributions [20].

The Support Vector Classifier: Identifies an optimal hyperplane to separate classes and maximize the margin between them. It's suitable for various classification tasks, including non-linear ones, through kernel techniques. Proper parameter tuning is crucial for its effectiveness [21].

The Random Forest Classifier: Is an ensemble learning method that builds multiple decision trees using random data and feature sampling. These trees are then combined to make predictions, effectively handling linear and non-linear relationships. It's known for its robustness, versatility, and insights into feature importance [22].

The Extra Trees Classifier: Is a variant of the Random Forest algorithm that emphasizes randomness in decision-making. By constructing multiple decision trees through random subsampling, it increases diversity among trees and offers faster training times than standard Random Forest. It also provides insights into feature importance [23].

AdaBoost Classifier: Is a boosting ensemble algorithm widely used in classification. It trains weak learners iteratively and combines their predictions using weighted voting. This approach corrects mistakes in each iteration, resulting in a strong classifier with improved accuracy [24].

Table 1 shows the performance metrics of various defect detection methods using diverse machine learning algorithms.

Table 1. The performance Metrics of using diverse machine learning algorithms.

	Precision	Recall	F1-Score	Accuracy
KNeighborsClassifier	0.99	1	1	**0.98**
Support Vector Classifier	0.97	1	0.98	**0.99**
GaussianNB	0.73	0.93	0.82	0.87
RandomForestClassifier	0.73	0.93	0.82	0.87
ExtraTreesClassifier	0.96	1	0.98	**0.99**
AdaBoostClassifier	0.47	1	0.64	0.64

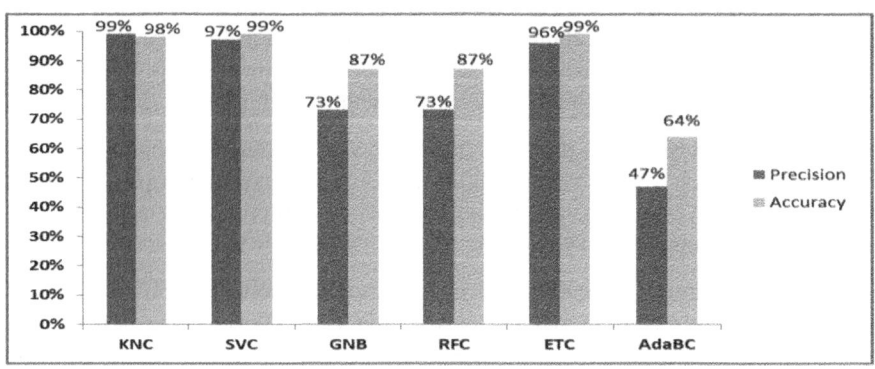

Fig. 2. Precision and Accuracy of diverse machine learning algorithms.

The experimental results showed the reliability of the developed methods to detect and classify common faults occurring in photovoltaic arrays. The results demonstrates that the KNeighborsClassifier(KNC), ExtraTreesClassifier(ETC) and,Support Vector Classifier(SVC) methods can classify and detect the defects with an high accuracy which achieved 99%, 97%, and 96% respectively, in comparison with GaussianNB(GNB) and RandomForestClassifier(RFC) which is only limited to 77%. Nevertheless, the AdaBoostClassifier(AdaBC) method shows the lower precesion achieved 47% as showed in Fig. 2.

3.2 Data Anomalies Detection Using ML and DL Methods

Data anomalies detection using machine learning and deep learning methods has emerged as a powerful and indispensable technique for identifying and handling irregularities in large datasets. These algorithms can be trained to recognize patterns and regularities within data, enabling them to differentiate between normal and anomalous observations. They show promising results in detecting anomalies in data sets [25].

XGBoost Is widely used in machine learning for anomaly detection tasks. Its exceptional accuracy and scalability make it a popular choice for detecting anomalies in large and complex datasets [26]. Moreover, XGBoost is a powerful tool for detecting anomalies in a wide range of applications, from fraud detection to predictive maintenance. By applying the GridSearch method, we improved the parameters of this algorithm, resulting in the optimal values shown in Table 2. The results of anomaly detection using the improved XGBoost method are presented in Fig. 3.

Table 2. The best parameters for the XGBOOST algorithm.

n_estimators	Max_depth	Learning_rate	Colsample_bytree
10000	7	0.1	0.8

AutoEncoder Long Short-Term Memory (AE_LSTM) approach: An autoencoder functions as an unsupervised neural network, aiming to proficiently learn the optimal encoding-decoding process from the provided data. The structure generally consists of essential components like an input layer, an output layer, an encoder neural network, a decoder neural network, and a latent space. When data is fed into the system, the encoder condenses it into the latent space, followed by the decoder's task of reconstructing this condensed representation back to the output layer. Various categories of autoencoders have been introduced in the literature, including classical, convolutional, regularized, and LSTM autoencoders. The architecture of an LSTM_AE is a powerful framework that combines the strengths of LSTM networks and Autoencoders, it consists of two main elements: the Encoder and the Decoder as shown in Fig. 4 [27]. LSTMs' proficiency in identifying patterns in extensive data sequences makes them apt for tasks like time series prediction and anomaly detection, capturing temporal dependencies in intricate datasets Table 3. Shows the Hyper-parameters of the proposed AE-LSTM algorithm. This approach suggested in this work to improve the performance of detecting anomalies Figure 5. Illustrates the results of the LSTM_AE algorithm in detecting anomalies.

XGBOOST

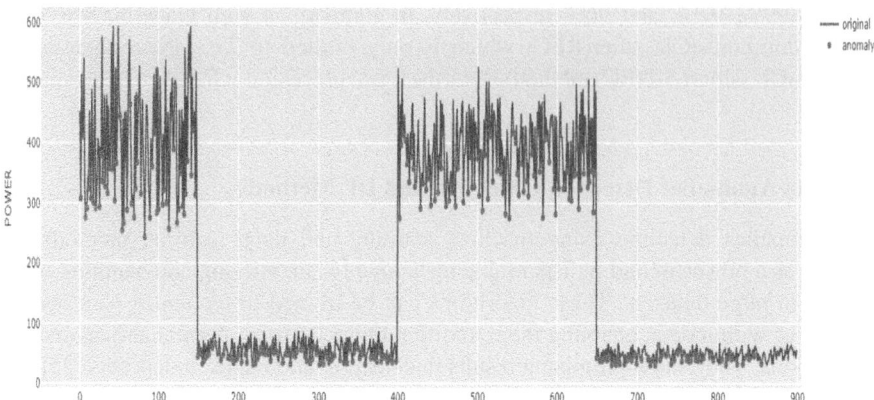

Fig. 3. Result of the anomalies detection using XGBoost method.

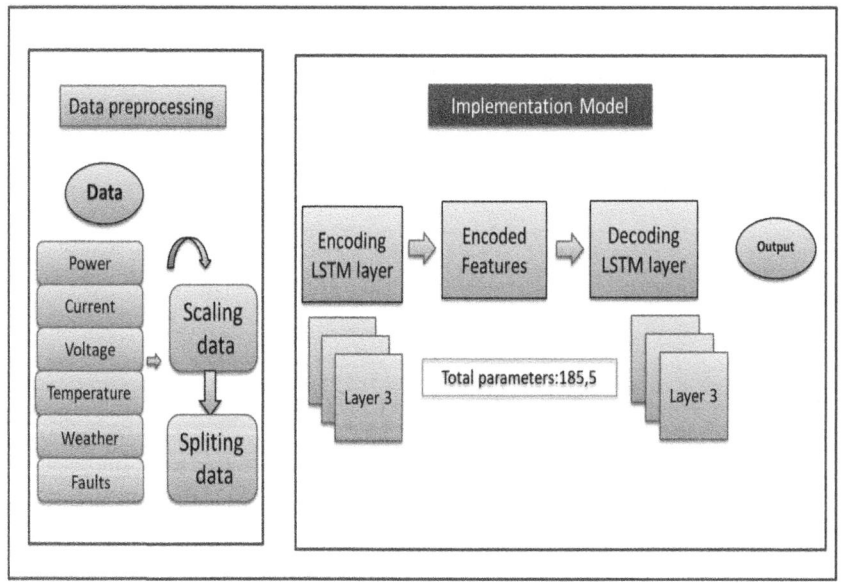

Fig. 4. Architecture of LSTM_AE approach.

The achieved results show that LSTM_AE method is able to detect more anomalies compared to XGBOOST method. The **XGBoost** algorithm typicaly identify only the minimum outliers. However, the LSTM_AE algorithm is able to detect the majority of the identified anomalies were situated in the higher and lower peaks as shown in Fig. 5. In comparing the methods applied in this work, it is noted that the classification methods for the detection of anomalies in a PV system is more efficient since it gives significantly

Table 3. Hyper-parameters of the proposed AE-LSTM algorithm.

Number of encoder layers	Number of decoder layers	Activation function	Optimizer	Learning rate	Batch size
3	3	ReLU	Adam	0,001	32

AE-LSTM

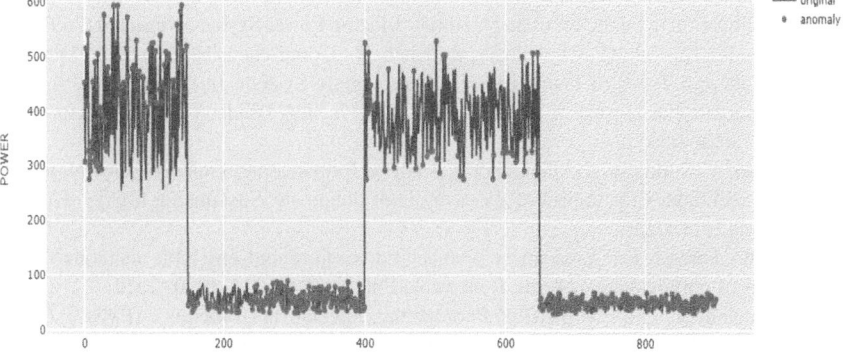

Fig. 5. Result of the anomalies detection using LSTM_AE algorithm.

better results. Nevertheless, this method requires a more detailed preparation of the data, compared to the anomaly detection methods in the data, which are used to extract outliers in the dataset. Overall, ML and DL-based anomaly detection techniques have significant potential in photovoltaic fault detection and monitoring, leading to increased energy efficiency, and enhanced safety in the renewable energy sector.

4   Conclusion

Anomaly detection in a solar system can lead to significant benefits such as minimizing downtime and optimizing equipment efficiency. As a conclusion, the demand for using more intelligent methods of faults detection and diagnosis has increased. These methods can be used instead of conventional approaches to improve the operational efficiency and safety of PV systems. In order to select the most effective Artificial Intelligence algorithm for this task, set of Machine Learning methods such as Isolation Forest, XGBOOST and other Deep Learning methods such as LSTM_AE are used to detect faults in this work. The results indicate that the AE-LSTM method outperforms XGBOOST in detecting anomalies in data. Concerning the Machine Learning methods KNeighborsClassifier, Support Vector Classifier and ExtraTreesClassifier are more efficients, they give an accuracy more than 97% compared to the AdaBoostClassifier method which gives a low accuracy less than 47%. As a perspective, it is recommended to work on other defects related to the photovoltaic field structure. Also introduce methods based on real-time image processing to allow preventive maintenance and minimize system downtime.

References

1. Ehsanul, K., Pawan, K., Sandeep, K., Adedeji A., Ki-Hyun, K.: Solar energy: Potential and future prospects. Renewable and Sustainable Energy (82), 894–900 (2018)
2. Raul A.B.: Fossil fuels, alternative energy and economic growth. Economic Modelling (75), 196–220 (2018)
3. Abbasi, A.R.: Fault detection and diagnosis in power transformers: a comprehensive review and classification of publications and methods. Electric Power Systems Research (209) (2020)
4. Prasanna, R., Karthik, C., Chowdhury, S., Khan, B.: Comprehensive Review on Modelling, Estimation, and Types of Faults in Solar Photovoltaic System. In: Thomas, K., Justin, R. (eds.) International Journal of Photoenergy 3053317. SCA Hindawi (2022). https://doi.org/10.1155/2022/3053317
5. Dhritiman, A., Soumesh, C., Chakraborty, A.K.: Performance assessment of selective machine learning techniques for improved PV array fault diagnosis. Sustainable Energy, Grids and Networks (29) (2022)
6. Mellit, A., Soteris, K.: Assessment of machine learning and ensemble methods for fault diagnosis of photovoltaic systems. Renewable Energy **184**, 1074–1090 (2020)
7. Hempelmann, S., et al.: 47th IEEE Photovoltaic Specialists Conference (PVSC). Calgary, AB, Canada **2020**, 2671–2674 (2020). https://doi.org/10.1109/PVSC45281.2020.9300481
8. Mehmood, A., Sher, H.A., Murtaza, A.F., Al-Haddad, K.: Fault Detection, Classification and Localization Algorithm for Photovoltaic Array. In: IEEE Transactions on Energy Conversion, vol. 36, no. 4, pp. 2945–2955 (2021). https://doi.org/10.1109/TEC.2021.3062049
9. Zyout, I., Oatawneh A.: Detection of PV Solar Panel Surface Defects using Transfer Learning of the Deep Convolutional Neural Networks. In: 2020 Advances in Science and Engineering Technology International Conferences (ASET), pp. 1–4. Dubai, United Arab Emirates (2020). https://doi.org/10.1109/ASET48392.2020.9118382
10. Hossam, A.E.,Elgebaly, A., Taha, I.: A New Monitoring Technique for Fault Detection and Classification in PV Systems Based on Rate of Change of Voltage-Current Trajectory. Int. J. Electr. Power & Energy Sys. (133) (2021)
11. Ibrahim, M., Alsheikh, A., Awaysheh, F.M., Alshehri, M.D.: Machine Learning Schemes for Anomaly Detection in Solar Power Plants. Energies (15), 1082 (2022)
12. Kim, D., Kim, S.M., Suh, J., Choi, Y.: Anomaly detection of photovoltaic systems installed in renewable energy housing support project sites by analyzing power generation data. Journal of the Korean Solar Energy Society **42**(1), 33–46 (2022)
13. Mellit, A., Herrak, O., Rus Casas, C., Massi Pavan, A.: A machine learning and internet of things-based online fault diagnosis method for photovoltaic arrays. Sustainability (13), 13203 (2021)
14. PV_fault_Python. https://github.com/benjamin2044/PV_fault_Python. Last accessed 27 Mars 2023
15. Welcome To Colaboratory. https://colab.research.google.com/. Last accessed 27 Mars 2023
16. Scikit-Learn. https://scikit-learn.org/stable//. Last accessed 27 Mars 2023
17. Keras. https://keras.io/. Last accessed 27 Mars 2023
18. Boubaker, S., Kamel, S., Ghazouani, N., Mellit, A.: Assessment of machine and deep learning approaches for fault diagnosis in photovoltaic systems using infrared thermography. Remote Sensor (15), 1686 (2023)

19. Tzanos, G., Kachris, C., Soudris, D.J.: Hardware Acceleration on Gaussian Naive Bayes Machine Learning Algorithm. 8th International Conference on Modern Circuits and Systems Technologies (MOCAST), pp. 1–5 (2019)
20. Elbaghdadi, A., Mezroui, S., El Oualkadi, A.: K-Nearest Neighbors Algorithm (KNN) (2021)
21. Nishat, M.M., et al.: An investigative approach to employ support vector classifier as a potential detector of brain cancer from MRI dataset. International Conference on Electronics, Communications and Information Technology (ICECIT), 1–4 (2021)
22. Roy, S.S., Dey, S., Chatterjee, S.: Autocorrelation Aided Random Forest Classifier-Based Bearing Fault Detection Framework. (Sensors Journal) **20**, 10792–10800 (2020)
23. Peng, L., Yuan, R., Shen, L., Gao, P., Zhou, L.: LPI-EnEDT: an ensemble framework with extra tree and decision tree classifiers for imbalanced lncRNA-protein interaction data classification. (BioData Mining) 14 (2021)
24. Gulati, K.: Comparative analysis of machine learning-based classification models using sentiment classification of tweets related to COVID-19 pandemic. (Materials Today: Proceedings) (2021)
25. Esmaeili, F., et al.: Anomaly Detection for Sensor Signals Utilizing Deep Learning Autoencoder-Based Neural Networks. Bioengineering (10), 405 (2023)
26. Park, M.-H., et al.: Anomaly detection based on time series data of hydraulic accumulator. Sensors (22), 9428 (2022)
27. Khala, M., Abouzid, H., Teidj, S., Eloutassi, O., Messaoudi, C.: LSTM deep learning method for radiation short and long-term prediction. In: Ben Ahmed, M., Boudhir, A.A., Santos, D., Dionisio, R., Benaya, N. (eds.) Innovations in Smart Cities Applications Volume 6. SCA 2022. Lecture Notes in Networks and Systems, vol 629. Springer, Cham (2023). https://doi.org/10.1007/978-3-031-26852-6_63

Raspberry Pi 4-Based Real-Time System for Solar Panels Soiling and Dust Detection Using Deep Learning and Computer Vision Approaches

Hajar Elkarch[1]($\boxtimes$), Rachid Elgouri[1] (ORCID), Mohamed Benally[2],
and Abdelkader Mezouari[2] (ORCID)

[1] Laboratory of Advanced Systems Engineering, National School of Applied Sciences,
Kenitra, Morocco
Hajar.elkarch@uit.ac.ma

[2] Faculty of Sciences, Lab of Electronic Systems, Information Processing, Mechanics and
Energetics Kenitra, Kenitra, Morocco

Abstract. Many studies have underscored the impact of depositions, soiling, and dust accumulation on the performance of photovoltaic (PV) systems, resulting in energy output reduction. Recent research studies have explored new techniques to detect soiling and dust on photovoltaic panels, integrating image processing, machine learning, and thermal imaging. This paper introduces a Real-time embedded system based on Neural Network Algorithms and image processing techniques to recognize soiling and dust depositions on PV panels. The system architecture integrates a Raspberry Pi 4 and an HD camera for PV panel image capture and acquisition. The proposed research outlines a comprehensive approach that combines Neural Network Algorithms (NNA), image processing techniques, and hardware platforms to build a high-performance, real-time embedded system for solar panels soiling and dust recognition and help to make intelligent maintenance decisions for optimal power production. According to the results, the proposed system achieves an accuracy of over 85%. The proposed framework offers a trade-off between speed and accuracy, making them suitable for Real-time processing applications compared to other object detection algorithms.

Keywords: Embedded system · Raspberry Pi4 · Deep Learning · CNN · Image processing · Yolov5 · PV panel inspection · Soiling detection

1 Introduction

Photovoltaic (PV) energy is one of the main options to serve the rising global energy needs with low negative effects on the environment [1]. The primary objective of research focused on photovoltaic (PV) systems is to enhance their performance, enabling them to generate increased electricity with elevated efficiency and in an ecological manner [2]. Several studies in the existing literature center on comparing electrical performance

H. Hagras et al. (Eds.): ISACS 2023, CCIS 2255, pp. 216–227, 2025.
https://doi.org/10.1007/978-3-031-93448-3_18

and the energy productivity of several PV modules within different environmental and operating conditions. One of the main considerations is the influence of dust and soiling accumulation on PV panels, an aspect explored through many studies.

Many research studies in this field have demonstrated that the deposition of dust particles on solar panels significantly declines their performance [3, 4]. The results of previous related research [5] concerning the electrical performance of photovoltaic (PV) panels indicate that the electrical performance of the panel with dust is reduced by an average of 39% compared to the reference PV panel. For the power output, it has been noticed that the PV panel with dust generates an average of 65% less energy than the clean PV panel. Another experimental work [4] about the effects of dust on azimuth tracking solar PV was conducted in the desert regions of Sharjah. This study demonstrated that the efficiency of solar energy technologies is reduced due to dust accumulation during daily exposure periods. Köntges et al. [6] indicate in a review of failures of photovoltaic modules that soiling negatively impacts power production and decreases the incident radiation transmittance through the cover glass of PV modules, reducing the quantity of solar radiation available to be converted into electricity. In recent years, different studies have employed novel techniques to identify faults in PV systems. In a literature review [7], a structured analysis was conducted to explore the application of Artificial Neural Networks (ANN) for the Fault Detection and Diagnosis (FDD) of photovoltaic systems. According to the existing literature overview, ANN has efficiently detected and diagnosed nearly all common PV faults, including electrical and permanent visible faults.

R. Cavieresa et al. [8] proposed one of the early contributions concerning the viability of novel methods for evaluating the condition of PV panels. It concerns a tool based on convolutional neural networks developed to estimate the power loss of PV modules in the field subject to soiling and partial shading. The proposed approach uses visible spectrum RGB images of multiple solar panels and environmental data to predict each module's performance individually. The algorithm can detect, segment, homogenize, and evaluate partial shading and soiling for each module displayed in the image. Another study [9] proposes a Denoising Convolutional Neural Networks DnCNN-based dust accumulation status evaluation of photovoltaic panels. The proposed approach in this paper is divided into three steps: preprocessing the images with DnCNN, stripping the noise background in the images, training different neural networks based on the processed images, and selecting the most appropriate model [9].

A recent paper [10] proposed a novel Cloud-Based IoT Solution to measure the Soiling Ratio of PV Systems. The approach involves utilizing Artificial Neural networks (ANN) and low-cost sensors to minimize hardware needs for a soiling station. The system adopts an Internet of Things (IoT) and cloud-based centralized architecture, enabling remote monitoring of soiling deposits on PV panels. The cloud server hosts the ANN model for detecting the soiling ratio and transmits the results to a graphical user interface. Image-processing techniques were utilized by W. Kean Yap1 et al. [11] and M. Unluturk et al. [12] to conduct quantitative analyses of dust and soiling on solar PV panels. Their approach involved employing an image-processing toolbox that incorporated techniques such as binarization, histogram modeling, statistical modeling, image matching, and texture matching. Both studies [11] and [12] performed simulations to evaluate diverse dust accumulations' influence. These studies highlighted the effective-ness of image matching and shallow neural networks using texture features extracted via a gray-level co-occurrence matrix. These techniques proved to be effective techniques for quantifying the degree of soiling on solar panel surfaces. In the PoChing Hwang et al. [13] study, image-processing techniques were employed to analyze Unmanned Aerial Vehicle (UAV) images to assess soiling rates on photovoltaic panels. However, integrating artificial intelligence and statistical algorithms to comprehensively evaluate the distribution of soiling across PV panel surfaces was deferred and identified as a potential area for future research work.

The paper is organized into the following sections: The first section presents an overview of previous research work on the effects of dust and soiling on PV panels. It also discusses the existing research related to the detection of soiling and dust in PV systems. The methodology section describes the novel PV status evaluation system based on the YOLOv5 algorithm for soiling recognition and image processing techniques for dust detection. The last section concerns the case study and the results analysis. Finally, the last section concludes this paper and mentions future work.

2   The Proposed System

In this paper, we propose a Real-time embedded system used for PV panel soiling and dust detection consisting of two main parts. The software is based on YOLOv5 Deep Learning Networks [14, 15, 27, 30], and image processing techniques using computer vision techniques [11, 12, 29]. The hardware setup for implementing the proposed algorithm in this work includes a Raspberry Pi4 as a processing unit and an HD camera device for PV panel image capturing. Figure 1 illustrates the proposed system architecture followed in this work for soiling and dust accumulation status evaluation on PV panels.

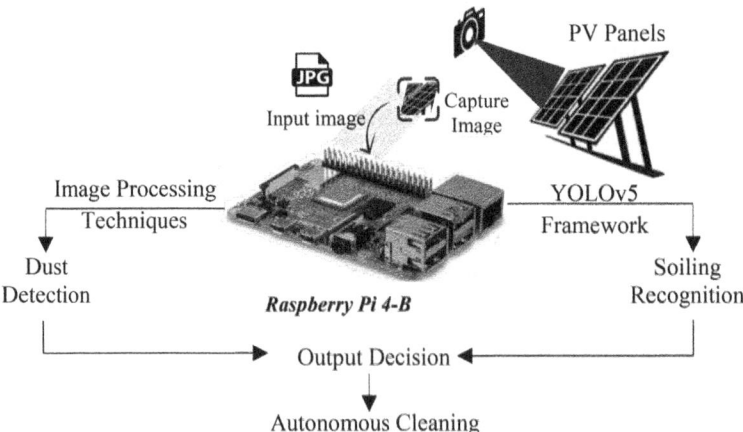

Fig. 1. The proposed system architecture for soiling and dust detection on solar panels

After image acquisition by the Raspberry Pi4. The YOLOv5 algorithm installed on the embedded device provided real-time soiling detection in each photovoltaic panel image by applying a Convolutional Neural Network (CNN) algorithm. Images processing techniques based on OpenCV were explored for dust layer detection.

The proposed system used YOLOv5 algorithms and image processing techniques to classify different types of soiling and quantify the dust coverage on the PV panel surface. The YOLOv5 algorithm was trained to classify different types of soiling commonly found on PV panels.

2.1 YOLO Algorithm Framework

YOLO Algorithm is a Real-time object detection based on YOLOv1 [20], YOLOv2 [21], YOLOv3 [22], and YOLOv4 [23] models [24]. Figure 3 illustrates the main idea of the YOLO network, which consists of segmenting the input image into an S × S grid. Each square is responsible for detecting and classifying the objects in that region. Each grid cell predicts B bounding boxes, and their confidence scores designate how confidence the bounding box contains an object, represented by $p(Objet)$ and how accurate the model addresses the spatial position of an object, represented by $IO \cup_{Pred}^{Truth}$ [25] (Fig. 2).

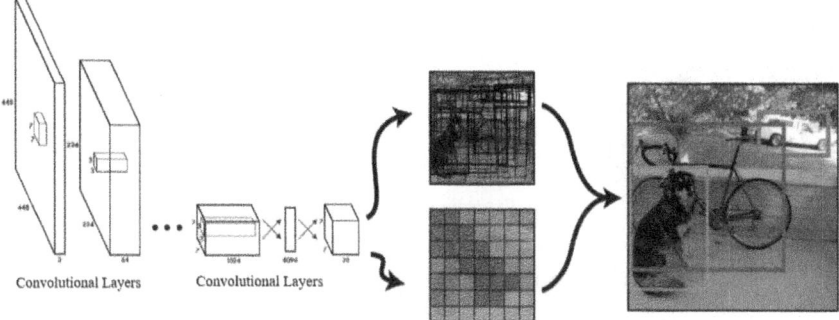

Fig. 2. The main Network architecture of the YOLO algorithm [25]

This confidence score indicates whether an object is present within the confines of the bounding box. The confidence score is expressed as follows:

$$Confidence\ score = p(Objet) * IO \cup_{Pred}^{Truth} \tag{1}$$

The $IO\cup_{Pred}^{Truth}$ signifies the IOU (Intersection of Union) between the predicted bounding boxes b_{pred} and the ground truth b_{truth}. This $IO \cup_{Pred}^{Truth}$ is mathematically defined as:

$$IO \cup_{Pred}^{Truth} = \frac{\cap(b_{pred}, b_{truth})}{\cup(b_{pred}, b_{truth})} \tag{2}$$

2.2 YOLOv5 Algorithm for Soiling Recognition

The YOLOv5 algorithm was proposed by Glenn Jocher [26] one month after the YOLOv4 [27]. YOLOv5 features four networks with different widths and depths. As the model size increases, its processing speed decreases, but its accuracy improves. The mean Average Precision (mAP) and inference speed on the COCO dataset demonstrate that YOLOv5 performs well, striking a balance between speed and accuracy [28].

This section describes the YOLOv5 network architecture [29] used in this study to identify and detect soiling. The Neural Network Algorithm (NNA) comprises three main parts that enable the detection process, as illustrated in Fig. 3. The initial step of the algorithm involves dividing the input image into an S × S grid. In the extraction and classification stage, each individual grid section of the grid is classified and localized. In the second step, classification-based algorithms are achieved through a two-step approach. The first step involves the identification of Regions of Interest, followed by applying a Convolutional Neural Network to the selected regions. In the final step, YOLO's regression algorithm predicts bounding boxes for the entire image in a single pass. The Non-Maximum Suppression (NMS) algorithm selects the bounding box with the highest class score. All the other bounding boxes having IOU greater than a predefined threshold will be discarded [30].

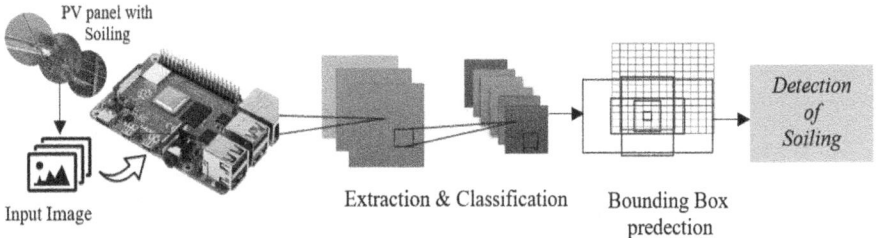

Fig. 3. The proposed YOLOv5 pipeline for soiling detection

Applying the YOLOv5-based object detection framework for dust layer detection on various surfaces led to unsatisfactory results due to the heterogeneous distribution of dust compared to the OpenCV-based image processing techniques. The YOLOv5 algorithm is optimized for object detection tasks, assuming a relatively uniform distribution of objects within the image. We achieved satisfactory results using appropriate image processing techniques by segmenting the regions of interest and isolating dust particles from the input image background.

2.3 Image Processing-Based Dust Detection

The second section of this work describes the proposed image processing techniques based on the OpenCV library [31, 32] for dust extraction and detection. The block diagram (see Fig. 4) describes the main processing techniques involved in dust area detection using the OpenCV library. After image acquisition, a series of image processing techniques are involved in preprocessing: thresholding, binarization, edge detection, and morphological transformations to improve the image quality and get accurate dust layer extraction from the input image. In the first step, the RGB matrix of the input image was converted to HSV (Hue, Saturation, and Value) space. Then, to identify the pixels within a desired range of values (pixels with dust) from the obtained HSV image, the cv2.inrange () function was used to perform basic thresholding in the second step. This function takes three parameters to extract the dust layer we are interested in. The Gaussian blur function removed a false detection along the image border. Gaussian filtering has been intensively studied in image processing and computer vision to reduce noise and preserve edges [33]. Finally, the canny edge detection method based on OpenCV was used for dust edge detection. First, erosion followed by dilatation was performed to preserve the shape and size of the dust area in the image [34]. To calculate the percentage of the dust-covered regions, the process involves converting the dust detection result (likely in the form of a binary image) into a percentage by counting the non-zero (dust-covered) pixels and dividing that count by the total number of pixels in the image. This helps quantify the extent to which dust covers the image. The covered dust area corresponds to the number of non-zero pixels in the binary image (2). Total pixels (3) is the number of white pixels (whose value is 255) and black pixels (whose value is 0) inside the binary image.

$$Dust\ percentage(\%) = NonZero_{pixels}/Total_{pixels} \qquad (3)$$

$$Total_{pixels} = Height * Width \qquad (4)$$

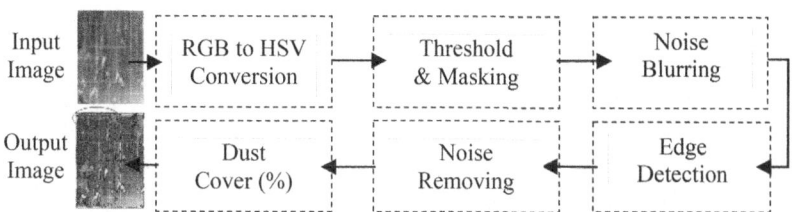

Fig. 4. The Block diagram of image processing techniques applied to the dusty panel

2.4 Experiment Field

The test facility included a stand-alone photovoltaic (PV) system consisting of four panels of poly-crystalline silicon (SolarWord SW-255 Poly). The configuration of the PV system used for the tests is shown in Fig. 5. This PV system is used as an auxiliary source of electricity and is located on the roof of the physics department building of the faculty of science at Ibn Tofail University.

The PV panels are being used to capture images under various conditions and levels of soiling for data collection to train our model. The data collection process involves taking images of the PV panels at different times and under different environmental conditions to create a diverse and representative dataset. This dataset was used to train our model to recognize and quantify the level of soiling on the panels.

Fig. 5. Field experiment of PV panel images for soiling and dust accumulation detection

2.5 YOLOv5 Training Dataset

For the training of our model, we assembled and manually annotated a database containing over 10000 images of size (1088 × 1920) pixels captured using a high-resolution camera. It covers a diverse range of more than ten distinct soiling types, effectively providing a rich dataset for our training model. We allocated 80% of the dataset for training the model and reserved the remaining 20% for test validation purposes. Indeed, using 80% of the dataset for training is common in machine learning. This allocation balances providing sufficient data to train our model effectively and reserving a substantial portion for testing and validation. By allocating 80% for training, we ensure that our model has ample exposure to the data's patterns, while the remaining 20% set aside for testing and validation serves as a robust measure of the model's performance on unseen data. We annotated the database using the image-labeling tool for object detection to create a dataset for the training model.

The data annotation step consists of labeling individual elements of training images. The obtained YOLO format files for the training model and image training with labeling are uploaded to the Google Drive Platform. Three distinct types of soiling were annotated to validate the YOLOv5 algorithm. These examples include tree-dropping leaves, tree branches, and bird droppings, one of the most aggressive types of soiling as it can burn into the glass surface and give rise to hotspots under high-intensity sunlight [35].

For our training dataset, we used Google Colab, a free Integrated Development Environment (IDE) for machine learning and deep learning tasks. Google Colab provides access to powerful hardware resources like Graphic Processing Units (GPUs) and Tensor Processing Units (TPUs) to accelerate computational tasks.

3 Results and Discussion

3.1 Processing System

The proposed method was implemented using Python 3.10 on a Raspberry Pi 4 platform with a quad-core Cortex-A72 (ARM v8) 64-bit SoC operating at 1.5 GHz and 8 GB of RAM. The Raspberry Pi 4 has sufficient computational power and memory to handle these algorithms, although the performance may vary depending on the complexity of the algorithms and the size of the images being processed.

The Raspberry Pi 4 shows high-energy consumption and a very long average processing time, two critical parameters to building a High-performance power system.

To identify a promising platform with high performance for embedded machine-learning systems. The comparison of Raspberry Pi4 to similar platforms like Jetson Nano, FPGA (Field-Programmable Gate Array), and VPU (Vision Processing Unit) will help to evaluate the advantages and limitations of each platform, and you can make an optimal decision on which platform will be the best suits for our embedded machine learning requirements (Table 1).

Table 1. Results and technical specifications of processing systems.

Processing Systems	Raspberry Pi 4
Processing System Features	Quad-core Cortex-A72 (ARM v8) 64-bit 1.5 GHz and 8 GB RAM
Energy Consumption	2,89−7,28 W
Average Processing Time for one frame	6.42 ms
Price	330$
FPS	32

3.2 YOLOv5 Performance Results

Three types of soiling were used to evaluate the proposed method results for soiling detection using a YOLOv5 detector. We conducted a manual simulation of soiling by introducing three distinct types of soiling onto the photovoltaic panel. Figure 6 displays the results of the soiling detection process, executed using the YOLOv5 algorithm. These images display the soiling detection on three types of soiling. Distinct colored Bounding Boxes surround every identified instance of soiling on the photovoltaic (PV) panel.

The results demonstrated that the YOLOv5 algorithm effectively identified each type of soiling on the input photovoltaic panel images. The accuracy of the YOLO algorithm for soiling detection was impressive, achieving a global rate of 85%. This means that in 85% of the cases studied, the algorithm correctly identified soiling on the photovoltaic panels.

Our study highlights the effectiveness of the YOLOv5-based approaches algorithm for efficient inspection and detection of soiling on photovoltaic panels. Compared to traditional detection methods, YOLO exhibited better accuracy and faster detection times. Applying the YOLOv5-based object detection framework for dust layer detection on various surfaces led to unsatisfactory results due to the heterogeneous distribution of dust. In this work, we used image-processing techniques to identify dust distributions and isolate the regions containing dust particles.

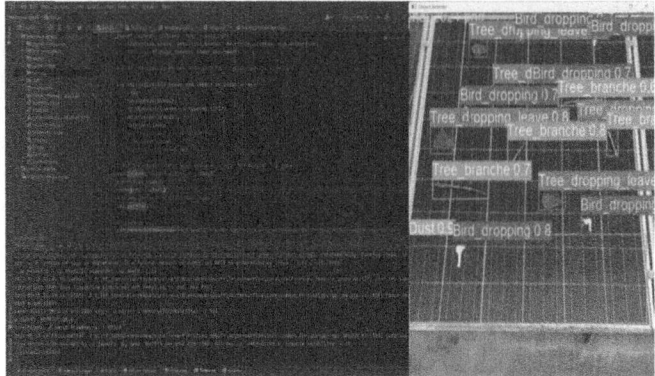

Fig. 6. Examples of the YOLOv5 algorithm detection results.

3.3 Image Processing-Based Dust Detection

The results of the proposed system achieved a successful detection of dust particles and obtained data about the state of the associated PV panel imagery. Figure 7 displays the results of a series of image processing techniques, using OpenCV, applied to a PV panel covered artificially with dust.

The visual results stemming from the dust detection process on these PV panel images are successful. By referring to Eqs. (4) and (5) mentioned above, the outcome of the percentage calculation is depicted in Fig. 8. The findings distinctly indicate that approximately more than 24% of the PV panel surface is covered by dust particles, thereby leading to a consequential loss in energy yield.

Panel efficiency and yield reduction can be estimated from the calculated percentage of the panel area covered by dust. As shown in Fig. 8, Dust coverage on more than 20% of three panels adversely affects their electrical performance, resulting in a significant decrease in voltage and current output compared to clean panels.

(a) Input image	(b)HSV image	(c)Thresholded image	(d) Grayscale image	(e) Dust edge Detection image

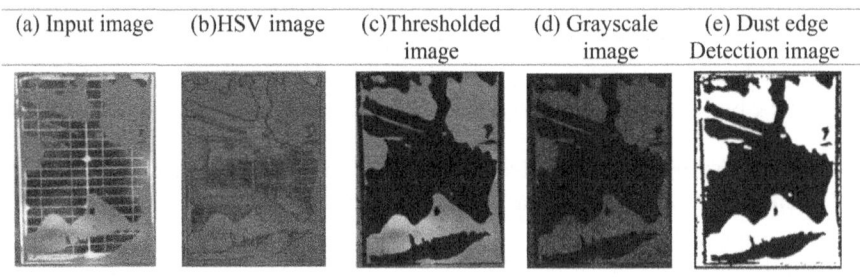

Fig. 7. Examples of dust image detection performed using OpenCV-Library

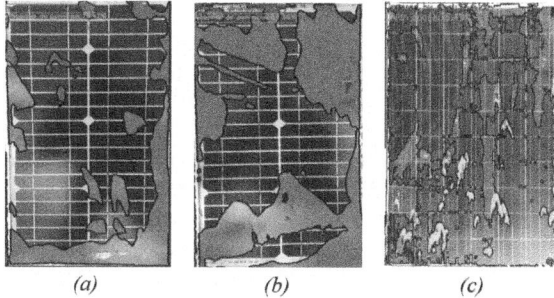

Fig. 8. The percentage calculation result of dust accumulation and dust cover % diagram using the matplotlib function of three PV panels using the OpenCV library.

The new proposed embedded system provides a quantification of dust on PV panels and facilitates rapid decision-making to perform intelligent maintenance. Based on the obtained results, we can make informed decisions and program a cleaning process according to the specific types of detected soiling. Future work will focus on exploring the implementation of the proposed system for autonomous photovoltaic cleaning robots. The robot employs various algorithms to analyze the type of soiling and extract relevant information, such as the severity of the soiling, the distribution of the soiling on the surface, and any other pertinent features to select and perform the suitable cleaning method.

4 Conclusion

Computer Vision and Deep Learning are establishing dominance across diverse application domains due to their higher accuracy advantages than traditional algorithms.

The proposed system in this paper provides a solution for the real-time inspection of photovoltaic panels, enabling the concurrent detection of dust and dirt. This is achieved by integrating two distinct methodologies. The suggested system boasts several benefits, including accelerated processing speeds, reduced resource demands, and enhanced suitability for diverse environmental conditions. We proposed a YOLOv5 framework to detect soiling on photovoltaic PV panels and perform operations on visible images and image processing techniques using the computer vision library OpenCV to extract the dust layer on the PV panel for the state PV panel evaluation. The results obtained in this work are favorable and can be used for further research to develop and conceive a robust Real-time system for photovoltaic module inspection. Furthermore, it can significantly improve the accuracy and efficiency of real-time PV panel inspection conditions. The YOLOv5 algorithm was tested on over 20 photovoltaic panels demonstrated and gave promising accuracy results with a global rate of 85% of soiling detection.

Raspberry Pi4 shows high energy consumption and a long average processing time. In future work, we will compare Raspberry Pi4 to similar systems, such as Jetson Nano, FPGA (Field-Programmable Gate Array), and VPU (Vision Processing Unit), to choose a promising platform with high performance for embedded Machine Learning and highlight their advantages and limitations.

References

1. Neherab, I., et al.: Impact of atmospheric aerosols on photovoltaic energy production scenario for the Sahel zone. Energy Procedia **125**, 170–179 (2017). https://doi.org/10.1016/j.egypro.2017.08.168
2. Jordan, D.C., Deline, C., Kurtz, S.R., Kimball, G.M., Anderson, M.: Robust PV degradation methodology and application. IEEE J. Photovoltaics **8**(2), 525–531 (2018). https://doi.org/10.1109/JPHOTOV.2017.2779779
3. Mohamed, A.M., et al.: Experimental study of the impact of dust on azimuth tracking solar PV in Sharjah. Int. J. Electr. Comput. Eng. **11**(5), 3671–3681 (2021). https://doi.org/10.1016/j.egypro.2017.09.010
4. Menoufia, K., Hamdy, F.M., Farghala, B., Ahmed, A.F., Khedrc, M.H.: Dust accumulation on photovoltaic panels: a case study at the East Bank of the Nile (Beni-Suef, Egypt). Energy Procedia **128**, 24–31 (2017). https://doi.org/10.1016/j.egypro.2017.09.010
5. Pulipaka, S., Kumar, R.: Analysis of soil distortion factor for photovoltaic modules using particle size composition. Sol. Energy **161**, 90–99 (2018). https://doi.org/10.1016/j.solener.2017.11.041
6. Köntges, M., Kurtz, S., Packard, C., Jahn, U.: Review of failures of photovoltaic modules. St. Ursen, Zwitzerland, IEA-PVPS (2014)
7. Li, B., Delpha, C., Diallo, D., Migan-Dubois, A.: Application of artificial neural networks to photovoltaic fault detection and diagnosis: a review. Renew. Sustain. Energy Rev. **138**, 170–179 (2021). https://doi.org/10.1016/j.rser.2020.110512
8. Cavieres, R., Barraza, R., Estay, D., Bilbao, J., Valdivia-Lefort, P.: Automatic soiling and partial shading assessment on PV modules through RGB images analysis. Appl. Energy **306**, 117964 (2022). https://doi.org/10.1016/j.apenergy.2021.117964
9. Yuanpeng, T., Kun, L., Xiaojing, B., Chunyu, D.: Denoising convolutional neural networks based dust accumulation status evaluation of photovoltaic panel. In: IEEE International Conference on Energy Internet (ICEI), Nanjing, China, pp. 560–566 (2019). https://doi.org/10.1109/ICEI.2019.00105
10. Ul Mehmood, M., Ulasyar, A., Ali, W., Zeb, K., Zad, H.S., Uddin, W., Kim, H.-J.: A new cloud-based IoT solution for soiling ratio measurement of PV systems using artificial neural network. Energies **16**(2), 996 (2023). https://doi.org/10.3390/en16020996
11. Yap, W.K., Galet, R., Yeo, K.C.: Quantitative analysis of dust and soiling on solar PV panels in the tropics utilizing image-processing methods. Solar Res. Conf. Asia-Pacific (2015)
12. Unluturk, M., Kulaksiz, A.A., Unluturk, A.: Image processing-based assessment of dust accumulation on photovoltaic modules. In: 2019 1st Global Power, Energy and Communication Conference (GPECOM), pp. 308–311 (2019)
13. PoChing Hwang, C., Ku, C.-Y., Chan, J.C.-C.: Soiling detection for photovoltaic modules based on an intelligent method with image processing. In: IEEE International Conference on Consumer Electronic-Taiwan (ICCE-Taiwan), pp. 1–2 (2020)
14. Shihavuddin, A.S.M., et al.: Image based surface damage detection of renewable energy installations using a unified deep learning approach. Energy Rep. **7**, .4566–4576 (2021). https://doi.org/10.1016/j.egyr.2021.07.045
15. Ruby Florence, J.A., Kirubasri, G.: Accident detection system using deep learning. In: Computational Intelligence in Data Science, pp. 301–310. Springer International Publishing, Cham (2022). https://doi.org/10.1007/978-3-031-16364-7_23
16. Girshick, R., Donahue, J., Darrel, T., Malik, J.: Rich feature hierarchies for accurate object detection and semantic segmentation, computer vision and pattern recognition. Columbus, pp. 580–587 (2014). https://doi.org/10.1109/CVPR.2014.81

17. He, K.M., Zhang, X.Y., Ren, S.Q., Sun, J.: Spatial pyramid pooling in deep convolutional networks for visual recognition. In: IEEE Transactions on Pattern Analysis and Machine Intelligence, pp. 1904–1916. Springer International Publishing, Cham (2014). https://doi.org/10.1007/978-3-319-10578-9_23

18. Ren, S.Q., He, K.M., Girshick, R., Sun, J., Faster R-CNN: Towards real-time object detection with region proposal networks. Advances in neural information processing systems. pp. 91–99, Montreal (2016). https://doi.org/10.48550/arXiv.1506.01497

19. Girshick, R.: Fast R-CNN. (2015). https://doi.org/10.48550/arXiv.1504.08083

20. Redmon, J., Divvala, S., Grishick, R., Farhadi, A.: You only look once unified, real-time object detection. In: Computer Vision and Pattern Recognition. Las Vegas, pp. 779-788 (2016). https://doi.org/10.48550/arXiv.1506.02640

21. Redmon, J., Farhadi, A.: YOLO9000: better, faster, stronger. In: Proceedings of the IEEE Conference on Computer Vision and Pattern Recognition, Honolulu, pp. 7263−7271 21−26 July 2017

22. Redmon, J., Farhadi, A.: Yolov3: an incremental improvement. Comput. Vis. Pattern Recognit. (2018). https://doi.org/10.48550/arXiv.1804.02767

23. Bochkovskiy, A., Wang, C.Y., Liao, H.Y.M.: YOLOv4: optimal speed and accuracy of object detection, computer vision and pattern recognition (2020)s

24. Xingkui, Z., Shuchang, L., Xu, W., Zhao, Q.: TPH-YOLOv5: improved YOLOv5 based on transformer prediction head for object detection on drone-captured scenarios. Comput. Vis. Pattern Recognit. 24 Feb. 2023. https://doi.org/10.48550/arXiv.2108.11539

25. Qingtian, W., Yimin, Z.: Real-time object detection based on unmanned aerial vehicle. IEEE 8th Data Driven Control and Learning Systems. May 2019. https://doi.org/10.1109/DDCLS.2019.8908984

26. Jocher, G., et al.: ultralytics/yolov5: v5.0 - YOLOv5-P6 1280 models, AWS, Supervise.ly and YouTube integrations. Apr. 2021

27. Wang, C.-Y., Bochkovskiy, A., Liao, H.-Y.-M.: Scaled-YOLOv4: scaling cross stage partial network. Proc. IEEE/CVF Conf. Comput. Vis. Pattern Recognit. (CVPR), pp. 13024–13033 Jun. 2021

28. Song, Y., Xie, Z., Wang, X., Zou, Y.: MS-YOLO: object detection based on YOLOv5 optimized fusion millimeter-wave radar and machine vision. IEEE Sensors J. **22**(15), 15435–15447 (2022). https://doi.org/10.1109/JSEN.2022.3167251

29. Chen, S., Chen, B.: Research on object detection algorithm based on improved Yolov5. In: Liang, Q., Wang, W., Mu, J., Liu, X., Na, Z. (eds.) Artificial Intelligence in China. Lecture Notes in Electrical Engineering, pp. 290–297. Springer Singapore, Singapore (2022). https://doi.org/10.1007/978-981-16-9423-3_37

30. Diwan, T., Anirudh, G., Tembhurne, J.V.: Object detection using YOLO: challenges, architectural successors, datasets and applications. Multimed. Tools Appl. **82**, 9243–9275 (2022). https://doi.org/10.1007/s11042-022-13644-y

31. Manjunath, A.A., et al.: Automated invoice data extraction using image processing. IAES Int. J. Artif. Intell. (IJ-AI) **12**(2), 514 (2023). https://doi.org/10.11591/ijai.v12.i2.pp514-521

32. Benallal, M.A., Tayeb, M.S.: An image-based convolutional neural network system for road defects detection. IAES Int. J. Artif. Intell. (IJ-AI) **12**(2), 577 (2023). https://doi.org/10.11591/ijai.v12.i2.pp577-584

33. Xu, Z., Baojie, X., Guoxin, W.: Canny edge detection based on Open CV. Key Laboratory of Modern Measurement and Control Technology Ministry of Education, Beijing Information Science and Technology University, Beijing 100192, China

34. Singh, H.: Practical Machine Learning and Image Processing. A press, Berkeley, CA (2019). https://doi.org/10.1007/978-1-4842-4149-3

35. Tommasoa, A.D., Bettia, A., Fontanellia, G., Michelozzia, B.: A multi-stage model based on YOLOv3 for defect detection

Variability Study for Balancing an Assembly Line: Dynamic Balancing

Youness Hillali[1,2]([⊠]), Najlae Alfathi[3] [iD], Samir Chafik[2] [iD], and Mourad Zegrari[1] [iD]

[1] Laboratory of Complex Cyber Physical Systems (LCCPS), ENSAM
Casablanca, Casablanca, Morocco
youness.hillali-etu@etu.univh2c.ma
[2] Pluridisciplinary Laboratory of Research and Innovation (LPRI), EMSI Casablanca,
Casablanca, Morocco
s.chafik@emsi.ma
[3] Laboratory Intelligent Systems and Applications (LSIA), EMSI Tanger, Tanger, Morocco
n.alfathi@emsi.ma

Abstract. The present study investigates the impact of highly variable characteristics on assembly line balance, with a focus on mass customization in modern manufacturing. The challenges of balancing assembly lines have intensified due to the increasing demand for customization, which has led to greater efficiency, productivity, product quality, and customer satisfaction. To address this issue, the study aims to identify the critical factors that significantly affect assembly line balance. Typical assembly lines are designed for the production of a single product or a narrow range of similar items in high volumes. Therefore, this research employs 3D matrix representation and graphical interpretation with the MATLAB tool to identify the highly variable parameters and their interactions that impact assembly line balance. The results of this analysis demonstrate that modifying the pilot parameters of the assembly line has a significant impact on line balance, necessitating dynamic balancing. The study applies this methodology primarily to the automotive industry, specifically to the wire harness manufacturing line.

Keywords: Dynamic balancing · assembly line · 3D matrix · high variability parameters

1 Introduction

The manufacturing industry is undergoing rapid changes in response to shifting market demands and technological advancements. One of the most prominent trends in modern production is the concept of mass customization, wherein firms alter product specifications to accommodate varying customer demands and production volumes [1]. To remain competitive in this increasingly digital and volatile environment, businesses must successfully forecast, adapt to, and cope with external changes in the market [2].

A key factor in meeting these challenges is the concept of manufacturing line balance, which involves optimizing the production process to minimize operator idle time and

H. Hagras et al. (Eds.): ISACS 2023, CCIS 2255, pp. 228–242, 2025.
https://doi.org/10.1007/978-3-031-93448-3_19

enhance efficiency [3]. Assembly lines, which consist of multiple workstations linked by conveyor belts, are a common method used in modern industry to produce standardized items. The challenge of balancing production lines is to assign operations to workstations in a manner that optimizes one or more objective functions, such as cost or capacity [4].

Mass customization is essential in meeting the diversified and personalized requirements of modern consumers, which include shorter product lifecycles, customized product configurations, and high production flexibility. To achieve mass customization, firms must possess the ability to generate a large number of diverse product alternatives for a broad market and quickly adjust product and process design in response to consumer demand, without sacrificing cost, delivery, or quality. Four components of mass customization capability include high-volume customization, customization cost efficiency, customization responsiveness, and customization quality [5].

While mass customization can lead to improved efficiency, production, product quality, and customer satisfaction, it also presents significant challenges, including increased complexity, higher downtime, and the need for new technologies and processes [6]. Assembly lines are a crucial industrial manufacturing method that can handle the expansion of customer expectations and product range in today's competitive environment. The assembly line balance problem (ALBP) is a critical concern in modern manufacturing, as it involves allocating tasks to sequentially linked stations while taking precedence connections into account [7]. Two broad types of assembly lines exist, each with its unique advantages and challenges. The use of assembly line arrangements can help firms optimize production processes and achieve mass customization goals. Overall, the ability to mass customize products is a crucial competitive advantage in today's fast-paced and ever-changing manufacturing landscape.

In this research paper, we introduce a novel methodology employing 3D statistical modeling represented as a 3D matrix to identify parameters with significant variability that affect the optimization of an assembly line's balance.

The rest of this essay is organized as follows. We begin by outlining the issues that this paper will address. The methodology that we will use to apply it in Sect. 3's case study is the main topic of Sect. 2. Discuss the conclusions, the research's ramifications, its limits, and future research directions before concluding.

2 Problematic

The present study aims to investigate the impact of a VUCA (Volatility, Uncertainty, Complexity, Ambiguity) environment on assembly line operations [8]. Specifically, we examine the interdependence between various parameters to gain a better understanding of how variations in these parameters can affect the balance of an assembly line [9]. In order to achieve this objective, we employ 3D matrix to identify the principal parameters that have the greatest influence on assembly line balance.

In a VUCA environment, the manufacturing industry faces significant challenges due to rapid changes in consumer demand, technical advancements, global economic conditions, supply chain disruptions, and market uncertainties [10]. These factors can make efficient production planning and scheduling difficult, thereby affecting the stability of assembly line operations. Furthermore, the increasing complexity of manufacturing processes and a rising range of goods and customization options can add to the difficulty of managing assembly line operations. To address these challenges, assembly lines must be adaptable, effective, and capable of handling a wide range of commodities and variations. Innovative manufacturing technologies and data analytics can be leveraged to improve production operations and optimize assembly line designs. Moreover, dynamic re-balancing procedures can help maintain a stable production process [11]. However, it is crucial to identify the key parameters that have a significant impact on productivity before implementing new balancing procedures. Such parameters may include operator skill levels [12], feeder line variability [13, 14], and other variables that could impact manufacturing line variability. By using graphical interpretation, we aim to determine which parameters require close monitoring and control to ensure stable assembly line operations.

Overall, the findings of this study can provide valuable insights into the design and optimization of assembly lines in a VUCA environment [15]. Effective parameterization of assembly lines can lead to improved efficiency and productivity in the manufacturing industry.

3   Methodology

The aim of this study is to identify the Y_i characteristics that influence the balance of assembly lines, resulting in the unpredictability of Y balancing $Y = F(Y_i)$, where Y represents the balancing parameter and Y_i refers to the sources of variability in Y. To achieve a comprehensive collection of significant parameters, we have examined both scholarly literature and industrial cases.

Our literature review focused on the variables that researchers have identified as directly related to assembly line balancing. On the other hand, data from industries, specifically those in the automotive sector, provided us with actual metrics used to manage production lines.

By analyzing both sources of information, we were able to create a representation that illustrates the relationship between Y (balance) and Y_i (the parameters generating a variability of the parameter Y). We present this representation in Table 1.

Table 1. The general parameter

Y	Y_1	Y_2	Y_3	....	Y_n

We note:

- Y = balancing
- Y_i = parameters that cause variability for the general parameter Y where i varies from 1 to n i = (1,.......,n)

To clarify the relationship between Y and Y_i, we have formulated Y as a set of parameters, where Y_i represents the sources that affect the variability of the general parameter Y. Alternatively, we can express Y as the balance of a production line, which can fluctuate due to various causes. Overall, our study provides insights into the characteristics that influence the balance of assembly lines. By identifying and understanding these variables, practitioners can take measures to improve assembly line efficiency and productivity. For example:

Y = Balancing, Y_1 = product specification.

The concept of balancing, denoted by Y, is a critical parameter in production processes. The balancing Y can be affected by various factors, denoted by Y_i, that cause variations in the final product's characteristics. For example, if the product specification changes, the production lines must be rebalanced to accommodate the new requirements. Therefore, it is crucial to identify the parameters Y_i that contribute to the variation in the balancing Y.

To achieve this, we define a new parameter, denoted by X_{ij}, where i varies from 1 to n and j varies from 1 to m. The parameter X_{ij} represents the root parameters that decompose each parameter Y_i after defining the balancing Y and the parameters Y_i that cause the variation in the balancing Y. Using the new parameter X_{ij}, we can create a straightforward representation of the relationship between the balancing Y and the parameters Y_i.

In Table 2 below, we illustrate this representation, where each row represents a parameter Y_i and its corresponding root parameters X_{ij}. By identifying the root parameters X_{ij}, we can determine the impact of each parameter Y_i on the balancing Y and adjust the production process accordingly to achieve the desired product specifications (Table 2).

Table 2. 2D Matrix

Y	Y_1	Y_2	Y_3	....	Y_n
	X_{11}	X_{21}	X_{31}		:
	X_{12}	X_{22}	X_{32}		:
	:	:	:		
	X_{1j}	X_{2j}	X_{3j}		X_{nm}

We note:

- Y = balancing
- Y_i = parameters that cause variability for the general parameter Y
- X_{ij} = the root parameters that decompose the parameters Y_i

In order to understand the relationship between the balancing Y and the parameters Y_i is essential for effective production processes. The new parameter X_{ij} provides a useful tool for decomposing each parameter Y_i and identifying its impact on the balancing Y, leading to efficient and optimized production processes.

We have the example:

Y = Balancing, Y_1 = product specification, X_{11} = mass customization.

In modern production processes, mass customization has become a critical capability, enabling the consistent production of a vast array of distinct product variants, each with its own set of specifications. This diversity in product specifications can cause variations in the balancing parameter Y, highlighting the importance of understanding the relationship between Y and the factors that contribute to its variability, denoted by Y_i.

To decompose each Y_i parameter, we define a new parameter, denoted by X_{ij}, which represents the root parameters. Additionally, we incorporate a new parameter called V_{ijk}, where k varies from 1 to t. V_{ijk} stands for the values that the root parameter X_{ij} can take. By incorporating V_{ijk}, we can model the three critical parameters (Y_i, X_{ij}, and V_{ijk}) as a 3D matrix, as shown in Fig. 1 below.

This matrix enables a comprehensive understanding of the complex relationships between the balancing parameter Y, its contributing factors Y_i, and the values that the

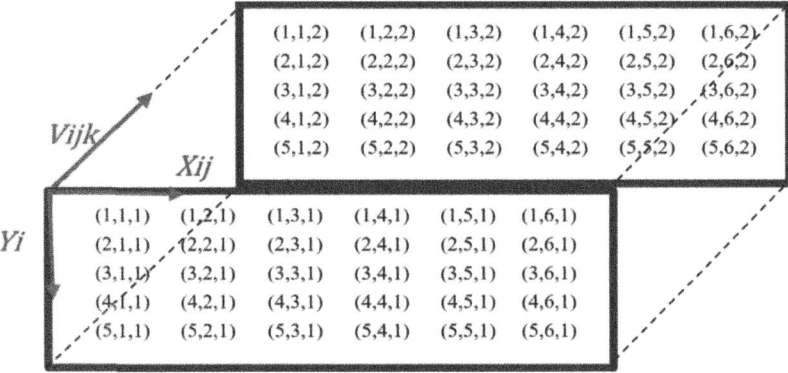

Fig. 1. 3D matrix

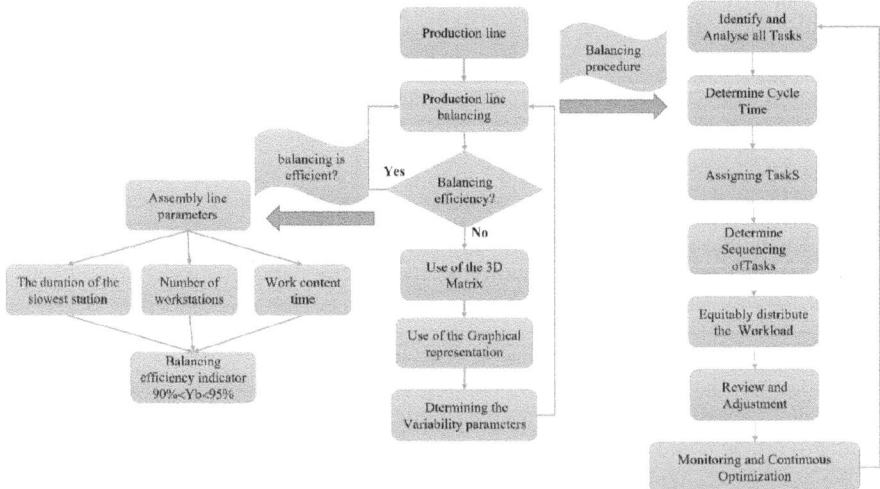

Fig. 2. Balancing procedure

parameter Y can take, as represented by V_{ijk}. By identifying the root parameters X_{ij} for each Y_i factor and analyzing the corresponding V_{ijk} values, we can optimize production processes to achieve the desired product specifications while maintaining a consistent balancing parameter Y (Fig. 2).

The balancing procedure delineates a structured sequence of actions for the seamless integration of the proposed approach aimed at efficiently realigning the production line. This methodology offers a conventional set of instructions for the operationalization of line balancing, concurrently streamlining the process through the utilization of a 3D matrix and graphical representations employing MATLAB. The primary objective is to establish a standardized protocol for the optimization of assembly line balancing through the employment of this procedural framework.

The 3D matrix acts as an intermediary between the balancing efficiency indicator and the Y_i and X_{ij} control parameters of the manufacturing line. This matrix serves as a tool to analyze the impact of various control parameters on the efficiency of the manufacturing line. By examining the relationship between the control parameters and the balancing efficiency indicator, the 3D matrix enables a deeper understanding of the performance of the manufacturing line. Furthermore, this tool provides insights into the factors that contribute to inefficiencies in the manufacturing process and facilitates the identification of opportunities for improvement. Overall, the 3D matrix plays a crucial role in the analysis and optimization of manufacturing line performance.

4 Application

In accordance with the established methodology, we shall now apply it to an industrial case within the automotive sector. Initially, we have collated a comprehensive database comprising information that is specific to the manufacturing line employed by the company under consideration. It is noteworthy that the company in question employs an assembly line that consists of a total of 29 manual stations, as illustrated in Fig. 3 below.

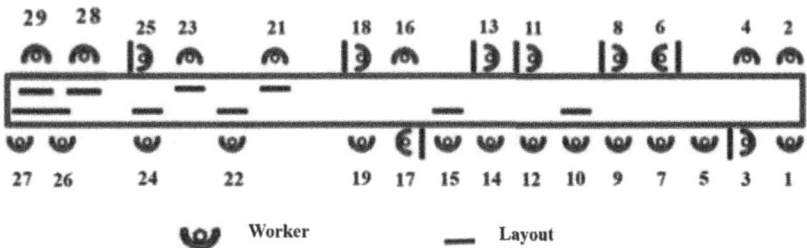

Fig. 3. Layout of the assembly line

After an analysis of the database chosen in the automotive sector and more precisely the wiring of automotive harnesses. We will follow the methodology proposed in the previous part.

4.1 Balancing the Assembly Line

Balancing an assembly line is a crucial process to maximize production and minimize costs. The key steps to balancing an assembly line are as follows for more information [16, 17]:

- Data collection: All relevant data about the assembly line, including cycle times, processing times, number of operators, and downtime, must be collected.
- Identifying bottlenecks: Using the collected data, bottlenecks in the line, i.e., steps in the line where the flow is limited, must be identified.
- Determining desired production rate: By determining the desired production rate, the necessary cycle time for each step in the line can be calculated.
- Balancing the line: Using the calculated cycle time for each step in the line, the line can be balanced by adjusting operations and redistributing operators to eliminate bottlenecks.
- Verifying results: It is crucial to verify the results of the line balancing to ensure production goals are met. If adjustments are necessary, they must be made to maintain line balance.
- Monitoring and improving: Regular monitoring of line performance is essential to detect potential problems and make improvements to maintain optimal production.

Our chrono analysis and variability study revealed that some stations were overburdened, leading to obstructions in the assembly process. Therefore, balancing the assembly line becomes necessary. Figure 4 below provides a visual representation of this balance.

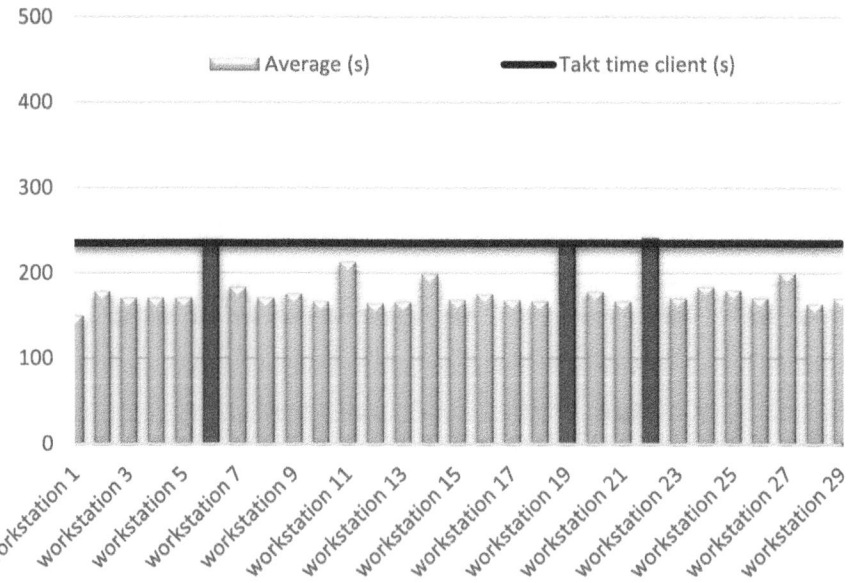

Fig. 4. Variability study of the assembly line before balancing

Through the utilization of one of the available balancing algorithms, as reported in the references [18–20], we have implemented the largest candidate rule algorithm to reallocate tasks and operations among each workstation, aiming to balance the assembly line. Following the application of the algorithm, we have analyzed the variability graph of the workstations and concluded that the line is now balanced, as all workstations exhibit an equivalent workload, as depicted in the figure below.

By using the formula (1) below, we calculated the balancing efficiency indicator to properly measure the quality of balancing used:

$$Y_b = T_{wc}/(m \times T_s)$$

We note:

- Y_b: Balancing efficiency indicator
- T_{wc}: Work content time
- m: number of workstations
- T_s: the duration of the slowest station

After implementing the largest candidate rule algorithm [18], we found that our line is well-balanced, with a calculated balancing efficiency indicator of 97%. Drawing from the assembly line's variability graph, it is discernible that the line is deemed balanced, given that each station's workload appears to be equitably distributed.

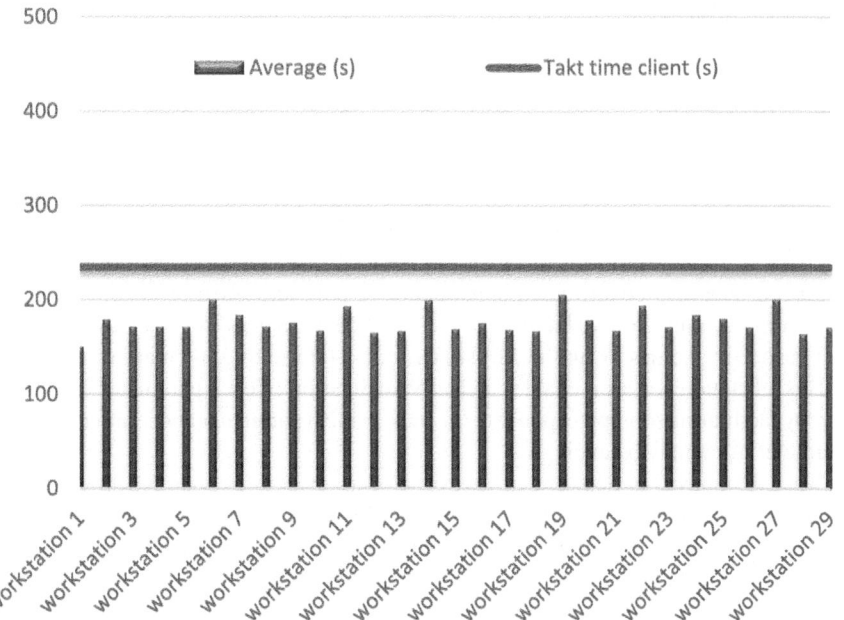

Fig. 5. Variability study of the assembly line after balancing

4.2 Matrix Representation

After balancing our assembly line, we will collect data that characterizes the line and its evolution post-balancing. With reference to the database collated from the automotive sector, and more specifically pertaining to the wiring of automobile harnesses, the techniques elucidated in the preceding section shall be implemented.

In fact, we have decided to focus on four factors called Y_i that are immediately included into the control of the manufacturing process for automotive harnesses. Namely:

Parameter Y_i and X_{ij}:

Y_1: Efficiency:

- X_{11}: Cadence: Number of conforming bundles made per time.
- X_{12}: Range time: fixed index which expresses the duration of a cycle of assembly until the final control
- X_{13}: Staff: number of staff present.
- X_{14}: Working hours

Y_2: The time allocated to manufacture a beam:

- X_{21}: Shift time bottleneck
- X_{22}: Shift time

Y_3: Takt time:

- X_{31}: Production time
- X_{32}: Daily demand

Y_4: Product specification:

- X_{41}: Routing time
- X_{42}: LAD frequency (product rotation frequency)

In adherence to the methodology outlined in the previous section, the parameters Y_n, which contribute to the variability of the overall parameter Y balance, as well as the root parameters X_{ij} that break down the parameter Y_i, are determined. Subsequently, the values V_{ijk} that may be attributed to parameter Y are established.

To represent the collated database, the selected Y_i and X_{ij} parameters are assigned their respective values using the MATLAB tool. The use of a 3D matrix within MATLAB is advantageous, as it enables a clear visualization of each parameter's variability, thereby facilitating prompt response to the most critical parameter concerning the general parameter Y, namely balancing.

The 3D matrix, as depicted in Fig. 6 below, serves to provide an illustrative representation of this approach. The 3D matrix illustrates that the control parameters of the assembly line exhibit temporal variability, thereby leading to fluctuations in the balancing process.

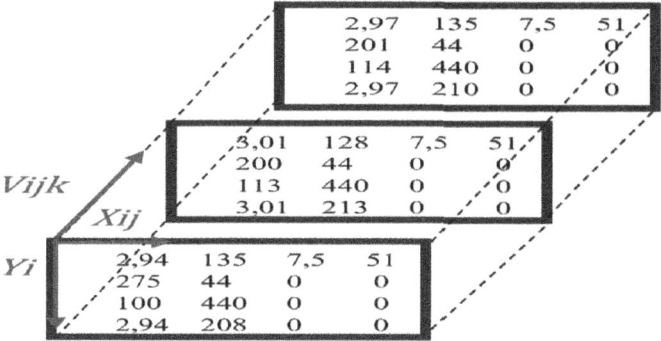

Fig. 6. Application of the 3D matrix

4.3 Result Interpretation

Once the selected parameters from the collated database are represented in a matrix, it becomes imperative to scrutinize the results utilizing the MATLAB tool and visually depict the findings derived from the 3D matrix. This approach facilitates the identification of parameters that exert a substantial influence on variability.

Subsequently, we proceed to isolate the parameter Y_i that exhibits the highest variability among the three that were previously identified. Figure 7 below provides a visual representation of this analysis.

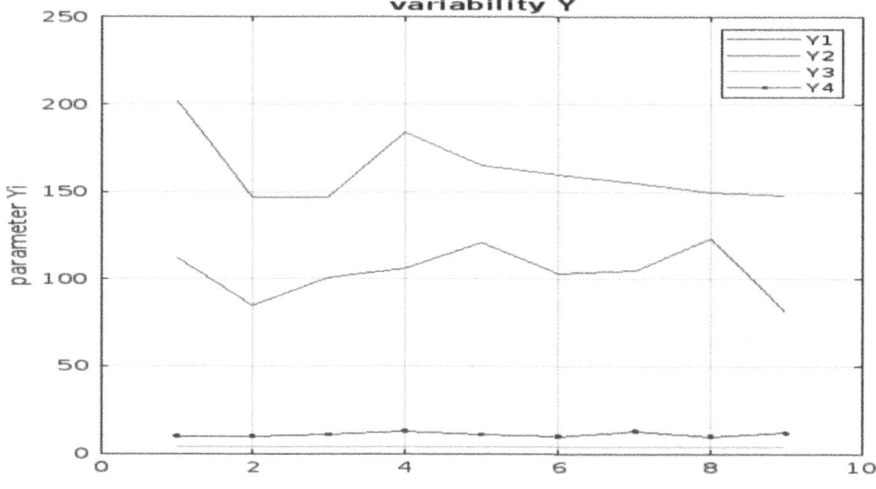

Fig. 7. Graph interpretation Yi

From the graph depicting the three curves of parameters Y_1, Y_2, and Y_4, it is evident that Y_1 (Efficiency) and Y_2 (time required for constructing a beam) have a substantial impact on the overall balancing parameter Y. These parameters exhibit a high degree of variability, as evidenced by the graph.

Further analysis reveals that the parameter X_{11} (speed) is primarily responsible for the variability in Y_1, whereas the parameter X_{21} (period of post-bottleneck) contributes significantly to the fluctuation observed in Y_2.

To investigate the influence of these parameters on the assembly line's balancing, we proceed to vary the two parameters identified in the previous step. The set of parameters Y_i is first examined to determine the X_{ij} parameter that contributes the most to the variability of Y_i. This analysis is depicted in Fig. 8, 9, 10 and 11, illustrating the fluctuation of Y_i versus X_{ij}.

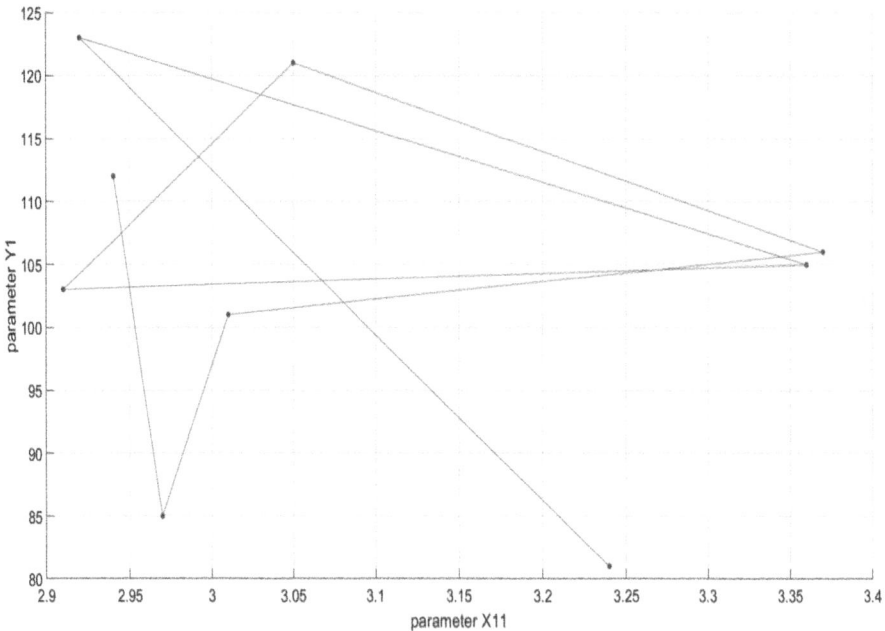

Fig. 8. Graph interpretation Y1, X11

This analysis is performed for all parameters Y_i present in the database, and it is apparent that X_{11} and X_{12} are responsible for the variability observed in Y_1, while X_{21} has a significant influence on the variability of Y_2. Additionally, the parameters X_{41} and X_{42} contribute to the variability of Y_4. However, Y_3 remains stable and constant throughout the analysis, leading to the conclusion that Y_1, Y_2, and Y_4 are the parameters with the most variability.

After identifying the parameters with strong variability and determining their root causes, the next step is to visualize the balance of the assembly line. To achieve this, we conducted a variability analysis based on a sample of 5 times [19]. Subsequently, we analyzed the results obtained to determine the bottleneck positions in the assembly line [20]. As per the variability graph shown in Fig. 12, we identified five bottleneck positions in the assembly line [21].

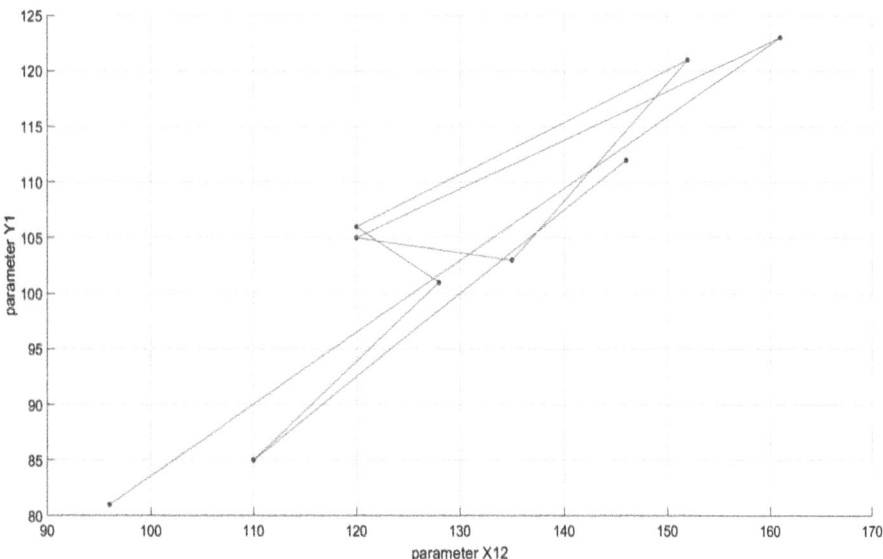

Fig. 9. Graph interpretation Y1, X12

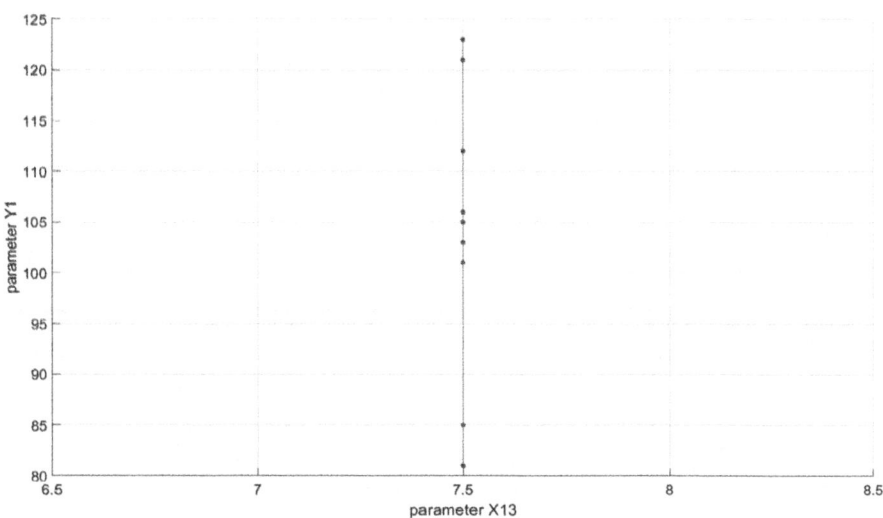

Fig. 10. Graph interpretation Y1, X13

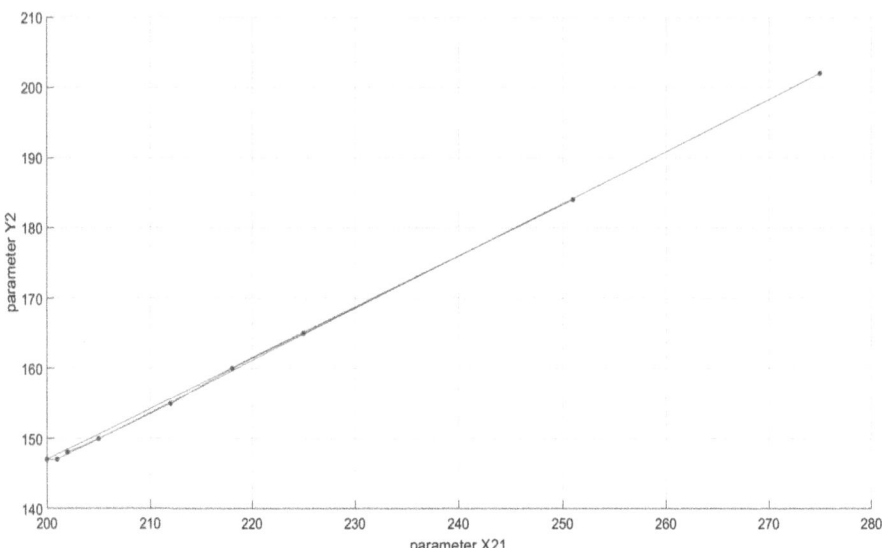

Fig. 11. Graph interpretation Y2, X21

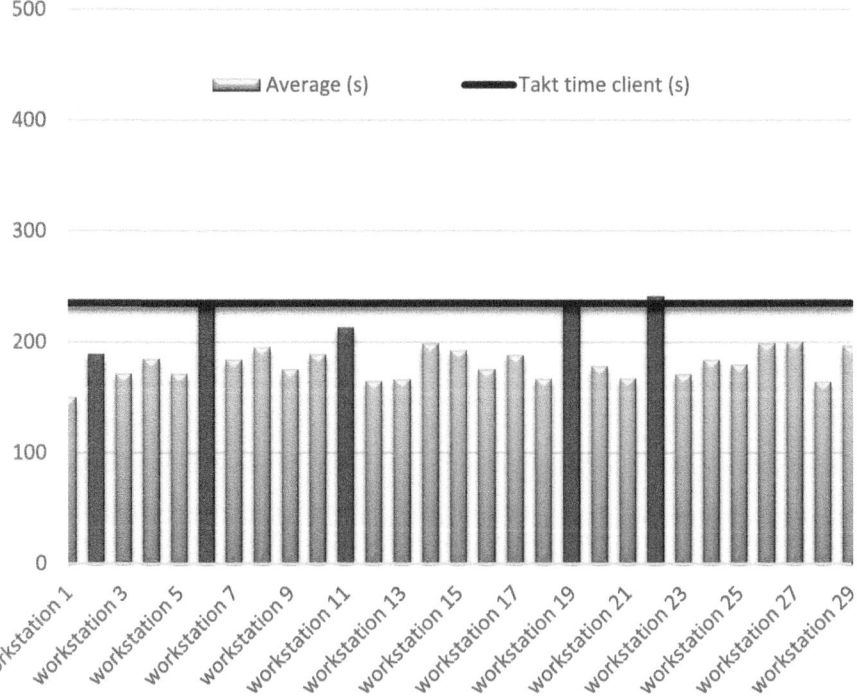

Fig. 12. Variability study of the assembly line after changing some parameters

5   Conclusion and Future Work

Due to the growing demand for customized products, assembly lines must adapt while responding to the assembly line control parameters. In actuality, the balance can change depending on how the parameters of the manufacturing line are altered. As a result, the approach used shows that the situation we are in involves dynamic balance [21].

The recommended approach comprises locating the critical factors with high variability that directly influence the balance of the manufacturing line then proposing a balancing procedure to achieve a maximum efficiency of balancing the assembly. There is a balanced variability created by these variables. The balance then ceases to be stable.

Now, these high variability characteristics are manually determined using the MATLAB tool's graphic interpretations and a 3D matrix representation.

This approach should be improved by recommending artificial intelligence algorithms [22] to automatically detect the qualities with high variability.

References

1. Ren, W., Wen, J., Guan, Y., Hu, Y.: Research on assembly module partition for flexible production in mass customization. Procedia CIRP **72**, 744–749 (2018). https://doi.org/10.1016/j.procir.2018.03.023
2. Tsutsui, S., Kaihara, T., Kokuryo, D., Fujii, N., Harano, K.: A proposal of production scheduling method with dynamic parts allocation for mass customization. Procedia CIRP **107**, 882–887 (2022). https://doi.org/10.1016/j.procir.2022.05.079
3. Bastos, N.M., Alves, A.C., Castro, F.X., Duarte, J., Ferreira, L.P., Silva, F.J.G.: Reconfiguration of assembly lines using lean thinking in an electronics components' manufacturer for the automotive industry. Procedia Manuf. **55**, 383–392 (2021). https://doi.org/10.1016/j.promfg.2021.10.053
4. Salveson, M.E.: The assembly-line balancing problem. MJ. Fluids Eng. **77**(6), 939–947(1955)
5. Pérez, E., Rossit, A.T., Alejandro, D., Fernando, T., Óscar, V. C.: Mass customized/personalized manufacturing in Industry 4.0 and blockchain: Research challenges, main problems, and the design of an information architecture. Inf. Fusion pp. 44–57 (2022)
6. Battaïa, O., Otto, A., Sgarbossa, F., Pesch, E.: Future trends in management and operation of assembly systems: from customized assembly systems to cyber-physical systems. Omega **78**, 1–4 (2018). https://doi.org/10.1016/j.omega.2018.01.010
7. Li, Z., Janardhanan, M.N., Rahman, H.F.: Enhanced beam search heuristic for U-shaped assembly line balancing problems. Eng. Optim. https://doi.org/10.1080/0305215X.2020.1741569(2020)
8. Bulińska-Stangrecka, H., Bagieńska, A., Iddagoda, A.: Organizational trust management in industry 4.0 in a VUCA world: a comprehensive review and future research directions
9. Romero-SilvaR,Hurtado-Hernández, The effects of supply variability on the performance of assembly systems Mhttps://doi.org/10.1080/00207543.2022.2086085 1–18(2022)
10. Troise, C., Corvello, V., Ghobadian, A., O'Regan, N.: How can SMEs successfully navigate VUCA environment: the role of agility in the digital transformation era. Technol. Forecast. Soc. Chang. **174**, 121227 (2022). https://doi.org/10.1016/j.techfore.2021.121227
11. Wei, Z., Liang, H., Roger, J.: Dynamic takt time decisions for paced assembly lines balancing and sequencing considering highly mixed-model production: an improved artificial bee colony optimization approach. Comput. Indust. Eng. (2021)

12. Gilles, M., Gaudez, C.: Do age and work pace affect variability when performing a repetitive light assembly task. Wild PAppl. Ergonomics **98**, 103601 (2022)
13. Gräßler, I., Roesmann, D.: Skill-based worker assignment in a manual assembly line. Procedia CIRP **100**, 433–438 (2021). https://doi.org/10.1016/j.procir.2021.05.100
14. Aslihan, K., Feristah, O.: Assembly line worker assignment and rebalancing problem: a mathematical model and an artificial bee colony algorithm. Comput. Indust. Eng. (2021)
15. Khan, S., Majid, A.: Yasir, Strategic renewal of SMEs: the impact of social capital, strategic agility and absorptive capacity. Manag. Decis. **59**(8), 1877–1894 (2020)
16. Andrés-López, E., González-Requena, I., Sanz-Lobera, A.: Lean service: reassessment of lean manufacturing for service activities. Procedia Eng. **132**, 23–30 (2015). https://doi.org/10.1016/j.proeng.2015.12.463
17. Nallusamy, S.: Execution of lean and industrial techniques for productivity enhancement in a manufacturing industry. Mater. Today Proc. **37**, 568–575 (2021). https://doi.org/10.1016/j.matpr.2020.05.590
18. Çelik, M.T., Arslankaya, S.: Solution of the assembly line balancing problem using the rank positional weight method and Kilbridge and Wester heuristics method: An application in the cable industry. J. Eng. Res. **11**(3), 182–191 (2023). https://doi.org/10.1016/j.jer.2023.100082
19. Kucukkoc, I., Zhang, D.Z.: A mathematical model and genetic algorithm-based approach for parallel two-sided assembly line balancing problem. Prod. Plann. Control Manage. Oper. **26**(11), 874–894. https://doi.org/10.1080/09537287.2014.994685(2015)
20. Eduardo, Á.-M., Jordi, P., et al.: Analysis of the simple assembly line balancing problem complexity, Comput. Oper. Res. (2023)
21. Johannes, S.M., Ferid, O.F.: Dynamic line balancing in unpaced mixed-model assembly lines: a problem classification. CIRP J. Manuf. Sci. Technol. 134–142 (2022)
22. Xingjian, L., Tianchen, Q., et al.: Predicting future production system bottlenecks with a graph neural network approach. J. Manuf. Syst. 201–212 (2023)

Efficient Energy Management for a Solar-Wind Microgrid Using Fuzzy Logic Control

Ouadiâ Chekira[1]([✉]) [iD], Abdelfettah El-ghajghaj[2], Younes Boujoudar[1] [iD],
Hassan EL Moussaoui[1], Tijani Lamhamdi[1] [iD], Ali Boharb[1] [iD],
and Hassan EL Markhi[1] [iD]

[1] Laboratory of Intelligent Systems, Faculty of Science and Technology, Geo-Resources and Renewable Energies, Sidi Mohamed Ben Abdullah University, Fez, Morocco
Ouadia.chekira@usmba.com
[2] Laboratory of Engineering, Systems and Applications, National School of Applied Sciences, Sidi Mohamed Ben Abdellah University, Fez, Morocco

Abstract. Microgrids are stand-alone power systems that can operate independently or in conjunction with the main grid. Achieving a balanced and reliable power supply in microgrids is a challenging issue due to the fluctuating nature of power generation and load demand. In this paper, we present a new fuzzy logic-based approach to control power flow in microgrids. To maintain the work reserve of the BSS and manage the charging and discharging conditions, this intelligent control system presented flexible operation in the microgrid, maximizing the benefits of renewable energy. The proposed approach uses real-time data to make decisions regarding electricity generation, storage, and consumption, which helps maintain a stable energy balance in the system. We demonstrate the effectiveness of our approach through simulation studies, which show an excellent contribution to reducing power fluctuations and improving the reliability of the microgrid, as well as a comparison between the fuzzy logic controller and PID control in terms of precision and stability. Our approach is flexible and can be adapted to different microgrids, including those based on renewable energy sources and hybrid systems. Overall, our approach represents a promising solution to improve the performance of microgrids and ensure a reliable energy supply in these systems. Simulation results show greater adaptability to voltage variations of the fuzzy logic controller and the ability to manage uncertainties and unpredictable variations in production and load demand.

Keywords: Microgrid · Fuzzy logic · Control · Power flow · Energy balance

1 Introduction

One of the most serious issues of our time is how to meet the rising demand for energy while minimizing the environmental harm caused by the production of electricity [1]. The world's reliance on conventional.

fossil fuel-based power-generating sources has resulted in serious environmental problems, including greenhouse gas emissions that fuel global warming and climate

H. Hagras et al. (Eds.): ISACS 2023, CCIS 2255, pp. 243–252, 2025.
https://doi.org/10.1007/978-3-031-93448-3_20

change [2], water pollution, air pollution, and water contamination. Because of this, there is an increasing demand for environ-mentally friendly alternatives to conventional power generation techniques that can lessen the effects of climate change. In contrast to conventional power generation techniques, renewable energy sources including solar, wind, and hydropower have shown promise in reducing climate change [3]. Renewable energy sources still confront obstacles that must be addressed in order to guarantee a steady and dependable power supply, notwithstanding their advantages for the environment. Intermittency, which describes how the output of renewable energy sources can change depending on the weather and other variables, is a significant obstacle [4]. Because of this, balancing the supply and demand of power can be difficult, particularly during periods of high demand or bad weather. Multiple distributed energy resources (DERs) must be integrated and balanced by efficient energy management systems in order to overcome this obstacle. DERs are grid-distributed, small-scale power production units like solar panels, wind turbines, and battery storage units.

The most important aspect of a microgrid is the control approach. Due to their simplicity and ease of use, traditional control methods like proportional integral-derivative (PID) control have been widely utilized to incorporate renewable energy sources into microgrids [5]. By modifying the control signal based on the discrepancy between the targeted setpoint and the actual output, PID control may control the power output of the microgrid. PID control, however, has limits when it comes to handling uncertain, im-precise, and complex nonlinear systems [6]. To enhance the control effectiveness of microgrid systems, researchers have suggested a number of modifications to the conventional PID control, including fuzzy-PID control and adaptive PID control [7]. To integrate renewable energy sources into a microgrid, for instance, a recent study offered a fuzzy-PID control-based solution, which enhanced the control effectiveness and stability of the system [8]. Another study suggested an adaptive PID control algorithm for a microgrid system that might modify the controller's settings in real-time to take into account of modifications in the system's operational conditions [9]. PID control systems still have shortcomings concerning handling un-certainty and disturbances despite recent advancements. To operate microgrids more effectively and dependably, researchers have been looking into more sophisticated control techniques like model predictive control and AI-based systems. Despite being frequently used in microgrid energy management systems, traditional control methods, such as PID control, have limitations when it comes to handling complex and nonlinear systems, uncertainties, and imprecise information. To get around these restrictions, fuzzy logic control has emerged as a promising technique. By allowing the use of linguistic variables and rule-based decision-making, fuzzy logic can handle ambiguous information and uncertainties effectively [10]. Fuzzy log-ic controllers are effective for managing microgrid energy in numerous studies.

To regulate the power flow in a hybrid AC/DC microgrid system, for in-stance, a study suggested a fuzzy logic-based control technique, which in-creased the system's power quality and stability [11]. In a different study, a fuzzy logic controller was created to reduce the running costs of a microgrid system with numerous energy storage devices [12]. It has been demonstrated to be successful at enhancing power quality, stability, and microgrid systems' efficiency in terms of cost. Additionally, we will discuss variable scenarios for solar radiation, wind speed, and dynamic, erratic load demands. We will give a full assessment of fuzzy logic's performance in extremely complicated microgrid settings by contrasting it with PID control, a popular conventional control technique. As a whole, our work makes a substantial addition to the subject of microgrid energy management since it tackles the problems brought on by complex power systems and highly fluctuating sources of renewable energy. The rest of this essay is organized as follows: A thorough explanation of the fuzzy logic controller employed in this investigation is provided in Sect. 2. The energy management system used to supply power to loads is described in Sect. 3. In Sect. 4, the results of the simulation study are presented, followed by a succinct analysis of the results. An overview of the research's major contributions and implications completes the publication.

2 Fuzzy Logic Controller

Due to its capacity to manage complicated, dynamic systems, uncertainties, and inaccurate information, fuzzy logic control has emerged as a viable method for managing the energy consumption of microgrids [15]. The major goal of this project is to integrate several renewable energy sources, including solar, wind, and hydropower, to offer a steady and dependable power supply. Due to the intermittent nature of renewable energy, the microgrid's fluctuating load requirements, and the unpredictability of weather conditions, integrating various sources can be difficult. These issues can be re-solved by fuzzy logic control, which offers a more adaptable and flexible control mechanism that can change in response to changing conditions in real-time. To regulate the power output of each renewable energy source and balance it with the microgrid's load demands, a controller based on fuzzy logic can be built and deployed in a microgrid project. The controller can also adapt the renewable energy sources' power output in real-time ac-cording to changes in the weather.

The charging and discharging of the battery, a crucial part of the microgrid energy management system, will be managed by the fuzzy logic controller. The intermittent and variable power produced by renewable energy sources like solar and wind might make it difficult to keep the loads' power supplies steady. The battery acts as a buffer between the supply and demand for electricity, storing surplus power when it is there and supplying it to the loads again when necessary. When deciding whether to charge or discharge the battery, the fuzzy logic controller will consider the inputs of the power produced by the renewable energy sources, the power demanded by the loads, and the battery's state of charge. The fuzzy logic controller will use a set of rules that describe how the inputs relate to the output of the battery charging and discharging control. These rules will be based on expert knowledge of the microgrid system and the characteristics of the battery. A set of rules that specify how the inputs relate to the output of the battery charging and discharging control will be used by the fuzzy logic controller as shown in Fig. 1.

These guidelines will be founded on the specialist understanding of the microgrid system and the battery's properties. The control strategy will be more adaptable and flexible thanks to the fuzzy logic controller's usage of membership functions and fuzzy sets to handle input variability and uncertainty. Defuzzification techniques are also employed by the fuzzy logic con-troller to turn the fuzzy output into a crisp value that may be used

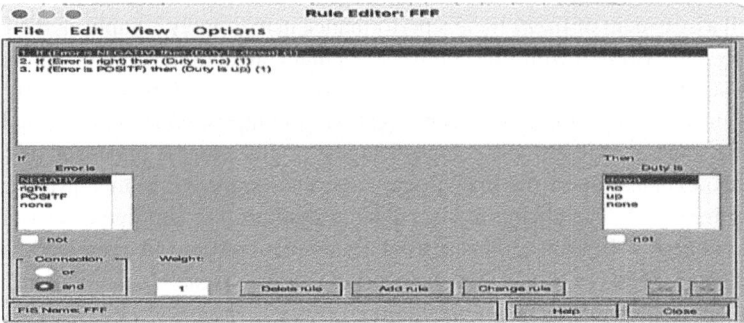

Fig. 1. Fuzzy logic controller rules.

to regulate battery charging and discharging. The capability of fuzzy logic control to manage complex and nonlinear systems is one benefit of adopting it in this microgrid project, uncertainty and inaccurate data. It may be challenging to maintain a steady power supply due to the variability and unpredict-ability of renewable energy sources and loads, which can lead to swings in power supply and demand. The battery charging and discharging method can be adjusted in response to these oscillations by the fuzzy logic controller, resulting in a dependable and stable power supply.

To improve the battery charging and discharging strategy and reduce the cost of electricity, the fuzzy logic controller may additionally include additional inputs, such as weather predictions and energy costs.

To provide a dependable and steady power supply, maximize the use of renewable energy sources, and reduce reliance on fossil fuels, the fuzzy logic controller in this microgrid project will play a crucial role. The microgrid can use fuzzy logic to combine various inputs and outputs for the best control strategy, respond fast and correctly to changes in power demand and supply, and adapt to the fluctuation and uncertainty of renewable energy sources and loads.

3   Energy Management System

This microgrid project's energy management system is built to maximize power production from solar PV and wind turbine sources while assuring a steady and dependable power supply to satisfy the demands of the dynamic loads. The power output of the solar PV and wind turbine systems are continuously adjusted based on changes in meteorological conditions using a maximum power point tracking (MPPT) algorithm based on the Perturb and Observe (P&O) method. The power generated by these sources is fed into the fuzzy logic controller along with the power required by the loads and the battery's state of charge (SOC).

The fuzzy logic controller's rules are established using expert knowledge of the system, and they can be modified to meet the unique needs of the microgrid. The guidelines for this project specify that the battery should be charged when the microgrid has excess power and discharged when the amount of power produced by renewable sources is insufficient to fulfill the demands of the loads. The precise control action to be executed, which is the charge of the battery or discharging current, is then determined using the output from the fuzzy logic controller, which has been defuzzified. The battery management system then executes the charging or discharging of the battery using the control actions determined by the fuzzy logic controller. The battery management system keeps track of the battery's state of charge (SOC) and modifies the charging or discharging current as necessary to keep the battery working safely at all times.

1. *Start*
2. *Set initial battery SOC*
3. *Continuously measure the power output of the solar PV and wind turbine sources, and adjust based on P&O MPPT algorithm*
4. *Continuously measure the power demand from the loads*
5. *Fuzzify the inputs (power produced, power demand, and battery SOC)*
6. *Use the fuzzy inference engine to determine the control action (charge or discharge) based on the rules defined in the fuzzy logic controller*
7. *Defuzzify the output to determine the precise control action (charging or discharging current)*
8. *Send the control action to the battery management system*
9. *The battery management system adjusts the charging or discharging current based on the battery SOC*
10. *Repeat steps 3-9 continuously to maintain a stable and reliable power supply in the microgrid*
11. *Stop*

4 Energy Management System

Figure 2 illustrates the components of the microgrid proposed in this study, which consists of a hybrid solar and wind system along with a battery storage system (BSS). The purpose of this microgrid will supply a reliable and sustainable source of power to the connected loads.

The solar system consists of 40 photovoltaic (PV) panels arranged in 4 strings of 10 panels each. The panels have a rated output of 320 Wp each, resulting in a total capacity of 12.8 kWp. The panels are connected to a DC converter and equipped with an MPPT algorithm, or maximum power point tracking that ensures the panels operate at their optimal operating point.

The wind turbine has a rated capacity of 5 kW and is connected to a wind inverter that converts the AC output of the turbine to DC, which is then fed into the microgrid. The wind inverter has an efficiency of 96% and is equipped with an MPPT algorithm that ensures the turbine operates at its optimal operating point. The battery storage system consists of a 200 V, 300 Ah lithium battery bank with a total capacity of 60 kWh. The battery bank is connected to a bidirectional inverter that allows it to charge and discharge as needed to balance the microgrid. The inverter has a maximum power output of 50 kW

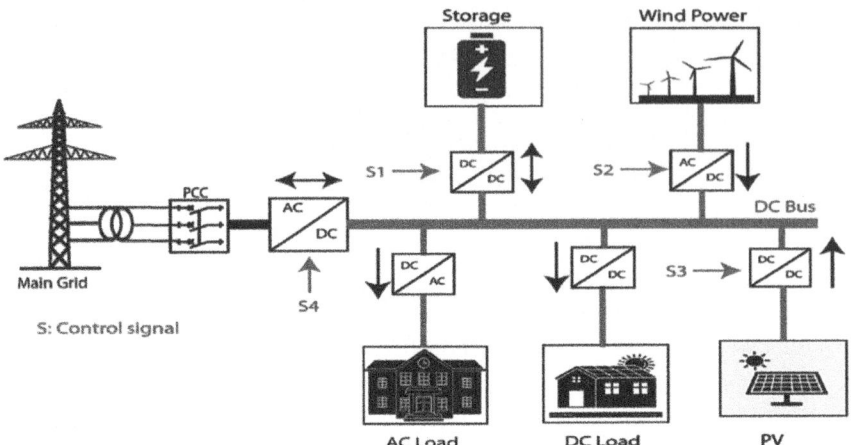

Fig. 2. Microgrid Proposed structure.

and an efficiency of 95%. A DC-DC converter connects the solar system and battery bank, a DC-DC converter connects the wind tur-bine and battery bank, a DC-DC bidirectional converter connects the battery and the microgrid, and a DC-AC converter connects the microgrid DC bus to the AC loads. All converters are 95% efficient and have control algorithms to regulate the microgrid's power flow. In order to maximize the utilization of renewable energy sources while reducing reliance on the grid, this microgrid was created. The components are chosen and set up to function together flawlessly and supply dependable, steady power to the loads. Taking into consideration changes in solar irradiation and wind speed, the solar system has a maximum power output of 60 kW and the wind turbine has a maximum output of 20 kW. For the microgrid to function independently of the grid, a high-capacity and effective energy storage option is provided by the lithium battery bank. The weather conditions used in this work are presented in Figs. 3 and 4. The power output is affected by weather conditions, as clear skies result in higher power generation compared to cloudy or overcast conditions as shown in Fig. 5. These findings highlight the importance of monitoring weather conditions and adjusting the microgrid's energy management strategy accordingly to ensure optimal performance and maximum energy efficiency. The observed power output of the wind turbine system is shown in Fig. 6.

The graph clearly shows that the wind speed directly affects the turbine's power production, with higher wind speeds producing more energy.

The measured power of the solar and wind turbines exhibited fluctuations caused by the variable nature of renewable energy sources. These fluctuations caused discontinuities in the microgrid's power supply, resulting in surplus power in some instances and a lack of power in others. The measured power of the DC and AC loads in the microgrid is shown in Figs. 7 and 8, respectively.

Figures 7 and 8 clearly demonstrate that the power generated from renewable energy sources is effectively meeting the power demand of the DC and AC loads.

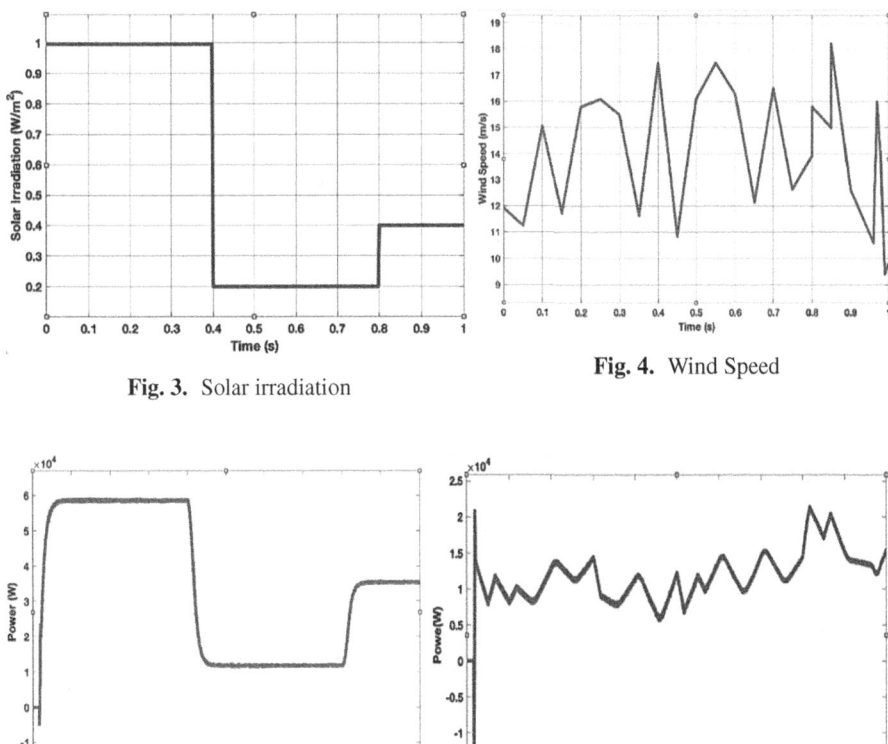

Fig. 3. Solar irradiation

Fig. 4. Wind Speed

Fig. 5. Produced power using solar panels

Fig. 6. Measured Wind turbine Power

The paragraph explains how an energy management system in a microgrid operates, concentrating on how excess electricity is managed under the direction of a battery. The usefulness of a fuzzy logic controller in controlling battery charging and discharging processes to provide a dependable power source is also covered.

The surplus of energy occurs when the microgrid's renewable energy sources, such as solar panels and wind turbines, produce more energy than is currently required. Instead of being wasted, this extra energy is used to charge a battery for later use. On the other hand, if the microgrid encounters a power deficit, meaning it needs more power than the renewable sources are currently able to supply, the battery gets drained. Throughout the operation of the microgrid, the energy stored in the battery is released to complement the power supply, maintaining a steady and balanced supply of electricity. The research's Figs. 9 and 10 probably provide graphical depictions of how the battery's charge and power levels alter over time. By displaying when the battery charges and drains, these graphs assist in seeing how the battery is managed.

According to the paragraph, the energy management technique under discussion has produced favorable outcomes. This indicates that the system successfully manages the

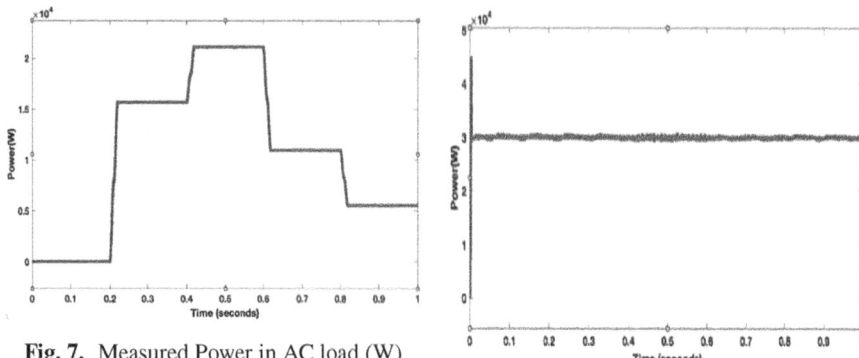

Fig. 7. Measured Power in AC load (W)

Fig. 8. Measured Power in DC load (W)

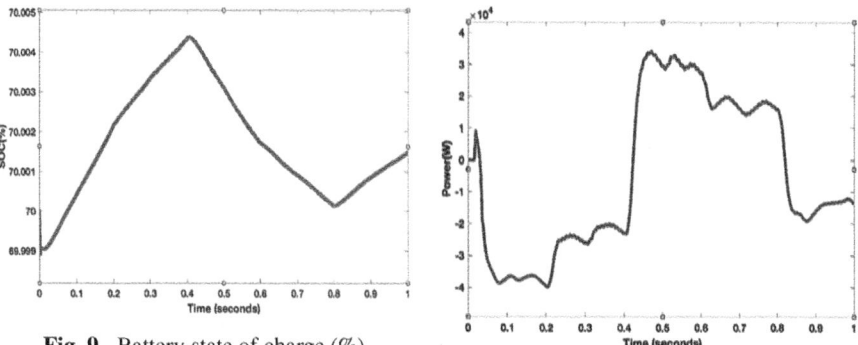

Fig. 9. Battery state of charge (%)

Fig. 10. Variation of Battery Power (W)

balance between the production of renewable energy and the consumption of electricity, resulting in efficient functioning. A fuzzy logic controller is emphasized as a crucial element of this energy management system. When determining when and how to charge or discharge the battery, it is crucial. In order to make the most use of the battery's stored energy, the controller modifies battery operations in response to current conditions and demand. The battery power shows how well the fuzzy logic controller handles the battery. When demand outpaces production, it helps renewable energy sources and saves extra energy when renewable sources generate more than is required. The dynamic management contributes to the stability of the power supply.

Battery State of Charge in Graph 9 shows how well the battery is maintained by the fuzzy logic controller. This is essential for the stability and dependability of the micro-grid. The battery will always be ready to supply power when required if it is kept in an ideal condition of charge. Figures 11 and 12 likely show a comparison between two control methods: PID (Proportional-Integral-Derivative) and fuzzy controllers. They demonstrate how well these control methods maintain the microgrid's voltage and frequency within acceptable ranges, further ensuring a stable and reliable power supply.

In summary, this passage provides insights into how an energy management system, with the assistance of a fuzzy logic controller, effectively handles surplus power, addresses power deficits, and ensures the stability and reliability of a microgrid's power supply by efficiently managing a battery's charging and discharging operations.

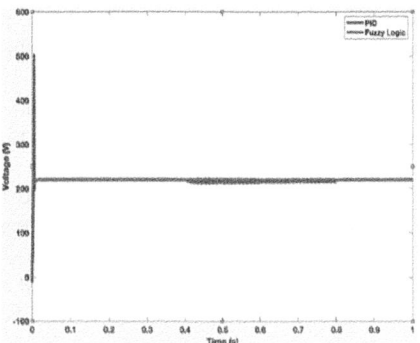 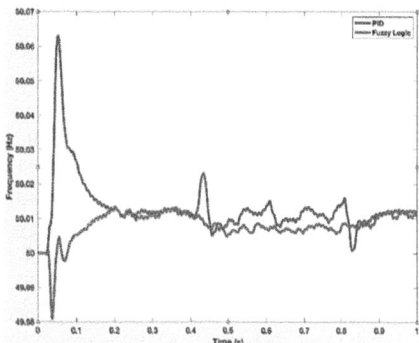

Fig. 11. Measured voltage at DC   **Fig. 12.** Measured frequency at AC Bus

Bus With PID and Fuzzy logic With PID and Fuzzy logic.

Comparing the results of the PID and Fuzzy controllers for regulating the DC bus voltage and frequency in the microgrid, it is evident that the Fuzzy logic controller outperforms the PID controller. The Fuzzy controller maintains a more stable DC bus voltage and frequency with minimal variation, even when load demand and the production of renewable energy fluctuate. In contrast, the PID controller shows slightly larger variations in both DC bus voltage and frequency. These results highlight the superior performance of the Fuzzy controller in ensuring a stable and reliable microgrid operation. Thus, it can be said that the suggested energy management system, especially when combined with the Fuzzy controller, successfully controls the DC bus voltage and frequency, adding to the microgrid system's overall stability and dependability.

5 Conclusion

This paper proposed an efficient energy management strategy for a microgrid system that utilizes renewable energy sources and energy storage. The proposed strategy employs a fuzzy logic controller to manage the charging and discharging of the battery and regulate the DC bus voltage and frequency. The results of the simulation showed that the proposed energy management system effectively balances the generation and demand of the microgrid and ensures a stable and reliable operation. Furthermore, the comparison between the results obtained using the fuzzy logic controller and the PID controller showed that the fuzzy logic controller outperformed the PID controller in terms of stability and accuracy. Overall, the proposed energy management strategy is an effective approach for ensuring the reliable operation of microgrid systems, especially those powered by renewable energy sources. Future work can focus on optimizing the strategy and expanding its implementation in other microgrid systems.

References

1. Rodriguez, M., Arcos-Aviles, D., Martinez, W.: Fuzzy logic-based energy management for isolated microgrid using meta-heuristic optimization algorithms. Appl. Energy **335**, 120771 (2023)
2. Chekira, O., Boharb, A., Boujoudar, Y., El Moussaoui, H., Lamhamdi, T., El Markhi, H.: An improved energy management control strategy for a standalone solar photovoltaic/battery system. Indonesian J. Electr. Eng. Comput. Sci. **27**(2), 647–658 (2022)
3. Boujoudar, Y., Azeroual, M., Elmoussaoui, H., Lamhamdi, T.: Intelligent control of battery energy storage for microgrid energy management using ANN. Int. J. Electr. Comput. Eng. **11**(4), 2760 (2021). https://doi.org/10.11591/ijece.v11i4.pp2760-2767
4. Sayigh, A.: Solar and wind energy will supply more than 50% of world electricity by 2030. In: Green Buildings and Renewable Energy. IRE, pp. 385–399. Springer, Cham (2020). https://doi.org/10.1007/978-3-030-30841-4_27
5. Chekira, O., Boharb, A., Lamhamdi, T., El Moussaoui, H., El Markhi, H., Beniss, M.A.: Frequency control and energy management of microgrid with distributed energy storage. E3S Web Conf. **351**, 01047 EDP Sciences (2022)
6. Regad, M., Helaimi, M.H., Taleb, R., Othman, A.M., Gabbar, H.A.: Frequency control of microgrid with renewable generation using PID controller based krill herd. Indonesian J. Electr. Eng. Inf. (IJEEI) **8**(1), 21–32 (2020)
7. Sumar, R.R., Coelho, A.A.R., dos Santos Coelho, L.: Computational intelligence approach to PID controller design using the universal model. Inf. Sci. **180**(20), 3980–3991 (2010)
8. Kheshti, M., Ding, L., Askarian-Abyaneh, H., Singh, A.R., Zare, S., Terzija, V.: Improving frequency regulation of wind-integrated multi-area systems using LFA-fuzzy PID control. Int. Trans. Electr. Energy Syst. **31**(3), e12802 (2021)
9. Behera, S., Choudhury, N.B.D.: Modelling and simulations of modified slime mould algorithm based on fuzzy PID to design an optimal battery management system in microgrid. Cleaner Energy Syst. **3**, 100029 (2022)
10. Zehra, S.S., Wood, M.J., Grimaccia, F., Leva, S., Mussetta, M.: Solar and grid power integration for dynamic energy management in electric vehicle charging and load fulfilment with fuzzy logic. In: 2023 AEIT International Conference on Electrical and Electronic Technologies for Automotive (AEIT AUTOMOTIVE) (pp. 1–6). IEEE
11. Kambalimath, S., Deka, P.C.: A basic review of fuzzy logic applications in hydrology and water resources. Appl. Water Sci. **10**(8), 1–14 (2020)
12. Saraswat, R., Suhag, S.: Type-2 fuzzy logic PID control for efficient power balance in an AC microgrid. Sustainable Energy Technol. Assess. **56**, 103048 (2023)

Evaluation of RANS Turbulence Models, Including the GEKO Model for Turbulent Flow Around a Wind Turbine Blade S809

Jawad El Marbouh[✉] and Nacer Eddine El Kadri Elyamani

Sciences Engineering Laboratory, University of Sidi Mohamed Ben Abdellah, Polydisciplinary Faculty of Taza, B.P.1223 Fez, Morocco
elmarbouhjawad@gmail.com,
nacereddine.elkadrielyamani@usmba.ac.ma

Abstract. Invaluable research efforts have been made to develop a standard turbulence model. However, researchers have failed to uncover the pitfalls being presented thus far. In this study, we have dealt with a two-dimensional flow, viscous and incompressible, around the subsonic profile S809 in a steady state, at Reynold's number of 1 million, from various angles of attack. Regarding the field's topological study, we have chosen a structured C-type mesh. The element shape is quadri-angular, and the resolution method is pressure-based. In the first part, a comparison for calculating the aerodynamic performance has been carried out between conventional RANS models (Spalart Almaras, $K - \varepsilon$ Realizable model, $k - \omega$ (SST) model) and the GEKO (Generalized $K - $ Omega) model in the light of varying the separation of coefficient Csep. According to the results obtained, GEKO models are considered the most effective for predicting drag and lift coefficients. The second part is devoted to highlighting the recently developed GEKO model, which has demonstrated its ability to accurately predict the wake phenomenon and the onset of separation. The GEKO model offered a flexible model that could be adapted to different flow cases without impacting the essential calibration.

Keywords: Horizontal axis wind turbine · **CFD** · **S809** Profile · **RANS** (Reynolds Averaged Navier-Stokes) turbulence models · **GEKO** turbulence model · aerodynamic performance · boundary layer separation

Nomenclature

ρ	Density, kg/m^3
k	Turbulent kinetic energy, m^2/s^2
δ_{ij}	Delta de Kronecker
ε	Dissipation rate of turbulent kinetic energy
μ	Dynamic viscosity, kg/m.s
μ_t	turbulent Dynamic viscosity
ω	Specific dissipation rate of turbulent kinetic energy,
C	Chord length, m
Re	Reynolds number
α	Angle of attack

© The Author(s), under exclusive license to Springer Nature Switzerland AG 2025
H. Hagras et al. (Eds.): ISACS 2023, CCIS 2255, pp. 253–264, 2025.
https://doi.org/10.1007/978-3-031-93448-3_21

Abbreviations

RANS Reynolds Averaged Navier-Stokes
SST   Shear Stress Transport
GEKO Generalized K-Omega
CFD   Computational Fluid Dynamics
HAWT Horizontal-axis wind turbine
CSEP Separation coefficient
CNW   Near Wall coefficient
CMIX Mixing coefficient
CJET Jet coefficient

1 Introduction

Taking into account the significant greenhouse effects and climate change, the innovation and sustainable development of renewable energies become necessary, in particular the improvement of wind energy's performance.

The effects of aerodynamic forces (drag and lift) are necessary for the performance and profitability of horizontal axis wind turbines (**HAWT**) and through **CFD** tools such as **ANSYS FLUENT**. Researchers are making great efforts to study them with precision and accuracy. Several factors influence **CFD** results, but the choice of turbulence.

model remains significant. That is why it is important to inspect with great care which hypotheses are based on these models and their limitations.

Below, some research has been carried out on the evaluation of turbulence models.

In 2005, Vance Dippold [1] studied different near-wall flow modelling methods available in the WIND CFD code and concluded that both two-equation turbulence models performed well in a neutral or favourable pressure gradient environment. However, the SST model performed better when an unfavourable pressure gradient was present.

In 2006, Guerri et al. [2] used a 2D Navier-Stokes simulation of a steady, unsteady flow for the S809 wing. They studied different turbulence models: the SST k-ω model and the RNG k-ε model. They established that the k-ω model better simulates the unsteady flow region than the k-ε model.

In 2017, Dimitra C. Douvi et al. [3] performed a 2D CFD analysis for the S809 airfoil using the FLUENT code. They concluded that the k-ε feasible model appears to be the most appropriate turbulence model for predicting aerodynamic performance degradation.

In 2019, B.abed et al. [4] conducted a numerical investigation under ANSYS CFX to evaluate the k-ε and k-ε RNG turbulence models, concluding that both models cannot predict aerodynamic performance in the pre-stall and post-stall zones.

In 2020, Khan et al. [5] Analyzed the NACA 0018 airfoil flow at positive angles of attack, ranging from 0 to 18 degrees for various Reynolds numbers with four different turbulence models in ANSYS Fluent. They concluded that the SST k-ω turbulence model more accurately predicted the lift coefficient for low angles of attack. In contrast, the Transition k-kl-ω model captured the flow separation and reattachment regions.

In 2021 Spyridon et al. [6] evaluated Spalart-Allmaras, the feasible k-ε and the standard $k - \omega$, concluding that the k-ω model is the most appropriate for stall conditions.

The study focuses on the numerical resolution of a two-dimensional, viscous and incompressible flow around the S809 subsonic profile in steady state, at Reynold's number of 1 million in order to evaluate the performance of the RANS models: Spalart Almaras, Model $K - \varepsilon$ realizable, Model $k - \omega$ (SST), and The Generalized $k - \omega$ model (GEKO), seeing that this model just saw the light of day in 2019 and that there is no excellent research elaborated to highlight it, we decided to work on it in order to issue an aerodynamic performance test. The results obtained will be validated by wind tunnel tests (Somers) [7].

The special feature of the (GEKO) model is its flexibility. Even if we vary one of its free coefficients, altering its basic calibration is not risky.

The current approach aims to establish a unique framework, using different coefficients to cover numerous fields of application, such as aerodynamics, hydrodynamics, and heat transfer.

2 Methodology

The simulation was carried out using ANSYS 2022 R2 STUDENT, a commercial software package based on the finite volume method. Figure 1 illustrates the approach adopted for the numerical resolution.

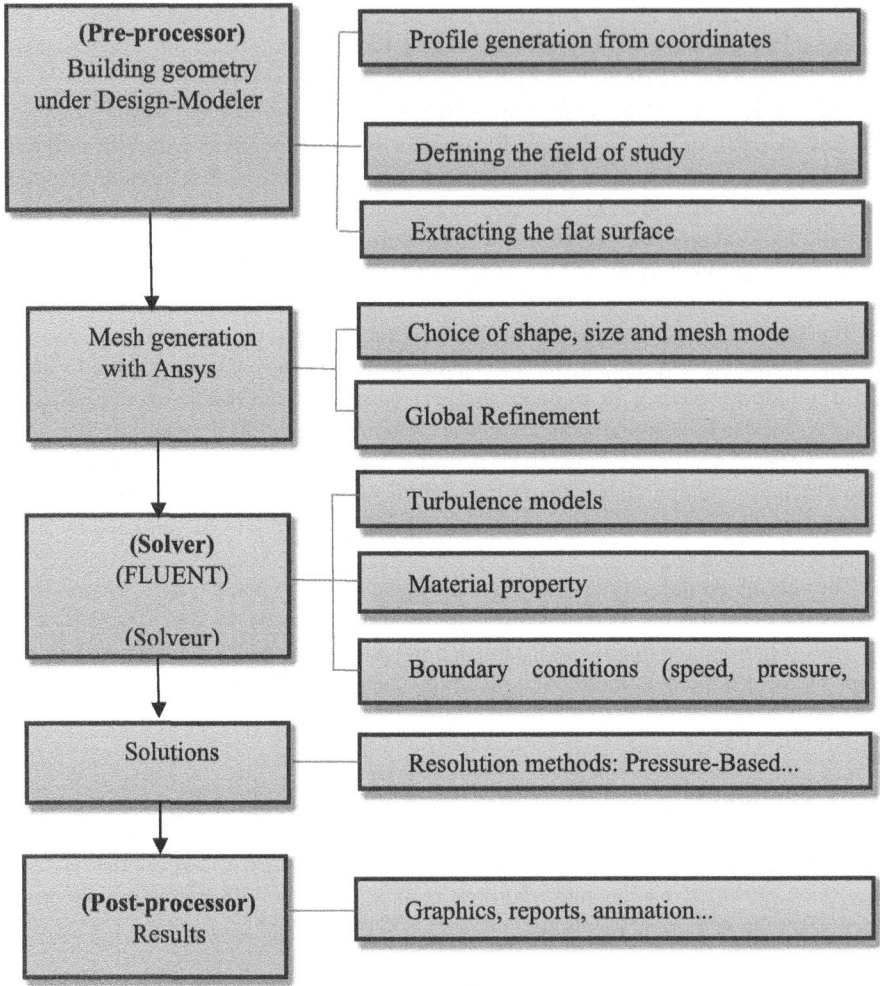

Fig. 1. Flow chart of the numerical solution approach.

3   Mathematical Modeling

3.1   The Turbulence Model k − ω

To overcome the weaknesses of the earlier model, **Wilcox** adopts the specific dissipation rate ω in place of the epsilon dissipation rate, as defined here (Table 1):

$$\rho\frac{\partial(k)}{\partial t} + \rho\frac{\partial(ku_i)}{\partial x_j} = \frac{\partial}{\partial x_j}\left[(\mu + \mu_t\sigma_k)\frac{\partial k}{\partial x_j}\right] + P_k - \beta^*\rho k\omega \qquad (1)$$

$$avecP_k = \tau_{ij}\frac{\partial u_i}{\partial x_j}$$

$$\rho \frac{\partial(\omega)}{\partial t} + \rho \frac{\partial(\omega u_i)}{\partial x_j} = \frac{\partial}{\partial x_j}\left[(\mu + \mu_t \sigma_\omega)\frac{\partial \omega}{\partial x_j}\right] + \frac{\gamma_1}{\upsilon_t}P_k - \beta_1 \rho k \omega^2 \qquad (2)$$

Table 1. The coefficients of the **wilcox 1988** model

Model	β^*	β_1	σ_k	σ_w
Wilcox (1988)	1.92	1.44	2	2

The main advantage of this model is that it can be used throughout the boundary layer without any modification. However, its main drawback is that it is very sensitive to values of k and omega in the free flow as they approach 0.

To solve this problem, **Menter** (1994) proposes the Shear Stress Tansport (**SST**) model [8].

3.2 The k-w (SST) Turbulence Model

This model is a hybrid of two models, of which the k-w model is used in the region close to the wall and the k-epsilon model in the region far from the wall, as shown in the Fig. 2:

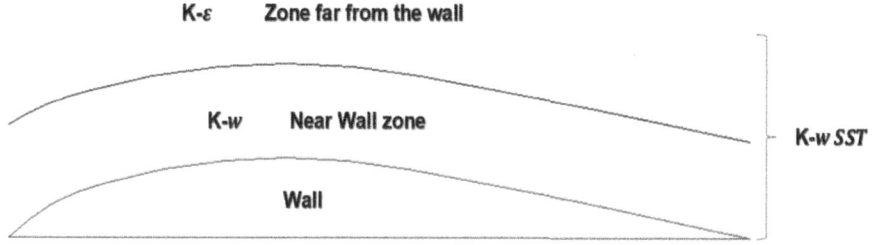

Fig. 2. k - w SST model.

It has been demonstrated that this model can be integrated up to this point under a viscous layer, without introducing any changes to the wall or damping functions.

$$\rho \frac{\partial(k)}{\partial t} + \rho \frac{\partial(k u_i)}{\partial x_j} = \frac{\partial}{\partial x_j}\left[(\mu + \mu_t \sigma_k)\frac{\partial k}{\partial x_j}\right] + P_k - \beta^* \rho k \omega \qquad (3)$$

$$\rho \frac{\partial(\omega)}{\partial t} + \rho \frac{\partial(\omega u_i)}{\partial x_j} = \frac{\partial}{\partial x_j}\left[(\mu + \mu_t \sigma_k)\frac{\partial \omega}{\partial x_j}\right] + \frac{\gamma}{\upsilon_t}P_k - \beta_1 \rho k \omega^2$$
$$+ 2\rho(1 - F_1)\sigma_{\omega 2}\frac{1}{\omega}\frac{\partial k}{\partial x_j}\frac{\partial \omega}{\partial x_j} \qquad (4)$$

The last term in the omega transport equation is an additional, non-conservative cross-diffusion term. The presence of this term means that the $k - \omega$ model returns the same results as the k-epsilon model in the region away from the wall.F1 is a mixing function defined as the distance from the wall and determines the regions where the k-epsilon and k-w models are used.

3.3 GEKO Model

It is a $k - \omega$ based model designed to consolidate two **RANS** models into a flexible and robust turbulence model for general use.

Compared to other RANS MODELS, the **GEKO** model is more easily calibrated for specific flow conditions. [9].

The GEKO model provides parameters for adjustment according to application type and specificity, with no negative impact on the model's basic calibration. In contrast, for conventional models, modification of these parameters can lead to loss of model calibration.

There are four free parameters:

- **CSEP**: this parameter controls the flux separation of smooth surfaces; increasing it leads to earlier and stronger separation.
- **CNW**: this parameter optimizes flow in regions close to the out-of-equilibrium wall; increasing it leads to higher heat transfer rates at stagnation points (leading edge, for example).
- **CMIX**: increase will lead to stronger mixing and free shear flows.
- **CJET**: optimizes free jets independently of the mixing layer, increasing this parameter will increase free jet spreading rates (Table 2).

Table 2. Recommended free coefficients (GEKO)

MIN		Parameter	MAX		Default
0.7	$\leq$	CSEP	$\leq$	2.5	1.75
−2.0	$\leq$	CNW	$\leq$	2.0	0.50
…0.5	$\leq$	CMIX	$\leq$	1.0…	CMixCor
0.0	$\leq$	CJET	$\leq$	1.0	0.90
0.0	$\leq$	CCORNER	$\leq$	1.5	1.00
0.0	$\leq$	CCURV	$\leq$	1.5	1.00

4 Geometry

The S809 shown in Fig. 3 is an airfoil supplied by the National Renewable Energy Laboratory (NREL). Suitable for laminar flows with a thickness of 21%, it is designed specifically for HAWT horizontal-axis wind turbine applications. The NREL Phase VI wind turbine, with a diameter of 10 m and a power output of 20 kW, also uses an S809 airfoil. Its inlet speed is 14.6 m/s, and it rotates at 72 rpm. Point coordinates are taken from the reference website [10].

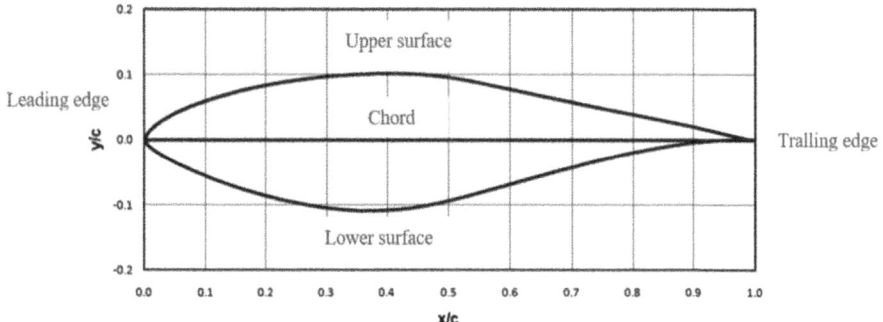

Fig. 3. Profile section S809

5   CFD Domain and Boundary Conditions

In order to avoid the influence of boundary conditions on the results obtained and to clearly describe the wake phenomenon, the boundaries must be sufficiently far apart. On the other hand, we must guard against an excessively large domain, which would require many computational elements, the chosen dimensions are shown in the Fig. 4.

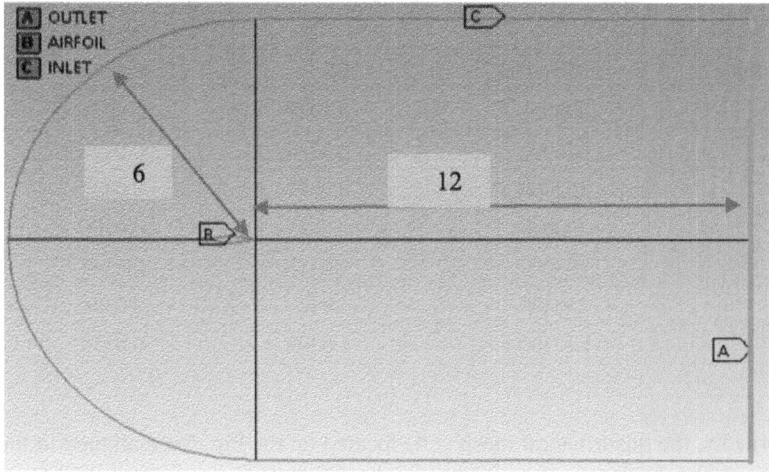

Fig. 4. CFD domain dimensioning and boundary conditions

Outlet (A): The pressure direction was taken to be normal to the boundary, with a value of 1atm (101325pas), a turbulent intensity of 2.84%.

Airfoil (B): Experience confirms that particle velocities close to the profile boundary are considered zero in the case of viscous fluids, and therefore the no-slip condition must be taken into account.

Inlet (C): The inlet flow velocity (V) is 14.6 m/s with a turbulent intensity of 2.84%, and a hydraulic diameter of 1.

$$Re = \frac{\rho VA}{\mu} \tag{5}$$

$\mu = 1.78 \times 10^{-5}\,\text{kg/ms}; \quad \rho = 1.225\ \text{kg/m}^2; \quad C = 1\ \text{m}; \quad Re = 10^6$

6   Meshing

The study domain is subdivided into 4 sub-domains. To guarantee greater precision and smooth handling, we have adopted a combination of edge dimensioning and face meshing, with a size ratio assigned to the edges so that they ensure convergent progression and consequently obtain a fine mesh along the aerodynamic profile and a coarse mesh in the far field. About the topology of the study domain, we chose a structured C-type mesh based on its effectiveness cited in the literature and in articles [11] and [12]. The Table 3 independence study shows that increasing the number of elements does not significantly increase Cl and Cd values. The Table 4 shows the characteristics of the selected grid.

Table 3. Study of mesh independence for α = 10.2.

Mesh num	Mesh size	Cl	Cd
1	40000	0.7921	0.0551
2	67600	0.8474	0.0496
3	102400	0.9082	0.0441
4	160000	1,002	0,0366
5	193600	1.031	0.0347
6	230400	1.042	0.0338
7	270400	1.0309	0.0338

Normally, the quadrilateral mesh cells located on the Fig. 5 are aligned in the flow direction, which leads to more accurate results and better convergence of CFD solvers. The tests of multiple mesh configurations performed in the article [13] demonstrated that the structured mesh gives more accurate drag predictions with fewer cells than the hybrid mesh.

Table 4. Mesh characteristics

Mesh type	Number of elements	Number of nodes	Order of elements	Distance of the first cells from the airfoil	Y +
Quadri angular	160000	160700	Linear	0.027 mm	1.18

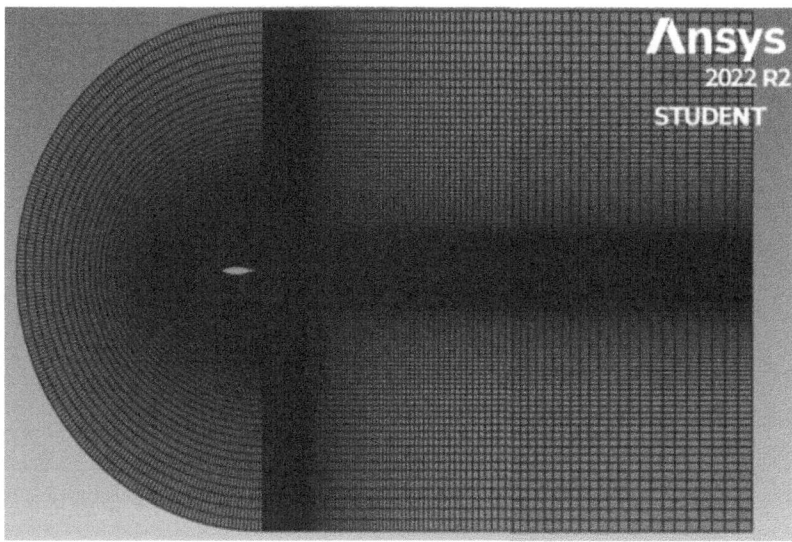

Fig. 5. Mesh grid for profile **S809**

7   Solver Tuning

The resolution method adopted is pressure-based; the mails are based on the Green-Gauss method, simulations have been carried out in steady state, with a discretization scheme coupled between pressure and velocity, and the equations are put in higher order to increase the accuracy of the calculations, the number of iterations is chosen to be 1000 to ensure convergence with a residual value of 0.0001.

In our case, a large part of the flow in the domain is far from being influenced by the blade; the velocity of most of the flow is independent of the blade velocity; therefore, solving them using the absolute velocity formulation is recommended.

8   Results and Discussion

8.1   Aerodynamic Coefficients

The curves in Fig. 6 show a comparison of the lift coefficient between the Spalart almaras turbulence models, K epsilon Realizable, $K - \omega$ SST, and the GEKO models by varying the separation coefficient Csep for different angles of attack concerning the SOMERS

262   J. E. Marbouh and N. E. E. K. Elyamani

Fig. 1 experimental results. The results obtained by the K − ω SST and GEKO (1.75) models are considered to be closer to the experimental results than the other models.

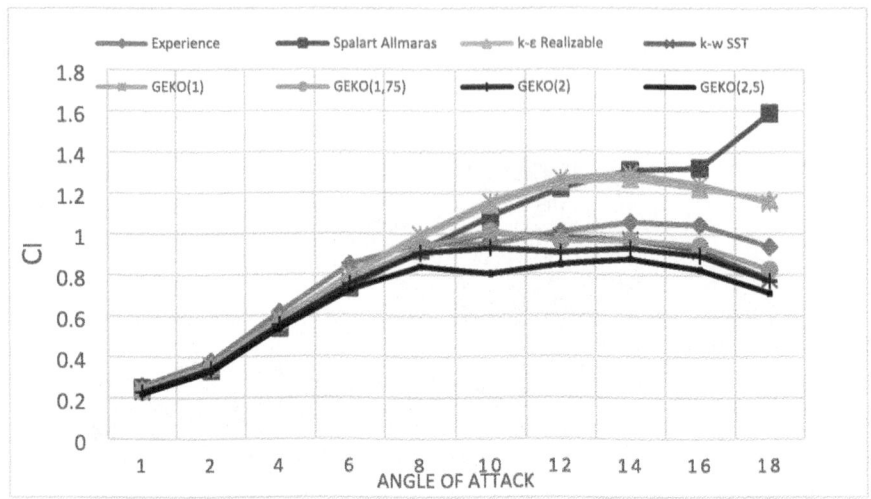

Fig. 6. Comparison curves between the Cl obtained by experiment and that obtained by CFD by varying the angle of attack (the value in brackets is the separation coefficient).

About the drag coefficient shown in Fig. 7, the G − ω SST model was more accurate for angles of attack between 1 and 10, and the GEKO (2.5) model for angles between 12

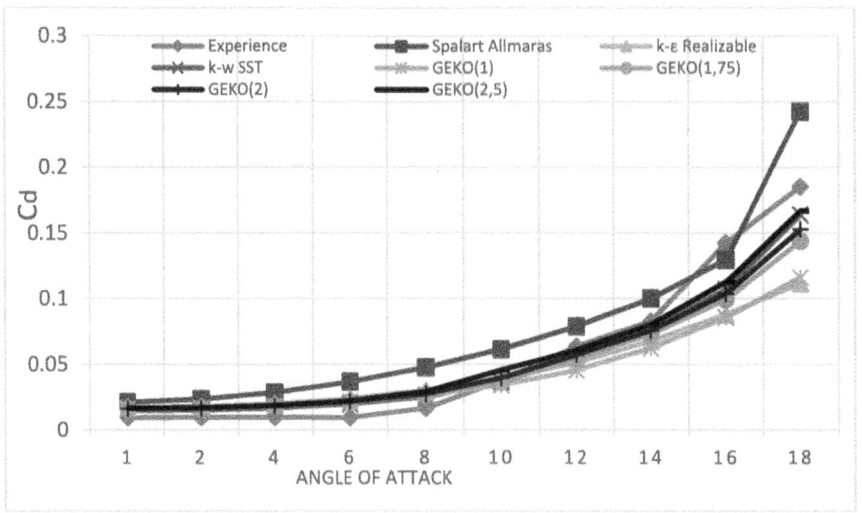

Fig. 7. Comparison curves between Cd obtained by experiment and that obtained by CFD by varying the angle of attack.

and 20. Generally speaking, the results of the $G - \omega$ SST and GEKO models are almost identical.

8.2 Velocity Contours for Wake Analysis

From the results obtained in Fig. 8, we can see that increasing Csep leads to an increase in the length of the wake zone, which makes the model capable of accurately predicting the wake phenomenon without having influenced other characteristics, and this asset is a strong point of the GEKO model. Moreover, the $k - w$ SST model has been placed at the last level of accuracy.

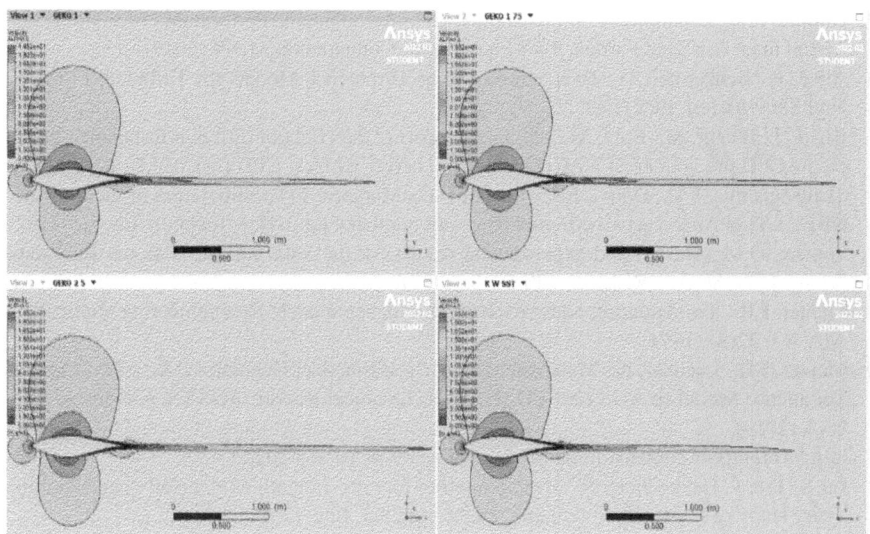

Fig. 8. Flow velocity contours of the 4 models for $\alpha = 0°$.

9 Conclusion

The present study seeks to evaluate the accuracy of conventional turbulence models, and the recently developed GEKO models through a CFD study launched on an S809 wind turbine blade.

The results showcase that for the calculation of lift coefficient, the $G - \omega$ SST and GEKO (1.75) models are considered the closest to the experimental results compared to the other models. Concerning drag coefficient, the $G - \omega$ SST model demonstrated its superiority compared to the GEKO models. That is to say, and it was more accurate for angles of attack ranging from 1 to 10 and the GEKO (2.5) model for angles between 12 and 20.

Also, from the results obtained for analyzing the wake for $\alpha = 0°$, we found that increasing Csep leads to an increase in the length of the wake zone, making the model capable of predicting the wake phenomenon accurately without having influenced other characteristics.

Thanks to its flexibility, this approach has considerably improved the accuracy of CFD study results.

References

1. Dippold. V.: Investigation of Wall Function and Turbulence Model Performance within the Wind Code. AIAA Aerospace Sciences Meeting and Exhibit (2005)
2. Guerri, O., Bouhadef, K., Harhad, A.: Turbulent flow simulation of the NREL S809 airfoil. Wind Eng. **30**(4), 287–301 (2006)
3. Dimitra. C.D., Dionissios. P.M., Aristeidis. E.D.: Aerodynamic Performance of a NREL S809 Airfoil in an Air-Sand Particle Two-Phase Flow. Computation,MDPI (2017)
4. Abed, B., Benzerdjeb, A.: Evaluation of Rans Turbulence Models for Turbulent Flow over Nrel S809 Airfoil. EPSTEM, (2019)
5. Khan, S., Bashir, M., Baig, M., Ali, F.: Comparing the effect of different turbulence models on the CFD predictions of NACA0018 airfoil aerodynamics. CFD Lett. **12**(3), 1–10 (2020)
6. Skaltsogiannis, S.D., Douvi, E.C., Douvi, D.C., Margaris, D.P.: Simulation of the Flow over NREL's S834 Airfoil at two different Reynolds numbers. Int. J. New Technol. Res. **7**(5) (2021)
7. Somers, D.M.: Design and experimental results for the S809 airfoil. National Renewable Energy Laboratory. NRELISR-440-6918 (1997)
8. Menter, F.R.: Two-equation eddy-viscosity turbulence models for engineering applications. AIA A J. **32**(8) (1994)
9. Menter, F.R., Lechner, R., Matyushenko, A.: Best Practice: Generalized k-ω Two-Equation Turbulence Model in ANSYS CFD (GEKO). Technical Report; ANSYS: Canonsburg, PA, USA (2019)
10. http://airfoiltools.com/airfoil/details?airfoil=s809-nr 10 Sep 2022
11. Lu, S., Liu, J., Hekkenberg, R.: Mesh properties for rans simulations of airfoil-shaped profiles, a case study of rudder hydrodynamics. J. Marine Sci. Eng. (2021)
12. El khchine, Y., Sriti, M.: Boundary layer and amplified grid effects on aerodynamic performances of S809 airfoil for horizontal axis wind turbine (HAWT). J. Eng. Sci. Technol. (2017)
13. Lu, S., Liu, J., Hekkenberg, R.: Mesh Properties for RANS Simulations of Airfoil-Shaped Profiles: A Case Study of Rudder Hydrodynamics. Journal of Marine Science and Engineering, MDPI (2021)
14. Spalart and Allmaras: A One-Equation Turbulence Model for Aerodynamic Flows (1992)
15. Launder, B.E., Spalding, D.B.: The numerical computation of turbulent flows. Comput. Methods Appl. Mech. Eng. **3**(2), 269–289 (1974). https://doi.org/10.1016/0045-7825(74)900 29-2
16. Fluent intro Release 15.0 L07 Turbulence available on line: http://www.ansys.com/
17. Thierry TARDIF and Adrian ILINCAmodélisation de l'écoulement d'air autour d'un profil de pale d'éolienne. Laboratoire de Recherche en Énergie Éolienne LREE (2008)
18. Ferziger , J.H., Perić, M., Street, R.L.: Computational Methods for Fluid Dynamics

Fuzzy-PI Controller Using Line Integral Lyapunov Fuzzy Function: Application to Electric Vehicle Powered by PMSM Motor

Elhoussein Elouardi[1]($\boxtimes$)(ID), Ismail Lagrat[2], Omar Mouhib[1], Ahmed Bentaleb[3], and Elouardi Brahim[4]

[1] Laboratory of Electronic Systems, Information Processing, Mechanics and Energetics, Faculty of Sciences, IBN TOFAIL University, Kenitra, Morocco
elhoussein.elouardi1@uit.ac.ma

[2] Laboratory of Advanced Systems Engineering, National School of Applied Sciences, IBN TOFAIL University, Kenitra, Morocco

[3] MIS Laboratory, University of Picardie Jules Verne, Amiens, France

[4] Department of Physics, LPMC-ERSA, Faculty of Sciences, Ben M'sik, Hassan II University, Casablanca, Morocco

Abstract. This paper proposes a robust control strategy for electric vehicles, equipped with a permanent magnet synchronous motor (PMSM), which aims to stabilize and guarantee the optimal tracking of the reference speed.

First, a model is formulated from the motor vehicle dynamics in the synchronous d-q frame. Then, Takagi-Sugeno (TS) fuzzy model is used to deal with the nonlinearities of this model.

Second, a proportional integral (PI) fuzzy controller is proposed to track the reference speed. To reduce conservatism in the conditions obtained, the Line Integral Lyapunov function (LILF) is used. The H_∞ approach is also employed to deal with large load torque variations considered as external disturbances. The linear matrix inequality (LMI) tool is utilized to determine the controller gains.

Finally, the performance of the suggested control strategy is confirmed by the simulation results.

Keywords: Line Integral Lyapunov Function · PMSM motor · Electric vehicle · Fuzzy control · Speed tracking · LMI · H_∞ performance

1 Introduction

The transport sector consumes around a third of total energy consumption, and is also the source of 20% of greenhouse gas emissions [1]. Electric vehicles (EVs) are environmentally friendly, quieter, more efficient and generally consume less energy [2]. So many countries see them as an alternative solution in this sector

H. Hagras et al. (Eds.): ISACS 2023, CCIS 2255, pp. 265–277, 2025.
https://doi.org/10.1007/978-3-031-93448-3_22

to protect the environment. As a result, the number of EVs is set to rise from 3 million to 120 over the next decade [3].

However, the main obstacles to integrating these vehicles into the transportation system are safety and energy management [2,4]. Several advanced control strategies are used to overcome these obstacles and boost the efficiency of these vehicles. driving comfort and improved start-up times are examined in [5] using a (PID) controller. In [6] Robust model predictive control (MPC) for direct yaw moment coordinated and path tracking is proposed. Zhang et al. [7] suggest a second-order sliding mode controller (SMC) for vehicle stability. [8] used the Linear-quadratic regulator (LQR) technique to study the effect of skid angle on vehicle stability, and a Model predictive control (MPC) is applied to optimise yaw moment and torque vector control in [9].

In this paper, used the Line Integral Lyapunov Fuzzy (LILF) function, T-S fuzzy models and H_∞ criteria and (LMI) technique we develop a proportional integral controller (PI) to track the desired speed of the EV. Consequently, with the proposed control strategy in this work, good tracking and regulation capabilities while the presence of disturbances can be obtained without adjusting any controller parameter compared to the standard PI controller.

The rest of the paper proceeds as follows: First, the EV configuration is introduced in Sect. 2. In Sect. 3, the non-linear dynamic model of the EV engine constituted by the (PMSM) is presented. Furthermore, the nonlinear system of the (PMSM) is approximated into several linear sub-systems via T-S Fuzzy approach. In Sect. 4, the Fuzzy Integral Lyapunov integral, H_∞ criteria and (LMI) technique are introduced and used to design the (PI) controller gains. Finally effectiveness of the proposed control strategy is verified by simulations in Sect. 5.

2   System Description

2.1   Electric Vehicle Model

Figure 1 shows the main powertrain components of an electric vehicle (EV). For an electric vehicle model to be representative, a variety of factors need to be taken into account, such as road conditions, aerodynamic drag etc.

The total tractive force required at the wheel can be expressed as follows [10]:

$$F = F_{rr} + F_{ad} + F_{hc} + F_i \tag{1}$$

Where $F_{rr} = sing(v)\mu_{rr}mgcos(\theta)$ is the resistance force of rolling, $F_{ad} = 0.5\rho C_d v^2$ is the aerodynamic drag force, $F_{hc} = mgsin(\theta)$ is the grading resistance force and $F_i = m\frac{dv}{dt}$ is the inertia force.

Where m is EV's mass, v the EV's velocity, g the gravity acceleration coeffiecent, ρ the air density, θ the hill climbing angle, A the area of frontal of EV, and C_d the drag coefficient.

Resultant force F will produce a counteractive torque $C_e = F\frac{r}{g}$ that will be transmitted to the wheels to move, r is the tire radius.

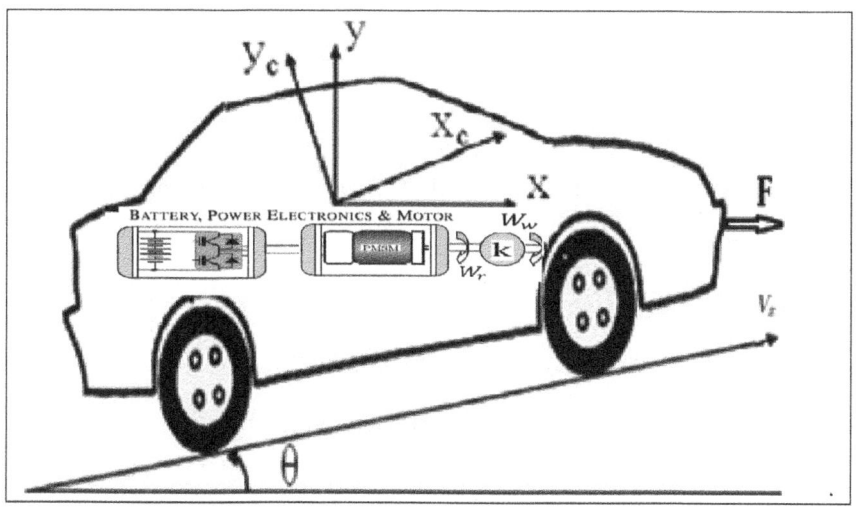

Fig. 1. The Electric vehicle drive train.

2.2   Motor Description

Rotating machines key element of electric vehicles. The PMSM is the type of machine most frequently used in electric vehicles thanks to its excellent efficiency [11].

Many control techniques are proposed to drive PMSM [12].

In this work, we are interested to study the electric vehicle model based on the PMSM. In this sense, the purpose of this section is to describe the dynamics of the PMSM.

The d-q Frame Dynamics of PMSM. In the d-q frame, the PMSM dynamic's can be described as:

$$\begin{cases} V_q = R_s i_q + L_q i_q + W_r L_d i_d + W_r \phi_m \\ V_d = R_s i_d + L_d i_d - W_r L_q i_q \end{cases} \tag{2}$$

Where V_q , V_d are dq-fram voltage, i_q, i_d are dq-fram current, R_s is winding resistance, L_q, L_d are dq-fram inductances, ϕ_m is flux linkage established by PMSM and W_r is electrical rotor rotation speed. Moreover, using the fundamental principle of dynamics, the mechanical equation governing the operation of the PMSM can be written as follows:

$$\dot{W_r} = \frac{-B}{J} W_r + \frac{3n_p^3 \phi_m}{8J} i_q + \frac{-n_p C_r}{2J} \tag{3}$$

The electromagnetic torque C_e generated by is given by:

$$C_e = J \frac{2}{n_p} \dot{W_r} + B \frac{2}{n_p} W_r + C_r \tag{4}$$

where B is the damping coeffiecent of PMSM system, J is the inertia coeffiecent, n_p is the number of magnetic poles C_r is the load torque. Moreover, C_e can be written as:

$$C_e = \frac{3n_p}{4}[\phi_m i_q + (L_q - L_d)i_q i_d] \tag{5}$$

In the PMSM with the surface-mounted ($L_q \cong L_d$) and by combining equations (2) and (3), the state representation of the PMSM system can be done as follows:

$$\begin{bmatrix} \dot{W}_r \\ \dot{i}_q \\ \dot{i}_d \end{bmatrix} = \begin{bmatrix} \frac{-B}{J} & \frac{3n_p^2 \lambda_m}{8J} & 0 \\ \frac{-\phi_m}{L_q} & \frac{-r_s}{L_q} & \frac{-L_d}{L_q}W_r \\ 0 & \frac{-L_q}{L_d} & \frac{-r_s}{L_d} \end{bmatrix} \begin{bmatrix} W_r \\ i_q \\ i_d \end{bmatrix} + \begin{bmatrix} 0 & 0 \\ \frac{1}{L_q} & 0 \\ 0 & \frac{1}{L_d} \end{bmatrix} \begin{bmatrix} v_q \\ v_d \end{bmatrix} + \begin{bmatrix} \frac{-n_p C_r}{2J} \\ 0 \\ 0 \end{bmatrix} \tag{6}$$

Which can be written in the following simplified form

$$\begin{cases} \dot{x}(t) = Ax(t) + Bu(t) + v(t) \\ y(t) = W_m = \begin{bmatrix} 1 & 0 & 0 \end{bmatrix} x(t) = Cx(t) \end{cases} \tag{7}$$

Where $v(t)$ are distrubances of the system that can be represented by:

$$v(t) = \begin{bmatrix} \frac{-n_p C_r}{2J} \\ 0 \\ 0 \end{bmatrix} = \begin{bmatrix} \frac{-n_p}{2J} & 0 & 0 \\ 0 & 0 & 0 \\ 0 & 0 & 0 \end{bmatrix} \begin{bmatrix} C_r \\ 0 \\ 0 \end{bmatrix} = D\psi(t)$$

Fuzzy T-S Model of PMSM. The Takagi-Sugeno fuzzy representation (T-S fuzzy) [13] is well known for dealing with nonlinearities arising from complex systems such as the (PMSM) model [14].

Acoording [12], the PMSM model described in (7) is nonlinear due to the existence of the variable W_r in the state matrix of the system.

Assuming that $W_r^{min} \leq W_r \leq W_r^{Max}$, W_r can be written as:

$$W_r = h_1(W_r(t))W_r^{min} + h_2(W_r(t))W_r^{max}$$

where W_r^{min} and W_r^{Max} are the maximum and minimum of the electrical rotor speed W_r, and

$$\begin{cases} h_1(W_r(t)) = \dfrac{W_r^{Max} - W_r}{W_r^{Max} - W_r^{min}} \\ h_2(W_r(t)) = \dfrac{W_r - W_r^{min}}{W_r^{Max} - W_r^{min}} \end{cases}$$

The global dynamics of the system (7) can be represented as follows:

$$S = \begin{cases} \dot{x}(t) = \sum_{i=1}^{2} h_i(W_r(t)))[A_i x(t) + B_i u(t) + D_i \psi(t)] \\ y(t) = \sum_{i=1}^{2} h_i(W_r(t)))C_i x(t) \end{cases} \tag{8}$$

Where $h_i(W_r(t))$ satisfy the following convexity conditions:

$$\sum_{i=1}^{r} h_i(W_r(t)) = 1 \qquad and \qquad 0 \leq h_i(W_r(t)) \leq 1; \qquad i = 1, 2.$$

3   Control Strategy

The main objective of the control strategy is to develop a control that allows the vehicle to follow the driver's desired longitudinal reference speed profile V_x^d. The idea is to reinforce the motor so that it rotates with an angular speed W_r^d which will be the image of the reference value V_x^d. The wheel angular speed can be expresed as $W_w = kW_r$, k gear ratio.

In this case, the relation between the longitudinal speed V_x and wheel rotation speed W_w are given as follows: $V_x = RW_w$, where R is the wheel radius.

3.1   Line Integral Lyapunov Function (LILF)

The Lyapunov function is usually used for stability analysis and control design for fuzzy systems whose constraints are expressed as LMIs.

Lyapunov's quadratic (CLF) involving finding a common matrix $P = P^T > 0$ that satisfies the constraints for each subsystem of the fuzzy set, which can be a very hard task and can lead to a conservative and time-consuming solution [15] [16].

The (LILF) function is defined as the integral of a scalar function along a trajectory of the system [17]. This technique is based on the analysis of the local stability for each system and, subsequently, the global function will be a fuzzy intersection between all these local functions [18], which leads to less restrictive stability conditions.

Consider the function:

$$V(x(t)) = 2 \oint_{\Gamma_{(0;x)}} f(\phi)d\phi \tag{9}$$

Rhee et al. [17] demonstrate that (9) is a lyapunove function if the following condition is verified

$$\frac{\partial f_n(x)}{\partial x_m} = \frac{\partial f_m(x)}{\partial x_n}, \qquad for \ any \ n \neq m; \ (n, m) = \{1, 2..., n\}^2.$$

$f(x) = \sum_{i=1}^{r} h_i(\theta(t))H_i x(t) > 0$; function of the state x(t) $H_i(x) = (H0 + \sum_{j=1}^{r} D_i)(x)$; the diagonal elements are different according to the fuzzy sets in the premise parts of the fuzzy rules [17].

$$H_0 = H_0^T = \begin{bmatrix} 0 & h_{12} & h_{13} & ... & h_{1n} \\ * & 0 & h_{23} & ... & h_{2n} \\ & & \ddots & & \vdots \\ * & * & & & \\ * & * & * & ... & 0 \end{bmatrix}, D_i = \begin{bmatrix} d_{11}^i & 0 & 0 & ... & 0 \\ * & d_{22}^i & 0 & ... & 0 \\ & & \ddots & & \vdots \\ * & * & & & \\ * & * & * & ... & d_{nn}^i \end{bmatrix}$$

The (CLF) Lyapunov function can therefore be considered a special form of (LILF). The following example illustrates the comparison between (LILF) and (CLF) stability regions.

Example 1 [16]. Let us consider the following nonlinear model:

$$\dot{x}(t) = \sum_{i=1}^{2} h_i(x(t))(A_i x(t) + B_i u(t)) \tag{10}$$

$$A_1 = \begin{bmatrix} -12 & -4 \\ 0.2(7a-6)+6a & -6 \end{bmatrix}, A_2 = \begin{bmatrix} -12 & -4 \\ 0.2(7a-1)+a & -1 \end{bmatrix}, B_1 = \begin{bmatrix} 0 \\ 1 \end{bmatrix}, \ a \in [0;50];$$

$$A_3 = \begin{bmatrix} -6 & -4 \\ 0.2(b-6)+6a & -6 \end{bmatrix}, A_4 = \begin{bmatrix} -6 & -4 \\ 0.2(b-1)+a & -1 \end{bmatrix}, B_2 = \begin{bmatrix} 0 \\ 1 \end{bmatrix}, \ b \in [0;80];$$

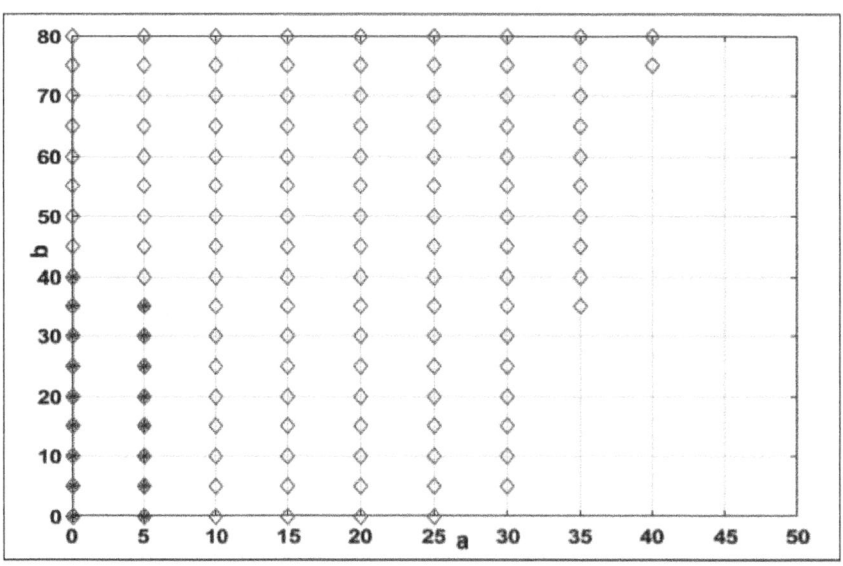

Fig. 2. Comparison of the feasibility fields via (LILF) and (CLF).

Figure 2 showing that the (CLF) Lyapunov function (*) produce restrictive results compared to the (FILF) (◇). This justifies its use in this work.

3.2   Structure of Proposed Controller

The structure of the proposed fuzzy controller is shown in Fig. 3 and is given as follows

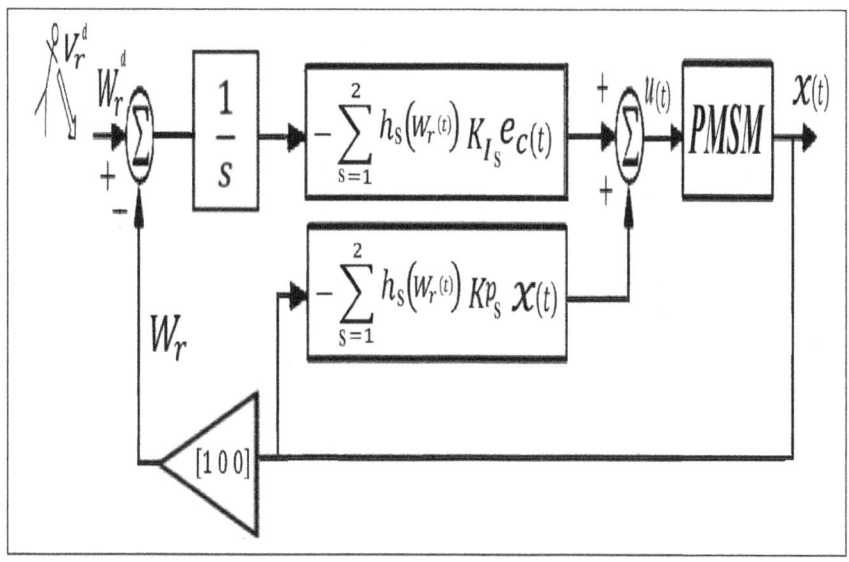

Fig. 3. Structure of the proposed fuzzy controller strategy.

$$U(t) = - \sum_{s=1}^{2} h_s(W_r(t))[K_{P_s}x(t) + K_{I_s} \int_{0}^{t} (W_r - W_r^d)] \tag{11}$$

Let's denote the tracking error dynamic: $\dot{e}_c = W_r - W_r^d$
Substituting (11) into (8) the following augmented system is obtained:

$$\begin{bmatrix} \dot{x} \\ \dot{e}_c \end{bmatrix} = \sum_{i=1}^{2} \sum_{s=1}^{2} h_i(W_r(t))h_s(W_r(t)) \begin{bmatrix} A_i - BK_{Ps} & -BK_{Is} \\ M & 0 \end{bmatrix} \begin{bmatrix} x \\ e_c \end{bmatrix} + \begin{bmatrix} A_i & D \\ 0 & 0 \end{bmatrix} \begin{bmatrix} W_r^d \\ \psi \end{bmatrix}$$

That it can be written as

$$\dot{\hat{x}}(t) = \sum_{i=1}^{2} \sum_{s=1}^{2} h_i(W_r(t))h_s(W_r(t))[(\hat{A}_i - \hat{B}K_s)x + \hat{D}\zeta(t)] \tag{12}$$

where
$$\hat{A}_i = \begin{bmatrix} A_i & 0 \\ N & 0 \end{bmatrix}; \quad \hat{B} = \begin{bmatrix} B \\ 0 \end{bmatrix}; \quad \hat{D} = \begin{bmatrix} A_i & D \\ 0 & 0 \end{bmatrix}; \quad N = [1\ 0\ 0]; \quad K_s = [K_{Ps}\ K_{Is}];$$
$$\zeta(t) = \begin{bmatrix} W_r^d \\ \psi \end{bmatrix}$$

In order to stabilize closed-loop T-S fuzzy model system (8) and design a robust controller, Lyapunov function and H_∞ approache will be used.

Let's consider the H_∞ performance related to the traching error e_c:

$$\int_0^\infty e_c(t)^T e_c(t)dt \le \gamma^2 \int_0^\infty \zeta(t)^T \zeta(t)dt$$

That also can be expressed as:

$$\int_0^\infty \hat{x}(t)^T M^T M \hat{x}(t)dt \le \gamma^2 \int_0^\infty \zeta(t)^T \zeta(t)dt; \qquad M = [1 \ 0 \ 0]. \tag{13}$$

The goal is to design the controller (11) such that the system (8) satisfies:

– The system (12) is globally stable with the controller (11).
– H_∞ performances (13) are satisfied for the system (12).

Corollary 1. *If there are symmetric positive definite matrices X_j, Y_{sj}, K_s and scalars $\gamma > 0$, can satisfy the following inequalities:*

$$\begin{bmatrix} \Xi_{isj} & \hat{D} & XN^T \\ * & -\gamma I & 0 \\ * & * & -I \end{bmatrix} < 0 \tag{14}$$

where $N = [1 \ 0 \ 0]$, I is the identity matrix,

$$\Xi_{isj} = \hat{A}_i X_j + X_j \hat{A}_i^T - \hat{B}Y_{sj} - Y_{sj}^T \hat{B}^T; \qquad Y_{sj} = K_s X_j$$

Then the system (8) is stable asymptotically and the H_∞ performances (13) are guaranteed with attenuation level γ^2.
Where X_j and Y_{sj} (thus $Ks = Y_{sj}X_j^{\frac{1}{}}$) can be easily obtained by solving (14).

Proof. In order to establish to the asymptotic stability of (12), The (LILF) (9) is used. Moreover

$$\dot{V}(\hat{x}(t)) < 0 \tag{15}$$

To account for the H_∞ performance related to the tracking error $e_c(t)$ (15) combined with (13) becomes:

$$\dot{V}(\hat{x}(t)) + \hat{x}(t)^T M^T M \hat{x}(t) - \gamma^2 \zeta^T \zeta < 0 \tag{16}$$

Substituting the expression for $\dot{V}(\hat{x}(t))$ by $\dot{\hat{x}}$.

Lemma 1 [12,19]. *The system (12) is globally asymptotically stable with H_∞ performance (13) if the following conditions are verified*

$$P_j(\hat{A}_i - \hat{B}_i K_s) + (\hat{A}_i - \hat{B}K_s)^T P_j + \frac{1}{\gamma^2} P_j \hat{D}\hat{D}^T P_j + M^T M < 0 ; \quad \{i, s, j\} = 1, 2. \tag{17}$$

Post- and pre-multiply (17), (X_j where $X_j = P_j^{-1}$ and $Y_s j = K_s X_j$), the inequality (17) can be expressed as:

$$\hat{A}_i X_j + X_j \hat{A}_i^T - \hat{B} Y_{sj} - Y_{sj}^T \hat{B}^T + \frac{1}{\gamma^2} \hat{D} \hat{D}^T + X_j M^T M X_j < 0 ; \quad \{i, s, j\} = 1, 2.$$

$$(18)$$

By using Schur's complement, LMI conditions (14) are obtained.

Remark 1. The approach developed in this document is compared with that used in [12], where the (CLF) is used.

4   Simulations and Results

To demonstrate the effectiveness of the proposed control strategy, simulations are carried out using the model (8) of (PMSM) motor. Its parameters are shown in Table 1.

Table 1. *PMSM and Vehicul parameters.*

Parametes of the PMSM	Values
Stator resistance	$RS = 2.875\Omega$
Direct axis inductance	$Ld = 7.5$ mH
Quadrature axis inductance	$Lq = 2.5$ mH
Moment of inertia	$J = 0.0008$ Kg.m^2
Coefficient of friction	$f = 0.0001$ N.m.s/rad
Flux linkage estabished by PMSM	$\phi_m = 0.175$
Numbre of magnetic poles	$np = 8$
Maximum PMSM rotor speed	$W_r^{max} = 1800$ rpm
Minimum PMSM rotor speed	$W_r^{min} = -1800$ rpm

By solving the LMIs (14), the control's gains of the PI fuzzy control law (11) are giving as:

$$KP1 = \begin{bmatrix} 5.7780 & 11.7586 & 6.4279 \\ 1.3747 & 2.4339 & 14.3841 \end{bmatrix} \qquad KI1 = 10^3 * \begin{bmatrix} 3.8664 \\ 1.0239 \end{bmatrix}$$

$$KP2 = \begin{bmatrix} 5.7780 & 11.7586 & -6.4279 \\ -1.3747 & -2.4340 & 14.3841 \end{bmatrix} \qquad KI2 = 10^3 * \begin{bmatrix} 3.8664 \\ -1.0239 \end{bmatrix}$$

The simulation results are shown in figures (Fig. 4) and (Fig. 5).

It's clear that, with both controllers, the speed of PMSM motor Wr tracked perfectly the reference speed Wr* and, consequently, the speed of the vehicle Vx, tracked the reference speed Vx*.

Fig. 4 show that the proposed (FILF) controller has better temporal responses, both in terms of rise time and in terms of compensation of disturbances, than the one developed by the (CLF) approach.

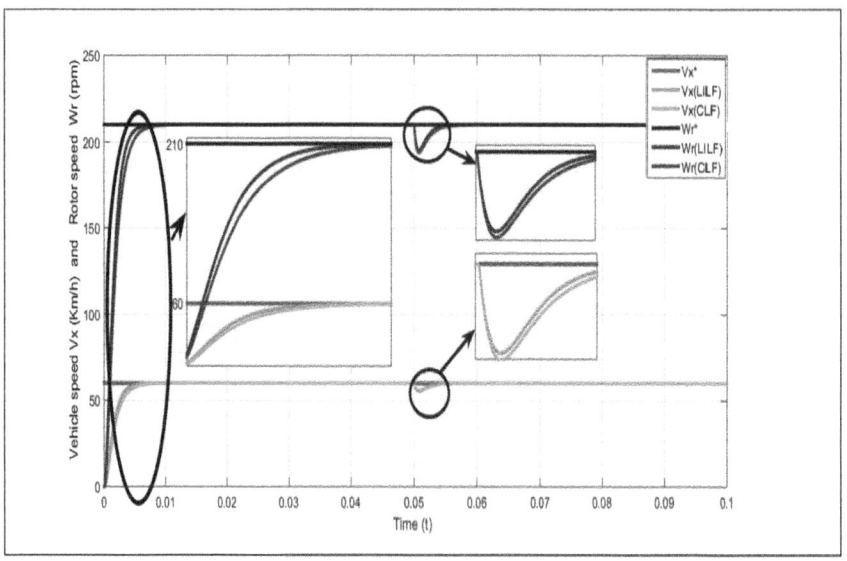

Fig. 4. Tracking references longitudinal Vx* and motor angular Wr* speeds.

In order to verify the dynamic performance of the proposed speed controller, assuming that the driver decides to change the speed of the vehicle. So the engine represented by PMSM needs to develop a couple adapted to the new situation. Fig. 5 shows that the developed controller has the ability to adapt perfectly to the speed variation. As a result, the vehicle tracks the variation of its reference speed Vx*.

Moreover, it is well known that the effect of an external disturbance degrades the performance of a system and can even render it unstable. To test the robustness of the proposed controller, a disturbance $Cr = 10N.m.s^{-1}$ (load torque), in the form of a step Fig. 6, was applied several times (at instances $t = 2s$ in Fig. 4 and Fig. 5, $t = 12.5s$ in Fig. 5 and $t = 22.5s$ in Fig. 5).

The simulations show that with the (LILF) approach, the controlled system is less sensitive and quickly compensates for the effect of this disturbance compared with the (CLF) approach.

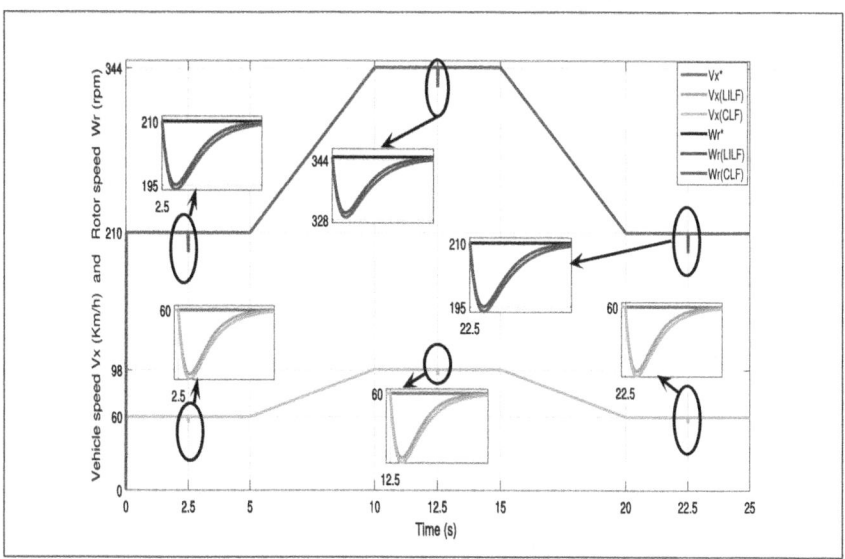

Fig. 5. Tracking references longitudinal Vx* and motor angular Wr* speeds.

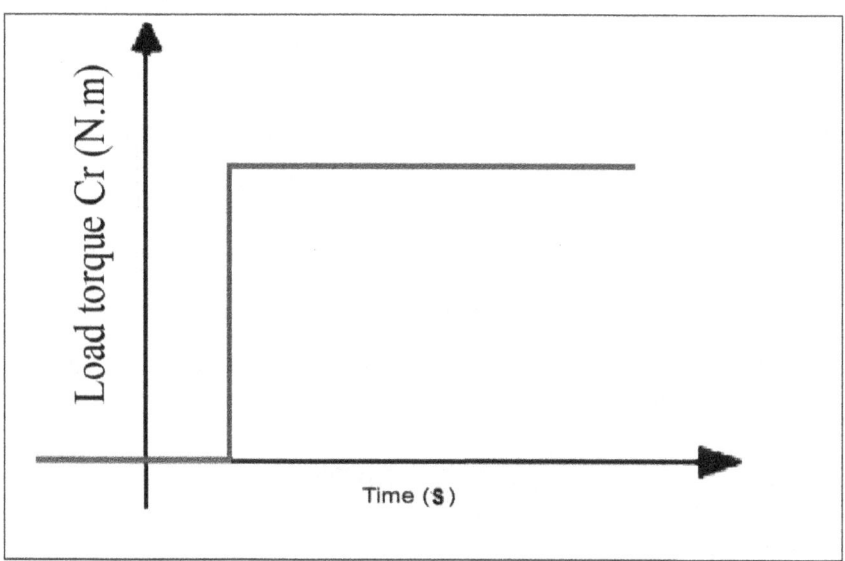

Fig. 6. Load torque profile.

5   Conclusion

In this paper, a robust H_∞ fuzzy control of the electric vehicle, whose motor is represented by a PMSM, is designed. The objective is to follow the desired longitudinal reference speed of the vehicle by generating an optimal motor torque. The FILF and the H_∞ performance criterion are used to build a PI fuzzy controller. The controller designed using (FILF) function is compared with (CLF). LMI tools are used to calculate the controller's gains. Results and numerical simulation show that the proposed (FILF) controller has better temporal responses, both in terms of rise time and reaction against disturbances, than the (CLF).

References

1. Saldaña, G., San Martin, J.I., Zamora, I., Asensio, F.J., Oñederra, O.: Electric vehicle into the grid: charging methodologies aimed at providing ancillary services considering battery degradation. Energies **12**(12), 2443 (2019)
2. Hossain, M., Kumar, L., El Haj Assad, M., Alayi, R.: Advancements and future prospects of electric vehicle technologies: a comprehensive review. Complexity **2022** (2022)
3. Gottumukkala, R., Merchant, R., Tauzin, A., Leon, K., Roche, A., Darby, P.: Cyber-physical system security of vehicle charging stations. In: 2019 IEEE Green Technologies Conference (GreenTech), pp. 1–5. IEEE (2019)
4. Ouyang, T., Wang, C., Xu, P., Ye, J., Liu, B.: Prognostics and health management of lithium-ion batteries based on modeling techniques and bayesian approaches: A review. Sustainable Energy Technol. Assess. **55**, 102915 (2023)
5. Xu, X., Liang, Y., Jordan, M., Tenberge, P., Dong, P.: Optimized control of engine start assisted by the disconnect clutch in a p2 hybrid automatic transmission. Mech. Syst. Signal Process. **124**, 313–329 (2019)
6. Peng, H., Wang, W., An, Q., Xiang, C., Li, L.: Path tracking and direct yaw moment coordinated control based on robust mpc with the finite time horizon for autonomous independent-drive vehicles. IEEE Trans. Veh. Technol. **69**(6), 6053–6066 (2020)
7. Zhang, L., et al.: An adaptive backstepping sliding mode controller to improve vehicle maneuverability and stability via torque vectoring control. IEEE Trans. Veh. Technol. **69**(3), 2598–2612 (2020)
8. Han, Z., Xu, N., Chen, H., Huang, Y., Zhao, B.: Energy-efficient control of electric vehicles based on linear quadratic regulator and phase plane analysis. Appl. Energy **213**, 639–657 (2018)
9. Peng, H., Wang, W., Xiang, C., Li, L., Wang, X.: Torque coordinated control of four in-wheel motor independent-drive vehicles with consideration of the safety and economy. IEEE Trans. Veh. Technol. **68**(10), 9604–9618 (2019)
10. Schaltz, E., Soylu, S.: Electrical vehicle design and modeling. Electr. Veh.-Model. Simul. **1**, 1–24 (2011)
11. Kim, S.-H.: Electric Motor Control: DC, AC, and BLDC Motors. Elsevier, Amsterdam (2017)
12. Elouardi, E., Mouhib, O., Lassioui, A., Bentaleb, A., El Ouardi, B., El Fadil, H.: Cruise control system of electric vehicle powered by pmsm motor using t-s fuzzy approach. In: International Symposium on Automatic Control and Emerging Technologies. Springer, Heidelberg (2023)
13. Takagi, T., Sugeno, M.: Fuzzy identification of systems and its applications to modeling and control. IEEE Trans. Syst. Man Cybern. **1**, 116–132 (1985)

14. Ounnas, D., Chenikher, S., Bouktir, T.: Tracking control for permanent magnet synchronous machine based on takagi-sugeno fuzzy models. In: 2013 Eighth International Conference and Exhibition on Ecological Vehicles and Renewable Energies (EVER), pp. 1–5. IEEE (2013)
15. Saenz, J.M., Tanaka, M., Tanaka, K.: Relaxed stabilization and disturbance attenuation control synthesis conditions for polynomial fuzzy systems. IEEE Trans. Cybern. **51**(4), 2093–2106 (2019)
16. Houili, R., Hammoudi, M.Y., Benbouzid, M., Titaouine, A.: Observer-based controller using line integral lyapunov fuzzy function for ts fuzzy systems: application to induction motors. Machines **11**(3), 374 (2023)
17. Rhee, B.-J., Won, S.: A new fuzzy lyapunov function approach for a takagi-sugeno fuzzy control system design. Fuzzy Sets Syst. **157**(9), 1211–1228 (2006)
18. Vafamand, N.: Global non-quadratic lyapunov-based stabilization of t-s fuzzy systems: a descriptor approach. J. Vib. Control **26**(19–20), 1765–1778 (2020)
19. Dahmani, H., Pagès, O., El Hajjaji, A., Daraoui, N.: Observer-based tracking control of the vehicle lateral dynamics using four-wheel active steering. In: 16th International IEEE Conference on Intelligent Transportation Systems (ITSC 2013), pp. 360–365. IEEE (2013)

Intelligent Control for Increasing Maximum Extracted Power of a Wind Generation System

I. Elidrissi[1]($\boxtimes$) (iD), F.-E. Lamzouri[1] (iD), A. Mouradi[2] (iD), and E.-M. Boufounas[1] (iD)

[1] REIPT Laboratory, Faculty of Sciences and Technology, Ismail University of Meknes, B.P. 509, Boutalamine, Errachidia, Moulay, Morocco
ledrissi.ibrahim@gmail.com

[2] Energy, Materials and Computing Physics Research Group, ENS, Abdelmalek Essaadi University, 93020 Tetouan, Morocco

Abstract. This study develops a robust nonlinear control, using an integral sliding mode control (ISMC) associated to an artificial neural network (ANN) approach for a variable-speed wind turbine (VSWT). At below rated speed of wind, the control aims to extract the maximum energy from the wind by the WT as well decreasing mechanical loads. Therefore, in the proposed controller, a modified sliding mode control (SMC) law with action of integral is elaborated to reach smoothly the optimal turbine speed. Moreover, the main problem of the controller design is that of external disturbances and uncertainties in the model of the dynamic system. To bridge this gap, a new technique based on ANN is employed to identify the uncertain dynamics of the wind turbine model. Thus, the system control stability was demonstrated by means of function Lyapunov analysis. The developed controller (NN-ISMC) efficiency was compared with the conventional ISMC and SMC techniques, and the simulation analysis show better performances and robustness of the developed NN-ISMC method regarding transition of response and error of tracking level.

Keywords: Variable Speed Wind Turbine · Power Capture Optimization · Artificial Neural Network (ANN) · Integral Sliding Mode Control (ISMC)

1 Introduction

Global energy consumption has risen sharply in recent years and will continue to do so, due to rising electricity consumption per capita and the effect of economic growth. The wind energy conversion system (WECS) is an attractive topic for research and innovation today, it's constantly evolving, due to their economic, social, and environmental benefits [1–3]. In the WES, the kinetic energy of wind is converted into electrical energy via a generator. Typically, two basic types of wind turbines (WTs) were adopted to respond to the growing trend in energy demand: vertical axis wind turbines (VAWT) and horizontal axis wind turbines (HAWT) [2]. Specifically, HAWTs can be divided into two famous prototypes like fixed speed wind turbines (FSWT) and variable speed wind turbines (VSWT) which remains widely used, thanks to their high capacity to extract electrical power with limited fluctuations [4–6].

H. Hagras et al. (Eds.): ISACS 2023, CCIS 2255, pp. 278–291, 2025.
https://doi.org/10.1007/978-3-031-93448-3_23

Against this backdrop, control techniques are key to make the installation fully exploited. In general, the WTs control strategy can be designed for a specific nominal wind speed, where two main operating zones can be identified ("below" and "above" the nominal speed of wind). So, when wind speed is below the nominal, torque control is applied to enhance the energy extraction from wind. On the other hand, pitch control is an excellent solution for maintaining the wind turbine rated power at its nominal value [2–4, 6, 7]. In this work, the controlling has been investigated for extracting maximum power at below the nominal speed of wind.

In literature, linear control, including Proportional Integral controller (PI controller), Proportional Integral Derivative controller (PID controller), and linear quadratic (LQR) controllers, has been widely used [8], but the controller's performance proved less robust concerning disturbances and nonlinearity of WECS. Further, non-linear control has been the topic of several studies aimed at extracting the maximum power of wind, due to the WT extremely nonlinear dynamics and its environs. Furthermore, it can be observed that sliding mode control (SMC) has involved significant consideration from researchers. This is mainly because of its robustness, efficiency, simplicity and ability to investigate progressively complex models and control laws [3, 5]. Reporting to [4], the authors investigate a classic SMC controller with the intention of increasing the extracted energy from the wind. This control law has shown robustness in presence of variations in system parameters and external disturbances. However, we found that the output response achieved was slow, and we get chattering and oscillation on the turbine shaft with high value of control gain. Therefore, when uncertainties are sufficiently large, the controller can have a high switching gain and, as a result, a high chattering amplitude [3, 9]. In the other hand, the ISMC can ensure greater robustness by reducing the static error because of the modified sliding surface by introducing the action of integral. The SMC and ISMC laws have been discussed using the WT one-mass model in [10]. Moreover, a systematic comparative study among conventional SMC and ISMC controllers has also been established in [11, 12], for the two mass model of WT. The well-known drawback of the previous control law (i.e., ISMC) remains in the sign function utilization and high value of control gain to reduce the chattering, which increases the oscillations and the drivetrain's mechanical loads.

The contribution of this paper, motivated by the existing works, consists of proposing an intelligent control for increasing maximum generation power efficiency of a VSWT. Thus, the proposed control strategy is constructed by combining non-linear ISMC control and the artificial neural network (ANN) approach. Generally, WT external disturbances are not predictable. In this work, a neural network [1, 7, 13], is used to approximate any nonlinear functions, uncertainties, and external disturbances without the need for detailed analytical models of the system. In the present work, ANN has been used to estimate the WT model uncertain part and therefore provides the utilization of a low gain of switching. The proposed NN-ISMC controller stability was examined using the Lyapunov method [1, 4–7].

Moreover, the results of several simulation tests are investigated to validate our system control efficiency in terms of power extraction, reduction of loads and improvement of steady-state error.

This study is planned as follows; the WT mathematical equation model is detailed in Sect. 2. Section 3 is devoted to design the proposed NN-ISMC nonlinear controller. Section 4 presents the simulation results and the proposed technique validation. Lastly, conclusions are shown in Sect. 5.

2 WT System Modeling

VSWTs are essentially consisted of an aeroturbine related to the generator by the mean of a gearbox. However, only part of the available wind energy can be captured. The aerodynamic power captured from wind can be defined in the non-linear equation given in Eq. (1) [3]:

$$P_a = \frac{1}{2}\rho\pi R^2 C_p(\lambda, \beta)v^3 \tag{1}$$

where ρ the density of air and R the rotor radius. We can see that P_a is proportionate to the speed of wind cubic value [1]. The coefficient of power $C_p(\lambda, \beta)$, is the turbine's capacity to extract energy from the wind, depending on the ratio of tip-speed λ and the angle of pitch β. Indeed, the expression of λ is the ratio among the linear speed of the blade tip $\omega_t R$ (ω_t is the speed of rotor) and the speed of wind v [3]:

$$\lambda = \frac{\omega_t R}{v} \tag{2}$$

The aerodynamic torque T_a is linked to the aerodynamic power by the relationship below:

$$P_a = \omega_t T_a \tag{3}$$

Then, the aerodynamic torque expression can be obtained as below:

$$T_a = \frac{1}{2}\rho\pi R^3 C_q(\lambda, \beta)v^2 \tag{4}$$

where, the torque coefficient $C_q(\lambda, \beta)$ expression is:

$$C_q(\lambda, \beta) = \frac{C_p(\lambda, \beta)}{\lambda} \tag{5}$$

The two-mass model of wind-turbine's mechanical part has been presented in several research works [1, 3], which has also been studied in the present work. The inertia J_r of the rotor is driven, through the aerodynamic torque T_a, at the turbine speed ω_t. The corresponding dynamics are defined using a first-order differential equation:

$$J_r\dot{\omega}_t = T_a - K_r\omega_t - T_{ls} \tag{6}$$

K_r and J_r are the coefficient of friction and inertia of the rotor, respectively, where the shaft torque at low speed T_{ls}, produces torsional and frictional effects as a result of the difference among ω_t and ω_{ls}, it is acting on the rotor as a decelerating torque [8]:

$$T_{ls} = B_{ls}(\theta_t - \theta_{ls}) - K_{ls}(\omega_t - \omega_{ls}) \tag{7}$$

with K_{ls} and B_{ls} are the coefficients shaft damping and shaft stiffness, respectively.

In addition, the generator side dynamics can be determined using the ensuing first order differential equation, where the inertia J_g of the generator is driven at the generator speed ω_g through the torque of the high-speed shaft T_{hs} and braking using the electromagnetic torque T_e:

$$J_g \dot{\omega}_g = T_{hs} - K_g \omega_g - T_e \tag{8}$$

The gearbox is assumed ideal, then transmission ratio N_g is given as follows:

$$N_g = \frac{T_{ls}}{T_{hs}} = \frac{\omega_g}{\omega_{ls}} \tag{9}$$

Furthermore, in the typical case where the low-speed shaft is perfectly rigid with $\omega_t = \omega_{ls}$, a one mass model can be considered for the wind turbine, consisting of a unique inertia and a unique friction coefficient grouping all external friction coefficients [4, 5]. We can get:

$$J_t \dot{\omega}_t = T_a - D_t \omega_t - T_g \tag{10}$$

$$J_t = J_r + N_g^2 J_g$$

where, $D_t = K_r + N_g^2 K_g$

$$T_g = N_g T_e$$

T_g, J_t and D_t are respectively, the generator torque, the total turbine inertia and the total turbine external damping.

Subsequently, the produced electric power by the generator is:

$$P_e = \omega_t T_g \tag{11}$$

On the other hand, the maximum power extraction of VSWTs has been achieved by operating in region II. Furthermore, the characteristics curve corresponding to the coefficient of power $C_p(\lambda, \beta)$ involved in the aerodynamic power expression (1) are highlighted in Fig. 1 for different values of β [3, 7]. Thus, $C_p(\lambda, \beta)$ has a single peak power point (i.e., C_{popt}) corresponding to the optimal capture of wind energy according to Fig. 1. Then,

$$C_{popt} = C_p(\lambda_{opt}, \beta_{opt}) \tag{12}$$

where,

$$\lambda_{opt} = \frac{\omega_{topt} R}{v} \tag{13}$$

with λ_{opt} is the optimal tip-speed ratio.

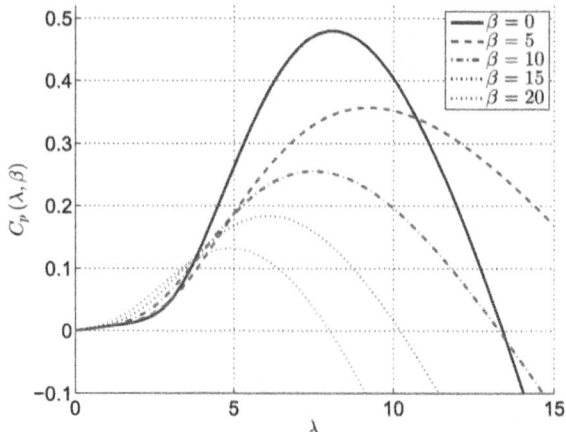

Fig. 1. WT power coefficient versus λ for different β [2].

3   Maximum Power Extraction Controller Design

This section presents a design of an NN-ISMC to achieve optimal wind energy extraction below rated power (Region II). The proposed method aims to force the VSWT rotor speed ω_t track its reference ω_{topt}. Indeed, the parameters of C_p must be maintained at their optimum values ($\beta = 0$ and $\lambda = \lambda_{opt}$) so that the maximum power is achieved, [3, 7, 8], so as to ensure that the power coefficient is always as high as possible. Moreover, the ω_{topt} is calculated in Eq. (14) according to the technique of Maximum Power Point Tracking (MPPT), given as [3]:

$$\omega_{topt} = \frac{\lambda_{opt}}{R}v \tag{14}$$

Further, the speed tracking error is given as below:

$$e_\omega(t) = \omega_{topt}(t) - \omega_t(t) \tag{15}$$

Using the Eq. (15) time derivative in Eq. (10), and reporting to [2], the representation in state space of the WT dynamic model is given as below:

$$\begin{cases} x_1(t) = e_\omega(t) = \omega_{topt}(t) - \omega_t(t) \\\\ \dot{x}_1(t) = \dot{\omega}_{topt}(t) - \dot{\omega}_t(t) = x_2(t) = \dot{\omega}_{topt}(t) - \left(\frac{T_a(t) - D_t\omega_t(t) - N_g T_e(t)}{J_t} \right) \\\\ \dot{x}_2(t) = \ddot{\omega}_{topt}(t) - \ddot{\omega}_t(t) = \ddot{\omega}_{topt}(t) - \left(\frac{\dot{T}_a(t) - D_t(\dot{\omega}_{topt}(t) - x_2(t)) - N_g \dot{T}_e(t)}{J_t} \right) \end{cases} \tag{16}$$

The dynamic model described by the above equation is also considered in this work. Nevertheless, to take into account the uncertainties, the external disturbances, the neglected terms and the unmodeled dynamics, an unidentified time-varying part $d(t)$ is introduced in the dynamic model. Consequently, the WT mechanical dynamics becomes as below:

$$\begin{cases} \dot{x}_1(t) = x_2(t) \\ \dot{x}_2(t) = \ddot{\omega}_{topt}(t) - \left(\dfrac{\dot{T}_a(t) - D_t(\dot{\omega}_{topt}(t) - x_2(t)) - N_g \dot{T}_e(t)}{J_t} \right) + d(t) \end{cases} \tag{17}$$

Consequently, the system eq. (17) can be transformed to a form of matrix as below:

$$\begin{bmatrix} \dot{x}_1(t) \\ \dot{x}_2(t) \end{bmatrix} = \begin{bmatrix} 0 & 1 \\ 0 & M_1 \end{bmatrix} \begin{bmatrix} x_1(t) \\ x_2(t) \end{bmatrix} + \begin{bmatrix} 0 \\ M_2 \end{bmatrix} u(t) + \begin{bmatrix} 0 \\ 1 \end{bmatrix} d(t) + \begin{bmatrix} 0 \\ 1 \end{bmatrix} h(t) \tag{18}$$

where, $M_1 = -\frac{D_t}{J_t}$, $M_2 = \frac{N_g}{J_t}$ and $h(t) = \ddot{\omega}_{topt}(t) - \frac{D_t}{J_t}\dot{\omega}_{topt}(t) - \frac{1}{J_t}\dot{T}_a(t)$ supposed known. $d(t)$ represents the part of uncertainties and external disturbances. The derivative of electromagnetic torque denotes the control law (i.e., $u(t) = \dot{T}_e(t)$), and $y(t) = x_1(t)$ is the system output.

Finally, the system representation in state space can be described by:

$$\begin{cases} \dot{x}(t) = Ax(t) + Bu(t) + Cd(t) + Dh(t) \\ y(t) = x_1(t) \end{cases} \tag{19}$$

with, $x(t) = \begin{bmatrix} x_1(t) \\ x_2(t) \end{bmatrix}$, $A = \begin{bmatrix} 0 & 1 \\ 0 & M_1 \end{bmatrix}$, $B = \begin{bmatrix} 0 \\ M_2 \end{bmatrix}$, $C = \begin{bmatrix} 0 \\ 1 \end{bmatrix}$ and $D = \begin{bmatrix} 0 \\ 1 \end{bmatrix}$.

As a result, the established model described by the Eq. (17) can be used in the next to design the NN-ISMC based torque control.

3.1 Sliding Mode Control with Integral Action Scheme

Besides the chattering behavior, the classic SMC response becomes slow and that because of the high switching gain. So, to guarantee fast error convergence and high robustness, the switching surface is modified by the action of integral as:

$$s(t) = x_2(t) + k_1 x_1(t) + k_2 \int_0^t x_1(\tau)d\tau \tag{20}$$

where k_1 and k_2 are the positive gains. The Eq. (20) time derivative gives:

$$\dot{s}(t) = \dot{x}_2(t) + k_1 \dot{x}_1(t) + k_2 x_1(t) \tag{21}$$

By substituting the dynamics of Eq. (17) in Eq. (21), we can obtain the subsequent expression:

$$\dot{s}(t) = \left(\ddot{\omega}_{topt}(t) - \left(\dfrac{\dot{T}_a(t) - D_t(\dot{\omega}_{topt}(t) - x_2(t)) - N_g \dot{T}_e(t)}{J_t} \right) + k_1 x_2(t) + k_2 x_1(t) + d(t) \right) \tag{22}$$

With the intention of suppressing the phenomenon of chattering resulting from the classic function *sign*, the method of quasi-sliding mode (function *sat*) is used [14] in this study, so that the state remains in the layer of boundary.

$$\dot{s}(t) = -k.sat(s(t)) - qs(t) \tag{23}$$

with k and q signify positive scalars and *sat* represents the function of saturation:

$$sat(s) = \begin{cases} s/L & \text{if } |s| < L \\ \text{sgn}(s) & \text{otherwise} \end{cases} \tag{24}$$

L refers to the layer of boundary width.

Further, to ensure the sliding mode presence on a switching surface in finite time, the ensuing condition must be assured [15]:

$$s\dot{s} < -\eta|s| \tag{25}$$

η is a positive constant.

To satisfy Eq. (25), the control law is considered as below:

$$\dot{T}_e = \frac{J_t}{N_g}\left(\left(\frac{\dot{T}_a(t) - D_t\dot{\omega}_{topt}}{J_t}\right) - \ddot{\omega}_{topt} - \left(k_1 - \frac{D_t}{J_t}\right)x_2(t) - k_2x_1(t) - ksat(s(t)) - qs(t)\right) \tag{26}$$

Thus, the torque control law can be obtained by taking the integration of the Eq. (26):

$$T_e(t) = A_1 \int_0^t \left(A_2(t) - A_3x_2(t) - A_4x_1(t) - A_5sat(s(t)) - A_6s(t) - \ddot{\omega}_{topt}\right)d\tau \tag{27}$$

where $A_1 = \frac{J_t}{N_g}$, $A_2(t) = \left(\frac{\dot{T}_a(t) - D_t\dot{\omega}_{topt}}{J_t}\right)$, $A_3 = \left(k_1 - \frac{D_t}{J_t}\right)$, $A_4 = k_2$, $A_5 = k$ and $A_6 = q$.

3.2 NN-ISMC Controller Design

The ISMC law is a robust control against variations of system parameters and external disturbances. Moreover, the integral action introduced in surface of switching, can theoretically ensure greater robustness by improving the steady state error, along with escaping the phase of reaching. Thus, the control signal generated in Eq. (27) can achieve the control objectives with small uncertainties. However, when the uncertainties are large, ISMC control technique may also generate chattering and oscillatory phenomena in the control signal, due to the higher required gain [16]. As a solution to this problem, the Radial Basis Function Neural Networks (RBFNN) technique is utilized to approximate the unknown part of the system model given in Eq. (17). Afterward, the error of prediction by RBFNN, can be determined as below:

$$d(t) - \hat{d}(t) = \varepsilon_d \tag{28}$$

where $\hat{d}(t)$ denote the estimated unknown nonlinear function of $d(t)$ by RBFNN and $|\varepsilon_d| < \varepsilon_d^*$, with ε_d^* refer to the superior bound of the neural network prediction error, supposed to be known.

Theorem: Below the nominal power, consider the system designed using Eq. (17) in the existence of significant disturbances and uncertainties. If the developed control law is given according to Eq. (26):

$$T_e(t) = A_1 \int_0^t \left(A_2(t) - A_3 x_2(t) - A_4 x_1(t) - A_5 sat(s(t)) - A_6 s(t) - \ddot{\omega}_{topt} - \hat{d}(t) \right) d\tau$$

(29)

with $\left(\varepsilon_d^* + \eta < k \right)$, hence, the tracking error convergence trajectory to zero within finite time will be achieved. Moreover, the developed wind generation system realizes a robust MPPT.

Proof: In this part, a Lyapunov theory is employed to demonstrate the closed loop system control stability. Accordingly, the candidate function of Lyapunov is formed as shown:

$$V(t) = \frac{1}{2} s^T(t) s(t)$$

(30)

The Eq. (26) time derivative is obtained as:

$$\dot{V}(t) = s^T(t) \dot{s}(t)$$

(31)

By substituting the expression of the surface dynamic given in Eq. (22), we get the following expression:

$$\dot{V}(t) = s^T \left(\ddot{\omega}_{topt} - \left(\frac{\dot{T}_a(t) - D_t(\ddot{\omega}_{topt} - x_2(t)) - N_g \dot{T}_e(t)}{J_t} \right) + k_1 x_2(t) + k_2 x_1(t) + d(t) \right)$$

(32)

By replacing the expression of the generator torque dynamic as defined in the theorem, we have:

$$\begin{aligned}
\dot{V}(t) &= s^T(t) \left(d(t) - \hat{d}(t) - A_5 sat(s(t)) - A_6 s(t) \right) \\
&= s^T(t)(\varepsilon_d - k sat(s(t)) - q s(t)) \\
&\leq |s(t)||\varepsilon_d| - k s sat(s(t)) - q s^2(t) \\
&< |s(t)|\varepsilon_d^* - k s sat(s(t))
\end{aligned}$$

(33)

If $|s| > L$, $sat(s) = sign(s)$, it is then easy to get $\dot{V}(t) < \left(\varepsilon_d^* - k \right)|s(t)|$ and that by choosing $\varepsilon_\tau^* + \eta < k$ we have $\dot{V}(t) < -\eta|s(t)|$.

If $|s| < L$, $sat(s) = \frac{s}{L}$, in a small origin L-vicinity [15], the trajectories of the system are restricted to a sliding mode manifold boundary layer $s = 0$.

Therefore, it was concluded that the designed NN-ISMC controller is asymptotically stable with external noises and uncertainties. Consequently, the tracking error convergence trajectory to zero within finite time is accomplished.

3.3 Neural Network Online Update Algorithm

The RBFNN is a type of ANN method which employ, as activation functions, radial basis functions for approximation of nonlinear function, prediction of time series as well as the control [17]. In particular, the RBFNN approach is used in this work to learn and estimate the unidentified nonlinear part of the WT system [18]. The basic RBFNN architecture is shown in Fig. 2, where a linear function is usually considered for the output layer. The hidden layer of RBF neural network involves a Gaussian function as activation function, represented as below:

$$h_j = \exp\left(-\frac{\|X - C_j\|^2}{2\xi_j^2}\right), \qquad j = 1, 2, 3, 4, 5 \tag{34}$$

where $h = [h_1, h_2, ..., h_5]^T$ is the vector of radial basis, $X = [x_1, x_2]^T$ design the input vector, $\xi = [\xi_1, \xi_2, ..., \xi_5]^T$ is the vector of basis width and $C_j = [c_{j1}, c_{j2}, ..., c_{j5}]^T$ denotes the jth neuron center vector. The RBFNN output is given by:

$$\hat{d} = \sum_{p=1}^{5} w_p h_p \tag{35}$$

where w_p is the pth hidden neuron weight toward the RBFNN output.

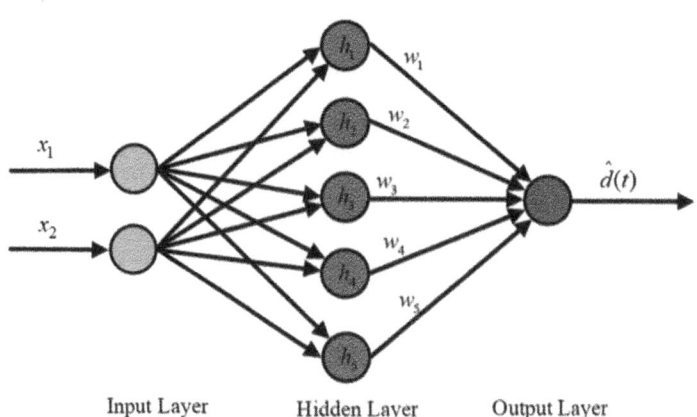

Fig. 2. The structure of the used RBFNN

The RBFNN weights are calculated on-line by means of the formula below [17]:

$$w_j(t+1) = w_j(t) + \rho \varepsilon_d h_j \quad ; j = 1, 2, ..., 5 \tag{36}$$

with ρ is the rate of learning.

4   Simulation Results

In this study, numerical simulations using the MATLAB/Simulink platform, have been implemented on a wind turbine one-mass model, whose parameters value are given in Table 1, with a low-speed shaft supposed perfectly rigid. To evaluate the performances of the developed strategy of control, several simulations were investigated for our model of WT. In addition, a comparison of the NN-ISMC method to the classical controllers is derived. Hence, the tests of simulation are investigated using similar conditions of operating and with the same controller parameters:

- A randomly changing sinusoidal wind speed profile with an average of 8 m/s is applied to the WT (see Fig. 3), which was described in the literature [3] by:

$$v(t) = 6.3 \left(1 - 0.1.x. \cos\left(\frac{\pi t}{5}\right) . e^{\frac{t}{30}} + 0.5 \sin\left(\frac{\pi t}{20}\right) \right) \tag{37}$$

- Presence of a reference additive term modeled with a white Gaussian noise, representing external disturbances and uncertainties of WT system on ω_t with a Signal-to-Noise Ratio (SNR) around 7 dB.

The numeric values used for the various controller parameters are shown in Table 2.

Table 1. Wind turbine characteristics [2].

Parameter	Value
Rated power P_n	4.8 MW
Rated wind speed v_n	11.63 m/s
Radius of rotor R	57.5 m
Density of air ρ	1.225 kg/m^3
Max power coefficient $C_{p,max}$	0.48
optimal ratio of tip-speed λ_{opt}	8.1
Turbine total external damping D_t	7.9×10^5 N.m/rad.s
Turbine total inertia J_t	$2.5 \cdot 10^8$ Kg $\cdot$ m^2
Gearbox ratio N_g	95
Maximum rotor torque T_g	162 kN $\cdot$ m

Table 2. Proposed controller parameters.

Parameter	Value
k_1	0.9
k_2	0.3
k	0.12
q	0.01

Figure 4 illustrates the curves of rotor speed. As shown, the proposed approach offers improved performance in term of response time. We observed a faster reached output response for the proposed NN-ISMC method compared to the standard SMC and ISMC controllers. Indeed, the transit times were around 7 s, 9 s and 15 s for NN-ISMC, ISMC and SMC, respectively. Thus, the NN-ISMC have fast convergence and good robustness with respect to disturbances. As illustrated in Fig. 5, the tracking error signals of the three methods are shown. It is clearly stated that the NN-ISMC technique can ensure a good response of tracking with a zero inaccuracy. Figure 6 illustrate the reference and the reel aerodynamic power curves by applying all controllers. It comes out that the NN-ISMC controller provides excellent power capture with less turbine shaft vibration. An illustration of the controller's torque input signals is shown in Fig. 7, which demonstrates the smoothness of the NN-ISMC control signal. What's more, the proposed controller can also reduce chattering phenomenon. Figure 8 depicts the ANN approximation error time evolution, we notice that the error of training is almost zero (it's only an order of magnitude of 10^{-16}), indicating that ANN was able correctly to estimate the external disturbances and uncertainties term of WT system, due to the effectiveness of the online parameter update law. Finally, obviously, the proposed NN-ISMC controller optimizes better the extracted power from WT, because of its superior robustness to the speed of wind variations and system uncertainties. Moreover, the developed controller ensures an enhanced rotor speed tracking to achieve optimal extraction of power from wind compared to the other methods.

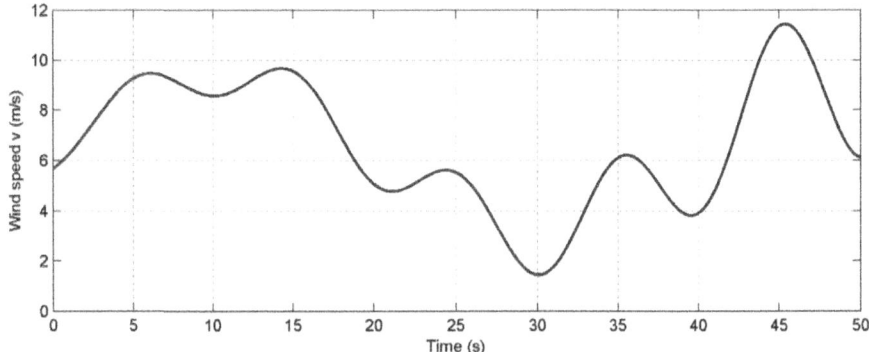

Fig. 3. Wind speed profile (Region-2)

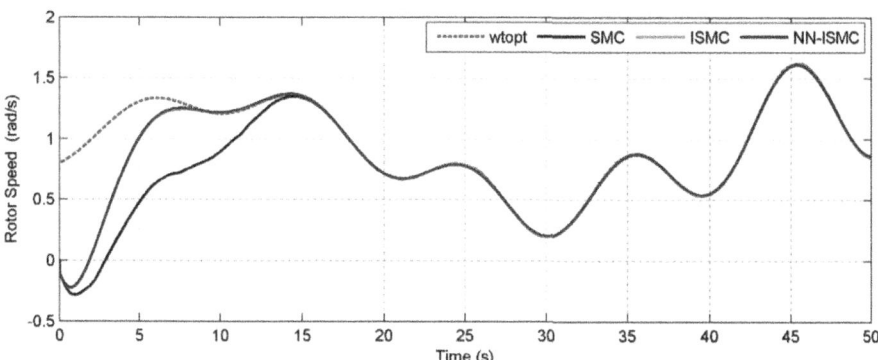

Fig. 4. Time evolution of the rotor speed

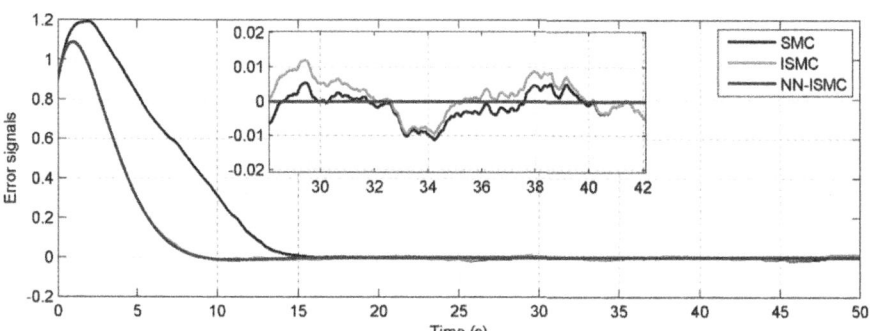

Fig. 5. Tracking error

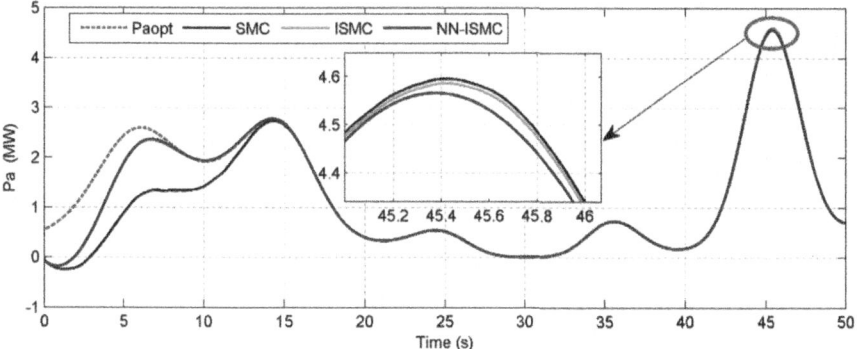

Fig. 6. The captured Aerodynamic power

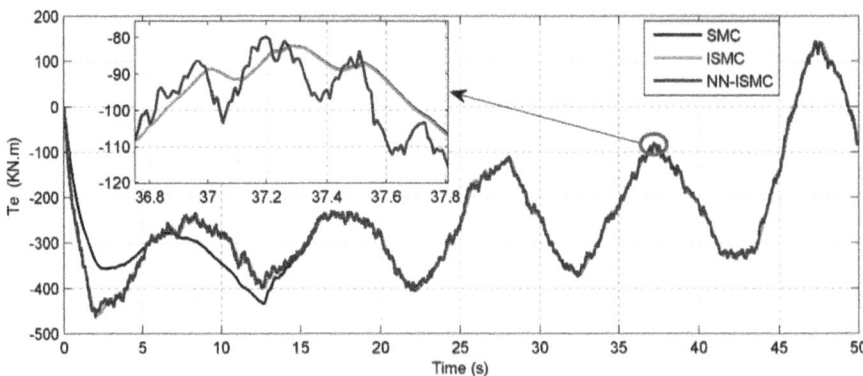

Fig. 7. Time evolution of applied torque

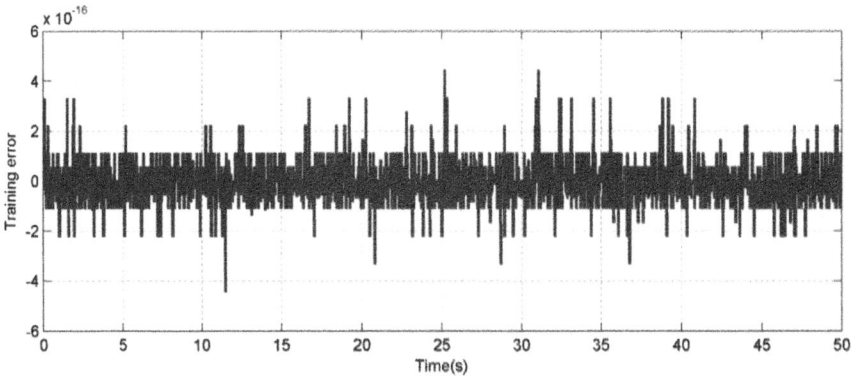

Fig. 8. Network training error

5 Conclusion

This study presents a practical combination of the ISMC controller and the ANN app-roach. As a result, the problem of uncertainties and exterior disturbances in the dynamic system has been taken into consideration for the proposed control law. Thus, the ANN approach is applied to identify the WT unknown nonlinear function using an online update algorithm for parameter adaptation, as this leads to a better description of the system. On the other hand, a comparative study, with conventional SMC and ISMC, shows that the proposed NN-ISMC deliver excellent power regulation, with completely deleting the steady state error, and enable the use of lower gain of switching despite the existence of strong disturbances. Moreover, the simulations result reveal that the designed NN-ISMC yields the best tracking results without any oscillation behaviour.

References

1. Boufounas, E., Boumhidi, J., Farhane, N., Boumhidi, I.: Neural network sliding mode controller for a variable speed wind turbine. Control Intell. Syst. **41**(4), (2013)
2. Periyanayagam, A.R., Joo, Y.H.: Integral sliding mode control for increasing maximum power extraction efficiency of variable-speed wind energy system. Int. J. Electr. Power Energy Syst. **139**, 107958 (2022)
3. Lamzouri, F.-E., Boufounas, E., El Amrani, A.: Backstepping integral sliding mode control for power capture optimization of wind turbine system. J. Mechatron. Syst. Control **47**(4), 225–234 (2019)
4. RAJENDRAN, S., JENA, D.: Backstepping sliding mode control of a variable speed wind turbine for power optimization. J. Modern Power Syst. Clean Energy **3**(3), 402–410 (2015). https://doi.org/10.1007/s40565-015-0106-2
5. Chehaidia, S.E., et al.: Robust nonlinear terminal integral sliding mode torque control for wind turbines considering uncertainties. IFAC-PapersOnLine **55**(12), 228–233 (2022)
6. Lamzouri, F.E.Z., Boufounas, E.M., El Amrani, A.: Power capture optimization of a wind energy conversion system using a backstepping integral sliding mode control. In: 4th International Conference on Optimization and Applications (ICOA) IEEE, pp. 1–6 (2018)
7. Lamzouri, F.E.Z., Boufounas, E.M., El Amrani, A.: A Robust double integral sliding mode control based neural network of a large wind turbine. In 2018 International Conference on Electronics, Control, Optimization and Computer Science (ICECOCS), pp. 1–6. IEEE(2018)
8. Boukhezzar, B., Siguerdidjane, H.: Comparison between linear and nonlinear control strategies for variable speed wind turbines. Control. Eng. Pract. **18**(12), 1357–1368 (2010)
9. Laina, R., Lamzouri, F.E.Z., Boufounas, E.M., El Amrani, A., Boumhidi, I.: Intelligent control of a DFIG wind turbine using a PSO evolutionary algorithm. Procedia Comput. Sci. **127**, 471–480 (2018)
10. Jena, D., Rajendran, S.: A review of estimation of effective wind speed based control of wind turbines. Renew. Sustain. Energy Rev. **43**, 1046–1062 (2015)
11. Slotine, J.J.E.: Sliding controller design for non-linear systems. Int. J. Control **40**(2), 421–434 (1984)
12. Rajendran, S., Jena, D.: Control of variable speed variable pitch wind turbine at above and below rated wind speed. J. Wind Energy **2014**, 1–14 (2014). https://doi.org/10.1155/2014/709128
13. Yin, X., Jiang, Z., Pan, L.: Artificial neural network based adaptive integral sliding mode power maximization control for wind power systems. Renew. Energy **145**, 1149–1157 (2020)
14. Hung, J.Y., Gao, W., Hung, J.C.: Variable structure control: a survey. IEEE Trans. Ind. Elect. **40**(1), 2–22 (1993)
15. Slotine, J.J.: Sliding controller design for non-linear systems. Int. J. Control **40**, 421–434 (1984)
16. Lamzouri, F.E.Z., Boufounas, E.M., Amrani, A.E.: Power control of a stand-alone electric generation hybrid system using integral sliding mode controller. Int. J. Autom. Control **16**(3–4), 388–409 (2022)
17. Yilmas, A.S., Ozer, Z.: Pitch angle control in wind turbines above the rated wind speed by multi-layer perceptron and radial basic function neural networks. Expert Syst. Appl. **36**(6), 9767–9775 (2009)
18. Lamzouri, F.E.Z., Boufounas, E.M., El Amrani, A.: Energy management and intelligent power control of a stand-alone wind energy conversion system with battery storage. Int. Trans Electr. Energy Syst. **31**(9), e13003 (2021). https://doi.org/10.1002/2050-7038.13003

An Intelligent MPPT Controller Based on Bald Eagle Search Optimization Algorithm for a Thermoelectric Generator System

I. Bekki$^{(\boxtimes)}$, F.-E. Lamzouri⬤, A. El Amrani⬤, and E.-M. Boufounas⬤

REIPT Laboratory, Faculty of Sciences and Technology, Moulay Ismail University of Meknes, B.P. 509, Boutalamine, Errachidia, Morocco
bekkiissam@gmail.com

Abstract. This paper considers a control strategy based on backstepping sliding mode control (BSMC) for maximizing the power generation efficiency of the thermoelectric generator (TEG) system. The considered system contains five series TEG modules connected to a resistive load through a boost converter. Thus, the principal objective of the developed method is to allow the TEG system to work to its required MPP by adjusting the boost converter duty cycle, under sudden change in temperature. In addition, in order to enhance the controller performances by optimizing BSMC parameters, the proposed controlling approach is further associated to an evolutionary algorithm based bald eagle search algorithm (BES). Finally, the results of simulation, illustrated to present the effectiveness and the feasibility of the developed control scheme, show that the proposed BSMC controller-based BES algorithm offers higher response speed, a lesser stable-state error and a fast feedback against varying temperature conditions, compared to the conventional SMC.

Keywords: Thermoelectric generator system · DC-DC boost converter · MPPT · Backstepping sliding mode control · BES algorithm

1 Introduction

The thermoelectric generator (TEG), as a renewable and eco-friendly power generator, has the capability to convert thermal energy directly into electrical power [1–4]. The idea of using thermoelectric generators to produce electricity from heat is consolidated; known as the Seebeck effect, the Thomson effect and the Peltier effect [5, 6]. Thus, the TEG generated voltage is proportional to the temperature difference, and as with the heat, a practical TEG modules number can be associated serially or in parallel in the aim of reach the desired levels of voltage and current. So as to fully exploit the energy captured from the TEG array, DC-DC converter based MPPT is being used to stabilize the output voltage produced from TEG as well as to guarantee maximum power generation from TEG system [7–9].

In order to maximize the output power from the TEG system in different temperature varying conditions, a MPPT strategy is required for the TEG modules. Indeed,

© The Author(s), under exclusive license to Springer Nature Switzerland AG 2025
H. Hagras et al. (Eds.): ISACS 2023, CCIS 2255, pp. 292–306, 2025.
https://doi.org/10.1007/978-3-031-93448-3_24

there exist several algorithms in literature for the MPPT with various power generation control schemes of the TEG system. As reported in [10], an artificial neural network algorithm was investigated to increase the TEG system performances. In addition, an MPPT method based on fuzzy logic control with a variable fractional order for power conversion enhancing of the TEG has been presented in [11]; the authors aim to enhance the efficiency of the energy conversion by the TEG which their operating point is rapidly progressing toward an optimal point to increase the efficiency of energy harvesting. A maximum power generation from a photovoltaic module and a TEG forming a hybrid electrical generation system was investigated in [12], where authors suggested a structure combining two sources for energy production from lost heat and solar radiation using a double-input topology of the boost converter to supply the DC load by the generated power. In [13] and [14], a MPPT based on sliding mode power control (SMC) was used for improving the stability and the performance of the TEG. However, the well-known drawback of this method is the occurrence of the chattering due to the high frequency switching control when both the parameter's variations and external disturbances are present.

This work presents a MPPT control strategy of a TEG system based on backstepping sliding mode control (BSMC). The considered TEG system contains five TEG array connected to a serial resistive charge by a DC-DC converter. Indeed, the aim of the controller is to allow the TEG system to work at the calculated MPP through regulating the converter duty cycle. In addition, the efficient bald eagle search optimization algorithm (BES), as a meta-heuristic global optimization technique, is applied to enhance the controller performances by selecting BSMC gains. Therefore, the suggested BES-BSMC control system preserves the performance of BSMC while improving its robustness. Thus, the stability of the proposed BES-BSMC is established by the application of Lyapunov theory, and the obtained results in the simulations illustrate the effectiveness of the developed method. Indeed, this research study constitutes an important contribution to the optimization and control of energy production and to the improvement of efficiency in relation to the available optimum power. On the other hand, this work can open up new fields and perspectives of applications in the clean energy production industry.

This paper has the following organization: The following part describes the modeling of the TEG system. The designed MPPT control strategy for the TEG system is developed in the third part. The simulation results are presented and discussed in the fourth part. Finally, the conclusion is given in part 5.

2   Thermoelectric Generator System Modeling

The TEG system structure is depicted in Fig. 1; it composed of the thermoelectric power generation system using a boost chopper to supply a resistive charge.

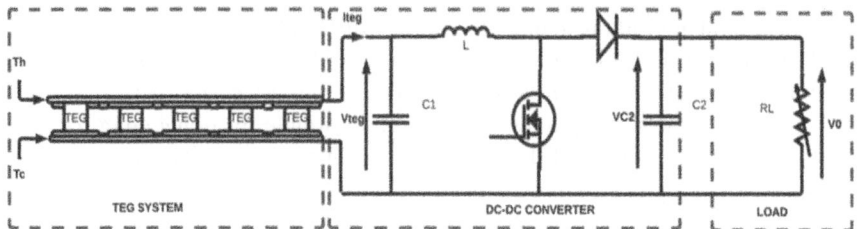

Fig. 1. The structure of Thermoelectric system

2.1 Thermoelectric Generator Module Modeling

A thermoelectric unit is primarily composed of n-type and p-type semiconductors. Figure 2 presents a typical structure of a thermoelectric module, whose output voltage is produced when a difference of temperature is created among two different surfaces; and are the hot side and the cold side temperatures, respectively.

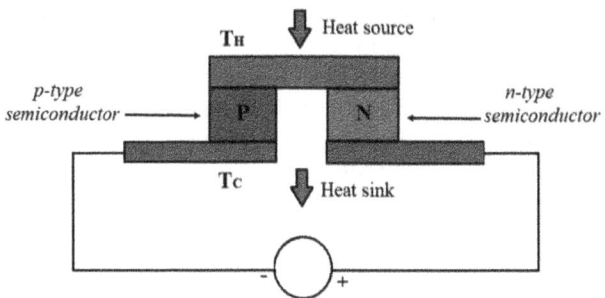

Fig. 2. Structure of a thermoelectric device [13]

A TEG module is normally formed by stacking number of thermoelectric units with the purpose of generating the required power. Thus, the TEG module equivalent circuit corresponds to a source of open circuit voltage connected to a serial internal resistor [15].

As reported in [16] and [17], the voltage expression is mainly related to the difference of the temperature among the TEG surfaces and the Seebeck coefficient as:

$$V_{TEG} = N\alpha_{pn}\Delta T = N\alpha_{pn}(T_H - T_C) \tag{1}$$

where $N\alpha_{pn}$ refers to the TEG module Seebeck coefficient (α_{pn} is the coefficient of thermocouple Seebeck between the PN junction) and N is the number of thermocouples.

The TEG array internal resistance R_{int} can be determined, using the open circuit voltage V_{OC} ratio to the short circuit current I_{SC}, as follows:

$$R_{int} = V_{TEG}/I_{TEG} \tag{2}$$

The generated current I_{TEG}, when a gradient of temperature is applied ΔT, is expressed as:

$$I_{TEG} = (V_{OC} - V_{TEG})/R_{int} \tag{3}$$

For the different gradients temperature, the variation in maximum power output of the TEG depends on the current-voltage requirements of the load. Therefore, an MPPT method is necessary for maximizing the produced energy by TEG system. For that reason, a boost converter based an adequate MPPT control is usually used as an interface among TEG source and its external charge to attain the desired objective.

2.2 DC-DC Boost Converter Modelling

By using the time average method [17–19], The mathematical model describing the dynamic of the boost converter with the TEG system is given as:

$$
\begin{cases}
\dot{V}_{TEG} = -\dfrac{1}{C_1} i_L + \dfrac{1}{C_1} I_{TEG} \\[3mm]
\dot{i}_L = \dfrac{1}{L} V_{TEG} - \dfrac{R_c(1-d)}{L\left(1+\frac{R_c}{R}\right)} i_L + \dfrac{1-d}{L}\left(\dfrac{R_c}{R_c+R} - 1\right) V_{C2} - \dfrac{V_D(1-d)}{L} \\[3mm]
\dot{V}_{C2} = \dfrac{(1-d)}{C_2\left(1+\frac{R_c}{R}\right)} i_L - \dfrac{1}{C_2(R+R_c)} V_{C2}
\end{cases}
\tag{4}
$$

where V_{TEG}, V_{C2}, and i_L are the TEG system voltage, the voltage of the capacitance C_2, and the current on the inductance L, respectively. R_C is the internal resistance on the capacitance C_2, V_D is the diode direct voltage and d is the duty cycle. R and R_c are the resistance of charge and the internal resistance of the capacity C_2, respectively.

By considering $x_1(t) = V_{TEG}$, $x_2(t) = i_L$, $x_3(t) = V_{C2}$ and $u(t) = d(t)$, the set of Eq. (4) can be expressed as below:

$$
\begin{cases}
\dot{x}_1(t) = \dfrac{1}{C_1}(-x_2(t) + I_{TEG}) \\[3mm]
\dot{x}_2(t) = f_1(x) + g_1(x)u(t) \\[3mm]
\dot{x}_3(t) = f_2(x) + g_2(x)u(t)
\end{cases}
\tag{5}
$$

where $x = \begin{bmatrix} x_1 & x_2 & x_3 \end{bmatrix}^T$ is the system state vector assumed to be available for measurement, and:

$$f_1(x) = \dfrac{x_1}{L} - \dfrac{R_c}{L\left(1+\frac{R_c}{R}\right)} x_2 + \dfrac{1}{L}\left(\dfrac{R_c}{R+R_c} - 1\right) x_3 - \dfrac{V_D}{L} \tag{6}$$

$$g_1(x) = -\dfrac{R_c}{L\left(1+\frac{R_c}{R}\right)} x_2 - \dfrac{1}{L}\left(\dfrac{R_c}{R+R_c} - 1\right) x_3 + \dfrac{V_D}{L} \tag{7}$$

$$f_2(x) = \frac{1}{C_2\left(1 + \frac{R_c}{R}\right)}x_2 - \frac{1}{C_2(R + R_c)}x_3 \tag{8}$$

$$g_2(x) = -\frac{1}{C_2\left(1 + \frac{R_c}{R}\right)}x_2 \tag{9}$$

3 Intelligent MPPT Controller Design

In order to maximize the produced energy through an MPPT technique for the TEG system, the backstepping sliding mode controller (BSMC) is envisaged to allow the TEG voltage V_{TEG} track the reference voltage V_{TEGref} for different gradients temperature of the TEG system.

3.1 Maximum Power Point Searching Algorithm

Reported to Eq. (3), the extracting power P_{TEG} from the TEG system is given as:

$$P_{TEG} = V_{TEG}I_{TEG} = V_{TEG}(V_{OC} - V_{TEG})/R_{int} \tag{10}$$

Then, the primary objective is to follow the MPP of the TEG, which means that the power P_{TEG} derivative with respect to V_{TEG} is equal to zero as follows [11]:

$$\left.\frac{dP_{TEG}}{dV_{TEG}}\right|_{MAX} = (V_{OC} - 2V_{TEG})/R_{int} = 0 \tag{11}$$

Consequently, the TEG output voltage at the MPP ($V_{TEG}|_{MAX}$) is expressed as:

$$V_{MPP} = V_{TEGref} = V_{TEG}|_{MAX} = \frac{V_{OC}}{2} \tag{12}$$

Therefore, the MPP current $I_{TEG}|_{MAX}$ is obtained as the following equation [20]:

$$I_{MPP} = I_{TEG}|_{MAX} = \frac{I_{SC}}{2} \tag{13}$$

3.2 Sliding Mode Control Method (SMC)

The principle of SMC method is to design switching surface firstly. Then, the second step present a conceiving of control law which is responsible to allow system trajectories towards this surface of state space and will maintain it in this one [20, 21].

The error of the voltage tracking can be expressed as:

$$e = x_1 - V_{TEGref} \tag{14}$$

Principally, the surface of sliding is determined as below:

$$\sigma(t) = \left(\gamma + \frac{d}{dt}\right)^{r-1} e(t) \tag{15}$$

where γ is a positive constant and r is order of the system.

The system order specified in Eq. (5) is 2. Therefore, the switching surface may be expressed as follows:

$$\sigma = \dot{e} + \gamma e \tag{16}$$

The function σ time derivative is given as:

$$\dot{\sigma} = \frac{1}{C_1}\left(-f_1(x) - g_1(x)u(t) + \dot{I}_{TEG}\right) - \ddot{V}_{ref} + \gamma\dot{e} \tag{17}$$

The following requirement is necessary for the SMC existence in finite time on a commutating surface [20]:

$$\sigma\dot{\sigma} < -\eta|\sigma| \tag{18}$$

The expression of control law which guarantees Eq. (18) can be written as follows:

$$u = \frac{1}{g_1(x)}\left[-f_1(x) + \dot{I}_{TEG} - C_1\ddot{V}_{ref} + \gamma C_1\dot{e} + kC_1 sign(\sigma)\right] \tag{19}$$

where k refers to the positive switching gain and $sign(.)$ is the function of sign, given by:

$$sign(\sigma) = \begin{cases} 1 & si\ \sigma > 0 \\ 0 & si\ \sigma = 0 \\ -1 & si\ \sigma < 0 \end{cases} \tag{20}$$

3.3 Backstepping Sliding Mode Control

Within this part, a robust Backstepping Sliding Mode Controller (BSMC) is developed for maximizing the produced power by the TEG system under changing temperature. The combination of both techniques allows to benefit from their advantages at the same time, and that by increasing the robustness of backstepping on the one hand, and reducing chattering behavior of the SMC on the other hand [22, 23]. The derivative voltage tracking error, given in Eq. (14) can be expressed as:

$$\dot{e} = \dot{x}_1 - \dot{V}_{TEGref} \tag{21}$$

Define the stable variable as follows:

$$\delta = h_1 e \tag{22}$$

where $h_1 > 0$.

Considering now a supplementary tracking error variable:

$$e_1 = \dot{e} + \delta \tag{23}$$

The first function of Lyapunov is selected as:

$$V_1 = \frac{1}{2}e^2 \tag{24}$$

Differentiating V_1 yield to,

$$\dot{V}_1 = e\dot{e} = e(e_1 - \delta) = ee_1 - h_1 e^2 \tag{25}$$

The augmented Lyapunov function is considered as:

$$V_2 = V_1 + \frac{1}{2}\sigma^2 \tag{26}$$

where σ is the commutating surface given by:

$$\sigma = e_1 + h_2 e \quad \text{with } h_2 > 0 \tag{27}$$

By deriving σ and using Eq. (25), the derivative of V_2 can expressed as follows:

$$\dot{V}_2 = \dot{V}_1 + \sigma\dot{\sigma} = ee_1 - h_1 e^2 + \sigma(\dot{e}_1 + h_2(e_1 - h_1 e)) \tag{28}$$

The derivative of e_1 is given by:

$$
\begin{aligned}
\dot{e}_1 &= \ddot{e} + \dot{\delta} \\
&= \ddot{x}_1 - \ddot{V}_{TEGref} + \dot{\delta} \\
&= -\frac{1}{C_1}[f_1(x) + g_1(x)u(t)] + \frac{1}{C_1}I_{TEG} - \ddot{V}_{TEGref} + \dot{\delta}
\end{aligned} \tag{29}
$$

Then,

$$\dot{\sigma} = h_2(e_1 - h_1 e) - \frac{1}{C_1}[f_1(x) + g_1(x)u(t)] + \frac{1}{C_1}I_{TEG} - \ddot{V}_{TEGref} + \dot{\delta} \tag{30}$$

We apply the next dynamic to the commutating surface as:

$$\dot{\sigma} = -h(\sigma + \beta sign(\sigma)) \tag{31}$$

where $h > 0$ and $\beta > 0$.

The commutating mode is taking place if $\dot{\sigma} = 0$. Thus, the control law is expressed by:

$$u(t) = \frac{1}{g_1(x)}(-f_1(x) + I_{TEG} - C_1\ddot{V}_{TEGref} + C_1\dot{\delta} + C_1 h_2(e_1 - h_1 e) + C_1 h(\sigma + \beta sign(\sigma))) \tag{32}$$

where $g_1(x) \neq 0$.

Optimizing the control parameters of BSMC using conventional or manual methods is often considered challenging and time-consuming. To address this issue, a novel approach is proposed in this study, which involves the utilization of swarm intelligence for real-time optimization of BSMC controller parameters. Specifically, the Bald Eagles Search Optimization (BES) algorithm is investigated in the next subsection.

3.4 Bald Eagles Search Online Update Algorithm

The bald eagles search (BES), introduced by [24], is a new meta-heuristic algorithm that draws inspiration from natural biological processes. To tackle complex real-world problems, individuals may develop personalized search strategies based on their individual experiences, whether local or global. More precisely, individuals navigate the search area by emulating the predatory practice. of bald eagles, which involves imitating their consumption of salmon at specific locations. Bald eagles employ a unique predation technique aimed at maximizing their success while minimizing energy expenditure.

- Selecting the space

  The hunting approach of the bald eagle involves three crucial components: the selection of a suitable search domain, a comprehensive survey of the chosen area, and maximizing the chances of capturing the prey. During the select phase, the defined the search area is influenced by the bald eagle's recent movement, which can be expressed as follows:

$$Pn(i) = Pb + \alpha.r.(Pm - Pi) \tag{33}$$

  where Pn is the i-th new position, Pb is the best obtained position, Pm is the mean position, P is the position of the i-th bald eagle, α is a control gain between 1.5 and 2 and r represents a random number falling within the range of [0, 1].

- Search stage

  The eagles use a spiral movement pattern in this stage of the procedure to speed up their hunt for prey inside the designated search area. Equation (34), which controls the update method, is used to dynamically modify the eagle's position.

$$pn = pi + yi \times (pi - pi + 1) + xi \times r(pi - pm) \tag{34}$$

  with:

$$xi = xr(i)\,max(|xr|)\,,\ yi = yr(i)\,max(|yr|)$$
$$xr(i) = ri \times sin(\theta i)\,,\ yr(i) = ri \times cos(\theta i)$$
$$\theta i = \alpha \times \pi \times rand$$
$$ri = \theta(i) \times R \times rand$$

  To calculate the bald eagle's positions in polar axis, the variables x(i) and y(i) assume values within the range of 0 to 1 in polar coordinates, ri and θi stand for the spiral flight's polar diameter and polar angle, respectively; R is for a parameter that regulates the search time and has a range of 0.2 to 2, a stands for a parameter that accepts a value in the range[0, 1], and rand represents a random number that falls in the range[0, 1].

- Swooping stage

  During stage, the eagles start to move in a motion similar to swinging from the perfect search position to their targeted prey, as described in Eq. (19):

$$Pn = rand \times Pb + xi_1 \times (Pi - c_1 \times Pm)$$
$$+ yi_1 \times (Pi - c_2 \times Pb) \tag{35}$$

where:

$$xi_1 = xr(i) \, max(|xr|), \; yi_1 = yr(i) \, max(|yr|)$$
$$xr(i) = ri * sinh[\theta i], \, yr(i) = ri \times cosh[\theta i]$$
$$\theta i = \alpha \times \pi \times rand, \, r(i) = \theta i$$

with the moving velocities c_1 and c_2, which are both between 1 and 2, are the optimal and central positions, respectively.

The objective function f to be minimized is chosen in this work as the Integral Square Error: $ISE = \int e^2 dt$, it determines the performance of any non-linear system. On the other hand, the variables to be selected is the parameters of the BSMC and SMC controllers. The BES is selected to solve this problem, since it can prevent local optimum and ensure that a global solution is reached. By take out the chosen optimum values of the parameters ($h_{1Optimum}$, $h_{2Optimum}$, $h_{Optimum}$ and $\beta_{Optimum}$,) that gives the fitness function's minimum value.

Theorem 1: *Consider the thermoelectric energy production system defined in Eq. (5). If the developed control law is established as per Eq. (32), with the parameters h_1, h_2, h, and β are selected off-line by BES algorithm, the controlled TEG system realizes a robust MPPT. In addition, the convergence of the maximum power point voltage tracking in finite time is ensured.*

Proof 1: By considering the Eq. (26), the following expression can be obtained:

$$\dot{V}_2 = \dot{V}_1 + \sigma \dot{\sigma} \tag{36}$$

By replacing the expression of the Eqs. (25) and (30) we can get:

$$\dot{V}_2 = e_1 e_2 - h_1 e_1^2 + \sigma \left[h_2(e_1 - h_1 e) - \frac{1}{C_1}[f_1(x) + g_1(x)u(t)] + \frac{1}{C_1} I_{TEG} - \dot{V}_{TEGref} + \delta \right] \tag{37}$$

By substituting the control law u expression in Eq. (32), we can have the following formula:

$$\begin{aligned}
\dot{V}_2 &= ee_1 - h_1 e^2 + \sigma(-h(\sigma + \beta sign(\sigma))) \\
&= ee_1 - h_1 e^2 - h\sigma^2 + \beta h\sigma \, sign(\sigma) \\
&\leq ee_1 - h_1 e^2 - h\sigma^2 + \beta h|\sigma| \\
&\leq -E^T P E - \beta|\sigma|
\end{aligned} \tag{38}$$

where $E = [e \quad e_1]^T$ and P is a symmetric matrix with the following form:

$$P = \begin{pmatrix} h_1 + hh_2^2 & -hh_2 - \frac{1}{2} \\ -hh_2 - \frac{1}{2} & h \end{pmatrix} \tag{39}$$

with the intention of making $\dot{V}_2 \leq 0$, the matrix P must be a positive symmetric. Otherwise, the determinant $|P| > 0$:

$$|P| = h(h_1 + hh_2^2) - (hh_2 + \frac{1}{2})^2 = h(h_1 - h_2) - \frac{1}{4} \tag{40}$$

Trough selecting precise values of h, h_1 and h_2, we get $|P| > 0$.

Then, an asymptotically stability of the optimized BSMC controller is guaranteed. Thus, the e and e_1 converge to zero in finite time. Thus, the optimized BSMC controller structure is illustrated in Fig. 4.

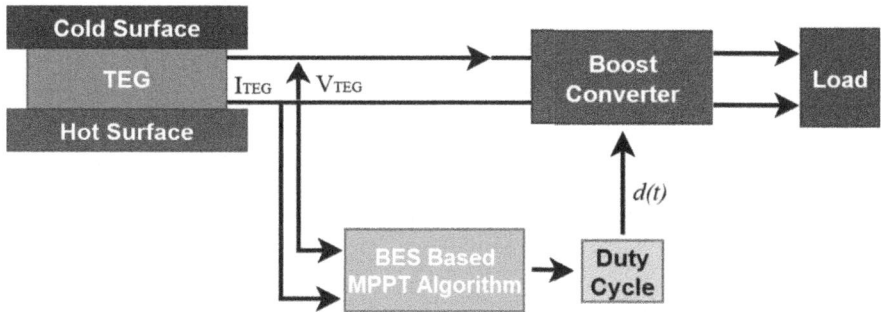

Fig. 4. Structure of the proposed BSMC controller based BES algorithm [19]

4 Simulation Results

In this part, numerical simulations were performed using MATLAB software to evaluate the performances of the suggested BES-BSMC controller. Furthermore, for the purpose to prove the proposed method efficiency, the obtained simulation results are compared to that of the conventional sliding mode control. Moreover, comparative studies had been conducted to prove the proposed controller effectiveness and feasibility under fast varying steps of temperature. Also, the designed controller's monitoring performance was studied for a TGM-199-1.4-0.8 TEG array [19]. The TEG system tested in this work, designed by connecting five TGM-199-1.4-0.8 modules in series [16], and the TGM-199-1.4-0.8 module manufacturer data consists of 199 thermocouples electrically arranged in serially and thermally in parallel. Furthermore, the TEG system main properties are shown in Table 1, and the parameter values of the DC-DC converter are mentioned in Tables 2 and 3, show the optimized parameters of the proposed controller that are selected off-line using the BES algorithm. In addition, the temperature of thermoelectric cold-side is fixed at $T_c = 30$ °C while that of the thermoelectric hot-side is varied according to a square signal as shown in Fig. 5.

To show the effectiveness of the proposed BES-BSMC controller, the comparison has been done in the presence of an abruptly varying temperature profile. Figures 6, 7 and 8 present a comparison of the suggested method and the standard SMC. Thus, the corresponding output voltages and powers are depicted in Figs. 6 and 7, respectively. We noticed that the developed controller attains the MPPT in finite time and shows high performance to abruptly varying in temperature. Also, we clearly observed that the proposed BES-BSMC approach provides better performance in term of transit response compared to the other method. The response times were found of about 0.6 s and 1.1 s for BES-BSMC and SMC, respectively. Besides, the suggested BES-BSMC ensure a very fast system response with a low tracking error without any chattering phenomena (Fig. 8), due to a low switching gain selected by BES algorithm and its search efficiency. This fluctuation proved in control signal (i.e. SMC) can obviously affect electrical power generation of the TEG system.

Table 1. Characteristics of TEG system [16]

Parameter	Numerical value
TE couples (N)	199
Thermoelectric modules	5 in series
Output Power at MPP (PMPP)	57 W
Open circuit voltage (VOC)	41 V
Short circuit current (ISC)	5.61 A
Internal Resistance	7.3 Ω
Hot-side temperature (TH)	200 °C
Cold-side temperature (TC)	30 °C
Seebeck coefficient	242.6 μV/K

Table 2. DC-DC boost converter characteristics

Parameter	Numerical value
Inductance L	0.22 mH
Capacitance $C_1 = C_2$	1000 μF
Resistance R_C	39.6 Ω
Resistance R	25 Ω
Diode voltage V_D	0.82 V

Table 3. Optimal BES-BSMC controller parameters

Parameter	Numerical value
$h_{1Optimum}$	100.00
$h_{2Optimum}$	1.0000
$h_{Optimum}$	1.1000
$\beta_{Optimum}$	0.0117

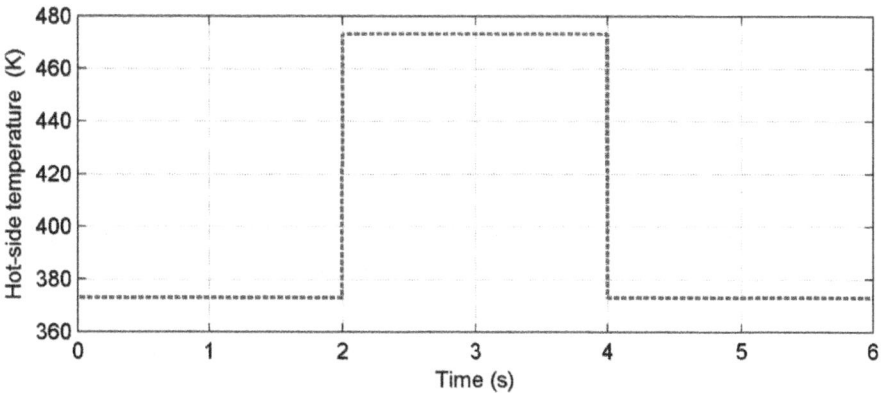

Fig. 5. The thermoelectric hot-side temperature T_h time evolution

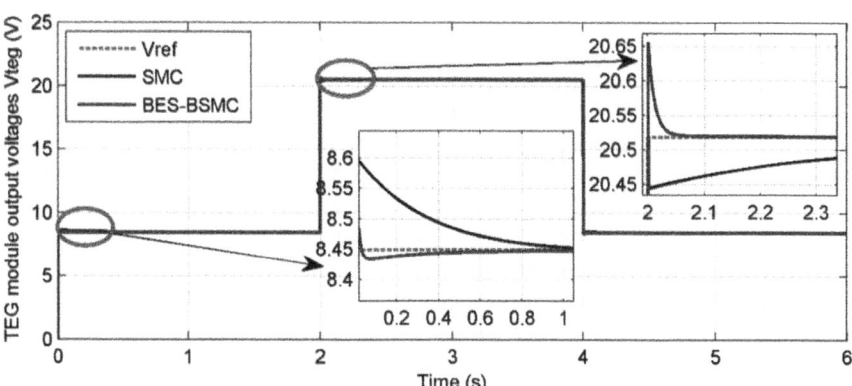

Fig. 6. The actual and desired voltage time evolution

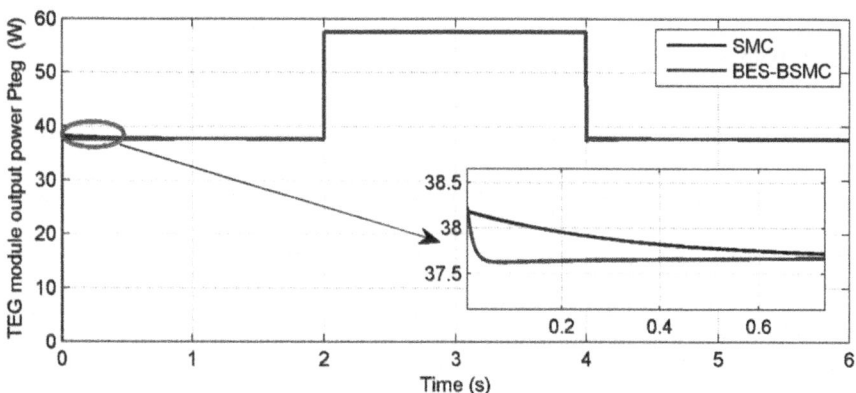

Fig. 7. The TEG power time evolution

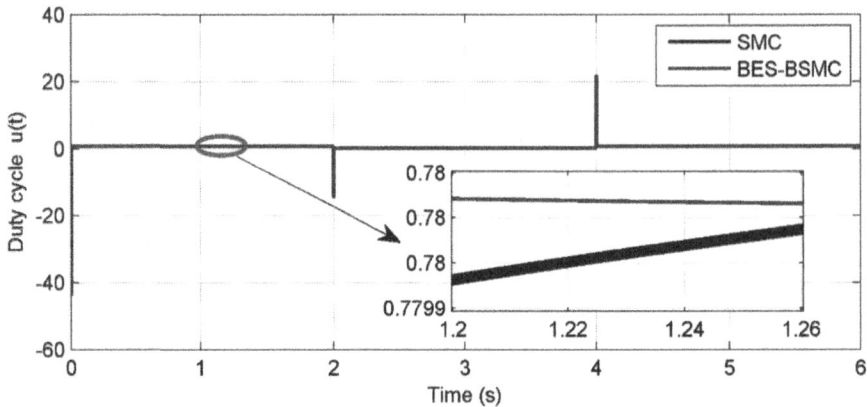

Fig. 8. The corresponding control signals

5   Conclusion

In this study, a robust and optimal control method that combines backestteping sliding mode control with the BES algorithm was developed, in order to increase maximum power generation efficiency of a TEG system. The BES based evolutionary algorithm was used in this work to select the BSMC parameters with a view to improve the proposed controller performances. The effectiveness of the designed method was demonstrated by simulation tests in a brutally varying temperature, and the obtained results show the feasibility and the superiority of the designed controller (BES-BSMC) compared to the standard SMC. The work reported in this study will be extended in the future to focus on efficient MPPT techniques with various power generation control strategies for a hybrid PV-TEG energy system. An experimental validation, using a real temperature variation profile for the thermoelectric hot side, of the proposed method-based BES algorithm is another topic that will be the focus of our further study.

References

1. Ahiska, R., Mamur, H.: A test system and supervisory control and data acquisition application with programmable logic controller for thermoelectric generators. Energy Convers. Manage. **64**, 15–22 (2012)
2. Kandil, A.A., Awad, M.M., Sultan, G.I., Salem, M.S.: Performance of a photo-voltaic/thermoelectric generator hybrid system with a beam splitter under maximum permissible operating conditions. Energ. Convers. Manag. **280**, 116795 (2023). https://doi.org/10.1016/j.enconman.2023.116795
3. Kumar, R., Montero, F.J., Lamba, R., Vashishtha, M., Upadhyaya, S.: Thermal management of photovoltaic-thermoelectric generator hybrid system using radiative cooling and heat pipe. Appl. Thermal Eng. **227**, 120420 (2023). https://doi.org/10.1016/j.applthermaleng.2023.120420
4. Gharzi, M., Kermani, A.M., Tash Shamsabadi, H.: Experimental investigation of a parabolic trough collector-thermoelectric generator (PTC-TEG) hybrid solar system with a pressurized heat transfer fluid. Renew. Energy **202**, 270–279 (2023). https://doi.org/10.1016/j.renene.2022.11.110

5. Yuan, D., Sha, A., Jiang, W., Wu, W., Xiao, J., Wang, T.: Technology method and functional characteristics of road thermoelectric generator system based on Seebeck effect. Appl. Energy (331), 120459 (2023)
6. Gould, C.A., Grainger, S., Shammas, N.Y.A.: Thermoelectric power generation: Properties, application and novel TCAD simulation. In: IEEE European Conference on Power Electronics and Applications, pp. 1–10 (2011)
7. Kim, S., Chou, P.H.: Size and topology optimization for supercapacitor-based sub-Watt energy harvesters. IEEE Trans Power Elec 28, 2068–2080 (2012)
8. Mamur, H., Ahiska, R.: Application of a DC-DC boost converter with maximum power point tracking for low power thermoelectric generators. Energy Convers. Manage. 97, 265–272 (2015)
9. Kanagaraj, N.: An enhanced maximum power point tracking method for thermoelectric generator using adaptive neuro-fuzzy inference system. J. Electr. Eng. Technol. 16, 1207–1218 (2021)
10. Saraireh, M., Saraereh, O., Maqableh, A.M., Jaradat, M.: A novel method for thermoelectric generator based on neural network. Comput. Mater. Continua 73, 2116–2133 (2022)
11. Kanagaraj, N., Rezk, Hegazy, Gomaa, Mohamed R.: A variable fractional order fuzzy logic control based MPPT technique for improving energy conversion efficiency of thermoelectric power generator. Energies 13(17), 4531 (2020). https://doi.org/10.3390/en13174531
12. Belkaid, A., Kayisli, K., Colak, I., Bulbul, H.I., Bayindir, R.: Maximum power extraction from a photovoltaic panel and a thermoelectric generator constituting a hybrid electrical generation system. In: 6th IEEE International Conference on Smart Grid, Japan (2018)
13. Belkaid, A., Kayisli, K., Colak, I.: Modeling and simulation of thermo electrical generator with MPPT, in: IEEE 6th International Conference on Renewable Energy Research and Applications (ICRERA) (2017)
14. Benhadouga, S., Meddad, M., Boukhetala, D., Eddiai, A., Riad, K.: Sliding mode control for MPPT of a thermogenerator. J. Electron. Mater. 48, 2103–2111 (2019)
15. Lineykin, S., Ben-Yaakov, S.: Modeling and analysis of thermoelectric modules. IEEE Trans. Ind. Applicat. 43(2), 505–512 (2007)
16. Üstüner, M., Mamur, H., Taskin, S.: Modeling and validation of the thermoelectric generator with considering the change of the Seebeck effect and internal resistance. Turk. J. Electr. Eng. Comput. Sci. 30, 2688–2706 (2022)
17. Mamur, H., Ahiska, R.: Application of a DC-DC boost converter with maximum power point tracking for low power thermoelectric generators. Energy Convers. Manage. 97, 265–272 (2015)
18. Kamran, A., et al.: Robust integral backstepping based nonlinear MPPT control for a PV system. Energies 12, 3180 (2019)
19. Yamada, H., Ishiyama, T., Kimura, K., Hanamoto, T., Takahashi, T., Sakaguchi, T.: A novel MPPT control method of thermoelectric power generation using state space averaging method, In: IEEE Ninth International Conference on Power Electronics and Drive Systems, Singapore (2011)
20. Slotine, J.J.: Sliding controller design for non-linear systems. Int. J. Control 40, 421–434 (1984)
21. Frih, A., Mrabti, M., Chalh, Z.: Wind turbine: bond graph modelling and sliding mode control. J. Mechatron. Syst. Control 46, 8–14 (2018)
22. Lamzouri, F.-E., El Amrani, A., Boufounas, E.-M.: Backstepping integral sliding mode control for power capture optimization of wind turbine system. J. Mechatron. Syst. Control 4(47), 225–234 (2019)

23. Lamzouri, F.-E., El Amrani, A., Boufounas, E.-M.: Nonlinear controller for MPPT based photovoltaic system under variable atmospheric conditions. Int. J. Model. Ident. Control **35**, 29–39 (2021)
24. Atlam, Z., Dndar, G.: A practical equivalent electrical circuit model for proton exchange membrane fuel cell (PEMFC) systems. Int. J. Hydrogen Energ. **46**, 13230–13239 (2021)

A Comparative Study of Neural Network and Fuzzy Logic Controller Approaches for BLDC Motor Speed Control

Meriem Megrini[✉], Ahmed Gaga, and Youness Mehdaoui

Polydisciplinary Faculty (FPBM), Research Laboratory of Physics and Engineers
Sciences (LRPSI), Research Team in Embedded Systems, Engineering, Automation,
Signal, Telecommunications and Intelligent Materials (ISASTM), Sultan Moulay
Slimane University (USMS), Beni Mellal, Morocco
megrinimeriem1@gmail.com

Abstract. In the last year, artificial intelligence has grown in popularity and is now being used in a variety of fields. Either be a well-known tool in the industry. This paper discusses two critical controllers that are used to regulate the speed of various motors in order to achieve the desired and recommended speed. These controllers are the Fuzzy Logic Controller (FLC), which employs fuzzy set theory, and the Artificial Neural Network Controller (ANNC), which is based on human brain logic. They are used to control the efficient and high-performance Brushless DC motor (BLDC). Because it does not have brushes like a DC motor, this motor requires no maintenance. This motor has become more efficient as a result of these controllers. Where they minimize settling time, eliminate peak time, and overshoot of system response speed.

Keywords: ANNC · FLC · BLDC · Speed control

1 Introduction

Currently, there are many applications for motors, including electric vehicles, robotics, elevators, home appliances, computer hard drives, heating, and ventilation [1]. The direct current (DC) motor was the first form of motor to be discovered. It is more effective, and has a straightforward speed regulating system [2]. But they have brushes that generate noise and increase pollution because to the carbon that construct the brushes [3]. The ongoing maintenance is another drawback. In order to get around these issues, BLDC motor has emerged. In recent years, BLDC motors have seen significant growth in industrial use [4]. It is a type of permanent magnet synchronous motor (PMSM) in which the back electromagnetic force (EMF) generated when the motor is powered is trapezoidal rather than sinusoidal as in classical one [5]. The operation of a BLDC motor is similar to that of a conventional PMSM [6]. BLDC motor is highly efficient, requires less maintenance due to its brushless architecture, and is small in size [7].

© The Author(s), under exclusive license to Springer Nature Switzerland AG 2025
H. Hagras et al. (Eds.): ISACS 2023, CCIS 2255, pp. 307–317, 2025.
https://doi.org/10.1007/978-3-031-93448-3_25

Many studies are conducted in order to develop position, speed, and/or torque control. A speed control is proposed in this paper to achieve the desired speed of a brushles DC motor. This control is such an important factor in the industry [8]. That why, it is mandatory to focus on and improve its regulatory process. To get the right controller design for the required speed, an accurate mathematical model of a bldc motor is required. As we all know, several researchers have worked in recent years to include Artificial Intelligence (AI) into a wide range of applications [9–11]. This paper will present two artificial intelligence-based controllers; Fuzzy Logic Controller (FLC) and Artificial Neural Network Controller (ANNC). A fuzzy logic controller can easily work with dynamic systems and eliminate the non-linearity problem, which is why it is becoming more popular in many applications [12]. This controller source is L.ZADEH's set theory [13,14]. Which regroups a flux of crisp values by flow values. It consists of a fuzzifier that converts crisp values into flow variables first, followed by a system engine that uses a mamdani system and some rule bases to join this input by output skipping by converting flow variables to crisp output values, which is known as defuzzification block. Because of their high learning trait and nonlinear mapping of various inputs and corresponding outputs of an electric motor drive system, artificial neural networks (ANN) are the most widely used and appreciated controller [15,16]. ANNs are computer models that were created with inspiration from research on how the human brain learns from observations and generalizes to data that has not yet been observed [17,18]. The following is an outline of the proposed work. Section 2 describes the materials and methods employed in this work. It is divided into two sections; the first explains the construction of the BLDC motor and provides the dynamic model used. The second explains the Fuzzy logic controller and artificial neural network controller, as well as how they can be used. Section 3 shows the results of these controllers' simulations in the MATLAB/SIMULINK environment, and explains them through discussion. Section 4 summarizes the work and evaluates each controller's performance.

2   Materials and Methods

2.1   BLDC Motor Dynamic Model

A brushless DC motor is a machine that converts electrical energy to mechanical energy. It has become widely used due to its high efficiency and controllability. Brushless DC motor is made up of a permanent magnet in rotor, a windings stator an inverter that corresponds to brushes, and commutators, changes the 3 winding phases. The energizing sequence of stator windings is used to control rotor speed.

Without taking into account the effects of saturation, hysteresis, and eddy current loss, as well as the effect of armature reaction on the air gap magnetic field. Figure 1 depicts the electromechanical model for each phase of a BLDC motor.

Applying Kirchoff Voltage Law (KVL) to the armture circuit, and balanced three-phase system. The BLDC motor's transfer function have a relationship between bus voltage and angular velocity expressed by:

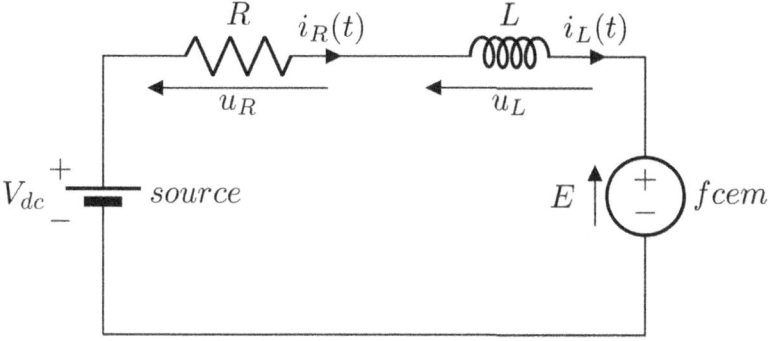

Fig. 1. Single phase electromechanical model of BLDC motor

$$H(S) = \frac{\Omega(S)}{V_{dc}(S)} = \frac{K_m}{J \cdot S + K} \tag{1}$$

where:

$$K_m = \frac{K_M}{R} \tag{2}$$

$$K = \frac{K_E \cdot K_M}{R} \tag{3}$$

The parameters of the BLDC motor used in this work are depicted in the Table 1:

Table 1. BLDC motor parameters.

Parameters	Values
Work voltage (V_{dc})	7–12 V
Internal resistor (R)	0.090 Ω
Shaft diameter (2r)	3.2 mm
Motor weight (M)	52.7 g
Rotation speed (K_V)	1000 RPM/V

Where:
The rotation speed is:

$$W_{max} = K_V \cdot V_{dc} \tag{4}$$

Mechanic constant:

$$K_M = \frac{1}{K_V} \tag{5}$$

Moment of inertia:

$$J = \frac{1}{2} \cdot M \cdot r^2 \tag{6}$$

Motor constant:

$$K_m = \frac{K_M}{R} \tag{7}$$

Friction constant:

$$K = \frac{K_E \cdot K_M}{R} \tag{8}$$

According to these parameters and Table 1, the transfer function using a numerical application become:

$$H(S) = \frac{\Omega(S)}{V_{dc}(S)} = \frac{10^2}{0,36 \cdot 10^{-2} \cdot S + 1} \tag{9}$$

Using the Z transformation, the BLDC motor model will be converted into discrete time. Using the pole-zero mapping discretization method with a sampling periode $T_{samp} = 0.001$, the BLDC motor model is declared as follows:

$$\frac{\Omega(S)}{V_{dc}(S)} = \frac{158.7}{Z - 0.841} \tag{10}$$

2.2   Fuzzy Logic Controller

Fuzzy set theory as a source of inspiration for the application of human practice knowledge [19]. It is widely used in the last center of industry to improve processes [20]. It is made up of: Fuzzification, which converts inputs data set to flow variables, defuzzification, which converts flow variables to output data set, an inference engine that uses the Mamdani system based on center of area equation, and the rule bases, which relate the inputs to the outputs by using logical statements (IF-THEN) to carry out the actions. Figure 2 resumes the blocks that make it up.

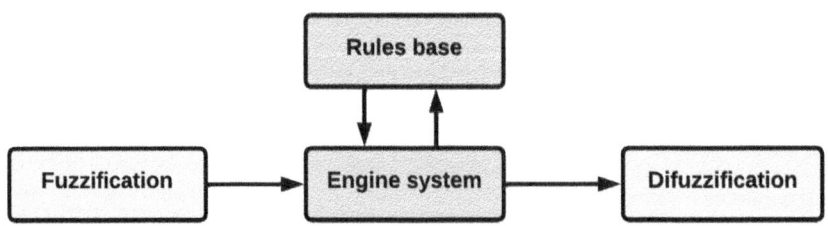

Fig. 2. Fuzzy logic controller blocks.

The main idea behind fuzzy logic controllers is membership functions, which are represented by linear functions. In this work, triangular linear functions are used to develop fuzzy controllers. In addition to all fuzzy logic processes, the fuzzy set membership functions are primarily based on linguistic variables (NB, NM, NS, Z, PS, PM, PB) as the Fig. 3 depicts:

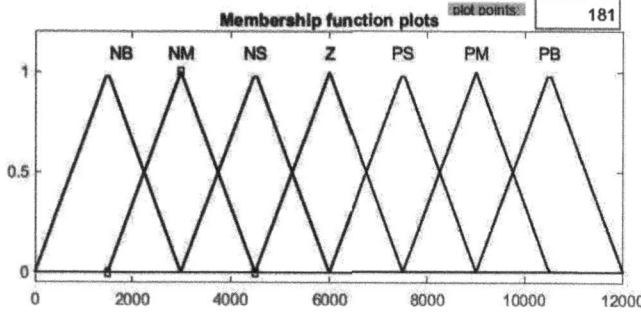

Fig. 3. Membership functions and linguistic variables of FLC.

This work focuses on MISO (Multiple Input Single Output) systems as the Fig. 4 depicts.

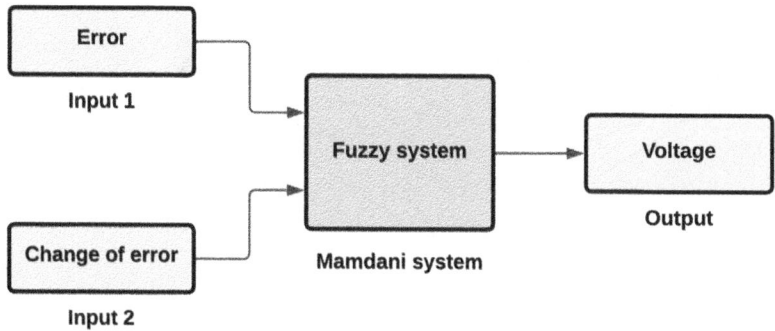

Fig. 4. Inputs and output of FLC.

Where the inputs are the error value (E) and the change of error DE. These are as follows:

$$E_i = \Omega_i - \Omega_{i-1} \tag{11}$$

$$DE_i = E_i - E_{i-1} \tag{12}$$

where error E is the difference between the desired speed and the actual one. The change of error DE is the error value's rate of change, and the output is the voltage applied to the BLDC motor. Triangular membership functions based on the Mamdani fuzzy inference system are used to present both inputs and outputs as the Fig. 3 shown. 49 rule bases (probability) get better response of the system, that's why 7 membership functions was used for each input and output. they have the following form: IF (error (E) is membership function 1) and (change of error (DE) is membership function 2) THEN (voltage (V_{dc}) is membership function 3) [12].

2.3   Artificial Neural Network

ANN has the same system as the human biological nervous system. It is made up of an input layer, an output layer, and a set of hidden layers, as shown in Fig. 5:

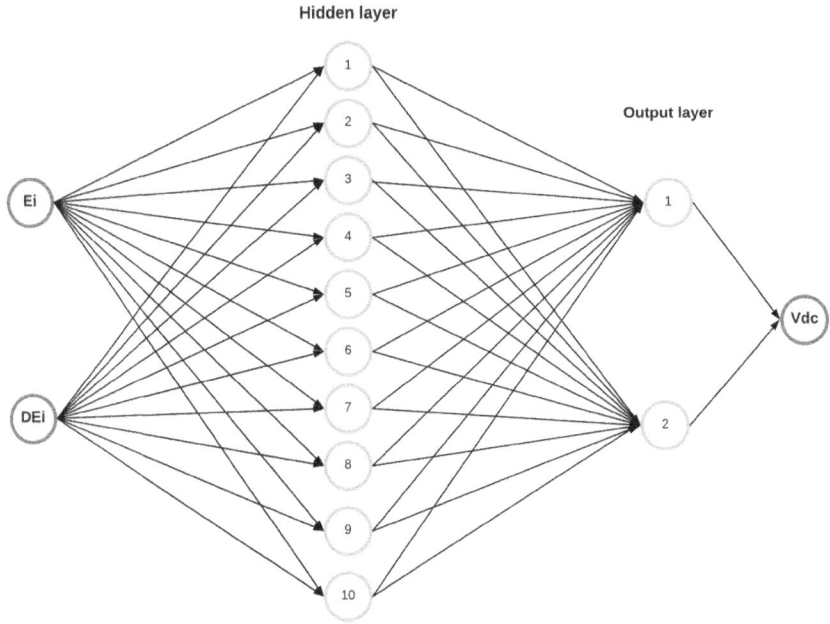

Fig. 5. Artificial neural network structure.

A network function is built by a relationship between the elements to produce an output that is equal to or close to the target output. This means that ANN learn from multiple experiments on the system's known training data set using neurons with activation and sum functions, as expressed by the Eq. 13 [21]:

$$y = \varphi \left(\sum_{i=1}^{n} W_i * x_i b \right) \tag{13}$$

where x is the input of the neuron, W is the weights, b is the bias of the neuron, and φ is the function, as well as y is the output. Iterative training can be used to find the output by eliminating the error between it and the target vector. This training is affected by the number of neurons, the number of layers, and the initial value of W.

In this work, data is collected using the SIMULINK model depicted in Fig. 6.

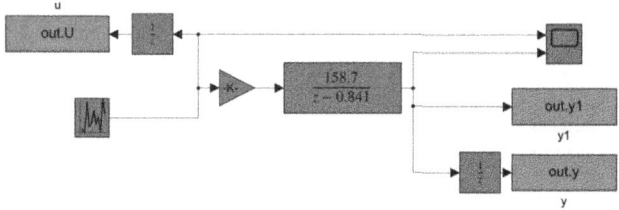

Fig. 6. SIMULINK model for ANN data collection.

Where, [y, y1] is the input of ANN training, u is the target. This data collection results in the identification of an inverse palnt model of the system, which will play the role of ANNC.

3 Results Discussions and Comparison to Other Works

3.1 Results Discussions

The system is simulated in MATLAB/SIMULINK as proposed in the Fig. 7, with the high part representing the closed loop using a fuzzy logic controller and the low part representing the closed loop using an ANN controller.

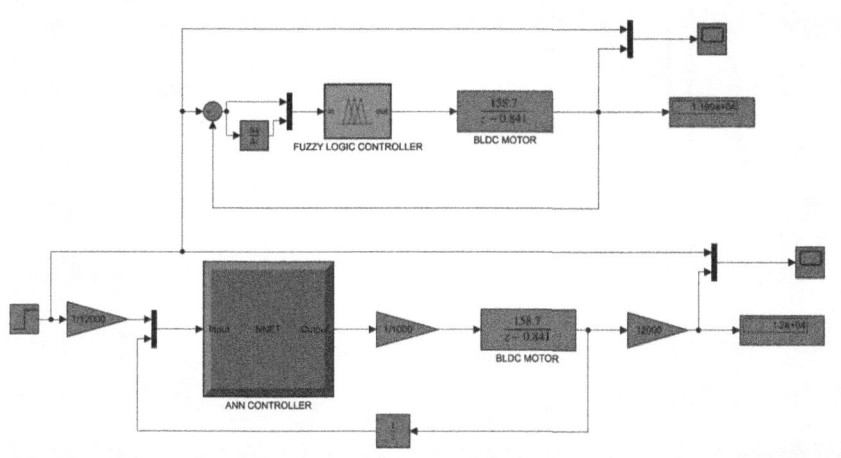

Fig. 7. SIMULINK model for FLC and ANNC.

Figure 8 displays the speed response of an FLC controller at 12000 rpm. Where, there is no overshoot, no peak time, and zero settling time, as shown by the zoom part in Fig. 8, yet there is a minor steady state inaccuracy of 5 rpm.

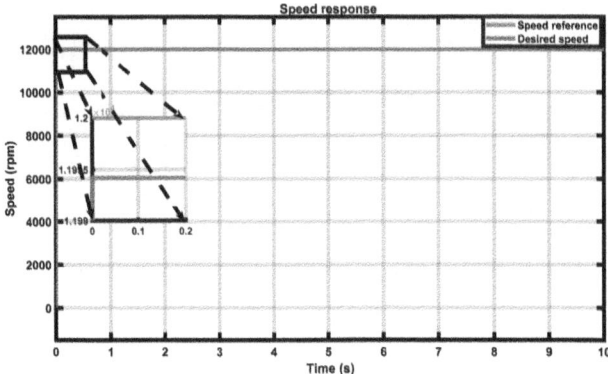

Fig. 8. FLC response at 12000 rpm speed.

Figure 9 depicts the speed response of a ANN controller at a speed of 12000 rpm. Where, there is an overshoot of 66 % ([((20000-12000)/12000)*100]), a peak time of 0.02 ms, a 0.01 ms rising time, and a 0.06 ms settling time as the zoom part depicts in Fig. 9, but there is no steady state error.

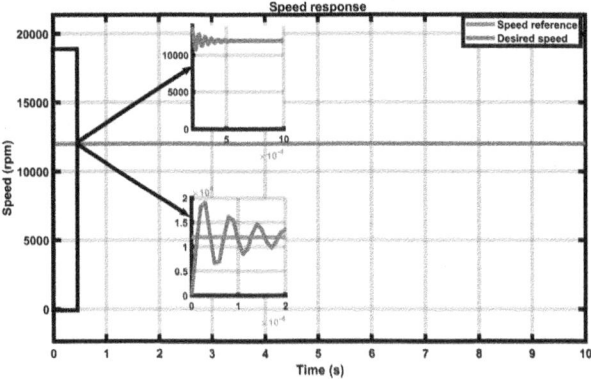

Fig. 9. ANNC response at 12000 rpm speed.

The response of each controller is depicted for a speed of 12000 rpm in the Fig. 10, which clearly shows the difference in response and performance of each controller. Thus, the application criteria that help to choose the right controller. Where there are some applications where this overshoot in ANNC does'nt present a problem and others where this petite steady state error presented by FLC do not present a problem.

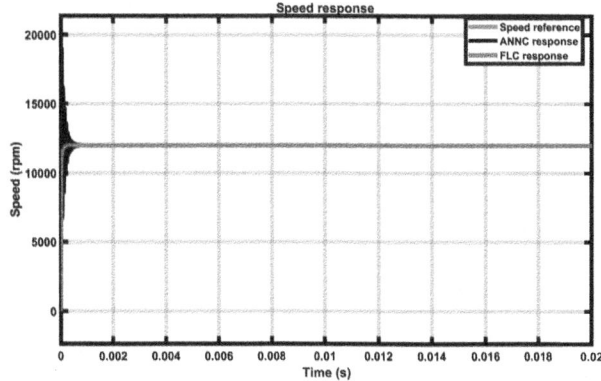

Fig. 10. Performance of FLC and ANNC at 12000 rpm speed.

3.2   Comparison with Other Works

In [22] authors found that the settling time using PID controller is 1.5 s, 0.3 ms using reference model, and 0.8 ms using ANN controller, Where the overshoot is 0 rpm for both last controllers and 3 rpm for PID controller. In [23] authors use model reference neural adaptive control, they found that the settling time is 1 ms and an overshoot close to 150 rpm. In comparison to our work, for the ANN controller gives better response where there is an overshoot but for a peak time equal to 0.02 ms and a small settling time of 0.06 ms, and for the FLC all these settings are better only a petite steady state error equal to 5 rpm. To summarize, the controllers employed in this paper are better due to the shorter periods for overshoot and settling.

4   Conclusion

This paper proposes two developed artificial intelligence-based controllers for controlling the speed of a BLDC motor. The first is based on a fuzzy logic controller that controls the speed of a BLDC motor and generates the motor's compatible winding voltage. The second is an artificial neural network controller, which requires a set of data from the system obtained through a system test using a default input. As a result of simulations of different controllers, it is clear that the speed response of ANNC hasn't a steady state error compared to FLC but a it has large overshoot that FLC doesn't have. Thus, we must select the appropriate and compatible controller for the appropriate application, which means that for applications where overshoot is not a major concern, we can use ANNC, but for applications where it is, we can use FLC. As a perspective, we can develop a controller based on FLC and ANNC at the same time to obtain a controller with all of these capabilities.

References

1. Pindoriya, R.M., Mishra, A.K., Rajpurohit, B.S., Kumar, R.: Analysis of position and speed control of sensorless BLDC motor using zero crossing back-EMF technique. In: 2016 IEEE 1st International Conference on Power Electronics, Intelligent Control and Energy Systems (ICPEICES), Delhi, India, pp. 1–6. IEEE (2016). https://doi.org/10.1109/ICPEICES.2016.7853072

2. Niapour, S., Danyali, S., Sharifian, M., Feyzi, M.R.: Brushless DC motor drives supplied by PV power system based on Z-source inverter and FL-IC MPPT controller. Energy Convers. Manag. **52**(8), 3043–3059 (2011). https://doi.org/10.1016/j.enconman.2011.04.016

3. Gobinath, S., Madheswaran, M.: Deep perceptron neural network with fuzzy PID controller for speed control and stability analysis of BLDC motor. Soft. Comput. **24**(13), 10161–10180 (2019). https://doi.org/10.1007/s00500-019-04532-z

4. Shifat, T.A., Jang-Wook, H.: Remaining useful life estimation of BLDC motor considering voltage degradation and attention-based neural network. IEEE Access **8**, 168414–168428 (2020). https://doi.org/10.1109/ACCESS.2020.3023335

5. Matsui, N.: Sensorless PM brushless DC motor drives. IEEE Trans. Ind. Electron. **43**(2), 300–308 (1996). https://doi.org/10.1109/41.491354

6. Monika, A.K.: Comparison of Fuzzy Logic and NEURO Fuzzy Algorithms for Load Sensor (2013). https://www.semanticscholar.org/paper/Comparison-of-Fuzzy-Logic-and-NEURO-Fuzzy-for-Load-Monika-Kaur/1fedeb0c43939a26d086fb55e742d493df3df136. Accessed 28 Mar 2023

7. Arivalahan, R., Venkatesh, S., Vinoth, T.: An effective speed regulation of brushless DC motor using hybrid approach. Adv. Eng. Softw. **174**, 103321 (2022). https://doi.org/10.1016/j.advengsoft.2022.103321

8. Sanatizadeh, M., Bigdeli, N.: The design of NMSS fractional-order predictive functional controller for unstable systems with time delay. ISA Trans. **92**, 49–64 (2019). https://doi.org/10.1016/j.isatra.2019.02.026

9. Karakuzu, C., Karakaya, F., Çavuşlu, M.A.: FPGA implementation of neuro-fuzzy system with improved PSO learning. Neural Netw. **79**, 128–140 (2016). https://doi.org/10.1016/j.neunet.2016.02.004

10. Magdy Saady, M., Hassan Essai, M.: Hardware implementation of neural network-based engine model using FPGA. Alexandria Eng. J. **61**(12), 12039–12050 (2022). https://doi.org/10.1016/j.aej.2022.05.035

11. Véstias, M.P., Duarte, R.P., de Sousa, J.T., Neto, H.C.: A fast and scalable architecture to run convolutional neural networks in low density FPGAs. Microproces. Microsyst. **77**, 103136 (2020). https://doi.org/10.1016/j.micpro.2020.103136

12. Controlling Speed of DC Motor with Fuzzy Controller in Comparison with ANFIS Controller. https://www.scirp.org/(S(i43dyn45teexjx455qlt3d2q))/journal/paperinformation.aspx. Accessed 5 Apr 2023

13. Enhancing The Performance Of DC Motor Speed Control Using Fuzzy Logic - IJERT. https://www.ijert.org/enhancing-the-performance-of-dc-motor-speed-control-using-fuzzy-logic. Accessed 28 Mar 2023

14. Control Systems Engineering. EasyEngineering (2019). https://easyengineering.net/control-systems-engineering-by-nagrath-nw. Accessed 28 Mar 2023

15. Leena, N., Shanmugasundaram, R.: Artificial neural network controller for improved performance of brushless DC motor. In: 2014 International Conference on Power Signals Control and Computations (EPSCICON), pp. 1–6 (2014). https://doi.org/10.1109/EPSCICON.2014.6887513

16. Kishor, K., Tiwari, S.: Speed Control of a Brushless DC Motor Using Neural Network Based MRAC (2018). https://www.semanticscholar.org/paper/SPEED-CONTROL-OF-A-BRUSHLESS-DC-MOTOR-USING-NEURAL-Kishor-Tiwari/b685fc40d6751613da517d08fdc4de2ceaa44d20. Accessed 28 Mar 2023

17. Zhang, Q.J., Gupta, K.C.: Neural Networks for RF and Microwave Design. Artech House (2000)

18. Sadrossadat, S.A., Rahmani, O.: ANN-based method for parametric modelling and optimising efficiency, output power and material cost of BLDC motor. IET Electr. Power Appl. **14**(6), 951–960 (2020). https://doi.org/10.1049/iet-epa.2019.0686

19. Classical Sets and Fuzzy Sets. Fuzzy Logic with Engineering Applications, pp. 25–47. Wiley (2010). https://doi.org/10.1002/9781119994374.ch2

20. Speed control of DC motor using Fuzzy Logic Controller. https://ieeexplore.ieee.org/document/7867673. Accessed 5 Apr 2023

21. van Assen, M., Lee, S.J., Cecco, C.N.D.: Artificial intelligence from A to Z: from neural network to legal framework. Eur. J. Radiol. **129** (2020). https://doi.org/10.1016/j.ejrad.2020.109083

22. Mamadapur, A., Unde Mahadev, G.: Speed control of BLDC motor using neural network controller and PID controller. In: 2019 2nd International Conference on Power and Embedded Drive Control (ICPEDC), pp. 146–151 (2019). https://doi.org/10.1109/ICPEDC47771.2019.9036695

23. Utomo, D.S.B., Rizal, A., Gaffar, A.F.O.: Model reference neural adaptive control based BLDC motor speed control. In: 2017 5th International Conference on Electrical, Electronics and Information Engineering (ICEEIE), Malang, pp. 49–54. IEEE (2017). https://doi.org/10.1109/ICEEIE.2017.8328761

Assessment of the Wind Power Capacity in the Taza Province of Morocco

Badr El Kihel[✉] ⓘ, Nacer Eddine El Kadri Elyamani ⓘ, and Abdelhakim Chillali ⓘ

Laboratoire Des Sciences de L'Ingénieur (LSI), Faculté Polydisciplinaire de Taza, Université Sidi Mohamed Ben Abdellah, Fès, route d'Oujda – B.P. 1223, Taza, Morocco
{badr.elkihel,nacereddine.elkadrielyamani}@usmba.ac.ma,
abdelhakim.chillali@usmb.ac.ma

Abstract. This article assesses the wind energy potential at two sites in the Taza province, northeastern Morocco: Tahla and Tizi Ouasli. The analysis is based on wind speed data measured from January 1, 2003, to December 31, 2022. Wind measurements were taken at heights of 50 m and 100 m above ground level. The aim of this study is to analyse the wind potential of the selected sites and assess their suitability for wind energy development. The Weibull distribution is used to determine the power density and energy output of wind turbines. The shape and scale parameters were estimated using the Energy Pattern Factor Method, with a wind speed class interval of 0.5 m/s. The statistical analysis includes the calculation of monthly mean wind speeds and the generation of wind rose diagrams. The results indicate that Tahla has the highest potential. At a height of 100 m, the average power density at this location is estimated at 197.3 W/m^2. Among the evaluated turbine models, the GoldWind GW 140/3.0 exhibits the highest capacity factor, making it the most economically advantageous option for both sites.

Keywords: Wind potential · Weibull function · Power density · Capacity factor · Energy pattern factor method.

1 Introduction

In the current era, climate change is one of the issues threatening the stability of populations worldwide. Ecologists warn of the danger posed by global warming [1].

At the international level, government policies increasingly favour more sustainable and accessible energy systems, such as renewable energy [2]. The European Commission has set a binding target of 32% renewable energy by 2030 [3]. This view stems from the COP 21 meeting in Paris, where the Kingdom of Morocco committed and set a target for electricity generation from renewable sources (52% by 2030) [4]. In addition, since adopting the new constitution in 2011, Morocco has strategically chosen to make advanced regionalisation an engine of socioeconomic development. Thus, each region must exploit its natural resources to achieve energy self-sufficiency.

In this sense, Morocco's geographical and climatic position allows it to benefit from a significant wind potential estimated at around 6 GW [5]. The regions in Morocco

© The Author(s), under exclusive license to Springer Nature Switzerland AG 2025
H. Hagras et al. (Eds.): ISACS 2023, CCIS 2255, pp. 318–332, 2025.
https://doi.org/10.1007/978-3-031-93448-3_26

characterised by solid winds encompass the northernmost section adjacent to the Strait of Gibraltar, the Tangier-Tetouan area, the Essaouira district, the southern Atlantic region of Tarfaya, as well as the Lagouira and Taza passages [4]. That said, it seems appropriate to conduct a study on the Taza area to verify its wind potential and to know to what extent we could use this potential to produce electrical energy. It should be noted that a wind project is already installed in the Twahar site of the commune of Ouled Chrif with a power of 87 MW. This power reaches 150 MW by installing another park in the communes of Meknassa Al Gharbia and Bab Marzouka.

The area in question has previously been the subject of a similar study published by El Khchine et al. [6], revealing a low power density with a value of 122.91 W/m^2. Nevertheless, given the narrowness of its field of investigation, the data is collected on a single site; our intervention then consists of multiplying the study points for better satisfaction. Indeed, two sites were studied: Tahla and Tizi Ouasli.

The Weibull distribution is used to model wind speeds at two locations. Estimate shape and size parameters using the Energy Configuration Factor algorithm to calculate power density and annual energy for different wind turbine tower heights.

Other similar studies were also performed: Alouhi et al. [7] for four years, he assessed the wind energy potential of his six coastal regions of the Kingdom of Morocco (Al Hoceima, Tetouan, Asila, Essaouira, Laayoune and Dakhla). The average wind energy density is higher in the southern regions of Morocco than in the northern regions. The maximum power densities at Dakhla and Laayoune in July were 532 W/m^2 and 494 W/m^2 at 50 m height and 633 W/m^2 and 588 W/m^2 at 75 m height.

Daoudi et al. [8] presented their studies on the Zagora province over nine years. The Weibull distribution method was used. The initial assessment indicates that higher wind speeds increase annual energy production and capacity factor. The production is estimated to be around 2.62 GWh/year.

Daoudi et al. [9] analysed the wind potential of the province of Tiznit with wind speed data over 24 years at a height of 10 m using a Weibull distribution. The results show that the best capacity factor is 36.91%, and the annual production reaches 3.0 GWh.

In contrast, the research conducted yielded the following results:

Alham et al. [10] present a study conducted at four sites in Egypt: Ras El-Hekma, Farafra, Nuweiba and Aswan. Calculate wind power density, energy density and other parameters based on the Weibull distribution function. Wind speed data was analysed using hourly measurements taken 10 m above sea level over five years. The results show that Ras El Hekma has a maximum wind energy density of 5207.9 kWh/m^2, while Farafra has a minimum wind energy density of 992.67 kWh/m^2.

A study by A-J Collaros-Lara et al. [11] Shows two valid methods for estimating the annual mean power density at a height of 10 m over 20 years in the province of Granada, Spain. Use Rayleigh and Weibull distributions to interpret shape and scale parameters. From January to April, the power density is between 44.25 and 53.80 W/m^2 but can vary greatly depending on location (minimum 3.47 W/m^2, maximum 2115.05 W/m^2). During the rest of the year, it fluctuates between a minimum of 1.90 and a maximum of 1609.98 W/m^2, depending on the region.

This document is structured as follows: Sect. 1 begins by providing a brief overview of the Taza province, focusing on existing or planned renewable energy systems. Section 2 presents the approach and methodology adopted for conducting the study. The analysis details are described in Sect. 3, while the results and discussions are presented in Sect. 4.

2 Description of the Region of Taza

The Taza province, situated in northeastern Morocco, spans an area of 7,101 square kilometres and has a population of 497,229 people as of 2021 [12]. Figure 1 displays the municipalities within the province of Taza. These municipalities are classified based on the similarity of data obtained from the POWER NASA site, which offers databases containing various physical measurements such as temperature, wind speed, and pressure at different elevations. Table 1 demonstrates the distribution of municipalities across zones 1 and 2. From this selection, two specific locations have been identified: Tahla and Tizi Ouasli.

Table 1. The chosen sites of each municipality

Zone	M	Municipalities (M)	Study site	Lat	Lon
Z1	11	**Tahla**, Bab Marzouka, Ghiata Al Gharbia, Oued Amlil, Bouhlou, Matmata, Bouchafra, Smiaa, Tazarine, Zrarda, Ait Saghrouchen, Bab Boudir	Tahla	34.050	−4.424
Z2	2	Sidi Ali Bourkba, **Tizi Ouasli**	Tizi Ouasli	34.764	−3.794

From a geographical perspective, the province of Taza exhibits diverse geomorphology. It has located in an area that connects the mountain ranges of the Rif and the Middle Atlas, with these two chains converging at the Twahar Pass, reaching an altitude of 559 m.

Regarding energy consumption, the Taza province consumed 121,855 MWh in 2022, representing a 3% increase compared to 2021. The province lacks hydroelectric or solar energy sources. However, it does have the Twahar wind farm located approximately 12 km northwest of the city. This wind farm consists of 27 wind turbines, each with a power capacity of 3.23 MW [13].

3 Approach and Methodology

This paper aims to study the feasibility of wind energy utilisation in Taza province and assess wind energy density and wind energy potential. The program chosen for this follows a structured three-stage approach.

First Stage: Data collection. The initial phase involves gathering data. The wind speed data from 1/1/2003 to 31/12/2022 is sourced from the NASA website, POWER I DATA ACCESS VIEWER [14], and downloaded in.csv format. The data is collected at regular one-hour intervals at 50 m and 100 m heights.

Second Stage: Data processing and analysis. The collected data is then processed using the POWER QUERY software, integrated into the Microsoft Office EXCEL application software [15]. This software facilitates the processing and analysis of the data.

Third Stage: Wind power selection. In this stage, the selection of wind power is determined by studying the various wind power options available in the market. Factors such as performance, reliability, and suitability are considered during this selection process.

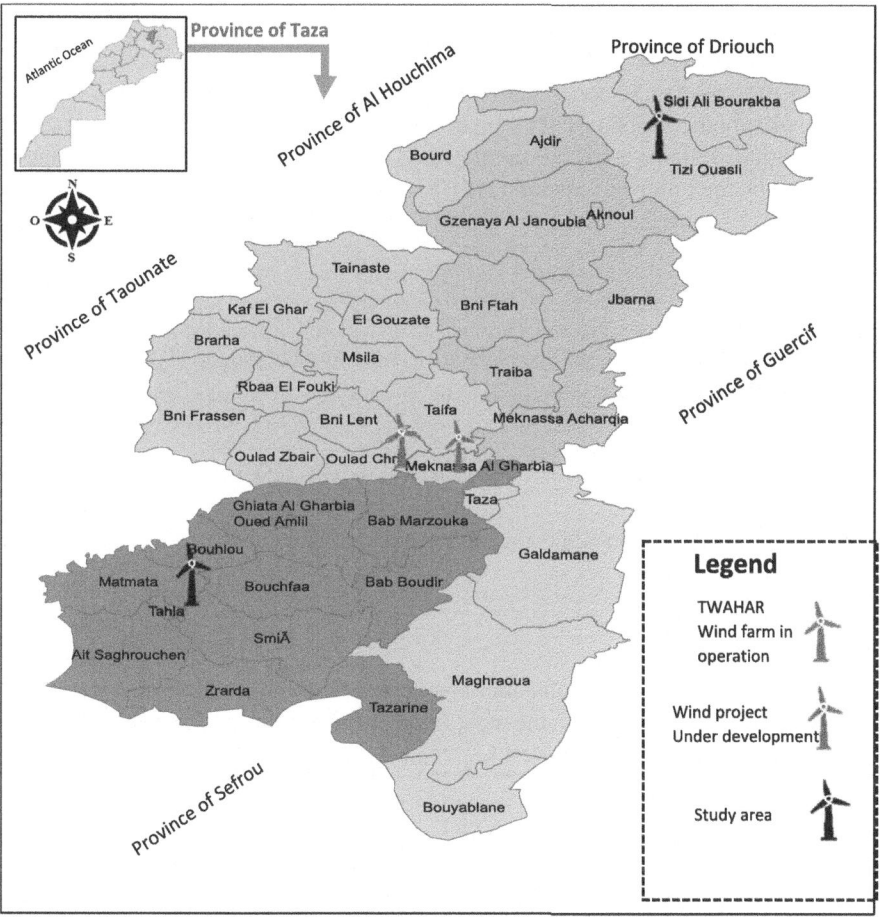

Fig. 1. The municipalities of the province of Taza in MOROCCO

4 Mathematical Analysis

4.1 Weibull Distribution and Calculation of Statistical Parameters

Different probability functions can be employed to depict the occurrence pattern of wind speeds. For example, Burr distribution, Gamma distribution, Weibull distribution, Rayleigh distribution, inverse Gaussian distribution, etc., may be mentioned. This study chose the Weibull distribution function for its simplicity and accuracy. Its formula is as follows [5–7, 16]:

$$f(v) = \frac{k.v^{k-1}}{c^k} e^{-(\frac{v}{c})^k} \tag{1}$$

Here, $f(v)$ symbolizes the probability of wind speed, where k and c respectively represent a shape parameter (dimensionless) and a scale factor (m/s). To determine the values of these two parameters, various approaches are possible. Among the iterative methods, the maximum likelihood and energy equivalent methods are notable. As for non-iterative methods, the empirical methods of Lysen or Jestus and the energy pattern factor method can be mentioned. In our study, we employ the latter to ascertain the values of k and c. It is defined by the following equation [17]:

$$E_{pf} = \frac{\overline{v^3}}{\overline{v}^3} = \frac{\frac{1}{n}\sum_{i=1}^{n} v_i^3}{\frac{1}{n}\sum_{i=1}^{n} \overline{v}_i} \tag{2}$$

where $\overline{v^3}$ is the mean cubic wind speed. Here, n. s the number data in 20 years. Then the Weibull shape parameter k is giving as [18]:

$$k = 1 + \frac{3.69}{E_{pf}^2} \tag{3}$$

The value of c is determined using the formula provided in [19].

$$c = \frac{\overline{v}}{\Gamma\left(1 + \frac{1}{k}\right)} \tag{4}$$

A crucial element in the wind potential assessment is the most probable wind speed, denoted as v_{mp}, corresponding to the most frequently oberved wind speed at any given point. This value is provided by [7]:

$$v_{mp} = c\left(1 - \frac{1}{k}\right)^{1/k} \tag{5}$$

Wind speed is another essential feature of turbine design, which produces maximum energy throughout the year. This parameter represents the annual maximum wind energy, which can be expressed by [20]:

$$v_{me} = c\left(1 + \frac{2}{k}\right)^{1/k} \tag{6}$$

To achieve optimal efficiency, the selection of a wind turbine should be based on its nominal wind speed to align with the one generating maximum energy. Furthermore, the formula below determines the probability of obtaining wind speeds between v_a and v_b [21]:

$$p(v_a < v < v_b) = \int_{v_a}^{v_b} p(v)dv \tag{7}$$

4.2 Analysis of Power and Energy Densities Associated with Wind

Wind energy, naturally produced by the wind, is highly sought-after resource by humanity. To quantify this resource, the measure of power density is often employed. This metric, usually expressed in watts per square meter (W/m^2), can be used to assess the wind energy potential of a given location. The higher the density of wind power generation, the more energy can be converted into electricity by wind turbines. Its formula is as follows [22]:

$$P_D = \frac{P}{A} = \frac{1}{2}\rho v^3 \tag{8}$$

Here, v represents the velocity, A represents the area perpendicular to the v vector, and $\rho = 1.225$ kg/m^3 corresponds to air density (at a temperature of 15 °C). Following the Weibull distribution function, the wind power density can be formulated as follows [5, 7]:

$$P_W = \frac{P}{A} = \frac{1}{2}\rho \int_0^{\infty} v^3 p(v)dv = \frac{1}{2}\rho c^3 \Gamma\left(1 + \frac{3}{k}\right) \tag{9}$$

Further, the average wind power density, can be determined as follows [23]:

$$\overline{P_D} = \frac{\overline{P}}{A} = \frac{1}{2}\rho \sum_{i=1}^{N} \frac{v_i^3}{N} \tag{10}$$

Similarly, the wind energy density for period time $N\Delta t$ is given by formula (11), where N is the number of time measurement periods Δt [5]:

$$\overline{E_D} = \frac{\overline{E}}{A} = \frac{1}{2}\rho\Delta t \sum_{i=1}^{N} v_i^3 = \left(\frac{\overline{P}}{A}\right)(N\Delta t) \tag{11}$$

4.3 Energy Production from Wind Turbines

This section aims to calculate the amount of energy produced by wind turbines, which is crucial for selecting the most efficient turbines in different study areas. A vital indicator of a wind turbine's efficiency is the capacity factor C_f, which measures the actual proportion of maximum energy a wind turbine can generate. The formula to calculate this factor is provided in reference [6].

$$C_f = \frac{E_{out}}{E_{rated}} = \frac{\overline{P_{out}}}{P_r} \tag{12}$$

P_r is the rated power of the wind turbine, $\overline{P_{out}}$ is the average output power over a specific period.

The energy captured from a wind machine, E_{out}, c be expressed as [6]:

$$E_{out} = C_f E_{rated} = C_f P_r T = \sum_{i=1}^{N} P_{out}(v_i)(\Delta t) \tag{13}$$

P_{out} is represented as a function of wind speed v_i.

5   Results and Discussion

5.1   Average Wind Speed

The average annual wind speed, over 20 years, at two heights is determined for the two areas of the province of Taza. With a value of 5.610 m/s, at 100 m, Tahla has the highest average annual speed. If we consider the classification made by EL HADRI et al. [24], this performance is considered marginal. As for the minimum wind speed, a value of 4.491 m/s is recorded at Tizi Ouasli (50 m) (Table 2).

Table 2. Mean annual wind speed (m/s) at two heights for two sites in Taza.

$v(m/s)$	$v_{50\,m}$	$v_{100\,m}$
Tahla	5.091	5.610
Tizi Ouasli	4.491	4.948

According to Fig. 2, the average monthly wind speeds at Tahla, at 50 m and 100 m, vary between 4.328–5.795 m/s and 4.77–6.386 m/s respectively. Generally, the maximum and minimum speeds occur in February and July for the Tahla and Tizi Ouasli sites.

5.2   Wind Speed Distribution

Table 3 shows the annual Weibull distribution parameters (k and c) for two elevations in two selected areas of Taza province, using the energy allocation factor method [6, 13, 25].

Figure 3 shows the Weibull distribution and its corresponding wind data at an altitude of 50 m. It is worth noting that the Weibull distribution in Fig. 3a fits the experimental data very well. However, for Fig. 3, an apparent discrepancy between the observed and

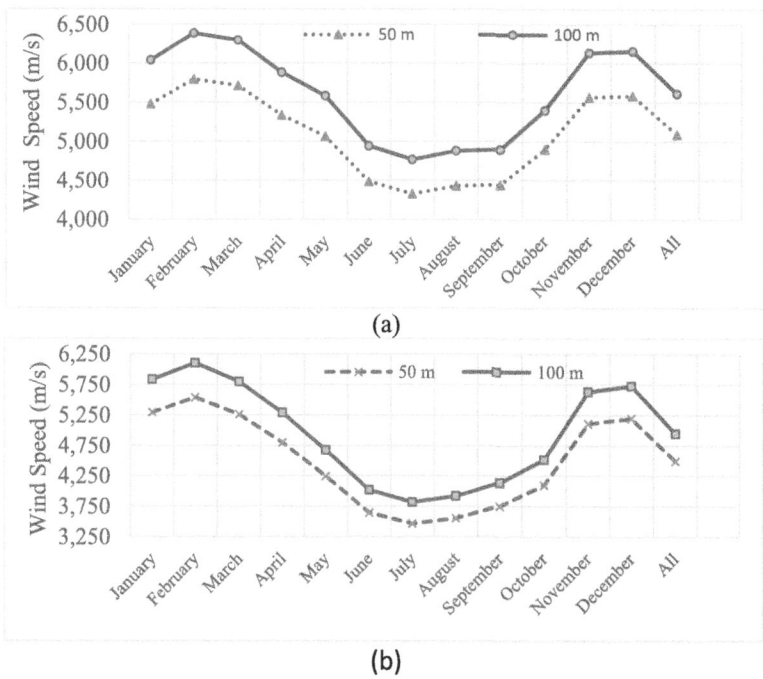

Fig. 2. Mean monthly wind speeds for two heights for the sites: (a) Tahla, (b) Tizi Ouasli

Table 3. Annual Weibull parameters k and c

	Tahla		Tizi Ouasli	
Height (m)	k	c (m/s)	k	c (m/s)
100	2.103	6.340	5.905	5.594
50	2.103	5.754	5.905	5.077

estimated Weibull curve is observed. This difference can be attributed to the inability of the Weibull function to handle low wind speed values, which account for almost 60% (see Table 5).

Table 4 shows the estimated values of v_{me} and v_{mp} for two heights. We find that the wind speed v_{me} and the most probable wind speed v_{mp} that produce the maximum energy are higher at the Tahla site throughout the year. Therefore, these results indicate that the site is more likely to generate electricity.

The table below illustrates the probability of wind speed exceeding 5 m/s. At the height of 100 m, the Tahla and Tizi Ouasli locations exhibit high probabilities, reaching 54.50% and 59.73%, respectively.

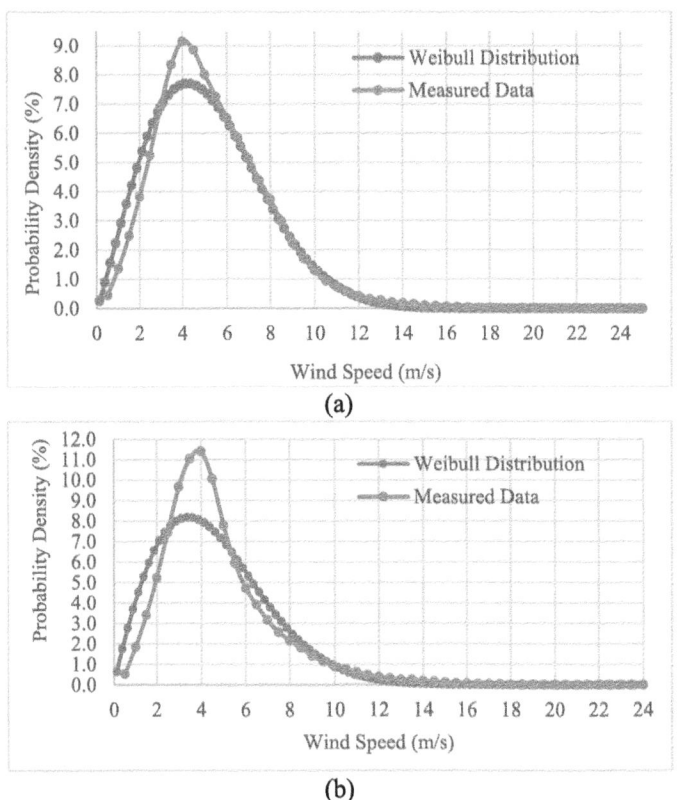

Fig. 3. Wind speed distribution for the different sites at 5, (a) Tahla and (b) Tizi Ouasli

Table 4. Values of v_{me} and v_{mp} at two heights for the two sites.

Location	v_{me} (m/s)		v_{mp} (m/s)	
	50 m	100 m	50 m	100 m
Tahla	7.907	8.712	4.234	4.665
Tizi Ouasli	5.334	5.877	4.920	5.421

5.3 Wind Direction Analysis

Another crucial aspect of a wind energy assessment is evaluating the wind speed's direction and frequency distribution in a specific direction. This step holds significance in determining the ideal placement of a wind farm. Figure 4 provides a visual representation of the mean wind direction recorded at a 50 m elevation monthly

A wind rose diagram is useful for displaying information about both the frequency and direction of the wind simultaneously [26]. Using the WRPLOT View software [27], the wind roses shown in Fig. 5 reveal that the most probable directions in Tahla and Tizi

Table 5. Probability of wind velocity P (v ≥ 5 m/s) at the dual locations.

Location	$P(v \geq 5\,\text{m/s})(\%)$	
	50 m	100 m
Tahla	47,51%	54,50%
Tizi Ouasli	40,10%	59,73%

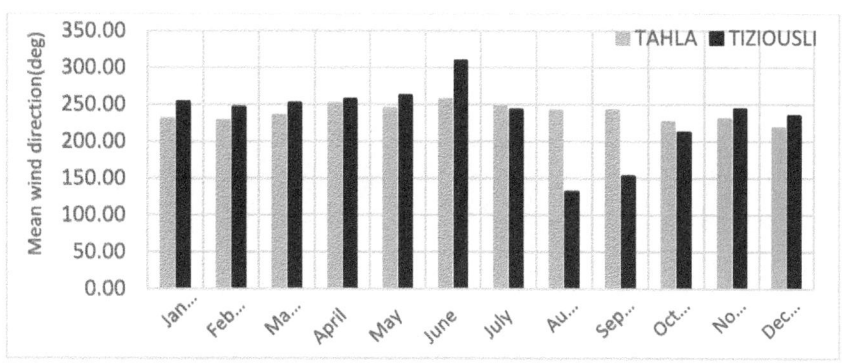

Fig. 4. The average wind direction per month at a height of 50 m.

Ouasli are South-West and West-South-West, respectively. For the Tahla site, the wind direction varies between West and South-East. It is essential to highlight that, among the sites under study, the least robust and infrequent wind direction originates from the North.

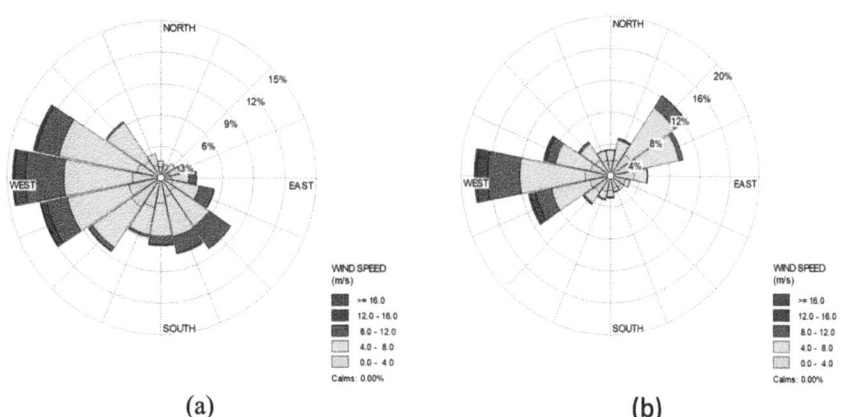

Fig. 5. Wind rose for the different sites: (a) Tahla, (b) Tizi Ouasli

5.4 Wind Power and Energy Density

Monthly Wind Power and Energy Density

The wind power density for each month is computed at two different heights, as depicted in Figs. 6 and 7. The graphs illustrate that the highest monthly peak power densities are observed in February and March. Conversely, the period from June to September exhibits lower power density.

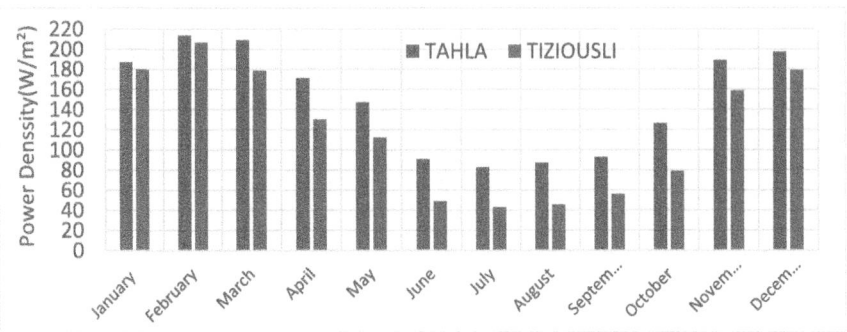

Fig. 6. Power density every month at a 50-m elevation

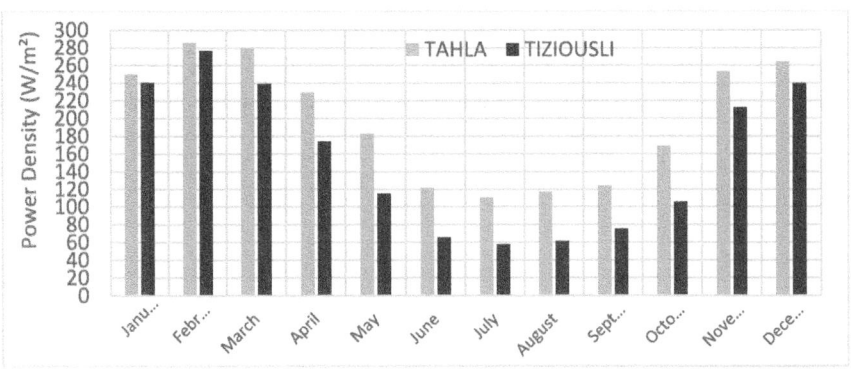

Fig. 7. Power density monthly at a 100-m elevation.

The annual power density is determined by comparing the actual measured data (Eq. 10) with the data generated by the Weibull distribution (Eq. 9). The histogram shown in Fig. 8 clearly shows the maximum power density observed at Tahla. According to the average wind energy density, wind characteristics and classes can be divided into the following categories:

$$\frac{\overline{P}}{A} < 100\frac{W}{m^2} \, is \, poor \qquad \frac{\overline{P}}{A} \approx 400\frac{W}{m^2} \, is \, good \qquad \frac{\overline{P}}{A} > 700\frac{W}{m^2} \, is \, excellent$$

According to the criteria mentioned above and the results presented in Figs. 6 and 7, Tahla is identified as a suitable location for large-scale turbines. However, the results indicate that the Tizi Ouasli site is not conducive to installing large-scale turbines. Nevertheless, small-scale wind turbines could be a suitable use for this site.

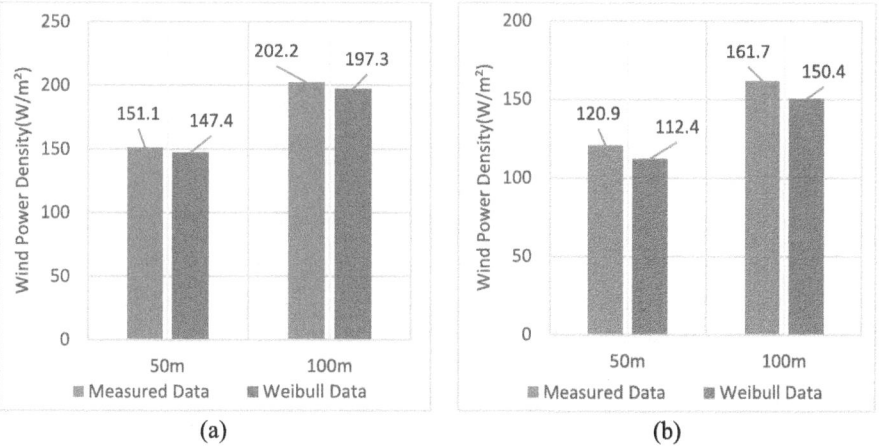

(a)   (b)

Fig. 8. Yearly wind density at elevations of 50 and 100 m in (a) Tahla, and (b) Tizi Ouasli.

5.5 Selection of Wind Turbines

To assess Taza province's performance, two turbines were selected with rated powers of 0.5 MW and 3.4 MW, respectively. Table 6 provides the technical specifications of the chosen turbines.

Table 6. Technical characteristics of specific wind turbines.

Sigle	Wind turbine model	Tower height (m)	Rated Power (KW)	Rated Speed (m/s)	Cut-In Speed (m/s)	Cut-Out Speed (m/s)	Rotor Diameter (m)
GW3.4	Goldwind GW 140/3.4	100/120	3400	10.1	2.5	20.0	140.0
EWT4	EWT DW54–500	40/50/75	500	10.0	2.5	25.0	54.0

Figure 9 illustrates the turbine power curves. The Weibull probability distribution function assessed the yearly capacity factor and the yearly energy output of the chosen turbines. Selected impellers are designed to operate at different hub heights.

However, in this study, the efficiency of the turbines was evaluated at two different altitudes (i.e., 50 m and 100 m), and the results clearly showed that the annual capacity factor increased as the altitude increased from 50 m to 100 m. As shown in Table 7,

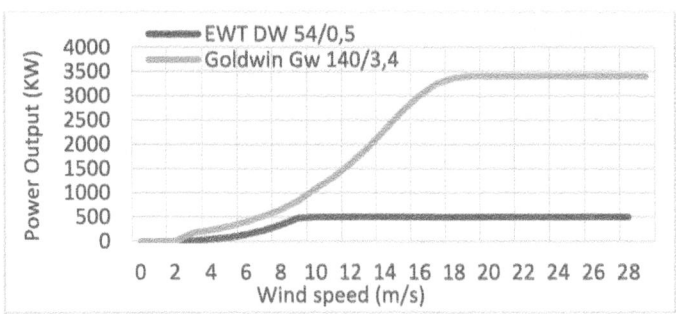

Fig. 9. Wind turbine power curves

Goldwind GW 140/3.4 unit has a nominal output power of 3400 kW and has the highest efficiency in terms of capacity factor. Therefore, it remains a lucrative choice. It is worth noting that, at a height of 100 m, the Tahla site demonstrates a high-capacity factor of 30.84%, while the Tizi Ouasli site registers a value of 24.21%.

Table 7. The annual capacity factor for the wind turbines considered.

Model	Height	Tahla		Tizi Ouasli	
		C_f (%)	E_{out} (KWh)	C_f (%)	E_{out} (KWh)
GW3.4	100 m	30.84	8.105	24.21	6.362
EWT4	50 m	23.21	6.100	17.78	4.673

Concerning energy production, the Tahla site, at a height of 100 m, generates the highest amount of energy (8.105 GWh) using the GOLDWIND GW 140/3.4 turbine. This turbine model continues to be the most suitable choice. On the other hand, the EWT DW54–500 turbine at the Tizi Ouasli site produces an average energy value of 4.673 MWh. It is important to emphasise that these two turbine choices were selected from ten options studied based on two critical criteria: the highest capacity factor and the most significant energy production.

6 Conclusions

Based on NASA data collected over 20 years, an analysis was conducted to examine the wind energy potential and its attributes in the province of Taza, located in Morocco. By studying the statistical data and performing calculations, several conclusions can be inferred:

The maximum annual average wind speed of 5.61 m/s at 100 m was recorded in Tahla, while the minimum wind speed of 4.948 m/s was observed in Tizi Ouasli. The monthly maximum wind speeds occur in February, while the minimum wind speeds are observed in July for Tahla and Tizi Ouasli. The Weibull probability distribution function and the energy configuration factor fitting algorithm were used to determine the shape k and scale c parameters that best fit the data. At 50 m, the parameter k ranges from 2.103 in Tahla to 5.905 in Tizi Ouasli, while the parameter c ranges from 5.754 m/s to 5.077 m/s for the exact locations. The power density estimation across all sites indicates that the highest values are recorded in February and March, while lower values are observed during the summer. At 100 m, the Tahla site exhibits a higher capacity factor of 32%, whereas the Tizi Ouasli site has a lower value of 12.62%. The Chinese turbine model named GOLDWIND GW 140, with a power capacity of 3.4 MW, remains the most suitable choice for both sites, with a minimum capacity factor value of 24.21%.

The results obtained make it possible to make excellent recommendations for wind turbine installation projects in the province of Taza.

References

1. Wang, L., Wang, L., Li, Y., Wang, J.: A century-long analysis of global warming and earth temperature using a random walk with drift approach. Dec. Anal. J. **7**, 100237 (2023). https://doi.org/10.1016/j.dajour.2023.100237
2. Chapman, A.J., Itaoka, K.: Energy transition to a future low-carbon energy society in Japan's liberalizing electricity market: Precedents, policies and factors of successful transition. Renew. Sustain. Energ. Rev. **81**, 2019–2027 (2018). https://doi.org/10.1016/j.rser.2017.06.011
3. Bartolucci, L., Cordiner, S., Mulone, V., Rocco, V., Rossi, J.L.: Hybrid renewable energy systems for renewable integration in microgrids: Influence of sizing on performance. Energy **152**, 744–758 (2018). https://doi.org/10.1016/j.energy.2018.03.165
4. Boulakhbara, M., et al.: Towards a large-scale integration of renewable energies in Morocco. J. Energy Storage **32**, 101–806 (2020). https://doi.org/10.1016/j.est.2020.101806
5. Kousksou, T., Allouhi, A., Belattar, M., Jamil, A., El Rhafiki, T., Zeraouli, Y.: Morocco's strategy for energy security and low-carbon growth. Energy **84**, 98–105 (2015). https://doi.org/10.1016/j.energy.2015.02.048
6. El Khchine, Y., Sriti, M., Eddine, N., Elyamani, E.K.: Evaluation of wind energy potential and trends in Morocco. Heliyon **5**(6), e01830 (2019). https://doi.org/10.1016/j.heliyon.2019.e01830
7. Allouhi, A., et al.: Evaluation of wind energy potential in Morocco's coastal regions. Renew. Sustain. Energy Rev. **72**, 311–324 (2017). https://doi.org/10.1016/j.rser.2017.01.047
8. Daoudi, M., Mou, A.A.S., Elkhomri, M., Elkhouzai, E.: Wind speed data and wind energy potential using weibull distribution in Zagora, Morocco. Int. J. Renew. Energy Dev. **8**(3), 267–273 (2019). https://doi.org/10.14710/ijred.8.3.267-273
9. Daoudi, M., Mou, A.A.S., Naceur, L.A.: Analysis of the first onshore wind farm installation near the Morocco-United Kingdom green energy export project. Sci. Afr. **17**, e01388 (2022). https://doi.org/10.1016/j.sciaf.2022.e01388
10. Alham, M.H., Gad, M.F., Ibrahim, D.K.: Potential of wind energy and economic assessment in Egypt considering optimal hub height by equilibrium optimizer. Ain Shams Eng. J. **14**, 101–816 (2023). https://doi.org/10.1016/j.asej.2022.101816
11. Collados-Lara, A.-J., Baena-Ruiz, L., Pulido-Velazquez, D., Pardo-Igúzquiza, E.: Data-driven mapping of hourly wind speed and its potential energy resources: a sensitivity analysis. Rene. Energy **199**, 87–102 (2022). https://doi.org/10.1016/j.renene.2022.08.109
12. Bank of Africa Homepage. https://www.bankofafrica.ma/. Last accessed 24 May 2023
13. ONEE Homepage: http://www.one.org.ma/. Last accessed 24 May 2023
14. POWER | Data Access Viewer Homepage: https://power.larc.nasa.gov/data-access-viewer/. 24 May 2023

15. Microsoft Homepage: https://www.office.com/. Last accessed 24 May 2023
16. Benazzouz, A., Mabchour, H., El Had, K., Zourarah, B., Mordane, S.: Offshore wind energy resource in the Kingdom of Morocco: assessment of the seasonal potential variability based on satellite data. J. Mar. Sci. Eng. **9**(1), 1–20 (2021). https://doi.org/10.3390/jmse9010031
17. Chaurasiya, P.K., Ahmed, S., Warudkar, V.: Study of different parameters estimation methods of Weibull distribution to determine wind power density using ground based Doppler SODAR instrument. Alex. Eng. J. **57**(4), 2299–2311 (2018). https://doi.org/10.1016/j.aej.2017.08.008
18. Al Zohbi, G., Hendrick, P., Bouillard, P.: Evaluation du potentiel d'énergie éolienne au Liban. J. Renew. Energ. **17**(1), 83–96 (2023). https://doi.org/10.54966/jreen.v17i1.425
19. Ouahabi, M.H., Elkhachine, H., Benabdelouahab, F., Khamlichi, A.: Comparative study of five different methods of adjustment by the Weibull model to determine the most accurate method of analyzing annual variations of wind energy in Tetouan – Morocco. Procedia Manuf. **46**, 698–707 (2020). https://doi.org/10.1016/j.promfg.2020.03.099
20. Akpo, A.B., Damada, J.C.T., Donnou, H.E., Kounouhewa, B., Awanou, C.N.: Evaluation de la production énergétique d'un aérogénérateur sur un site isolé dans la région côtière du Bénin. Revue des énérgies renouvelables **18**(3), 457–468 (2015)
21. Dabar, O.A., Awaleh, M.O., Waberi, M.M., Adan, A.B.I.: Wind resource assessment and techno-economic analysis of wind energy and green hydrogen production in the Republic of Djibouti. Energy Rep. **8**, 8996–9016 (2022). https://doi.org/10.1016/j.egyr.2022.07.013
22. Jangamshetti, S.H.: Site matching of wind turbine generators : a case study. IEEE Trans. Energy Convers. **14**(4), 1537–1543 (1999)
23. Dabbaghiyan, A., Fazelpour, F., Abnavi, M.D., Rosen, M.A.: Evaluation of wind energy potential in province of Bushehr, Iran. Renew. Sustain. Energ. Rev. **55**, 455–466 (2016). https://doi.org/10.1016/j.rser.2015.10.148
24. El Hadri, Y., Khokhlov, V., Slizhe, M., Sernytska, K.: Wind energy land distribution in Morocco in 2021–2050 according to RCM simulation of CORDEX-Africa project. Arabian J. Geosci. **12**(24) (2019). https://doi.org/10.1007/s12517-019-4950-7
25. Tiam Kapen, P., Jeutho Gouajio, M., Yémélé, D.: Analysis and efficient comparison of ten numerical methods in estimating Weibull parameters for wind energy potential: application to the city of Bafoussam, Cameroon. Renew. Energy **159**, 1188–1198 (2020). https://doi.org/10.1016/j.renene.2020.05.185
26. Zhang, M., Zhang, J., Chen, H., Xin, X., Li, Y., Jiang, F.: Probabilistic wind spectrum model based on correlation of wind parameters in mountainous areas: Focusing on von Karman spectrum. J. Wind Eng. Ind. Aerodyn. **234**, 105337 (2023). https://doi.org/10.1016/j.jweia.2023.105337
27. Lakes Environmental software Homepage: https://www.weblakes.com/software/freeware/wrplot-view/. Last accessed 24 May 2023

Computer Vision

Advancing Visual Relationship Detection: Comparative Analysis of ResNet101 vs. ResNet152

Meryem Ouazzani Chahdi[1]([✉]) [iD], Afafe Annich[1,2] [iD], Adnane Ouazzani Chahdi[1] [iD],
Abdellatif El Abderrahmani[1] [iD], and Khalid Satori[1] [iD]

[1] Computer Science Department, LISAC Laboratory, Sidi Mohamed Ben Abdellah University,
FSDM 22MF+97C, 30050 Fez, Morocco
{meryem.ouazzanichahdi,Abdellatif.elabderrahmani,
khalid.satori}@usmba.ac.ma
[2] ISIC-Rabat, Higher Institute of Information and Communication. Avenue Allal El Fassi
Madinat Al Irfane - Rabat Institutes, Rabat, Morocco
afafe.annich@isic.ac.ma

Abstract. Scene understanding refers to the ability of a computer system to analyze and interpret a given scene, by extracting meaningful information from visual elements, such as images or videos. The objective is to achieve a higher level of comprehension and enumeration of the various objects present in the scene, their attributes, the visual relationships between them, and then expressing such understanding by providing an accurate and complete description of the given scene in natural language. Scene understanding plays a crucial role in enabling machines to perceive, analyze, and interpret their environments, empowering them to make intelligent decisions and facilitate natural and intuitive communication with humans. This has significant implications for the advancement of scientific research that relies heavily on visual data, particularly in medicine, industry, and astronomy. Several techniques and methodologies have been developed to achieve a deeper understanding of the environment, the best known and commonly used are Deep learning models, particularly CNNs, GNNs, and neural language generation models, such as (RNNs) or transformer-based models like GPT. As the volume of visual data continues to grow, the number and diversity of visual relationships between objects also increase, which presents a significant challenge in discovering and quantifying these relationships, taking into consideration the complexity of the used techniques and the available material resources. With the aim of addressing this issue, our research focuses on exploring alternative methods that can enhance the visual relationship detection accuracy, while reducing the computational time using available material rather than acquiring more efficient ones. Our approach involves comparing two CNN models, namely resnet101 and resnet152, to determine their effectiveness in enhancing visual relationship detection.

Keywords: Scenes semantic understanding · deep learning · Visual relationships recognition · human language scene description · Scene Graph representation

© The Author(s), under exclusive license to Springer Nature Switzerland AG 2025
H. Hagras et al. (Eds.): ISACS 2023, CCIS 2255, pp. 335–345, 2025.
https://doi.org/10.1007/978-3-031-93448-3_27

1 Introduction

Deep learning is a subfield of artificial intelligence [1–3] that focuses on building and training neural networks using large amounts of data with the aim of giving her the ability to anticipate the future and make decisions. It has revolutionized various domains, including computer vision, natural language processing, robotics, and speech recognition. When it comes to computer vision, deep learning has made significant advances in what is known as the axis of semantic understanding of 3D scenes. This not only includes understanding and analyzing images and video clips by discovering and recognizing their basic components and extracting their visual, spatial and semantic features and eliciting the visual relationships that bind them [4–8] but goes deeper to the understanding of the scene structure, the functions of objects and hidden relationships that connect them. By employing deep learning techniques, researchers and engineers have recently been able to develop algorithms and models that can quickly learn and automatically infer such complex relationships and semantics from 3D scene data. Among the most popular deep learning models used in this field are convolutional neural networks (CNN) [9] and recurrent neural networks (RNNs) [10, 11] in addition to the Graph neural network (GNN). To process spatial and temporal information in the visual data, these networks can be trained on large datasets that include annotated scene information, allowing them to learn to recognize objects, segment scenes, predict their properties, and even infer higher-level concepts like scene affordances or human intentions. In this paper, we have introduced on comparison of two CNN models, namely resnet101 and resnet152, to determine their effectiveness in enhancing visual relationship detection.

2 Related Work

In the context of semantic understanding of 3D scenes using Deep learning models, several approaches have been developed.

In their work, Yan et al. [12] proposed SAFNet, a network that utilizes a structural Deep Metric Learning approach on points and pixels leading to improved relationship detection, and the existing data fusion methods 'effectiveness. The utilization of these relationships enables the representation and alignment of 2D images and point clouds in a shared canonical space, and facilitates prediction tasks. Their method demonstrated competitive competence on widely-used datasets such as S3DIS and ScanNetV2 for the understanding of the 3D work space.

J. Wald et al. [13] employed a scene graph structure to comprehend 3D scenes, representing objects as nodes and relationships as edges. They proposed a novel architecture that utilizes PointNet and GCN network models to learn and predict the scene graph from point cloud data. They introduced the 3DSSG dataset, which contains rich semantic relations in 3D scene graphs generated semi-automatically. Their method exhibited a high level of performance in accomplishing scene retrieval tasks.

J. Moon et al. [14] presented a novel method for scene understanding using natural language, particularly, within the realm of human-robot-Interaction. They generated work environments' human language descriptions based on Object-directed 3D semantic graphs constructed from RGB-D images, utilizing Graph Convolutional Neural network and Recurrent Neural Network (RNN) to produce sentences. The graph vortex represented semantic and spatial region features, while the edges captured object relationships. The proposed method's performance was evaluated on SUN360 (Scene Understanding 360° panorama) and NYU-Depth-V2 datasets.

Lu C. et al. [15] addressed the challenge of associating multiple predicates with objects in visual relationships. They trained visual models for objects and predicates separately and merged them to predict multiple relationships per scene using RCNN [10]. A visual appearance and language modules were utilized to score each object pair, and a threshold mechanism produced a relationships labels set. In addition they introduced a new 37,993 relationships database. Although the training dataset is small; their method successfully detects 1000 relationships and improves Image recovery based on the content.

An alternative approaches [16, 17] employed deep convolutional neural networks (CNNs) [18, 19] to detect objects and predicates separately in input images. The detected objects' features (visual, spatial, and semantic) and predicates (relations between ROI) were merged into low-dimensional feature vectors for triplet detection. Liang, K. et al. [16] proposed a method utilizing structure ranking loss to prioritize annotated relationships, taking into account the occurrence and limited information of visual relationships. Le Zhang et al. [17] addressed the topological relationships between regions of interest by converting input images into weighted graphs using GNN model, with the objective of improving the visual relationship detection efficiency.

Botao Zhong et al. [20] have introduced a framework based on the attention mechanism to extract complex semantic information from videos captured by construction site cameras, aiming to enhance safety in construction sites. This framework comprises two primary stages: initially, an image extraction model employs an inter-image difference mechanism to derive images from construction videos. Subsequently, an image scene understanding model is proposed, which integrates a ResNet101 "encoder" and an LSTM + Attention "decoder" to identify semantic information and generate natural language descriptions from these images. Finally, this innovative framework's validity is confirmed through multiple experiments utilizing datasets containing construction scene images.

Ming-Gang Gan et al. [21] and his team improved visual relationship detection in real 3D space by creating Depth VRDs, an extension of the VRD dataset incorporating essential depth information from 2D images. They introduced the Adaptive Depth Aware Visual Relationship Detection Network (ADVRD) to effectively utilize this additional depth data. The depth-aware visual fusion module guided RGB visual data within bounding boxes, reducing background noise and enhancing object details. Their adaptive depth spatial location method accurately extracted object depth spatial positions, minimizing irrelevant information within bounding boxes. Extensive experiments validated the improved network performance with the inclusion of depth information. Comprehensive comparative experiments were conducted to evaluate the effectiveness of their depth-aware visual fusion module and adaptive depth spatial location method.

Our study focuses on assessing the performance of two approaches: the VRTS framework, which is based on ResNet101 [17], and our approach, which utilizes ResNet152.

We specifically evaluate their ability to detect various relationships within a visual element, with particular emphasis on their capability to identify zero-shot relationships.

3   Methodology

Visual relationships detection refers to the task of identifying and understanding the relationships or interactions between objects in an image or a visual scene. It involves detecting the semantic connections, dependencies, or spatial arrangements between pairs or groups of objects (Fig. 1). The goal is to recognize and classify the relationships into different categories, such as "behind", "in", "in front of," or more complex relationships like "hanging on", "under" or " inside". Visual relationships detection aims to provide a comprehensive understanding of the scene by analyzing the contextual relationships between objects, enriching the interpretation and representation of visual information by detecting the triplets like (Picture, Hanging on, wall).

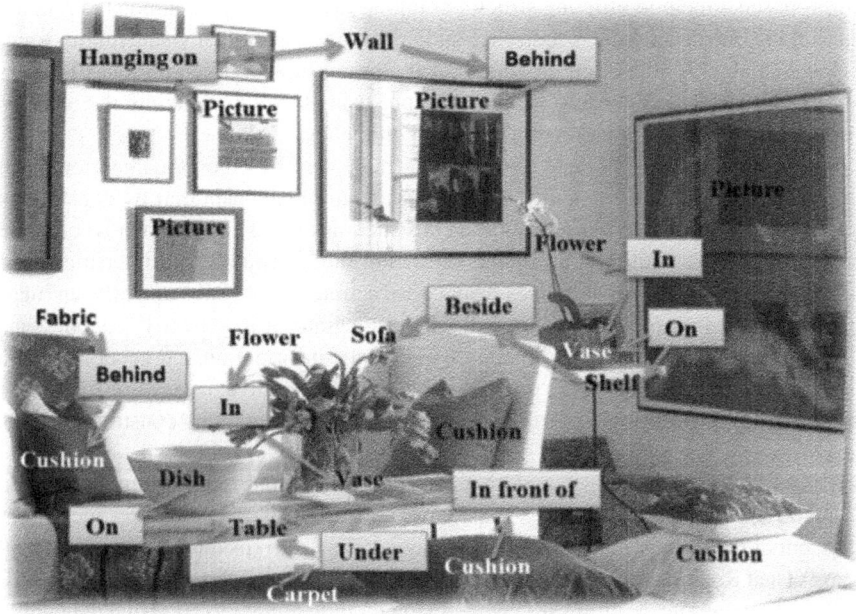

Fig. 1. Representing the visual relationships among different image objects

In order to improve research in this particular field, we have developed our approach by inspiring methods previously found in the literature [13, 16, 17], which leverages the benefits of three deep learning modules to enhance the visual relationships detection task (Fig. 4).

Initially, we applied basic image treatment techniques such as resizing and normalization to manipulate the database.

Subsequently, ResNet152 (Fig. 2) was used to segment the input images and extract the regions of interest, as well as their visual, semantic and spatial characteristics to compare its performance with those obtained by the ResNet101[1] model (Fig. 3) used by Le Zhang et al. [17] in their VRTS framework by evaluating the effectiveness of two models in improving the detection of visual relationships (Fig. 4).

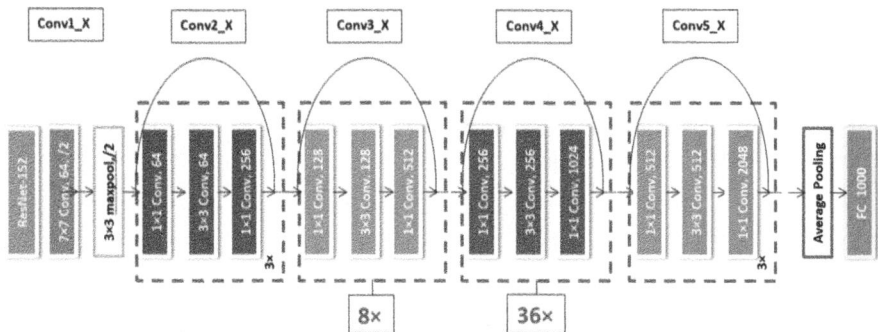

Fig. 2. Resnet152 Architecture with 152 layers for Features extraction

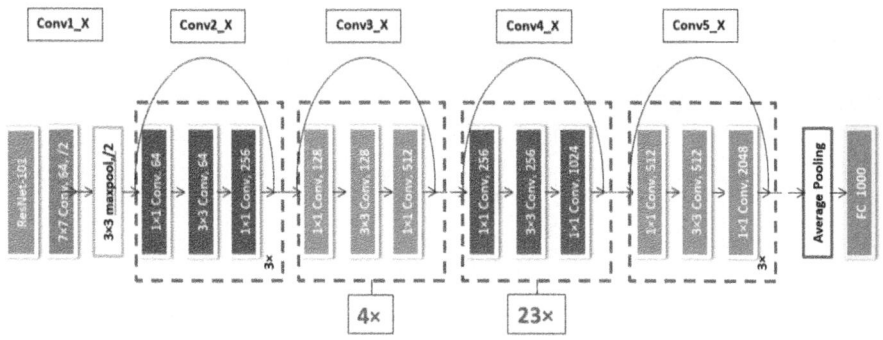

Fig. 3. Resnet101 Architecture with 101 layers for features extraction

Next, the extracted features were fed into a Graph Neural Network (GNN), which transformed them into a weighted visual object digraph denoted as G(V, E, W). In this graph, the nodes $v_i^{obj} \in V$ represent the regions of interest (objects like Screen, Table, PlayStation,...), V is the set of objects detected in the scene, $v_k^{pred} \in E$ the predicates between them (such as: Under, Behind, on,..) and E is the predicates set; when the edges

---

[1] ResNet-101 and ResNet-152 are two deep neural network architectures used in computer vision. The main difference lies in their depth: ResNet-101 has 101 layers, while ResNet-152 has 152 layers. Generally, ResNet-152 has a higher modeling capacity, meaning it can capture more complex features, but it also requires more resources in terms of memory and computational power. ResNet-152 is used for demanding computer vision tasks, while ResNet-101 may suffice for simpler tasks. The choice depends on the specific task and available resources

represent the pathway objectpredicate and W is the dependency probability between an object and a predicate (Fig. 4), and can be calculated by the formula (Eq. 1).

$$P(v_k^{pred}|v_i^{obj},v_j^{obj}) = \frac{\sqrt{P\left(v_k^{pred},v_i^{obj},v_j^{obj}\right)}}{v_i^{obj}} \cdot \frac{\sqrt{P\left(v_k^{pred},v_i^{obj},v_j^{obj}\right)}}{v_j^{obj}} = w_{ik} \cdot w_{kj} \quad (1)$$

In addition, we employed a pre-trained model called Word2Vec for word embedding to encode the labels of object and subject categories. The word embedding vector for the predicate is derived by merging the vectors of the subject and object (Fig. 4).

Finally, the outputs of the three modules ware combined to extract the final low-dimensional feature vector (Fig. 4).

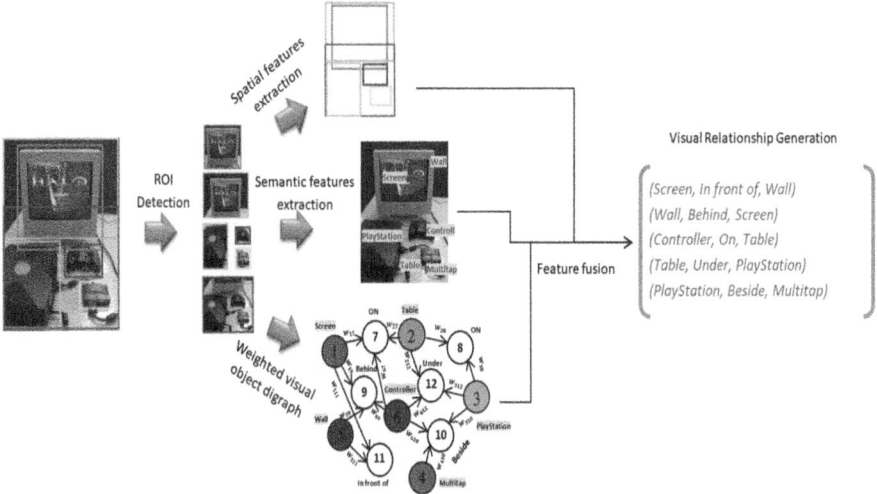

Fig. 4. Visual Relationship Detection Approach (ROI: region of interest).

It is difficult for a model to detect all the visual relationships present in a given visual element, due to the long-tail distribution problem[2] (the visual relationship occurrence probability). For this reason, a model must be able to detect zero-shot visual relations.

Zero-shot relationship detection refers to the ability of a model to detect and understand relationships between object categories that were not seen during the training phase. Since zero-shot relationship detection involves generalizing to unseen relationships, its performance may be lower compared to conventional relationship detection

---

[2] In statistics and business, the "long tail" refers to the portion of a distribution that contains a large number of occurrences far from the central or popular part of the distribution. This concept can be applied to various scenarios, such as the popularity of items, random occurrences with different probabilities, and more. The term is often used informally, without a specific definition, but it can be precisely defined in certain cases. The long tail phenomenon highlights the presence of numerous rare or less popular occurrences that extend beyond the dominant or central part of the distribution.(https://en.wikipedia.org/wiki/Long_tail)

methods that are trained. The performance can be influenced by factors such as the complexity of relationships, the quality and diversity of the training data, the choice of feature representations, and the efficiency of the learning algorithm's performance.

In our work, we evaluate the performance of two approaches: the VRTS framework based on ResNet101 [17] and our approach based on ResNet152, in detecting various relationships within a visual element, focusing on their ability to detect zero-shot relationships.

4 Obtained comparison result

4.1 VG dataset

The Visual Genome dataset consists of over 108,000 medium-sized images (600 x 800), and split into two sets: 73,796 images are allocated for training, while 25,857 images are reserved for testing. It consists of 100 categories for predicate relationships and 200 categories for objects.

4.2 Work equipment

The working environment utilized in this study involved an HPZ820 workstation with an Intel(R) Xeon(R) CPU E5-2680 v2 @ 2.80 GHz (40 CPUs), ~2.8 GHz processor, and a single NVIDIA Quadro P4000 graphics card. The code was implemented using PyTorch library, Anaconda navigator and Spyder editor.

Note: Due to hardware limitations, it was not feasible to handle the entire Visual Genome dataset. We worked with only 25% of the training and testing image set size to ensure reasonable processing time.

4.3 The models setting

Regarding the adjustment of the GNN model, we have employed the same hyper parameters as those utilized in [17] (N° Epoch=7, N° Iterations=5, N° Layers=2, Batch-size=1, LR=0.0001). We use the pre-trained models ResNet101.weights and ResNet152.weights from the ImageNet dataset to initialize the weights of the two models, ResNet101 and ResNet152 respectively.

4.4 Performance metric

To evaluate the performance of the two models, we employ the Recall[3] metric, specially Recall@50 and Recall@100. These metrics represent the percentages of true positive triplets found among the top 50 and 100 predictions, respectively.

4.5 Results and comparisons

It is important to emphasize that the process of uncovering visual relationships involves two distinct tasks: identifying predicates and detecting triplets (object, predicate, subject). In (Table 1), we provide a comparison of the results obtained by our proposed approach for predicates detecting task, utilizing ResNet152 as the feature extractor, with those achieved by the VRTS framework [17] tested in the same work environment, which employs ResNet101. Furthermore, we assess the proficiency of both models in detecting zero-shot relationships, as shown in (Table 2).

Table 1. Performance (%) of Predicate Detection Task on the (25%) VG dataset during the training phase:

Training phase	R@50	R@100	Training time
VRTS(Resnet101)	81.60	86.56	2 d 8 h 24 m 43 s
Our Approach(Resnet152)	81.84%	86.52%	20 h 18 m 07 s

Table 2. Zero-Shot Predicate detection Task on the (25%) VG dataset during the training phase

Training phase	R_{ZS}@50	R_{ZS}@100
VRTS(Resnet101)	29.16	38.25
Our Approach(Resnet152)	29.92%	39.77

In this paper, our primary objective was to enhance the performance of visual relationship detection while reducing the training time of the model. To achieve this, we conducted preprocessing (scaling, standardization, normalization ...) of the database images and selected ResNet152 as the feature extraction model. We compared our results with those obtained by the VRTS framework [17] that is tested in our workstation. With these modifications, we have successfully reduced the training time to 20 hours, 18 minutes, and 7 seconds. This marks a significant improvement compared to the previous duration of 2 days, 8 hours, 24 minutes, and 43 seconds. (Fig. 6).

---

[3] Recall metric, also known as sensitivity or true positive rate, is a measure of a model's ability to identify positive instances correctly from the total number of actual positive instances in a dataset.(https://en.wikipedia.org/wiki/Precision_and_recall)

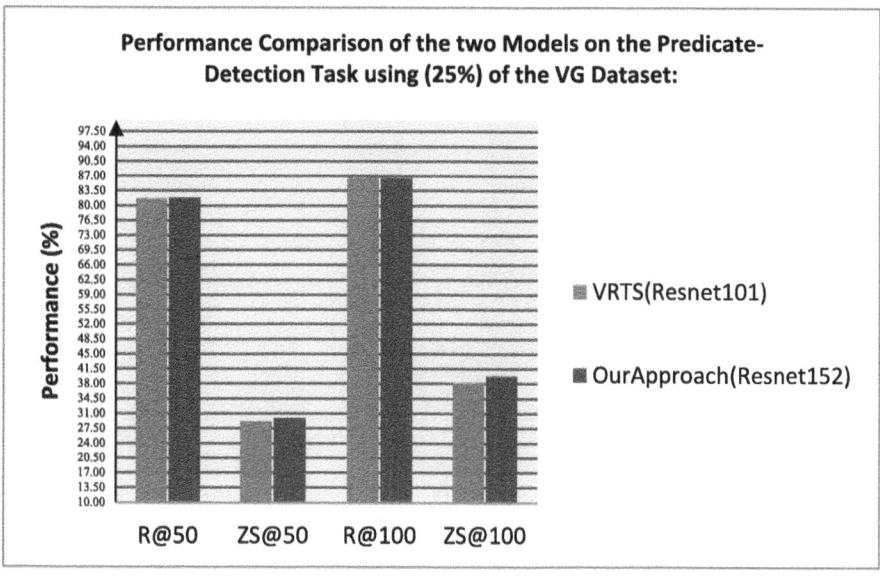

Fig. 5. Performance Comparison of the two Models on the Predicate-Detection Task using (25%) VG Dataset

In addition, our approach demonstrated significant improvements in the predicate-detection task, surpassing the performance of the VRST framework, especially in detecting zero-shot relationships. The results we obtained outperformed the VRST framework by 0.76% in $Recall_{ZS}$@50 and 1.52% in $Recall_{ZS}$@100 (Fig. 5).

Table 3. Testing task performance on the (25%) VG Dataset

Testing Phase	R@50	R_{ZS}@50	R@100	R_{ZS}@100	Testing time
VRTS(Resnet101)	81.60%	29.16%	86.56%	38.25%	3 h 45 m 40 s
Our Approach(Resnet152)	81.84%	29.92%	86.52%	39.77	1 h 08 m 38 s

Farther more, we have achieved a successful reduction in the testing time (Fig. 6) to 1 hour, 8 minutes, and 38 seconds (Table 3). This represents a notable improvement from the duration (3 h 45 m 40 s) achieved by VRTS framework [17].

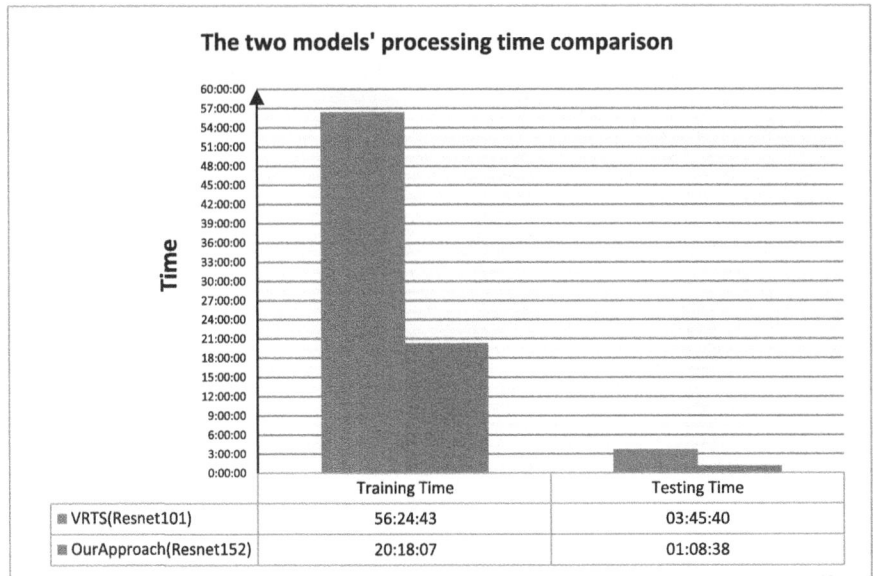

Fig. 6. A comparison of the processing times between the two models

5 Conclusion

This study aims to enhance scene understanding by analyzing and interpreting visual elements. In our approach, the ResNet152 deep learning model was utilized to extract the features, GNNs to generate the weighted visual object digraph, and Word2Vec for word embedding, in order to improve the accuracy of visual relationship detection. Comparing our approach with the VRST framework, which uses ResNet101, we achieved notable advancements in detecting zero-shot relationships. Additionally, the training time was substantially reduced from 2 days and 8 hours to approximately 20 hours. These findings contribute to a deeper understanding of scenes, enabling machines to make informed decisions and facilitating effective communication with humans.

References

1. LeCun, Y., Bengio, Y., Hinton, G.: Deep learning. Nature **521**(7553), 436–444 (2015). https://doi.org/10.1038/nature14539
2. Shinde, P.P., Shah, S.: A review of machine learning and deep learning applications. In: 2018 Fourth International Conference on Computing Communication Control and Automation (ICCUBEA), pp. 1–6. Pune, India (2018). https://doi.org/10.1109/ICCUBEA.2018.8697857.
3. Janiesch, C., Zschech, P., Heinrich, K.: Machine learning and deep learning. Electron. Mark. **31**, 685–695 (2021). https://doi.org/10.1007/s12525-021-00475-2
4. Fan, J., Zheng, P., Li, S.: Vision-based holistic scene understanding towards proactive human–robot collaboration. Robot. Comp.-Integr. Manuf. **75**, 102304 (2022)
5. Arashpour, M., Ngo, T., Li, H.: Scene understanding in construction and buildings using image processing methods: A comprehensive review and a case study. J. Build. Eng. **33**, 101672 (2021)

6. De Cesarei, A., Loftus, G.R., Mastria, S., Codispoti , M.: Understanding natural scenes: Contributions of image statistics. Neurosci. Biobehav. Rev. **74**(Part A), 44–57 (2017)

7. Kojima, R., Sugiyama, O., Nakadai, K.: Audio-visual scene understanding utilizing textinformation for a cooking support robot. IEEE/RSJ Int. Conf. Intel. Rob. Sys. (IROS) **2015**, 4210–4215 (2015)

8. Husain, F., Dellen, B., Torras, C.: Scene understanding using deep learning. Handbook of Neural Computation, 373-382 (2017)

9. Li, Z., Liu, F., Yang, W., Peng, S., Zhou, J.: A survey of convolutional neural networks: analysis, applications, and prospects. In: IEEE Transactions on Neural Networks and Learning Systems, vol. 33(12), pp. 6999–7019 (2022). https://doi.org/10.1109/TNNLS.2021.3084827

10. Cebollada, S., Payá, L., Flores, M., Peidró, A., Reinoso, O.: A state-of-the art review on mobile robotics tasks using artificial intelligence and visual data. Expert Sys. Appl. **167**, 114195 (2021). https://doi.org/10.1016/j.eswa.2020.114195

11. Medsker, L., Jain, L.C., (eds.): Recurrent Neural Networks: Design and Applications, 1st ed. CRC Press (1999). https://doi.org/10.1201/9781003040620.

12. Yan, H., Lv, Y., Liong, V.E.: Structure-aware fusion network for 3D scene understanding. Chinese J. Aeronaut. **35**(5), 194–203 (2022). https://doi.org/10.1016/j.cja.2021.07.012

13. Wald, J., Dhamo, H., Navab, N., Tombari, F.: Learning 3D Semantic Scene Graphs From 3D Indoor Reconstructions. 2020 IEEE/CVF Conference on Computer Vision and Pattern Recognition (CVPR), pp. 3960–3969 (2020)

14. Moon, J., Lee, B.: Scene understanding using natural language description based on 3D semantic graph map. Intel. Serv. Rob. **11**, 347–354 (2018). https://doi.org/10.1007/s11370-018-0257-x

15. Lu, C., Krishna, R., Bernstein, M., Fei-Fei, L.: Visual relationship detection with language priors. In: Leibe, B., Matas, J., Sebe, N., Welling, M. (eds.) Computer Vision – ECCV 2016. ECCV 2016. Lecture Notes in Computer Science, vol 9905. Springer, Cham.

16. Liang, K., Guo, Y., Chang, H., Chen, X.: Visual relationship detection with deep structural ranking. Proceedings of the AAAI Conference on Artificial Intelligence **32**(1), (2018). https://doi.org/10.1609/aaai.v32i1.12274

17. Zhang, L., Wang, Y., Chen, H., Li, J., Zhang, Z.X.: Visual relationship detection with region topology structure. Info. Sci. 564, pp. 384–395. Elsevier (2021)

18. Lin, C., et al.: Scene recognition using multiple representation network. Appl. Soft Comp. **118**, 108530 (2022)

19. Lu, C., Krishna, R., Bernstein, M., Fei-Fei, L.: Visual relationship detection with language priors. In: European Conference on Computer Vision, pp. 852–869. Springer (2016)

20. Zhong, B., Shen, L., Pan, X., Lei, L.: Visual attention framework for identifying semantic information from construction monitoring video. Safe. Sci. **163**, 106122 (2023). https://doi.org/10.1016/j.ssci.2023.106122

21. Gan, M., He, Y.: Adaptive depth-aware visual relationship detection. Knowl. Based Sys. **247**, 108786 (2022). https://doi.org/10.1016/j.knosys.2022.108786

Exploration of the Integration of Artificial Intelligence in Decision-Making Process: A Thematic Literature Review

Wijdane Merioumi[✉] [ID], Ghita Ibrahimi [ID], and Bouchra Benchekroun [ID]

Economic Science and Management Department, ERMOT Laboratory, Faculty of Legal, Economic, and Social Sciences, Sidi Mohammed Ben Abdellah University, P.O. Box 42, 30000 Fez, Morocco
{wijdane.merioumi,ghita.ibrahimi,
bouchra.aiboudbenchekroun}@usmba.ac.ma

Abstract. Artificial intelligence (AI) has emerged as a transformative technology with the potential to revolutionize the decision-making process. To fully investigate the integration of AI in decision-making and its implications, we performed a thematic literature review. We selected 79 articles from an initial pool of 4,645 papers. These articles underwent a quality assessment to identify papers that are more relevant to explore the research contexts and themes related to AI and decision-making. The findings reveal four key themes, including the Role of Artificial Intelligence in Enhancing the Decision-Making process, the Impact of Artificial Intelligence on Decision-Making Processes, AI's Ability to Transform Consumer Decision-Making Processes, and AI's ethical dimensions and implications for society. Thus, this review provides valuable insights to academics and practitioners willing to assess the advancements of AI in decision-making, its influence on societal dynamics, and ethical concerns. Finally, this study advocates for further empirical evidence, investigation of specific ethical issues, and effective strategies for incorporating AI into decision-making processes to improve the quality of human judgment.

Keywords: Artificial intelligence · Decision-Making Process · Thematic Literature Review

1 Introduction

1.1 Background

Few advancements in technology have caught the public attention and hold the potential for significant change as keenly as artificial intelligence (AI). It carries out unlimited possibilities and executes tasks that were previously thought only possible for human intelligence effectively and rapidly [1]. It refers to the integration of computer science and physiology to make computers behave like humans [2, 3]. To better comprehend artificial intelligence, it may be divided into two concepts: "artificial" and "intelligence."

H. Hagras et al. (Eds.): ISACS 2023, CCIS 2255, pp. 346–357, 2025.
https://doi.org/10.1007/978-3-031-93448-3_28

"Artificial" refers to the synthetic nature of the technology itself, meaning something made by humans. While "intelligence" refers to the necessary mental capabilities to acquire knowledge, reasoning, understanding, and make decisions. By combining these two together, Artificial Intelligence can be understood as making machines capable of simulating intelligence [2]. This dynamic synergy between human creativity and AI tools (e.g., machine learning and deep learning) enables firms to detect, understand, infer, and learn from data in order to make informed decisions.

Traditionally, decision-making has relied on human intuition, experience, and cognitive abilities. However, the advent of AI has introduced a paradigm shift in this fundamental process. Accordingly, we conducted a thematic literature review to explore the integration of artificial intelligence in the decision-making process.

1.2 Research Questions

To achieve this aim, the following questions were formulated: (1) How does the integration of artificial intelligence enhance the decision-making process? (2) What impact does artificial intelligence have on the decision-making process? (3) How can artificial intelligence, particularly context-aware AI, facilitate decision-making in complex and dynamic environments? (4) How does the integration of artificial intelligence transform consumer decision-making processes? And, (5) what are the ethical dimensions and implications of using artificial intelligence in decision-making processes?

1.3 Contribution

This thematic literature review enriches our understanding of integrating artificial intelligence in decision-making by offering valuable insights. It provides:

A Holistic Examination of AI's Influence on Decision-Making Process: This thematic analysis provides a comprehensive investigation into the integration of artificial intelligence (AI) within decision-making process. By delving into a wide array of domains, ranging from smart city development to waste management, the study elucidates the multifaceted ways in which AI can potentially revolutionize decision-making. This holistic perspective offers a valuable foundation for further exploration into the transformative potential of AI technologies.

Insights into Enhanced Decision-Making and Ethical Considerations: The study highlights AI's potential to enhance outcomes and efficiency across sectors like finance, emergencies, and supply chains. The analysis also addresses biases, moral issues, and human involvement in AI decisions. By highlighting the need for transparent frameworks and accountability, the study furnishes a substantial resource for navigating the ethical intricacies of AI integration.

Balanced Approach and Future Research Agenda: This analysis not only illuminates the current landscape but also extends its significance into the future. By stimulating critical questions on the symbiotic relationship between AI and human decision-making, the study advocates for an approach that capitalizes on AI's strengths while upholding the expertise and ethical considerations of human decision-makers.

This thematic analysis offers a comprehensive examination of AI's impact on decision-making processes, shedding light on the dual facets of enhanced outcomes and ethical considerations. Through these insights, the analysis propels the discourse forward by advocating for a balanced approach and providing a roadmap for future research endeavors in this dynamic field.

This paper is divided into five sections. Section 2 outlines the methodology and review process. Section 3 presents the results along with the analysis. Section 4 provides the discussion and outlines the limitations. Finally, Sect. 5 presents the conclusion and suggestions for future work.

2 Materiel and Methods

2.1 Search Strategy and Data Collection

In this paper, we conducted a thematic literature review to assess the current state of art of "Artificial Intelligence" and "decision-making process". Thus, we used Web of Science and Scopus electronic databases to access relevant articles. The initial search query resulted in a total of 4 645 papers. Whereas, limiting the search to Business and Management subject areas resulted in 417 papers (see Fig. 1).

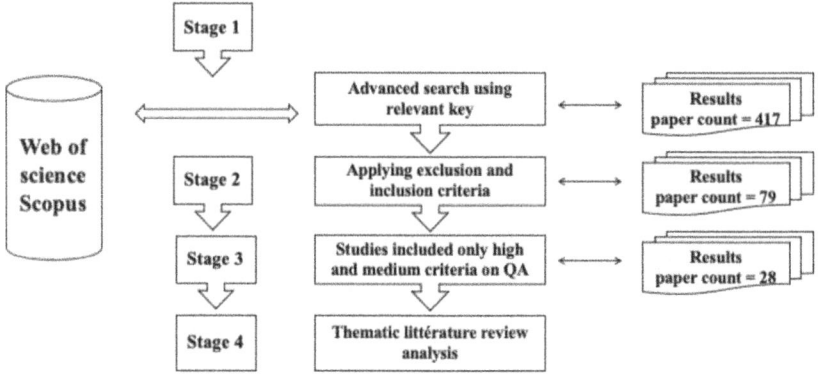

Fig. 1. Review selection process

Afterward, we applied inclusion and exclusion criteria to determine the relevance of each paper. Accordingly, we limited our findings to fully available papers written in English related to the research core themes. As a result, 79 articles met the inclusion criteria.

2.2 Quality Assessment Criteria

The 79 selected papers underwent a quality-based assessment (QA) to evaluate the relevance of the study's findings (see Table 1). Following this assessment, 28 articles remained (see Fig. 1).

In order to enhance the credibility assessment of the findings within this review, three quality ratings have been determined: "high," "medium," and "low". Consequently, the

Table 1. The five quality assessment criteria

Number of Quality Assessments	Questions
Q1	Are the topics discussed in the paper related to key themes?
Q2	Is it clear in what context the research was conducted?
Q3	Is the research methodology sufficiently explained?
Q4	Is the process and methodology for data collection described in sufficient detail in paper?
Q5	Is the Data Analysis approach evaluated accurately?

quality of each article can be evaluated through a resulting score. The results are divided into three categories:

If a study fully meets the quality criteria, it receives a score of 2.

If a study partially fulfills the quality criteria, a score of 1 is given for that criterion.

If a study fails to meet the quality criteria, a score of 0 is assigned for that criterion. Hence, considering the five quality criteria, the highest possible score for an article is 10 (or 5×2), while the lowest score is 0 (or 5×0). Within this review, a paper is.

classified as having high quality if its score is equal to or greater than 6. Papers with a score of 5 are considered medium quality, while those with a score below 5 are deemed low quality (see Fig. 2).

3   Results

3.1   Quality Assessment Score Results

This study's findings analysis included an in-depth review of numerous scenarios within the core research themes of artificial intelligence and the decision-making process. The findings show that the study included a wide range of research themes and settings.

In the quality assessment, each of the 79 papers underwent scoring and rating based on the criteria outlined in QA1-QA5 (see Table 1). This evaluation process determined the quality assessment scores for each selected study, identifying those suit able for thematic analysis.

The majority of articles had relatively low ratings based on the quality evaluation criteria. 22 items received high ratings, while 6 received medium ratings (see Table 2).

3.2   Thematic Analysis

The Role of Artificial Intelligence in Enhancing Decision-Making Process
Venkatachalam and Ray (2002) conducted research on the role of AI in decision-making within Recommender Systems, particularly in the fitness domain. Their study highlights the enhancement of contextuality in Context-aware RS (CARS) algorithms through the application of AI techniques [4]. In a similar vein, Herath and Mittal (2020) investigated the role of AI in smart city development, emphasizing the potential of AI and the Internet of Things (IoT) to drive the transformation of cities into sustainable smart cities [5].

Table 2. Quality assessment count related to key themes.

Category	Article number	Count of papers related to key theme
High quality assessment	S1, S2, S3, S4, S5, S6, S7, S8, S9, S10, S11, S12, S13, S14, S16, S17, S18, S19, S20, S22, S23, S25	22
Medium quality assessment	S15, S21, S24, S26, S27, S28	6
Low quality assessment	S29, S30, S31, S32, S33, S34, S35, S36, S37, S38, S39, S40, S41, S42, S43, S44, S45, S46, S47, S48, S49, S50, S51, S52, S53, S54, S55, S56, S57, S58, S59, S60, S61, S62, S63, S64, S65, S67, S68, S69, S70, S71, S72, S73, S74, S75, S76, S77, S78, S79	51
	Total	79

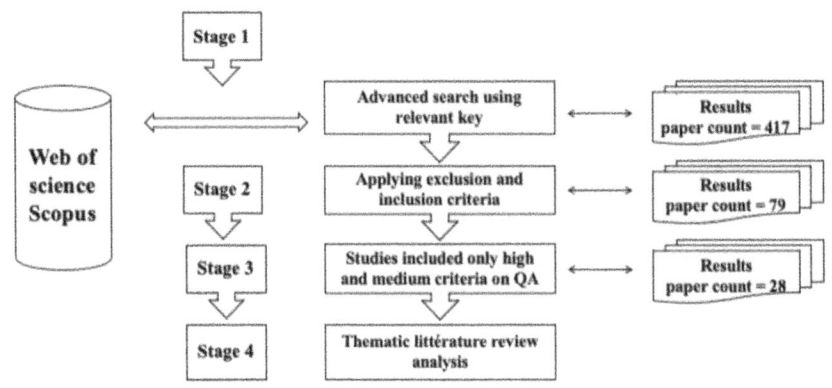

Fig. 2. Distribution of articles based on quality assessment.

Moving beyond urban contexts, Mac Carthy and Pasley (2021) examined the role of AI in decision-making within Product Lifecycle Management (PLM) systems. They propose principles for enhancing decision-making by capturing and reusing decision knowledge [6]. Furthermore, Lu et al. (2020) shed light on the role of AI in decision-making through the development of digital twins (DTs) for buildings and cities, demonstrating how AI in DTs enhances data analysis, decision-making, and asset management [7].

Shifting focus to the financial sector, Waliszewski and Warchlewska (2020) analyzed the role of AI in decision-making within this domain and its impact on consumer satisfaction [8]. Expanding on the theme of decision-making support, Hogan et al. (2020)

implemented Decidio, an AI-based software tool, to facilitate collaborative decision-making among student teams. They highlight the effectiveness of Decidio and explore correlations between personality traits and decision-making behaviors [9].

Turning attention to waste management, Paul and Bussemaker (2020) investigated the role of AI in decision-making within this field, proposing a web application as a decision support system. Their application provided valuable insights into waste quantity and flows, contributing to strategic waste valorization, waste conversion technologies, and recycling options [10].

Similarly, Huang et al. (2020) introduced the Multi-Actor Multi-Criteria Analysis (MAMCA) methodology, emphasizing the integral role of AI in the decision-making process. Through efficient data analysis, visualization, and collaborative decisionmaking. The MAMCA software facilitates stakeholder engagement and consensus-building [11].

Moving on to transport emergencies, Raikov et al. (2020) explored the role of AI in enhancing decision-making processes in such situations. Their paper proposed the use of AI, big data analysis, and deep learning methods to improve efficiency and support decision-making during emergencies [12]. Moreover, Abuova et al. (2019) demonstrated the role of AI in the decision-making process for analyzing railway emergencies. By employing intelligent computer technologies and decision support systems, their research highlighted the automation and efficiency improvements in managing railway emergencies [13].

Another study by Psarras et al. (2022) explores how AI, specifically the integration of the Balanced Scorecard (BSC) and Artificial Neural Networks (ANNs), can enhance decision-making in EU funding programs by utilizing non-financial measures and forecasting outcomes [14]. Finally, in the airline industry, the application of Data Mining and AI for dynamic market surveillance has been investigated by Pérez-Campuzano et al. (2022) showcasing the potential of data-driven decision-making in understanding and responding to market dynamics [15].

Exploring the Impact of Artificial Intelligence on Decision-Making Processes
Dubey et al. (2022) focused on humanitarian supply chains and investigated the influence of AI-driven big data analytics on agility and resilience. Their study argued that traditional theories are insufficient in this context and proposed the practice-based view as a suitable perspective. Moreover, their findings revealed that AI-driven big data analytics significantly enhance agility, resilience, and overall performance in humanitarian supply chains, emphasizing the potential of AI in improving coordination and relief operations [16].

In a similar vein, Shrestha (2021) delved into the integration of deep learning algorithms in organizational decision-making. The study introduced the concept of deep learning-augmented decision-making (DLADM) and discussed its underlying principles, promises, and challenges. By presenting real-world case studies, the author illustrated the practical applications of DLADM and underscored the importance of understanding deep learning while addressing ethical concerns. Furthermore, the study proposed future research directions to explore the integration of deep learning into decision making processes and evaluate its overall impact [17].

In exploring the combination of human and AI in strategic organizational decision making, Trunk et al. (2020) investigated the challenges and benefits of integrating AI in uncertain environments. The study emphasized the importance of clear task division and role definitions, as well as addressing pre-conditions and consequences.

Moreover, the research discussed the evolving role of human decision makers in the presence of AI support. The findings provided valuable insights into the potential of AI as a valuable tool for supporting strategic decision-making [18].

Furthermore, Stylos investigated the influence of AI applications on tourist decision making through a new theoretical framework that account for cognitive technologies, the study highlighted the impact of digital technologies on tourists' decisionmaking processes. The research envisioned scenarios in which AI support assists tourists, emphasizing the complementary relationship between tourists and AI agents [19].

Lastly, Alkraiji (2022) explores the role of top management in enhancing the efficiency of Decision Support Systems (DSSs) in the government sector of Saudi Arabia [20].

Harnessing the Power of AI: Transforming Consumer Decision-Making Processes
In recent research, Santos and Gonçalves (2021) focus on the consumer decision journey and its relationship with artificial intelligence (AI). Through a literature review, they identify gaps in the existing understanding of how AI technologies impact the consumer journey, emphasizing the incorporation of sensory inputs and autonomous shopping systems to enhance consumer experiences [21].

Tassiello et al. (2021) explore the interaction between consumers and voice assistants (VAs) and investigate the role of psychological power in the decision-making process. They find that consumers' willingness to purchase is influenced by their level of involvement and the psychological condition of power during VA interactions [22].

Building on this, Dellaert et al. (2020) examine the impact of Artificially Intelligent Voice Assistants (AIVAs) on consumer decision-making, highlighting the shift towards voice-based dialogs facilitated by AI. They suggest further research to explore the potential changes brought about by AIVAs and provide insights into the unique consumer experience of interacting with these systems [23]. Sindhu and Vadivu (2019) emphasize the use of AI algorithms to extract sentiment and attitudes from customer feedback, condensing insights into concise statements for informed decision-making [24].

Lastly, Kim (2020) explores the value of AI-driven recommendation agents (AIRAs) in the decision-making process. The author highlights their positive impact on attitudes and outcomes. AIRAs utilize AI algorithms to provide personalized recommendations, improving consumer decision-making, customer relationships, and business performance [25].

Ethical Dimensions of Artificial Intelligence in Decision-Making: Implications for Society and Accountability
Tamò-Larrieux (2021) explores the challenges and concerns associated with the shift from machines supporting human decision-making to machines making decisions on behalf of humans. The article emphasizes the need for new paradigms for policymaking and ongoing monitoring to address unintended side-effects and societal shifts caused by automated decision-making systems [26].

Coombs et al. (2021) report on a workshop focused on applying human freedom principles in the development and use of intelligent machines. They highlight the critical examination of AI design, human involvement in decision-making processes, and the ability to interpret and explain those processes as essential attributes of humanity [27]. Serafimova (2020) examines the moral implications of decision-making based on algorithms and questions the feasibility of developing strong "moral" AI scenarios. The article analyzes normative theories in machine ethics and raises important ethical considerations [28].

Krupiy (2020) analyzes the impact of AI decision-making processes from a social justice perspective, emphasizing the potential reconfiguration of relationships and the perpetuation of social inequalities. The article highlights the need for human decision-making and structural reform to address inequality [29]. Kilani et Haikal (2020) explore the impact of expert systems on ethical decision-making within organizations. They emphasize the importance of human involvement and ethical considerations in decision-making, even when utilizing expert systems, and recommend additional ethical surveillance measures [30].

Vakkuri et al. (2019) evaluate the RESOLVEDD strategy for incorporating ethical considerations into AI projects. The study finds that an ethical tool positively influences ethical considerations and increases developers' sense of responsibility. The research emphasizes the importance of group discussions and suggests tailored practices to enhance transparency, responsibility, and accountability in AI development [31].

4 Discussion

The role of artificial intelligence (AI) in enhancing decision-making processes has been extensively explored across various domains, as evidenced by the studies discussed. These studies have shed light on the potential, challenges, and implications of integrating AI into decision-making contexts. Several key themes emerge from the literature, encompassing the areas of context-aware recommendations, smart city development, product lifecycle management, waste management, transport emergencies, humanitarian supply chains, organizational decision-making, social justice considerations, tourist decision-making, and consumer decision journeys.

One significant finding is the enhancement of contextuality in decision-making through the application of AI techniques. Studies focusing on context-aware recommender systems (CARS) [4] and smart city development [5] illustrate how AI can improve decision-making by incorporating contextual information and leveraging the Internet of Things (IoT). Similarly, studies in product lifecycle management [6] and waste management [10] demonstrate how AI can capture and reuse decision knowledge, providing valuable insights for more informed decision-making processes.

The studies also highlight the potential of AI in improving decision outcomes and efficiency across different sectors. Research in the financial domain [8] shows how AI can impact consumer satisfaction by simplifying decision-making processes and providing AI-based recommendations. In transport emergencies [12] and railway emergencies [13], AI and intelligent decision support systems enhance decision-making efficiency and automation. Additionally, studies in humanitarian supply chains [16] reveal that

AI-driven big data analytics can significantly enhance agility, resilience, and overall performance.

Ethical considerations emerge as a crucial aspect of AI-driven decision-making. Scholars have raised concerns regarding biases and the potential perpetuation of inequality [29], the lack of moral enhancement in AI algorithms [28], and the need for human involvement and ethical surveillance in decision-making processes [27]. The studies emphasize the importance of transparency, accountability, and the development of robust ethical frameworks in the design and implementation of AI systems.

The integration of AI and human decision-making is a prevalent theme in the literature. Studies underscore the importance of understanding the evolving role of human decision-makers in the presence of AI support and the complementary relationship between tourists and AI agents [19]. The research emphasizes that AI should augment human judgment rather than replace it, with human decision-makers providing context, interpretation, and considering ethical implications.

Another important aspect highlighted by the studies is the impact of AI on consumer decision journeys and behavior. AI-driven recommendation agents [25] and voice assistants [23, 24] have been found to enhance consumer experiences, expedite information search and evaluation, and improve overall business performance. These findings emphasize the value of AI in shaping consumer decision-making processes and fostering customer relationships.

The literature also acknowledges the challenges and concerns associated with AI-driven decision-making. These include the need for new paradigms for policymaking, ongoing monitoring, and interpretation of automated decision-making systems [26]. The moral implications of AI algorithms and the feasibility of developing "moral" AI scenarios are subjects of critical examination. The ethical considerations, social justice implications, and the importance of human involvement in decision-making processes involving AI technologies are also emphasized [29–31].

In summary, the studies discussed provide valuable insights into the role of AI in decision-making processes. They highlight the potential of AI to enhance decision outcomes, increase efficiency, and provide valuable insights across various domains.

5   Conclusion

This paper provides a thematic literature review that explores the potential of integrating artificial intelligence (AI) to enhance decision-making. The findings are the outcome of an in-depth analysis of papers collected from Scopus and Web of Science databases with a focus on Business and Management areas. The results divided the literature into four key themes: The first theme discussed the role of Artificial Intelligence in enhancing the Decision-Making process in different fields (e.g. supply chain, smart cities, finance, education, and transportation). The findings highlighted the role of Artificial intelligence in facilitating collaborative decision-making and stakeholder engagement. They also underlined the role of AI in promoting sustainability and preventing waste. The second theme focused on the impact of Artificial Intelligence on the Decision-Making process in various sectors. The results highlight the potential of AI tools to support organizations diving in uncertain environments. However, we noticed that papers focus more on private sectors than public ones. Thus, future studies must imperatively explore the influence of AI on public decision-making, especially with the succession of crises disrupting global economic systems (e.g. Covid-19). In addition, the third theme emphasizes the aptitude of AI technologies to transform consumer's decision-making processes (e.g. voice assistants and recommendation agents). However, the fourth theme raises the ethical considerations related to the utilization of AI in decision-making (e.g. social inequalities, human slavery, and poor morality). Thus, the findings underlined the need for new policies and regulations, as well as the need for spreading awareness among developers and decision-making teams to ensure transparency and accountability. Whereas, while ethical considerations are acknowledged, a deeper exploration of specific ethical challenges, such as bias, transparency, privacy, and fairness, is needed. Moreover, Future research should look on viable techniques for implementing AI to assist human decision-making without completely replacing it. As each study has its own limitations, ours is no exception. It encompasses methodological limitations as we only relied on two databases. However, scrolling other databases might have provided insights that are more relevant. Future studies might also extend the key themes used for search query, adding machine learning and deep learning among others as part of AI to enrich their findings. In addition, inclusion and exclusion criterion, as well as quality assessment might have limited our results. To sum up, Artificial intelligence is a two-edged sword that is revolutionizing the way organizations operate and make decisions. However, it presents an array of ethical and societal challenges that must be addressed.

References

1. Cockburn, I., Henderson, R., Stern, S.: The Impact of Artificial Intelligence on Innovation. National Bureau of Economic Research, Cambridge, MA (2018). https://doi.org/10.3386/w24449
2. Bunod, R., Augstburger, E., Brasnu, E., Labbe, A., Baudouin, C.: Intelligence artificielle et glaucome : une revue de la littérature. Journal Français d'Ophtalmologie. **45**, 216–232 (2022). https://doi.org/10.1016/j.jfo.2021.11.002
3. Edwin: Advantages and Disadvantages of Artificial Intelligence and Machinelearning: a Literature Review. (2022). https://doi.org/10.17605/OSF.IO/GV5T4
4. Venkatachalam, P., Ray, S.: How do context-aware artificial intelligence algorithms used in fitness recommender systems? a literature review and research agenda. Int. J. Info. Manage. Data Insights **2**, 100139 (2022). https://doi.org/10.1016/j.jjimei.2022.100139
5. Herath, H.M.K.K.M.B., Mittal, M.: Adoption of artificial intelligence in smart cities: a comprehensive review. International J. Info. Manage. Data Insights **2**, 100076 (2022). https://doi.org/10.1016/j.jjimei.2022.100076
6. MacCarthy, B.L., Pasley, R.C.: Group decision support for product lifecycle management. Int. J. Prod. Res. **59**, 5050–5067 (2021). https://doi.org/10.1080/00207543.2020.1779372
7. Lu, Q., et al.: Developing a digital twin at building and city levels: case study of west cambridge campus. J. Manage. Eng. **36**, 05020004 (2020). https://doi.org/10.1061/(ASCE)ME.1943-5479.0000763
8. Waliszewski, K., Warchlewska, A.: Attitudes towards artificial intligence in the area of personal financial planning: a case study of selected countries. JESI. **8**, 399–420 (2020). https://doi.org/10.9770/jesi.2020.8.2(24)

9. Hogan, K., et al.: Decidio: A Pilot Implementation and User Study of a Novel Decision-Support System. In: Morais, D.C., Fang, L., Horita, M. (eds.) Group Decision and Negotiation: A Multidisciplinary Perspective, pp. 192–204. Springer International Publishing, Cham (2020). https://doi.org/10.1007/978-3-030-48641-9_14

10. Paul, M., Bussemaker, M.J.: A web-based geographic interface system to support decision making for municipal solid waste management in England. J. Clean. Prod. **263**, 121461 (2020). https://doi.org/10.1016/j.jclepro.2020.121461

11. Huang, H., Lebeau, P., Macharis, C.: The Multi-Actor Multi-Criteria Analysis (MAMCA): New Software and New Visualizations. In: Moreno-Jiménez, J.M., Linden, I., Dargam, F., Jayawickrama, U. (eds.) Decision Support Systems X: Cognitive Decision Support Systems and Technologies, pp. 43–56. Springer International Publishing, Cham (2020). https://doi.org/10.1007/978-3-030-46224-6_4

12. Raikov, A.: Accelerating decision-making in transport emergency with artificial intelligence. Adv. Sci. Technol. Eng. Syst. J. **5**, 520–530 (2020). https://doi.org/10.25046/aj050662

13. Abuova, A., Lakhno, V., Oshanova, N., Yagaliyeva, B., Anosov, A.: Conceptual model of the automated decision-making process in analysis of emergency situations on railway transport. In: Doucek, P., Basl, J., Tjoa, A.M., Raffai, M., Pavlicek, A., Detter, K. (eds.) Research and Practical Issues of Enterprise Information Systems, pp. 153–162. Springer International Publishing, Cham (2019). https://doi.org/10.1007/978-3-030-37632-1_14

14. Psarras, A., Anagnostopoulos, T., Salmon, I., Psaromiligkos, Y., Vryzidis, L.: A change management approach with the support of the balanced scorecard and the utilization of artificial neural networks. Administrative Sciences. **12**, 63 (2022). https://doi.org/10.3390/admsci120 20063

15. Pérez-Campuzano, D., Rubio Andrada, L., Morcillo Ortega, P., López-Lázaro, A.: Visualizing the historical COVID-19 shock in the US airline industry: a Data Mining approach for dynamic market surveillance. J. Air Transp. Manag. **101**, 102194 (2022). https://doi.org/10.1016/j.jai rtraman.2022.102194

16. Dubey, R., Bryde, D.J., Dwivedi, Y.K., Graham, G., Foropon, C.: Impact of artificial intelligence-driven big data analytics culture on agility and resilience in humanitarian supply chain: A practice-based view. Int. J. Prod. Econ. **250**, 108618 (2022). https://doi.org/10.1016/ j.ijpe.2022.108618

17. Shrestha, Y.R., Krishna, V., Von Krogh, G.: Augmenting organizational decision-making with deep learning algorithms: principles, promises, and challenges. J. Bus. Res. **123**, 588–603 (2021). https://doi.org/10.1016/j.jbusres.2020.09.068

18. Trunk, A., Birkel, H., Hartmann, E.: On the current state of combining human and artificial intelligence for strategic organizational decision making. Bus. Res. **13**, 875–919 (2020). https://doi.org/10.1007/s40685-020-00133-x

19. Stylos, N.: Technological evolution and tourist decision-making: a perspective article. TR. **75**, 273–278 (2020). https://doi.org/10.1108/TR-05-2019-0167

20. Alkraiji, A.I.: Top management's role in promoting decision support systems efficiency: an exploratory study in government sector in Saudi Arabia. J. Cases on Info. Technol. **22**, 38–56 (2022). https://doi.org/10.4018/JCIT.2020010103

21. Santos, S., Gonçalves, H.M.: The consumer decision journey: a literature review of the foundational models and theories and a future perspective. Technol. Forecast. Soc. Chang. **173**, 121117 (2021). https://doi.org/10.1016/j.techfore.2021.121117

22. Tassiello, V., Tillotson, J.S., Rome, A.S.: Alexa, order me a pizza!: The mediating role of psychological power in the consumer–voice assistant interaction. Psychol. Mark. **38**, 1069–1080 (2021). https://doi.org/10.1002/mar.21488

23. Dellaert, B.G.C., et al.: Consumer decisions with artificially intelligent voice assistants. Mark. Lett. **31**, 335–347 (2020). https://doi.org/10.1007/s11002-020-09537-5

24. Sindhu, V,.: Sentiment Analysis and Opinion Summarization of Product Feedback. ijrte. **8**, 59–64 (2019). https://doi.org/10.35940/ijrte.B1011.0782S419
25. Kim, J.: The influence of perceived costs and perceived benefits on AI-driven interactive recommendation agent value. J. Glob. Scholars Market. Sci. **30**, 319–333 (2020). https://doi.org/10.1080/21639159.2020.1775491
26. Tamò-Larrieux, A.: Decision-making by machines: Is the 'Law of Everything' enough? Comput. Law Secur. Rev. **41**, 105541 (2021). https://doi.org/10.1016/j.clsr.2021.105541
27. Coombs, C., et al.: What is it about humanity that we can't give away to intelligent machines? A European perspective. Int. J. Inf. Manage. **58**, 102311 (2021). https://doi.org/10.1016/j.ijinfomgt.2021.102311
28. Serafimova, S.: Whose morality? which rationality? challenging artificial intelligence as a remedy for the lack of moral enhancement. Humanit. Soc. Sci. Commun. **7**, 119 (2020). https://doi.org/10.1057/s41599-020-00614-8
29. Krupiy, T.: (Tanya): A vulnerability analysis: Theorising the impact of artificial intelligence decision-making processes on individuals, society and human diversity from a social justice perspective. Comput. Law Secur. Rev. **38**, 105429 (2020). https://doi.org/10.1016/j.clsr.2020.105429
30. Kilani, Y.M.M., Haikal, E.K.: Exploitation of expert system in identifying organizational ethics through controlling decision making process, 1417–1426 (2020). https://doi.org/10.5267/j.msl.2019.12.026
31. Vakkuri, V., Kemell, K.-K., Abrahamsson, P.: Ethically aligned design: an empirical evaluation of the RESOLVEDD-strategy in software and systems development context. In: 2019 45th Euromicro Conference on Software Engineering and Advanced Applications (SEAA), pp. 46–50. IEEE, Kallithea-Chalkidiki, Greece (2019). https://doi.org/10.1109/SEAA.2019.00015

HyIDS: A Hybrid Intrusion Detection System in IaaS Cloud

Meryem Ec-Sabery$^{(\boxtimes)}$, Adil Ben Abbou, Abdelali Boushaba, Fatiha Mrabti, and Rachid Ben Abbou

Intelligent Systems and Applications Laboratory, Faculty of Sciences and Technology, Sidi Mohamed Ben Abdellah University, Fez, Morocco
{meryem.ecsabery,adil.benabbou,abdelali.boushaba,fatiha.mrabti, rachid.benabbou}@usmba.ac.ma

Abstract. The migration to cloud computing has increased exponentially with its measured, available and scalable services, as many companies have subscribed to the IaaS model to freely address their IT needs. However, the security of their data, especially if the cloud is public, remains a major concern for them. Therefore, an intrusion detection system can be developed as a defense mechanism to monitor, detect and prevent threats. In this field, the researchers were interested in the algorithms used in the mechanism of detection, in addition to the location of IDS in cloud computing. These two main points aim to reach high detection accuracy and reduce the false alarms of internal and external, as well as known and unknown intrusions. In this paper, we propose an adaptable solution to IaaS cloud using a hybrid method, which is based on Snort and majority voting technique. Our proposed method provides high detection accuracy and low number of false alarms and confirms its reliability for IaaS cloud.

Keywords: cloud security · signature-based detection · anomaly-based detection · majority voting

1 Introduction

In recent years, many companies have hosted their IT resources on cloud computing in order to take advantage of the technical and business benefits of the cloud. However, the security and privacy of their data remains a serious concern [1]. According to National Institute of Standards and Technology (NIST) the cloud services are divided into three models: Software as a Service (SaaS), Platform as a Service (PaaS) and Infrastructure as a Service (IaaS). PaaS model provides development or application platforms, such as middleware, databases, file storage, etc.... SaaS model offers an application hosted and managed by the cloud provider. IaaS model provides the customers with computing resources such as storage, compute, and network and gives them more freedom to create virtual machines, run applications and deploy different operating systems. Each

© The Author(s), under exclusive license to Springer Nature Switzerland AG 2025
H. Hagras et al. (Eds.): ISACS 2023, CCIS 2255, pp. 358–372, 2025.
https://doi.org/10.1007/978-3-031-93448-3_29

of these service models has its own challenges that must be handled to provide security to customer. In the IaaS model the client is responsible for tuning and securing its virtual environment while the Cloud Service Provider's (CSP) responsibilities are limited to the hypervisor layer and below [2–4].

IaaS model is exposed to plenty and varied risks, which are inherited from the distributed and dynamic nature of cloud, virtualization technology, multitenancy and remote accessibility [1]. Hence, the landscape of threats keeps expanding, and the probability of injecting malicious mining code, unknown malware, phishing, DoS/DDoS attacks and illegal activities is increased [5,6]. So enhancing IaaS security is of utmost importance, an intrusion detection system is one of the most widely adopted methods by the CSP and the customer to detect and prevent attacks from entering to the infrastructure [7]. By NIST, intrusion is an attempt to access to a system without having authorization to compromise the CIA of resources, i.e., confidentiality, integrity and availability.

Intrusion detection systems are commonly classified into two principal categories: anomaly-based detection and signature-based detection. In the signature-based detection (misuse detection), rules (signatures) are created for known attacks, these rules are used to inspect the received data and they are maintained and updated periodically [8]. The most important advantage of using signature-based detection system (SIDS) method is its high efficiency in detecting the known intrusions. i.e., high rate of true positive [9]. In contrast, SIDS can not detect attacks such as unknown and zero-day attacks. Traditional design of SIDS is unable to analyze a massive volume of traffic and identify a dynamic change of attacks, which is why it is not suitable for cloud computing [7]. In anomaly-based detection system (AIDS) [10], the traffic behavior is examined to build a normal baseline and then use it to decide the nature of the events. Hence, combination of these techniques can provide inclusive security for the cloud. IDSs are also classified based on their locations [7]: host based IDS (HIDS), an intelligent agent installed on the host machine, which analyzes OS events files, system calls, audit files, application events file, etc...., and network-based IDS (NIDS) monitors and detects network malicious activities.

The pressing need for robust intrusion detection in cloud ever-evolving threat landscape, prompts many researchers in [11–16] to combine signature and anomaly detection to identify unknown and known attacks and enhance the detection rate. However, the hybrid systems proposed have some shortcomings in terms of architecture clarity, SIDS positioning, detection speed and datasets. In these works, the authors have given the full control of IDS to the cloud provider, ignoring that in the case of IaaS, the customer is responsible for their own virtual machines since he is the one who knows better what services are used. They did not specify the placement of the Snort agent in cloud infrastructure and missed the process to be followed in case of an IDS overload, which is very common in cloud environment, as well as the use of old datasets, created and collected before 2010.

The main motivation behind this article is to propose an intrusion detection system for IaaS model, which detects efficiently and effectively the known

and unknown attacks, shares the security responsibility between the CSP and
the customer and analyzes a huge amount of traffic. Our approach consists of
a hybrid intrusion detection system (HyIDS), which is a serial combination of
adaptable Snort instances to block patterns of newly detected and known attacks
and ensemble model to prevent unknown and zero-day attacks. The ensemble
model makes decisions about the packet nature using majority voting on predictions from Naive Bayes, Support vector machine, Decision Tree and k-Nearest
Neighbor classifiers. In our experiment, the classifiers are trained on CICIDS2017
dataset, which encompasses a comprehensive range of attacks and majority voting performed better than did individual classifiers in terms of detection accuracy
and false alarms.

The rest of this paper is organized as follows: In Sect. 2, we present some
related studies focused on hybrid intrusion detection. In Sect. 3, we propose an
approach for detecting attacks in IaaS environment. In Sect. 4, we discuss the
experiment and the results of the study and Sect. 5 concludes this paper and
presents some perspectives at this work.

2   Related Works

In this section, we mention some related works that aimed to improve the
IDS design in cloud environment; their main objective is disclosing known and
unknown intrusions with high accuracy detection and minimal false warnings.
Many researchers in Table 1 published about hybrid approaches of network based
intrusion to benefit from the advantages of a misuse detection system and an
anomaly detection system.

The authors, In [11] proposed a hybrid network intrusion system in order to
trap both known and unknown intrusions. They used Snort as misuse detection
engine that correlates captured packets with rules and sends normal packets to
Decision Tree (DT) to predict the final class label of the preprocessed packets. In
the two phases, an alert is generated whether the packet is malicious. The components of this system are packet capture, packet preprocessing, which prepare
data by removing outlier and redundant packets, intrusion detection process,
which analyzes packets by snort engine and then by decision tree classifier and
finally alerts the system about the presence of attack.

The authors, In [12] proposed a hybrid approach called Hybrid Intrusion
Detection in Cloud Computing (HIDCC), which is carried out in four steps:
First step uses snort module which contains rules to detect the known intrusions,
and the attacks detected by anomaly module. The anomaly detection module
modeled by C4.5 algorithm and vector quantization algorithm (LVQ), processes
the traffic judged normal by snort and start detecting the final class of the packet.
After that, if the packet is malicious, a warning is generated and the packet is
dropped, finally a new rule about this attack is added to the derived database
of snort module.

The authors, In [13] proposed a hybrid approach based on machine learning
algorithm appropriate to cloud computing. The intrusion system proposed is for

known and zero-day attacks and it contains tree layers: Data acquisition layer, which is responsible of capturing and preprocessing the traffic and extracting needed features to transform packets to data vectors. Detection layer, which is based on snort detection engine first, and then on check of normal traffic baseline, it is built by machine learning model. Machine learning layer permits the system to train a model by using DT algorithm, Multilayer Perceptron (MLP), Naïve Bayes (NB) and Random Forest (RF). DT reached the highest accuracy with 99.9%.

The authors, In [14] presented a hybrid intrusion system approach to detect attacks. For the first phase, they proposed installing IDS in each layer of the cloud environment. i.e., network layer, application layer and host layer and then collecting logs generated by these IDSs to have a comprehensive visibility. In the second phase, they prepared data of application layer and applied anomaly detection based on C4.5 to uncover the unknown attacks.

The authors, In [15] proposed a collaborative and hybrid IDS for cloud environment. They used Snort as signature detection system and a cascade of DT and Support Vector Machine (SVM) as anomaly detection system; the authors combined two machine learning techniques to remove the limitations of each other and then reach a high accuracy of detection. They also established a central correlation unit, which helped the NIDSs to collaborate and reduce the impact of the coordinated attacks.

The authors, in [16] proposed an anomaly-based NIDS to detect several types of attacks (Probe, DoS, U2R and R2L) in cloud computing, the model is created by training SVM classifier coupled with Particle Swarm Optimization (PSO) technique on NSL-KDD dataset, the model showed its effectiveness in recognizing the normal behaviors and detecting the attacks.

Table 1. Research works related to intrusion detection system in cloud computing.

Ref	SIDS	AIDS	Dataset	Best accuracy
[11]	Snort	C4.5	NSL-KDD, KDD	95%
[12]	Snort	LVQ + C4.5	NSL-KDD	99.7%
[13]	Snort	C4.5	CICIDS2017	99.9%
[14]	Snort Ossec Modsecurity	C4.5	PCAP files CSIC2010 HTTP	62%
[15]	Snort	SVM + C4.5	NSL-KDD, KDD, ITOC	98.9%
[16]	Snort	SVM + PSO	NSL-KDD	99.10%

3   A Hybrid IDS in IaaS Cloud: HyIDS

HyIDS in IaaS environment performs the detection mechanism in three stages, as shown in Fig. 1:

- The first stage is to detect known patterns, thereby immediately blocking those attacks by Snort engine, which uses rules from two databases: Known attacks database and detected attacks database and then an alert is raised.
- The second stage is to uncover attacks that were not detected in the first stage, there is a risk of them increasing due to the nature of cloud computing. At this stage, the preprocessing module prepares the packets to be used by the majority voting module, and then, this voting classifier predicts the class of the network packet based on the baseline model, which is created by training the ensemble classifier on CIC-IDS2017 dataset. Majority voting classifier combines the performances of multiple base classifiers to make decisions, it serves as means to improve the accuracy detection.
- The third stage consists of generating a new rule if an attack is detected by the second stage, the rule is sent to a central database and thus the database of detected attacks in Snort engine is updated.

3.1 HyIDS Design in IaaS Cloud

In IaaS model, which is a multi-tenant environment, security and privacy are a shared responsibility between the customer and the cloud provider and should be discussed in the service level agreement (SLA) as important as the resources to be leased. As shown in Fig. 2, multiple instances of our proposed HyIDS are deployed to meet cloud needs. CSP manages the central database and all HyIDS instances except those installed on the client resources.

CSP side: HyIDS must be emplaced at the frontend to detect external attacks and at the backend to track internal ones coming from malicious tenants. The design has four properties:

- Self-adaptable, HyIDS automatically adapts its components according to the changes in physical and virtual infrastructure such as server addition, VM creation, migration and destruction;
- Highly scalable, it initiates new HyIDS instances when the network's load increases and the existing HyIDS capacity is submerged, Fig. 3 represents, the proposed process to share traffic between HyIDS, the need to have a load-balancer is paramount in order to manage and track the HyIDS performance. Initially, only two instances of HyIDS are created and if there is a need, the number will increase until it reaches its maximum, which is set by the CSP to avoid the cloud resources interpolation. After a period of inactivity, the new HyIDS must be deleted.
- Comprehensive, it detects known and newly detected attacks. In each HyIDS instance there is a combination of AIDS and SIDS. AIDS uncovers the new attacks, blocks them, then generates the signature and send it to the central database, if the same signature is generated by 51% of the number of HyIDS, It must be added to the detected attacks database of all HyIDS instances, otherwise no update is requested. SIDS contains the known attacks database and the detected attacks database. The known attacks database is downloaded by

Snort engine and contains the patterns of the attacks already uncovered by security communities and updated automatically. The most generated signatures in the central database feed the detected attacks database.

- Affordable cost, the implementation cost is affordable because HyIDS components are shared between tenants.

Client side: HyIDS should be installed on VMs to prevent malicious traffic coming from semi-reliable CSP or suspicious tenants. HyIDS on client resources has two properties:

- Customizable, it allows tenant to include rules in order to monitor vulnerabilities targeting their deployed services, if the tenant adds new services or deletes them, the database get updated.
- Interactive, it periodically updates its known attacks database from trusted security communities and from the central database, which contains the rules of detected attacks shared by the CSP.

3.2 Known Attacks Detection Stage in IaaS Cloud

At this stage, Snort is used as signature-based intrusion detection system (SIDS), adapted to operate efficiently in IaaS cloud. Snort is a powerful open source intrusion detection and prevention system, which provides data packet logging and real-time network traffic analysis; it uses signature-based detection techniques and a rule-based language. Snort takes the packets and compares their contents to its predefined signatures in the known attacks database and the detected attacks database.

3.3 Unknown Attacks Detection Stage

At this stage, majority voting technique is used as anomaly-based detection system (AIDS) to classify network packets received from the SIDS module. The motivation for using the ensemble technique is to enhance the accuracy detection and reduce the number of false alarms. Ensemble methods are a machine learning technique that combines the results of several base classifiers. These classifiers can be the same type or not in order to produce an optimal predictive model.

The proposed approach uses CICIDS2017 dataset [17], to build model that can accurately distinguish malicious from benign network traffic. It can help intrusion detection solution to uncover new and unknown attacks that are not detected through traditional SIDS. Figure 4 depicts the architecture of the proposed approach. It is divided into five sections: data collection, data preprocessing, feature selection, base classifiers, and majority voting technique.

- Data Collection: the dataset CIC-IDS2017 is used in this study, which is one of the most modern labelled datasets for intrusion detection. It is developed by gathering network traffic from heterogeneous sources for five days. CIC-IDS2017 include Web attack, Infiltration, Heartbleed, Brute Force FTP, DoS, Brute Force SSH, Botnet and DDoS attacks and normal traffic.

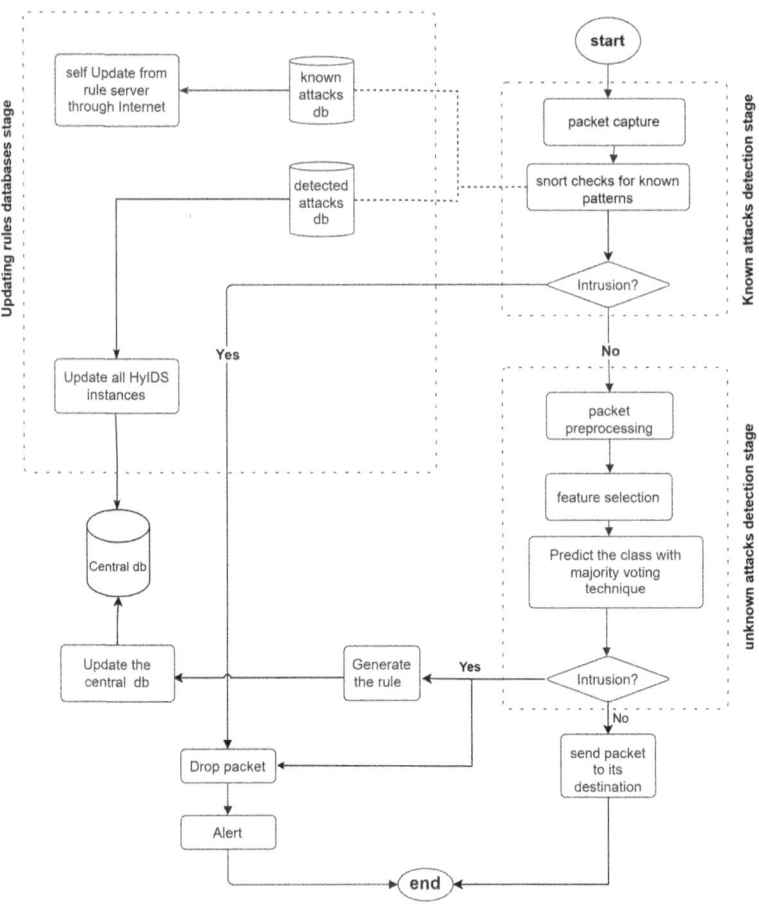

Fig. 1. Flowchart of our proposed HyIDS

- Data preprocessing: this step helps cleaning, formatting, and organizing the raw data, thereby making it ready for machine learning models, it involves: Data cleaning, which seeks for cleaning the data by smoothing the noises, removing outliers, filling in missing values, and resolving the inconsistency. Data Transformation, which aims to consolidate the data into alternate forms by changing the value, structure, or format [18].
- Feature Selection, this step reduces the number of input variables when developing a predictive baseline. It is recommended to only select the features that contribute mostly to the accuracy of the model; the reason is to reduce the computational cost of the modeling and in some cases to improve the performance of the model. The original dataset consists of 77 features. In this study, we chose chi square algorithm after having tested information gain algorithm to select only the 20 most relevant features. In our experiment, chi square algorithm provided better results and its formula is given by Eq. 1.

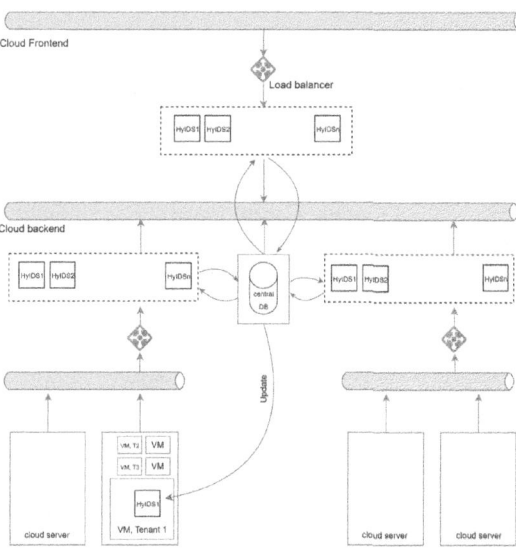

Fig. 2. HyIDS architecture

$$\chi^2 = \sum \frac{(Oi - Ei)^2}{Ei} \qquad (1)$$

where Oi = observed value and Ei = expected value.

- Base Classifier, this step evaluates the proposed AIDS approach, the ensemble technique is created by means of some classifiers given in the literature for intrusion detection, namely decision tree, naive Bayes, k-nearest neighbors, and support vector machine, the output of these base classifiers is combined through majority voting.
- The majority vote technique is one of the simplest and most effective forms of combining predictions produced by several classifiers. In a majority vote, the class that receives the most votes, i.e. that exceeds 50%, is chosen. As shown in Fig. 4, we have a training set and a set of classifiers (C1, C2...Cn), each classifier after the step of training on training set, produces the prediction class yi(x). At this point we have n predictions and thus a majority voting scheme have to decide what is the final prediction Y, for that it uses the mode of the predicted classes.

$$Y = mode\{C1(x), C2(x), ..., Cn(x)\} \qquad (2)$$

where Ci(x) = yi(x)

3.4 Updating the Detected Attacks Database

After detecting unknown attacks at the second stage, it is necessary to add rules to the central database in Fig. 2 and if the same rules are generated by 51% of

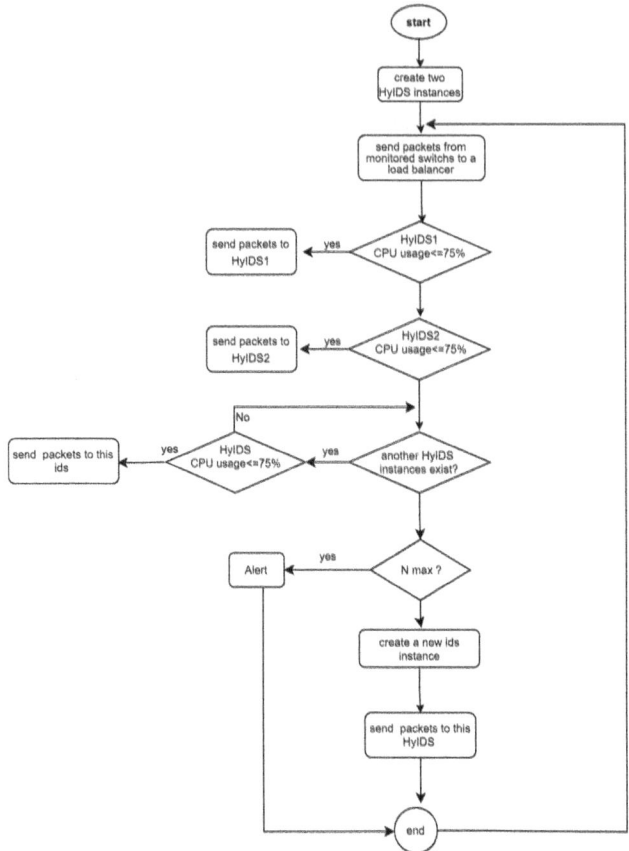

Fig. 3. Process of load balancing between HyIDSs

the number of HyIDS instances, launch an update to add them to the detected attacks database of all HyIDS instances. So that in the future, when a similar attack occurs, HyIDS can immediately detect and prevent them from accessing the infrastructure.

4   Experiment and Results

4.1   Experiment

In the experiment, Sci-kit learn tool and CIC-IDS2017 dataset were used on HP computer with intel core i5, CPU 1.70 GHZ and 16GB of RAM. Scikit-learn is a free machine learning library in Python that performs data mining tasks. The experiment used a balanced subset of CIC-IDS2017 dataset, which have 78 features and one class label. After removing the redundant feature, only 77 features are available to be analyzed by chi square algorithm. 20 features are selected,

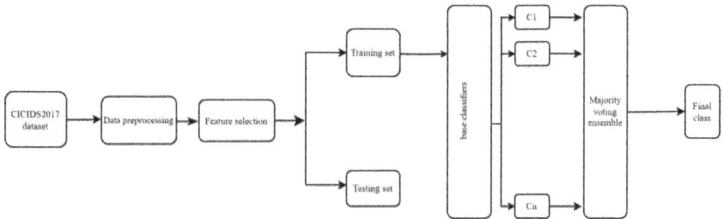

Fig. 4. Ensemble approach for our AIDS

no data transformation is required because data are already in numerical type except the label column, we use LabelEncoder to convert intrusion class to 1 and benign to 0, and we use StandardScaler to standardize the range of the inputs. The dataset is divided into training and testing set, Table 2 shows the used subset of CIC-IDS2017 dataset.

Table 2. The used subset of CIC-IDS2017 dataset.

Total records	Benign records	Intrusion records
566149	280000	286149

4.2 Classification Evaluation Metrics

The evaluation criteria are defined to process the performance of majority voting model, which combines DT, SVM, Naïve Bayes and KNN models; they are based on the parameters bellow:

A: True positive, which is a number of instances accurately classified as intrusions, in fact are intrusions.
B: True negative, which is a number of instances accurately classified as benign, in fact are benign.
C: False positive, which is a number of instances classified as containing intrusion but in fact, it is a benign.
D: False negative, which is a number of instances that ML algorithm classifies as benign but in fact, it is an intrusion.

These parameters are used to calculate the precision, recall, the F1 score and the accuracy:

$$Precision = \frac{A}{A+B} \tag{3}$$

$$Recall = \frac{A}{A+D} \tag{4}$$

$$F1 = \frac{2*Recall*Precision}{Recall+Presicion} \tag{5}$$

$$Accuracy = \frac{A+B}{A+B+C+D} \tag{6}$$

4.3   Evaluation and Result

At first, the training data, which represent 80% of the optimized CIC-IDS2017 dataset are delivered to the KNN, Naïve Bayes, SVM, Decision Tree, which represent the most commonly used algorithms for intrusion detection in the literature and then majority voting classifier. Tables 3, 4, 5, 6, 7 and 8 represent the results of the tested classifiers.

In Table 4, the SVM classifier performed very poor with 51% of accuracy. The algorithm classified nearly all instances as intrusion, which is definitely not suitable for our anomaly detection system, as shown in Table 3, 55631 instances are classified as intrusion while in fact, are benign. This model was unsuitable for our system with 55634 false alarms.

Table 3. Confusion matrix of SVM classifier

	Benign	Intrusion
Benign	156	55631
Intrusion	3	57440

Table 4. Evaluation metrics of SVM classifier

Metrics	Rate
precision	50%
recall	99.9%
F-score	66.6%
accuracy	51%

Table 5. Confusion matrix of Naïve Bayes classifier

	Benign	Intrusion
Benign	47439	8348
Intrusion	19612	37831

Table 6. Evaluation metrics of Naïve Bayes classifier

Metrics	Rate
precision	81%
recall	95.7%
F-score	85%
accuracy	75%

Table 7. Confusion matrix of KNN classifier

	Benign	Intrusion
Benign	55170	617
Intrusion	25	57418

Table 8. Evaluation metrics of KNN classifier

Metrics	Rate
precision	98.9%
recall	99.9%
F-score	98%
accuracy	99.4%

In Table 5, the results of Naïve Bayes classifier was moderately good compared to SVM classifier with 85%, especially in detecting benign traffic. The precision rate is 81%, which means that a lot of normal traffic is classified as intrusion and then blocked, which affects the reliability of the anomaly detection system. As shown in Table 6, 19612 instances are incorrectly classified as benign while more than 8348 instances are incorrectly classified for benign traffic. The accuracy is relatively poor with 75%.

Table 9. Confusion matrix of Decision Tree classifier

	Benign	Intrusion
Benign	55641	146
Intrusion	10	57433

Table 10. Evaluation metrics of Decision Tree classifier

Metrics	Rate
precision	98.9%
recall	99.9%
F-score	98%
accuracy	99.8%

Table 11. Confusion matrix of majority voting classifier

	Benign	Intrusion
Benign	55757	30
Intrusion	21	57422

Table 12. Evaluation metrics of majority voting classifier

Metrics	Rate
precision	99.9%
recall	99.9%
F-score	99.9%
accuracy	99.95%

In Table 8, the KNN classifier performed very well with 99% of accuracy. It was increased by 22% compared to Naïve Bayes classifier. This algorithm reaches 98.8% in detecting benign traffic, which is relatively good result for anomaly detection system, as shown in Table 7, 617 instances are classified intrusion while in fact, are benign. This model produces 632 false alarms.

In Table 10, the decision tree classifier also performed very well with a high rate of detection 99.8%. This algorithm reaches 99.7% in detecting benign traffic. According to the confusion matrix in Table 9, a total number of false alarms equal to 156 (10 False Negatives and 146 False Positives), which is relatively very low compared to Naives Bayes and SVM.

In Table 12, the ensemble technique combined the following four base classifiers: DT, SVM, Naïve Bayes and KNN, majority-voting technique performed very well with 99.9% in detecting benign traffic, which was the highest rate we obtained. According to the confusion matrix in Table 11, only 30 instances are incorrectly classified as intrusion. Thus, ensemble technique is very appropriate to create a baseline for normal traffic in our AIDS.

Our ensemble approach performed better than did individual classifiers in terms of accuracy with 99.95% accuracy, 99.9% precision, and 99.9% recall and low number of false warnings equal to 51 instances.

Figure 5 shows that our ensemble approach performed better than did the works in Table 1 in terms of accuracy with 99.95%. There is a small improvement over [13], which is very interesting in high traffic environment like cloud computing. Ensemble technique is much better in identifying benign traffic and thus creating a model for anomaly detection system. However, there was an increase in processing time, which was very normal in ensemble technique.

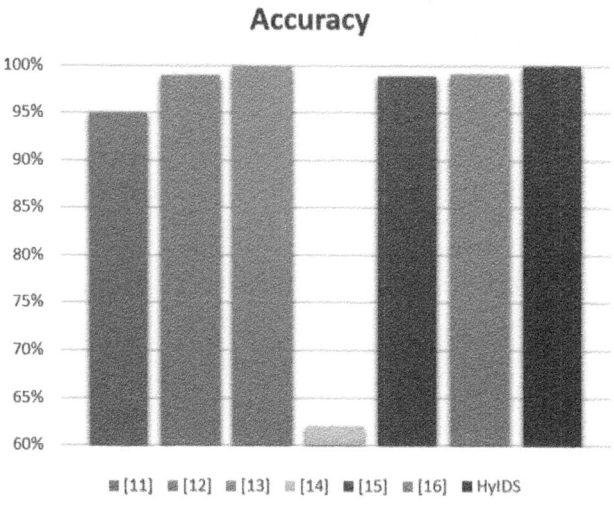

Fig. 5. Accuracy metric for HyIDS and related works

5   Conclusion

The efficiency of intrusion detection mechanisms is defined as the ability to identify intrusions in the shortest time and the lowest rate of false warnings. Generating a large number of false alarms may lead to block normal traffic, thus affecting the cloud services availability and the intrusion detection system's reliability. In this article, a network intrusion detection system is proposed to detect the known and unknown attacks. To increase the efficiency, a serial combination of signature and anomaly detection technique is applied. First, we applied adapted Snort instances to find patterns of known attacks and then ensemble technique to identify unknown and zero-day attacks. After preprocessing CIC-IDS2017 dataset, it is trained by Naive Bayes, Support vector machine, Decision Tree, k-Nearest Neighbor classifiers and majority vote ensemble to select the most efficient in terms of accuracy of detection and false alarms. Our proposed ensemble approach performed better than did individual classifiers with a reduced dataset and limited features size, it gave a detection accuracy of 99.95% and low number of false warnings. In the future work, we intend to accomplish the following tasks: Applying advanced features selection techniques to use the most relevant features and using other machine learning/deep learning techniques to find the most accurate ones for cloud computing.

References

1. Kumar, R., Goyal, R.: On cloud security requirements, threats, vulnerabilities and countermeasures: a survey. Comput. Sci. Rev. **33**, 1–48 (2019)
2. Pahl, C., Xiong, H.: Migration to PaaS clouds - migration process and architectural concerns. In: 2013 IEEE 7th International Symposium on the Maintenance and Evolution of Service-Oriented and Cloud-Based Systems, pp. 86–91 (2013)
3. Modisane, P., Jokonya, O.: Evaluating the benefits of cloud computing in small, medium and micro-sized enterprises (SMMEs). Procedia Comput. Sci. **181**, 784–792 (2021)
4. Hussein, N., Khalid, A.: A survey of Cloud Computing Security challenges and solutions (2016)
5. Khan, M.: A survey of security issues for cloud computing. J. Netw. Comput. Appl. **71**, 11–29 (2016)
6. Belal, M., Sundaram, D.: Comprehensive review on intelligent security defences in cloud: taxonomy, security issues, ML/DL techniques, challenges and future trends. J. King Saud Univ. Comput. Inf. Sci. **34**, 9102–9131 (2022)
7. Patel, A., Taghavi, M., Bakhtiyari, K., Celestino Júnior, J.: An intrusion detection and prevention system in cloud computing: a systematic review. J. Netw. Comput. Appl. **36**, 25–41 (2013)
8. Mehmood, Y., Shibli, M., Habiba, U., Masood, R.: Intrusion detection system in cloud computing: challenges and opportunities. In: 2013 2nd National Conference on Information Assurance (NCIA), pp. 59–66 (2013)
9. Lata, S., Singh, D.: Intrusion detection system in cloud environment: literature survey & future research directions. Int. J. Inf. Manag. Data Insights **2**, 100134 (2022)
10. Yang, Z., et al.: A systematic literature review of methods and datasets for anomaly-based network intrusion detection. Comput. Secur. **116**, 102675 (2022)
11. Modi, C., Patel, D., Borisanya, B., Patel, A., Rajarajan, M.: A novel framework for intrusion detection in cloud. In: Proceedings of the Fifth International Conference on Security of Information and Networks, pp. 67–74 (2012)
12. Hatef, M., Shaker, V., Jabbarpour, M., Jung, J., Zarrabi, H.: HIDCC: a hybrid intrusion detection approach in cloud computing. Concurr. Comput. Pract. Exp. **30**, e4171 (2018)
13. Ouiazzane, S., Addou, M., Barramou, F.: A multiagent and machine learning based hybrid NIDS for known and unknown cyber-attacks. Int. J. Adv. Comput. Scie. Appl. **12** (2021)
14. Jelidi, M., Ghourabi, A., Gasmi, K.: A hybrid intrusion detection system for cloud computing environments. In: 2019 International Conference on Computer and Information Sciences (ICCIS), pp. 1–6 (2019)
15. Singh, D., Patel, D., Borisaniya, B., Modi, C.: Collaborative IDS Framework for Cloud (2016)

16. Sakr, M.M., Tawfeeq, M.A., El-Sisi, A.B.: Network intrusion detection system based PSO-SVM for cloud computing. Int. J. Comput. Netw. Inf. Secur. **11**, 22–29 (2019)
17. Sharafaldin, I., Habibi Lashkari, A., Ghorbani, A.: Toward generating a new intrusion detection dataset and intrusion traffic characterization. In: Proceedings of the 4th International Conference on Information Systems Security and Privacy, pp. 108–116 (2018)
18. Alexandropoulos, S., Kotsiantis, S., Vrahatis, M.: Data preprocessing in predictive data mining. Knowl. Eng. Rev. **34**, e1 (2019)

Comparative Analysis of Deep Learning-Based Generative Models Used for Recommendation Systems

Sanae Filali Zegzouti[1]([✉]), Oumayma Banouar[2] [iD], and Mohamed Benslimane[1] [iD]

[1] Laboratory of Innovative Technologies, Sidi Mohamed Ben Abdellah University, Fez, Morocco
sanae.filalizegzouti@usmba.ac.ma
[2] Laboratory of Computer Science Engineering and Systems, Cady Ayyad University, Marrakesh, Morocco

Abstract. Recommendation systems have evolved significantly over the years. Companies employing these systems aim to boost their profits by suggesting customized products that users may not have initially considered but are likely to enjoy and eventually purchase, view, or try. Their applications can be observed in various sectors such as e-commerce, media, social media platforms, banking, healthcare, tourism, education, and travel. While traditional recommendation systems have a long history, their integration with Deep Learning techniques and generative models has substantially enhanced their efficiency. In this paper, we trace the evolution of recommender systems from traditional models to those employing generative models based on Deep Learning. Additionally, we delve into a qualitative comparative analysis of three generative models: VAE, GAN, and Diffusion. This study compares these algorithms on the basis of a number of criteria, including components, complexity, training process, nature of input data, data generation, requirements, and cost.

Keywords: Machine Learning · Deep Learning · Recommendation systems · Generative models · VAE · GAN · DIFFUSION

1 Introduction

Recommendation systems have experienced significant growth in recent years, thanks to advances and research in this field. Numerous algorithms have been proposed to introduce new models or enhance existing ones. This phenomenon can be attributed to the widespread use of the internet in nearly every aspect of our daily lives.

Within recommendation system models, there are algorithms that utilize data on user behavior [1, 2], preferences [3], and interactions [1, 2, 4], to suggest items or actions that would interest the user. These systems are commonly employed in e-commerce giants like Amazon, Alibaba, and Netflix, as well as in media platforms such as YouTube and Spotify, and on social media platforms including Facebook, Instagram, and LinkedIn. They can be used also in other industries such as banking, healthcare [5], tourism [6,

7], education [8, 9], or travel. Recommendation systems may use different techniques such as Collaborative filtering [1, 2, 10, 11], or Deep Learning [12–17]. Collaborative filtering is a popular technique in recommendation systems that is based on the collective behavior of users to make predictions and offer personalized recommendations. Deep learning models includes techniques that involve neural networks with multiple layers. To optimize and increase the capabilities of collaborative filtering in recommender systems, the integration of deep learning models is a powerful approach that has yielded good results.

In the context of recommendation systems, generative models [12–17] are deep learning models that used to generate new items or predict user preferences. Despite these advantages, they face several challenges such as data requirements, complexity, and training processes.

In this study, we conduct a qualitative comparative analysis of generative models based on Deep Learning for recommendation systems. We present three of these models, each of which has demonstrated strong performance in recent years. We discuss their strengths and limitations and compare them based on several criteria, including their components, complexity, and training processes.

The remaining of this article is organized as the following. Section 2 presents traditional types of Machine Learning models vs Deep Learning models. While Sect. 3 summarizes the different categories of recommendation systems. Section 4 presents Generative models used for recommendation systems. The conclusion closes the paper.

2 Traditional Types of Machine Learning Models vs Deep Learning Models in Recommendation Systems

There are several different types of models, including Supervised Learning, Unsupervised Learning, Semi-supervised Learning, and Reinforcement Learning.

Supervised Learning is where the model is trained on labeled data to predict outcomes for new, unseen data. There are two types of supervised Learning, Classification, and Regression. Examples of supervised learning algorithms include linear regression, logistic regression, and KNN [18, 19, 25].

Unsupervised Learning, the model is trained on unlabeled data to find out patterns or structures in the data. Some types of unsupervised learning are Clustering, Dimensionality reduction, and Association rule learning. Examples of unsupervised learning algorithms include k- means [2, 7, 18], and PCA (Principal Component Analysis) [10, 20, 22]. In [2], the main advances concern the classification of users according to their attributes using an adapted k-means algorithm, and then using a fuzzy best-worst method (F-BWM) to treat opinions of users. In [20], the authors used K-means to segment customers and PCA to reduce dimensionality of different features of products and customers.

Semi-supervised Learning [23] is a combination of supervised and unsupervised learning. In this case, the algorithm is trained on a dataset that contains both labeled and unlabeled data to improve the performance of a model. The model is generally trained on a small amount of labeled data and a large amount of unlabeled data. In many recommendation systems cases, data are sparce with a big volume of implicit feedback.

In this case, As explain in [23], Semi-supervised Learning can help integrate the large volume of implicit and unlabeled reviews into the recommendation model.

Reinforcement Learning [24], the model learns to make decisions by receiving rewards or penalties for certain actions. Some examples of reinforcement Learning models are Q-Learning, SARSA (State-Action-Reward-State-Action), and Monte Carlo (MC).

On the other hand, Deep learning is a subset of machine learning, called also Artificial Neural Network. Deep learning is often used for complex tasks and relies on neural networks comprising multiple layers of interconnected nodes, known as artificial neurons, for information processing and transmission. The performance of Deep Learning algorithms improves as both the volume of data and the number of layers in the neural network increase. Deep Learning-based methods excel in handling extensive and complex datasets They often outperform traditional methods in terms of accuracy. However, they may necessitate a substantial amount of data for model training, and they can be computationally intensive and challenging to interpret. Deep Learning-based methods can be viewed as an advancement or alternative to traditional techniques.

Deep learning models can be broadly categorized into two main categories: Generative models [12–17] and Discriminative models. Generative models aim to generate new data samples resembling the training data, while discriminative models are primarily used for supervised classification or regression tasks, focusing on making predictions related to class labels or categories. (See Fig. 1 for a visual classification of machine learning and Deep Learning models regarding recommendation systems).

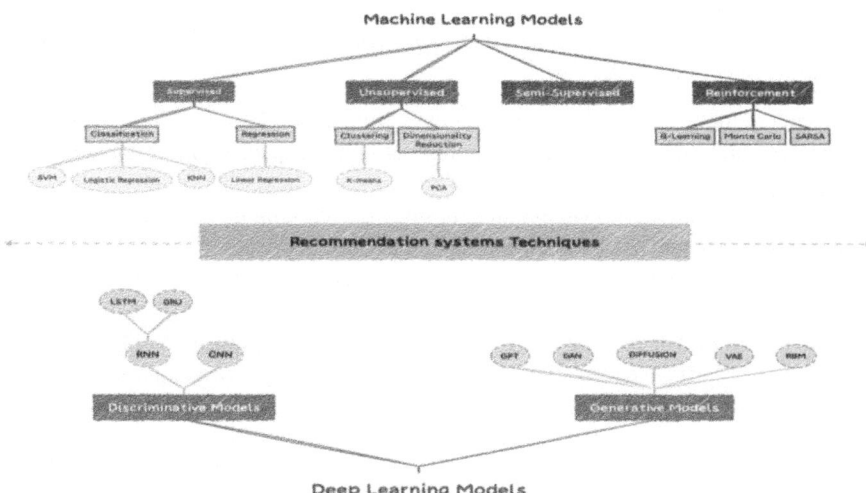

Fig. 1. Classification of machine learning and Deep Learning models regarding recommendation systems

Combining various models can allow to leverage the strengths of each, often leading to improved performance. For instance, using a combination of clustering and classification for customer segmentation. First, clustering is used to group similar customers together, and then a supervised learning model is trained to classify each cluster into specific segments. Another example involves integrating a Deep Learning model with recommendation systems by using generative models.

3 Recommendation Systems

Recommendation systems are techniques that use Machine Learning and/or Deep Learning models to perform the recommendation made. These recommendations encompass collaborative filtering, content-based, Popularity-based Recommendation, hybrid systems, and those relying on generative Deep Learning models.

In Collaborative Filtering (CF) [1, 2], the past behavior of users is collected, analyzed, and used to predict recommendations. The algorithm's basic principle here is that users with the same interests will have the same preferences and like the same items. Collaborative filtering can be classified into two categories: memory-based and model-based approaches.

In memory-based models, there are two types of approach: user-based and item-based.

- User based [1]: For example, if user 1 and user 2 have a similar behavioral history. Then, there is a high probability that they will be interested in the same products in the future. So later, when user 1 is interested in a product, that product will be recommended to user 2.
- Item based [1]: in this approach, a user will certainly like similar products to those he has already liked in the past.

In general, memory-based models are not complicated. There are intuitive and easy to implement, although they can become computationally expensive as the data set grows or is sparce.

In model-based models, mathematical or machine learning models are built in order to capture latent factors or patterns from the data. These models perform well cold start problem or when data is sparce. They include a variety of techniques, such as Bayesian models, clustering algorithm, and matrice factorization (MF) [4, 21]. Some common techniques used in MF includes SVD (Singular Value Decomposition) [4, 21], NMF (Non-negative Matrix Factorization) [28], ALS (Alternating Least Squares) [25] and SGD (Stochastic Gradient Descent) [26, 27].

Content-based (CB) [1, 3, 19] systems, less popular than CF, focus on the characteristics or attributes of the items, that a user had shown interest in them, in order to make recommendations for him. For example, if a user has already shown interest in a movie or a song, a content-based recommendation system could recommend videos of the same actor, genre, etc. Popularity-based Recommendation [30] makes recommendations based on the popularity of items, which is simple but can be effective in some cases.

Hybrid Systems [6, 10, 11] combine all the approaches above to make recommendations (Fig. 2).

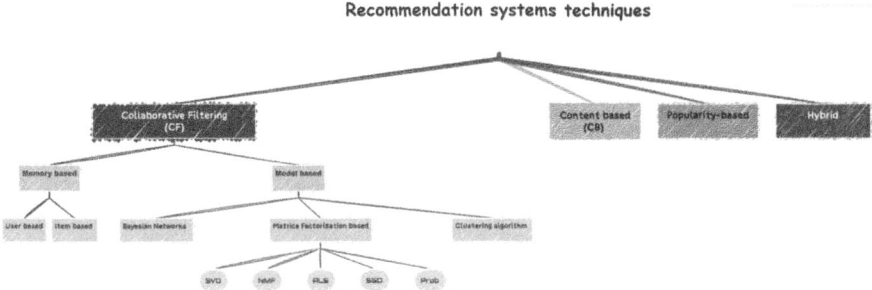

Fig. 2. Classification of recommendation systems techniques

To summarize, Collaborative filtering is good for handling a large number of users and items. While Content-based filtering is good for handling new users and items with no past interactions. Hybrid systems are good for taking advantage of the strengths of those different methods, overcoming the limitations of each method used individually. Nevertheless, they are more complex to implement and to evaluate than the individual methods. They require more data and computer resources, and the results can be difficult to interpret in many cases. According to Hyeyoung Koet et al. in [31], there has been a big interest in research on hybrid recommendation systems since 2014, which has resulted in an increase in the number of studies and research on this topic since this year.

In the upcoming section, we will focus on generative models for recommendation systems.

4 Generative Models for Recommendation Systems

In this case, Generative models can be used to generate new recommendations for users based on their past behavior by using complex Deep Learning algorithms. There are several types of generative models using Deep Learning. Table 1 below list Recent works using Generative models based on Deep Learning.

In the following section, we will focus on the models: VAE, GAN, and DIFFUSION.

VAE is a type of generative model that learns to generate new data by learning a compact representation of the input data in the form of a continuous latent variable. The VAE consists of two main neural network: an encoder and a decoder (see Fig. 4a).

The encoder is a neural network that takes the input data and maps it to a lower-dimensional, continuous latent space. The encoder learns to compress the input data into a compact representation by maximizing the likelihood of the input data given the latent variables. The decoder is another neural network that maps the latent variables to the original input space. The decoder learns to generate new samples by sampling from the latent space and then mapping them back to the input space. VAEs are trained to minimize the difference between the generated samples and the real samples. It can be used for tasks such as an image or speech generation, anomaly detection, and feature extraction. In [12], authors use a VAE model, upstream of other ML Algorithms (XGBoost, CatBoost and LightGBM), to recommend an optimal Nitrogen rate for rice growers. As data related to environmental and agricultural resources suffer usually from discrepancy and noise.

Table 1. Recent works using Generative models based on Deep Learning.

Generative models	Name of Generative models	Year
RBM	Restricted Boltzmann Machines	2006
VAE	Variational Autoencoder	2013
GAN	Generative Adversarial Network	2014
cGANs	Conditional GANs	2014
DIFFUSION	Diffusion	2015
AAE	Adversarial Autoencoder	2016
FBGM	Flow-based generative models	2016
DCGANs	Deep Convolutional GANs	2016
InfoGANs	InfoGANs	2016
Cycle GANs	Cycle GANs	2017
WGAN	Wasserstein GAN	2017
Transformer-based models	Transformer-based models	2017
GPT	Generative Pre-training Transformer	2018
StyleGAN	Style-Based Generator Architecture	2018
BigGAN	BigGAN	2019
GPT-3	GPT-3	2020
DALL-E	DALL-E	2021

Using VAE to reconstruct data, which means generate clean data, has allowed increasing of 4.32% yield compared to using normal data (without VAE).

It is based on a dataset of 4884 records that contains characteristics of soil and climatic data, remote sensing indices, and farming practices. That information is collected from extended surfaces cultivated intensively with rice for the last 5 years prior to the article (2017–2021). The Neural Network is composed of 1024 nodes, and a 128-dimension hidden representation was obtained for the encoder. Here, some variants and extensions of VAE: Conditional VAE (CVAE), Adversarial Autoencoder (AAE), Wasserstein VAE, VQ-VAE, and Flow-based VAE model.

GAN consists of two neural networks: a generator and a discriminator (see Fig. 4b). The generator creates new data samples, and the discriminator attempts to distinguish between the generated samples and the real samples from the training dataset. The two networks are trained together in an adversarial way.

GAN is used to generate realistic things that have never existed as images, video, text, and music,…. It can be used to generate synthetic data to train the recommendation model with more data, and then be more performant. One example in the medical field is about generating 3D synthetic lung [13]. It is used to solve the problem of lack of healthy lungs, to better train the model and so have good results, by using a 3D Progressive Growing GAN, named PGGAN, capable of generating unreal healthy lungs with good resolution.

In the fashion field [14], the authors proposed a multimodal transformer-based GAN with cross-modal attention. It explores simultaneously visual features and textual attributes. This model applied in fashion recommendation allows to generate a complete set of outfits and decides the number of items in the set. This model does not consider audio features, which could be a possible improvement to have better performance.

GAN can generate top-N recommendation with implicit feedback of users. It's the case in social media platforms [17]. In this article, the authors used Matrix factorization, which is a technique used in recommendation systems by capturing latent factors. In social media platforms [17], authors built a model, named GANMF, that generate top-N recommendation with implicit feedback of users.

In this model, the latent factors are learned through a two-part process involving a discriminator and a generator. On one hand, the discriminator is trained to minimize a hinge loss function, this loss function encourages the discriminator to minimize the reconstruction error for real profiles and maximize it for generated profiles. On the other hand, the generator, based on matrix factorization (MF), is trained to minimize the reconstruction error of the discriminator on generated profiles.

To stabilize the training process and ensure that the generator produces user-specific profiles, an additional loss term called "feature matching" is introduced. Feature matching encourages the generated profiles to match the statistics of real profiles in the latent space induced by the encoder of the discriminator. This loss is added to the generator loss. Unlike SVD [4, 21, 31] and NMF [21] (other techniques used to capture latent factors), which have predefined constraints and assumptions, GANMF enables the incorporation of additional components like adversarial training, feature matching, regularization and conditioning attributes.

There are many variants and extensions of GANs that have been proposed recently, including Conditional GANs, Deep Convolutional GANs, Wasserstein GANs, Info-GANs, Cycle GANs, and each of these algorithms has their strengths and weaknesses. Their use will depend on the problem and the types of input data (Fig. 3).

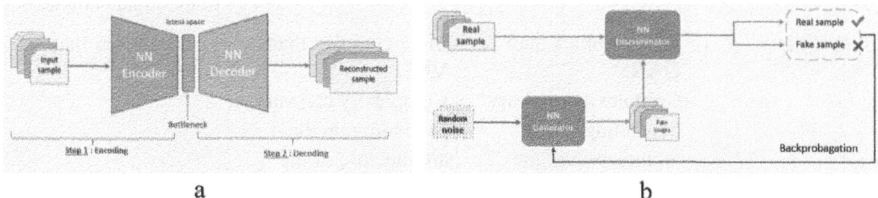

a   b

Fig. 3. Architecture of VAE (a), and GAN (b) models

DIFFUSION [15, 16] model's purpose is to generate data similar to the data on which they are trained, by adding gaussian noise to image until having only noise. And then learning to recover the data by reversing this noising process. DIFFUSIONs are used in tasks like image-to-image translation, image synthesis, anomaly detection, Video Generation, ... The model is composed of 2 steps: Forward Diffusion process, and Backward/Reverse diffusion process.

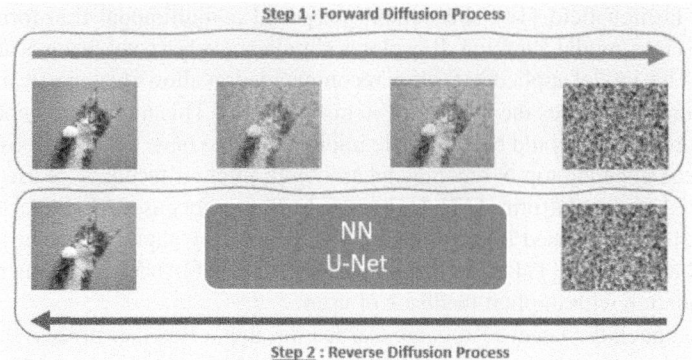

Fig. 4. Architecture of DIFFUSION model

As opposed to GANs, for which two models are required for learning, DIFFUSION only require one model. Also, Unlike GANs for which, the generator model has noise as input noise, DIFFUSION's models use image as input. And this is one of the sources of the unstable training of GAN compared to DIFFUSION. Below is a comparative study of the generative models presented above, based on components, complexity, training process, nature of input data, data generation, requirements, and cost (Table 2).

Table 2. Comparative study of generative models VAE, GAN, and DIFFUSION

Criteria / Model	VAE	GAN	DIFFUSION
Components	Two neural networks: an encoder and a decoder	Two neural networks: a generator and a discriminator	One neural network (U-net) with a preceding process of adding Gaussian noise to the input samples
Complexity	Less complex than GAN Complexity can vary depending on the architecture of the encoder and decoder networks	More complex than VAE Complexity can vary depending on the architecture of the generator and discriminator	Less complex than GAN
Nature of input data	Any kind of data (images, video, audio, text, etc.)	Any kind of data (images, video, audio, text, etc.)	Any kind of data (images, video, audio, text, etc.)

(continued)

Table 2. (*continued*)

Criteria / Model	VAE	GAN	DIFFUSION
Training process	consists of two steps: the first step is to train the encoder to map the data to the latent space, and the second step is to train the decoder to generate the data from the latent space	consist of two steps: the first step is to train the generator to generate new samples, and the second step is to train the discriminator to distinguish the generated samples from the real ones	Consist of two steps: Step 1: Forward Diffusion Process → add noise to the image until having only noise Step2: Reverse Diffusion Process → remove noise from the image until producing high-quality synthetic data
Data generation	used to generate new images, texts, or other types of data, but it generates data that is similar to the training data	GANs are capable of generating data that is very realistic and can be used to generate new data that is not similar to the training data	Diffusion models generate more realistic images than GANs
Requirement	Require smaller number of parameters and less training data than other generative models	Require a larger number of parameters and more training data to generate new data samples	Require smaller number of data
Cost	Relatively cost-efficient → Can be done on a standard personal computer or a GPU	More computationally expensive than VAE → Require a more powerful GPU than VAE	

Below, Strengths vs Weaknesses of the generative models presented above (Table 3).

Table 3. Strengths vs Weaknesses of generative models VAE, GAN, and DIFFUSION

Criteria / Model	VAE	GAN	DIFFUSION
Strengths	- Easier to train than GAN - Can be used for unsupervised learning, as they can learn to generate data without the need for labeled examples	- Can generate high-quality, realistic-looking images, videos, and audio - Can be used for unsupervised learning, as they can learn to generate data without the need for labeled examples	- not requiring adversarial training - need small number of training examples - benefits of scalability and parallelizability - Better then GANs on Image Synthesis

(*continued*)

Table 3. (*continued*)

Criteria / Model	VAE	GAN	DIFFUSION
Weaknesses	- May not generate images that are as realistic as those generated by GANs - Black-box model: difficult to understand how decisions are done, which can make it hard to debug or improve the model - Sensitive to the quality of the training data which may result in poor performance if the data is not cleaned properly	- Can be Difficult to train and require a lot of computational power, to find the right hyperparameters and architecture to produce good results - Can suffer from mode collapse, where generated samples are very similar or even identical - Black-box model: difficult to understand how decisions are done, which can make it hard to debug or improve the model - High computational cost - Require a large amount of data to produce good results, which can be a limitation in some cases - Sensitive to the noise in the data (quality of the training data) which may result in poor performance if the data is not cleaned properly	- Slow generation process: Diffusion models rely on a long Markov chain of diffusion steps to generate samples, so it can be quite expensive in terms of time and compute. New methods have been proposed to make the process much faster, but the sampling is still slower than GAN

5 Conclusion

Generative models have been around since the early years of machine learning and artificial intelligence. But their growth has multiplied since the progress that Deep Learning models have achieved. Much recent research has combined Deep Learning and generative models to develop new architectures and techniques. These models have shown promising results in improving the performance of recommendation systems and providing more personalized recommendations.

In this paper, we introduced traditional types of Machine Learning models vs Deep Learning models and their application in recommendation systems. We conducted a qualitative comparison of three generative Deep Learning models, the most used in recommendation systems recently i.e., Variational Autoencoder (VAE), Generative Adversarial Network (GAN), and DIFFUSION. We discussed their strengths and weaknesses.

In future work, we will implement those models in order to make a quantitative comparison study. This will help to assess their performance under specific conditions, datasets, and goals.

References

1. Hameed, M.A., et al.: Collaborative Filtering Based Recommendation System: A survey. Int. J. Comp. Sci. Eng. **4**(5) (2012)
2. Jing, H.: Application of Improved K-Means Algorithm in Collaborative Recommendation System. J. Appl. Math. Article ID 2213173 (2022). https://doi.org/10.1155/2022/2213173
3. Javed, U., et al.: A review of content-based and context-based recommendation systems. Int. J. Emerg. Technol. Learn. (iJET) **16**(3), 274–306 (2021). Kassel, Germany: International Journal of Emerging Technology in Learning. Retrieved August 24, 2023 from https://www.learntechlib.org/p/219036/
4. Liu, N., Zhao, J.: Recommendation system based on deep sentiment analysis and matrix factorization. IEEE Access **11**, 16994–17001 (2023). https://doi.org/10.1109/ACCESS.2023.3246060
5. Varoquaux, G., Cheplygina, V.: Machine learning for medical imaging: methodological failures and recommendations for the future. npj Digital Medicine **5**, 48 (2022)
6. Forouzandeh, S., Rostamib, M., Berahmand, K.: A Hybrid Method for Recommendation Systems based on Tourism with an Evolutionary Algorithm and Topsis Model, 26–50 (2022). https://doi.org/10.1080/16168658.2021.2019430
7. Samani, N., Aliyari, S., Jelokhani, M.: Developing a group urban tourism recommendation system based on the modied k-means algorithm and fuzzy bestworst method. Researchsquare (2023). https://doi.org/10.21203/rs.3.rs-2500314/v1
8. Ali, S., et al.: Enabling recommendation system architecture in virtualized environment for elearning. Sciencedirect **23**(1), 33–45 (2022). https://doi.org/10.1016/j.eij.2021.05.003
9. Dahdouh, K., Dakkak, A., Oughdir, L., Ibriz, A.: Large-scale elearning recommender system based on Spark and Hadoop. Journal of Big Data **6**(2) (2019). https://doi.org/10.1186/s40537-019-0169-4
10. Oumayma, B., Said, R.: Enriching SPARQL queries by user preferences for results adaptation. Int. J. Software Eng. Knowl. Eng. **28**(8), 1195–1221 (2018)
11. Oumayma, O., Oumayma, B., Salah, E., Said, R.: Intelligent recommender system based on quantum clustering and matrix completion. Concurrency and Computation Practice and Experience **34**(3) (2022). https://doi.org/10.1002/cpe.6943
12. Iatrou, M., Karydas, C., Tseni, X., Mourelatos, S.: Representation learning with a variational autoencoder for predicting nitrogen requirement in rice. Remote Sensing **14**(23) (2022). https://doi.org/10.3390/rs14235978
13. Artur, F., et al.: Synthesizing 3D Lung CT scans with Generative Adversarial Networks. Proceedings of Annu Int. Conf. IEEE Eng. Med. Biol. Soc., pp. 2033–2036 (2022). https://doi.org/10.1109/EMBC48229.2022.9871481
14. Valery, V., Klavdiya, B.: Content-aware generative model for multi-item outfit Recommendation, Content-Aware Generative Model for Multi-item Outfit Recommendation. In: Groen, D., de Mulatier, C., Paszynski, M., Krzhizhanovskaya, V.V., Dongarra, J.J., Sloot, P.M.A. (eds.) Computational Science – ICCS 2022. ICCS 2022. Lecture Notes in Computer Science, vol 13350. Springer, Cham (2022). https://doi.org/10.1007/978303108751612
15. Croitoru, F.-A., et al.: Diffusion models in vision: a survey. IEEE Transactions on Pattern Analysis and Machine Intelligence **45**, 10850–10869 (2022)
16. Yang, L., et al.: Diffusion Models: A Comprehensive Survey of Methods and Applications. **1**(1), 49 (2022). https://doi.org/10.48550/arXiv.2209.00796
17. Dervishaj, E., Cremonesi, P.: GAN-based matrix factorization for recommender systems. SAC '22: Proceedings of the 37th ACM/SIGAPP Symposium on Applied Computing, pp. 1373–1381 (2022). https://doi.org/10.1145/3477314.3507099

18. Ahuja, R., Solanki, A., Nayyar, A.: Movie Recommender System Using K-Means Clustering AND K-Nearest Neighbor. 9th International Conference on Cloud Computing, Data Science Engineering (Confluence), pp. 263–268. Noida, India (2019). https://doi.org/10.1109/CONFLUENCE.2019.8776969

19. Airen, S., Agrawal, J.: Movie recommender system using K-nearest neighbors variants. Nation. Acad. Sci. Lett. **45**, 75–82 (2022). https://doi.org/10.1007/s40009-021-01051-0

20. Bandyopadhyay, S., Thakur, S.S., Mandal, J.K.: Product recommendation for e-commerce business by applying principal component analysis (PCA) and K-means clustering: benefit for the society. Innovations Syst. Softw. Eng. **17**, 45–52 (2021)

21. Rahman, S.: Extended Collaborative Filtering Recommendation System with Adaptive KNN and SVD (2023). https://doi.org/10.31033/ijemr.13.4.14

22. Vozalis, M.G., Margaritis, K.G.: A Recommender System using Principal Component Analysis. Published in 11th Panhellenic Conference in Informatics, pp. 271–283. Patras, Greece (2007)

23. Matuszyk, P., Spiliopoulou, M.: Stream-based semi-supervised learning for recommender systems. Mach. Learn. **106**, 771–798 (2017). https://doi.org/10.1007/s10994-016-5614-4

24. Mehdi Afsar, M., Crump, T., Far, B.: Reinforcement Learning based Recommender Systems: A Survey, arxiv.org, Version, v2 (2022). https://doi.org/10.48550/arXiv.2101.06286

25. Adyatma, H.A.: Book Recommender System Using Matrix Factorization with Alternating Least Square Method (2023). https://doi.org/10.47065/josh.v4i4.3816

26. Abubaker, N., Caglayan, O., Karsavuran, M.O., Aykanat, C.: Minimizing staleness and communication overhead in distributed SGD for collaborative filtering. In: IEEE Transactions on Computers. https://doi.org/10.1109/TC.2023.3275107

27. Qin, W., Wu, H., Lai, Q., Wang, C.: A parallelized, momentum-incorporated stochastic gradient descent scheme for latent factor analysis on high-dimensional and sparse matrices from recommender systems. In: 2019 IEEE International Conference on Systems, Man and Cybernetics (SMC), pp. 1744–1749. Bari, Italy (2019). https://doi.org/10.1109/SMC.2019.8914671

28. Cremonesi, P., Koren, Y., Turrin, R.: Performance of recommender algorithms on top-n recommendation tasks. In: Proceedings of the fourth ACM conference on Recommender systems, pp. 39–46 (2010)

29. Al-Nafjan, A., Alrashoudi, N., Alrasheed, H.: Recommendation System Algorithms on Location-Based Social Networks: Comparative Study (2022). https://doi.org/10.3390/info13040188

30. Bressan, M., Leucci, S., Panconesi, A., Raghavan, P., Terolli, E.: The Limits of Popularity-Based Recommendations, and the Role of Social Ties (2016). https://doi.org/10.1145/2939672.2939797

31. Ko, H., Lee, S., Park, Y., Choi, A.: A Survey of Recommendation Systems: Recommendation Models, Techniques, and Application Fields, Electronics **11**(1) (2022). https://doi.org/10.3390/electronics11010141

Physiological Indicators Estimation Through Photoplethysmography Wave Analysis Using Serial-EMD and Fast PCA Methods

Zakaria El Khadiri[1]([✉]), Rachid Latif[1], and Amine Saddik[1,2]

[1] Laboratory of Systems Engineering and Information Technology LiSTi, National School of Applied Sciences, Ibn Zohr University, Agadir, Morocco
zakaria.elkhadiri@edu.uiz.ac.ma
[2] Faculty of Applied Sciences, Ibn Zohr University, Ait Melloul, Morocco

Abstract. An RGB camera or webcam can be used to accurately estimate the physiological features of the biomedical symptomatic issue from the signals received. In this regard, our current work proposes a method based on the most well-known image and multi-dimensional signal processing algorithms to estimate the pulse and breathing rates from facial skin by photoplethysmography wave examination. The current study uses signal processing and image processing techniques to eliminate noise that can be caused by head movements, poor signal strength, changes in lighting, or acquisition devices. To collect the most PPG data feasible, we will base our image processing on the three distinct color spaces: RGB band, Luv band, and Lab band on the one hand, and skin detection on the other. Afterward, the signal processing part combines two well-known methods: fast-PCA, a distributed PCA algorithm, and serial-EMD, a method for multi-dimensional signal decomposition. The latter method can achieve higher accuracy and a decomposition time that is more reduced compared with the existing methods. Our results of the extracted PPG waves and the IMF modes signals are depicted further in the result section.

Keywords: Photoplethysmography · Serial-EMD · Fast PCA · Physiological signs · Non-contact

1 Introduction

1.1 Motivation

Remote vital measurement is very useful for biomedical diagnostics and monitoring, whereas it conducts a crucial duty of cardiovascular health by prior predicting the malady linked to cardiovascular disease and instantaneously surveilling

Supported by organization Laboratory of Systems Engineering and Information Technology LiSTi.

H. Hagras et al. (Eds.): ISACS 2023, CCIS 2255, pp. 385–398, 2025.
https://doi.org/10.1007/978-3-031-93448-3_31

the chronic disorder circumstances [1, 2]. Besides, through physiological waves such as photoplethysmography and ballistocardiography concepts, several physiological parameters, including heart rate, respiratory rate, blood pressure, arterial oxygen saturation, and others, could be accurately estimated in order to provide sufficient information related to the cardiovascular mechanism [3–11], based on the latter vital sign components, the physiological and pathological conditions of a human being can be predicted. Minutely, the heart organ is among the most important parts of the physical body because it allows blood to flow out of the body by beating roughly between 60 and 100 beats per minute [12]. Contrarily, it can be treated as an abnormality whether it is below 60 bpm (termed bradycardia) or above 100 bpm (termed tachycardia) [13], the latter alteration depends on several factors that can influence physiological parameters, including age, air temperature, body position, emotions, and so forth.

Simple digital filtering techniques have been used to estimate the respiratory and cardiac rates using the PPG data [14, 15]. However, the performance is very reliant on the filter's cutoff frequency. Nevertheless, it was chosen empirically. Despite the fact that there are analytical techniques, these techniques are particularly susceptible to the nature of the noise. Therefore, if a motion artifact taints the PPG signal, the outcome is subpar. The wavelet transform method [16], and other estimating techniques based on time frequency analysis approach [17], were presented as solutions to this problem. The empirical mode decomposition was recently put out as a flexible technique for processing both nonstationary and nonlinear signals. As the sum of their intrinsic mode functions and residues, many signals in practice can be described. The center frequencies of these components are located in the frequency bands, and their indices are used to order the center frequencies. Due to this advantageous trait, a number of empirical mode decomposition-based techniques [18, 19], were created to breakdown the PPG signals and estimate the respiratory and cardiac rates. In 2021, we will develop a straightforward and original signal serialization method that will allow us to combine multivariate or multidimensional signals into a one-dimensional signal. This opens the door for using one-dimensional empirical mode decomposition (EMD) methods for multi-signal decomposition. Most advantageously, this concatenation method can reduce computation time without changing the current EMD algorithms. Additionally, it can offer a fresh approach to improving existing EMD algorithms by changing the structure of input signals rather than creating new envelope identification methods or new multi-EMD algorithms. The rapid serial-EMD method that has been described can therefore be a good substitute because it offers effective signal analysis and mode decomposition.

1.2   Our Contribution

The current work's primary goal is to suggest a reliable method for estimating vital signs with low-cost RGB cameras using modern signal processing and decomposition methods while taking into account the significant amount of input data. In detail, the suggested methodology is based on a number of bands extracted from facial skin, including the RGB, Luv, and Lab bands. The latter color spaces have an important rule to gather the most PPG data from facial skin imaging, and the latter conversion will be combined with a skin detection function to prevent the unwanted areas generated by the user's environment from being included in face frames. An additional conversion from the RGB band to the HSV and YCbCr color spaces will be carried out in order to accomplish skin detection.

The first basic PPG signal will then be extracted by calculating the average of the frame's pixels, and this signal will serve as the input to the signal processing phase. On the other hand, the signal processing component took up the largest portion of the entire proposed approach; in fact, after extracting the first noisy PPG signal, a signal decomposition method needs to be applied to all 7 PPG signals (which are according to R, G, B, u, v, a, and b bands); for this purpose, we will base our approach on the serial-EMD approach, which is proposed in 2021 for the signal-serialization method. Then, using a decomposed multi-dimension signal, the Fast-PCA will be used to reduce the signal's dimensionality and identify the signal that is most prominent. We may then estimate the heart rate and respiratory rate based on the latter one-dimensional signal by applying the Fourier transform method to convert the final PPG signal from time domain to frequency domain.

1.3 Organization

The remainder of this work is organized as follows: Sect. 2 illustrates some related works. Section 3 depicts the prominent methods used in the present paper and the corresponding proposed approach for physiological indicators extraction. Section 4 provides the experiments conducted. Section 5 provides the conclusion, followed by a discussion and future directions in Section 6.

2 Related Works

Traditionally, a contact sensor has been employed to monitor the most physiological signs, such as the respiratory rate, heart rate variability (HRV), arterial blood oxygen saturation, body temperature, and blood pressure [20,21]. [22], placed on human skin. However, several studies have demonstrated that the latter functions can be simply estimated from remote video recordings of patients in ambient light. For instance, an approach that was put forth in 2014 by Xiaoib et al. [23], served to lessen the environmental illumination artifacts from RGB color space signals. The latter study's main foundation was the normalized least square (NLMS) adaptive filter, and the authors were successful in getting good agreement and correlation between the reference sensor and the suggested approaches. In the same year, Guo et al. [24], used the independent vector analysis (IVA) method to extract HR from a driver's facial video without taking into account the lighting artifacts. In 2015, the author [25], also uses a multiset canonical

correlation analysis (MCCA) method to extract the same physiological parameters, such as HR and HRV, from drivers' facial videos. By taking into account
motion artifacts, this method produced results that were higher performing and
superior to the ICA, Independent Components Analysis.

Recently, in 2020, R. Lei et al. [26], put forth a framework for estimating
the physiological parameters from the photoplethysmography (PPG) signal that
combines the complementary ensemble empirical mode decomposition technique
with both independent component analysis and non-negative matrix factorization. With improved accuracy and reliability for estimating physiological markers, the authors' important conclusion outperforms both the digital filtering
approach and the traditional empirical mode decomposition-based methods. In
the same year, according to H. Sharma [27], a straightforward method based on
the ensemble empirical mode decomposition (EEMD) and Kalman filter coupling
may accurately estimate the respiratory rate (RR) from a photoplethysmogram
(PPG). The authors used CapnoBase and MIMIC, two separate datasets, and
they were able to estimate with less inaccuracy.

The BCG concept, however, which stands for ballistocardiography, is utilized
to gauge and extract the respiratory and heart rates from a person's face. Indeed,
after being found in the 19th century, it attracted researchers' attention from
the 1940s until the 1980s. While the cardiac ejection of blood causes a stiff
motion across the entire body. The physiological signals received through BCG
are therefore more closely tied to characterizing the blood flow within the heart,
inside the arteries (mostly the aorta), and the movement of the heart itself. In
2016, Haque et al. [28], developed a method for estimating heart rate based
on BCG by merging the corner feature points of useful characteristics [29], the
drawbacks of [30], involving loss of features owing to movement or occlusion of
the face were overcome by the authors using the feature fusion-based approach.
Using the KLT tracking technique, the feature points were tracked, and the
vertical components of the trajectories were recovered as raw BCGtraces. Using
an eight order Butterworth band-pass filter with operating frequencies ranging
from 0.75 Hz to 5 Hz, the authors significantly improved the raw traces.

3   Proposed Methodology

3.1   Methods

Empirical Mode Decomposition. The standard EMD [31], is a technique
used for a non-linear and non-stationary signal unidimensional decomposition
into several constituent signal components termed Intrinsic Mode Functions
(IMFs), by which, this decomposition is founded on amplitude and frequency-
modulated linear fusion functions, together with the IMFs functions, this method
generates moreover a residue signal which can be expressed in the following equation:

$$x(t) = \sum_{i-1}^{N} IMF_i(t) + r(t) \tag{1}$$

On a mathematical part, the standard one-dimensional EMD method can be depicted as follows:

1. Find the local minima and maxima of the original signal x(t).
2. Obtain the lower and upper signal envelope by interpolating between local minima and maxima (env)min(t) and (env)max(t).
3. Compute the local mean m(t) = ((env)max(t) + (env)min(t))/2.
4. Compute the IMF candidate y(t) = x(t) − m(t).
5. If the y(t) fulfills the below stopping criterion, then (IMF)i = y(t), otherwise, consider the x(t) = y(t), and repeat all steps starting from 1.

The stopping criterion can be defined as follows:

a. The number of zero crossings and extrema points should be the same or different by at least one.
b. The average envelope should be zero at all points.

Serial Empirical Mode Decomposition. Over the past decade, the amount of data has increased gradually in the physics and engineering fields, which require significant requirements for real-time signal treatment and data speed examination. The latter limitations are considered the biggest obstacles for the EMD's variants. Thus, in order to trade off the growth of data dimension along with respecting the real time constraints in a faster speed manner, J. Zhang et al. [32] have proposed a novel signal-serialization approach termed Serial-EMD, which is mainly based on the multi-dimensional signals concatenation into a one-dimensional signal and uses various one-dimensional EMD algorithms to decompose it. This method has significantly overpassed the existing multi-EMD methods in terms of the quality of IMFs and is highly considered as the fast alternative for multi-dimensional signal analysis with a dramatically reduced processing time. The multi-dimensional signal can be thought of as being made up of many vectors (one-dimensional signals). The multi-dimensional signal can then be serialized by utilizing a transition that is calculated using a portion of the data from each dimension. After that, the conventional one-dimensional EMD or one of its variants is used to decompose the serialized one-dimensional signal, and the IMFs for the serialized signal are determined. The IMFs of the original multi-signals are then recovered from the IMFs of the serialized signal by reshaping and slicing after the redundant transitions have been removed. Typically, the serial-EMD is based mainly on three blocks as below:

1. Generate the serialized signal by making a serial signal concatenation by inserting a transition signal, the concatenated signal maintains the continuity and characteristics of the original signals.
2. Generate the intrinsic modes functions of the serialized signal using the EMD or its variants.
3. The fast IMFs de-concatenation algorithm and transition removal in order to conclude the IMFs for original multidimensional signals.

The following Fig. 1 illustrates the lain blocks used for the Serial-EMD:

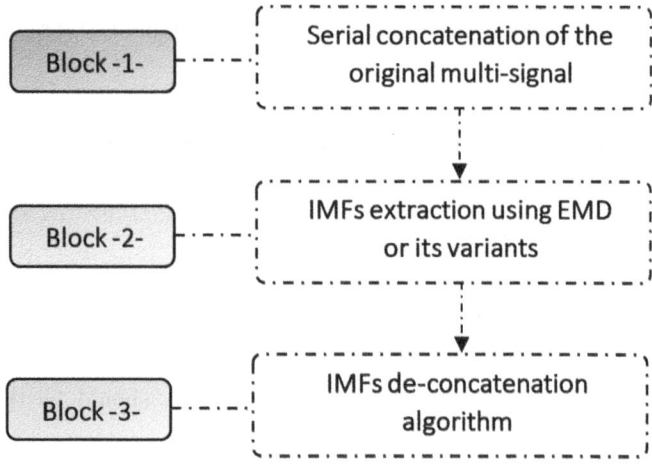

Fig. 1. Main blocks of Serial-EMD method

Fast Principal Components Analysis. Massive dimensional datasets are starting to act as a barrier to the widespread use of a number of current techniques. Principal Components Analysis (PCA), which is frequently simplified to dimension reduction for this purpose, actually has two goals: feature learning and dimension reduction. Since it is based on a few mathematical ideas like Eigenvalues, Eigen-factors, Variance, and Covariance, it is in fact frequently used for evaluating big datasets with a lot of dimensions or specific attributes [33]. On the other hand, Fast-PCA is much faster than PCA implementation for high-dimensional data, especially when implemented in Python [34]. The latter optimization in treatment time is described on how to compute the PC from the "small" sample-sample covariance matrix rather than the larger feature-feature covariance matrix, PCs from both covariance matrices can be converted into each other.

3.2   Proposed Approach

Our suggested vital signs extraction, as previously indicated, is primarily based on two significant components that are extensively used by the image and signal processing community. The first function is devoted to transforming each frame from an RGB band to Lu*v* and Lab through the CIE XYZ space after gathering human face frames. The HSV and YCrCb areas are used for the second purpose, which is skin detection. Then, the previous block will produce the raw PPG signal using the average of each frame; according to Equation. 2 below, the brute PPG signal was subjected to an amplitude normalization operation, where n is the PPG signal's sample number:

$$Normalized_{PPG_{Signal}} = \frac{PPG(n)}{max(|PPG(n)|)} \qquad (2)$$

The normalized signal will next be used for signal decomposition using the modern technique known as serial-EMD. This technique will produce a number of intrinsic mode functions, or IMFs, which will serve as the foundation for the subsequent operation. After that, we will use the fats-PCA method to decompose the mixed PPG signal into its constituent sub-signals. At the conclusion, the Fast Fourier Transform is used to convert from the time domain to the frequency domain in order to extract the appropriate index for the purposes of HR and RR calculations. The stacking blocks of the complete strategy are shown in more detail in Fig. 2 below:

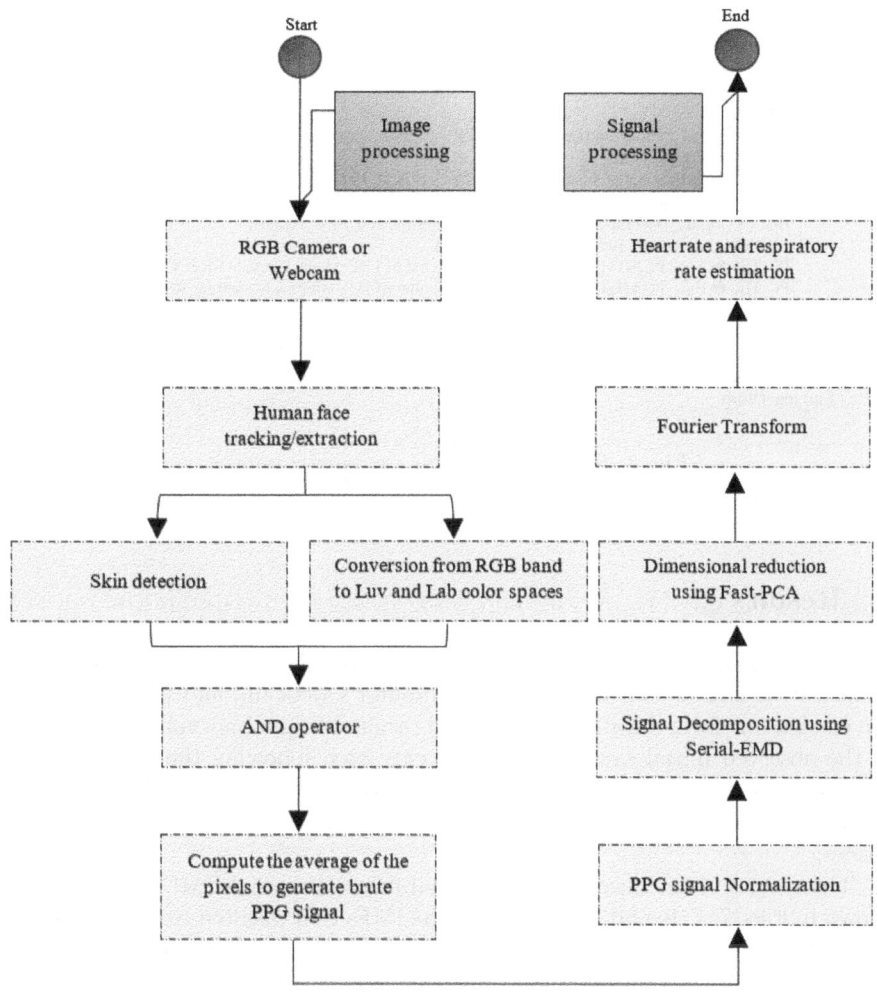

Fig. 2. Proposed Algorithm for heart rate and respiratory rate estimation

In addition, the following pseudo-code (Fig. 3) illustrates the suggested strategy:

```
Proposed approach
Start algorithm
    //// Tracking and detection human faces using CascadeClassifier
    RGB_frames = cv2.CascadeClassifier("haarcascade.xml")
    Function Main_function(Input : RGB_frames, Output : HR_RR_values)
      Function Image_Processing(Input : RGB_frames, Output : Brut_PPG_signal)
        Luv_frame ← FromRGB2Lub(RGB_frames);
        Lab_frame ← FromRGB2Lab(RGB_frames);
        //// Skin detection function
        YCrCb_frame ← cvtColor(RGB_frames, cv2.COLOR_BGR2YCrCb);
        HSV_frame ← cvtColor(RGB_frames, cv2.COLOR_BGR2HSV);
        //// Skin area can be extracted based on YCrCb_frame and HSV_frame and the thresholds
        //// Extracting the brute PPG signal
        Brut_PPG_signal ← ANDoperationWithAverage(frame, skin):
      END function
      Function Signal_Processing(Input : Brut_PPG_signal, Output : HR_RR_values)
        //// Signal normalization
        Normalized_PPG_signal ← signal_Normalization(Brut_PPG_signal);
        //// Signal decomposition using Serial-EMD
        IMFs ← signal_Decomposition_Serial_EMD(Normalized_PPG_signal);
        //// Multi-dimensional reduction using fast-PCA
        PC_HR ← Fast_PCA(IMFs[:,n,:]); //n : the number of IMF which adequate for HR information.
        PC_HR ← Fast_PCA(IMFs[:,m,:]); //m : the number of IMF which adequate for RR information.
        //// The HR and RR can be estimated based on the spectral power dominance
        //// of the modes using Fourier Transform
      END function
    END function
End algorithm
```

Fig. 3. Pseudo-code of the proposed approach

4   Results

Our physiological sign monitoring system is primarily tested on several experimental PPG signals extracted from a computer's webcam, and the simulations are carried out for a duration of 30 s. The results of signal normalization on one of the observed initial raw PPG signals, extracted following the normalization process carried out in accordance with Equation (2) in the time domain, are presented in the following Figs. 4, 5, and 6 with the RGB, Lab, and Lu*v* color spaces:

The results of the decomposition signal using the serial-EMD technique are shown in Figs. 7, 8, 9, and 10. These are the IMFs that resulted from the normalized PPG signal outlined in the above figures. From our side, we have depicted only the intrinsic mode functions that can provide respiration and heart rate information. Indeed, the IMF's choice comes after transforming the signal modes from time domain to frequency domain using the Fast Fourier transform; the

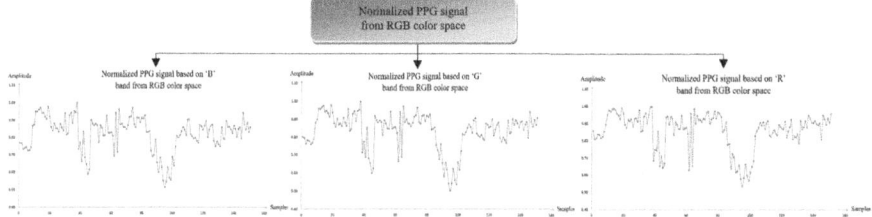

Fig. 4. Normalized PPG signal from RGB color space

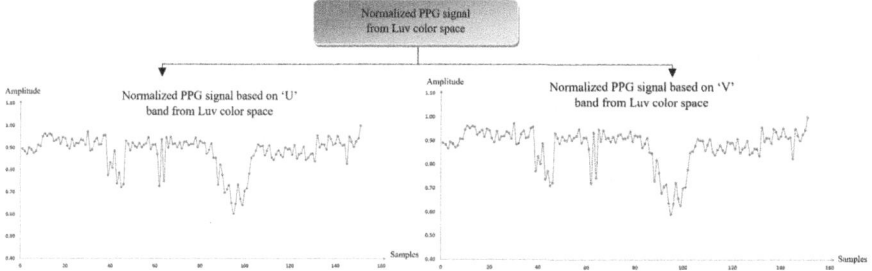

Fig. 5. Normalized PPG signal from Luv color space

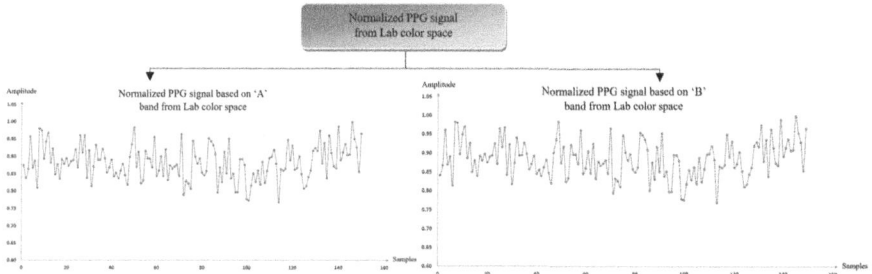

Fig. 6. Normalized PPG signal from Lab color space

results of the latter technique in each mode illustrated differences in the power spectral at different frequency intervals and ranges. Typically, from our side, an IMF candidate that can provide respiratory rate information, i.e., IMF-7, has a breathing frequency feature, while IMF-5 has a heart frequency characteristic. From the implementation side, our system was wholly implemented and programmed using the Python programming language, and our simulation process was carried out on a Python tool through several PPG signals extracted from the real data (Figs. 9 and 10).

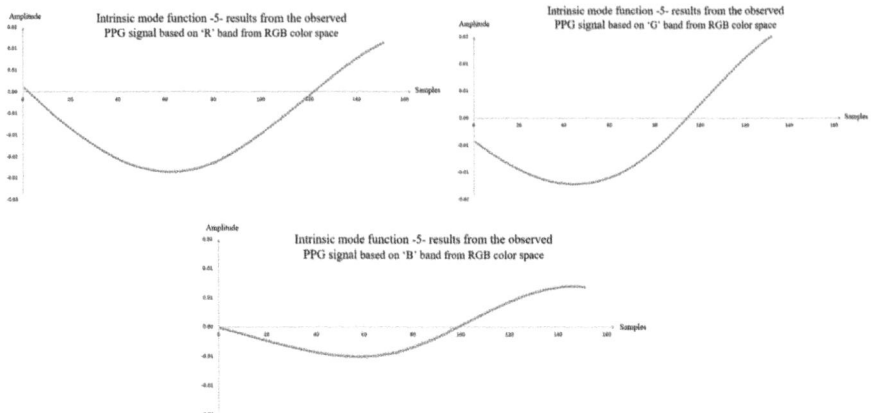

Fig. 7. Intrinsic mode function -5- results from the observed PPG signal based on RGB color space

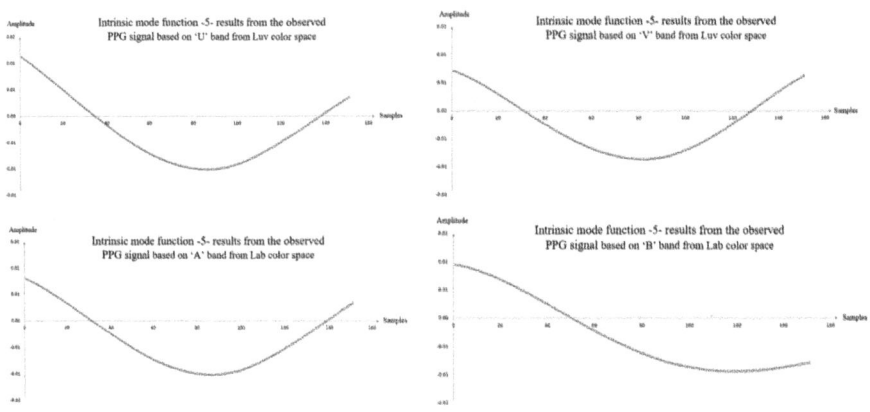

Fig. 8. Intrinsic mode function -5- results from the observed PPG signal based on Luv and Lab color spaces

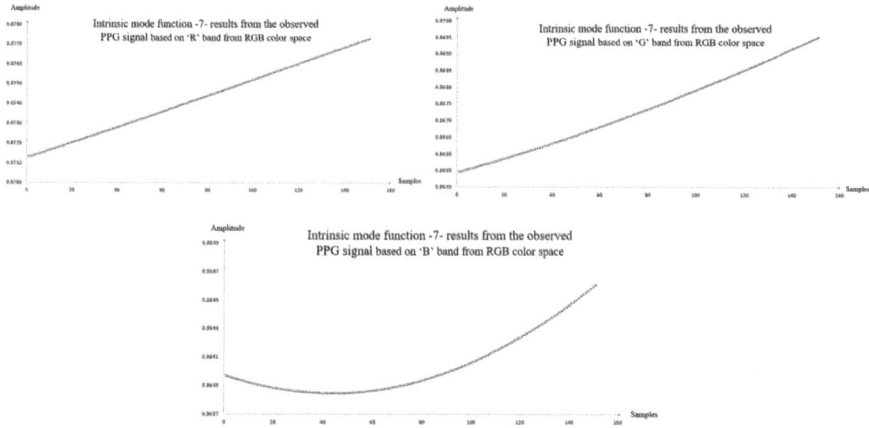

Fig. 9. Intrinsic mode function -7- results from the observed PPG signal based on RGB color space

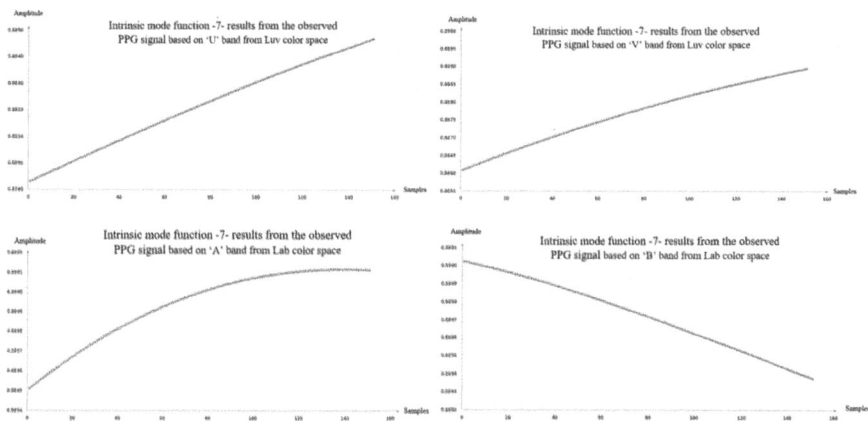

Fig. 10. Intrinsic mode function -7- results from the observed PPG signal based on Luv and Lab color spaces

5   Conclusion

The current proposed method is in fact based on several image and signal processing algorithms to gather the necessary PPG data elements and eliminate the unwanted noise generated by many factors linked to users' movements and artifacts in the environment. The latter approach is primarily based on the serial-EMD methodology, which has superior performance in many areas. This study describes a comprehensive approach to determining physiological indicators, particularly the heart rate and respiratory rate. The Python programming language was used to run the current simulation. By the time this study is finished, the techniques that were employed could be used to establish additional critical metrics, including heart rate (HR), arterial blood oxygen saturation, and HRV, among others. In order to enhance the quality of the face's frame and lessen the unexpected noises from the first PPG noisy signal, further picture pre-processing algorithms and signal filtering can be applied to the proposed system.

6   Discussion

We built the current study's physiological parameter extraction strategy on recently developed methods that are often employed in the signal processing field. From our perspective, the first stage of our system is mostly based on the serial-EMD method, which was presented to decompose the multi-dimensional signal in order to lessen the computing load during the multi-variate sifting process. The authors of serial-EMD have demonstrated experimental results for both real and synthetic signals regarding the quality of IMFs and the computational load that is quite proportional to the signal decomposition algorithm itself (EMD's variants). They have also demonstrated that the serial-EMD method has higher accuracy and better performance than GiT-BEMD at separating noise from the synthetic images, as well as a significant reduction in computational load that allows it to be used on real-time systems. However, to produce a better decomposition performance, the transition generation process still needs to be improved. On the other hand, the Fast-PCA technique was proposed for accelerating the PCA method and is highly recommended in cases involving large data matrices that can take a long computation time. It is applied after decomposing the multi-dimensional PPG signal. According to the experimental investigation, the Fast PCA approach greatly outperforms the PCA implementations in terms of processing speed, and this success is due to how the main component computation is done and its manner of determining the PCs. In our upcoming work, we intend to compare our approach to the existing approaches that have recently been introduced by the biomedical engineering community, such as the EMD, EEMD, VMD, and SVMD techniques. We also intend to evaluate the processing time of the entire system and compute the complexity rate, which are crucial metrics to take into account for real-time constraints and conditions.

Acknowledgements. We owe a debt of gratitude to the Ministry of National Education, Vocational Training, Higher Education and Scientific Research (MENFPESRS) and the National Centre for Scientific and Technical Research of Morocco (CNRST) for their financial support for the project Cov/2020/109.

References

1. Allen, J.: Photoplethysmography and its application in clinical physiological measurement. Physiol. Meas. **28**(3), R1 (2007)
2. Cook, S., Togni, M., Schaub, M.C., Wenaweser, P., Hess, O.M.: High heart rate: a cardiovascular risk factor? Eur. Heart J. **27**(20), 2387–2393 (2006)

3. Yan, Y., Ma, X., Yao, L., Ouyang, J.: Non-contact measurement of heart rate using facial video illuminated under natural light and signal weighted analysis. Bio-Med. Mater. Eng. **26**(s1), S903–S909 (2015)

4. El Khadiri, Z., Latif, R., Saddik, A.: Breathing pattern assessment through the empirical mode decomposition and the empirical wavelet transform algorithms. In The 3rd International Conference on Artificial Intelligence and Computer Vision (AICV2023), 5–7 March 2023, pp. 262–271. Springer, Cham (2023)

5. El Boussaki, H., Latif, R., Saddik, A.: A review on video-based heart rate, respiratory rate and blood pressure estimation. In: Advances in Machine Intelligence and Computer Science Applications: Proceedings of the International Conference ICMICSA 2022, pp. 129–140. Springer, Cham (2023)

6. Bella, A., Latif, R., Saddik, A., Jamad, L.: Review and evaluation of heart rate monitoring based vital signs, a case study: Covid-19 pandemic. In: 2020 6th IEEE Congress on Information Science and Technology (CiSt), pp. 79–83. IEEE (2021)

7. El Khadiri, Z., Latif, R., Saddik, A.: An efficient hybrid algorithm for non-contact physiological sign monitoring using plethysmography wave analysis. Comput. Methods Biomech. Biomed. Eng.: Imaging Vis. (2023)

8. Latif, R., Addaali, B., Saddik, A.: Real-time SPO2 monitoring based on facial images sequences. In Digital Technologies and Applications: Proceedings of ICDTA 2023, Fez, Morocco, vol. 1, pp. 474–483. Springer, Cham (2023)

9. Bella, A., Latif, R., Saddik, A., Guerrouj, F.Z.: Monitoring of physiological signs and their impact on the Covid-19 pandemic. In: E3S Web of Conferences, vol. 229, p. 01030. EDP Sciences (2021)

10. El khadiri, Z., Latif, R., Saddik, A.: Remote heart rate measurement using plethysmographic wave analysis. In: Advances in Machine Intelligence and Computer Science Applications: Proceedings of the International Conference ICMICSA 2022, pp. 254–267. Springer, Cham (2023)

11. Hassan, M.A., Malik, A.S., Fofi, D., Saad, N., Karasfi, B., Ali, Y.S., Meriaudeau, F.: Heart rate estimation using facial video: a review. Biomed. Signal Process. Control **38**, 346–360 (2017)

12. Bauer, A., et al.: Heart rate turbulence: standards of measurement, physiological interpretation, and clinical use: international society for Holter and noninvasive electrophysiology consensus. J. Am. Coll. Cardiol. **52**(17), 1353–1365 (2008)

13. Kazemi, S., Ghorbani, A., Amindavar, H., Li, C.: Cyclostationary approach to Doppler radar heart and respiration rates monitoring with body motion cancelation using Radar Doppler System. Biomed. Signal Process. Control **13**, 79–88 (2014)

14. Nilsson, L., Johansson, A., Kalman, S.: Monitoring of respiratory rate in postoperative care using a new photoplethysmographic technique. J. Clin. Monit. Comput. **16**, 309–315 (2000)

15. Nakajima, K., Tamura, T., Miike, H.: Monitoring of heart and respiratory rates by photoplethysmography using a digital filtering technique. Med. Eng. Phys. **18**, 365–372 (1996)

16. Leonard, P.A., Beattie, T.F., Addison, P.S., Watson, J.N.: Standard pulse oximeters can be used to monitor respiratory rate. Emerg. Med. J. **20**, 524–525 (2003)

17. Chon, K.H., Dash, S., Ju, K.: Estimation of respiratory rate from photoplethysmogram data using time-frequency spectral estimation. IEEE Trans. Biomed. Eng. **56**, 2054–2063 (2009)

18. Garde, A., Karlen, W., Dehkordi, P., Ansermino, J.M., Dumont, G.A.: Empirical mode decomposition for respiratory and heart rate estimation from the photoplethysmogram. Comput. Cardiol. Conf. **40**, 799–802 (2013)

19. Labate, D., La Foresta, F., Occhiuto, G., Morabito, F.C., Lay-Ekuakille, A., Vergallo, P.: Empirical mode decomposition vs. wavelet decomposition for the extraction of respiratory signal from single-channel ECG: A comparison. IEEE Sens. J. **13**, 2666–2674 (2013)
20. Kinkeldei, T., Zysset, C., Cherenack, K.H., Tröster, G.: A textile integrated sensor system for monitoring humidity and temperature. In: 2011 16th International Solid-State Sensors, Actuators and Microsystems Conference, pp. 1156–1159. IEEE (2011)
21. Pantelopoulos, A., Bourbakis, N.G.: A survey on wearable sensor-based systems for health monitoring and prognosis. IEEE Trans. Syst. Man Cybern. Part C (Appl. Rev.) **40**(1), 1–12 (2009)
22. Nemati, E., Deen, M.J., Mondal, T.: A wireless wearable ECG sensor for long-term applications. IEEE Commun. Mag. **50**(1), 36–43 (2012)
23. Li, X., Chen, J., Zhao, G., Pietikainen, M.: Remote heart rate measurement from face videos under realistic situations. In: Proceedings of the IEEE Conference on Computer Vision and Pattern Recognition, pp. 4264–4271 (2014)
24. Guo, Z., Wang, Z. J., Shen, Z.: Physiological parameter monitoring of drivers based on video data and independent vector analysis. In: 2014 IEEE International Conference on Acoustics, Speech and Signal Processing (ICASSP), pp. 4374–4378. IEEE (2014)
25. Qi, H., Wang, Z. J., Miao, C.: Non-contact driver cardiac physiological monitoring using video data. In: 2015 IEEE China Summit and International Conference on Signal and Information Processing (ChinaSIP), pp. 418–422. IEEE (2015)
26. Lei, R., Ling, B., Feng, P., Chen, J.: Estimation of heart rate and respiratory rate from PPG signal using complementary ensemble empirical mode decomposition with both independent component analysis and non-negative matrix factorization. Sensors **20**(11), 3238 (2020)
27. Sharma, H.: Extraction of respiratory rate from PPG using ensemble empirical mode decomposition with Kalman filter. Electron. Lett. **56**(13), 650–653 (2020)
28. Haque, M.A., Irani, R., Nasrollahi, K., Moeslund, T.B.: Heartbeat ratemeasurement from facial video. IEEE Intell. Syst. **31**(3), 40–48 (2016)
29. Tomasi, C., Kanade, T.: Detection and tracking of point features. School of Computer Science, Carnegie Mellon University, Pittsburgh (1991)
30. Balakrishnan, G., Durand, F., Guttag, J.: Detecting pulse from head motions in video. In: Proceedings of the IEEE Conference on Computer Vision and Pattern Recognition, pp. 3430–3437 (2013)
31. Wu, Z., Huang, N.E.: Ensemble empirical mode decomposition: a noise-assisted data analysis method. Adv. Adapt. Data Anal. **1**(01), 1–41 (2009)
32. Zhang, J., et al.: Serial-EMD: fast empirical mode decomposition method for multidimensional signals based on serialization. Inf. Sci. **581**, 215–232 (2021)
33. Jolliffe, I.T., Cadima, J.: Principal component analysis: a review and recent developments. Philos. Trans. Roy. Soc. A: Math. Phys. Eng. Sci. **374**(2065), 20150202 (2016)
34. Bishop, C.M., Nasrabadi, N.M.: Pattern Recognition and Machine Learning. Springer, New York (2006)

Human-Computer Interaction: A Bibliometric Analysis

Samhale Soukaina$^{(\boxtimes)}$ ⓘ, Louzaoui Khadija ⓘ, and Benlhachmi Khalid ⓘ

Ibn Tofail University, Kenitra, Morocco
{soukaina.samhale,khadija.louzaoui1,khalid.benlhachmi}@uit.ac.ma

Abstract. Human-computer interaction (HCI) has made remarkable progress in recent years, transforming the way we interact with technology. This article presents a bibliometric analysis study conducted on HCI publications, using the Scopus database as the primary source. Initially, we obtained 187 435 publications and applied filters and inclusion/exclusion criteria to refine the selection, resulting in a final dataset of 20 085 publications. These publications cover the period from 2018 to 2022. The primary goal of this study is to offer researchers and scientists valuable insights into HCI research. By examining publication patterns, this study aims to illuminate the current state of research, highlight emerging trends, and assist researchers in prioritizing their future investigations in HCI.

Keywords: Bibliometric Analysis · Computer Vision · Gesture Recognition · HCI · Human-Computer Interaction · Visualization

1 Introduction

Recently, we have observed a significant development in the relationship between machines and humans. This relationship has become more intelligent and effective. This increased connectivity and interactive communication between people and their devices is what we refer to as human-computer interaction (HCI). The rapid development of technologies and computers has led to a closer bond in this relationship, facilitating seamless collaboration between humans and machines. Across numerous scientific articles, researchers have used various modern technologies to create perfect connections. Among them are artificial intelligence (AI), gesture recognition, voice recognition, virtual reality (VR), and augmented reality (AR). AI empowers computers to learn from how people behave and make interactions smarter using machine learning [1], deep learning [2], etc. Gesture recognition enables machines to understand human movements, making interaction with computers easier. In [3], authors created an interactive system, utilizing camera-based technology, that empowers users to engage with computers through simple hand gestures without using additional devices. An innovative framework that combines the human gaze and hand gestures for robot interaction is proposed in [4]. This framework is designed for construction sites with various machines. Voice Recognition transforms spoken words into actionable commands, fostering effortless communication [5]. The application of VR [6] and AR [7] led to better HCI by creating immersive digital experiences that engage users with technology.

H. Hagras et al. (Eds.): ISACS 2023, CCIS 2255, pp. 399–409, 2025.
https://doi.org/10.1007/978-3-031-93448-3_32

Scientists have provided different definitions of HCI based on their perspectives. In [8], the authors define it as the study and design of how humans interact with computers and how to create user-friendly computer systems. HCI enables humans to interact with computers in a natural and intuitive way, bridging the gap between users and technology [9].

The key concepts of HCI are functionality and usability. Functionality refers to the capabilities and features of a system, while usability focuses on how easily and effectively users can interact with it. Balancing functionality and usability is critical to HCI's success [10].

There are several research papers concerning numerous applications of HCI across various fields, including sports [11], gaming [12], Education [13], healthcare [14], Smart city [15], Automotive industry [16] … These applications of HCI aim to make technology more accessible, enjoyable, and efficient for users in different aspects of their lives.

When scientists want to research a topic, they must read and analyze many scientific articles. Some articles may not be relevant, so researchers often read the abstracts to decide. Bibliometric analysis solves this issue by providing scientists with a global view of articles on a specific topic. Bibliometric analysis uses statistical methods to help researchers understand patterns and the importance of different articles [17]. It makes their research process more efficient and informed.

Several bibliometric analyses have been done to investigate research trends in HCI. For example, in the study [18], authors examined and evaluated literature on interaction design of HCI between 1985 and 2020, and in [19] researchers provided a comprehensive overview of HCI research conducted from 1969 to early 2017.

The purpose of this study is to analyze HCI publications using visualization and bibliometrics analysis in the period of the last five years, from 2017 to 2022. All the data used in this study have been collected from Scopus database. In this article, we intended to answer the following research questions through bibliometric analysis:

- What is the distribution of human-computer interaction publications by year for the last five years?
- What are the 10 most relevant journals in human-computer interaction research?
- What are the 10 most relevant authors in human-computer interaction research?
- What are the most relevant affiliations in human-computer interaction research?
- What are the most productive countries in human-computer interaction research?

2 Materials and Methods

In this paper, we employed a bibliometric analysis approach utilizing the Scopus database to explore the research trends in the field of HCI. In the initial search, we obtained 187 435 documents by conducting a keyword search using "human-computer interaction". To ensure the relevance and quality of our analysis, we applied several filters and inclusion/exclusion criteria. In Fig. 1, a comprehensive representation of the applied filters on the initial articles' dataset is presented. These filters help us sort and organize the information in the articles. Each filter focuses on certain aspects of the articles. Firstly, we limited the dataset to articles published within the last five years to maintain the currency of information. Secondly, articles were filtered based on language for clarity. Thirdly, specific types were selected, including conference paper, article, review, and conference review. Fourthly, we selected publications from reputable sources like academic journals and conference proceedings to enhance the reliability of the dataset. Additionally, articles were filtered based on keywords, specifically focusing on those related to " human-computer interaction". Lastly, the subject area filter narrowed down the dataset to articles specifically related to computer vision, to ensure the contextual alignment of the chosen publications with our research objectives.

Table 1 serves as an essential reference for understanding the specific inclusion and exclusion criteria that were applied during the filtration process. This table comprehensively outlines the parameters used to determine whether an article was included or excluded from the refined dataset.

After applying these filters and inclusion/exclusion criteria, we obtained a final dataset of 20 085 publications that formed the basis of our comprehensive bibliometric analysis.

Table 1. The inclusion and exclusion criteria for data screening.

Inclusion criteria	Exclusion criteria
Documents published between 2012 and 2022	Documents not categorized under the subject area of Computer Science
Articles, Conference Proceedings, Conference Reviews, Reviews	
Documents published in English language	
Keywords: Human Computer Interaction, Human-Computer Interaction, Machine Learning, Artificial Intelligence, Computer Vision, Human Robot Interaction, Human Computer Interaction (HCI), Interactive Computer Systems	

To visualize the bibliometric networks, we employed specialized software VOSViewer that facilitated the analysis and interpretation of our dataset. By utilizing this tool, we were able to map and visualize the relationships between relevant countries, authors, and keywords.

3 Findings

3.1 Research Question 1

What is The distribution of human-computer interaction publications by year for the last five years?

Figure 2 displays the number of publications in the field of HCI from 2018 to 2022. The histogram displays the distribution of publication counts per year, allowing for a visual understanding of the variations in research output over a period of five years. It

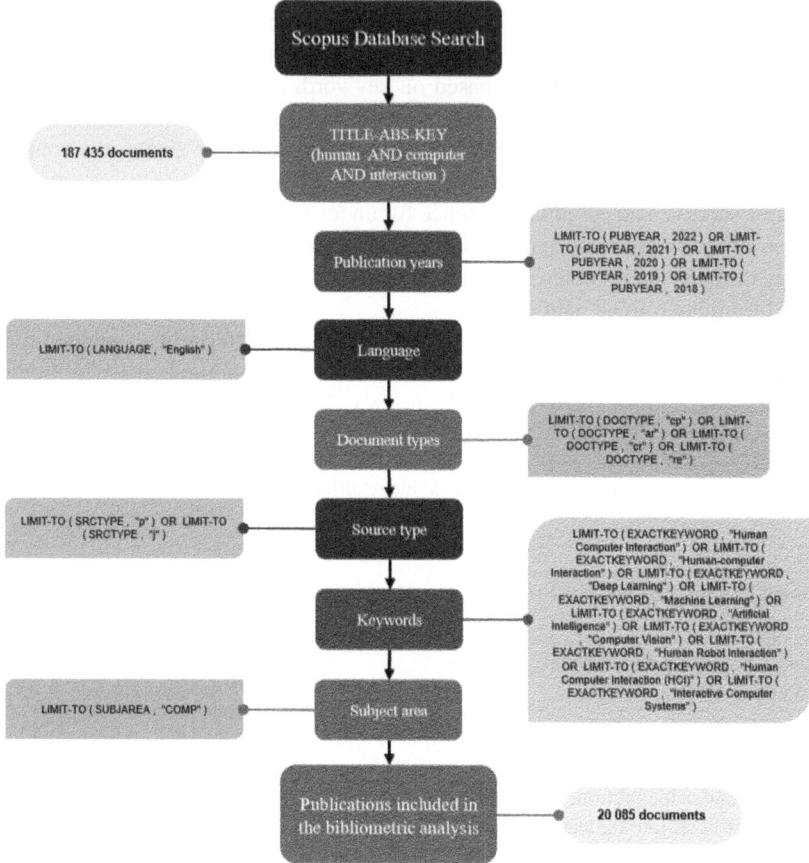

Fig. 1. Analytic Framework of The Study

shows that the number of publications has not always increased over the years. Notably, the year 2019 had the highest number of publications, indicating a significant surge in research and scholarly output during that period.

3.2 Research Question 2

What are The 10 Most Relevant Journals in Human-Computer Interaction Research?

Table 2 presents the top 10 most productive journals in HCI research during the five-year period from 2018 to 2022. The "ACM International Conference Proceeding Series" tops the list with 1 802 publications, signifying its high productivity and influence in the field. The "Conference on Human Factors in Computing Systems Proceedings" follows closely with 1 605 publications. Additionally, "Computers in Human Behavior" contributed 534 publications, and "IEEE Access" published 402 papers.

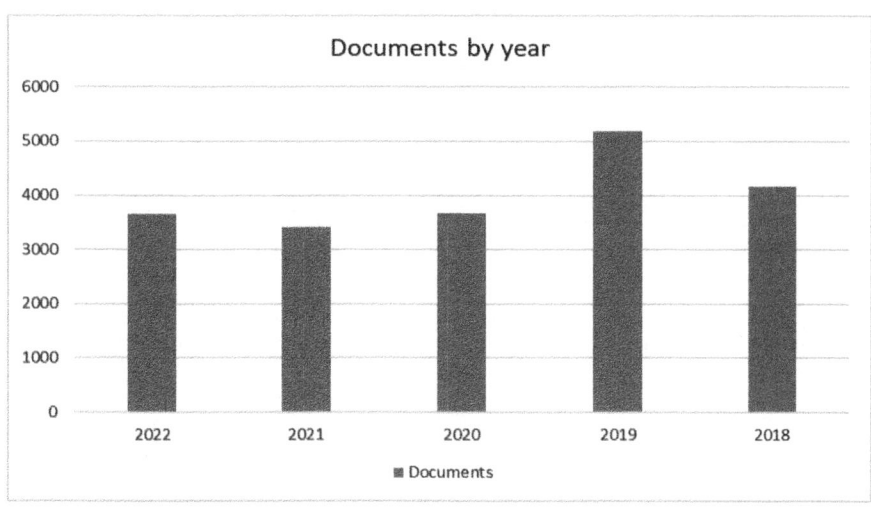

Fig. 2. Distribution of publications by years (2018–2022).

Table 2. The top 10 relevant journals in HCI.

Journal	Documents	TP	TC	Cite score
-ACM International Conference Proceeding Series	1 802	44 179	44 929	1.0
-Conference On Human Factors in Computing Systems Proceedings	1 605	3 496	29 095	8.3
-Computers In Human Behavior	534	1 607	23 983	14.9
-IEEE Access	402	50 910	341 106	6.7
-CEUR Workshop Proceedings	373	20 716	22 097	1.1
-Proceedings of the ACM on Human Computer Interaction	291	929	5 181	5.6
-International Journal of Human Computer Interaction	232	512	3 725	7.3
-Multimedia Tools and Applications	151	6 085	32 104	5.3
-Proceedings of SPIE the International Society for Optical Engineering	151	45 811	41 709	0.9
-Sensors	142	25 441	163 891	6.4

Note: TP = Total Publications, TC = Total Citation

3.3 Research Question 3

What are The 10 Most Relevant Authors in Human-Computer Interaction Research?

Table 3 presents the top 10 authors in HCI research from 2018 to 2022, based on the number of publications. "Billinghurst, Mark" is the most prolific author in this list, he published 39 documents and received a total of 17 650 citations. "Brereton, Margot" is the second most productive author with 34 publications and 2 536 citations.

Table 3. The top 10 relevant authors in HCI.

Authors	Documents	TP	TC	h-index	Current affiliation
-Billinghurst, Mark	39	599	17 650	60	University of South Australia, Adelaide, Australia
-Brereton, Margot	34	209	2 536	25	Queensland University of Technology, Brisbane, Australia
-Schmidt, Albrecht	31	527	12 657	55	Ludwig – Maximilians -Universität München, Munich, Germany
-Togelius, Julian	31	309	7 907	46	Modl.ai, Copenhagen, Denmark
-Henze, Niels	30	213	4 225	32	Universität Regensburg, Regensburg, Germany
-Alt, Florian	29	253	4 737	37	Universität der Bundeswehr München, Neubiberg, Germany
-Kumar, Neha	29	116	1 837	25	Georgia Institute of Technology, Atlanta, United States
-Orji, Rita	29	200	2 888	27	Dalhousie University, Halifax, Canada
-Malaka, Rainer	28	222	1 830	23	Universität Bremen, Bremen, Germany
-Steinicke, Frank	24	264	3 886	32	Universität Hamburg, Hamburg, Germany

Note: TP = Total Publications, TC = Total Citation

Figure 3 provides a visual representation of the collaboration network between authors, each one is represented as a node. The connections between nodes indicate that authors have co-authored publications together. The size of each node corresponds to the number of co-authored works by that author. Colors are used to group nodes into clusters based on their collaborations. Authors in the same cluster have worked closely together, contributing to similar areas within HCI research. This map helps visualize the collaborative relationships and research focus among authors, making it easier to identify key contributors, influential clusters, and the overall structure of the HCI research network. The figure demonstrates that there is a significant presence of authors actively contributing to the HCI field. The strong connectivity in the graph highlights a prevalent culture of collaboration among HCI researchers.

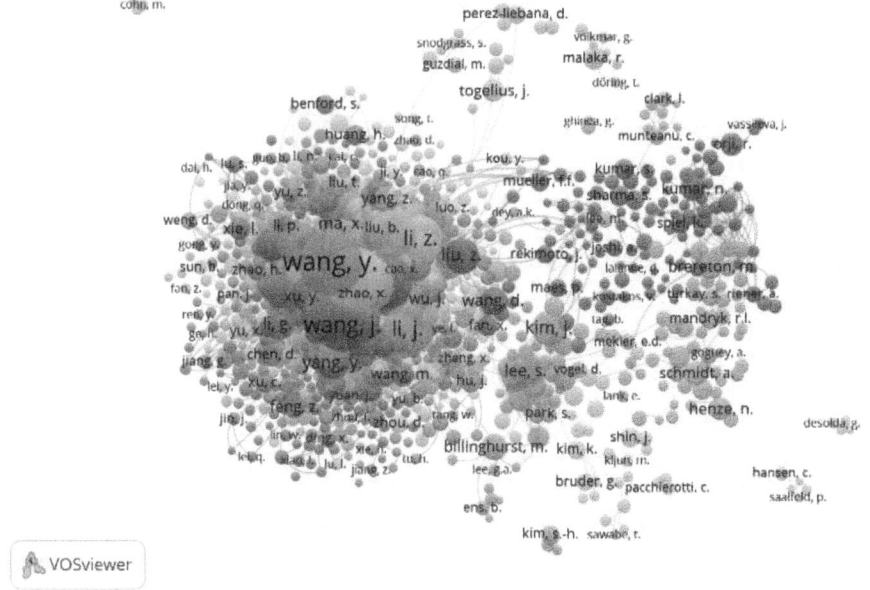

Fig. 3. Analysis results of relevant authors in HCI research

3.4 Research Question 4

What are The Most Relevant Affiliations in Human-Computer Interaction Research?

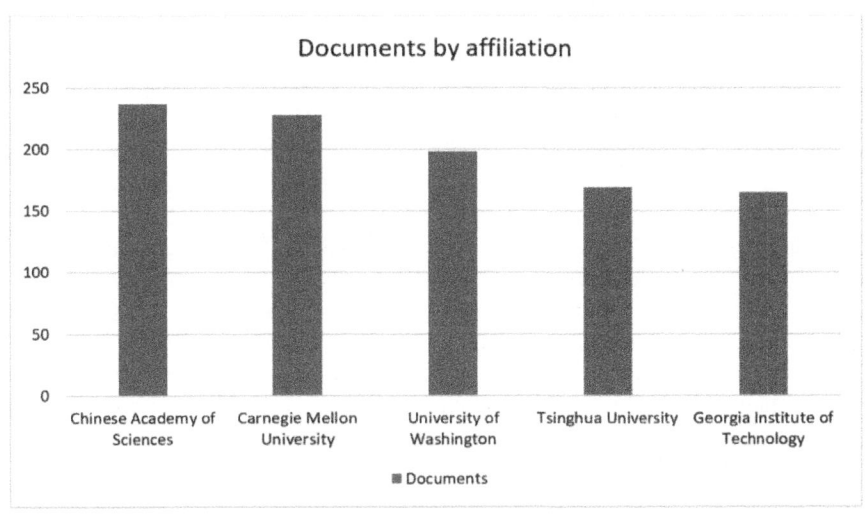

Fig. 4. The most 5 relevant affiliations in HCI.

Figure 4 shows the top five affiliations based on the number of publications they have contributed to HCI research. The figure can be helpful in identifying which institutions are contributing the most to research in HCI. For example, "Chinese Academy of Sciences" is the most productive affiliation in this field, which published 237, followed by "Carnegie Mellon University" with 228 publications.

3.5 Research Question 5

What are The Most Productive Countries in Human-Computer Interaction Research?

Table 4. The most 5 productive countries in HCI.

Rank	Country	TP	Most productive Academic Institution
1	United States	4 127	Carnegie Mellon University
2	China	3 646	Chinese Academy of Sciences
3	United Kingdom	1 785	University College London
4	Germany	1 529	Ludwig-Maximilians-Universität München
5	India	1 137	Indian Institute of Technology Bombay

Table 4 provides an overview of the top five most productive countries in the field of HCI research during the period from 2018 to 2022. It showcases the significant number of publications contributed by each country, emphasizing their notable productivity. United States stands out with 4 127 publications, led by the most productive affiliation, Carnegie Mellon University. Following closely behind is China with 3646 publications, primarily associated with the affiliation Chinese Academy of Sciences.

Figure 5 shows countries that are highly productive in HCI research, with the connections between them representing co-authorship collaborations. Each country is represented by a node. The lines connecting the nodes indicate that researchers from these countries have worked together on research projects. The size of each node corresponds to the volume of collaborative research output from that country. Colors are used to group countries with similar collaborative patterns. These clusters highlight regions of intense collaboration and shared research interests. Overall, this map helps to identify the countries that have established strong collaborative relationships in HCI research, and it can be used to guide future collaboration efforts. As we can see, the map reveals that the United States and China stand out as the largest nodes, signifying their significant contributions to HCI research. This prominence suggests that these countries have played pivotal roles in fostering substantial international collaborations and shaping the advancement of knowledge in this field.

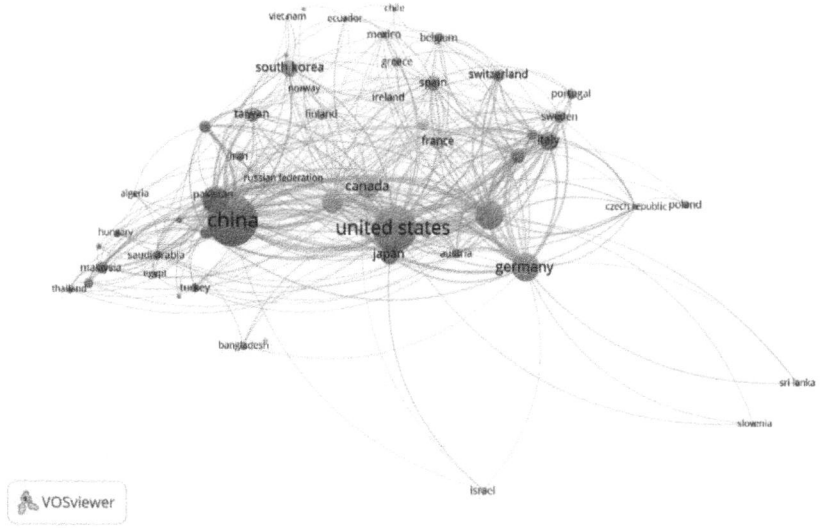

Fig. 5. Analysis results of productive countries in HCI research

4 Discussion

Based on the 20 085 research publications collected from the Scopus database, this study provides an overview of research conducted on HCI. This analysis demonstrates that the field of HCI is highly significant, with numerous studies indicating a strong interest among researchers. Moreover, HCI is applied across diverse domains, highlighting its broad applicability and relevance.

The results of the study indicate a significant number of publications during the period from 2018 to 2022 in the field of HCI. Several countries have shown notable productivity in this research domain. Figure 6 presents the number of publications per country in HCI research from 2018 to 2022. As seen, the United States has the highest number of publications with 4 127, followed by China with 3 646 publications. The United Kingdom also has a high number of publications with 1 785. This histogram provides an overview of the countries that have been highly active in publishing research in the field of HCI. It can be useful for identifying potential collaborators for future research.

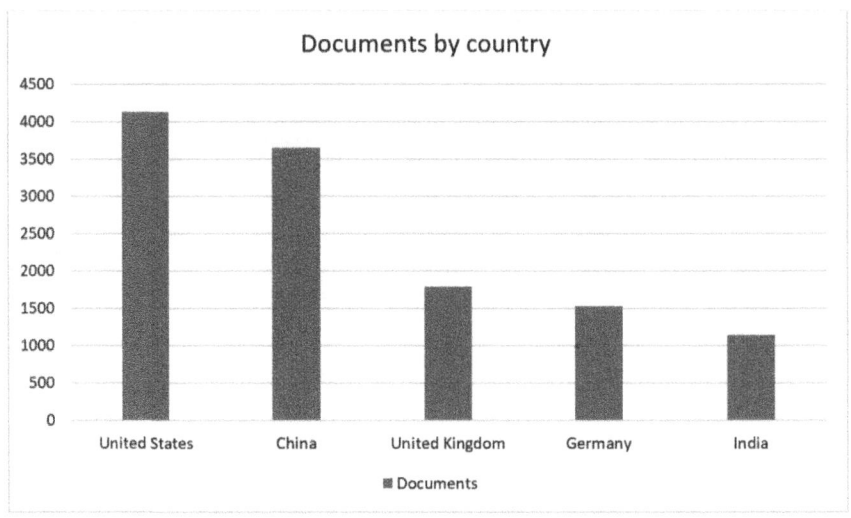

Fig. 6. Distribution of publications by countries

5 Conclusion

Human-computer interaction has rapidly advanced in recent years, leading to significant changes in our lives and deepening the relationship between humans and machines. It has transformed the way we interact with technology, making it more user-friendly, intuitive, and integrated into our daily routines. Through this bibliometric analysis study, we aimed to highlight the significance of HCI research and provide valuable insights into the research trends and priorities in this area. This paper serves as a valuable resource for researchers, offering valuable inspiration for future investigations and collaborations in this exciting and evolving field.

6 Perspectives

In conducting a bibliometric analysis of HCI, we've gained valuable insights into patterns of publication, collaboration, and research impact. However, this method has its limitations, as it focuses primarily on quantitative aspects. To address this, incorporating a content analysis perspective holds immense importance. Content analysis allows us to delve deeper, exploring the actual themes, methodologies, and emerging trends within these publications. By combining these two approaches, we can present a more comprehensive view of HCI research, identifying research gaps and future directions more effectively.

References

1. Semeraro, F., Griffiths, A., Cangelosi, A.: Human-robot collaboration and machine learning: a systematic review of recent research. Robot. Comput.-Integr. Manuf. **79**, 102432 (2023)

2. Saad, Mohamed, A.A.: An integrated human computer interaction scheme for object detection using deep learning. Comput. Electr. Eng. **96**, 107475 (2021)
3. Zahra, R., et al.: Camera-based interactive wall display using hand gesture recognition. Intell. Syst. Appl. **19**, 200262 (2023)
4. Wang, X., Veeramani, D., Zhu, Z.: Gaze-aware hand gesture recognition for intelligent construction. Eng. Appl. Artif. Intell. **123**, 106179 (2023)
5. Ameer, B., Alia, A.-H.: A review on voice-based interface for human-robot interaction. Iraqi J. Electr. Electr. Eng. **16**(2), 91–102 (2020)
6. Lteif, F.C., Daher, K., Angelini, L., Mugellini, E., Khaled, O.A., Hajj, H.E.: Virtual reality to improve human computer interaction for art. In: Human Interaction, Emerging Technologies and Future Applications IV: Proceedings of the 4th International Conference on Human Interaction and Emerging Technologies: Future Applications (2021)
7. Qiu, S., Liu, H., Zhang, Z., Zhu, Y., Zhu, S.-C.: Human-robot interaction in a shared augmented reality workspace. In: 2020 IEEE/RSJ International Conference on Intelligent Robots and Systems (IROS) (2020)
8. Himanshu, B., Rizwan, K.: A review paper on human computer interaction. Int. J. Adv. Res. Comput. Sci. Softw. Eng. **8**(4), 53 (2018)
9. Munmun, D.C., Min, K., Haiyi, Z., David, A.S.: Introduction to this special issue on unifying human computer interaction and artificial intelligence. Hum.-Comput. Inter. **35**(5–6), 355–361 (2020)
10. Mathew, R., Al Hajj, A., Al Abri, A.: Human-computer interaction (HCI): an overview. In: 2011 IEEE International Conference on Computer Science and Automation Engineering (2011)
11. Pan, .T.-Y., Tsai, W.-L., Chang, C.-Y., Yeh, C.-W., Hu, M.-C.: A hierarchical hand gesture recognition framework for sports referee training-based EMG and accelerometer sensors. IEEE Trans. Cybern. **52**(5), 3172–3183 (2020)
12. Nasri, N., Orts-Escolano, S., Cazorla, M.: An sEMG-controlled 3d game for rehabilitation therapies: Real-time time hand gesture recognition using deep learning techniques. Sensors **20**(22), 6451 (2020)
13. Dingli, A., Caruana Montaldo, L.: Human computer interaction in education. In: Stephanidis, C. (ed.) HCII 2019. CCIS, vol. 1034, pp. 226–229. Springer, Cham (2019). https://doi.org/10.1007/978-3-030-23525-3_29
14. D'Auria, D., Persia, F., Siciliano, B.: Human-computer interaction in healthcare: how to support patients during their wrist rehabilitation. In: 2016 IEEE Tenth International Conference on Semantic Computing (ICSC) (2016)
15. Kashef, M., Visvizi, A., Troisi, O.: Smart city as a smart service system: human-computer interaction and smart city surveillance systems. Comput. Hum. Behav. **124**, 106923 (2021)
16. Shaikh: An interactive design using human computer interaction for autonomous vehicles. Int. J. Eng. Trends Technol. (IJETT) **10**(1), 160–172 (2020)
17. Su, M., Peng, H., Li, S.: A visualized bibliometric analysis of mapping research trends of machine learning in engineering (MLE). Expert Syst. Appl. **186**, 115728 (2021)
18. Wang, D., Xu, Z.: Bibliometric analysis of the core thesis system of interaction design research on human-computer interaction. In: 2020 International Conference on Big Data and Social Sciences (ICBDSS) (2020)
19. Koumaditis, K., Hussain, T.: Human computer interaction research through the lens of a bibliometric analysis. In: Human-Computer Interaction. User Interface Design, Development and Multimodality (2017)

About the Reliability Analysis by Stochastic Petri Net and Markov Model: Comparative Study

Hamid EL Moumen$^{(\boxtimes)}$ ⓘ and Nabil EL Akchioui ⓘ

Faculty of Sciences and Technology Al Hoceima, University Abdelmalek Essaadi, Tétouan, Morocco

hamid.elmoumen@etu.uae.ac.ma, n.elakchioui@uae.ac.ma

Abstract. This article presents an approach for the reliability analysis of discrete event systems, aiming to address the challenge of combinatorial explosion of states. The proposed method utilizes stochastic Petri nets and introduces an estimation technique based on average marking and throughput, which yields relevant results. This approach specifically tackles the limitations encountered by Markov models in systems with interdependent components. The introduced stochastic estimator demonstrates a convergence behavior similar to that of the Markov model in the steady state regime while eliminating the need to determine the marking graph. However, it is worth noting that the marking and throughput estimation convergence may be slower. This approach improves the reliability analysis of complex systems by taking interdependencies, by overcoming the limitations of traditional models, it offers improved prospects for reliability analysis in various fields.

Keywords: Petri Net · Stochastic Petri Net · Steady State · Combinatorial Explosion · Reliability Analysis · Markov Model

1 Introduction

Discrete event systems, ubiquitous in various fields such as production, communication, and traffic control, can be modeled using discrete event stochastic models [1]. Stochastic models, including Markov models and stochastic Petri nets (SPNs), are commonly used to study the reliability of complex systems, particularly those involving repairs [2, 3]. SPNs are of particular interest as, under certain conditions, they can be considered equivalent models to the Markov model [4, 5].

The analysis and simulation of stochastic discrete event systems pose challenges when using the Markov Model, especially for large-scale systems [4, 6]. To address these limitations, Petri nets (PNs) offer an appealing alternative by enabling the construction of equivalent models. SPNs, introduced by G. Florin and S. Natkin, associate random durations with transitions, typically following an exponential distribution [7]. This allows for a homogeneous representation of the stochastic nets marking as a Markov model [8,

© The Author(s), under exclusive license to Springer Nature Switzerland AG 2025
H. Hagras et al. (Eds.): ISACS 2023, CCIS 2255, pp. 410–421, 2025.
https://doi.org/10.1007/978-3-031-93448-3_33

9]. Consequently, the stochastic behavior of the Petri Net can be analyzed based on the corresponding Markov model. These approaches constitute valuable tools for evaluating the reliability of industrial systems.

However, in the case of large marking graphs, the SPN can be viewed as an estimator of the Markov model [4, 6], enabling the determination of asymptotic average rates and markings through simulation [10]. This approach offers the advantage of not requiring an explicit determination of the marking graph, but it may suffer from slow convergence, particularly in the presence of rare events [11]. In this study, we propose a method to estimate the average marking and flow of the Markov model based on information about the marking of places in the SPN, to highlight the advantages and limitations of these two models.

This article explores the reliable operation of repairable systems and the fundamental concepts associated with reliability. We focus on the reliability of large-scale discrete systems. These studies can be based on the Markov model or SPN, commonly used for analysis and synthesis throughout different phases of a system's life cycle. These modeling tools allow for deriving the average behavior of the system, such as average markings and average throughputs, and obtaining performance indicators through calculation or estimation. A presentation of Markovian analysis of the system with a finite state space and its estimator obtained using SPN will be presented, analyzed, and discussed.

2 Background

2.1 Reliability Definition

The capacity of a system to perform a required function under specified conditions for a specified period is known as reliability [3, 12, 13]. Reliability is the probability of having no failure during a given period. Performance measurements are used to characterize the system's robustness or validate productivity requirements, and the choice of these measures depends on the system's function and use.

Two categories of measures can be distinguished [12, 14]:

The first category pertains to non-repairable systems, where the system under study is subject only to the failure process without any possibility of repair. For example, this category could apply to assessing the consequences of catastrophic failure in critical systems within the automotive field.

The second category concerns repairable systems, which can transition from a failed state to an operational state. These systems are subject to both failure and repair processes. Examples of this category include studying a production line or an industrial computer network. Measures in this category include availability and maintainability.

In the case of non-repairable systems, if failures are unpredictable and occur randomly, the number of failures over time is solely determined by the number of occurrences. The failure rate λ (number of failures per unit of time) remains constant, resulting in an exponential distribution for the reliability law [14]. Each failure reduces the probability of experiencing a failure in the next unit of time. The reliability law is expressed as:

$$R(t) = \mathrm{e}^{-\lambda t} \tag{1}$$

This exponential function is utilized to calculate the Mean Time to Failure (*MTTF*), given by the reciprocal of the failure rate:

$$MTTF = \int_0^{+\infty} R(t).dt = 1/\lambda \qquad (2)$$

Conversely, λ represents the inverse of the average time before failure. In the case of an exponential law, regardless of the duration of successful operation already achieved, the probability of a circuit failure between time t and $(t + dt)$ remains constant and equal to $dt / MTTF$ (a fundamental property of the exponential distribution). It is evident that regardless of the *MTTF*:

-At $t = 0$, the reliability is always *1*, indicating that no system fails during commissioning.
-As time (t) approaches infinity, the reliability tends to *0*, signifying that systems have a limited lifespan.

2.2 Markov Model

A Markov model is a mathematical structure, named after Andrey Markov that involves transitioning between a finite or countable number of possible states [15]. It is a memoryless random process, meaning that the next state is determined solely by the current state and independent of the events preceding it. This property is known as the Markov property and characterizes the "Memorylessness" of the process. Markov model finds wide-ranging applications as a mathematical model for real-world systems [16].

In the context of reliability analysis, Markovian models can be employed to evaluate and quantify the performance indicators of repairable systems [17]. Markov processes are often utilized to assess the functioning of systems, particularly when the transition rates remain constant. In such cases, the occurrence of failure and repair events for system components follow exponential distributions [12, 17].

Using Markovian analysis, the reliability of systems can be systematically studied, allowing for the analytical assessment of various performance metrics. By considering the constant transition rates and memoryless nature of the Markov model, these models provide valuable insights into the behavior and reliability of complex systems.

2.3 Petri Net (PN)

A PN consists of three main components: a set of n places P_i, a set of q transitions T_j, and the incidence matrix W, denoted as $< P, T, W^{PR}, W^{PO} >$ [11, 18, 19]. The places represent finite states, while transitions represent events or actions that can occur in the system. The incidence matrix captures the relationships between places and transitions, indicating the throughput of tokens (or markings) between them.

The incidence matrix is divided into two parts: the pre-incidence matrix, W^{PR}, and the post-incidence matrix, W^{PO} [5]. W^{PR} contains the weights of the arcs from places to transitions, while W^{PO} contains the weights of the arcs from transitions to places [20, 21]. These weights define the strength or significance of the connections between the places and transitions in the PN.

The marking of a place P_i at a given time t is denoted as $M(t, P_i)$, representing the number of tokens or markings in that place [5]. The PN marking vector, $M(t)$, represents the overall marking of the PN at time t. The initial marking, M_I, defines the initial distribution of tokens in the PN.

PNs also exhibit important characteristics such as T-semi-flows and P-semi-flows. T-semi-flows refer to the right normal annular of the token flow matrix W, while P-semi-flows refer to the left normal annular. A PN is considered conservative if the product of the T-semi-flows and the incidence matrix is zero, indicating the preservation of the total number of tokens. Conversely, a consistent PN is one where a vector x satisfying the condition $W.\, x = 0$ represents a repeated sequence or a possible steady state behavior in which all transitions can fire [7, 22].

These fundamental concepts and properties of PNs play a crucial role in analyzing and understanding the behavior and dynamics of systems modeled using this formalism. By examining the incidence matrix, marking, and firing of transitions, one can gain insights into the throughput and transformations occurring within the PN model [23].

2.4 Stochastic Petri Net (SPN)

An SPN is a variation of a timed PN where the firing periods of transitions are characterized by random distributions. Specifically, these distributions are based on the exponential distribution with a parameter that varies according to $(round(n_j(M)) \times \mu_j)$, where $n_j(M)$ represents the enabling degree of transition T_j for a given marking M_I. The concept of SPNs was introduced by Molloy [24], and subsequent extensions have been developed for the analysis of reliability in repairable systems [11, 25–27].

In an SPN, denoted as $< PN, \mu >$, the underlying PN is associated with a firing rate vector $\mu = (\mu_j) \in (R^+)^q$. Each transition T_j in the SPN is characterized by a firing rate μ_j, which represents the likelihood of T_j firing within a small-time interval dt, given that it has been activated with degree 1 at time t. The marking process of an SPN is described using various elements, including the PN incidence matrices, the initial marking, the firing rates, the firing policy, the server policy, and the execution policy [6, 18, 22].

In this paper, we consider an SPN that satisfies the following assumptions:

(A_1) The firing policy follows a race policy, where the transition with the shortest firing time is considered to be the one that will fire next.

(A_2) The server policy is infinite, meaning that each transition T_j has a minimal period determined by a stochastic length characterized by an exponential distribution with a parameter that varies according to $round(n_j(M)) \times \mu_j$ [1, 28]. The enabling degree of transition T_j for a marking M is represented by Eq. (9) [29]:

$$n_j(M) = \min\left(m_i/w_{ij}^{PR}\right), for\ all\ P_i \in {}^\circ T_j \qquad (3)$$

where ${}^\circ T_j$ represents the set of places upstream of T_j. The function "$round(.)$" denotes the integer part of a number.

(A_3) The execution policy is of the form of "resampling memory," where at the start of labeling, all transitions that were previously enabled have their remaining firing time reset.

By considering these assumptions, we can effectively model and analyze the behavior of an SPN, particularly in terms of its marking evolution and the timing of transition firings. The stochastic nature of SPNs allows for the incorporation of randomness and variability, making them suitable for studying complex systems in various domains.

2.5 Average Markings and Throughputs of SPNs

For live SPNs that satisfy the above assumptions and when the state space is finite, the SPN has a marking graph that is isomorphic to the state space of a Markov model [30]. In this case, the stationary state of the SPN can be deduced from the state probabilities of the Markov model. The vector of stationary state probabilities which is the solution of Eq. (4), is given by [4, 11]:

$$\Pi_{SS}.A(\mu) = 0 \text{ and } \Pi_{SS}.(1_N) = 1. \tag{4}$$

With $\Pi_{SS} = (\pi_{ss}(k)) \in [0, 1]^{(1 \times N)}$, the vector of stationary state probabilities of the Markov model related to N states, $A(\mu) \in (R)^{(N \times N)}$ as the Markov model generator associated with the SPN is a square matrix of dimension $N \times N$, N being the finite number of states of the linked Markov model, $(1)_N = (1,.....,1)^T \in (R^+)^N$ represents a vector of dimension N whose all components are equal to 1.

Let $X_s = (x_{s(j)}) \in (R^+)^q$ represent the average throughputs vector, and $M_s = (m_{si}) \in (R^+)^n$ represent the average SPN markings vector. As a consequence, from the vector Π_{SS}, we will deduce the average throughputs of transitions as well as the average markings of places as shown in Eq. (5) and Eq. (6) [10, 22]:

$$x_{s_j} = \mu_j.\left(\sum_{k=1..N} n_j(M_k) \cdot \pi_k \right) \tag{5}$$

$$M_{si} = \sum_{k=1..N} (m_{ki} \cdot \pi_{k_i}) \tag{6}$$

$M_k = (m_{ki}) \in (R^+)^n$ means, marking vector matching state k of the Markov model. When it comes to the ergodic Markov model, This method yields an analytical solution to the stationary state probabilities, but it necessitates the calculation of the $A(\mu)$ [17, 31], as a result, the SPNs reachability graph A(PN, M_1) [26, 32–34]. N is the number of states rising exponentially, for large system dimensions the calculation time and memory needs to evaluate A (PN, M_1) becomes more relevant. In this case, for the Markov model, SPN can be thought of as a stochastic estimator [35, 36]. The benefit of this estimator is that it eliminates the need to determine A(PN, M_1), but, the stochastic estimator is sluggish to converge, especially for rare events [6].

2.6 SPNs Algorithm

The simulation of stochastic systems provides a valuable tool for estimating operational safety indicators such as reliability, mean time to failure state, and availability. Markov analysis often becomes impractical when dealing with large systems due to the challenge of Combinatorial State Explosion resulting from the state graph [12, 14]. However, by utilizing SPNs, we can overcome this issue as SPNs serve as an estimator of the Markov model without the need for calculating the state graph. Figure 1 presents the algorithm of the stochastic estimator, which determines the Equivalent States and allows for comparing the random behavior of the SPN with that of a homogeneous Markov model possessing a finite state space.

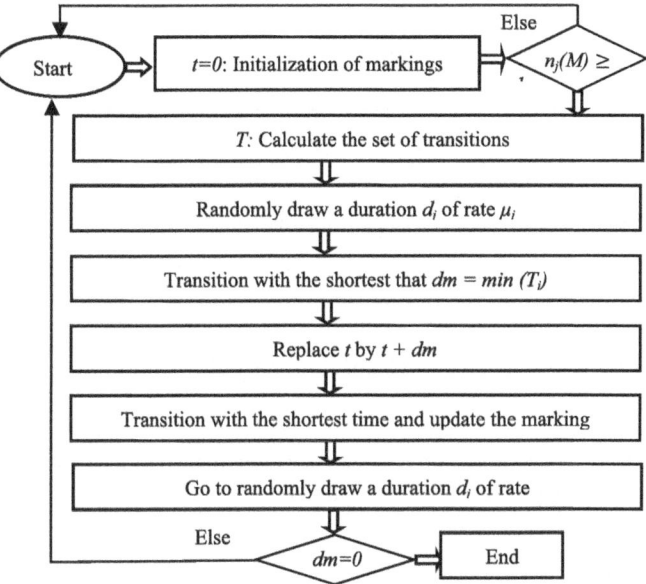

Fig. 1. Steady state by SPNs algorithm.

2.7 Complexity of the Reachability Graph

To illustrate these concepts, let's examine an example presented by [28] in Fig. 2. The model represents a manufacturing system consisting of five types of machinery $(T_1$ to $T_5)$ and three tools with limited resources $(P_1$ to $P_3)$. In this PN model, the parameters of the transitions and the initial marking are defined respectively by the vector: $\mu = (1,1,1,1,1)^T$, $M_1 = (6k,6k,4k,0,3k,0,3k,0,0)^T$ where $k \in IN$ (the set of natural numbers).

Table 1 illustrates the rapid increase in the number of states N and the computation time as a function of the parameter k. The computation time required to generate the reachability graph increases exponentially, making Markov analysis arduous, if not unfeasible [25].

The analysis of large-scale systems using traditional Markov analysis becomes impractical due to the problem of combinatorial state explosion arising from the traversal of the marking graph. In contrast, SPN simulation offers an alternative approach that does not require explicit computation of the marking graph, making SPNs a suitable estimator for Markov model [37, 38]. To address this problem, we will take advantage of

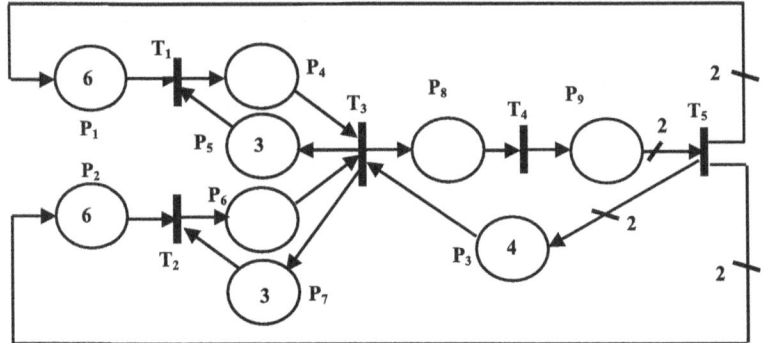

Fig. 2. Manufacturing system.

Table 1. The number of states and calculation time of the reachability graph depend on k.

Coefficient k	1	2	3	4	5
Number of states (N)	205	1885	7796	22187	50801
Calculation Time (s)	0.113	8.304	164.665	1321.804	6959.09

simulation to track the comparison between principal markings and average throughputs by the Markov model and the SPN estimator.

3   Case Study

We will consider the example of Silva and Recalde [33]. Figure 3 shows a manufacturing system with four machines (T_1 to T_4), and three tools with limited resources (P_1 to P_3). In this model of SPN, the initial marking $M_1 = (5, 0, 0, 0, 4)^T$, and the vector of the parameters of the transitions $\mu = (1,1,1,1,1)^T$.

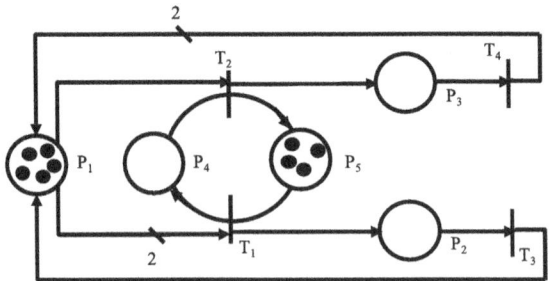

Fig. 3. Large industrial system.

The simulation of the SPN enables the computation of approximate values for average throughputs, markings, and standard reliability indicators. It is considered a stochastic estimator for the Markov Model. The major advantage of this estimator is that the determination of the SPNs steady state no longer necessitates the calculation of the reachability graph, which can be laborious [6]. This is particularly relevant in the case of the Markov model, where determining the probabilities of the stationary regime requires solving a system of linear equations of considerable size, typically associated with a large number of states. Consequently, it demands significant computation time.

To illustrate this, let's consider Fig. 3, which depicts a high-dimensional model requiring extensive computation time and memory space. The cost associated with finding all the states in this model is more substantial (Fig. 4).

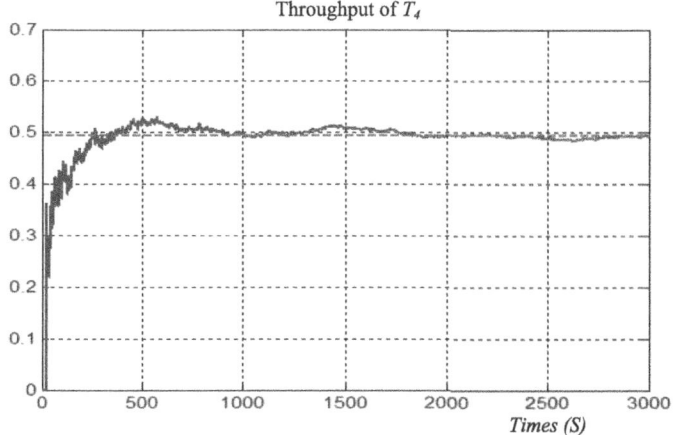

Fig. 4. Average throughput for transition T_4 of Fig. 3.

This estimator exhibits behavior similar to that of the Markov model. Its advantage lies in eliminating the need for determining the reachability graph. However, its major drawback is its slow stochastic convergence, particularly in systems involving rare events that occur across multiple domains. These events are characterized by exceedingly small probabilities. Simulation methods face significant challenges in these situations as the low probability of the event makes its observation highly unlikely in practice, resulting in poor estimation accuracy. Typically, simulations require extensive time to yield satisfactory results.

For instance, let's consider Fig. 3 with a new initial marking of k. The Markov model with $k = 4$. Figure 5 demonstrates the convergence of average asymptotic throughput towards that of the Markov model but only after a long computation time, indicating slow convergence.

Finally, Fig. 6 illustrates the asymptotic Average markings of places P_1 and P_2, which also converge towards the values obtained through Markovian analysis. However, these simulations require more intricate handling due to their delicate nature.

The performance of Markovian analysis is constrained by the size of the state space under study or the increasing mathematical complexity of the problem, leading to extensive and time-consuming computations. Similarly, the stochastic estimator faces a significant limitation in terms of slow convergence during simulations. This limitation arises

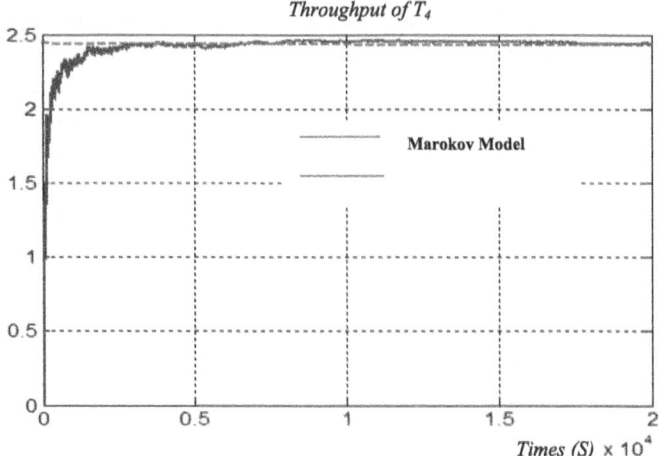

Fig. 5. Average throughput for T_4 transition of Fig. 3.

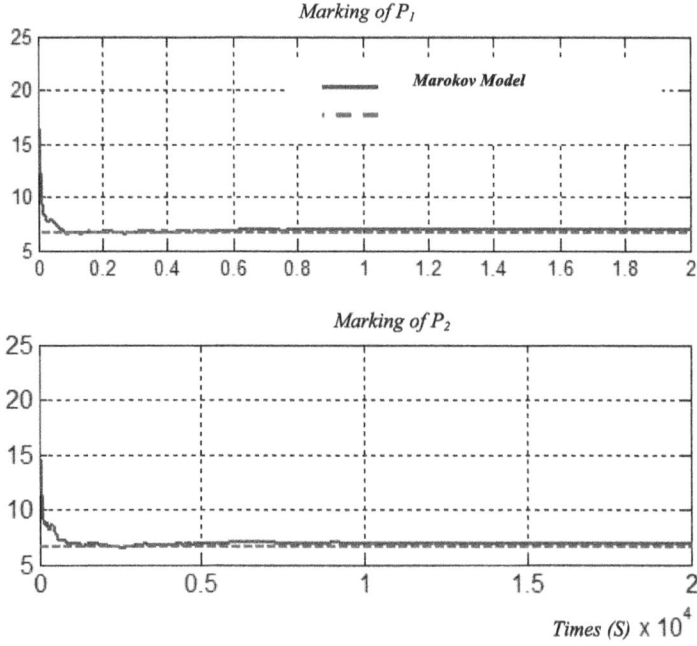

Fig. 6. Average markings for places P_1 and P_2 in the system are shown in Fig. 3.

due to the inherent difficulty of accurately estimating rare events with very small probabilities. The stochastic estimator's convergence rate is notably affected when dealing with such events, making it challenging to achieve precise and reliable results within reasonable simulation times. As a consequence, the accuracy and efficiency of the estimator may be compromised in practical applications.

4 Conclusions

In summary, Markovian analysis offers an analytical solution for assessing system performance indicators in cases where the system is ergodic and the state space is manageable. However, the computational time and memory requirements become prohibitive when dealing with complex systems, leading to limitations in its applicability. The exponential growth of the state space makes it challenging to exhaustively identify all states, rendering the study of such systems virtually impossible using the Markovian approach.

An alternative approach involves utilizing Stochastic Petri Nets (SPNs) as estimators for Markov models through simulation. This eliminates the need for reachability graph calculation but introduces the drawback of slow convergence rates, especially for rare events. Achieving accurate results through simulation requires significant time or excessive memory capacity, further constraining the approach.

While the Markovian approach may have slightly longer computation times compared to simulation, its usage remains relevant due to its ability to provide precise results. There exists a threshold where simulation time becomes more efficient. Recognizing the limitations, researchers have focused on addressing the issue of state explosion. The subsequent paper will delve into investigating industrial systems by utilizing the fluidification of SPNs, aiming to overcome these challenges.

References

1. Vázquez-Serrano, J.I., Peimbert-García, R.E., Cárdenas-Barrón, L.E.: Discrete-event simulation modeling in healthcare: a comprehensive review. Int. J. Environ. Res. Public Health **18**(22), 12262 (2021). https://doi.org/10.3390/ijerph182212262
2. Haas, P.J., Shedler, G.S.: Stochastic petri net representation of discrete event simulations. In: IEEE Transactions on Software Engineering, vol. 15, no. 4, pp. 381–393 (1989). https://doi.org/10.1109/32.16599
3. Pinto, C.A., Farinha, J.T., Singh, S.: Contributions of Petri Nets to the Reliability and Availability of an Electrical Power System in a Big European Hospital - A Case Study. WSEAS Transactions on Systems and Control **16** (2021). https://doi.org/10.37394/23203.2021.16.2
4. El Moumen, H., Nabil, E.A., Zerrouk, M.H.: About the Reliability Analysis of Complex Dynamical Systems via Fluidification: A Numerical Approach. Int. J. Reliab. Saf. **1**(1) (2023). https://doi.org/10.1504/IJRS.2023.10057771
5. El Moumen, H., Nabil, E.A., Zerrouk, M.H.: Stochastic and continuous petri nets approximation of markovian model. Int. J. Model Identif. Contr. **1**(1) (2023). https://doi.org/10.1504/IJMIC.2023.10057520
6. El Moumen, H., El Akchioui, N., Zerrouk, M.H.: Reliability analysis by Markov model and stochastic estimator of stochastic petri nets. Int. J. Reliab. Saf. **16**(1/2), 110 (2022). https://doi.org/10.1504/IJRS.2022.128614
7. Florin, G., Fraize, C., Natkin, S.: Stochastic petri nets: properties, applications, and tools. Microelectron. Reliab. **31**(4), 669–697 (1991). https://doi.org/10.1016/0026-2714(91)90009-V
8. Bobbio, A., Puliafito, A., Telek, M., Trivedi, K.S.: Recent developments in non-Markovian stochastic petri nets. J. Circ. Sys. Comp. **8**(1), 119–158 (1998). https://doi.org/10.1142/S0218126698000067
9. Vázquez, C.R., Silva, M.: Hybrid approximations of Markovian petri nets. IFAC Proceedings Volumes **42**(17), 56–61 (2009). https://doi.org/10.3182/20090916-3-ES-3003.00011

10. El-Moumen, H., El Akchioui, N., Zerrouk, M.H.: Limits of Direct Fluidification of Stochastic Petri Nets by Timed CPNs, 040012 (2023). https://doi.org/10.1063/5.0148812
11. Lefebvre, D., Leclercq, E., Khalij, L., de Cursi, E.S., El Akchioui, N.: Approximation of MTS stochastic petri nets steady state by means of continuous petri nets: a numerical approach. IFAC Proceedings Volumes **42**(17), 62–67 (2009). https://doi.org/10.3182/20090916-3-ES-3003.00012
12. Chung, W.K.: Reliability analysis of repairable and non-repairable systems with common-cause failures. Microelectron. Reliab. **29**(4), 545–547 (1989). https://doi.org/10.1016/0026-2714(89)90343-0
13. Rozenburg, G., Engelfriet, J.: Elementary Net Systems. In: Reisig, W., Rozenberg, G. (eds.) Lectures on Petri Nets I: Basic Models – Advances in Petri Nets (Lecture Notes in Computer Science, Vol. 1491, pp. 12–121. Springer (1998)
14. Tirumala Devi, M., Sumathi Uma Maheswari, T.: Reliability and availability for non-repairable & repairable systems using markov modelling. [Online]. Available: www.ije rt.org
15. Hiraishi, K.: Simulating markovian stochastic petri nets by difference equations with interval parameters. Discret. Event Dyn. Syst. **25**(3), 365–386 (2015). https://doi.org/10.1007/s10 626-014-0188-4
16. Vazquez, C.R., Silva, M.: Stochastic hybrid approximations of Markovian petri nets. IEEE Trans Syst. Man Cybern. Syst. **45**(9), 1231–1244 (2015). https://doi.org/10.1109/TSMC. 2014.2387097
17. Reisig, W., Rozenberg, G.: Lectures on petri nets i: basic models. Lecture Notes in Computer Science (1998). https://doi.org/10.1007/3-540-65306-6
18. Kalaiarasi, S., Marceline Anita, A., Geethanjalii, R.: Analysis of System Reliability Using Markov Technique. (2017). [Online]. Available: http://www.ripublication.com
19. David, R., Alla, H.: Discrete, Continuous and Hybrid Petri Nets, 2nd ed., Springer. Berlin, Heidelberg (2005). ISBN 3-540-22480-7
20. Giua, A., Silva, M.: Petri nets and automatic control: a historical perspective. Annu. Rev. Control. **45**, 223–239 (2018). https://doi.org/10.1016/j.arcontrol.2018.04.006
21. David, R.: Petri nets and grafcet for specification of logic controllers. IFAC Proceedings Volumes **26**(2), 683–688 (1993). https://doi.org/10.1016/S1474-6670(17)49215-9
22. El Akchioui, N., Choukrad, S.: Approximations of stochastic nets by means of continuous petri nets. Int. J. Comput. Appl. **155**(4), 26–31 (2016). https://doi.org/10.5120/ijca2016912292
23. EL Moumen, H., EL Akchioui, N.: Fluidization of stochastic petri nets via continuous petri nets: comparative study. J. of Control. Autom. Electr. Syst. **35**(2), 401–414 (2024). https:// doi.org/10.1007/s40313-024-01066-0
24. EL Moumen, H., EL Akchioui, N., Toukmati, A.: Continuous-time markov processes for reliability analysis: a comprehensive study. Presented at the 4th International Conference on Innovative Research in Applied Science, Engineering and Technology (IRASET 2024), pp. 1–8. IEEE, FEZ, Morocco, 16–17 May (2024). https://doi.org/10.1109/IRASET.2024. 10549235
25. Molloy: Performance Analysis Using Stochastic Petri Nets. IEEE Transactions on Computers **C–31**(9), 913–917 (1982). https://doi.org/10.1109/TC.1982.1676110
26. Júlvez, J., Recalde, L., Silva, M.: Steady-state performance evaluation of continuous Mono-T-Semiflow petri nets. Automatica **41**(4), 605–616 (2005). https://doi.org/10.1016/j.automa tica.2004.11.007
27. Gribaudo, M., Sereno, M., Bobbio, A.: Fluid Stochastic Petri Nets: An Extended Formalism to Include Non-Markovian Models. In: Proceedings - 8th International Workshop on Petri Nets and Performance Models, PNPM 1999, pp. 74–81. Institute of Electrical and Electronics Engineers Inc. (1999). https://doi.org/10.1109/PNPM.1999.796554

28. Vazquez, C.R., Recalde, L., Silva, M.: Stochastic continuous-state approximation of marko-vian petri net systems. In: 2008 47th IEEE Conference on Decision and Control, pp. 901–906, IEEE (2008). https://doi.org/10.1109/CDC.2008.4739075

29. Silva, M., Recalde, L.: On fluidification of petri nets: from discrete to hybrid and continuous models. Annu. Rev. Control. **28**(2), 253–266 (2004). https://doi.org/10.1016/j.arcontrol.2004.05.002

30. Lefebvre, D., Leclercq, E.: Piecewise constant timed continuous PNs for the steady-state estimation of stochastic PNs. Discrete Event Dynamic Systems: Theory and Applications **22**(2), 179–196 (2012). https://doi.org/10.1007/s10626-011-0114-y

31. Murata, T.: Petri nets: properties, analysis, and applications. Proc. IEEE **77**, 541–580 (1989). https://doi.org/10.1109/5.24143

32. EL Moumen, H., EL Akchioui, N.E., Zerrouk, M.H.: Continuous approximation of stochastic petri nets: adaptive maximal firing speeds. In: Bendaoud, M., El Fathi, A., Bakhsh, F.I., Pierluigi, S. (eds) Advances in Control Power Systems and Emerging Technologies. ICESA 2023. Advances in Science, Technology & Innovation, Springer, Cham.https://doi.org/10.1007/978-3-031-51796-9_16

33. Kara, R., Loiseau, J.J., Djennoune, S.: Quantitative analysis of continuous weighted marked graphs. Nonlinear Anal. Hybrid Syst. **2**(4), 1010–1020 (2008). https://doi.org/10.1016/j.nahs.2008.07.001

34. Recalde, L., Teruel, E., Silva, M.: Autonomous Continuous P/T Systems, pp. 107–126 (1999). https://doi.org/10.1007/3-540-48745-X_8

35. Marsan, M.A., Chiola, G.: On Petri Nets with Deterministic and Exponentially Distributed Firing Times, pp. 132–145 (1987). https://doi.org/10.1007/3-540-18086-9_23

36. Desel, J., Juhás, G.: What is a petri net? informal answers for the informed reader. In: Ehrig, H., Padberg, J., Juhás, G., Rozenberg, G. (eds.) Lecture Notes in Computer Science, pp. 1–25. Springer (2001)

37. Maione, G., Mangini, A.M., Ottomanelli, M.: A Generalized Stochastic Petri Net Approach for Modeling Activities of Human Operators in Intermodal Container Terminals. IEEE Trans-actions on Automation Science and Engineering **13**(4) (2016). https://doi.org/10.1109/TASE.2016.2553439

38. Navarro-Gutiérrez, M., Ramírez-Treviño, A., Silva, M.: Dual perspectives of equilibrium throughput properties of continuous Mono-T-Semiflow petri nets: firing rate and initial mark-ing variations. Automatica **136**, 110074 (2022). https://doi.org/10.1016/j.automatica.2021.110074

Emerging Mobile Apps for Enhancing L2 Listening: A Case Study of Moroccan Students

Hassane Benlaghrissi[(✉)] [ID] and L. Meriem Ouahidi [ID]

Department of English, Sultan Moulay Slimane University, Beni Mellal, Morocco
benlaghrissi@gmail.com

Abstract. Recently, learners and instructors widely utilise a wide range of educational mobile-assisted language learning (MALL) applications, making MALL the best potential framework for improving language skills and enhancing language learning and teaching quality. Despite the rising popularity of several popular apps to support language learning and teaching, empirical research on their pedagogical potential in improving language skills, mainly listening skills, still needs to be researched. Equally important, though recent evidence has proven the effectiveness of MALL, such as Podcasts and TED Talks, in boosting learners' listening skills, more research is needed into the implementation of other recent applications, such as English Listening Step by Step. Given this, this experimental study analysed the potential benefits of a mobile application in enhancing the listening skills of Moroccan EFL secondary school students. The study included a control group (n = 30) and an experimental group (n = 30). While students in the control group were taught listening traditionally, the experimental group used a mobile application (English Listening Step by Step) for one semester. A listening pre- and post-test was used to compare the participants' performance in both groups. For data analysis, independent sample t-tests (SPSS-26) were used to determine if there was a difference in the scores of the groups before and after the intervention. The results showed that the experimental group outperformed the control group's overall listening performance and sub-skills: listening for gist and detail. As a result, it was found that utilising English Listening Step by Step app boosted students' listening skills more effectively than traditional instruction.

Keywords: English Listening Step by Step · experimental study · listening skills · MALL · mobile apps · pedagogical potential

1 Introduction

Listening is crucial in everyday life and academic settings (Deveci, 2018; Purdy and Borisoff, 1997; Yildirim and Yildirim, 2016). Learning a language involves mastering four language skills: listening, speaking, reading, and writing (Aydoğan and Akbarov, 2014; Kumar and Shankar, 2021; Sadiku, 2015). However, "listening is perhaps the most critical for language learning" (Vandergrift, 1997, p. 387) of these four skills. Listening plays a critical role in students' language acquisition and enhancement since it provides intelligible input, and thus, it is the key to acquiring a language (Hamouda, 2013).

© The Author(s), under exclusive license to Springer Nature Switzerland AG 2025
H. Hagras et al. (Eds.): ISACS 2023, CCIS 2255, pp. 422–434, 2025.
https://doi.org/10.1007/978-3-031-93448-3_34

Nunan (1997) describes listening as the basic skill for learning a language. Learners will never develop communication skills without effective listening since over 50% of students' time spent functioning in a foreign language is devoted to this skill. According to research, regular listening instruction can help students comprehend spoken language better, which, in effect, facilitates and improves language learning (Ahmadi, 2016).

Despite the significant role listening plays in L2 acquisition, it remains the least researched (Vandergrift, 2007), the most neglected (Kline, 1996), and thus a secondary skill (Nunan, 1997). In the words of Nunan (2002), listening is "the Cinderella skill in second language learning" (p. 238) since speaking and writing are often prioritised above listening and reading. Equally important, EFL learners find enhancing listening skills challenging due to the diverse critical processes to comprehend the spoken language with distinct features from the written language (Goss, 1982). Goh (2000) found several linguistic problems encountered by learners during the cognitive processing steps of perception, parsing, and utilisation. For the perception phase of listening comprehension, learners have difficulties recognising words they already know, neglect the following parts when they think about the meaning, have difficulties chunking streams of speech, miss the beginning of the text, and have concentration problems. In the parsing phase, learners quickly forget what is heard, have difficulties forming mental 13 representations from words heard, and thus cannot comprehend subsequent input parts due to previous problems. During the last phase, learners can understand words but not the intended meaning and are confused about critical ideas in the message.

In addition to the above difficulties, sociolinguistic, psychological, and environmental features may also develop or impede listening comprehension. Sociolinguistic elements include students' cultural backgrounds and regional accents. Psychological features include the extent to which students use both listening processes, bottom-up and top-down, their ability to decode the spoken message, and their use of metacognitive strategies to regulate their learning (Walker, 2014). Environmental conditions such as room temperature, background, and listening equipment also play a role in listening performance (Wilson, 2008).

Aiming at stimulating EFL listening and addressing the above challenges learners encounter, generating an innovative model of teaching listening becomes pre-requisite. Correspondingly, mobile-assisted language learning (MALL), as an alternative to the traditional teaching of listening, is believed to support the skill, connect classroom learning with out-of-class learning, and provide learners with unlimited opportunities for enhancing listening comprehension thanks to the unique characteristics of mobile devices. Mobile phones, for example, have a variety of functionalities that facilitate language learning, including SMS, MMS, Facebook, Twitter, internet access, MP3/MP4 players, a digital camera, and a video recorder. They also provide a variety of built-in educational applications, such as electronic dictionaries, speech recording, and listening (El Hariry, 2015; Chinnery, 2006).

With their unique properties, these new tools are precious for enhancing overall language ability, including proficiency in listening comprehension. Learners are exposed to audio and video recordings of spoken texts to practice listening, emphasising material from native speakers, which is a significant contribution of modern technologies. Additionally, the devices provide a variety of Help Options that clarify, expand, and change the spoken text. They also prepare, guide, and show learners effective listening techniques and tips (Hubbard, 2017). In this context, Blake (2016) asserts that the explosion of native-speaker-authored content on the web has been the most significant recent change in listening practice (p.132). YouTube, in particular, continues to be a never-ending supply of authentic material spanning a wide range of genres. Undoubtedly, one of the most effective methods for promoting second language learning and, more specifically, listening ability is using authentic language materials produced by native speakers.

English Listening Step by Step is a recent app currently being researched to improve EFL students' listening skills and overcome listening difficulties. The app is free and released in 2018 with an updated 2023 version. The app covers several topics in grades, ranging from family to story listening. Each lesson includes a test and transcript to help learners check their listening skills and follow native speakers. Students can translate any word in their mother language. They can also hear English American or British American.

In a nutshell, strengthening learners' listening comprehension continues to be one of MALL's most crucial contributions to foreign language acquisition. Recent evidence has proven MALL's effectiveness in boosting learners' listening skills through Podcasts and TED Talks. Nevertheless, further study is required to implement recent applications, such as English Listening Step by Step. Therefore, this study aims to broaden our understanding of MALL research in listening by investigating the pedagogical role of the English Listening Step by Step application in improving Moroccan secondary school students' listening skills, thus providing an essential opportunity for furthering our understanding of MALL research.

2   Literature Review

Although extensive research has been carried out on using mobile technologies to enhance English language skills, the literature has shown a need for MALL research on listening (Kukulska-Hulme and Shield, 2008). However, what has been published thus far suggests that mobile devices effectively support collaborative listening and speaking activities. In his one-group investigation, Gonulal (2020) investigated how podcasts and vodcasts improved the overall listening skills of college students in Turkey. The year-long study revealed that learners improved their overall listening skills considerably. Listening tests and log assignments also demonstrated noticeable progress in students' pronunciation.

Alzieni (2020) studied the effect of MALL on Dubai Men's College students' listening skills. The results obtained from IELTS (International English Language Testing System) indicated a substantial difference in pre- and post-test scores between the experimental and control groups favouring the experimental group. One year later, Sofiyan and Lidiyatul (2021) conducted a one-group experimental study in Indonesia to consider whether ELLLO Application improved senior high school students' listening skills. The pre and post-test scores confirmed a significant difference between students' pre-tests and post-tests. Thus, ELLLO Application improved students' listening skills.

In their quasi-experimental study, Mallampalli et al. (2021) examined the role of MALL in enhancing second-language listening. Further, the research sought to elucidate the difficulties encountered by both learners and instructors, as well as stakeholders' perspectives on the usage of MALL to improve listening skills. Participants were divided into an experimental group (n = 59) who brought their own devices (BYOD) and a control group (n = 60) who used desktop computers. The researcher worked with the experimental group using a variety of applications, including YouTube, TED Talks, WhatsApp, Learn English Podcasts, and English Listening Practice Apps. Listening pre- and post-test findings demonstrated a considerable change in the experimental group's performance.

In another quasi-experimental study, Yuniarti and Rakhmawati (2022) questioned whether the use of Genius Application affected the listening skills of 41 Indonesian university students. Based on the results of the pre and post-tests, the authors found an improvement in the experimental group in terms of understanding and questioning practice as well as in phoneme words. Likewise, Vera de la Torre et al. (2022) performed a similar study in Ecuador to assess students' acceptance of mobile technology for learning and enhancing listening skills using two mobile apps: English Listening and 6 min English. The authors concluded that the two apps improved students' listening comprehension by 95%.

Given all that has been mentioned, one may suppose there is still a scarcity of listening MALL studies, especially in the Arab world. In addition, research thus far provides evidence that fewer have been undertaken in secondary schools. Also, it is noteworthy that much of recent research on MALL in listening focused on the effectiveness of podcasts and TED Talks or the most common apps such as ELLO and 6 min English. In contrast, very little is known about the role of other recent apps, such as English Listening Step by Step, in boosting learners' listening skills. Therefore, this study sets out to obtain data to help address some of these research gaps by examining the pedagogical role of implementing English Listening Step by Step app in enhancing secondary school students' listening performance. Accordingly, the following research questions were addressed:

1. Is the implementation of English Listening Step by Step app more effective in enhancing students' overall listening performance than conventional teaching?
2. Is the implementation of English Listening Step by Step app more effective in enhancing students' listening sub-skills than conventional teaching?

Accordingly, the hypotheses were formulated as follows:

Hypothesis one:

H0: Participants who taught listening via English Listening Step by Step app showed no difference in their overall listening performance from participants in the control group.

H1: Participants who taught listening via English Listening Step by Step app scored significantly higher in their overall listening performance than participants in the control group.

Hypothesis two:

H0: Participants who taught listening via English Listening Step by Step app showed no difference in their listening sub-skills from participants in the control group.

H1: Participants who taught listening via English Listening Step by Step app scored significantly higher in their listening sub-skills than participants in the control group.

3 Methods and Procedures

A pre-test-post-test equivalent group design was used in this true experimental research. The experimental and control groups were chosen and assigned randomly through a lottery method, and the data were compared quantitatively. There are two variables in this study: one independent and one dependent. The independent variable is the listening mobile app English Listening Step by Step (X1) for the experimental group and traditional teaching of listening for the control group. In contrast, the dependent variable is students' listening performance (Y1).

3.1 Participants

The participants of this study were sixty common core EFL secondary school students (14–16 years old) studying in a high school in the Directorate of Khenifra, Benni-Mellal-Khenifra Academy, Morocco. The sixty students were randomly and equally assigned to the experimental group (n = 30) and control group (n = 30).

3.2 Data collection instruments

To consider the impact of English Listening by Step by Step mobile app on EFL learners' listening performance, a listening test was used as a pre and post-test to assess the participants' listening performance in both groups. The listening test comprised two sections. Section one included two questions targeting listening for general information. In the second section, the focus was on listening for specific information, involving two questions. The researcher designed the listening test based on students' textbooks and was graded out of 20.

3.2.1 Validity of the Pre-test

Content Validity Index (CVI) was used to confirm the instrument's validity. The listening pre-test was given to eight field experts: four MALL researchers, two English language supervisors, and two experienced teachers. However, the judges rated the test to be calculated at 0.902, which is a high value (higher than 0.80) (Rubio et al., 2003), confirming the validity of the test.

3.2.2 Reliability of the Pre-test

To ensure the reliability of the listening test, test re-test reliability was examined. A sample of 22 students not participating in the study undertook the listening test twice (two weeks following the initial test-taking). The Intraclass Correlation Coefficient (ICC), as presented in Table 1, suggested a value of 0.964, implying a very significant positive correlation between the two scores in the two tests. Therefore, the findings show that the listening pre-test is hugely reliable.

Table 1. Test-retest Reliability of the Listening Test

Cronbach's Alpha	Cronbach's Alpha Based on Standardised Items	N of Items
,964	,964	2

3.3   Procedure and Implementation

The investigation lasted one semester during the school year 2022–2023. Before the implementation, the researcher ensured all experimental group participants had smartphones. Then, the listening mobile application to be utilised: English Listening Step by Step, was presented to the participants. The researcher assisted all participants in installing the application and downloading the discussions, audio, talks, tales, and interviews to be utilised offline. Both groups took part in the study using different teaching methods. The control group received conventional instruction, whereas the experiment group received mobile-assisted language learning. The experiment group had to complete a listening task within a time limit every two weeks corresponding to the curriculum's five units.

Following the treatment, the two groups were given a post-test compared to the pretest to assess whether utilising the mobile app influenced learners' listening performance. As a final point, to date, students in both groups took the posttest without prior notice. Also, the researcher ensured the same examination conditions for both groups. The instructional and data-gathering procedures are summarised in Table 2:

Table 2. Instructional and Data Gathering Procedures

Weeks	The Experimental Group	The Control Group
Week 1	took the pre-test	
Week 2	Introduced to English Listening Step by Step application	Introduced to conventional teaching of listening
Weeks 3 and 4	Lesson 1: Study for Exams	Taught listening conventionally through students' textbooks
Weeks 5 and 6	Lesson 2: Doctor's Visit	
Weeks 7 and 8	Lesson 3: Making Plans	
Week 9 and 10	Lesson 4: Book Club	
Weeks 11 and 12	Lesson 5: A Night at the Theater	
Week 13	took the post-test	

3.4   Data Analysis

The analysis of the data collected began with confirming that the scores of each group in the pre-test and post-test were distributed normally. The homogeneity was then verified in both tests. The findings of the Kolmogorov-Smirnov and Shapiro-Wilk tests both revealed a normal data distribution. Furthermore, according to the results of Levene's test, the control and experimental groups were homogenous. As a result, parametric statistical analysis was performed using independent sample t-tests to compare the two groups' listening pre-test and post-test scores.

4 Results

4.1 Research Question 1

Is the implementation of English Listening Step by Step app more effective in enhancing students' overall listening performance than conventional teaching?

Attempting to answer the first research question, an independent-sample t-test was applied to compare the listening pre-test's scores between the control and experimental groups to determine whether there were any differences between the two prior to treatment. The group statistics are shown in Table 3.

Table 3. Group Statistics on Pre-test of the Control and Experimental Groups

Groups	N	Mean	Std. Deviation	Std. Error Mean
Control	30	8,87	2,726	,498
Experimental	30	9,13	2,488	,454

From the data in Table 3, the mean value of the control group was 8.37 with a standard deviation of 2.726 and 9.13 with a standard deviation of 2.488 in the experimental group. Therefore, these values showed no significant difference between the two groups, as the p-value was higher than 0.05 (See Table 4 below). Moreover, these values support the literature review that students have serious problems in listening comprehension.

As homogeneity of variance is a vital assumption of the Independent T-test, the researcher had to ensure that the variances of the two groups were equal. From Table 4, the p-value is 0.750, higher than 0.05. Thus, the variance of the data was homogeneous. Table 3 illustrates a p-value (2-tailed) of .694, which was higher than 0.05 (T = −.396; df = 58; p > .05). This suggests that there were no significant differences between the control and experimental groups in their overall listening performance before the intervention.

After one semester of implementation, an independent-sample t-test was performed to compare the control and experimental groups' listening post-test scores to consider whether there were differences in the post-test scores. The group statistics are reported in Table 6.

Table 6 illustrates that the control group had a mean score of 9.40 (SD = 3.820) compared to 13.70 (SD = 2.842) for the experimental group. Even though the experimental group outperformed the control group, a further analysis with an independent t-test was essential for assessing whether or not the difference was statistically significant (See Table 7).

Table 4. Independent Samples T-test on Pre-Test of the Two Groups

	Levene's Test for Equality of Variances		t-test for Equality of Means							
	F	Sig	T	df	Sig. (2-tailed)	Mean Difference	Std. Error Difference	95% Confidence Interval of the Difference		
								Lower	Upper	
Equal variances assumed	,103	,750	−,396	58	,694	−,267	,674	−1,615	1,082	
Equal variances not assumed			−,396	57,522	,694	−,267	,674	−1,616	1,082	

Table 6. Group Statistics on Post-test of the Control and Experimental Groups

Groups	N	Mean	Std. Deviation	Std. Error Mean
Control	30	9,40	3,820	,697
Experimental	30	13,70	2,842	,519

At first, Levene's test for equality of variances was run to determine whether or not the group variances were equal. The results show that ($p = 0.086$, with $\alpha > 0.05$), which confirms the assumption that the variances of the two groups were equal. In the t-test, as Table 7 shows, there is a significant difference between the mean scores of the post-tests of the control group ($M = 9.40$) and experimental group ($M = 13.70$), with a mean difference of 4.300. Moreover, Table 9 illustrates a p-value (2-tailed) of .000, which was smaller than 0.05 ($T = -4.946$; $df = 58$; $p > .05$). Overall, these results indicate the positive effect of using English Listening Step by Step app in improving students' overall listening performance after the treatment.

4.2 Research Question 2

Is the implementation of English Listening Step by Step app more effective in enhancing students' listening subskills than conventional teaching?

Two independent sample t-tests were run to consider if the implementation of MALL affected students' listening sub-skills: listening for general information and specific information. The results are presented in Table 8.

Table 7. Independent Samples T-test on Post-Test of the Two Groups

	Levene's Test for Equality of Variances		t-test for Equality of Means							
	F	Sig	T	Df	Sig. (2-tailed)	Mean Difference	Std. Error Difference	95% Confidence Interval of the Difference		
								Lower	Upper	
Equal variances assumed	3,049	,086	−4,946	58	,000	−4,300	,869	−6,040	−2,560	
Equal variances not assumed			−4,946	53,578	,000	−4,300	,869	−6,043	−2,557	

Table 8. Independent T-tests on Listening subskills in the Pre-test

	Control Group	Experimental Group	
	Mean	Mean	Sig. (2-tailed)
Listening for gist	4.2000	4.7667	**.228**
Listening for detail	4.6667	4.3667	**.376**

From the above table, we can see that the mean score for the control group in listening for gist was 4.2000 and 4.6667 in listening for detail. In contrast, the experimental group had a mean score of 4.7667 in listening for gist and 4.3667 in listening for detail. The pre-test mean scores, as a result, were equal in listening sub-skills as the p-value was greater than 0.05 ($p > .05$). Table 9 presents the post-test results.

Table 9. Independent T-tests on Listening subskills in the Post-test

	Control Group	Experimental Group	
	Mean	Mean	Sig. (2-tailed)
Listening for gist	4.6667	6.8000	.000
Listening for detail	4.7333	6.9000	.000

The control group's mean scores in the two subskills were 4.6667 in listening for gist and 4.7333 in listening for detail. Meanwhile, the experimental group had mean scores of 6.8000 and 6.9000 in listening for gist and listening for detail, respectively.

Accordingly, a statistical difference was found in favour of the experimental group, with a p-value (2-tailed) of 0.000 that was less than 0.05. Therefore, unlike traditional teaching, implementing English Listening Step by Step helped improve students' sub-skills: listening for gist and listening for detail.

All in all, the above findings illustrate that the experimental group taught listening using MALL outperformed the control group who received traditional teaching of listening. These findings proved the pedagogical potential of utilising English Listening Step by Step application in enhancing listening skills of the experimental group after the treatment. Therefore, the implementation of English Listening Step by Step application was more effective in developing EFL learners' overall listening and sub-skills than conventional teaching. Thus, the null hypotheses were rejected, and the alternative hypotheses were accepted.

These findings, however, are unsurprising since English Listening Step by Step allowed students in the experimental group to practice listening skills anytime, anywhere, using authentic materials produced by native speakers. In addition, learners could find various curriculum-related topics at different levels, thus meeting students' needs and learning styles. The study focused on five listening lessons, but students could still freely practice their listening skills by selecting other themes of interest. The app features allow learners to practice what they have learned through multiple exercises, assess their listening abilities, and get immediate feedback. This allowed individual scaffolding and keeping mistakes personal. For checking pronunciation, the app enabled US or UK pronunciation feature. These unique features provided a wonderful opportunity for students to easily and freely practice their listening skills and reflect on their learning.

5   Discussion

Independent t-tests indicated no difference in the pre-test of the two groups' overall listening performance (p = 0.694 > 0.05), while it showed a significant difference in the post-test (p = 0.000 < 0.05). Likewise, the analysis of listening sub-skills revealed a substantial difference in the posttest, with a p-value of 0.000 in listening for gist and detail. This suggests that the experimental group that utilised the listening mobile application: English Listening Step by Step outperformed the control group with conventional ways of teaching. The more remarkable results in the experimental group's post-test were undoubtedly due to the listening tasks using the given mobile app. Therefore, the present study agrees with several other studies (Al-Shamsi et al., 2020; Alzieni, 2020; Gonulal, 2020; Vera de la Torre et al. 2022; Yuniarti and Rakhmawati, 2022) that confirmed the effectiveness of implementing mobile-assisted language learning in enhancing EFL English listening skills. This is certainly due to the unique features of mobile devices that provide learners with various functionalities that facilitate and assist language learning.

The successful outcomes of the implementation has several possible explanations. Admittedly, enhancing students' listening skills results from the unique pedagogical affordances of mobile-assisted language learning that allow learners to boost self-confidence, self-direction, and engagement. They can also provide greater access to teaching/learning resources, make learning a personalised experience, and enhance performance (Zhang and Cristol, 2019). Equally important, Burston (2014) adds that extending classroom learning to out-of-class learning and the "anytime" and "anywhere" added value have outstanding contributions to language learning. Further, these affordances can open up new learning opportunities, a more flexible atmosphere, constant and fast access to information, and enhanced chances for learners to make their own choices and decisions (Darmi and Albion, 2014).

Another explanation of the success of the implementation is due to the features of English Listening Step by Step app. These features allow learners to practice listening skills in various contexts and with different native speakers. Unlike conventional teaching, learners can practice and evaluate their listening abilities, check and practice pronunciation, follow subtitles, and get instant feedback. These features make learning listening more enjoyable since learners control their learning using mobile technologies they are much familiar with. In this regard, many studies confirmed that students using MALL devices enhanced their English learning due to the enjoyable learning atmosphere these devices can provide (Mallampalli et al., 2021; Sofiyan and Lidiyatul, 2021).

6   Conclusion and Pedagogical Implications

This experimental study investigated the effectiveness of implementing mobile apps in enhancing the listening performance of Moroccan EFL secondary school students. The results showed that using English Listening Step by Step mobile app helped improve students' overall listening performance and sub-skills: listening for gist and listening for detail. Thus, this quantitative analysis is congruent with the literature review suggesting that MALL positively affects learners' outcomes. Accordingly, the findings provided positive answers to the research questions.

With respect to the positive outcomes of the present investigation, implications for students, teachers, syllabus designers, and educational authorities are suggested. First, EFL students can utilise mobile apps to enhance their listening skills for self-study. Teachers can also encourage and utilise mobile apps with their students. This facilitates the language process and helps overcome some problems in language learning, especially in a critical language area, such as listening. This way, teachers revise their teaching techniques and strategies and bridge the gap between out-of-class and classroom learning. Moreover, the study's findings can help syllabus designers and educational authorities incorporate new technology and social networks into teaching practices. Undoubtedly, incorporating modern mobile technologies makes learning more enjoyable, boosts learners' motivation, and performance, and improves learning quality (Zhang and Zhang, 2023).

Though the present study came to important conclusions within mobile-assisted language learning research, it has some limitations. First, the investigation is purely quantitative examining one English skill. The study was also conducted in one secondary school with limited number of participants. Accordingly, future researchers are recommended to mix quantitative data with qualitative data, such as conducting focus group discussions or interviews with students to explore their attitudes toward the impact of implementing mobile apps on their learning, thus having an in-depth analysis. In addition, future research should investigate the effectiveness of mobile apps on different English skills in different contexts using large samples.

References

Ahmadi, M.: The importance of listening comprehension in language learning. Int. J. Res. Eng. Educ. **1**(1), 7–10 (2016)

Al-Shamsi, A., Al-Mekhlafi, A.M., Busaidi, S.Al, Hilal, M.M.: The effects of mobile learning on listening comprehension skills and attitudes of omani EFL adult learners. Int. J. Learn. Teach. Educ. Res. **19**(8), 16–39 (2020). https://doi.org/10.26803/IJLTER.19.8.2

Alzieni, H.: The Impact of Mobile-Assisted Language Learning (MALL) in Developing the Listening Skill: A Case of Students at Dubai Men's College, the United Arab Emirates. Arab World English Journal **2**, 84–95 (2021). https://doi.org/10.24093/awej/mec2.6

Aydoğan, H., Akbarov, A.A.: The four basic language skills, whole language & intergrated skill approach in mainstream university classrooms in Turkey. Mediterr. J. Soc. Sci. **5**(9), 672–680 (2014). https://doi.org/10.5901/mjss.2014.v5n9p672

Blake, R.J.: Technology and the Four Skills. Lang. Learn. Technol. **20**(2), 129–142 (2016)

Burston, J.: MALL : The Pedagogical Challenges. Comput. Assist. Lang. Learn. **27**(4), 344–357 (2014). https://doi.org/10.1080/09588221.2014.914539

Chinnery, G.M.: Going to the MALL: Mobile Assisted Language Learning. Language Learning & Technology **10**(1), 9–16 (2006). http://www.llt.msu.edu/vol10num1/pdf/emerging.pdf

Darmi, R., Albion, P.: A review of integrating mobile phones for language learning. In: Proc. The 10th International Conference on Mobile Learning (2014)

Deveci, T.: Student perceptions on collaborative writing in a project-based course. Universal J. Educ. Res. **6**(4), 721–732 (2018). https://doi.org/10.13189/ujer.2018.060415

El Hariry, N.A.: Mobile phones as useful language learning tools. European Scientific Journal **11**(16), 298–317 (2015). https://eujournal.org/index.php/esj/article/viewFile/5870/5593

Goh, C.C.M.: A cognitive perspective on language learners' listening comprehension problems. System **28**(1), 55–75 (2000). https://doi.org/10.1016/S0346-251X(99)00060-3

Gonulal, T.: Improving listening skills with extensive listening using podcasts and vodcasts. Int. J. Contemporary Educ. Res. **7**, 311–320 (2020)

Goss, B.: Listening as Information Processing. Commun. Q. **30**(4), 304–307 (1982). https://doi.org/10.1080/01463378209369465

Hamouda, A.: An investigation of listening comprehension problems encountered by Saudi students in the El listening classroom. Int. J. Acad. Res. Progressive Educ. Develop. **2**(2), 113–155 (2013)

Hubbard, P.: Technologies for Teaching and Learning L2 Listening. In: Carol A., (ed.) Chapelle; Shannon, Sauro: Handbook of Technology and Second Language Teaching and Learning, pp. 93–106. John Wiley and Sons (2017)

Kline, J.A.: Listening Effectively. Air University Press (1996)

Kukulska-Hulme, A., Shield, L.: An overview of mobile assisted language learning: from content delivery to supported collaboration and interaction. ReCALL **20**(3), 271–289 (2008). https://doi.org/10.1017/S0958344008000335

Kumar, R.N., Shankar, L.R.: The importance of listening skill in language acquisition- the problems experienced & strategies adopted in teaching listening skill. Int. J. Innov. Res. Technol. **7**(12), 309–314 (2021)

Mallampalli S.M., Anumula, V.S.S., Akkara S.: Enhancing second language listening skills through smartphones: a case study. In: Auer, E., Tsiatsos, M. (eds.) Throsyvoulos. Internet of Things, Infrastructures and Mobile Applications. In: Proc. The 13th IMCL Conference. Spring Nature Switzerland AG (2021)

Nunan, D.: Approaches to teaching listening in the language classroom. In: Proc. The 1997 Korea TESOL Conference

Nunan, D.: Listening in language learning. In: Richards, J.C., Renandya, W.A. (eds.) Methodology in Language Teaching (2002). https://doi.org/10.1017/CBO9780511667190.032

Purdy, M., Borisoff, D.: Listening in Everyday Life: A Personal and Professional Approach, 2nd ed. University Press of America, Inc (1997)

Rubio, M.D., Marla, B.-W., Susan, S.T., Suzanne, L.E., Shannon, R.: Objectifying content validity: conducting a content validity study in social work research. Social Work Research **27**(2), 1869–1876 (2003). https://doi.org/10.1016/b0-12-227055-x/00351-5

Sadiku, L.M.: The importance of four skills reading, speaking, writing, listening in a lesson hour. European Journal of Language and Literature Studies **1**(1), 29–31 (2015)

Sofiyan, M., Lidiyatul, I.S.M.F.: The use of ELLLO in improving teaching listening to students. Ethical Lingua **8**(1), 86–98 (2021). https://doi.org/10.30605/25409190.256

Vandergrift, L.: Recent developments in second and foreign language listening comprehension research. Lang. Teach. **40**(3), 191–210 (2007). https://doi.org/10.1017/S0261444807004338

Vandergrift, L.: The Comprehension Strategies of Second Language (French) Listeners: A Descriptive Study. Foreign Lang. Ann. **30**(3), 387–409 (1997). https://doi.org/10.1111/j.1944-9720.1997.tb02362.x

Vera de la Torre, A.J., Mendoza Chavarria, V.C., Escalante Gamazo, M.C., Cumbe Coraizaca, D.M.: Building up the English Language Listening Skill through M-Learning Tools. A Preliminary Study. ConcienciaDigital **5**(1.1), 983–994 (2022). https://doi.org/10.33262/concienciadigital.v5i1.1.2045

Walker, N.: Listening: the most difficult skill to teach. Encuentro **23**, 167–175 (2014)

Wilson, J.: How to Teach Listening. Pearson Rducation Limited (2008)

Yildirim, S., Yildirim, O.: The importance of listening in language learning and listening comprehension problems experienced by language learners: a literature review. Abant İzzet Baysal Üniversitesi Eğitim Fakültesi Dergisi **16**(4), 2064–2110 (2016)

Yuniarti, F., Rakhmawati, D.: Genius application mobile learning on listening skills and attitudes of EFL adult learners. Journal of English Language Teaching and Applied Linguistics **8**(1), 62–71 (2022). p-ISSN: 2356-2048 e-ISSN: 2356-203x

Zhang, J., Zhang, P.: Influence of APP-assisted teaching on teaching quality in mobile learning. Int. J. Emerg. Technol. Learn. (iJET) **18**(9), 4–16 (2023). https://doi.org/10.3991/ijet.v18i09.37827

Zhang, Y., Cristol, D.: Handbook of Mobile Teaching and Learning. In: Spring (2019). https://doi.org/10.1007/978-981-13-2766-7_134

Security and Information Processing

Unveiling Blockchain Technology: A Comprehensive Exploration of Types and Variants

Fdilat Ismail$^{(\boxtimes)}$ ⓘ, Louzaoui Khadija ⓘ, and Benlhachmi Khalid ⓘ

Laboratory for Computer Science Research, Ibn Tofail University, Kenitra, Morocco
{fdilat.ismail,khadija.louzaoui,khalid.benlhachmi}@uit.ac.ma

Abstract. Blockchain technology has evolved as a transformative innovation with wide-ranging applications across industries. This article provides a comprehensive overview of blockchain technology and its various types. The article begins by elucidating the fundamental principles underlying blockchain, including decentralization, immutability, and cryptographic security. It explores the three main kinds of blockchain networks: public, private, and consortium. The characteristics, use cases, and advantages of each type are discussed, providing insights into their suitability for different scenarios. Furthermore, the article delves into the prominent blockchain variants, including permissioned, permissionless, and hybrid blockchains. It examines their unique features, such as consensus mechanisms, governance models, scalability, and privacy considerations. The comparative analysis enables readers to understand the trade-offs associated with different blockchain types and choose the most appropriate one for their specific requirements. Additionally, the article highlights notable blockchain platforms and protocols, including Bitcoin, Ethereum, Hyperledger Fabric, and Corda, elucidating their distinctive features and industry applications. The exploration of these platforms equips readers with valuable knowledge to navigate the evolving blockchain landscape. Finally, the article concludes with a discussion on the future prospects and challenges facing blockchain technology. It emphasizes the need for continued research and innovation to address scalability, interoperability, and regulatory concerns, ultimately unlocking the full potential of blockchain for a decentralized and transparent future.

Keywords: blockchain technology · types of blockchains · public blockchain · private blockchain · consortium blockchain · permissioned blockchain · permissionless blockchain · hybrid blockchain · consensus mechanisms · blockchain platforms · nodes · genesis block

1 Introduction

Blockchain technology has revolutionized various industries, offering a decentralized and secure framework for digital transactions. Its potential to transform traditional processes and enhance transparency has garnered significant attention from researchers, businesses, and governments worldwide. This article provides an in-depth exploration

H. Hagras et al. (Eds.): ISACS 2023, CCIS 2255, pp. 437–446, 2025.
https://doi.org/10.1007/978-3-031-93448-3_35

of blockchain technology and its diverse types, drawing insights from notable articles and research. Blockchain, at its core, is a distributed ledger that enables the secure and transparent recording of transactions across various participants. The foundational principles of decentralization, immutability, and cryptographic security form the bedrock of this technology. As highlighted in a study by Swan (2015) [1], blockchain's decentralized nature eliminates the need for intermediaries, allowing for peer-to-peer transactions while maintaining data integrity. To better understand the landscape of blockchain technology, it is essential to explore its various types. Public blockchains, exemplified by Bitcoin, provide an open and permissionless network where anyone can participate in the consensus process [2]. As opposed to that, private blockchains restrict access and participation, catering to specific organizations or entities [1]. A consortium blockchain, operates within a controlled network of trusted participants, making it suitable for industries requiring collaboration and shared governance [3]. The types of blockchains extend beyond their accessibility and permissioning. Permissioned blockchains impose access controls, granting specific participants varying degrees of authority and roles [4]. Permissionlessblockchains, offer an open participation model without centralized control, enabling a high standard of security through consensus algorithms [5]. Hybrid blockchains, a fusion of private and public characteristics, provide flexibility in balancing transparency and privacy [3]. This versatility allows industries to tailor blockchain solutions to their unique requirements, as demonstrated in the study by Zhang et al. (2018) [6] on healthcare data management. Prominent blockchain platforms and protocols have emerged to assist in the implementation of these various types. Bitcoin, the pioneering cryptocurrency based on blockchain technology, showcases the potential of public, permissionless networks [2]. Ethereum, a versatile blockchain platform, introduced the concept of smart contracts, enabling the development of decentralized applications [7]. Hyperledger Fabric, an open-source framework, focuses on private and permissioned blockchains, targeting enterprise use cases [8]. Corda, another prominent platform, specializes in facilitating secure and private transactions among trusted parties [9]. As blockchain technology in a continuous development, addressing challenges such as scalability and interoperability remains crucial [3]. Furthermore, regulatory frameworks must adapt to accommodate this disruptive technology and foster its widespread adoption [4]. In conclusion, this article serves as a comprehensive guide to blockchain technology and its diverse types, drawing from a range of scholarly articles and research. By understanding the principles, characteristics, and applications of various blockchain types, readers can navigate the ever-expanding blockchain landscape and harness its potential for their respective domains.

2   Objective of the Study

Clarify Fundamental Principles: To illuminate the fundamental principles underlying blockchain technology, including its core characteristics such as decentralization, immutability, and cryptographic security, offering readers a robust understanding of the foundational aspects that drive blockchain's functionality.

Categorize and Analyze Blockchain Types: To categorize and analyze the different types and variants of blockchain technology public, private, consortium, permissioned, permissionless, and hybrid blockchains, critically assessing their unique features, applications, and trade-offs.

Evaluate Prominent Platforms and Protocols: To evaluate prominent blockchain platforms and protocols like Bitcoin, Ethereum, Hyperledger Fabric, and Corda, with a focus on delineating their distinctive characteristics and the industries they predominantly serve.

Discuss Future Prospects and Challenges: To provide insights into the forthcoming avenues and challenges for blockchain technology, emphasizing scalability, interoperability, and regulatory adjustments that are quintessential to foster the technology's growth and adoption.

Incorporate Recent Research on Security Aspects: To integrate recent research findings, particularly focusing on the security challenges and solutions elucidated in the 2023 study by Asad Ali, into the discussion to offer a contemporary perspective on the blockchain technology's security paradigm, including potential vulnerabilities and the strategies to mitigate them.

3 Types of Blockchains

3.1 Public Blockchains

Public blockchains, exemplified by Bitcoin, provide an open and permissionless network where anyone can participate in the consensus process [2]. These blockchains are characterized by their transparency, immutability, and robustness, making them suitable for applications such as peer-to-peer transactions and decentralized finance. However, they face challenges regarding scalability and energy consumption.

3.2 Private Blockchains

Private blockchains restrict access and participation, catering to specific organizations or entities. These blockchains prioritize privacy and control, making them suitable for enterprises seeking to leverage blockchain technology within a closed ecosystem. Private blockchains provide faster transaction processing and increased efficiency, but they sacrifice some decentralization and transparency compared to public blockchains [1].

3.3 Consortium Blockchains

Consortium blockchains operate within a controlled network of trusted participants, often forming collaborations between multiple organizations. Consortium blockchains strike a combination between the openness of public blockchains and the control of private blockchains. They offer shared governance, scalability, and improved privacy compared to public blockchains. Consortium blockchains find applications in industries such as supply chain management and healthcare [3].

3.4 Hybrid Blockchains

In the ever-evolving landscape of blockchain technology, hybrid blockchains emerge as a potent solution that amalgamates the strengths of both public and private blockchains. They offer a flexible and customizable platform that maintains a balance between open access and controlled permission, enabling selective transparency which can be pivotal in industries like healthcare and supply chain management. These blockchains inherit robust security features from public blockchains, ensuring secure and verifiable transactions, while also allowing for controlled access akin to private blockchains, thus enhancing privacy and efficiency (Paul et al., 2019). Moreover, the adaptive and user-friendly nature of hybrid blockchains positions them as a future-ready solution capable of catering to diverse organizational needs, fostering a harmonized approach that encapsulates security, transparency, and flexibility. As indicated by industry experts, they are envisioned to play a critical role in the future developments of blockchain technology, potentially revolutionizing sectors with their balanced and versatile approach (Paul & Jacobs, 2021). This dynamic integration represents a promising pathway towards leveraging blockchain technology to its fullest potential, navigating the challenges posed by purely public or private blockchains [3] (Fig. 1).

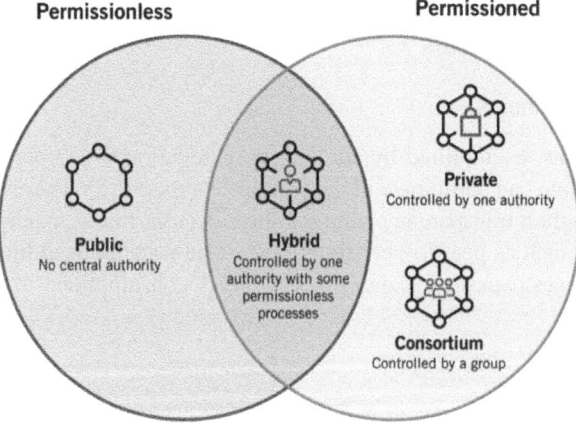

Fig. 1. The Rise of Hybrade Blockchain: Fusing Private and Public elements for Enhanced Efficiency and Security.

3.5 Public vs Private Blockchains

Both private and public blockchain networks operate in a decentralized manner, allowing users to collectively record peer-to-peer transactions without relying on a credible third party for authorization [10]. However, there are distinct characteristics that differentiate public and private blockchains. Private blockchains have a higher transaction processing rate and involve a limited number of authorized participants. This leads to faster consensus within the network and enables a higher volume of transactions to be processed per second. On the contrary, public blockchains have a limited transaction processing rate. Consensus mechanisms like Bitcoin's Proof-of-Work (PoW) in public blockchains require the entire network to agree on the state of transactions. Additionally, public blockchains have inherent risks to information privacy. They rely on an append-only data process, resulting in immutable data storage [3]. Every node in a public blockchain must agree on any changes made, which then need to be recorded in all subsequent blocks. Consequently, mining a single block onto the blockchain takes more time [4]. Furthermore, all blocks in public blockchains are linked back to the genesis block (The first block of a blockchain network, it records the initial state of the system) to maintain the reliability of the blockchain. Private blockchains offer strong data privacy, allowing changes to be made when there is consensus among all participating nodes [1]. On the other hand, controlling the upload of information is a challenge in public blockchains. If sensitive information is uploaded by anyone into the system, it cannot be altered. In a public blockchain, although there is an unlimited number of anonymous nodes, secure communication is ensured through cryptographic techniques. Each node possesses a pair of private and public keys, eliminating the need to trust any individual using the network. All participants are incentivized to adhere to the contract rules to achieve the best outcomes for the network. Consequently, transaction validation and verification can occur without relying on a trusted third party. Transparency is a key strength of public blockchains, as all transactions are publicly accessible for verification. In contrast, private blockchains restrict network access to trusted parties who can validate and verify transactions. Public blockchains are more decentralized due to a higher number of nodes, making it difficult for malicious actors to manipulate the network. However, private blockchains have less nodes, making it easier for a bad actor to gain control, thereby increasing the possibility of hacking and data manipulation. In terms of security, public blockchains are considered more secure. Furthermore, public blockchains doesn't need any infrastructure costs for network setup [13], whereas private blockchains require widespread adoption and operational costs. A federated blockchain merges features from both private and public blockchains [13]. In a federated system, instead of a single entity, a designated leader is assigned to verify transaction processes. This approach represents a partially decentralized blockchain [3], bridging the gap between public and private blockchains. In other words, federated blockchains establish a hybrid network that incorporates elements of low-trust public blockchains and the highly trusted entity model of private blockchains Table 1.

4   Variants of Blockchain

4.1   Permissioned Blockchains

Permissioned blockchains impose access controls, granting specific participants varying degrees of authority and roles. These blockchains are favored in enterprise settings where the network participants are known and trusted. Permissioned blockchains provide improved scalability, efficiency, and regulatory compliance compared to permissionless blockchains. They are suitable for industries requiring controlled access and data privacy [4].

Table 1. Comparative Analysis of Public and Private Blockchains: Key Characteristics and Differences

Criteria	Public Blockchain	Private Blockchain	hybrid Blockchain
Access	Open to everyone	Restricted access, generally to a specific organization or group	Selective access allowing both public transparency and private permissions
Trust	Trustless, consensus based on proof-of-work or proof-of-stake	Trust required, often permissioned and managed by a central authority	Combines decentralized and centralized trust models, offering customizable solutions
Security	High level of security due to decentralization	Depends on the security measures ofthe controlling organization	Enhances security through a combination of public verifiability and permissioned access controls
Transaction Speed	Slower due to network size and consensus mechanism	Faster because of a smaller network size and simplified consensus	Offers adjustable transaction speeds, potentially optimizing between private and public blockchain characteristics
Scalability	Limited by the network size and consensus mechanism	Greater scalability due to fewer nodes participating in the consensus process	Offers balanced scalability, capable of optimization to suit specific needs
Use Case	Cryptocurrencies like Bitcoin, Decentralized apps, Initial Coin Offerings	Interbank transactions, Supply Chain Management, Private Enterprise Operations	Ideal for scenarios requiring both public accessibility and controlled privacy
Transparency	Highly transparent - all transactions are public	Varying levels of transparency - can be audited if required, but transactions are generally private	Provides selective transparency, allowing a mix of public and private verifications
Anonymity	Anonymity can be maintained but all transactions are traceable	Typically not anonymous due to the identity requirement for network participation	Enables customizable anonymity levels, facilitating a balance between transparency and privacy

4.2 Permissionless Blockchains

Permissionless blockchains, also known as open blockchains, allow anyone to take part in the network without requiring permission. They offer a high level of decentralization, immutability, and security through consensus algorithms such as Proof of Work (PoW) or Proof of Stake (PoS). Permissionless blockchains, like Bitcoin and Ethereum, enable global participation and foster innovation but face challenges related to scalability and energy consumption [5].

4.3 Permissioned vs Permissionless Blockchains

The two different blockchain network types, permissioned and permissionless, each have unique properties and use cases. So we can explain those in two big titles. First permissioned blockchain, in order to participate in a permissioned blockchain, often referred to as a private blockchain or a consortium blockchain, members must first seek authorization from a central authority or network administrator. Its main aspects are Access Control which means Permissioned blockchains the private network that gives access to the users and these autorisation are given to individuals known in this network and the administration members. Then we have Centralized Governance. This central authority puts major protocols for the network and it can change them if needed. Next we have Enhanced Privacy Permissioned blockchains gives and offers more privacy than permissionless counterparts members may have restricted visibility of transactions within the network. In addition we also have Higher Scalability and Efficiency: permissioned blockchains achieve higher transaction throughput and faster consensus mechanisms because they do not require the extensive computational power. For the second model Permissionless Blockchain known as public blockchains its major is giving access to anyone who wants to participate in the network. Some of its characteristics are Decentralized Governance; it's the fact that there is no central authority controlling the system. And also Public Accessibility: the openness of this network allows for a high level of inclusivity and transparency. Then Transparency and Audibility provide complete transparency, and all transactions are visible to every participant. Then we'll have Security and Resilienceness: Permissionless uses consensus mechanisms such as Proof of Work (PoW) or Proof of Stake (PoS) in order to achieve safety and prevent malicious activity. Permissionless blockchains' decentralized nature enables them to respond better to attacks Table 2.

5 Blockchain: Platforms, Protocols, and Prospects

5.1 Prominent Blockchain Platforms

Bitcoin: Bitcoin is the pioneering cryptocurrency based on blockchain technology. It showcases the potential of public, permissionless networks. Bitcoin's blockchain facilitates peer-to-peer electronic transactions without the need for intermediaries, ensuring transparency and security [2].

Table 2. Differentiating Permissionless and Permissioned Blockchains: An Analysis of Key Features and Applications

Criteria	Permissionless Blockchain	Permissioned Blockchain
Participation	Anyone can join and participate	Only authorized participants can join and participate
Consensus Mechanism	Proof-of-Work or Proof-of-Stake commonly used	Typically uses faster consensus mechanisms such as PBFT (Practical Byzantine Fault Tolerance), PoA (Proof of Authority)
Governance	Typically community driven	Typically governed by one organization or a consortium
Data Visibility	Complete transparency; all transaction data is visible to all	Selective visibility; transaction data visibility can be controlled and is usually visible only to involved parties
Use Cases	Cryptocurrencies like Bitcoin, Ethereum, etc	Interbank transactions, supply chain management, voting systems, and many enterprise solutions
Speed and Scalability	Generally slower due to large network and complex consensus mechanism	Generally faster and more scalable due to fewer nodes and lighter consensus mechanisms
Identity Privacy	Anonymity can be maintained but all transactions are traceable	Participants are known and identifiable, offering accountability

Ethereum: Ethereum introduced the concept of smart contracts, enabling the development of decentralized applications (DApps) on its blockchain. Ethereum's programmable blockchain platform allows developers to create and execute smart contracts, enabling a wide range of decentralized applications and tokenized ecosystems (Wood, 2014) [7].

Hyperledger Fabric: Hyperledger Fabric is an open-source blockchain framework that focuses on private and permissioned blockchains. It provides a modular and flexible architecture, allowing enterprises to customize their blockchain networks to meet specific requirements. Hyperledger Fabric emphasizes privacy, scalability, and modular consensus mechanisms. It is particularly well-suited for use cases in industries such as supply chain management, healthcare, and finance [8].

Corda: Corda is a distributed ledger platform designed for secure and private transactions among trusted parties. It emphasizes the concept of "smart agreements" rather than smart contracts, ensuring that sensitive business data remains confidential to involved participants. Corda's architecture enables interoperability, regulatory compliance, and efficient transaction processing, making it suitable for use cases in areas such as trade finance, insurance, and healthcare [9].

5.2 Future Prospects and Challenges

As blockchain technology continues to evolve, there are several key areas that require attention:

Scalability and Interoperability: Scalability and interoperability are critical challenges facing blockchain technology. It describes a blockchain network's capacity to handle a large number of transactions efficiently. The consensus mechanisms and the requirement for every participant to validate transactions can limit scalability. Interoperability, on the other hand, involves enabling communication and data exchange between different blockchain platforms. Establishing standards and protocols is crucial to achieving seamless interoperability. overcoming these challenges is essential for broader adoption and integration of blockchain technology across Industries.

Regulatory Frameworks: The regulatory framework for blockchain technology is still evolving globally. Governments and regulatory bodies face challenges in establishing consistent regulations due to the global nature of blockchain. Key considerations include anti-money laundering (AML) and know your customer (KYC) compliance, consumer protection, data privacy, legal recognition of smart contracts, regulations around initial coin offerings (ICOs) and tokens, and the exploration of central bank digital currencies (CBDCs). Collaboration between stakeholders is essential to strike a balance between innovation and protecting individuals and society [12].

Security Challenges and Solutions: In light of recent advancements and studies [14], this section underscores the prevailing security challenges faced by the blockchain technology. The blockchain networks, although robust, are not immune to vulnerabilities, and the degree of susceptibility varies among public, private, and consortium blockchains.

The modern landscape of blockchain is witnessing the emergence of strategies aimed at mitigating these vulnerabilities, fostering a more secure environment. These strategies are predominantly focused on innovation and the development of new protocols to enhance network security.

Moreover, numerous real-world applications and cases demonstrate the successful implementation of these strategies, instilling trust and reliability in blockchain technology. As we move forward, the trajectory indicates a concerted effort towards creating a resilient blockchain ecosystem, with ongoing research playing a pivotal role in shaping a secure future.

6   Conclusion

In conclusion, blockchain technology has emerged as a transformative force with various types catering to diverse requirements. Public, private, consortium, permissioned, permissionless, and hybrid blockchains offer unique features and benefits. Prominent platforms and protocols such as Bitcoin, Ethereum, Hyperledger Fabric, and Corda have demonstrated the potential of blockchain technology across different sectors. As the technology continues to evolve, addressing scalability, regulatory challenges, and advancing research efforts will unlock its full potential for disruptive innovation.

References

1. Swan, M.: Blockchain: Blueprint for a New Economy. O'Reilly Media (2015)
2. Nakamoto, S.: Bitcoin: A Peer-to-Peer Electronic Cash System (2008)
3. Tapscott, D., Tapscott, A.: Blockchain Revolution: How the Technology Behind Bitcoin is Changing Money, Business, and the World. Portfolio (2016)
4. Bashir, I.: Mastering Blockchain. Packt Publishing (2017)
5. Christidis, K., Devetsikiotis, M.: Blockchains and Smart Contracts for the Internet of Things. IEEE Access **4**, 2292–2303 (2016)
6. Zhang, P., White, J., Schmidt, D.C., Lenz, G.: Blockchain Technology Use Cases in Healthcare: A Comprehensive Review. Healthcare Information Management Systems **7**(1) (2018)
7. Wood, G.: Ethereum: A Secure Decentralized Generalized Transaction Ledger (2014)
8. Androulaki, E., et al.: Hyperledger fabric: a distributed operating system for permissioned blockchains. In: EuroSys'18: Proceedings of the Thirteenth EuroSys Conference (2018)
9. Brown, R., Crespi, V., Singh, R., Spiegelhalter, D.: Corda: An Introduction (2016)
10. Hawlitschek a, F., Notheisena, B., Teubner, T.: The limits of trust-free systems: a literature review on blockchain technology and trust in the sharing economy (2018)
11. Hamida, E.B., Brousmiche, K.L., Levard, H., Thea, E.: Blockchain for enterprise: overview, opportunities and challenges. In: The Thirteenth International Conference on Wireless and Mobile Communications (ICWMC 2017) (2017)
12. "The Legal and Regulatory Challenges Facing Blockchain Technology" by the World Economic Forum
13. Yanga, R., et al.: Public and private blockchain in construction business process and information integration (2020)
14. Ali, A.: Dep. of computer science, UOL. Blockchain Security: Challenges and solutions related to the security of blockchain technology and cryptocurrencies (2023)
15. Paul, S., Jacobs, E.: Hybrid blockchains: the next frontier in blockchain technology. Journal of Blockchain Research **2**(1), 123–135 (2021)
16. Paul, L., Smith, A.: Bridging the Gap: Hybrid Blockchain Solutions for Enterprise Environments. Blockchain Technology Symposium, pp. 324–336 (2019)

A Comparative Study on Signature Algorithms of Blockchain 2.0-Based Applications

Adil Marouan[1(✉)], Morad Badrani[1], Nabil Kannouf[2], and Abdelaziz Chetouani[1]

[1] LaMAO Laboratory, ORAS team, ENCG, Mohammed First University, Oujda, Morocco
{adil.marouan,m.badrani,a.chetouani}@ump.ac.ma
[2] LSA Laboratory, SOVAI Team, ENSA, Abdelmalek Essaadi University, Tetouan, Morocco

Abstract. Blockchain (BC) technology has gained much attention due to its promising, disruptive, and revolutionary technology. It consists of creating numerous chains of consecutive blocks of transactions. This way, all blocks are encrypted and cannot be interpreted by anyone without consensus. There are five main stages of BC technology; however, in this paper, we will focus on BC 2.0 (smart contract). That is mainly utilized to ensure proper access control and contract enforcement. In smart contracts, digital signatures in transactions are signed using different signature algorithms such as the Elliptic Curve Digital Signature Algorithm (ECDSA) and the Edwards-curve Digital Signature Algorithm (EdDSA). Our principal objective is to compare the two digital signatures and their level of security and complexity to settle on the most performant one.

Keywords: Blockchain · Smart contract · ECDSA · EdDSA · Signature

1 Introduction

Blockchain technology (BCT) has garnered significant interest due to its benefits, including autonomy, cost savings, precision, redundancy, and trustworthiness. Smart contracts (SCs) can change different domains. SCs will be most effective in several areas, such as finance, insurance, e-commerce, audit and tax, election, and education. This framework came in light of the overall status of concentrated frameworks. Not at all like others, BC is a decentralized, circulated, and strong record that tracks all exchanges with checks straightforwardly and securely. The advancement of BC applications could be separated into five phases; BC 1.0, 2.0, 3.0, 4.0, and 5.0 [1], as displayed in Fig. 1.

BC 1.0 is the organization of cryptocurrencies as a peer-to-peer cash install-ment framework. BC 2.0 is a greater BC application than basic money exchanges,

H. Hagras et al. (Eds.): ISACS 2023, CCIS 2255, pp. 447–459, 2025.
https://doi.org/10.1007/978-3-031-93448-3_36

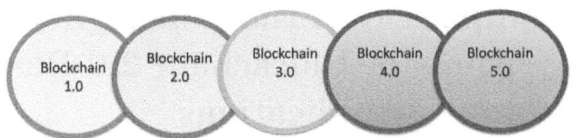

Fig. 1. The evolution of BCT

including stocks, securities, credits, perceptive property, and SCs. BC innovation permits individuals to trade resources and perform exchanges without an outsider. Resources are not generally put away in a focal spot yet circulated across a worldwide record, utilizing the most significant level of cryptography. At the point when an exchange is directed, it is posted across a huge number of PCs all over the planet. BC isn't successful only for resources; it likewise stretches out to contracts. BC 3.0 is growing BC applications past money, money, and markets, like government, well-being, science, education, culture, and workmanship. These three BC stages are not simply defined by changing or including certain characteristics that, in turn, affect a given BC functionality.

Additional features also allow for creating new markets that would otherwise be impossible, thereby increasing the potential value of the overall use of BC. The latest and emerging BC iterations-BC 4.0 result from the combined use of BC and artificial intelligence [2]. This allows the system to make decisions and respond without direct human intervention. BC 5.0: utilizes machine knowledge and information examination to robotize processes for smart applications [3]. The most notable system of SCs is Ethereum; it examines the security weaknesses of Ethereum SCs, giving a scientific classification of normal programming entanglements that might prompt weaknesses. Be that as it may, a few security weaknesses in Ethereum SCs have been found by involved improvement experience, and by static examination of the relative multitude of agreements on the Ethereum, BC [4]. These weaknesses have been taken advantage of by a few genuine assaults on Ethereum contracts, causing misfortunes of cash. In the mid-90 s, SC was instituted by Nick Szabo, who supported that the conditions of exchange could be programmed. However, there was not much reaction at the time, and, naturally, few developments followed. In the last few years, SCs have been introduced with BCT.

SC is an agreement that runs on a BC. It is a transaction stored, replicated, and updated in distributed BCs. Since discovering SC, developers can grant access to any function in the contract. Once the conditions in the SCs are met, the triggered instruction automatically executes the appropriate function predictably. SC ensures proper access control and contract enforcement [5], as shown in Fig. 2. In SCs, transactions are signed using public-key cryptography. Ethereum, Tron, Ontology, Neo, Solana, Cardano, and Stellar are some of the most known ones. These contracts use ECDSA [6] or EdDSA [7] to authorize payments. The two components of the algorithm are elliptic curves and cryptographic hash functions, e.g., SHA256. This paper studies and compares the security and complexity of different signature algorithms of BC 2.0-based applications and determines the most secure and reliable among them. We choose to divide our work into three sections: the first one presents a rundown on BC 2.0. The second one is dedicated to all the different platforms of SCs. The third section introduces the concept of signing and its effectiveness and mechanism. The last one announces the most well-known digital signature: ECDSA and EdDSA. Lastly, our work is summed up in the conclusion.

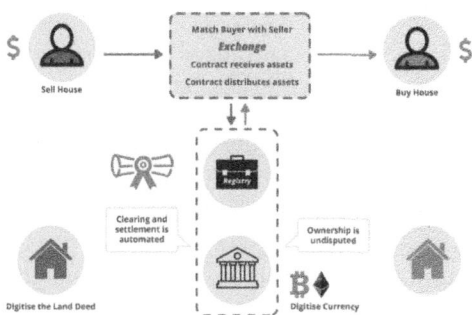

Fig. 2. Use of SCs

2   Related Work

In the upcoming section, we will delve into previous research conducted by various authors in the domain of comparing the Elliptic Curve Digital Signature Algorithm (ECDSA) and the Edwards-curve Digital Signature Algorithm (EdDSA). It is crucial to scrutinize the pertinent literature to acquire insights into the strengths and weaknesses of each algorithm and ascertain which might be better suited for specific applications. By delving into the contributions of these authors, we can enhance our grasp of the fundamental principles and intricacies associated with ECDSA and EdDSA, enabling us to make informed decisions based on their discoveries.

(Bergsma, Niek J. Bouman, and Oscar Garcia-Morchon) [18] presents a comparative study of the performance and security of ECDSA and EdDSA, including an evaluation of key generation, signing, and verification speeds.

(Denis Butin and Leon Groot Bruinderink) [19] focuses on comparing the performance of ECDSA and EdDSA in the context of secure messaging applications.

(Daniel J. Bernstein and Tanja Lange) [20] focuses on the comparison of ECC and RSA, it also provides insights into the performance of ECDSA, which can be useful for a broader perspective.

3   Rundown on BC 2.0

SCs are based upon BC innovation guaranteeing the right execution of the agreements. we initially give a short foreword to BC innovation in Sect. 3.1. We further give an outline of SCs in Sect. 3

3.1   BC Characteristics

BCT has the following main characteristics [8].

– Decentralization: A BC is a decentralized common public record where all Nodes are interconnected in a lattice network where all information and choices are put away Productions are set and circulated to various nodes.
– Traceability: BC traceability highlights improve the discernibility of occasions to store data in blocks safeguarded by a one-way encryption Hash capability. Mining pools keep up with the total BC and give a cloud-based site to investigate blocks.
– Consensus mechanism: alludes to the common understanding of everybody's Nodes related to the BC organization. So it doesn't rely upon, the middle person. POW [9], POS [10], DPOS [11] are a few procedures of consensus instrument.
– Immutability: The BC stores information as a record, and if changed by an outer node, the hash key worth changes because these keys are cryptographically connected to past and past blocks, and changing the information obliterates the key diligence
– Currency: BC innovation has the properties of cryptocurrencies, computerized or virtual cash that ensures start-to-finish exchanges, making them secure and reliable. Different mining calculations produce the development of this money. Thus, the associated types of BC and cryptocurrencies can be utilized in a few perspectives, like money and bookkeeping.

Blockchain technology (BC) can be categorized into three distinct types: public, consortium, and private. Here are the characteristics of each:

– **Public BCs:** These are accessible to anyone, and any individual can partake in the decision-making process by joining as a node. However, no single entity in the network has sole ownership of the ledgers, and access is unrestricted to all participants in the network.
– **Consortium BCs:** are not open to everybody but rather semi-private. Just pre-chosen members are acknowledged. As such, some piece of the BC is private and constrained by a gathering or associations, and the rest is available to general society for anybody to cooperate.
– **Private BCs:** are not open to general society and are available to just a gathering or associations, and the record is imparted to individuals who take part, as it were.

3.2 Smart Contract

We find creative technologies such as SC as we switch to newer and modern BCs. It is a computer protocol put away inside the BC and is planned to carefully work with, check, or implement the exchange or execution of an agreement. They allow us to combine old ideas to establish a new solutions platform. SCs are likely to be found in insurance policies, wills, copyrighted content, trusts, and lending.

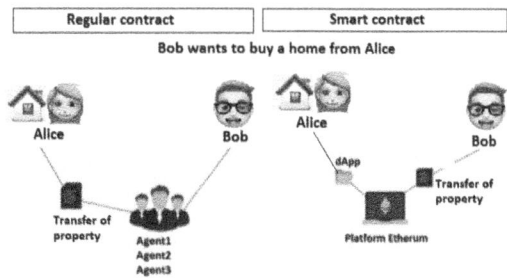

Fig. 3. Comparison between regular contract and SC

SCs [5] can be considered a major advancement in BCT. In the 1990s, SCs were proposed as mechanized exchange arrangements that authorize the authoritative terms of the understanding. Contract terms embedded in SCs are automatically enforced when certain conditions are met (e.g., a party that violates the contract is automatically penalized).

BC supports SCs [21]. SCs are implemented on top of BC. Supported agreement terms are changed over into executable programs. The legitimate associations between contract terms are likewise safeguarded in the program as consistent streams (such as if-else-if statements). The execution of each contract declaration is stored on the BC as an immutable transaction. Thanks to SCs, engineers can give admittance to any capability in the contract. Therefore, this agreement guarantees sufficient access control.

When the conditions in the SC are met, the setting off articulation naturally executes the fitting capability typically. For instance, two individuals settle on an agreement. If the initial party breaches the contract, the stipulated penalty (as defined within the contract) will be automatically deducted from their deposit as depicted in Fig. 3. In SCs, transactions are signed using public-key cryptography. Some of the most known ones are Ethereum (eth), Tron (trx), Ontology (ont) [13], and Neo. To authorize payments, these contracts use ECDSA [6]. The two components of the algorithm are elliptic curves and cryptographic hash functions. Eth, Trx uses the elliptic curve secp256k1 [12] and the hash function SHA256 recommended by the Standard Efficient Cryptography Group. Solana (Sol), Cardano (Ada), Stellar (Xlm) use EdDSA Algorithm [7]. EdDSA has high efficiency and low requirements for computing power, but it is easy to cause double-spending problems. Before checking the security level of ECDSA

[6]using the curves and hash functions above, we would like to make some general remarks.

The two prominent digital signature schemes that have gained widespread recognition are ECDSA and EdDSA [13]. In contemporary software development, EdDSA signatures, as opposed to ECDSA signatures, are frequently favored. This preference stems from the fact that EdDSA signatures employ 32-byte public and private keys and deliver faster signature generation and verification [7], requiring 64 bytes for the signature itself. Nevertheless, it's important to highlight that in the blockchain networks of Bitcoin (BTC) and Ethereum, ECDSA signatures demonstrate superior performance compared to EdDSA signatures as depicted in Table 1.

Table 1. Cryptocurrencies use SCs.

BC 2.0	Hash	Signing Algorithm	ECC curve	Program Language	Consensus	Value Usdt[a]
Eth	Keccak-256	ECDSA	secp256k1	Solidity	POS	1844.25
Sol	Sha3-256	EdDSA	curve25519	Rust C, C++	POH	18.77
ADA	Sha3-256,BLAKE2	EdDSA	Curve25519	Plutus	POS	0.3267
TRX	SHA-256	ECDSA	secp256k1	Solidity	DPOS	0.07740
XLM	SHA-256 and SHA-512	EdDSA	ed25519	Cross-platform	SCP	0.0872
ONT	3x SHA-256	ECDSA	nist256p1	OWL	POS	0.1946
NEO	SHA-256	ECDSA	secp256r1	C#	POS	9.01

[a]These results were last seen on 08 June 2023.

- Hash: What hash function to use to hash the transaction data and then sign it
- Signing algorithm: All current cryptocurrencies use elliptic curve cryptography, regardless of the signature algorithm used
- ECC Curve: What elliptic curve does the underlying signature algorithm use?
- Program language: which language to use to program
- Consensus: Which consensus to use Worth
- Value usdt: value for the current month

4   BC 2.0 Based Applications

SCs have a large number of uses, from the supply chain to the sharing of cryptocurrencies. Particularly, we, for the most part, order the top brilliant agreement applications. There are three sorts of based applications. We next depict them exhaustively.

4.1   Education

In the contemporary digital landscape, data security plays a pivotal role in safe-guarding essential certificates for graduates pursuing employment or further academic goals. Conventional certificate storage methods are prone to vulnerabilities, such as loss or damage, leading to inconveniences and disruptions.

To address this issue, a procedure leveraging Blockchain Technology (BCT) has been developed to issue digital certificates as depicted in Fig. 4. This process involves creating a digital copy of the paper certificate, computing its hash value, and storing it within the blockchain [14].

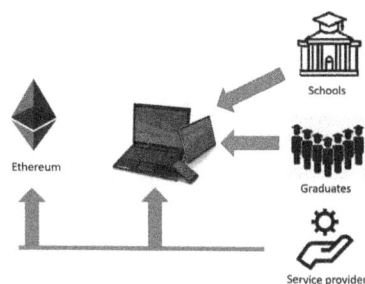

Fig. 4. The procedure of issuing digital certificates

Additionally, QR codes and query string codes are linked to the physical certificate, enhancing its authenticity and reducing the risk of loss.

Graduates can easily request digital certificates by providing identity verification information, which is verified through the blockchain system [22], streamlining the application process and ensuring data security.

To further bolster the security and integrity of digital certificates, the integration of ECDSA and EdDSA signatures [15], based on elliptic curve and Edwards curve cryptography, is recommended. These cryptographic signature algorithms provide robust security, fortifying graduates' certifications against tampering or unauthorized changes, guaranteeing the authenticity and unaltered state of certificate data stored within the blockchain.

4.2   Internet of Things

The Internet of Things (IoT) is an emerging innovation that has the potential to transform various applications, including e-learning, libraries, stock control systems, merchants, and supply chain management. IoT connects everyday objects to the internet, providing enhanced functionalities and services [23]. When combined with Smart Contracts (SCs), IoT can fully automate business transactions and processes.

One prominent application of IoT is in the smart home environment. In a blockchain system, SCs are stored as scripts with unique addresses. When a transaction is directed to a specific SC [15], it can be automatically triggered and executed, enabling secure and seamless interactions. This capability allows for general-purpose computations on the blockchain, eliminating the need for centralized systems and safeguarding users' private data.

To enhance the security of the smart home ecosystem, incorporating ECDSA and EdDSA signatures within the blockchain system is advisable. These signature algorithms, based on elliptic curve and Edwards curves cryptography, are widely used in blockchain applications. Integrating both ECDSA and EdDSA signatures in the blockchain system enhances the security and trustworthiness of the IoT network, ensuring the authenticity and integrity of transactions and data, thereby elevating security standards for IoT applications.

4.3   Cryptoccurencies

Cryptocurrency systems, as introduced in Satoshi Nakamoto's pioneering paper, aim to establish a decentralized framework for peer-to-peer money transfers, eliminating the need for intermediaries like governments or financial institutions. These systems predominantly rely on Blockchain Technology (BCT), providing a communal, publicly accessible ledger that ensures the transparency and immutability of transactions. In a cryptocurrency system built on blockchain [16], all transactions associated with a specific coin are open to anyone due to the public nature of the blockchain. BCT prevents double spending of the same coin, ensuring security and preventing fraudulent activities.

Smart Contracts (SCs) play a pivotal role in cryptocurrency systems, offering cost-effective transactions and reduced legal expenses compared to conventional financial agreements. SCs enable users to engage with contracts and facilitate fund transfers through authenticated data, referred to as transactions, within the cryptocurrency network. This network [15,17], comprised of nodes or miners, disseminates information, stores data, and verifies transactions by incorporating them into the blockchain.

To ensure the safety and trustworthiness of transactions within cryptocurrency systems, cryptographic signature algorithms like ECDSA and EdDSA are frequently used. ECDSA, based on elliptic curve cryptography, and EdDSA, built on Edwards curves, provide robust digital signature methods that validate and verify transaction integrity within the blockchain network.

Incorporating ECDSA and EdDSA signatures into cryptocurrency systems verifies the legitimacy and unaltered state of transactions, reinforcing the security and reliability of the blockchain network.

5   Signing Algorithm ECDSA and EdDSA

5.1   ECDSA Algorithm

ECDSA is the elliptic curve analog of the Digital Signature Algorithm (DSA). It optimizes security against numerous attacks. In addition, it improves performance to obtain efficiencies.

A Comparative Study on Signature Algorithms   455

Algorithm 1. ECDSA signature generation

Require: K_public,K_secret and h
1: $r \leftarrow 0$
2: $s \leftarrow 0$
3: **if** $r = 0$ or $s = 0$ **then**
4:     choose a random int k $\in$ [1,n-1]
5: Compute P1=K.H
6:     **if** $r \neq 0$ **then** $s = k^{-1} (h + rK\_secret) (mod\ n)$
7:         **if** $s \neq 0$ **then return** (r, s)
8:         **else**
9:             $r \leftarrow 0$
10:        **end if**
11:    **end if**
12: **end if**
Ensure: (r, s)

if $p > 3$ is an odd prime, then. An equation of this type describes an elliptic curve E over F_p

$$y^2 \equiv x^3 + ax + b \ (mod\ p) \tag{1}$$

where $4a^3 + 27b^2 \neq 0 \ (mod\ p)$ and a,b $\in F_p \ (mod\ p)$.

All points $(x, y), x \in F_p, y \in F_p$ that meet the defining equation (1) are included in the set $[F_p]$, together with a unique point θ known as the point at infinity. Here, we provide the key generation, signature creation, and verification algorithms that make up the ECDSA.

5.2   EdDSA Algorithm

The public-key signature algorithm known as EdDSA, which was created, bears similarities to ECDSA [7]. EdDSA is documented for two specific twisted Edwards curves, namely edwards25519 and edwards448, in RFC 8032, although it can also be applied to other curves. In a broader context, when a point $P = (x, y)$ satisfies the subsequent equation:

$$ax^2 + y^2 = 1 + dx^2y^2 \tag{2}$$

where a, d are two unique, non-zero elements of the field K over which E is defined, then it is said that the point $P = (x, y)$ resides on E, a twisted Edwards curve. Like Curve25519, Edwards25519 is defined over F_p with $(p = 2^{255} - 19)$. Edwards25519 is birationally equal to Curve25519, as showed; and as a result, the difficulty of solving the Discrete Logarithm Problem is the same for both curves. Edwards448 is also developed to provide a security level of 224 bits and is defined over F_q with $q = 2^{448} - 2^{224} - 1$.

Algorithm 2. EdDSA signature

Require: K_secret and msg
1: Compute a,prefix=$secret - exp(K\_secret)$
2: Compute A=$point - compr(point - mul(a, G))$
3: Compute Rs = $point - compr(R)$
4: Compute h = $sha512 - modq(Rs + A + msg)$
5: Compute s = $(r + h * a)\ (mod\ q)$
Ensure: $(Tableau)Rs, int.to - bytes(s, 32)$

Algorithm 3. secret-exp

Require: K_secret
1: **if** $len(K\_secret <> 32$ **then** "Bad size of private key"
2: **end if**
3: Compute h = $sha512(K\_secret)$
4: Compute a = $int.from - bytes(h[0 : 32])$
5: Compute a =$a\&(1 << 254) - 8$
6: Compute a = $a|(1 << 254)$
Ensure: $(Tableau)(a, h[32 :])$

---

6   Implementation Results and Discussion

In this section, we carried out a real-world application of the digital signa-ture techniques ECDSA and EdDSA, utilizing the elliptic curves secp256k1 for ECDSA and ed25519 for EdDSA. We aimed to evaluate and conduct a compara-tive evaluation of the efficiency of these methods in the key generation, signature generation, and verification processes.

The intricacy of ECDSA can be analogized to that of the Euclidean algo-rithm, possessing a time complexity denoted as $O(q)$, wherein q denotes the quotient of P and the key K. On the other hand, the complexity of EdDSA is expressed as $O((r+hash(r)*a)\% q)$, where r is the result of hashing the con-catenation of pref and msg. A represents the output of the secret-exp(secret) function. After completing the implementation, as depicted in Fig. 5, we gath-ered the subsequent outcomes: Throughout all phases of the digital signature procedure, encompassing key generation, signature generation, and verification, we noted a consistently superior performance of the ECDSA algorithm in both speed and efficiency when compared to the EdDSA algorithm.

These findings indicate that, for the chosen elliptic curves and experimental setup, the ECDSA algorithm exhibits superior performance compared to EdDSA in terms of execution time and computational efficiency. It is worth noting that the choice between ECDSA and EdDSA depends on specific requirements, such as the desired level of security, the available computational resources, and the target platform. Additional research and analysis are required to ascertain the optimal algorithm for a specific use case.

The algorithms have been implemented in Python on a Raspberry Pi 1.

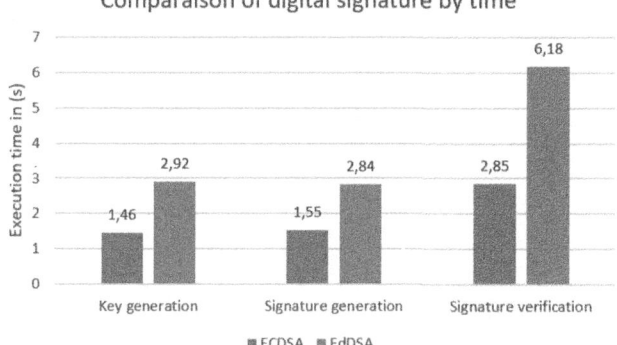

Fig. 5. Execution time in seconds of digital signature for ECDSA & EdDSA

7 Conclusion and Future Work

In this paper, we have undertaken an examination of the signing algorithms employed within BC 2.0-centric applications. To commence our study, we offered an introductory overview of BC 2.0, shedding light on its prominent features and operational capabilities. We then presented several BC 2.0-based applications to showcase the practical use cases of this technology.

Subsequently, we delved into the two most commonly employed signing algorithms in BC 2.0-based applications: ECDSA and EdDSA. We discussed the underlying principles and cryptographic techniques employed by these algorithms. Furthermore, we conducted theoretical and implementation-based analyses to compare their performance characteristics.

The results obtained from our study indicated that ECDSA outperforms EdDSA in terms of speed, with ECDSA being approximately two times faster than EdDSA. This finding suggests that ECDSA is a more efficient choice for signing operations in BC 2.0-based applications. As a direction for future work, we propose the integration of these signature algorithms in the field of education, mainly focusing on Electronic Voting in Moroccan universities. By leveraging the robustness and security provided by ECDSA and EdDSA, we can enhance the integrity and trustworthiness of the electronic voting systems, ensuring transparent and tamper-resistant elections within the academic environment.

Through the integration of these cutting-edge signing algorithms into the sphere of education, we have the potential to advance the creation of more dependable and secure systems. This, in turn, can promote democratic principles and guarantee equitable electoral procedures.

Acknowledgments. N/A.

Conflict of Interest. The authors confirm no conflict of interest exists.

Funding. The study did not receive any grants from public, commercial, or not-for-profit sectors.

Availability of Data. The corresponding author can provide the datasets analyzed during the study upon request and takes responsibility for the data's integrity and accuracy of the analysis.

References

1. Aggarwal, S., Kumar, N.: Blockchain 2.0: smart contracts. Adv. Comput. **121**, 301–322 (2021)
2. Angelis, J., Silva, E., Adoption, B.: A value driver perspective. Bus. Horiz. **62**(3), 307–314 (2019)
3. Choi, T.-M., Siqin, T.: Blockchain in Logistics and Production from Blockchain 1.0 to Blockchain 5.0: An Intra-Inter-organizational Framework. Transp. Res. Part E: Logist. Transp. Rev. **160**, 102653 (2022)
4. Kushwaha, S.S., et al.: Systematic review of security vulnerabilities in ethereum blockchain smart contract. IEEE Access **10**, 6605–6621 (2022)
5. Zheng, Z., et al.: An overview on smart contracts: challenges, advances, and platforms. Futur. Gener. Comput. Syst. **105**, 475–491 (2020)
6. Aumasson, J.-P., Hamelink, A., Shlomovits, O.: A survey of ECDSA threshold signing. Cryptology ePrint Archive (2020)
7. Basha, S.J., et al.: Security enhancement of digital signatures for blockchain using EdDSA algorithm. In: 2021 Third International Conference on Intelligent Communication Technologies and Virtual Mobile Networks (ICICV). IEEE (2021)
8. Yumna, H., Khan, M.M., Ikram, M., Ilyas, S.: Use of blockchain in education: a systematic literature review. In: Nguyen, N.T., Gaol, F.L., Hong, T.-P., Trawiński, B. (eds.) ACIIDS 2019. LNCS (LNAI), vol. 11432, pp. 191–202. Springer, Cham (2019). https://doi.org/10.1007/978-3-030-14802-7_17
9. Guo, H., Yu, X.: A survey on blockchain technology and its security. Blockchain Res. Appl. **3**(2), 100067 (2022)
10. Li, W., Andreina, S., Bohli, J.-M., Karame, G.: Securing proof-of-stake blockchain protocols. In: Garcia-Alfaro, J., Navarro-Arribas, G., Hartenstein, H., Herrera-Joancomartí, J. (eds.) ESORICS/DPM/CBT -2017. LNCS, vol. 10436, pp. 297–315. Springer, Cham (2017). https://doi.org/10.1007/978-3-319-67816-0_17
11. Do, T., Nguyen, T., Pham, H.: Delegated Proof of Reputation: A Novel Blockchain Consensus. In: Proceedings of the 1st International Electronics Communication Conference (2019)
12. Alouffi, B., et al.: A systematic literature review on cloud computing security: threats and mitigation strategies. IEEE Access **9**, 57792–57807 (2021)
13. Benabdallah, A., et al.: Analysis of blockchain solutions for E-voting: a systematic literature review. IEEE Access (2022)
14. Centobelli, P., et al.: Blockchain technology for bridging trust, traceability, and transparency in circular supply chain. Inf. Manage. **59**(7), 103508 (2022)
15. Conti, M., et al.: A survey on security challenges and solutions in the IOTA. J. Netw. Comput. Appl. **203**, 103383 (2022)
16. Stoll, C., Klaaßen, L., Gallersdörfer, U.: The carbon footprint of bitcoin. Joule **3**(7), 1647–1661 (2019)

17. Zaid, G., et al.: Efficiency through diversity in ensemble models applied to side-channel attacks: a case study on public-key algorithms. IACR Trans. Cryptogr. Hardw. Embed. Syst. 60–96 (2021)
18. Bergsma, F., Bouman, N.J., Garcia-Morchon, O.: Performance and security of ECDSA and EdDSA: a comparative study (2021)
19. Butin, D., Bruinderink, L.G.: Performance Comparison of ECDSA and EdDSA for Secure Messaging Applications (2021)
20. Bernstein, D.J., Lange, T.: Comparing elliptic curve cryptography and RSA on 8-bit CPUs (2022)
21. Kannouf, N., et al.: Security on RFID technology. In: 2015 International Conference on Cloud Technologies and Applications (CloudTech). IEEE (2015)
22. Badrani, M., et al.: Smart techniques for Moroccan students' orientation. In: Al-Sharafi, M.A., Al-Emran, M., Al-Kabi, M.N., Shaalan, K. (eds.) ICETIS 2022. LNNS, vol. 573, pp. 361–366. Springer, Cham (2022). https://doi.org/10.1007/978-3-031-20429-6_33
23. Fartitchou, M., et al.: Security on blockchain technology. In: 2020 3rd International Conference on Advanced Communication Technologies and Networking (Comm-Net). IEEE (2020)

A New Image Crypto-Compression Scheme Using Hybrid Approach with DWT and ECC for Emerging IoT Applications

Khadija El Kinani[1]([✉]) [iD], Salma Bendaoud[1], and Fatima Amounas[2] [iD]

[1] Faculty of Sciences and Technics, Moulay Ismail University of Meknes, Errachidia, Morocco
`k.elkinani@edu.umi.ac.ma`
[2] RO.AL&I Group, Computer Sciences Department, Faculty of Sciences and Technics, Moulay Ismail University of Meknes, Errachidia, Morocco
`f.amounas@umi.ac.ma`

Abstract. Today, multimedia content is widely used in several applications with the emerging of the Internet of Things. A digital image is one of the most commonly used forms of multimedia and their usage has exhibited an exponential growth in recent years. However, the need for securing digital images has become more pressing due to this increase in usage. Several cryptographic systems have been put in place to address this issue, but an effective and secure solution is required because IoT devices have limited power, processing capability, and network bandwidth. The proposed solution involves using elliptic curve cryptography (ECC), which is well-suited for such devices. Along with cryptographic systems, compression techniques can also be employed to enhance digital image security. Compression reduces the size of the image, making it easier to store and transmit securely. This research suggests an efficient solution for securing digital images by using ECC-encryption and compression techniques. This process provides a sequence of steps by compressing the input image using the discrete wavelet transforms algorithm, then using the ECC algorithm to encrypt the compressed data. After that, the cipher image is scrambled using Rubik's cube to achieve fast confusion. The simulation outcomes demonstrate that the suggested method provides high protection for different transmitted images. Moreover, the joint use of multiple techniques can achieve the highest performance, which makes it an effective approach for securing transmitted images in a wide range of IoT fields.

Keywords: Image Encryption · Elliptic Curve Cryptography · Discrete Wavelet Transform· Rubik's Cube

1 Introduction

The Internet of Things, a rapidly emerging technology is expected to revolutionize the way we live and work. With the potential to connect billions of devices, IoT technology has the capacity to generate vast amounts of data [1]. However, with the enormous amount of digital data that IoT devices produce and the universal application of multimedia technology, security is now a crucial problem that needs to be solved by us.

H. Hagras et al. (Eds.): ISACS 2023, CCIS 2255, pp. 460–471, 2025.
https://doi.org/10.1007/978-3-031-93448-3_37

Cryptography remains one of the most widely used methods to ensure the confidentiality of information [2–4]. While existing standards offer effective encryption for text files, they often fall short when it comes to securing multimedia content like digital images and videos. The exchange of image data over public networks presents two key challenges: the growing size of digital image and the vulnerability of image data during transmission. Both these issues can be effectively addressed by applying a compression and encryption method to the image data [5–7]. The merging of compression and encryption methods will be an effective approach for enhancing the security of data transmission while also ensuring high-quality and fast transmission. Image encryption has become an increasingly important area of research in cryptography due to the growing use of digital images in various applications and the need to protect sensitive information from unauthorized access. There are several techniques available for image encryption, including symmetric, asymmetric, and chaotic encryption [8–11]. In the last few years, the compression technique has shown its effectiveness in reducing the complexity of encryption and improving security. For instance, Peiya Li et al. proposed an efficient scheme for image compression and encryption, which employs a lossy compression approach [12]. This scheme uses a combination of block-based discrete cosine transform (DCT) compression and permutation-substitution-based encryption to achieve high security and compression performance. This scheme aims to improve encryption while maintaining JPEG compression efficiency. Next, Nasrullah et al. proposed another example of crypto-compression scheme to secure digital images [13]. The set partitioning in hierarchical trees (SPIHT) algorithm, a well-known method of image compression, serves as the foundation for their strategy. The authors demonstrate that the proposed method provides a high level of security by using multiple chaotic maps and optimizing the SPIHT algorithm for compression efficiency. However, like any encryption scheme, it is important to carefully evaluate its security before using it in sensitive applications. Following that, Gong et al. developed an innovative approach to combine image compression and encryption. This method leverages hyper-chaotic systems in conjunction with the discrete fractional random transform [14]. Their scheme involves transforming the original image into a spectrum using the discrete cosine transform. The spectrum is then compressed using a technique called spectrum cutting, which involves discarding the high-frequency components of the spectrum. The proposed method offers a high level of security by using multiple encryption techniques and optimizing the compression process for the encrypted data. However, it is important to note that the method may be vulnerable to certain attacks. After that, M. Al Duhayyim et al. presented a novel "encryption then compression" technique that can be used in resource-limited IoT environments where both compression efficiency and data secrecy are important considerations [15]. The authors adopt three processes: compression, encryption and IoT-based image acquisition. The results show that their approach provides a high level of security and compression efficiency in IoT environment. Recently, Elliptic Curve Cryptography (ECC) has been mostly used to efficiently overcome the security and privacy issues in application areas of the IoT [16]. The complexity of solving the Elliptic Curve Discrete Logarithmic Problem (ECDLP) determines the security of elliptic curve cryptosystems, especially those used for multimedia information protection in Internet of Things applications [17–20]. Therefore, the IoT requires a consistent crypto-compression system based

ECC for securing the transmitted data in resource-limited IoT environment. In this context, this paper attempts to adopt ECC-based mechanism with compression technique for multimedia information protection in IoT applications. ECC is a crucial security element for many IoT applications because it provides strong security guarantees while being computationally efficient, making it suitable for resource-constrained IoT devices. More precisely, this research aims to design a compression-encryption method by combining the compression technique with the elliptic curve cryptosystem ECC, in which the wavelet transform (DWT) is employed to achieve high security and good compression performance. The proposed approach additionally employs a scrambling technique to boost the cryptosystem's security.

The subsequent sections of the current paper are structured in the following manner: Sect. 2 investigates the basic theory of three different topics: elliptic curve, compression technique, and the principle of Rubik's cube. In Sect. 3, the suggested approach is introduced along with a flowchart of the proposed system. Thereafter, Sect. 4 shows the experimental results. Whereas, evaluation performance is furnished in Sect. 5. Finally, Sect. 6 comes to a conclusion and makes some recommendations for future research.

2 Background Detail

In this section, we provide an introduction to the fundamental concepts of elliptic curves cryptography, wavelet transform and rubik's cube.

2.1 ECC-Encryption

Neal Koblitz and Victor Miller introduced a public key cryptosystem called Elliptic Curve Cryptography (ECC) [21]. It is an alternative to conventional public-key cryptosystems like RSA. The efficient performance of ECC is due to the fact that it can provide the same level of security as RSA with considerably smaller key sizes. ECC is a cryptographic system that relies on the properties of elliptic curves over finite fields [22]. It is widely used for key exchange protocols, digital signatures and secure data transmission. The security of systems built on ECC relies on the Elliptic Curve Discrete Logarithm Problem (ECDLP), a mathematical problem that is thought to be difficult to effectively solve. ECC uses a private and public key pair to encrypt and decrypt data. The public key is made available to others for encryption, while the private key is kept secret and used for decryption. ECC is a very promising solution for applications that require secure and efficient encryption, especially on devices with limited resources like mobile phones and IoT devices.

– **Mathematical Basics of the elliptic curve**

An elliptic curve is a mathematical structure defined over a field F_p as the collection of points satisfying the equation(Eq. 1):

$$y^2 = x^3 + ax + b \bmod p \tag{1}$$

where a and b are constants satisfying the condition $4a^3 + 27a^2 \bmod p \neq 0$. p is a prime number that represents the characteristic of the field F_p. The ECC points are generated by substituting different values for x and y in Eq. (1). An abelian group is formed by this collection of points on E with the addition operation. The point at infinity Ω serves as the identity element for this group.

– *Rules for Addition*

There is specific rule for how to add two points on an elliptic curve, which can be defined as following:

Let $M(x_M, y_M)$ and $N(x_N, y_N)$ be two points on the elliptic curve E, and let $R(x_R, y_R)$ be their sum, i.e., $R = M + N$. The addition operation is defined as follows:

$$x_R = \left(\frac{y_N - y_M}{x_N - x_M} \right)^2 - x_M - x_N$$

and

$$y_R = \left(\frac{y_N - y_M}{x_N - x_M} \right)(x_M - x_R) - y_M$$

If $M = (x_M, y_M) \in E$ and $M \neq -M$, then $2M = (x_R, y_R)$

$$x_R = \left(\frac{3x_M^2 + a}{2y_M} \right)^2 - 2x_M$$

and

$$y_R = \left(\frac{3x_M^2 + a}{2y_M} \right)^2 (x_M - x_R) - y_M$$

2.2 Discrete Wavelet Transform

The discrete wavelet transform is a commonly employed method for achieving image compression. It can decompose an image into different frequency subbands, each representing a different level of detail in the image. This multi-resolution approach allows for efficient compression and analysis of images [23, 24]. In DWT-based image compression, the image is decomposed into different frequency subbands, and then the high-frequency subbands with less important information are discarded, while the low-frequency subbands with important information are kept. The remaining subbandsare then compressed using standard compression techniques like Huffman coding or arithmetic coding. DWT can effectively capture important image features and details at different resolutions, making it a powerful tool for image compression and other image processing applications.

2.3 Scrambling with Rubik's Cube

The Rubik's Cube is a 3D puzzle that consists of a $3 \times 3 \times 3$ cube with six faces as shown in Fig. 1. Each face divided into 9 smaller facelets. The complexity of the Rubik's Cube is due to the numerous combinations that it can have. This has led to the development of many cryptography solutions that use this concept. In this work, the Rubik's Cube structure has been extendedto scramble encrypted images [25].

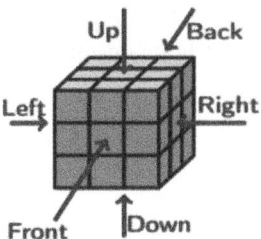

Fig. 1. Rubik's cube

3 Proposed Methodology

This section introduces a novel hybrid compression-encryption scheme using discrete wavelet transform and scrambling technique. The ECC Mecanism-based matrix approach is adopted to achieve fast computations. The proposed method employs the Rubik's cube technique to achieve good confusion and diffusion properties. This process involves first compressing and encrypting the image, and then applying a series of rotations to the faces of the cube, which further generate a highly disordering transformation of the encrypted image. The proposed approach consists of three main processes as represented in Fig. 2. The proposed methodology can be implemented by carrying out the subsequent actions:

- *Step 1.* Select the original image as input.
- *Step 2.* Apply the wavelet transform to perform the compression process.
- *Step 3.* Load a compressed image that requires encryption. After the image is loaded, it needs to be resized so that it can be divided into six smaller sub-images.
- *Step 4.* Embedding the pixel

  First, every pixel in the image is assigned a mapping point on an elliptic curve. The obtained points are then arranged into a data matrix called M.

- *Step 5.* Encryption using ECC technique

  ECC technique based on matrix approach can be used to encrypt the mapping points. This involves performing matrix multiplication between the PM matrix and a randomly generated encryption keymatrix. The resulting matrix is the encrypted matrix.7

- *Step 6.* Divide the encrypted matrix into sub-matrices (SM1, SM2, SM3, SM4, SM5, and SM6). Then, map the sub-matrices on the faces of a magic cube according to the following scheme (SM1 → Up, SM2 → Front, SM3 → Right, SM4 → Left, SM5 → Down and SM6 → Back).
- *Step 7.* By rotating randomly the Rubik's cube faces, the cipher image can be scrambled.

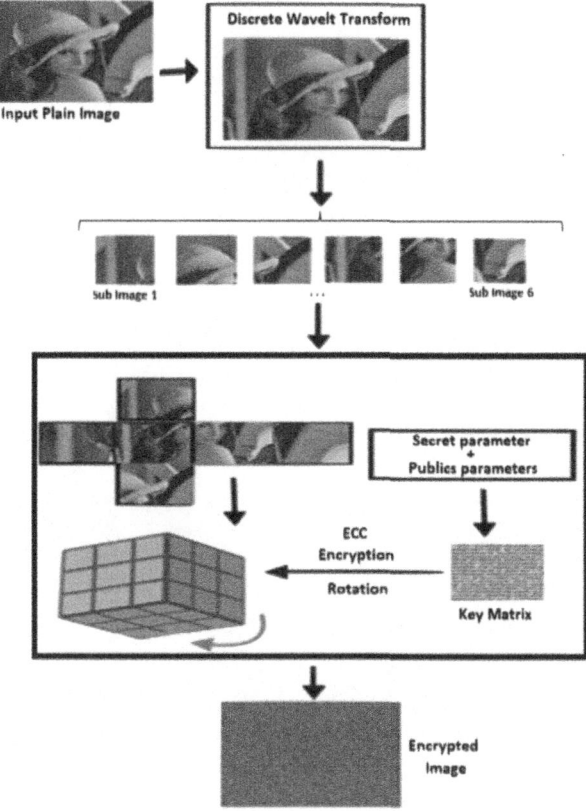

Fig. 2. Architecture of the proposed approach

4   Experimental Results

To analyze the security level and efficiency of the proposed image crypto-compression system, we can use Grayscale, Lena, and Peppers images as testing plain images. The simulation of the proposed method by using Matlab programming software can provide valuable insights into the scheme's effectiveness and level of security. The outcomes achieved through the application of the proposed algorithm on the Grayscale, Lena, and Peppers images are displayed in Fig. 3, where (a) show the original images, (b) shows the corresponding encrypted images and (c) shows the reconstructed images obtained after decryption. The encrypted images do not visually reveal any useful information about the original images, as seen in Fig. 3.

5   Statistical Analysis

In this section, we conduct some common statistical analyses, like histogram analysis and correlation analysis, to assess the efficacy of the suggested strategy.

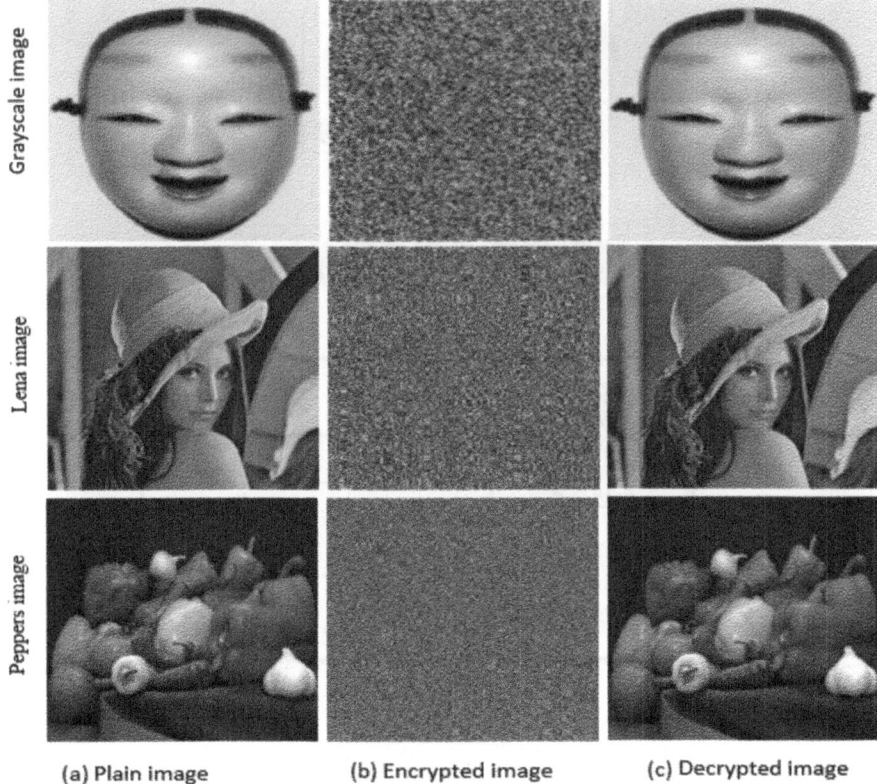

(a) Plain image   (b) Encrypted image   (c) Decrypted image

Fig. 3. Experimental simulation results.

5.1 Histogram Analysis

Histogram is a fundamental component of a digital image. It displays how the image's pixel gray values are distributed. The first test and best method for determining the distribution of all pixel values in the image is the histogram analysis. A more uniform distribution of pixel values in the encrypted image indicates that the encryption scheme has effectively randomized the pixel values, making it di-cult to recover the original image without the secret key. Figure 4 show the histograms for different plain and cipher images. It can be seen from the results that the encrypted image is distributed uniformly over the entire histogram interval. Further, it can be concluded that the proposed method is effective in randomizing the pixel values and covering the regularity of the original image's distribution. Therefore, encrypted images have strong cryptographic characteristics and can resist statistical attacks.

From our experiments, our proposed method has produced promising results and uniform histogram, as shown in Figs. 3 and 4. The evaluation's findings demonstrate that the cipher image's histogram is evenly distributed throughout the entire evaluation interval. Therefore, the original image's distribution pattern is covered. So, it can be concluded that the encryption has been implemented effectively. The cipher image

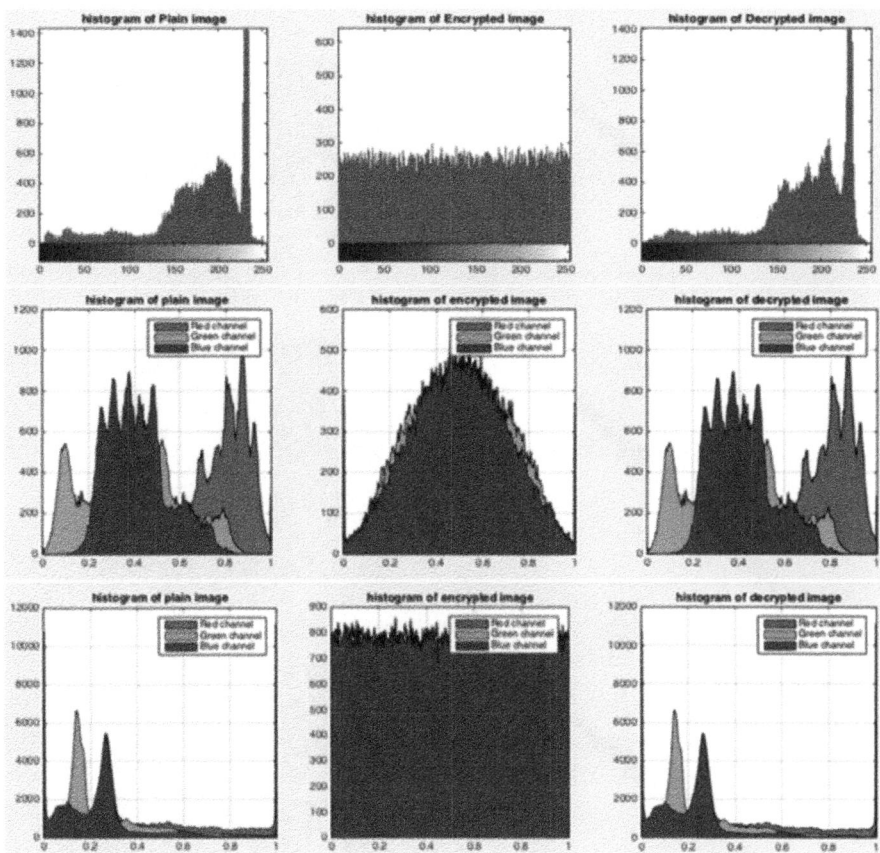

Fig. 4. Histograms of different plain and encrypted images respectively (Grayscale, Lena and Peppers).

histogram distributions are also uniform. This shows that the suggested solution has effectively concealed the statistical characteristics of the original images, making it difficult for attackers to use statistical attacks on the algorithm.

5.2 Correlation Analysis

Besides conducting histogram analysis, measuring the correlation between two adjacent pixels in the input image and the cipher image can provide further insights into the encryption process. Table 1 displays the correlation coefficient values obtained during the evaluation. Figure 5 illustrates the relevance of adjacent pixels in in various directions (H, V, D).

According to the experimental finding, the correlation coefficients of the original image are close to 1, while the correlation coefficients of cipher images are close to 0. As a result, the suggested method can successfully eliminate the correlation between

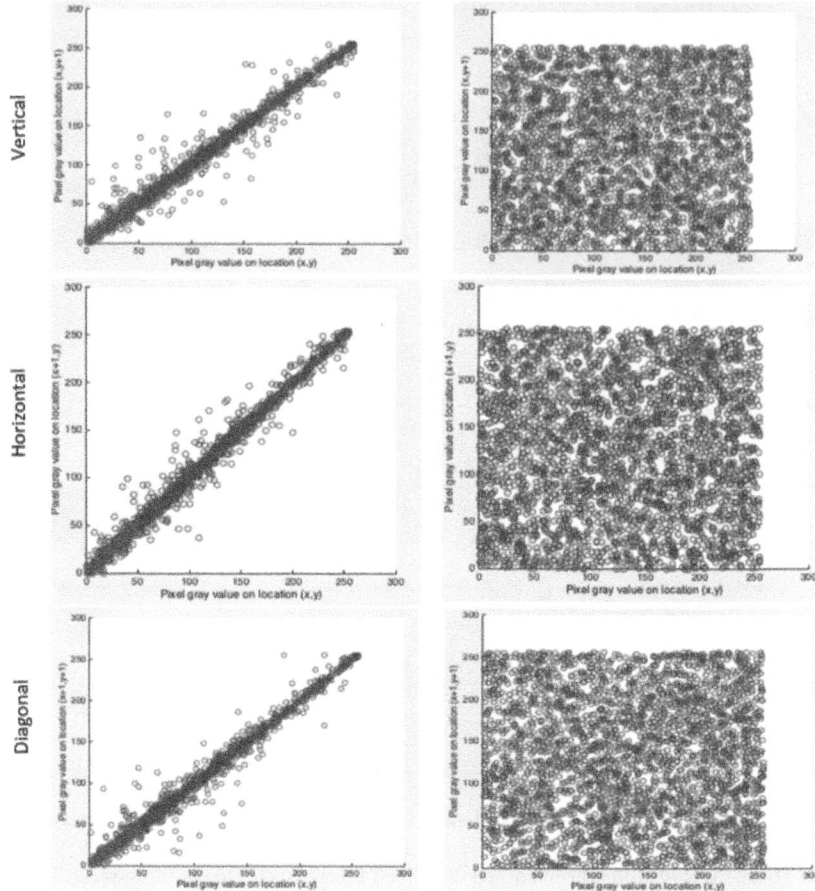

Fig. 5. Correlation plot of input and encrypted images in the Peppers image (Left and Right).

Table 1. Correlation coefficients.

	Image	H	V	D
plain image	Grayscale	0.9986	0.9986	0.9601
	Lena	0.9574	0.9792	0.9493
	peppers	0.9932	0.9886	0.9847
Encrypted image	Grayscale	0.0027	−0.0019	−0.008
	Lena	0.0099	0.0051	−0.0033
	peppers	−0.0042	−7.7246e-04	1.9007e-04

adjacent pixels. This shows the robustness of our approach against correlation-based attacks.

6 Comparison and Discussion

This section includes a comparison of our approach to other methods [26–28]. The evaluation of NPCR, UACI and the entropy values will be used to compare our method to other strategies in Table 2.

There are two significant indicators in cryptography [27]: the unified average intensity change (UACI) and the pixel number change rate (NPCR). The UACI is skewed towards measuring the intensity of the changes in pixel values at related spots, while the NPCR can quantify the amount of pixels that have been modified by inputting different plaintext images.

Table 2. Comparison of our method and the existing techniques

	Our method	[26]	[27]	[28]
NPCR	99.6056	99.4700	99.5941	99.6043
UACI	33.4612	33.1800	33.4078	33.4603
Entropy	7.9963	7.9955	7.9954	7.9961

Accordingly, Table 2 reveals that the entropy values approximate the ideal value of 8. The proposed algorithm exhibits greater entropy value compared to the other algorithms. Additionally, the parameters NPCR and UACI in accordance with international standards. Therefore, our method is effective in resisting against statistical and differential attacks.

7 Conclusion

Multimedia content is widely used in several IoT applications nowadays. This paper deals with a new image crypto-compression scheme using the discrete wavelet transform and the Rubik's cube principle. Firstly, a compression technique is performed to generate the compressed image. Secondly, an ECC encryption algorithm is implemented based on a matrix approach. The scrambling technique is employed to scramble the encrypted image during encryption. The proposed scheme shows good cryptographic properties and a high security level that depends on the difficulty to solve the ECDLP. According to the findings of our experiments, the suggested method can produce effective encryption and can resist any cryptanalytic attacks. Therefore, the proposed method may be employed to secure multimedia data in various IoTfields. The implementation of the suggested approach in healthcare, which is a particularly promising area of IoT applications, will be the main focus of our future study.

References

1. Hammoudi, S., Aliouat, Z., Harous, S.: Challenges and research directions for Internet of Things. Telecommun. Syst. **67**(2), 367–385 (2018). https://doi.org/10.1007/s11235-017-0343-y

2. Thakor, V.A., Razzaque, M.A., Khandaker, M.R.A.: Lightweight Cryptography Algorithms for Resource-Constrained IoT Devices: A Review, Comparison and Research Opportunities. In: IEEE Access, vol. 9, pp. 28177–28193 (2021). https://doi.org/10.1109/ACCESS.2021.3052867

3. Shahzad, K., Zia, T., Qazi, E.: A Review of Functional Encryption in IoT Applications. Sensors 22(19), 7567 (2022). https://doi.org/10.3390/s22197567

4. Hosny, K.M., Zaki, M.A., Lashin, N.A., Fouda, M.M., Hamza, H.M.: Multimedia security using encryption: a survey. In: IEEE Access, vol. 11, pp. 63027–63056 (2023). https://doi.org/10.1109/ACCESS.2023.3287858

5. Wen, H., Huang, Y., Lin, Y.: High-quality color image compression-encryption using chaos and block permutation. J. King Saud Univ. Comp. Info. Sci. 35(8) (2023). https://doi.org/10.1016/j.jksuci.2023.101660

6. Kuldeep, G., Qi, Z.: Design prototype and security analysis of a lightweight joint compression and encryption scheme for resource-constrained IoT devices. IEEE Internet of Things Journal 9, 165–181 (2023)

7. Vishwakarma, S., Gupta, N.K.: An efficient color image security technique for IoT using fast RSA encryption technique. 10th IEEE International Conference on Communication Systems and Network Technologies (CSNT), pp. 717–722. Bhopal, India (2021). https://doi.org/10.1109/CSNT51715.2021.9509697

8. Pourasad, Y., Ranjbarzadeh, R., Mardani, A.: A new algorithm for digital image encryption based on chaos theory. Entropy 23(3), 341 (2021). https://doi.org/10.3390/e23030341

9. Arab, A., Rostami, M.J., Ghavami, B.: An image encryption method based on chaos system and AES algorithm. J. Supercomput. 75(10), 6663–6682 (2019). https://doi.org/10.1007/s11227-019-02878-7

10. Milani, M., Ceyhan, S.: An efficient method for digital image encryption based on improved chaotic map. Electron. Lett. Sci. Eng. 18(2), Art. No 2 (2022)

11. Tarabay, S.Y., Twakol, A., Samrah, A.S., Yasser, I.: A secure and efficient cryptography system based on chaotic maps for securing data image in fog computing. Int. J. Comput. Netw. Inf. Secur. 15(1), 64–80 (2023)

12. Li, P., Lo, K.-T.: A content-adaptive joint image compression and encryption scheme. IEEE Trans. Multimed. 20(8), 1960–1972 (2018). https://doi.org/10.1109/TMM.2017.2786860

13. Nasrullah, J., Sang, M.A., Akbar, B., Cai, H.X., Hu, H.: Joint image compression and encryption using IWT with SPIHT, Kd-Tree and Chaotic Maps. Appl. Sci. 8(10), 1963 (2018). https://doi.org/10.3390/app8101963

14. ZheNie, Z.-X.L., He, X.-T., Gong, L.-H.: Image compression and encryption algorithm based on advanced encryption standard and hyper-chaotic system. Opt. Appl. 49(4) (2019). https://doi.org/10.37190/oa190402

15. Duhayyim, M., et al.: Novel image encryption and compression scheme for IoT environment. Comput. Mater. Contin. 71(1), Art. No 1 (2021). https://doi.org/10.32604/cmc.2022.021873

16. Mahajan, H.B., Junnarkar, A.A.: Smart healthcare system using integrated and lightweight ECC with private blockchain for multimedia medical data processing. Multimed Tools Appl. (2023). https://doi.org/10.1007/s11042-023-15204-4

17. Hasan, M.K., et al.: Lightweight encryption technique to enhance medical image security on internet of medical things applications. In: IEEE Access, vol. 9, pp. 47731–47742 (2021). https://doi.org/10.1109/ACCESS.2021.3061710

18. Aiyshwariya Devi, R., Arunachalam, A.R.: Enhancement of IoT device security using an Improved Elliptic Curve Cryptography algorithm and malware detection utilizing deep LSTM. High-Confidence Computing 3(2), 100117 (2023). https://doi.org/10.1016/j.hcc.2023.100117

19. Abduljabbar, Z.A., et al.: Elliptic curve cryptography-based scheme for secure signaling and data exchanges in precision agriculture. Sustainability **15**(13), 10264 (2023). https://doi.org/10.3390/su151310264

20. Goulart, A., Chennamaneni, A., Torre, D., Hur, B., Al-Aboosi, F.Y.: On Wide-Area IoT Networks, Lightweight Security and Their Applications—A Practical Review. Electronics **11**, 1762 (2022). https://doi.org/10.3390/electronics11111762

21. Narayan, S.: A review on elliptic curve cryptography. Int. J. Emerg. Technol. Innov. Eng. **4**(12) (2018)

22. Hayat, Uazam, N.A.: A novel image encryption scheme based on an elliptic curve. Signal Process **155**, 391–402 (2019). https://doi.org/10.1016/j.sigpro.2018.10.011

23. Khatke, R.N.: Image compression using wavelet transform. Imp. J. Interdiscip. Res. **2**(9), 82–84 (2016)

24. Latha, H., Ramaprasath: HWCD: a hybrid approach for image compression using wavelet, encryption using confusion, and decryption using diffusion scheme. J. Intel. Sys. **32**(1), 20229056 (2023). https://doi.org/10.1515/jisys-2022-9056

25. Abdullatif, A.A., Abdullatif, F.A., Naji, S.A.: An enhanced hybrid image encryption algorithm using Rubik's cube and dynamic DNA encoding techniques. Period. Eng. Nat. Sci. PEN **7**(4), Art. No 4 (2019). https://doi.org/10.21533/pen.v7i4.885

26. Zhu, S.Q., Zhu, C.X., Yu, F., Zhang, W.M., Wu, X.T.: A secure image encryption scheme with compression-confusion-diffusion structure. Multimedia Tools and Applications **79**, 31957–31980 (2020). https://doi.org/10.1007/s11042-020-09699-4

27. Wang, J., Song, X., El-Latif, A.A.A.: Efficient entropic security with joint compression and encryption approach based on compressed sensing with multiple chaotic systems. Entropy **24**, 885 (2022). https://doi.org/10.3390/e24070885

28. Song, X., Shi, M., Zhou, Y., Wang, E.: An image compression encryption algorithm based on chaos and ZUC stream cipher. Entropy (Basel) **24**(5), 742 (2022). https://doi.org/10.3390/e24050742

Toward a DoS and DDoS Detection Using eXtreme Gradient Boosting

Mohamed Loughmari$^{(\boxtimes)}$ ⓘ and Anass El Affar ⓘ

Engineering Sciences Laboratory (LSI), Multidisciplinary Faculty of Taza, Sidi Mohamed Ben Abdellah University, B.P. 1223, Taza, Morocco
mohamed.loughmari@usmba.ac.ma

Abstract. In today's interconnected world, ensuring the security of computer networks is crucial and massively important. One of the major threats faced by network administrators is the occurrence of Denial-of-Service (DoS) and Distributed Denial-of-Service (DDoS) attacks. Detecting and containing these attacks in a timely manner is crucial to maintaining network availability and preventing service disruptions. This paper presents a comprehensive approach for detecting DoS and DDoS attacks using the eXtreme Gradient Boosting (XGBoost) algorithm on a powerful and recent dataset. We focus on a subset of a dataset containing only normal DoS and DDoS attacks, and we perform extensive preprocessing and feature selection techniques. Our approach incorporates variable encoding, elimination of columns with only one value, normalization, besides correlation-based feature selection. Finally, we apply the XGBoost algorithm to classify the attacks. The experimental results demonstrate promising and insightful findings in terms of various performance metrics.

Keywords: Intrusion Detection · DoS · DDoS · Machine Learning · XGBoost

1 Introduction

Due to the ongoing development of sophisticated threats and intrusions, network and computer security have been major concerns in recent years. For many years, Denial of Service (DoS) and Distributed Denial of Service (DDoS) attacks have been a prevalent and rising threat, causing serious business disruption and continuing to be a major issue, with the number of attacks growing by 150% in 2022 [1], according to the "Radware Global Threat Analysis Report."

Denial-of-Service (DoS) is among the most damaging attacks in which attackers try to overwhelm the target's system or network with a large volume of traffic until it becomes unreachable to its legitimate users. This causes legitimate users to lose access and can cause serious financial and reputational harm to enterprises. Distributed Denial of Service (DDoS) attack is a harmful variation of the DoS attack; due to the usage of numerous devices often infected devices or botnets that are coordinated to launch simultaneous attacks from multiple locations, it is more challenging to protect against.

© The Author(s), under exclusive license to Springer Nature Switzerland AG 2025
H. Hagras et al. (Eds.): ISACS 2023, CCIS 2255, pp. 472–480, 2025.
https://doi.org/10.1007/978-3-031-93448-3_38

An intrusion detection system (IDS) [2] is a piece of equipment or software that scans a system or a network for unusual behavior. IDSs typically come in three different forms:

- NIDS (Network Intrusion Detection System): performs monitoring of all the traffic passing through; NIDS is widely deployed as they are cross-platform and more scalable than other IDS types.
- HIDS (Host Intrusion Detection System): deployed as an agent on individual hosts and performs intrusion detection to defend them from internal and external threats.
- Application-based IDS(AIDS): it's a particular type of HIDS deployed to monitor a specific application.

IDSs can also be classified based on the detection method used [3], as Signature-based or Anomaly-based. The first one detects harmful traffic based on predetermined rules and is excellent for recognizing known threats. Conversely, the latter detects malicious traffic by comparing its pattern to normal traffic, usually, anomaly-based IDS can identify more sophisticated and unidentified attacks more effectively than signature-based IDS.

Detecting and mitigating these attacks efficiently is a challenging task that requires robust intrusion detection systems. In this research paper, we focus on the detection of DoS and DDoS attacks in the CIC-IDS2017 dataset which is considered a recent and powerful dataset for intrusion detection, we employ the eXtreme Gradient Boosting (XGBoost) machine learning algorithm to classify attacks, after performing multiple preprocessing tasks such as normalization and feature selection techniques, our experimental results demonstrate promising findings in terms of all metrics with more than 99% achievement.

The remainder of this paper is organized as follows: Sect. 2 "Related Work" provides a state-of-the-art of the current research. Section 3 "Methodology" goes into detail about the dataset and methods employed. Section 4 "Results and Discussion" presents and discusses the results obtained, followed by the "Conclusion" section.

2 Related Work

In recent years, numerous approaches have been proposed in a variety of ways to protect all the different types of networks against denial-of-service attacks.

A vast amount of research is being conducted on the detection of DDoS attacks using artificial neural networks (ANNs), with an emphasis on packet characteristics to distinguish between legitimate and illegitimate traffic [4, 5]. These parameters are often "packet sequence number", "packet arrival time" and "protocol".

Aktar and Yasin Nur [6] evaluated their proposed contractive autoencoder model on three different datasets, NSLKDD, CIC-IDS2017, and CIC-DDoS2019, and compared their results against other deep learning approaches, including the basic autoencoder approach, which they found to be higher.

Asad et al. [7] proposed a feed-forward back-propagation deep neural network detection for the purpose of discovering multiple application layer DDoS attacks. Their designed neural network architecture effectively captures and leverages essential high-level features from packet flows, achieving an accuracy of 98%.

Kim et al. [8] presented a deep-learning CNN-Based NIDS designed to combat DoS attacks. Their experimental approach involves utilizing both the KDD dataset and the CSE-CIC-IDS2018, their results demonstrated the higher accuracy achieved using the RGB images in comparison with the grayscale, they also compared their findings to an RNN model to confirm that the CNN model exhibited superior performance for both binary and multiclass classification tasks.

In [9], Zhuo et al. focus on DDoS attack detection in the SDN-based cloud using the XGBoost classifier, and their result confirms the performance and the scalability of the classifier compared to others.

Sabeel et al. [10] proposed two Deep Learning based techniques, DNN and LSTM focusing on the prediction of DoS and DDoS attacks, in a binary classification, using the CIC-IDS2017 dataset, and a newly generated dataset, ANTS2019.

Huynh et al. [11] introduced a DNN-based feature selection technique for IDSs to extract the most significant features. They evaluated their approach on the UNSW-NB15 and CIC-IDS2017 datasets and compared their findings with those of other feature selection techniques.

In [12], Diego et al. present a developed new type of intrusion detection model based on image recognition and classification, where they first convert each dataset record to an image before employing convolutional neural networks (CNN) for feature extraction, then SVM for attack classification. The proposed model is evaluated with the CIC-IDS2017 dataset.

Yuening et al. [13] present a hybrid model that combines an autoencoder network (AN) with a long short-term memory (LSTM). The AN is used to reduce the dimensionality of the input data, while the LSTM is used to predict intrusion types.

3 Methodology

In this section, we outline the procedure and steps used in our research. The entire process includes dataset selection, preprocessing, feature selection, and application of the Extreme Gradient Boosting (XGBoost) algorithm on the random-shuffled dataset, testing the results, and evaluating performance. Figure 1 summarizes the flowchart of our work.

The data preprocessing phase began with the identification of our three classes: Normal, DoS, and DDoS. Subsequently, we addressed categorical data, managed missing values, eliminated duplicate entries and features with a single static value, and concluded by normalizing the data.

In the feature selection phase, we examine two different techniques, including "SelectKBest" and "Correlation", with 0.8 as the threshold.

Since the dataset is sufficiently large, we opted to perform an 80/20 split. This division retains a substantial volume of data for training while also ensuring a satisfactory amount of data for evaluation purposes.

The final two steps involve applying the selected algorithm and conducting testing and performance evaluation.

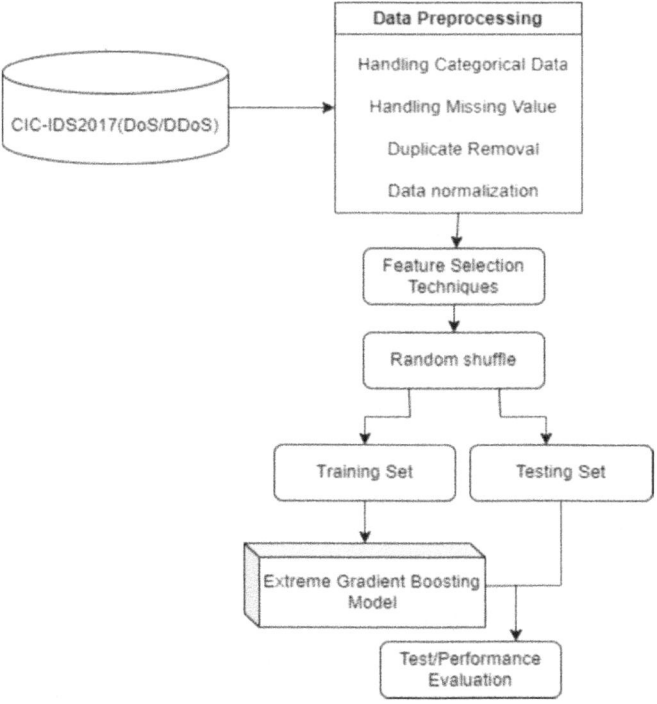

Fig. 1. Flow chart of work

3.1 Dataset

Effective intrusion detection research depends on the use of an appropriate and representative dataset, that has the ability to provide accurate and reliable information for the detection of DoS and DDoS attacks. In this study we leverage the CIC-IDS2017 dataset, specifically focusing on DoS and DDoS attacks.

The Canadian Cybersecurity Institute (CIC) is the organization that created the CIC-IDS2017 [14]. This dataset contains realistic benign traffic and the most recent DoS/DDoS attacks. It includes a variety of attack types and protocol types.

Our Dataset subset covers two types of attacks, **DoS** and **DDoS,** besides the **normal** pattern, as well as **68** features. As shown in Table 1, the selected dataset portion has the number of **918437** records was divided into an approximate 80%: 20% ratio of the training and testing data sets, respectively.

3.2 Feature Selection Process

Feature selection is an important phase for most machine learning problems, especially when the dataset is dimensionally large. The aim is to identify the most pertinent features of the dataset that contribute effectively to the model [15]. Feature selection can positively affect the model in several ways, such as preventing learning from noise, improving the model performance, and reducing the overall computational cost.

Table 1. Distribution of Dataset classes

Category	Training set	Testing set
Normal	430 199	107 550
DoS	202 129	50 532
DDoS	102 421	25 606
Total Records	734 749	183 688

The SelectKbest method selects the K best features relevant to the target variable by calculating the score of each feature based on statistical metrics. In this research, we used Scikit-Learn [16] SelectKBest library 31 with k = 40 and f_classif as the scoring function.

We also investigated Correlation-based Feature Selection (CFS), where we used the correlation matrix to find and remove highly correlated features after setting a threshold of 0.8, resulting in only 32 features.

3.3 Extreme Gradient Boosting

Extreme Gradient Boosting (XGBoost) is a strong and widely used machine learning algorithm that excels in a variety of predictive modeling applications. XGBoost is a boosting technique that combines the strength of multiple weak learners [17], such as decision trees, to create a robust and accurate predictive model. It employs a gradient boosting framework, where subsequent models are built to correct the errors of the previous models, leading to continuous improvement in prediction accuracy.

XGBoost incorporates several innovative features, including regularization techniques, parallel processing, and advanced tree construction algorithms, to enhance its efficiency and generalization capabilities. XGBoost has emerged as a popular option for many applications, including classification, regression, and ranking tasks, thanks to its capacity to handle large-scale datasets, manage missing values, and deliver interpretable results.

Its versatility, speed, and high accuracy make XGBoost a worthy tool for professionals seeking state-of-the-art intrusion detection performance.

3.4 Evaluation Metrics

Several performance metrics were employed to evaluate our suggested model: Precision, Recall, F1-Score, Accuracy, and False Alarm Rate, in addition to training and testing time. These metrics are calculated using the measures of the confusion matrix: true positive (TP), true negative (TN), false positive (FP), and false negative (FN):

• TP: when an attack instance is correctly labeled.
• FP: when a normal instance is marked as an attack.
• TN: when a normal instance is marked as normal.
• FN: when an attack instance is marked as normal.

Precision: Metric that measures the proportion of correctly classified attack samples out of all instances classified as attacks.

$$\text{Precision} = \frac{TP}{TP + FP} \tag{1}$$

Recall: Ratio of correctly classified anomalous instances to the total number of actual anomalous instances.

$$\text{Recall} = \frac{TP}{TP + FN} \tag{2}$$

Accuracy: Metric that considers both correctly categorized abnormal and normal instances in relation to all other instances.

$$\text{Accuracy} = \frac{TP + TN}{TP + FP + TN + FN} \tag{3}$$

F1-score: Metric that combines precision and recall into a single value by taking their harmonic average.

$$F1 - \text{score} = 2*\left(\frac{\text{Precision} * \text{Recall}}{\text{Precision} + \text{Recall}} \right) \tag{4}$$

False Positive Rate (FPR): The probability of reporting a positive test result when the true value is negative.

$$\text{FPR} = \frac{FP}{FP + TN} \tag{5}$$

4   Result and Discussion

Numerous features are often present in intrusion detection datasets, and not all of them contribute significantly to the model's predictive performance. To enhance model performance and reduce computational overhead, in addition to the elimination of features with only a single value, we applied two different feature selection techniques (FS), SelectKBest and Correlation-based Feature Selection. Table 2 presents the performance of our XGBoost model as well as a comparison that demonstrates the impact of the feature selection approach.

All experiments were conducted in a uniform manner concerning data splitting ratios and computational resources, and we ran several trials with various hyperparameter values in order to select the optimal one. The problem was approached as a multiclass classification involving three classes: Normal, DoS, and DDoS. However, while calculating the False Positive Rate (FPR), the analysis was transformed into a binary classification scenario, specifically comparing normal samples to DoS/DDoS attack samples. This approach ensured consistency and enabled a focused evaluation of the model's performance in detecting attacks against normal network behavior.

Figure 2 shows the confusion matrix for the method we use, including the three classes, Normal as the legitimate traffic, DoS and DDoS attack as the malicious traffic.

Table 2. Model performance evaluation and FS techniques comparison

	Dataset shape	Accuracy	Precision	Recall	F1-Score	FPR	Time-to-train(s)	Time-to-test(s)
No FS	918437, 68	0.99772	0.99773	0.99772	0.99773	0.00229	146.58	0.4035
SelectKbest	918437, 40	0.99711	0.99773	0.99772	0.99773	0.00613	129.03	0.3928
Correlation	918437, 32	0.99787	0.99787	0.99787	0.99787	0.00290	65.151	0.1391

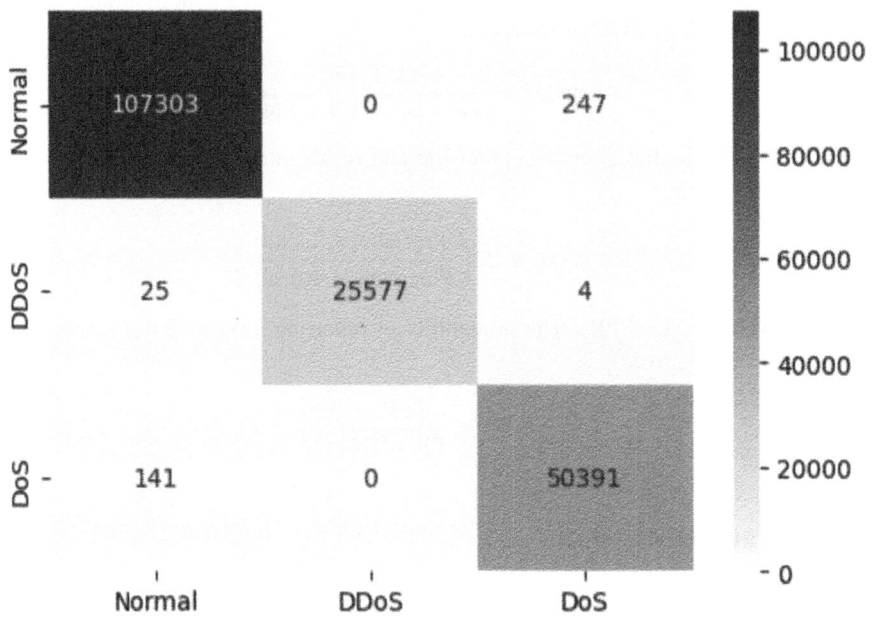

Fig. 2. Confusion Matrix for the three classes

Extreme Gradient Boosting shows a remarkable performance, with an accuracy of more than 99,78%. It also has a low False positive rate of 0,29%, which is very important because even high false positive rates would protect the system from attacks, but they also block out legitimate users, causing a disturbance. The time consumption is also very low considering the size of our dataset, which has 918437 entries.

In terms of accuracy, the result outperformed some of the related work, as summarized in Table 3.

The results also reveal the impact of feature selection, which enhances all the metrics investigated and also reduces the computational overhead. The correlation-based feature selection technique gave the best results and maximized the effectiveness of the model.

Table 3. Comparison between Our approach and related work

Reference	Dataset	Technique	Accuracy %
Aktar and Yasin Nur [6]	CIC-IDS2017	contractive autoencoder	92.45
Sabeel et al. [10]	CIC-IDS2017, ANTS2019	DNN, LSTM	99.68
Asad et al. [7]	CIC-IDS2017	ANN	98
Our approach	CIC-IDS2017	XGBoost	99,78

5 Conclusion

DoS and DDoS attacks are among the most serious threats faced by network administrators; they are becoming more sophisticated every day, and traditional intrusion detection systems fail to detect them due to their unexpected patterns. This paper presents a comprehensive approach to detect these attacks using the CIC-IDS2017 dataset and the eXtreme Gradient Boosting Model Classifier. The experimental results demonstrate promising findings indicating the potential for effective attack detection, with high metrics and an accuracy of up to 99.78%.

References

1. Radware® : Radware's 2022 Global Threat Analysis Report (2022)
2. Farahnakian, F., Heikkonen, J. A deep auto-encoder based approach for an intrusion detection system. International Conference on Advanced Communication Technology, ICACT, vol. 2018-February, pp. 178–183 (2018). https://doi.org/10.23919/ICACT.2018.8323688
3. Fenanir, S., Semchedine, F., Baadache, A.: A machine learning-based lightweight intrusion detection system for the internet of things. Revue d'Intelligence Artificielle 33(3), 203–211 (2019). https://doi.org/10.18280/ria.330306
4. Kale, M., Choudhari, D.M. : DDOS Attack Detection Based on an Ensemble of Neural Classifier (2014)
5. Preetha, G., Devi, B.S.K., Shalinie, S.M.: Autonomous agent for DDoS attack detection and defense in an experimental testbed. Int. J. Fuzzy Syst. 16, 520–528 (2014)
6. Aktar, S., Yasin Nur, A.: Towards DDoS attack detection using deep learning approach. Comput. Secur. 129, 103251 (2023). https://doi.org/10.1016/j.cose.2023.103251
7. Asad, M., Asim, M., Javed, T., Beg, M.O., Mujtaba, H., Abbas, S.: DeepDetect: detection of distributed denial of service attacks using deep learning. Comput. J. 63(7), 983–994 (2020). https://doi.org/10.1093/comjnl/bxz064
8. Kim, J., Kim, J., Kim, H., Shim, M., Choi, E.: CNN-based network intrusion detection against denial-of-service attacks. Electronics (Basel) 9(6), 916 (2020). https://doi.org/10.3390/electronics9060916
9. Chen, Z., et al.: XGBoost Classifier for DDoS Attack Detection and Analysis in SDN-Based Cloud. Proceedings - 2018 IEEE International Conference on Big Data and Smart Computing, BigComp 2018, pp. 251–256 (2018). https://doi.org/10.1109/BIGCOMP.2018.00044
10. Sabeel, U., et al.: Evaluation of Deep Learning in Detecting Unknown Network Attacks. In: 2019 International Conference on Smart Applications, Communications and Networking (SmartNets), pp. 1–6. IEEE (2019). https://doi.org/10.1109/SmartNets48225.2019.9069788

11. Huynh, M.-T., Le, H.-T., Nguyen, X.-H., Le, K.-H.: Deep Feature Selection for Machine Learning based Attack Detection Systems. In: 2022 IEEE International Conference on Communication, Networks and Satellite (COMNETSAT), pp. 339–344 (2022). https://doi.org/10.1109/COMNETSAT56033.2022.9994376

12. Munoz, W.Y.C. , Rueda Diego, D.F. and Caviedes, J.C.: A Hybrid Intrusion Detection Approach Based on Deep Learning Techniques. In: X., Pandian, H.W., Pasumpon, A., Fernando, (ed.) Computer Networks, Big Data and IoT, pp. 863–878. Singapore: Springer Nature Singapore (2022)

13. Zhang, Y., Zhang, Y., Zhang, N., Xiao, M.: A network intrusion detection method based on deep learning with higher accuracy. Procedia Comput. Sci. **174**, 50–54 (2020). https://doi.org/10.1016/j.procs.2020.06.055

14. Sharafaldin, I., Habibi Lashkari, A., Ghorbani, A.A.: Toward Generating a New Intrusion Detection Dataset and Intrusion Traffic Characterization. In : Proceedings of the 4th International Conference on Information Systems Security and Privacy, SCITEPRESS - Science and Technology Publications, pp. 108–116 (2018). https://doi.org/10.5220/0006639801080116

15. Naveed, M., et al.: A deep learning-based framework for feature extraction and classification of intrusion detection in networks. Wirel. Commun. Mob. Comput. 2022 (2022). https://doi.org/10.1155/2022/2215852

16. Pedregosa Fabianpedregosa, F., et al.: Scikit-learn: Machine Learning in Python Gaël Varoquaux Bertrand Thirion Vincent Dubourg Alexandre Passos PEDREGOSA, VAROQUAUX, GRAMFORT ET AL. Matthieu Perrot. Journal of Machine Learning Research **12**, 2825–2830 (2011). Accessed: 20 Aug. 2023. [Online]. Available: http://scikit-learn.sourceforge.net

17. Dhaliwal, S.S., Al Nahid, A., Abbas, R. : Effective intrusion detection system using XGBoost. Information (Switzerland) **9**(7) (2018). https://doi.org/10.3390/info9070149

Author Index

H. Hagras et al. (Eds.): ISACS 2023, CCIS 2255, pp. 481–482, 2025.
https://doi.org/10.1007/978-3-031-93448-3

The manufacturer's authorised representative in the EU is Springer
Nature Customer Service Centre GmbH, Europaplatz 3, 69115 Heidelberg,
Germany. If you have any concerns regarding our products, please
contact ProductSafety@springernature.com

Printed and bound by CPI Group (UK) Ltd, Croydon, CR0 4YY
28/04/2026
02098527-0007